Open Source SOA

Open Source SOA

JEFF DAVIS

MANNING
Greenwich
(74° w. long.)

For online information and ordering of this and other Manning books, please visit www.manning.com. The publisher offers discounts on this book when ordered in quantity. For more information, please contact

Special Sales Department
Manning Publications Co.
Sound View Court 3B fax: (609) 877-8256
Greenwick, CT 06830 email: orders@manning.com

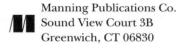

♾ Recognizing the importance of preserving what has been written, it is Manning's policy to have the books we publish printed on acid-free paper, and we exert our best efforts to that end. Recognizing also our responsibility to conserve the resources of our planet, Manning books are printed on paper that is at least 15 percent recycled and processed without the use of elemental chlorine.

Manning Publications Co.
Sound View Court 3B
Greenwich, CT 06830

Development Editor: Cynthia Kane
Copyeditor: Liz Welch
Typesetter: Krzysztof Anton
Cover designer: Leslie Haimes

ISBN 978-1-933988-54-2
Printed in the United States of America
1 2 3 4 5 6 7 8 9 10 – MAL – 16 15 14 13 11 10 09

brief contents

contents

preface

Only if you have been in the deepest valley can you ever know how magnificent it is to be on the highest mountain.

—Richard Nixon

I'm not sure exactly at what point I decided to write this book. I think the moment of inspiration came one night while sitting in the hot tub a couple years back. That day, I had spent considerable time working with the newest release (at the time) of JBoss jBPM. I was extremely fired up as I had explored its capabilities, and the more I dug under the covers, the more excited I became. Technically, as I considered its features, it provided all the capabilities we were looking for at HireRight for a business process management (BPM) product. However, the real challenge was, how would we integrate the solution with our existing products and applications?

Like a lot of companies, HireRight uses a mix of open source and commercial products. One of the main benefits of commercial products is that they tend to be all-inclusive in their feature set, and provide a consistent, and often comprehensive, set of capabilities. Open source products, however, tend to be more narrowly focused for solving specific needs. Thus, while jBPM may be an excellent BPM product, it's not obvious how you might integrate that with a services and component framework such as provided by Apache Tuscany. Further, building a complete SOA stack or environment using open source products can be challenging, because SOA itself can be a nebulous objective. Mixing and matching the best-of-breed open source products into a single, consistent SOA platform is a tall order, as I've discovered. Devoting time to studying the benefits of SOA and putting those concepts into practice using open source products are what formed the basis for the knowledge I share in this book. My motivation was to contribute in some small way to the success of open source.

Like a lot of folks, I often felt guilty for using these outstanding open source products, yet I seldom found the time to contribute back to the community. Each time I presented a question in a forum or mail list and got back a plethora of responses, the guilt level went up. Not only was I using the product for free, but I was also receiving free, high-quality advice to boot (granted, HireRight does believe in assisting open source companies by purchasing support for products used in production, but that usually occurs long after our initial evaluation, when most questions and issues arise). Being a believer in the quality of open source products and the outstanding efforts of individuals who support them, I figured it was time to give something back—this was my motivation for writing this book.

When a debate emerges whether to go with an open source offering, I often point out that open source, contrary to popular belief, represents substantially less risk to the adopting company than going with a commercial alternative. Why? As we've seen lately, commercial companies often go out of business or get acquired. When either happens, it's not uncommon for the products to be discontinued, or awkwardly merged into some other offering. Further, many commercial products have a very limited user base, if only because they charge so much to use the products that only large enterprises adopt them. Because the user base is smaller, the quality of the product is often substandard compared with comparable open source products, which enjoy a much broader user base (more users = more feedback). When working with commercial products, how often is it that you can communicate directly with the developers responsible for the code? Such interaction in the open source community is common. Of course, with open source, you also have access to the source code, and the hidden gems in the form of JUnit test cases—one of the best ways to learn an open source product.

My hope is that, by writing this book, I can help advance the adoption of these open source products, and the companies, organizations, or individuals that support them. I believe the benefits of SOA are real, and can be realized entirely through integrating best-of-breed open source products.

acknowledgments

People who work together will win.

—Vince Lombardi

I'm tremendously grateful to the Manning Publications team for the hard work they contributed to bring this book to fruition—it was truly a team effort! Cynthia Kane was instrumental in holding my hand (okay, prodding me) along the way with marvelous suggestions for improvement; the copyediting and proofreading work of Liz Welch and Katie Tennant transformed the readability of the work; and the review coordination efforts by Karen Tegtmeyer resulted in further improvements. Lastly, Marjan Bace's insights provided me with encouragement throughout the process. To others I didn't mention, your contributions were also greatly appreciated!

Special thanks are extended to the reviewers. They took time in their very busy schedules, usually under tight timelines, to review what was often rough copy. Their suggestions and ideas, while not always welcome by me at the time, helped make the book tighter in messaging and improved its content. The reviewers are Peter Johnson, Irena Kennedy, Francesco Goggi, Doug Warren, Davide Piazza, Ara Abrahamian, Alberto Lagna, Rick Wagner, Jonathan Esterhazy, Chuck Lee, Madhav Vodnala, Edmon Begoli, Valentin Crettaz, Andy Dingley, Glenn Stokol, Deiveehan Nallazhagappan, Christian Siegers, Michele Galli, Patrick Steger, Ramnath Devulapalli, and Marco Ughetti.

I would also like to highlight the efforts by Paul King, who was the technical reviewer. His thorough work at validating the source code and suggestions for improvement were outstanding and testimony to his breadth of experience.

Lastly, none of this would have been possible without the patience, understanding and support of my family. When I first mentioned to them that I was contemplating writing a book, they were a bit dubious of my plans. However, as weeks turned into months, and months into a year, they endured lost weekends, evenings, and vacations. None of this would have been possible without their encouragement; my guilt would have gotten the better of me.

To my friends and colleagues, my apologies if I was sometimes curt when you inquired about when the book would be done—this was a bit of a sore spot with me. All kidding aside, I appreciated your enthusiasm for the book. Stefano Malnati, my boss, was a constant source of inspiration, and his leadership and integrity provided a solid foundation for my efforts.

about this book

The audience for the first two chapters (part 1) of this book is broad, and can range from technically savvy business users who want to learn more about service-oriented architecture (SOA) to programmer analysts and architects. For the remaining chapters, some prior knowledge of Java is assumed, and numerous code samples are sprinkled throughout those remaining chapters. That said, there is material in the introductory chapters in each technology area covered that can be easily digested by non-developers. While the products covered are all written in Java, it's likely that if you are a C++ or C# developer, you'll be able to follow the examples sufficiently enough to understand the key concepts being imparted.

All of the products we cover in depth in the book undergo frequent updates. This may range from minor dot releases to major new versions. I will make every effort to make sure the examples provided in the sample code are kept up to date with the latest releases. Please visit http://jdavis.open-soa.info/wordpress/ regularly, as it houses the latest versions of the source code and will be used to highlight any significant new releases as they pertain to the products covered.

Roadmap

Part 1 of the book focuses on what constitutes SOA, the advantages gleaned by adopting this architectural pattern, and what technologies contribute or compliment the move to SOA. This part really establishes the foundation for the technologies we describe moving forward in the book, so I encourage you not to skip it!

Chapter 1 provides some historical perspective to SOA—why it came about, and why it's important. It also describes the essential characteristics of SOA, and separates the wheat from the chaff in identifying what is really most important for adopting SOA.

Chapter 2 explores which technologies products contribute or compliment the adoption of SOA. This discussion then provides the basis for evaluating and selecting the open source products that are covered in depth in the chapters that follow. If you're curious as to why I selected Apache Synapse instead of Apache ServiceMix or Mule for the ESB, this chapter will provide the justification.

Part 2 of the book describes the Service Component Architecture (SCA) framework, and how it can be used to develop components that can be exposed as low-level or composite services. We then move into SCA implementation using the open source Apache Tuscany product. Given the central role that services play in SOA, this is obviously an important section.

Chapter 3 introduces the SCA framework, its history, concepts, and benefits. The SCA assembly model, which is core to the framework, is described in detail. Specific examples are provided using Apache Tuscany, the SCA implementation chosen for use within the book.

Chapter 4 delves into advanced Apace Tuscany features. This includes how to use scripting languages such as JRuby and Groovy for building components, and how more complex interaction models such as conversations and callbacks are supported. We also introduce Service Data Objects (SDOs) along with their features and benefits. Part 3 explores how the services created through Apache Tuscany can be combined together to form a complete business process. This is accomplished by way of business process management (BPM), which is defined and examined. JBoss jBPM is introduced as the BPM tool used within the book, and its features and capabilities are explored in depth.

Chapter 5 introduces the role of BPM within SOA, and why we consider it to be the "secret sauce" of SOA. We follow that with an introduction to JBoss jBPM where we describe its key concepts, nomenclature, and how to construct a simple process using the product.

Chapter 6 examines the role of tasks within jBPM. A task represents a human activity that needs to be performed within a business process, such as an approval. The functionality provided by the jBPM Console is explored, as it provides a graphical interface to managing tasks and processes. Lastly, we illustrate how to use the jBPM API to programmatically interact with business processes and tasks.

Chapter 7 dives into some of the advanced capabilities of jBPM, including how to manage larger processes through using superstates and subprocesses. We also look at how to manage exceptions within a process, and the role of asynchronous continuations for distributed processing. Lastly, we look at how jBPM can be integrated with Apache Tuscany and SCA, and how this combination can be used to service-enable jBPM for integration with other platforms and languages.

Part 4 switches gears, and covers the emerging field of complex event processing (CEP). This is illustrated through the use of Esper, an open source event stream processing application. Detailed examples are provided for using Esper, and we describe how Esper can be used in tandem with jBPM and how to service-enable Esper using Apache Tuscany. The remaining chapters then address enterprise service buses (ESBs), and Apache Synapse is introduced and examined in depth using a real-life case study.

Chapter 8 provides an overview of CEP, and then introduces Esper, which is an open source application for event stream processing (ESP). The functionality and features of Esper are described using detailed examples, and we also illustrate how to integrate with Esper by service-enabling it through Apache Tuscany.

Chapter 9 describes the appropriate role ESBs play in SOA, along with the core features commonly found in all ESBs. Then, Apache Synapse is introduced as the ESB of choice for the book, and some quick-and-dirty examples are provided to demonstrate its capabilities.

Chapter 10 takes a deep dive into Synapse using a real-life case study. Advanced features such as transport switching, enterprise integration patterns, and quality of service mediation are described in detail.

Part 5 concludes the remaining chapters of the book by addressing the role played by a business rules engine, and how SOA acts as an enabler for realizing the great benefits that can be achieved by adopting an enterprise decision management approach. JBoss Drools is introduced as the open source business rule engines for the examples in the book, and its features are described in great detail through samples and a detailed case study.

Chapter 11 provides an overview of what constitutes business rules and the business rules approach, and why it is so beneficial, especially when married with SOA. We then explore the history and overview of JBoss Drools, which was selected as the rule engine of choice for the book. Simple examples are used to illustrate the key concepts behind Drools, such as how to construct rules and activate the engine.

Chapter 12 takes a more in-depth look into Drools, and in particular, how to use Guvnor, the Business Rule Management System (BRMS) that comes with the product. A real-life case study is provided to explore advanced Drools capabilities such as RuleFlow. Lastly, we illustrate how to service-enable Drools using Apache Tuscany.

A bonus chapter, available online at www.manning.com/OpenSourceSOA, will cover the role of registries, and how they can be used for cataloging services and assisting in SOA governance and best practices. An implementation of a registry product is provided through examples of using WSO2's Registry product.

Code conventions and downloads

All source code in listings or in text is in a `fixed-width font like this` to separate it from ordinary text. Code annotations accompany many of the listings, highlighting important concepts. In some cases, numbered bullets link to explanations that follow the listing.

Source code for all working examples in this book is available for download at http://jdavis.open-soa.info/wordpress/ as well as from the publisher's website at http://www.manning.com/OpenSourceSOA.

The source code is packaged as an Eclipse project. There are two different download options. One, which is referred to as "Source with no libraries," is a very small download and does not include any JAR libraries. Instead, an Ant target can be run that will automatically pull down all required libraries from various Maven public directories. The other download, which tops out at around 125MB, does include all of the JAR libraries pre-packaged. There is also a link to the installation instructions, which provides detailed instructions for setting of the source. The prerequisites (which are minimal) are described within the instructions PDF. Every effort will be made to keep the source code examples working with updated versions of the applications.

Author Online

The purchase of *Open Source SOA* includes free access to a private web forum run by Manning Publications, where you can make comments about the book, ask technical questions, and receive help from the author and from other users. To access the forum and subscribe to it, point your web browser to http://www.manning.com/OpenSourceSOA. This page provides information about how to get on the forum once you're registered, what kind of help is available, and the rules of conduct on the forum.

The Author Online forum and the archives of previous discussions will be accessible from the publisher's website as long as the book is in print.

About the cover illustration

The figure on the cover of *Open Source SOA* is captioned "L'épicier," which means storekeeper, grocer, or purveyor of fine foods. The illustration is taken from a 19th-century edition of Sylvain Maréchal's four-volume compendium of regional dress customs published in France. Each illustration is finely drawn and colored by hand. The rich variety of Maréchal's collection reminds us vividly of how culturally apart the world's towns and regions were just 200 years ago. Isolated from each other, people spoke different dialects and languages. In the streets or in the countryside, it was easy to identify where they lived and what their trade or station in life was just by their dress.

Dress codes have changed since then and the diversity by region, so rich at the time, has faded away. It is now hard to tell apart the inhabitants of different continents, let alone different towns or regions. Perhaps we have traded cultural diversity for a more varied personal life—certainly for a more varied and fast-paced technological life.

At a time when it is hard to tell one computer book from another, Manning celebrates the inventiveness and initiative of the computer business with book covers based on the rich diversity of regional life of two centuries ago, brought back to life by Maréchal's pictures.

Part 1

History and principles

Service-oriented architecture (SOA) has emerged over the past several years as one of the preferred approaches for systems design, development, and integration. Leveraging open standards and the ubiquity of the internet, SOA is premised on the notion of reusable services that correspond to self-contained, logical units of work. The promise is that these services can be quickly pieced together using common patterns to form new applications that are tightly aligned with the needs of the business. The upshot? Improved business agility and cost-effective utilization of IT resources and assets.

In part 1, we'll examine the history behind SOA and explore some of the commonalities that it shares with earlier architectural and technology approaches. We'll then identify some of the core characteristics of SOA, and explain how they're manifested in actual technologies that can be used in your own enterprise. Collectively, these technologies will combine to form what we are calling the *Open SOA Platform*. Once these technologies, such as business process management (BPM), are identified, our attention will turn to surveying the landscape of possible open source products that can be used to satisfy these technology requirements.

The maturity and adoption of open source products within the enterprise has become widespread. Many of these products are now suitable for use in crafting a technology stack that can support SOA. Some of the major challenges that have precluded more widespread adoption of these solutions in the past pertain to how they can be rationally assessed, and then integrated, within an organization. We'll present requirements for analyzing the product categories of the SOA technology stack, and using them, select what we consider to be the "best of breed" open source solutions for each category. The selection criteria, as we'll see, are also based on how well they can be integrated to form a complete SOA solution. What's more, this can be accomplished at a fraction of the cost of commercial alternatives—an important consideration in today's challenging economic environment.

1 SOA essentials

This chapter covers

- Origins of SOA in distributed computing
- Requirements of a SOA environment
- Key technologies supporting SOA

Ponce de León's early quest to find the "Fountain of Youth" in Florida is one of the most frequently told stories of American folklore. Although he failed in his journey to find the "healing waters," it turns out that he was in good company, for throughout history we can find tales of similar adventures that never materialized. The history of computing bears some resemblance. Every decade or so, a new "silver bullet" emerges that promises to heal the problems that have plagued software development in the past. Those problems include protracted development cycles; solutions that fail to achieve expectations; high maintenance costs; and, of course, the dreaded cost overruns.

The quest is to find a solution that simplifies development and implementation, supports effective reuse of software assets, and leverages the enormous and low-cost computing power now at our fingertips. While some might claim that service-oriented architecture (SOA) is just the latest fad in this illusive quest, tangible results have been achieved by those able to successfully implement its principles.

According to a recent article in the *Harvard Business Journal*, companies that have embraced SOA "have eliminated huge amounts of redundant software, reaped major cost savings from simplifying and automating manual processes, and realized big increases in productivity" [HBJ]. Further, SOA has achieved greater staying power than many earlier alternatives, which does say something of its merits. Perhaps this is because SOA is a more nebulous concept and embraces technologies as much as it does principles and guidelines—thus refuting its benefits becomes more difficult.

Until recently, achieving a technology infrastructure capable of sustaining a SOA generally required purchasing expensive commercial products. This was especially true if an enterprise desired a well-integrated and comprehensive solution. While several early SOA-related open source products were introduced, they tended to focus on specific, niche areas. For example, Apache Axis was first introduced in 2004 and became a widely adopted web services toolkit for Java. As we'll discover, however, web services represent only a piece of the SOA puzzle. Fast-forward to 2008 and we now see commercially competitive open source products across the entire SOA product spectrum. The challenge now for a SOA architect wanting to use open source is how to select among the bewildering number of competing products. Even more challenging is how to integrate them.

The goal of this book is to help you identify the core technologies that constitute a SOA and the open source technologies that you can use to build a complete SOA platform. Our focus will be on how to integrate these core technologies into a compelling solution that's comparable in breadth and depth to the expensive offerings provided by the commercial vendors. SOA is now attainable for even the smallest of enterprises using high-quality open source software. This book will present a technology blueprint for open source SOA. Of course, thanks to the plethora of high-quality open source solutions, you can naturally swap out the solutions I'm advocating with those you deem appropriate.

Before jumping headfirst into the technology stack, let's establish some context for where SOA originated and develop a common understanding of what it is.

1.1 Brief history of distributed computing

The mainframe systems of the 1960s and '70s, such as the IBM System/360 series, rarely communicated with each other. Indeed, one of the main selling points of a mainframe was that it would provide you with everything necessary to perform the computing functions of a business. When communications were required, the process usually amounted to transferring data by way of tape from one system to another. Over time, though, real-time access between systems became necessary, especially as the number of systems within an organization multiplied. This need was especially apparent in financial markets, where trading required real-time transactional settlements that often spanned across companies.

Initially, real-time access was accomplished via low-level socket communications. Usually written in assembly language or C, socket programming was complex and required a deep understanding of the underlying network protocols. Over time, protocols such as Network File System (NFS) and File Transfer Protocol (FTP) came on the scene that abstracted out the complexity of sockets. Companies such as TIBCO emerged that developed "middleware" software explicitly designed to facilitate messaging and communications between servers. Eventually, the ability to create distributed applications became feasible through the development of remote procedure calls (RPCs). RPCs enabled discrete functions to be performed by remote computers as though they were running locally. As Sun Microsystems' slogan puts it, "The Network is the Computer."

By the 1980s, personal computers had exploded onto the scene, and developers were seeking more effective ways to leverage the computing power of the desktop. As the price of hardware came down, the number of servers within the enterprise increased exponentially. These trends, coupled with the growing maturity of RPC, led to two important advances in distributed computing:

- *Common Object Request Broker Architecture (CORBA)*—Originated in 1991 as a means for standardizing distributed execution of programming functions, the first several releases only supported the C programming language. Adoption was slow, as commercial implementations were expensive and the ambiguities within the specification made for significant incompatibilities between vendor products. The 2.0 release in 1998 was significant in that it supported several additional language mappings and addressed many of the shortfalls present in the earlier standards. However, the advent of Java, which dramatically simplified distributed computing through Remote Method Invocation (RMI), and finally, through XML, has largely led to the demise of CORBA (at least in new implementations).
- *Distributed Computing Object Model (DCOM)*—DCOM is a proprietary Microsoft technology that was largely motivated as a response to CORBA. The first implementations appeared in 1993. While successful within the Microsoft world, the proprietary nature obviously limited its appeal. The wider enterprise class of applications that were emerging at the time—Enterprise Resource Planning (ERP) systems—generally used non-Microsoft technologies. Later, Java's Enterprise JavaBeans (EJB) platform could be construed as Java's alternative to DCOM, as it shared many of the same characteristics.

By the late 1990s, with the widespread adoption of the internet, companies began recognizing the benefits of extending their computing platform to partners and customers. Before this, communications among organizations were expensive and had to rely on leased lines (private circuits). Leased lines were impractical except for the largest of enterprises. Unfortunately, using CORBA or DCOM over the internet proved to be challenging, in part due to networking restrictions imposed by firewalls that only permitted HTTP traffic (necessary for browser and web server communications). Another reason was that neither CORBA nor DCOM commanded dominant market share, so companies attempting communication links often had competing technologies.

When the Simple Object Access Protocol (SOAP) first arrived (in January 2000), it was touted as a panacea due to its interoperable reliance on XML. SOAP was largely envisioned as an RPC alternative to CORBA and DCOM. Since RPCs were the predominant model for distributed computing, it naturally followed that SOAP was originally used in a similar capacity. However, RPC-based solutions, regardless of their technology platform, proved nettlesome. (It is worth noting that SOAP's RPC was an improvement over earlier RPC implementations, as it relied on XML as the payload, which facilitates a much higher degree of interoperability between programming languages.)

1.1.1 Problems related to RPC-based solutions

While RPC-based distributed computing was no doubt a substantial improvement over earlier lower-level socket-based communications, it suffered from several limitations:

- Tight coupling between local and remote systems requires significant bandwidth demands. Repeated RPC calls from a client to server can generate substantial network load.
- The fine-grained nature of RPC requires a highly predictable network. Unpredictable latency, a hallmark of internet-based communications, is unacceptable for RPC-based solutions.
- RPC's data type support, which aims to provide complete support for all native data types (arrays, strings, integers, etc.), becomes challenging when attempting to bridge between incompatible languages, such as C++ and Java. Often, incompatibilities result, greatly complicating its use.

SOAP RPC-style messages also suffered from the same inherent limitations as those mentioned here. Fortunately, SOAP offers alternative message styles that overcome these shortcomings.

1.1.2 Understanding SOAP's messaging styles

In addition to the RPC-style SOAP messaging, the founders of the standard had the foresight to create what is known as the document-style SOAP message. As pointed out earlier, the RPC style is for creating tightly coupled, distributed applications where a running program on one machine can rather transparently invoke a function on a remote machine. The intention with RPC is to treat the remote function in the same way as you would a local one, without having to dwell on the mechanics of the network connectivity. For example, a conventional client-server application could utilize SOAP RPC-style messaging for its communication protocol.

Document style, on the other hand, was envisioned more as a means for application-to-application messaging, perhaps among business partners. In other words, it was intended for more "loosely coupled" integrations, such as document or data transfers. The differences between the two styles are defined within the SOAP standard and are reflected in the Web Service Definition Language (WSDL) interface specification that describes a given service.

After the initial flirtation with RPC-based web services, a coalescing of support has emerged for the document-style SOAP messaging. Microsoft was an early proponent of the document style, and Sun likewise embraced it completely when introducing the Java API for XML Web Services (JAX-WS). Web services became viewed as a panacea to achieving SOA. After all, a linchpin of SOA is the service, and a service requires three fundamental aspects: implementation; elementary access details; and a contract [MargolisSharpe]. A SOAP-based web service, with its reliance on the WSDL standard, appeared to address all three. The implementation is the coding of the service functionality; the access details and contract are addressed within the WSDL as the port type and XML schema used for document-style messaging. So if you simply expose all your internal components as SOAP-based services, you then have the foundation by which you can (a) readily reuse the services, and (b) combine the services into higher-level business processes—characteristics that eventually would become cornerstones of SOA. So what exactly is SOA?

1.1.3 Advent of SOA

The concepts that today are associated with SOA began to emerge with the widespread adoption of the internet, and more specifically, HTTP. By 2003, Roy Schulte of Gartner Group had coined the term SOA, and it quickly became ubiquitous. What it was, exactly, remained somewhat difficult to quantify. Through time, some commonalities appeared in the various definitions:

> *Contemporary SOA represents an open, agile extensible, federated, composable architecture comprised of autonomous, QoS-capable, vendor diverse, interoperable, discoverable, and potentially reusable services, implemented as Web services. [Erl2005]*

> *Service-Oriented Architecture is an IT strategy that organizes the discrete functions contained in enterprise applications into interoperable, standards-based services that can be combined and reused quickly to meet business needs. [BEA]*

As you can see, the common theme is the notion of discrete, reusable business services that can be used to construct new and novel business processes or applications. As you learned earlier, however, many past component-based frameworks attempted similar objectives. What distinguishes these approaches from the newer SOA?

- As discussed earlier, CORBA, EJB, and DCOM are all based on RPC technologies. In many ways, this is the exact opposite of SOA, since it introduces highly coupled solutions by way of using distributed objects and remote functions. A central theme of SOA, on the other hand, specifically encourages loosely coupled services (I'll address this concept in greater detail later in this chapter).
- In the case of EJB and DCOM, they are both tied to specific platforms and are thus not interoperable. Unless a homogenous environment exists (which is rare in today's enterprises, as they are often grown through acquisition), the benefits from them couldn't be achieved easily. SOA-based web services were designed with interoperability in mind.

- CORBA, EJB, and, to a lesser degree, DCOM were complicated technologies that often required commercial products to implement (at least in their earliest incarnations). In particular, CORBA required use of Interface Description Language (IDL) mappings, which were tedious to manage, and until recently with the 3.0 release of EJB, complex XML descriptor files were required for its implementation. SOA can be introduced using a multitude of off-the-shelf, open source technologies.
- SOA relies on XML as the underlying data representation, unlike the others, which used proprietary, binary-based objects. XML's popularity is undeniable, in part because it is easy to understand and generate.

Another distinction between a SOA and earlier RPC-based component technologies is that a SOA is more than technology per se, but has grown to embrace the best practices and standards that are rooted in the lessons found through decades of traditional software development. This includes notions such as governance, service-level agreements, metadata definitions, and registries. These topics will be addressed in greater detail in the sections that follow.

So what does a SOA resemble conceptually? Figure 1.1 depicts the interplay between the backend systems, exposed services, and orchestrated business processes.

As you can see, low-level services (sometimes referred to as fine-grained) represent the layer atop the enterprise business systems/applications. These components allow the layers above to interact with these systems. The composite services layer represents more coarse-grained services that consist of two or more individual components. For example, a *createPO* composite service may include integrating finer-grained services

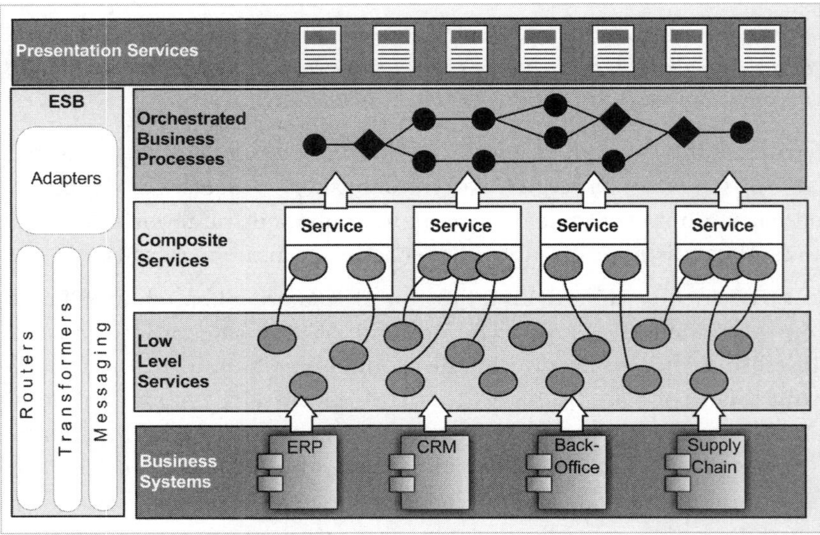

Figure 1.1 Illustration of a SOA environment. Notice the relationships between services and business processes.

such as *createCustomer, createPOHeader,* and *createPOLineItems.* The composite services, in turn, can then be called by higher-level orchestrations, such as one for processing orders placed through a website.

What is interesting is that, in many respects, SOA is a significant departure from older distributed computing models, which centered around the exchange of distributed objects and remote functions. SOA instead emphasizes a loosely coupled affiliation of services that are largely autonomous in nature.

The benefits achieved from embracing SOA are now being realized by the early adopters. When monolithic applications are replaced by discrete services, software can be updated and replaced on a piece-by-piece basis, without requiring wholesale changes to entire systems. This strategy improves flexibility and efficiency. An often-overlooked benefit is that this then enables a company to selectively outsource nonprimary activities to specialists who can perform the function more efficiently and at the lowest cost. Thanks to the advances in connectivity, where a service is housed can be largely transparent to the enterprise.

However, SOA is clearly no silver bullet. According to a recent InformationWeek survey [IW], 58 percent of respondents reported that their SOA projects introduced more complexity into their IT environments. In 30 percent of those projects, the costs were more than anticipated. Nearly the same percentage responded that their SOA initiatives didn't meet expectations. SOAP-based web services do introduce some added complexity to the SOA equation, despite their hype.

1.2 The promise of web services for delivering SOA

The SOAP standard, with its reliance on WSDLs, appeared to address many of the fundamental requirements of a SOA. That being the case, SOA, in many individuals' eyes, became rather synonymous with web services. The major platform vendors, such as Sun, IBM, Microsoft, BEA (now Oracle), and JBoss, developed tools that greatly facilitated the creation of SOAP-based web services. Companies began to eagerly undertake proof-of-concept initiatives to scope out the level of effort required to participate in this new paradigm. Web commerce vendors were some of the earliest proponents of exposing their API through SOAP, with eBay and Amazon.com leading the way (more than 240,000 people have participated in Amazon Web Services). Software as a Service (SaaS) vendors such as Salesforce emerged that greatly leveraged on the promise of web services. Indeed, Salesforce became the epitome of what the next generation of software was touted to become.

Within organizations, the challenge of exposing core business functionality as web services turned out to be daunting. Simply exposing existing objects and methods as web services often proved ill advised—to do so simply embraces the RPC model of distributed computing, not the SOA principles of loosely coupled, autonomous services. Instead, façade patterns or wrappers were often devised to create the desired web services. This approach often entailed writing significant amounts of new code, which contrasted with the heady promises made by vendors. The challenges were compounded by the vast number of choices that were available, even within a particular language environment. In the Java world alone, there were a bewildering number of choices for creating web services: Apache Axis (and Axis 2); Java-WS; Spring-WS, JBossWS, and CXF (previously known as XFire)—and these are just the open source products! Knowing which technology to use alone required significant investment.

Other factors also served to dampen the interest in SOAP web services. The perceived complexity of the various WS-* standards led to a movement to simply use XML-over-HTTP, as is the basis for Representational State Transfer (REST)-based web services (for more on this raging controversy between REST and SOAP, see [RESTvs-SOAP]). The nomenclature found in the WSDL specification, such as port types and bindings, is alien to many developers and strikes them as overly convoluted, especially for simple services (in the WSDL 2.0 standard, some of this arcane nomenclature has been removed, for instance, replacing *port type* with *interface* and *port* with *endpoint*, which is a big improvement, especially for Java and C# developers who are already familiar with such terms and their meaning). Interestingly enough, some convergence between REST and SOAP is taking place, such as the acknowledgment among some REST advocates that the metadata description capabilities of a WSDL are important. Towards this end, REST advocates have devised a new metadata specification for REST-based web services called the Web Application Description Language (WADL) [WADL]. While I may sometimes appear to be a bigot of SOAP, that's primarily because of the metadata features of WSDL, and REST coupled with WADL creates a compelling alternative.

The early enthusiasm for SOAP-based web services as the springboard for SOA began to wane as alternatives such as Web-Oriented Architecture (WOA) began to emerge, which promises a simpler, non-SOAP-based SOA architecture (see [Hinchcliffe]). Truth be told, there's likely room for both, with large enterprises opting for the WS-* stack due to its well-defined interface support, security, and reliable messaging provisions.

1.3 Understanding the core characteristics of SOA

As it turns out, achieving SOA requires more than SOAP-based web services. The characteristics of SOA transcend a particular technology. SOA is an amalgamation of technologies, patterns, and practices, the most important of which I'll address in this section.

1.3.1 Service interface/contract

Services must have a well-defined interface or contract. A contract is the complete specification of a service between a service provider and a specific consumer. It should also exist in a form that's readily digestible by possible clients. This contract should identify what operations are available through the service, define the data requirements for any exchanged information, and detail how the service can be invoked. A good example of how such a contract can be crafted can be found in a WSDL. Apart from describing which operations are available through a given network "endpoint," it also incorporates XML Schema support to describe the XML message format for each of the service operations. Figure 1.2 illustrates the relationship between WSDL and XML Schema.

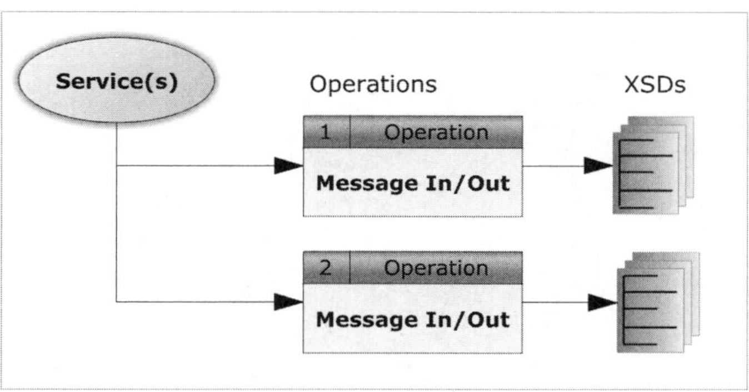

Figure 1.2 WSDL usage of XML Schema for defining the specification of an operation

Multiple operations can be defined, each of which can have its own schema definition associated with it. While the WSDL nomenclature can be confusing (particularly the 1.1 specification, with its rather arcane concepts of ports and bindings), it has, arguably, been the most successful means for defining what constitutes an interface and contract for a service. Commercial vendors, in particular, have created advanced tooling within their platforms that can parse and introspect WSDLs for code generation and service mapping. The WSDL 2.0 specification is intended to simplify the learning curve and further advance its adoption.

One of the early criticisms of the WSDL specification was that the specific service endpoint was "hardwired" into the specification. This limitation was largely addressed in the WS-Addressing standard, which has achieved widespread adoption. It supports dynamic endpoint addressing by including the addressing information within the body of the SOAP XML message, and not "outside" of it within the `SOAPAction` HTTP header. The endpoint reference contained with the WS-Addressing block could also be a logical network location, not a physical one. This enables more complex load-balancing and clustering topologies to be supported. We'll explore the issue of why such "service transparency" is beneficial next.

1.3.2 Service transparency

Service transparency pertains to the ability to call a service without specific awareness of its physical endpoint within the network. The perils of using direct physical endpoints can be found in recent history. Nearly all enterprise systems began offering significant API support for their products by the mid-1990s. This trend allowed clients to begin tapping into the functionality and business rules of the systems relatively easily. One of the most immediate, and undesirable, consequences of doing this was the introduction of point-to-point interfaces. Before long, you began seeing connectivity maps that resemble figure 1.3.

An environment punctuated by such point-to-point connections quickly becomes untenable to maintain and extremely brittle. By making a change in something as simple as the endpoint connection string or URI, you can break a number of applications,

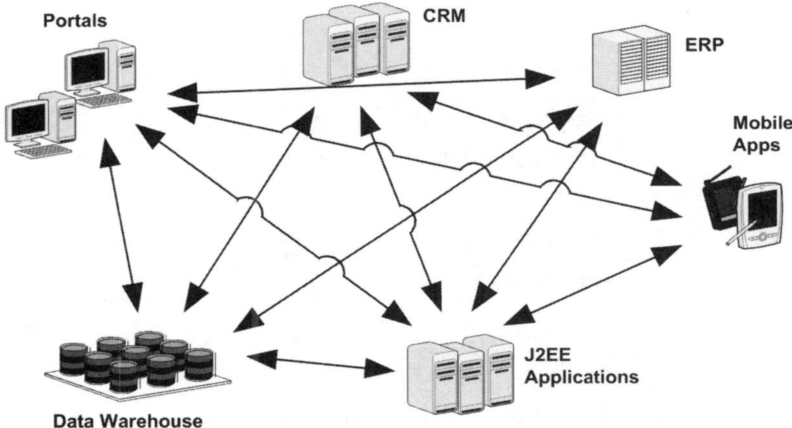

Figure 1.3 Example of how point-to-point connections greatly complicate service integration

perhaps even unknowingly. For example, in figure 1.3 imagine if the CRM system's network address changed—a multitude of other apps would immediately break.

An enterprise service bus (ESB) is often touted as the savior for avoiding the proliferation of such point-to-point connections, since its messaging bus can act as a conduit for channeling messages to the appropriate endpoint location. It no doubt performs such functionality admirably, but the same thing can be accomplished through a simple service mediator or proxy. The scenario depicted in figure 1.3 could then be transformed to the one shown in figure 1.4.

Obviously, figure 1.4 is an improvement over figure 1.3. No longer does the client application or API user have to explicitly identify the specific endpoint location for a given service call. Instead, all service calls are directed to the proxy or gateway, which, in turn, forwards the message to the appropriate endpoint destination. If an endpoint address then changes, only the proxy configuration will be required to be changed.

The WS-Addressing specification, one of the earliest and most well-supported of the WS-* standards, defines an in-message means for defining the desired endpoint or action for SOAP-based web services. It is significant in that, without it, only the transport protocol (typically HTTP) contains the routing rules (it's worth noting that SOAP supports more transports than just HTTP, such as JMS). WS-Addressing supports the use of logical message destinations, which would leave the actual physical destination to be determined by a service mediator (to learn more about WS-Addressing, see the [WSAddressing] reference in the Resources section at the end of this book).

Until fairly recently, no true open source web service proxy solution was available. However, Apache Synapse, although sometimes positioned as an ESB, is designed largely with this capability in mind. It supports outstanding proxy capabilities and can also serve as a protocol switcher. For instance, Synapse can be easily configured to receive a SOAP HTTP message and deposit it for internal consumption by a Java JMS queue. Synapse will be covered in depth in upcoming chapters.

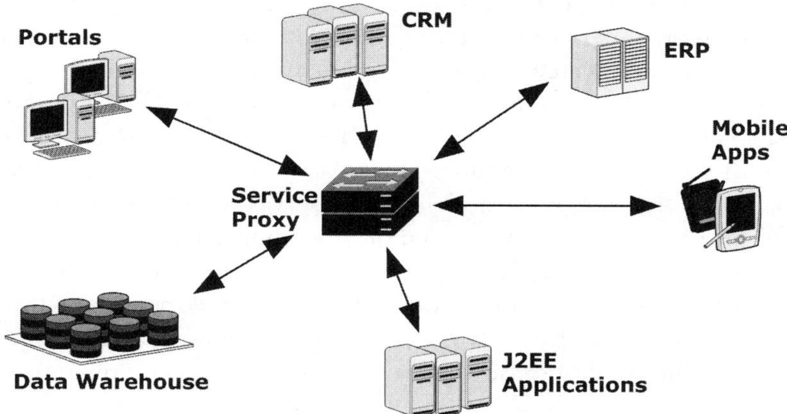

Figure 1.4 Example of mediator or proxy-based service endpoint environment

1.3.3 Service loose coupling and statelessness

Simply exposing a service as a SOAP-based web service, defined by a WSDL, does not, by itself, constitute service enablement. A key consideration is also whether the service is sufficiently self-contained so that it could be considered stand-alone. This factor is sometimes referred to as the level of "service coupling." For example, let's assume that we want to create a new service to add a new customer to your company's CRM system. If in order to use the service you must include CRM-specific identifiers such as `OrganizationId`, you have now predicated the use of that service on having a prior understanding of the internals of the CRM. This can greatly complicate the use of the service by potential consumers and may limit its audience potential. In this case, it would be preferable to create a composite service that performs the `OrganizationId` lookup first, and then performs the call to insert the new customer.

Related to this issue is granularity, which refers to the scope of functionality addressed by the service. For instance, a *fine-grained* service may resemble something like *addCustomerAddress*, whereas a *coarse-grained* service is more akin to *addCustomer.* The preponderance of literature advocates the use of coarse-grained services, in part for performance reasons as well as convenience. If the objective is to add a new customer to your CRM system, calling a single service with a large XML payload is obviously preferable to having to chain together a multitude of lower-level service calls. That said, maximizing reusability may sometimes warrant the construction of finer-grained services. In our example, having the ability to *addCustomerAddress* can be used in a variety of cases, not limited to just creating a new customer. Indeed, composite services that are coarser grained in function can then be crafted based on the lower-level services.

Finally, if possible, a service should be *stateless.* What would be an example of a *stateful* service? Imagine a service that includes a *validation* operation that first must be called prior to the actual action operation. If successful, the validation call would return a unique identifier. The action operation would then require that validation ID as its input. In this scenario, the data input from the validation call would be stored in a session state awaiting a subsequent call to perform the desired activity. While this solution avoids forcing the client user to resubmit the complete data set twice (one for the operation, the other for the action), it introduces additional complexity for the service designer (though various service implementations, both open source and proprietary, do attempt to simplify building stateful services). In particular, scalability can be adversely impacted, as the application server must preserve session state and manage the expiration of unused sessions. Performance management is complicated if appliance-based load balancing is being used, as it must pin the session calls to specific application servers (software clustering can overcome this, but it introduces its own challenges).

In the previous scenario, *statefulness* can be avoided by requiring the client to again send all relevant data when making the action call, along with the validation ID retrieved from the validation call. The validation ID would be persisted in a database and provided a timestamp. The action call would have to take place within a given number of minutes before the validation ID became invalidated.

1.3.4 Service composition

One of the main objectives of a SOA is the ability to generate composite services and/or orchestrations using service components as the building blocks. A *composable service* is largely a function of how well it is designed to participate in such a role. As was illustrated in figure 1.1, there are two general types of composite services. The first type, which could be classified as *simple* or *primitive*, simply wraps one or more lower-level services together into a more coarse-grained operation. This process can usually be accomplished by defining a simple data flow that stitches together services and then exposes the new functionality as a new service. Another goal may be to simply impose a new service contract for an existing service while leaving the underlying target endpoint unchanged. In any case, the underlying service or services participating in the simple composition must adhere to these attributes we've already addressed (and some of which will follow). They include a well-defined service contract; stateless in design, loosely coupled, and offer high availability. A composite service should be no different, and should be treated like any other service, as shown in figure 1.5.

The second type of composite services is the *complex* or workflow-type business processes, often referred to as business process management (BPM). These processes are generally multistep creations that may optionally include long-running transactions. The WS-BPEL (Business Process Execution Language) set of standards defines an XML-based language for describing a sequence flow of activities, or process. Within a process definition, a rich set of nodes can be used for routing, event handling, exception management (compensation), and flow control. The core WS-BPEL standard is tailored for working with SOAP-based web services. Because of this orientation, the

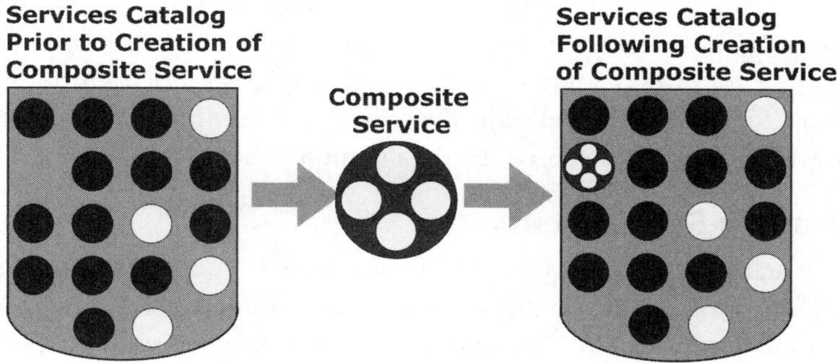

Figure 1.5 A composite service is added to an existing catalog of services.

entry point for invoking a WS-BPEL process is most typically a SOAP web service (other possibilities may include a timer service, for example). This can be either a blessing or a curse, depending on whether SOAP services are a standard within your environment.

How does a composite service author have visibility into which services are available for use when constructing such processes? This is the role of the service registry, which we'll cover next.

1.3.5 Service registry and publication

Unlike in the movie *Field of Dreams*, "if you build it, they will come" doesn't apply to services. Clients must be aware of the existence of a service if they're expected to use it. Not only that, services must include a specification or contract that clearly identifies input, outputs, faults, and available operations. The web services WSDL specification is the closest and most well-adopted solution for service reflection. The Universal Description, Discovery, and Integration (UDDI) standard was intended as a platform-independent registry for web services. UDDI can be used as both a private or public registry. Further, using the UDDI API, a client could theoretically, at least, "discover" services and bind to them. Unfortunately, UDDI suffered from an arcane and complex nomenclature, and its dynamic discovery features were myopic and predicated on naive assumptions. Today, relatively few enterprise customers are using UDDI and fewer still public registries. In practice, UDDI is rarely used today, except behind the scenes in a handful of commercial products where its complexity can be shielded from the user. Unfortunately, no standards-based alternative to UDDI is in sight.

The failure of UDDI doesn't obviate the need for a registry, and most companies have instead devised a variety of alternatives. For SOAP-based web services, a comprehensive WSDL can often be adequate. It can list all the available services and operations. Others have used simple database or Lightweight Directory Access Protocol (LDAP) applications to capture service registry information. Simply storing a catalog of services and their descriptions and endpoints in a wiki may suffice for many companies. Recently, there has also been an emergence of new open source registry solutions, such as MuleSource's Galaxy and WSO2's Registry, which attempt to fill this void; we'll discuss these solutions in the next chapter.

Now that we've identified some of the core characteristics of SOA, let's turn our attention to how those higher-level objectives can be decomposed into specific technologies that, when combined, can comprise a complete SOA technology platform.

1.4 Technologies of a SOA platform

As pointed out earlier, it's a mistake to assume that SOA is all about technology choices. Issues like governance, quality of service, and so forth are all major contributors to crafting a complete SOA. That said, our intention is to focus on the technical aspects, as the other areas largely fall outside the scope of this book. Figure 1.6 depicts the various technologies that constitute a SOA technology platform, which, moving forward, I will refer to as the Open SOA Platform. We'll explore each in greater detail along with an explanation of how the technologies tie together.

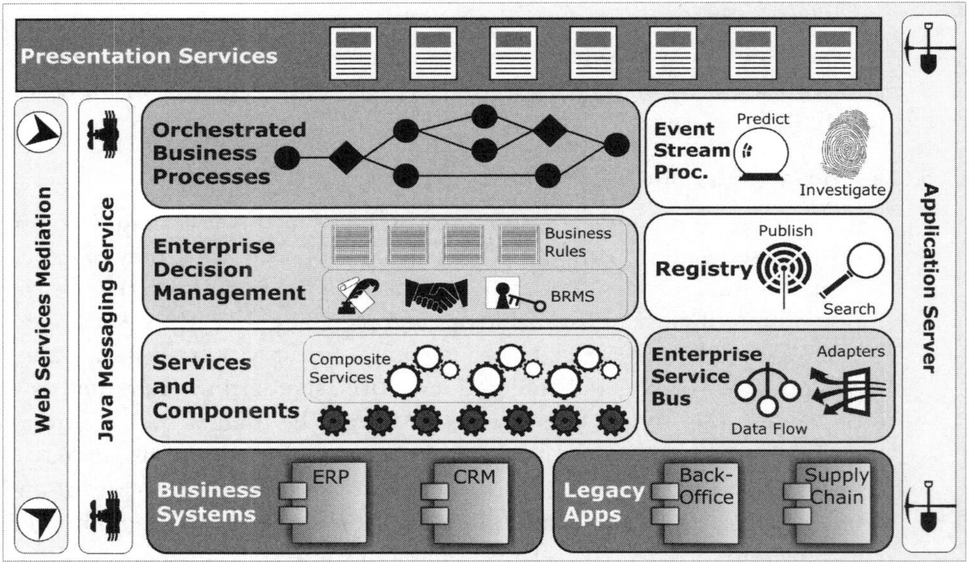

Figure 1.6 SOA technology platform. In chapter 2, we begin identifying applicable technologies for many of these areas.

1.4.1 Business process management

Business process management (BPM) is a set of technologies that enables a company to build, usually through visual flow steps, executable processes that span across multiple organizations or systems. In the past, such systems were less elegantly referred to as workflow processing engines. The promise of BPM, as optimistically stated by Howard

Where are the applications?

In looking at figure 1.6, you may be wondering, "Where are the applications?" The presentation layer can be considered your typical application, but with such a variety of different delivery models (mobile, web, gadgets, hybrids like Adobe AIR, RSS feeds, and so forth), the very notion of what constitutes an application is changing. Hence, we use "Presentation Services," which represent anything that can be considered an interface to computing services.

Smith and Peter Finger is that, "BPM doesn't speed up applications development; it eliminates the need for it" [SmithFinger]. This is because business applications, in this historical context, create stovepipes that are separated by function, time, and the data they use. The *process* in BPM refers to a holistic view of the enterprise, which incorporates employees, partners, customers, systems, applications, and databases. This also serves to extract the full value of these existing assets in ways never before possible.

Many consider BPM to be the "secret sauce" of SOA, insofar as the benefit it provides to companies that adopt it. In the book *The New Age of Innovation*, the authors identify business processes as the "key enablers of an innovation culture" [Prahalad]. To be competitive in a dynamic marketplace, business processes must change at a rapid pace, and this can only be achieved through BPM systems that enable defining, visualizing, and deploying such processes.

For a system to participate in a BPM process, services or functionality must be made externally accessible. For this reason, SOA is often considered a prerequisite for BPM, since SOA is fundamentally about exposing services in a way that enables them to participate in higher-level collaborations. Theoretically at least, BPM allows business users to design applications using a Lego-like approach, piecing together software services one-upon-another to build a new higher-level solution. In reality, it's obviously not quite so simple, but skilled business analysts can use the visual design and simulation tools for rapid prototyping. These design primitives can also be highly effective at conveying system requirements.

The fundamental impetus behind BPM is *cost savings* and *improved business agility*. As TIBCO founder Vivek Ranadivé notes, "The goal of BPM is to improve an organization's business processes by making them more efficient, more effective and more capable of adapting to an ever-changing environment" [Ranadivé]. Integrating many disparate systems and linking individuals across organizational boundaries into coherent processes can naturally result in significant return on investment (ROI). A useful byproduct of such efforts is improved reporting and management visibility. Agility, or the ability of a company to quickly react to changes in the marketplace, is improved by enabling new business processes to be created quickly, using existing investments in technology.

1.4.2 Enterprise decision management

An enterprise decision management (EDM) system incorporates a business rule engine (BRE) for executing defined business rules and a Business Rule Management

System (BRMS) for managing the rules. What exactly is a business rule? It is a statement, written in a manner easily digestible by those within the business, which makes an assertion about some aspect of how the business should function. For example, a company's policy for when to extend credit is based on certain business rules, such as whether the client has a Dun & Bradstreet number and has been in business for *x* number of years. Such rules permeate most historical applications, where literally thousands of them may be defined within the application code. Unfortunately, when they are within application code, modifying the rules to reflect changing business requirements is costly and time consuming.

A rules-based system, or BRMS, attempts to cleanly separate such rules from program code. The rules can then be expressed in a language the business user can understand and easily modify without having to resort to application development changes. This also serves to make business rules an "enterprise asset" that represents the very lifeblood of an organization. Figure 1.7 illustrates how a centralized decision service can be used by services and applications.

One of the biggest challenges when building applications is bridging the knowledge gap that exists between the subject matter experts (SMEs) who have an intimate understanding of the business, and the developers who often possess only a cursory awareness (and sometimes desire no more than that). Developers are faced with translating business requirements into abstract representations in code. This gap is often responsible for the disappointing results that too often surround the rollout of new applications. As Taylor and Raden note, "Embedding business expertise in the system is hard because those who understand the business can't code, and those who understand the code don't run the business" [TaylorRaden].

What differentiates a BRMS from an EDM? To be honest, it's probably mostly semantics, but EDM does emphasize centralized management of *all* business rules, including those considered operational, which may range in the thousands for a given company. According to Taylor and Raden, this includes heretofore "hidden" decisions that permeate a company, such as product pricing for a particular customer, or whether a customer can return a given product.

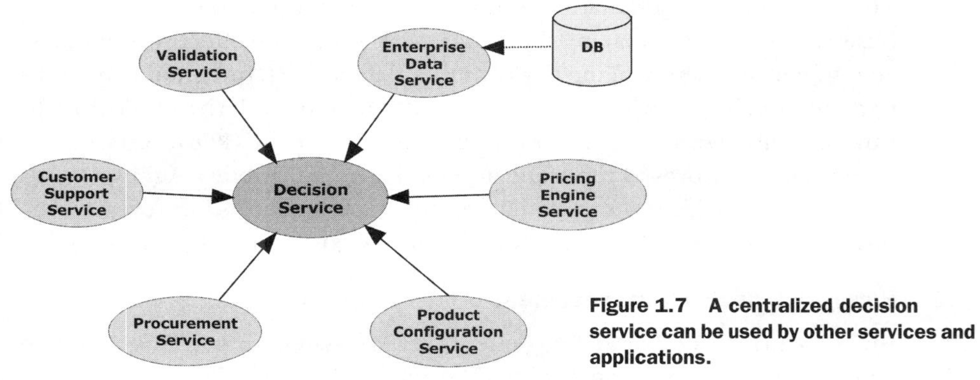

Figure 1.7 A centralized decision service can be used by other services and applications.

In chapters 11 and 12 we cover EDM in more detail, and describe how the use of domain-specific languages (DSLs) can be used to create business-specific, natural language representations of rules most suitable for maintenance by SMEs.

1.4.3 Enterprise service bus

An enterprise service bus (ESB) is at its core a "middleware" application whose role is to provide interoperability between different communication protocols. For example, it's not uncommon for a company to receive incoming ASCII-delimited orders through older protocols such as FTP. An ESB can "lift" that order from the FTP site, transform it into XML, and then submit internally to a web service for consumption and processing. Although this can all be done manually, an ESB offers out-of-the-box adapters for such processing, and most commonly, event-flow visual modeling tools to generate chained *microflows*. The cost savings over conventional code techniques is often substantial.

How does such a microflow (or what could be alternatively called a *real-time data flow*) differ from a BPM-type application? After all, at first glance they may appear similar. One key distinction is that BPM applications are typically designed for support of long-running transactions and use a central orchestration engine to manage how the process flow occurs. A real-time data flow, however, typically uses a model more akin to what's known as choreography. In a choreographed flow, each node (or hop) encapsulates the logic of what step to perform next. In addition, a real-time data flow typically passes data by way of message queues, and thus there's a single running instance of the process, with queues corresponding to each node that consume those messages. A BPM, on the other hand, typically instantiates a separate process instance for each new inbound message. This is because, as a potentially long-running transaction, the sequential queuing method would not be appropriate. To keep the number of running processes to a reasonable number, a BPM engine will "hydrate" or "dehydrate" the process to and from running memory to a serialized form, which can then be stored in a database.

Table 1.1 describes a typical set of services provided in an ESB. Because of the number of services provided by an ESB, it sometimes is described as a "backplane" or central nervous system that ties together the various SOA technologies.

Table 1.1 Core ESB features and capabilities

Feature	Description
Data Connectivity/Adapters	HTTP (SOAP, XML), FTP, SFTP, File, and JMS connectivity.
Data Transformation	XSLT for XML-based transformations.
Intelligent Routing	Content-based routing based on message properties or inline XML via XPath. Some include additional, more advanced rule-based routing using a rules engine.

Table 1.1 Core ESB features and capabilities *(continued)*

Feature	Description
Service Management	Administrative tools for managing deployments, versioning, and system configuration.
Monitoring & Logging	The ability to monitor, in real time, document and message flows. Beneficial is the capability to put inline interceptors between nodes and specifically target individual nodes for more verbose logging.
Data-flow Choreography	The ability to visually (or through editing declarative XML files) create graphs or chains to describe a sequence of steps necessary to complete a data flow.
Custom API	The ability to add custom adapters or components to the ESB.
Timing Services	The ability to create time-based actions or triggers.

Figure 1.8 depicts the role that an ESB plays in integrating various protocols and how they can be exposed through a standard messaging bus.

The flexibility of an ESB to tap into a variety of communication protocols lends some merit to an ESB-centric architecture. However, if an organization can successfully expose its business services as web services, the central role that an ESB plays is diminished (in any case, it certainly has a role in a SOA technology stack).

Let's now turn our attention to how analytical information can be drawn by the messages that flow through an ESB.

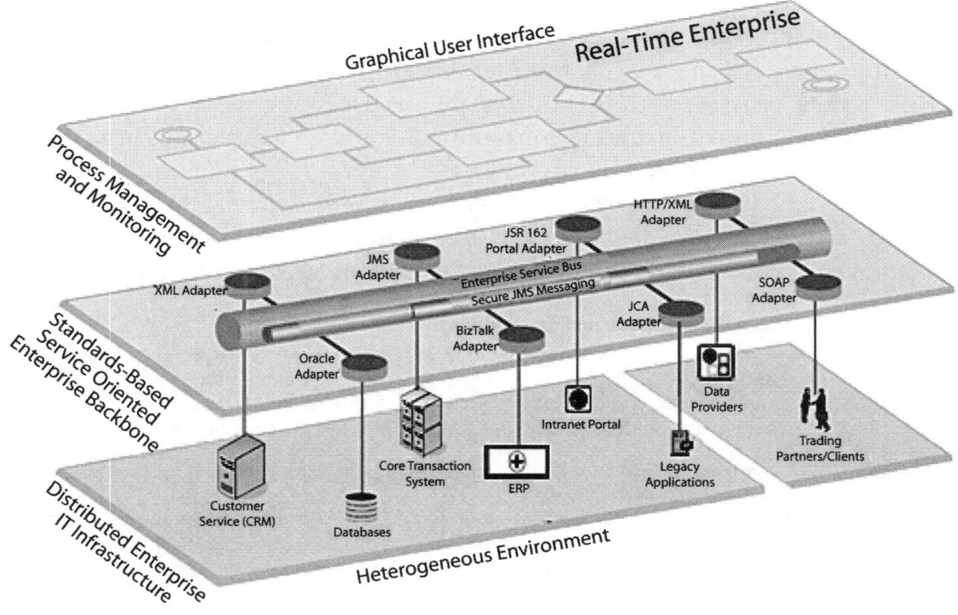

Figure 1.8 Example of an ESB-centric approach for enterprise architecture

1.4.4 Event stream processor

An *event* is simply something of interest that happens within your business. It may be expected and normal, or abnormal. An event that doesn't occur may have as much importance as those that do. Too many events may also indicate a problem. Why is it relevant to SOA? Event stream processing (ESP) support can be integrated into the implementation of your services so that real-time visibility into systems becomes a reality. This operational intelligence arms your enterprise with the ability to quickly spot anomalies and respond accordingly. Adding such capabilities into legacy solutions is often not feasible, and instead you must rely on data warehouse and business intelligence tools, neither of which provides real-time visibility.

Event stream processing is considered part of a relatively new technology sometimes referred to as complex event processing (CEP). TIBCO's Ranadivé defines it as

> *...an innovative technology that pulls together real-time information from multiple databases, applications and message-based systems and then analyzes this information to discern patterns and trends that might otherwise go unnoticed. CEP gives companies the ability to identify and anticipate exceptions and opportunities buried in seemingly unrelated events. [Ranadivé]*

The role of an ESP is to receive multiple streams of real-time data and to, in turn, detect patterns among the events. A variety of filters, time-based aggregations, triggers, and joins are typically used by the ESP to assist in pattern detection. The interpreted results from the ESP can then be fed into business activity monitoring (BAM) dashboards.

In *Performance Dashboards*, Wayne Eckerson identifies three types of business intelligence dashboards: operational, tactical, and strategic [Eckerson]. *Operational dashboards* generate alerts that notify users about exception conditions. They may also utilize statistical models for predictive forecasting. *Tactical dashboards* provide high-level summary information along with modeling tools. *Strategic dashboards*, as the name implies, are primarily used by executives to ensure company objectives are being met. Operational dashboards rely on the data that event stream processors generate. As the saying goes, you can't drive forward while looking in your rearview mirror. For a business to thrive in today's competitive landscape, real-time analysis is essential. This provides a company with the ability to immediately spot cost savings opportunities, such as sudden drops in critical raw materials; proactively identify problem areas, such as a slowdown in web orders due to capacity issues; and unleash new product offerings.

An event architecture strategy must be part of any SOA solution and must be designed from the get-go to be effective. Bolting on such capabilities later can result in expensive reengineering of code and services. Service components and backbone technologies (such as the ESB) should be propagating notable events. While a process may not be immediately in place to digest them, adding such capabilities later can be easily introduced by adding new Event Query Language (EQL) expressions into the ESP engine. We'll examine EQL in more detail in chapter 8.

The messages that carry event data that flow into an ESP are, within a Java environment, most likely to arrive by way of the Java Message Service (JMS), which is addressed next.

1.4.5 Java Message Service

The Java Message Service is one of the fundamental technologies associated with the Java Platform Enterprise Edition. It is considered message-oriented middleware (MOM) and supports two types of message models: (1) the point-to-point queuing model, and (2) the publish and subscribe model. The queuing model, which is probably used most frequently, enables a broadcaster to publish a message to a specific queue, whereby it can then be consumed by a given client. It is considered point-to-point because once the message is consumed by a client, it is no longer available to other clients. In the publish/subscribe model, events are published to one or more interested listeners, or observers. This model is analogous to broadcast television or radio, where a publisher (station) is sending out its signal to one or more subscribers (listeners).

JMS typically is ideally suited for asynchronous communications, where a "fire-and-forget" paradigm can be used. This contrasts with SOAP-based web services, which follow a request/response type model (this isn't a concrete distinction—there are variations of JMS and SOAP that support more than one model—but a generalization). JMS is typically used as one of the enabling technologies within an ESB and is usually included within such products.

Since JMS is rather ubiquitous in the Java world and well documented through books and articles, I won't cover it directly in this book. It is, however, a critical technology for Java-based SOA environments. Let's now address an often-overlooked but critical technology for building a SOA platform: a registry.

1.4.6 Registry

The implementation artifacts that derive from a SOA should be registered within a repository to maximize reuse and provide for management of enterprise assets. Metadata refers to data about data, so in this context, it refers to the properties and attributes of these assets. Assets, as shown in figure 1.9, include service components and composites, business process/orchestrations, and applications. It may also include typical LDAP objects such as users, customers, and products.

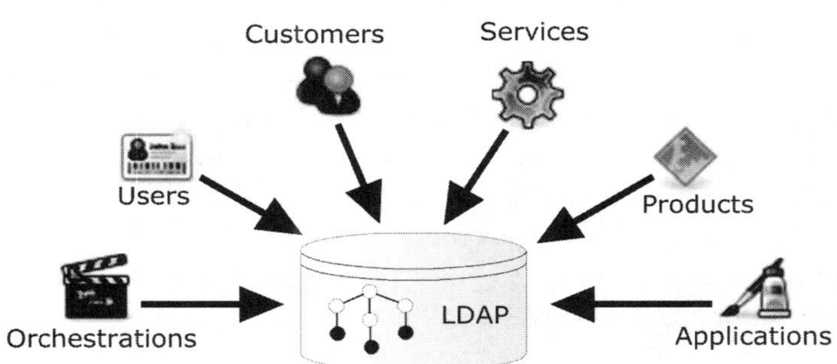

Figure 1.9 Example of an LDAP repository used as a registry. Notice that it's not just used for users, but also for products and even applications.

For smaller organizations, more informal repositories may be utilized and could be as simple as wiki articles or a simple database that describes the various assets. As organizations grow in size, however, having an appropriate technology like LDAP simplifies management and assists in reporting, governance, and security profiling. It's important to treat the SOA artifacts as true corporate assets—this represents highly valuable intellectual property, after all.

The metadata attributes for a given asset type will vary, so a flexible repository schema is essential. For example, a service component's attributes include the following:

- Service endpoint (WS-Addressing)
- Service description
- WSDL location
- Revision/version number
- Source code location
- Example request/response messages
- Reference to functional and design documents
- Change requests
- Readme files
- Production release records

Orchestrations and application may share a similar, if expanded, set of attributes, whereas those relating to a user will obviously vary significantly. A bonus chapter available at http://www.manning.com/davis includes coverage of registries.

We're nearly completed with our whirlwind overview of critical SOA technologies. One essential technology, indeed a cornerstone of SOA, is addressed next: services.

1.4.7 Service components and compositions

Service components and composites represent the core building blocks for what constitutes a SOA platform. A service can be construed as an intelligent business function that combines data and logic to form an abstract interaction with an underlying business service. This service is often a discrete piece of functionality that represents a capability found within an existing application. An example of such a service might be a customer address lookup using information found within a CRM system. The service component, in this instance, "wraps" CRM API calls so that it can be called from a variety of clients using just a customer name as the service input. If the CRM API had to be called directly, a multistep process of (a) first identifying the `customerId` based on the customer name, (b) performing code-list lookups for finding coded values, and (c) using the `customerId` to then call a `getAddress` operation may be necessary. The service component abstracts the methods and objects of the CRM into generic methods or objects and makes the underlying details transparent to the calling client. An illustration of such a service façade or wrapper is shown in figure 1.10.

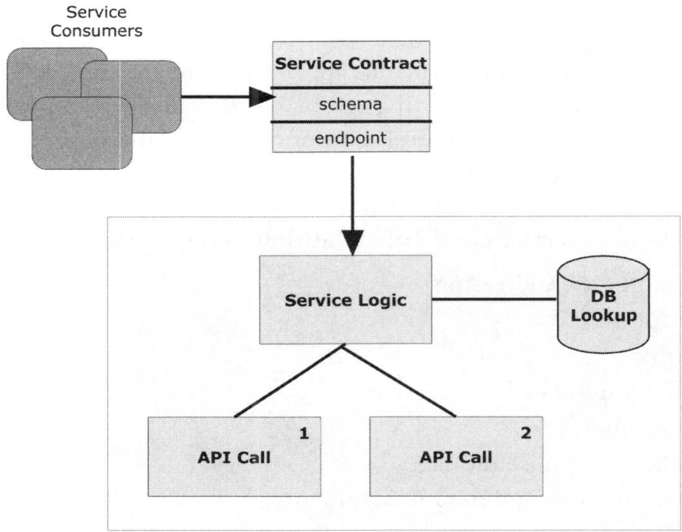

Figure 1.10 Using a façade/wrapper pattern for exposing service functionality

A service must support two fundamental requirements: a well-defined interface and binding. The interface is the contract that defines the service specification and is represented as a WSDL for SOAP-based web services. The binding is the communications protocol for how the client will interact with the service. Examples of such protocols are SOAP over HTTP; JMS; Java RMI (RMI); and EJB. Using a combination of those two requirements, a developer who wants to create a client that uses a service should be able to do so. Of course, how well the interface is designed will dictate how truly useful the service is.

A composite service, as the name suggests, is created by combining the functionality of one or more individual components. Composites may serve to further abstract functionality and are often considered coarse-grained services (such as a service to create a new customer). A composite service, in turn, may then be combined with other services to create even higher level composites. In any event, composites share the same requirements as components—an interface and binding.

Thomas Erl classifies compositions into two distinct types: primitive and complex [Erl2007]. A *primitive* type might be used for simple purposes such as content filtering or routing and usually involves two or three individual components. A *complex* composition could be a BPEL-based service that contains multiple nodes or sequence steps. Chapters 3 and 4 provides in-depth coverage of service components and composites.

Regardless of what protocol and standards your services use, there will likely be scenarios, particularly when integrating with outside organizations, that deviate from your best laid plans. One way to bridge such differences, and to improve service availability and performance, is through web service mediation technology—the topic of the next section.

1.4.8 Web service mediation

Mediation refers to bridging the differences between two parties. Consistent with that definition, web service mediation (WSM) refers to bridging between different communications protocols, with the result being a SOAP-based web service that can be redirected to an appropriate endpoint. For example, a web mediation engine might be used to process authenticating the credentials of inbound calls from an external partner's SOAP message using WS-Security (WSS). If approved, the message can then be forwarded, minus the WS-Security heading, to an internal web service to process the request. Or, perhaps a partner is unwilling or unable to use SOAP, and instead prefers a REST (XML over HTTP) solution. Using a mediator, the inbound REST call can be easily transformed into SOAP by adding the appropriate envelope. Even transformations between entirely different protocols, such as FTP to SOAP, are typically possible. Figure 1.11 depicts the role of the mediator.

A mediator serves other purposes as well, such as logging of all requests and responses, internal load balancing, advanced caching, and support of advanced WS-* features such as WS-ReliableMessaging. Another important feature is the ability to act as a proxy server. This allows the WSM to transparently intercept outbound messages, log them, and apply a WS-Security envelope, for example. The publisher of the originating message can let such policies be applied externally in a consistent fashion and not have to worry about implementing such complex details. Compliance and security can be managed independently of the application—a major benefit.

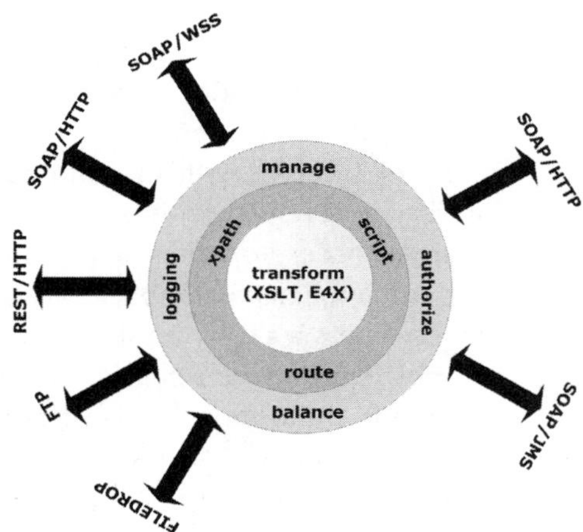

Figure 1.11 The role of web services mediator in bridging between protocols

Many of the web mediation capabilities we've talked about can now be found in modern-day ESBs. In fact, as you'll see moving forward, the ESB we've selected from the Open SOA Platform can perform both conventional ESB duties as well as the mediation features we've identified.

Does implementing SOA require all of the technologies we've alluded to in this section? Of course, the answer is no. In large part, it depends on your particular needs and requirements, so let's explore this further.

1.5 Introducing a SOA maturity model

A maturity model can be useful when you're analyzing the readiness of an IT organization in embracing the various levels of SOA that can be achieved. Figure 1.12

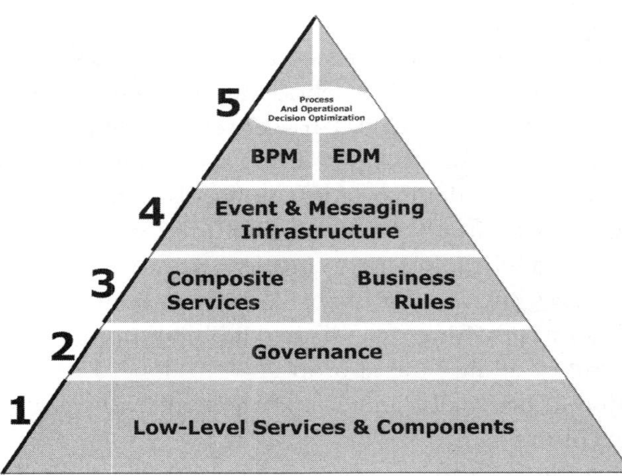

Figure 1.12 SOA maturity model. Not all levels are required for every environment

depicts such a model, and as the pyramid suggests, each stage, at least in part, depends on the former.

Level 1 begins with the foundation of services and related components. Moving forward to level 2 requires a governance program to ensure that these services are consistently developed using a common framework, along with associated security policies and a means for publication (i.e., think registry). After all, a service isn't really a service unless it's discoverable and reusable. The next tier, level 3, is where significant benefits begin to be realized. With a governance program in place, it now becomes possible to build more coarse-grained, composite services, whose audience may span beyond just the technical team. Business "power users" may begin consuming the services by using simple, end-user integration products like Jitterbit (http://www.jitterbit.com), OpenSpan (http://www.openspan.com), or Talend (http://www.talend.com). While using a business rule engine may make sense at any level, it often becomes a requirement when composite services become introduced, which is why it's also shown in level 3. This is because composite services often require business rule logic to determine how to logically combine lower-level services.

Similar to business rules, a message- and event-driven architectural orientation can be introduced earlier in the pyramid—it's a requirement for those aspiring to level 5. The ability to monitor, in real time, events that occur within your enterprise is essential for optimizing business processes and operational decisions. This capability represents level 4, and without it, decisions and processes are optimized in a vacuum and may not accurately reflect either the business bottom line or relevant trends.

This brings us to level 5, which is where BPM and EDM can really flourish. Although you can attempt to introduce these technologies lower in the maturity model, both benefit immensely by having the prior layers in place. BPM almost always requires the ability to tightly integrate with applications, data, and business rules, and when these assets are exposed as services using SOA principles, implementing BPM is greatly simplified. Centrally managing business rules through EDM exposes business rule assets to a wider audience of business users, who are best positioned to align them to the dynamic changes of the marketplace, which can detect more accurately when events can be assessed in real time through complex event processing (CEP) filters.

For those just undertaking their first SOA projects, attempting to embrace all of the technologies we talk about in this book may seem overly ambitious. By treating SOA as a journey, you begin benefiting quickly as you build reusable services and marry them with the introduction of a business rule engine. Since SOA isn't just about technology but also process, wrapping a governance layer is essential but not difficult (it just requires some discipline). Once these pieces are in place, you can decide whether you want to move further up the pyramid. If you achieve layer 5 on an enterprise basis, the benefits through tighter alignment between IT and business will make your organization much more agile, productive, and frankly, a more fun place to work!

1.6 Summary

In this chapter, we covered the historical origins of SOA, dating back from its roots in earlier distributed computing architectures. The emergence of SOAP-based web services is a critical enabler for a SOA, but it turns out that it's only one, albeit critical, part. Simply "exposing" an application's operations as a web service provides little more than earlier RPC-based models. Instead, a deeper dive into what constitutes SOA revealed five main technologies and principles that are the bedrock of a SOA environment: service interfaces; service transparency; service loose-coupling and statelessness; service composition; and service registry and publication. With that broad understanding of what constitutes a SOA, we then focused on the technical requirements to form the Open SOA Platform. Nine specific technologies were identified that were essential platform building blocks: application server; business process management; enterprise decision management; enterprise service bus; event stream processing; Java Message Service; metadata repository; service composition and composites; and web service mediation.

Until recently, there hasn't been a robust and complete set of open source technologies that addressed each of these nine areas. Instead, only the commercial vendors, with their deeper pockets and pricy products, appeared able to provide a comprehensive SOA environment. That has changed. Compelling open source solutions now exist for each of those eight technologies, and the next chapter provides an overview of them. Following that, we revisit these eight core technologies individually, with substantive examples provided so that you can implement your comprehensive open source SOA platform. The benefits of SOA are no longer limited to big companies with big budgets. Instead, even the smallest of enterprises can participate in this exciting new paradigm by enjoying the fruits of dedicated, and very bright, open source developers. In chapter 2 we assess the open source landscape for the SOA technology platform and identify those that will be focus for the remainder of the book.

2 Defining the Open SOA Platform

> ***This chapter covers***
> - Evaluating open source products
> - Selecting the products

In chapter 1 we explored some of the history behind SOA, and then we examined the key technology underpinnings of a SOA environment. Now we'll focus on identifying a suitable open source product for each of these technology areas. Collectively they'll comprise what we're calling the *Open SOA Platform.*

The open source community includes many early advocates of the recent wave of emerging SOA-related technology projects. Historically, open source has sometimes been considered a "late-follower," with commercial products first to hit the market, and then followed by "me-too" open source alternatives. One reason often cited by critics of open source is that open source projects are often not innovators but imitators (of course, some might argue Microsoft has done very well by following the imitation model). There may be some truth to that criticism, but many of the products we'll be examining are innovative and cutting edge. In some instances, the reason development has lagged vis-à-vis commercial offerings is simply because of resource challenges—open source projects are often supported and staffed by a small team of developers, many of whom have full-time responsibilities elsewhere.

Overall, it did take some time before a comprehensive collection of open source projects achieved sufficient breadth and maturity to offer a compelling alternative to the highly priced commercial alternatives. Now, you can choose among many options for crafting an entirely open source SOA environment. This chapter forms the basis for the remainder of the book—it identifies the open source products that we'll be exploring in greater detail in the chapters that follow. The selected products will form the basis for our Open SOA Platform, and we'll illustrate how these products can be integrated together in a coherent fashion so that, combined, they'll equal or surpass in value the offerings by the commercial SOA vendors. Figure 2.1 recaps the technologies involved in the Open SOA Platform and highlights (in double-width lines) those that we'll investigate moving forward (as you recall, JMS, application servers, and GUIs are covered thoroughly by other publications or are fairly commoditized in functionality).

Over the past five years I've had the opportunity to participate in "real-life" projects that have used many of the open source products discussed in this chapter. In choosing which ones will constitute our Open SOA Platform, I had to select a single product within each product category. This isn't intended to suggest those that aren't selected are any less worthy. As with any evaluation process, the final choice is based on some combination of objective and subjective facts (obviously, we all want to believe we only use objective facts, but human nature often dictates against such logic).

Before we dive into each of the technology categories and the open source possibilities within each of them, let's first establish some general, universal criteria that we can use when evaluating any of the products.

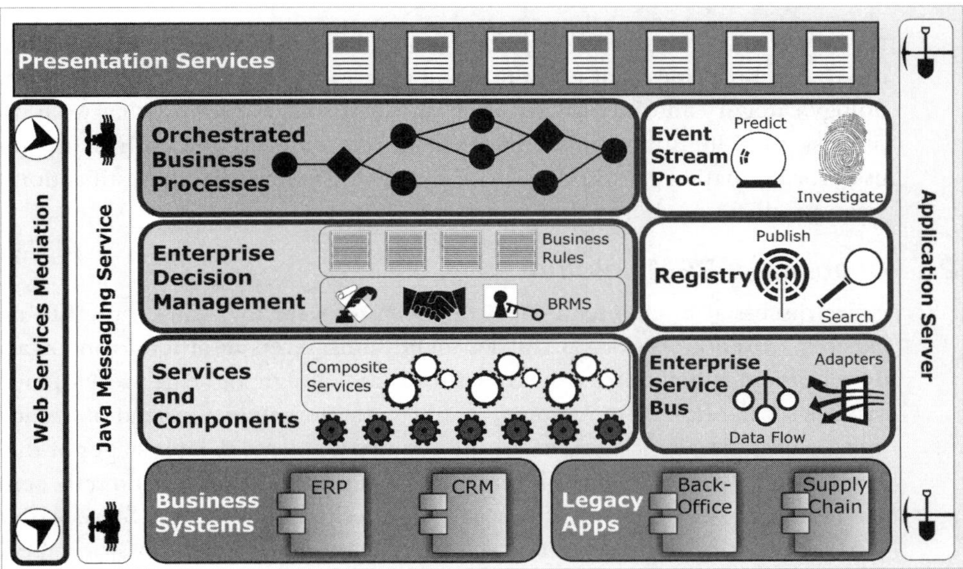

Figure 2.1 Open SOA Platform technologies. Those surrounded in double-width lines represent what's covered in this book.

2.1 Evaluating open source products

Some general criteria exist for examining all of the technology products that constitute the Open SOA Platform. They're described in table 2.1.

Table 2.1 Open source selection criteria, general guidelines

Criteria	Comments
Viability	Is the product widely used, and does it enjoy a strong user community? Is the solution well documented? Are sufficient development resources committed to the project?
Architecture	Is the architecture of the product complementary to the other products we are evaluating? Is it well documented and logical, and does it adhere to common best practices and patterns?
Monitoring and management	Does the product provide off-the-shelf monitoring and management tools? Since we are mostly evaluating Java products, does it utilize JMX, which is the standard for instrumentation and monitoring of Java applications?
Extensibility	Can the off-the-shelf solution be extended to add new functionality? Does a pluggable framework exist for adding new functionality?
"True" open source	This is a sensitive topic, but we want to consider only products that are licensed using one of the common open source licenses: GPL, LGPL, BSD, Apache, or Mozilla Public License. We want to avoid, if possible, "free" or "community" versions that retain restrictions in usage or modification.

Now that we've identified the general evaluation criteria that we can apply to evaluating the technologies that constitute the Open SOA Platform, let's look at each technology category and identify for each an open source product that we'll use. In this process, we'll identify competing open source solutions and address (a) the criteria used for evaluating the products within a category, and (b) the justification for why a given product was chosen. Let's start with BPM.

2.2 Choosing a BPM solution

As we discussed in chapter 1, BPM refers to software that can be used to model and execute workflow processes. BPM can be considered another form of application development, albeit more visual in nature. Also, design and early development of BPM processes can often be performed by subject matter experts instead of hardcore developers (that said, the latter is often still required, at least in later stages of the development cycle). Why is BPM considered part of SOA? It is because it directly benefits, and is enabled by, the exposing of reusable services that is central to SOA. With BPM, you can create business processes that span across multiple, previously stovepiped, applications. In this sense, BPM applications are often fundamentally different from traditional applications, and are less focused on performing a specific task and more oriented toward an entire business process. For example, a new hire process within a company may involve setting up the individual in a multitude of different systems, from benefits and payroll to a 401(k) system. A BPM process models that entire workflow and isn't isolated to populating just one of the applications with data.

> **What is a "stovepiped" application?**
> A *stovepiped* application, by its design, is completely isolated and self-contained. Legacy applications, which were often developed with little notion of integrating with external data or systems, are often considered stovepiped. SOA tools provide the ability to unlock the business rules and operations of these stovepiped applications into services that can be invoked externally. Existing investments can be leveraged without having to resort to replacing critical business systems.

It's worthwhile to distinguish between some of the terms used in BPM, as the terminology can sometimes be rather confusing:

- A *workflow* is generally understood as series of human and/or automated tasks that are performed to produce a desired outcome. A fancier name for workflow that is commonly used is *orchestration*.
- Closely related to workflow is a *process*. It's defined as "a set of activities and transactions that an organization conducts on a regular basis in order to achieve its objectives… It can exist within a single department, run throughout the entire enterprise, or extend across the whole value chain" [BPMBasics]. A process may involve one or more workflows.
- A *task* represents a specific work item that must be performed, most typically by a user. Tasks constitute the work within the workflow.
- A *node* is a generic command or step within a process. It can be a task, a wait state, or a decision. A business process consists of nodes.
- A *transition* (or, in XML Process Definition Language [XPDL] nomenclature, *edge*) defines how nodes are connected.

BPM systems, by their nature, involve modeling what can be complex processes. Mathematical algorithms are often used as the basis for implementation and can be fairly arcane to understand for those not steeped in its principles. The requirement to visually model workflows also represents a significant development challenge. These are perhaps the reasons why open source BPM solutions were, at first, slow to emerge. Recently that has changed, and you can now choose among several excellent open source BPM systems. We'll discuss how to make a wise choice in the next section.

2.2.1 BPM product evaluation criteria

As you recall, in section 2.1 we discussed general criteria for evaluating open source SOA software. There are obviously some additional BPM-specific criteria that we'll want to consider; they are listed in table 2.2.

What's the difference between BPM and BPEL?

BPEL (Business Process Execution Language) can be considered a subset of BPM. BPEL provides a semantically rich language for creating business processes that are composed of SOAP-based web services. It's a specification for how to materialize a business process that's composed of SOAP-based web services. BPEL, by itself, has no specific provisions for human activity–based tasks or queues (though the emerging BPEL4People—WS-BPEL Extension for People—will address some of these deficiencies), which are typically associated with workflow-based BPM processes. The BPEL standard also doesn't specifically address reporting, analysis, or monitoring, though some BPEL vendors have augmented their offerings to include such features. In other words, the term BPM is typically used when referring to complete product offerings whereas BPEL is typically used to refer to the web service orchestration standard.

Obviously, this only scratches the surface of the underlying functionality typical in any BPM solution. However, it does touch on some of the most important features and provides us with guidance on identifying what constitutes a BPM. That way, we can identify possible open source products, which is our next topic.

Table 2.2 BPM evaluation criteria

Criteria	Comments
Simplicity	BPM solutions, particularly those by commercial vendors, have a history of being very complicated to learn and even more difficult to deploy. Circumstantial evidence suggests many solutions become expensive "shelf-ware" and never live up to the promises anticipated. We want our solution to be simple to learn, deploy, and manage.
Lightweight/embeddable	In part related to simplicity, this criterion refers to the ability, if need be, to incorporate the BPM "engine" directly into an application. For example, you might be building a new loan processing application and want the ability to embed a workflow engine directly within it without having to manage it externally.
Process nodes	Are all standard process nodes available out of the box? This would include decision/conditional routing, human-interface task support, forks/splits, and joins/merges. Can callout nodes or capabilities exist to invoke Java and web services?
Transactional requirements	Do auditing, logging, and rollback/compensation features exist? Are long-running transactions supported? Are roles and users supported?

2.2.2 Open source BPM products

As we pointed out earlier, BPM solutions tend to be fairly complex in nature. This is both because of the visual modeling requirements and the complex workflow algorithms that drive the BPM engine. Fortunately, within the past few years, we've seen exciting developments in the open source community surrounding BPM, and there are now several excellent products to choose from. Table 2.3 lists the most active BPM open source products available today.

Table 2.3 BPM open source product overview

Product	Comments
Intalio BPMS (Community Edition)	Feature-rich BPM that uses business process modeling notion (BPMN) to generate BPEL-based orchestrations. Unfortunately, only parts of Intalio's solution are open source, with some confusing licensing restrictions. Also, since BPMN is converted to BPEL (with that code being proprietary), extending the product seems problematic, and reliance on BPEL means support for only SOAP-based web services.
ActiveBPEL Engine	An efficient and highly regarded BPEL engine. Models can be designed using the free, but not open source, Designer. Important functionality such as persisting process instances to a database, or versioning of processes, is only supported out of the box in the commercial Enterprise version. My experience using the product suggests that the open source release isn't suitable for production usage.
Apache ODE	Apache ODE (Orchestration Director Engine) is a runtime BPEL engine. Its API is such that you can extend it in new and interesting ways, and thus aren't tied to the SOAP-only invocation of BPEL. The licensing model is very attractive, and the engine is lightweight and can be exposed, via Java Business Integration (JBI), to ServiceMix, an excellent open source ESB, which we cover later. Apache ODE doesn't come with a designer per se, but you can use the beta of the Eclipse BPEL editor.
Enhydra Shark and Java Workflow Editor (JaWe)	Shark is a workflow engine that adheres to the XPDL workflow standard that's supported by the Workforce Management Coalition (WfMC). JaWe is an XPDL editor, but has some limitations compared with its commercial cousin, Together Workflow Editor. Documentation specific to Shark was difficult to locate, and the emphasis, like with Intalio and ActiveBPEL, is to push you toward commercial products.
JBoss jBPM	A mature, efficient, and lightweight process/workflow engine with a usable Eclipse-based modeler. Uses its own terse XML graph notation language known as jPDL (jBPM Process Definition Language), and includes support for all core modeling nodes, such as decision and fork. Can be easily extended and isn't tied to a particular deployment framework. Unlike several others, there is no commercial "upgrade," and no functionality is specifically excluded.
ObjectWeb Bonita	Powerful, XPDL-compliant workflow engine. Well documented and mature. Includes excellent human-task UI integration (i.e., form generator). Doesn't come with an open source editor, and requires the JOnAS (Java Open Application Server) application server.
WSO2 Business Process Server	The WSO2 Business Process Server is based upon Apache ODE, and adds a web-based administrative interface along with simulation capabilities.

While the overview in table 2.3 doesn't delve deeply into the feature sets of each available solution, the criteria we established does point to Apache ODE, JBoss jBPM, or Bonita as the most appealing of the solutions. We'll address the reasons for this next.

2.2.3 Selecting a BPM solution

For several of the products listed in table 2.3, licensing issues were a major consideration in their exclusion from further consideration. In the case of Intalio, only some portions of their product are truly open source. With several others, the open source releases are more of a teaser to encourage upgrading to a commercial product (Shark/JaWe, ActiveBPEL). While Apache ODE can be fairly easily extended, it doesn't come with any built-in support for human-interface tasks, which (though not a part of the core BPEL standard) are an essential part of a BPM. Also, given that it's a BPEL execution engine, it's limited to working with SOAP-based web services, and can't, for example, directly invoke a Java class or populate a JMS message (granted, you could extend it to support this, but then it's no longer truly supporting the BPEL standard). For these reasons, we didn't select ODE, or WSO2's Business Process Server, which is based on ODE, as the BPM product.

ObjectWeb's Bonita offers an attractive open source solution. It has a proven heritage dating back to its 1.0 release, and with the release of Version 2, added support for XPDL. Unfortunately, Bonita doesn't come with an XPDL editor. Instead, Bonita suggests using one of the available open source or commercial editors. This raises a concern, as the open source XPDL editors don't appear to be sufficiently robust (at least compared with their commercial alternatives). An additional concern is the newer version's reliance on the JOnAS application server. This will limit the ability to embed the engine within other applications. Because of these reasons, we didn't consider Bonita moving forward.

This leaves JBoss jBPM. It's a simple-to-use, but very powerful, workflow engine. As mentioned, jPDL is the XML vocabulary used to express business processes, and they can be created visually using the jPDL Designer, an Eclipse-based plug-in. Further, centralized administration of jBPM processes can be managed through the jBPM Console, which is a web-based management tool. jBPM has the financial backing of JBoss and enjoys a fairly vibrant user community, based on forum and mail list activity. It also is being extended to support those who want to use BPEL scripts for workflow execution (at its core, it's a graph-based process engine). For these reasons, we selected it as the BPM solution for our SOA technology stack. Let's take a more in-depth look at jBPM.

2.2.4 Introducing JBoss jBPM

The jBPM project's first official release was in early 2004, followed by the 2.0 release later in the year. At approximately the same time, the jBPM team merged with JBoss, officially making jBPM a part of the JBoss family of products. Since the merger, the product has been managed and led by largely the same team, which has resulted in a solid, robust, and time-tested product. At the time of this writing, the 3.3 release of jBPM was the latest production version, with 4.0 in early alpha (we didn't use the 4.0 release for this book as it remains very fluid).

JBoss describes jBPM as "a flexible, extensible framework for process languages," or alternatively as a "platform for graph-based languages." The jBPM Process Definition Language (jPDL) was the first, or "native," process language developed on this framework. jBPM comes with the jPDL Eclipse plug-in Designer for easily creating business processes, along with a web application page-flow framework for creating human-based tasks. It supports persistence of process instances by storing them within nearly any open source or commercial database (using the well-respected Hibernate object-relational database mapping framework). Chapters 5, 6, and 7 will delve into great detail on jBPM.

2.3 Choosing an enterprise decision management solution

Enterprise decision management (EDM) is an approach to automating and improving the decisions a business makes on a day-to-day basis. It plays an important role in our Open SOA Platform, as it provides the centralized management for all of the business rules and logic associated with each of the applications.

Fundamentally, an EDM is about extracting the decisions and rules that are today embedded into applications or people and systematically exposing them as rule assets that can be centrally managed and authored. Some have gone so far as to proclaim a "Business Rule Revolution" is under way, insofar as it "represents an emerging undeniable need for the right people to know what a business's rules are, to be able to change those rules on demand according to changing objectives, to be accountable for those rules, and to predict, as closely as possible, the impact of rule changes on the business, its customers, its partners, its competition, and its regulators" [VonHalleGoldberg].

What's the difference between BRMS and EDM ?

EDM, besides sounding a bit sexier and less boring than *Business Rule Management System* (BRMS), is also considered to be a superset of BRMS. By that, it also includes leveraging analytical models that can be derived from data warehouse or business intelligence capabilities to conceivably create self-tuning rulesets. The reason we chose EDM for this book was that EDM is becoming the more recognized acronym for rule-based systems. Consider it similar to how *workflow* slowly became subsumed by the more *glitzy sounding business process management* (after all, workflow does sound pretty dry).

The value of managing business rules in a centralized fashion, and making them maintainable by business users instead of developers, has long been recognized as a laudable goal. Unfortunately, tapping into those rules from external applications and processes was often a considerable challenge. Early business rule vendors had their own proprietary API, often in one or two supported languages. This made integrating the business rules difficult and ensured vendor lock-in. The advent of web services and SOA opened up a vast new opportunity for incorporating a BRMS. Since web services are designed to be language and platform neutral, centralized business rules can now be accessed by virtually any application. Further, composite applications, such as business processes designed using a BPM, can easily tap into a BRMS for decision-based content routing rules. Perhaps the hyperbole of a "Business Rules Revolution" isn't such an exaggeration after all. In this case, the foundations of SOA become an enabling force to this exciting, even enterprise-changing, technology.

Figure 2.2 depicts the main components of an EDM.

In figure 2.2, we see a repository of rules broadly categorized according to the types of rules they are, such as "Constraint Rules," which serves, for instance, to impose limits such as the maximum amount of credit to extend to a customer. These various types of rules constitute the rule repository, which obviously has a central role in a rules system. The *Rule Engine* component, sometimes referred to as the *inference* or *execution* engine, represents the algorithms and logic that define how the engine works. The *API/Web Service* layer defines how you interface with the system. Many EDMs include multiple language-specific libraries and APIs, and often a SOAP- or REST-based web service interface. The *Authoring IDE* is the tool for writing, editing, testing, and categorizing rules. An important aspect of the authoring environment is whether support for domain-specific languages (DSLs) is available. This refers to the ability to express rules in a language that's natural to the business user yet has rigorous semantics. Consider it analogous to building your own programming language using a business vocabulary (hence, it's sometimes referred to as "language-oriented programming"). The *External Apps* are those applications that are utilizing the rules engine.

What's the role of EDM in SOA? One of the principal tenets of SOA is designing systems that are flexible and agile. Rules engines are instrumental in advancing this concept, as they allow business rules to be changed independently of making application modifications. This effectively eliminates having to go through drawn-out development and testing cycles, thus improving agility. This obviously also contributes to loose coupling (another tenet of SOA), as the binding between an application and its business rules is no longer as tight. The next section delves more deeply into the criteria used for evaluating an EDM offering.

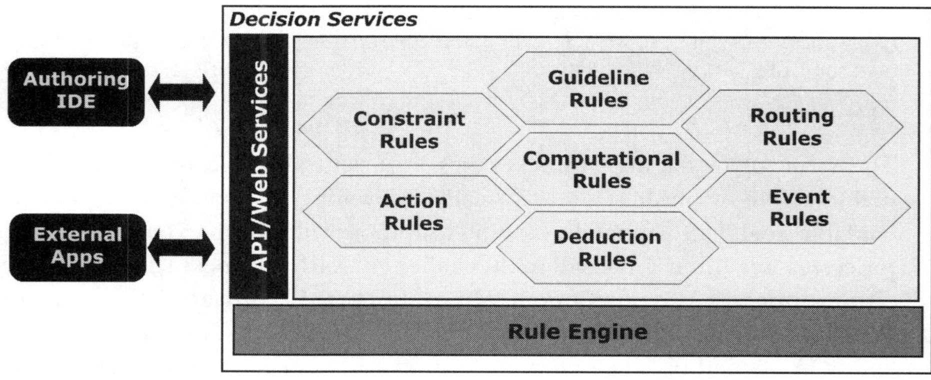

Figure 2.2 The components of an EDM, and its relationship to API services and rule engine

2.3.1 EDM product evaluation criteria

Section 2.1 identified some general criteria for evaluating the various SOA technologies, and an EDM obviously has some additional product-specific requirements. Table 2.4 identifies some key requirements we'll use when analyzing the suitability of the various open source rule systems.

Table 2.4 Open source selection criteria, general guidelines

Criteria	Comments
Centralized rule repository and classification	Central to the concept of EDM is a repository that enables rules to be classified, managed, and versioned. This should include the ability to add custom metadata and properties to each rule and ruleset. Security and access control are also important requirements.
Auditing and logging	In a time of increasing regulatory and compliance demands, the ability to audit the frequency and outcome of rule actions is essential. This can also provide analytical feedback to rule authors, allowing them to refine and improve their rules over time.
Integrated development environment (IDE)	A complete authoring environment for design, creating, testing, and publishing rules. Usually should include "wizards" or other forms of assistance for those new to the system.
Domain-specific language (DSL) support	We alluded to this briefly earlier: the ability to create a language based on business or domain nomenclature. An example of a rule expressed using a DSL is, "If Order is greater than $10,000, then sales manager approval is required." That, in turn, would be translated into a form that the rules engine could understand.
Robust API	Refers to the ability to integrate with the rules engine. This means not only providing programmatic access to the rule engine, but also whether it includes support for reading/writing data from popular SQL databases, where most fact-related data resides. In addition, the API should support multiple languages and/or have strong web services support.
Performance	Although performance was listed in section 2.1, it is worth reiterating because of the importance performance plays within an EDM. It's not uncommon to develop thousands of rules, and a highly efficient engine must be used since many rules must be fired in a real-time capacity.

Now that we have a foundation for assessing an EDM, we can turn to identifying the possible open source EDM candidates.

2.3.2 Open source EDM products

While commercial business rule solutions have been around for a decade or more, it's only been within the past five years or so that open source alternatives have become available. This is no doubt because of the increased visibility that has become associated with the "business rule approach," along with the success stories presented by the commercial vendors. Table 2.5 identifies the open source EDM products.

Table 2.5 EDM open source product overview

Product	Comments
Mandarax	Primarily just a rules engine with limited IDE support (Oryx, a UI editor for Mandarax, is maintained by a third party, and is a bit buggy and unrefined). Doesn't include a repository.
OpenLexicon	Fairly new product (2006) with limited documentation. Favorable license (modified Mozilla). Includes a polished management interface and repository. Can create rules through a web-based interface. DSL support is somewhat limited. Doesn't appear to be easily embeddable.
JBoss Rules (Drools)	Highly mature rules engine that has undergone several significant enhancements recently, which include the addition of BRMS repository functionality. DSL support is limited but useful. Highly efficient rules engine and decent Eclipse-based authoring environment. Lightweight and embeddable.
OpenRules	Restrictive license for commercial use (for example, you must purchase a non-GPL license if you're using OpenRules in a SaaS or ASP model). For this reason, it wasn't considered a viable selection for our Open SOA Platform. That said, it's a highly capable BRMS with a strong support community.
Jess	Jess, an early and highly respected rules engine, isn't open source or free, though it's commonly assumed to be (it's very affordable).
TermWare	Primarily targeted as an embedded solution. Doesn't include repository, management features, or IDE.

Based on the results in table 2.5, it appears as though the only two real choices are OpenLexicon and JBoss Rules (hereafter referred to as *Drools*, its historical name). Let's examine the reasons next.

2.3.3 Selecting an EDM

Mandarax, while maintained by a fairly small team of developers, does offer some innovative features. They include an elegant way of tapping into working memory from a variety of data sources, as well as a novel API approach to creating functions and predicate-style clauses using standard Java classes. Documentation is adequate. The biggest concern with Mandarax is that it's maintained by a small team and appears to have a limited user base. The concern is that, over time, without a strong user base the project could fall into quiescence and would no longer be actively maintained (a fate that afflicts the majority of open source projects). For this reason, we didn't consider Mandarax.

Both OpenRules and Jess were excluded from consideration due to their licensing restrictions. OpenRules, while proclaiming itself as open source, doesn't fit my criteria of open source: using it in certain commercial capacities requires purchasing a license. Although we are advocates of purchasing support for those open source applications that have a sponsoring company whose revenue model is based on that (such as JBoss), we think it's disingenuous to pitch a product as open source when a license must be purchased for commercial use. On the other hand, Jess clearly doesn't aim to mislead and doesn't position itself as open source (free versions for certain types of usage are available).

OpenLexicon shows great long-term promise, but the fact remains that it's still relatively new and lacks comprehensive documentation. Its nicely integrated BRMS features and well-designed user interface should definitely place it on anyone's open source short list. This leaves Drools, which has a long and proven track record and has been enhanced with more enterprise BRMS features, such as repository management.

2.3.4 Introducing JBoss Rules (Drools)

The Drools project began in 2001, and the first production-ready release was the 2.x version that appeared in 2003. By 2005, Drools had become a popular open source rules engine, so much so that in October of that year, it joined the JBoss family of products. With the deeper pockets afforded by JBoss (and then Red Hat, which, in turn, acquired JBoss in 2006), the 3.0 release of Drools offered significant performance enhancements and introduced an authoring/IDE Eclipse environment. In addition, a new rule language, DRL, simplified rule creation. Even more substantial improvements accompanied the 4.0 release. The rule language was enhanced; a Hibernate framework was introduced for populating working memory; performance was further improved; and, perhaps most significantly, BRMS functionality was added. The 5.0 release, which will be available by the time of this publication, adds further enhancements, related to process flow and includes complex event processing features (we are using the 5.0 release for the examples presented in this book). Drools can now claim to be a true feature-rich alternative to commercial BRMS offerings.

The Drools team at JBoss now includes over 12 full-time staffers, along with a fairly large contingent of non-JBoss contributors. The project has excellent documentation, which can be somewhat of a rarity in the open source world. The mailing list is also quite active.

If there's a knock against Drools, it's that a prebuilt web services interface isn't available. We address this deficiency in chapter 11, where you'll learn how to easily expose Drools rules as SOAP-based web services.

2.4 Choosing an ESB

As discussed in chapter 1, an enterprise service bus (ESB) is considered middleware that lies between business applications and routes and transforms messages along the way. Since the ESB acts as a messaging bus, it eliminates the need for point-to-point connectivity between systems. Instead, when one system needs to communicate with another, it simply deposits a message to the bus, and the ESB is then responsible for determining how to route the message to its destination endpoint. Any necessary transformations are performed along the way. Figure 2.3 illustrates the central role an ESB can play.

An important role an ESB plays is bridging between different protocols. For instance, an interface to an ERP system may require SOAP, but an internal CRM may only support XML over JMS. An ESB can translate between these protocols and lift JMS messages originating from the CRM and into a SOAP web service call understood by the ERP (and vice versa). Typically, ESB "adapters" perform the function of communicating with a disparate group of protocols, such as SOAP, CORBA, JMS, MQ Series, MSMQ, FTP, POP3, and HTTP, among others. We'll examine the ESB evaluation criteria next.

Figure 2.3 Central role of an ESB within the enterprise

2.4.1 ESB product evaluation criteria

In selecting which open source ESB to use for the SOA technology platform, let's consider several ESB-specific requirements, as shown in table 2.6.

Table 2.6 Open source selection criteria, general guidelines

Criteria	Comments
Protocol adapters	An ESB should support, at a minimum, adapters for the following protocols: POP3/SMTP, HTTP, FTP, SOAP, JMS and File.
Data-flow processing/ choreography	An ESB must often perform a series of tasks as part of a data gathering, routing, and transformation process. This requires the ability to chain together multiple steps into a processing pipeline that may require content-based routing, splitting, aggregating, and exception logic. For real-time processing, an ESB event-flow choreography may eliminate the need for BPM-type orchestrations (which are more suitable for long-running transactions).
Clustering and failover	Given the central role an ESB plays within a SOA environment, it must feature clustering and failover capabilities. In addition, the ability must exist to distribute, among a number of different servers, the various ESB services. For example, XSLT transformations can be very CPU intensive, so it may be desirable to isolate such processing on a separate server or servers.

Table 2.6 Open source selection criteria, general guidelines *(continued)*

Criteria	Comments
Transformations	Most ESBs, if not all, are XML-centric. That is, the messages that flow through the bus must typically be in XML format (binary data can be addressed through Base-64 encoding). As such, the ability to transform from one XML format to another is essential. While every ESB supports XSLT transformations, not all support XQuery, which adds significant query and transformational capabilities.
Service extensibility	A well-defined API should exist that easily permits creation of new services or adapters.

Although disagreement exists as to who invented the ESB (both Sonic Software, now a division of Progress, and TIBCO claim that honor), the first real mature commercial products began to appear around 2002. Emerging in 2004 was the first real open source ESB, Mule. It was closely followed by ServiceMix, which in turn was succeeded by several others. Now, there are at least half a dozen compelling open source ESBs. Indeed, it's difficult to make a clear-cut decision based on competing features, as several possess nearly identical capabilities (and this is no small feat, given how comprehensive these products are). Instead, the decision simply may come down to personal preference. In other words, you can't go wrong by picking nearly any of the top-tier ESBs.

What is the different between choreography and orchestration?

In a *choreographed* process flow, each node within the process determines which path to proceed moving forward. For example, each node could reside within its own Java virtual machine. It receives a message through some in-port queue, performs its processing, and then determines which out-port queue to deposit the message. The node is, in a sense, oblivious to its role within the larger process. With an *orchestration*, however, the process flow is managed centrally and typically within a single Java virtual machine. In the case of BPEL, each time a process is initiated, an "instance" of the process is created, and managed by the BPEL engine. If it is long-running, the instance may be persisted to a database (a process known as *dehydration*). Within a choreographed service, there's no concept of a "process instance," and the messages instead reside, somewhere, within the process nodes.

There's one distinction that can be made between some of the competing products—those that support the *Java Business Integration* (JBI) specification and those that don't. What is JBI? It's a Java Community Process (JSR 208) specification for building a runtime integration architecture and was formally approved in summer 2005. It expands on WSDL 2.0's message patterns to create a container that can house services and the consumers of those services. Without getting too immersed now into the technical nomenclature of JBI, suffice to say that it represents a standard for creating ESB components and its runtime messaging environment. Although it originally began with much fanfare, several early proponents such as IBM and BEA (now Oracle) soured on the JBI, and the follow-up version of the standard, intended to address many of its perceived inadequacies, has languished.

How important is JBI? That's a matter of great debate. Obviously the proponents of ServiceMix and OpenESB would argue that it's an important differentiator, as you are then not tied into a potentially proprietary solution. However, non-JBI implementations, such as Mule, could rightly point out that their product is based on open standards, just not JBI (though they do now offer JBI integration capabilities). It arguably also makes their products easier to use and configure, as JBI has some fairly abstruse configuration and deployment requirements. JBI does appear to be gaining some momentum, especially as the 2.0 specification (JSR 312) works its way through the approval process (it's purported to address some of the biggest deficiencies in the 1.0 spec).

With the JBI considerations in mind, let's take a look at the open source ESB products.

2.4.2 Open source ESB products

While the product category known as ESB is a fairly recent development, several open source products were quick to emerge. In part this was because a community of experienced developers already existed with great familiarity with messaging solutions such as JMS. There's a now a solid selection of products from which to choose, with several very mature. The open source ESBs are identified in table 2.7.

As table 2.7 indicates, there are several excellent choices. Let's take a closer look.

Table 2.7 Open source ESB product overview

Product	Comments
ServiceMix	Early (2005) JBI-compliant ESB. Has dozens of components/adapters and supports nearly every protocol. Allows creation of fairly complex data flows using enterprise integration pattern components. Active project with frequent releases.
MuleSource Mule	Broad connectivity options and is strong in transformation, routing, and security. Like ServiceMix, supports common enterprise integration patterns for real-time choreography. Vast array of components/adapters. Well documented, mature, and proven. Broad range of app servers supported.
Apache Synapse (WSO2 ESB)	Positioned as a lightweight ESB that, while supporting essential ESB functionality, is simple to use by way of XML configuration. In addition, it's designed with high performance and availability features that make it especially suitable for web mediation.
JBoss ESB	A fairly new entrant that still appears to be maturing. Not a greatly active user community, and using web services is tedious. Does provide nice integration with other JBoss middleware products.
OpenESB	Like JBoss ESB, a fairly new project that's still maturing. Version 2 promises to offer significant enhancements. Good IDE support through NetBeans plug-in. GlassFish App Server v2 has built-in support for OpenESB, but support for other app servers is lacking. Documentation is fairly sparse.

Table 2.7 Open source ESB product overview *(continued)*

Product	Comments
Jitterbit	Positioned more as an "end-user ESB" that's simple to use without being a developer. However, lacks broad protocol support. The concept of JitterPaks is novel and makes exchange of prebuilt integrations feasible. Backend written in C++, which limits appeal to Java shops. Strong LDAP integration capabilities.
Bostech ChainBuilder ESB	Adds polished user interface and management features to JBI containers such as ServiceMix or OpenESB. Eliminates a good portion of the tedium in configuring and packaging JBI assemblies. Documentation is adequate, though the project doesn't appear to have a lot of downloads, which raises concern about viability.
OpenAdapter	Mature, elegant, and lightweight ESB. Although it's been around for a long time, documentation is poor. Project activity is low, although a dedicated group of developers keeps the release cycle frequent. Maybe best suited for embedded-type applications.

2.4.3 Selecting an ESB

Both OpenESB and JBoss ESB are fairly new entrants into the space. While it's true that JBoss ESB has been around prior to JBoss purchase of the solution, it only recently introduced SOAP-based web services support. Sun's OpenESB appears to be gaining some momentum, but overall it lacks in documentation and mindshare (there's also confusion about its role in Sun vis-à-vis the SeeBeyond ESB that was acquired with Sun's purchase of SeeBeyond). At this point, we consider both OpenESB and JBoss ESB too immature, at least compared with some of the others, to consider as viable options.

Jitterbit, while very interesting, isn't positioned as a full-fledged ESB in the vein of the others. That said, it has a clever, user-friendly interface that's intended for technical business users and not necessarily developers. It supports the most common transport protocols and has excellent database connectivity with easy-to-use extraction wizards. On the negative side, documentation remains relatively weak, and there are some licensing restrictions introduced through its own Jitterbit Public License (which is unfortunate). Given the end-user orientation of the product, it isn't well suited for the complex ESB routing and transformational abilities that our Open SOA Platform demands. As such, it was excluded from consideration.

OpenAdapter is one of the easier ESB products to learn and use. It's very mature, and is lightweight and fast. It also has a devoted development team that provides frequent releases. Notwithstanding these positive attributes, it doesn't appear to have significant momentum or user adoption. Disappointingly, its documentation is poor, with only a few of their adapters adequately documented. Because of these reasons, we determined that OpenAdapter wasn't a good fit for the platform.

Both ServiceMix and Mule represent excellent choices. They both offer a broad range of functionality and support a wide range of transport protocols. A strong case can be made for either product. However, we believe that for most environments,

Apache Synapse is the better choice. Why? The main reason is one of simplicity. Most of the ESBs we've talked previously about include relatively complicated configurations. This is particularly true of ServiceMix, which, by its JBI heritage, has a complex deployment structure. The same, albeit to a lesser degree, applies to Mule.

One of the earliest, and still most popular uses of an ESB, is to service-enable existing legacy applications. Common usage scenarios include exposing legacy services with a SOAP or HTTP wrapper. As you'll learn, however, this can be better accomplished using the Service Component Architecture (SCA). That being the case, the role of an ESB becomes less pronounced and instead is used primarily as a protocol bridge. Indeed, JMS solutions such as ActiveMQ, which is the default messaging product for many open source ESBs, now incorporate enterprise integration patterns, via Apache Camel, that can perform many tasks traditionally left to the ESB. This includes functionality such as routing, transformations, message splitting/aggregation, and content filtering. It may well be that the central role that ESBs have typically played within a SOA environment will reduce in next-generation architectures.

In light of these developments, we believe that Apache Synapse, because of its dual capacity as both a lightweight ESB and service mediation (discussed in section 2.8) is a prudent choice for most enterprises. For those requiring more sophisticated ESB capabilities, such as advanced routing features or more esoteric protocols adapters, consider using Mule or ServiceMix.

2.4.4 Introducing Synapse as a lightweight ESB

Synapse originated in 2005 from the X-Broker source code denoted by Infravio, which subsequently was purchased by WebMethods, which was then sold to Software AG. While the motivations for the donation are unclear, it likely was because Infravio was a vendor within the SOA registry space, and the X-Broker code wasn't considered a key offering. What is interesting is that, more recently, Synapse has become closely affiliated with WSO2, which has re-branded Synapse as WSO2's ESB. Most of the project members for Apache Synapse belong to WSO2. WSO2's ESB, which is also open source, tracks closely with the official Apache Synapse releases, and offers some nifty graphical front-end management and monitoring enhancements to Synapse. However, we won't demonstrate the use of WSO2's version, since learning the essentials of Synapse is the most important consideration (and matches our desire to keep things as lightweight as possible).

The initial Apache incubator proposal submitted by Synapse definitely positions it as an ESB-type product, with highlights citing multiprotocol connectivity, transformation features, and high performance, and management. Special emphasis is placed on proving support for the WS-* standards stack, which includes WS-Addressing, WS-ReliableMessaging, WS-Security, and WS-Policy. This is noteworthy, as Synapse will be used for such purposes within our Open SOA Platform. The latest release as of this writing is 1.2, which added numerous enhanced capabilities as well as improvements for scalability and robustness. That release builds upon the 1.1

> **WSO2's ESB 2.0 and Carbon**
> As we pointed out, WSO2 has largely provided the financial and development resources behind Apache Synapse. As this book neared production, WSO2 released a significantly upgraded version of their ESB product, upon which the future version of Synapse will likely be based. In this new 2.0 release, the WSO2 ESB was rewritten using their new Carbon framework, which is a modular, OSGi-based solution. Unfortunately, we didn't have an opportunity to evaluate this product yet, but please visit our SOA blog at http://jdavis.open-soa.info/wordpress for ongoing and updated information.

release, which added task scheduling, XQuery support, file system support through Apache VFS, and database mediation.

A simplified view of the Synapse architecture is shown in figure 2.4.

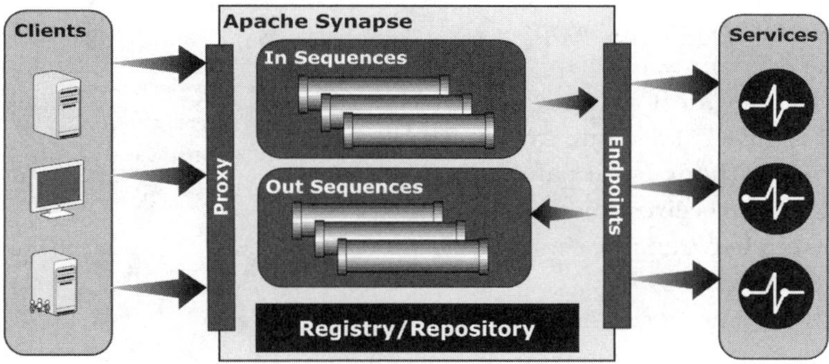

Figure 2.4 Simplified Apache Synapse architecture

As shown in figure 2.4, a request arrives from a client, and the proxy configuration determines which processing sequence to apply to the inbound message. Sequences are then applied to perform transformations, credential mapping, caching, security processing, and the like. Sequences can be applied to both the inbound and outbound messages, thus providing great flexibility. A remote or local registry can be used to facilitate reuse of commonly used sequences. Chapter 9 will go into much greater detail with code samples on the use of Apache Synapse.

2.5 Choosing an ESP solution

Event stream processing (ESP) is an emerging field that has begun to gather a lot of interest. It's considered a part of a broader trend known as *Event-Driven Architecture* (EDA). EDA is a style of application architecture that's centered on asynchronous, "push-based" communications. It's entirely complementary to SOA and uses asynchronous messages, in lieu of RPC-style function calls, to perform distributed computing. An *event* is simply an act of something happening, be it a new order, shipping notice, or employee termination. The system that records the event (or *sensor*) generates an *event object*, which is sent by way of a *notification*. The consumer of the notification (or *responder*) may be another system that, in turn, uses the event to initiate some action as a response. This is where the concept of ESP comes into play (which alternatively is sometimes called *complex event processing*, or CEP). Since ESP is a fairly nascent technology, let's take a closer look at it.

2.5.1 What is event stream processing?

ESP involves building or using tools to design, manage, and monitor the events that flow through an EDA-oriented environment. *Event patterns* are used to filter event data in order to detect opportunities or anomalies. An ESP solution must be able to support a high volume of events, perhaps millions daily, in order for it to be a viable offering. A business rule engine can be used in tandem with the event patterns to determine who receives what alerts. The relationship between these entities is shown in figure 2.5.

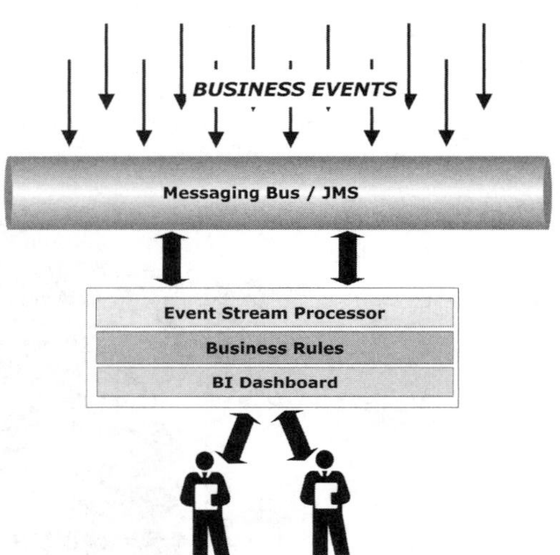

Figure 2.5 Event stream processing used for receiving business event notifications

In figure 2.5, messages that arrive into the JMS bus are interrogated by the ESP (sometimes referred to as *wire-tapping*). The business rules in the illustration may be contained directly within the ESP or externally managed, and drive the logic that occurs when certain patterns are detected. The results can then be fed into a BI dashboard.

> **BI, BAM, and ESP: are they all the same thing?**
>
> *Business intelligence* (BI) refers broadly to the technologies and applications used to analyze and present business information to targeted business consumers. *Business activity monitoring* (BAM), though similar to BI, tends to focus on real-time analysis of information. BI, on the other hand, often works in conjunction with data warehousing technologies to present analytics on historically gathered data. ESP shares the same real-time monitoring emphasis as BAM, but the source of data is derived directly from event streams. Historically, BAM solutions might cull real-time data from transaction records or BPM systems, but now are being enhanced to support ESP. So, BAM can be considered a super-set of ESP.

Perhaps because ESP is a fairly new concept, there's a dearth of open source solutions currently available that specifically address ESP. Esper is the only widespread open source ESP currently available. Some others are currently in development, including Pion. Several open source BI tools, which can be used in conjunction with an ESP to create executive dashboards, have become popular. Pentaho is perhaps the most recognized open source BI vendor, but others have successfully used tools such as JasperReports and Eclipse Foundation's Business Intelligence and Reporting Tools (BIRT) to create effective BI solutions. Though not open source, SeeWhy Software offers a "Community Edition" BI product that contains significant ESP capabilities. It can be used in production but is limited to a single release on any single-processor server.

Given that Esper is the only open source Java ESP currently available, let's examine it in greater detail.

2.5.2 Introducing Esper

The Esper project (whose name was derived from ESP-er, someone born with telepathy or paranormal mental abilities) was first released in August 2006. However, the project founder, Thomas Bernhardt, had developed earlier prototypes of ESP type solutions while working at a large financial institution. Since its initial release, a steady stream of updates has been provided (the most recent release, as of this writing, was 3.0). Beyond typical bug fixes, the main focus of enhancements relate to the Event Query Language (EQL), which is an SQL-like language for developing query expressions against inbound events. With EQL, you register prebuilt queries into the ESP engine, and as data is received, it's evaluated against those queries. Because events often must be viewed within the context of time (that is, no order in 15 minutes at night may be normal, but during the day, may indicate a website outage, for example), EQL provides "temporal window" syntax that allows time-period queries to be defined.

The documentation for Esper is quite good, especially since it's a fairly new project. This is likely because the founders of Esper have created a sponsoring company called EsperTech, which aims to build on the open source code base to introduce high availabilities and management features to Esper. This model is, admittedly, less than ideal for open source advocates, as it may mean some advanced features likely won't find their way into the open source release (this model contrasts with JBoss, who make their revenue entirely from support and do not limit the features found in their open source products).

Let's now turn our attention to the registry, which is used to store reference information about the artifacts that comprise a SOA.

2.6 Choosing a registry

The registry's role in our Open SOA Platform is to store the various software artifacts that are used in achieving a SOA environment. Historically, the *Lightweight Directory Access Protocol* (LDAP), which is a specification for directory services, was commonly used for registry purposes. It has become nearly ubiquitous in the enterprise because of Microsoft's Active Directory (AD) product, which is LDAP based. Most people mistakenly assume, in fact, that AD/LDAP is just intended for user and group management. Clearly, this is an excellent use of LDAP, but it's capable of considerably more. LDAP is ideally suited for any type of hierarchical directory where high-performance queries are required (with less emphasis on transactional updates and inserts).

Figure 2.6 depicts how LDAP could be used for managing a variety of artifacts, from individuals to BPM processes.

Although LDAP can be configured to support the management of software artifacts, it isn't necessarily ideally suited for this function. In particular, storing of the actual artifacts themselves, with the ability to query its contents, isn't easily accomplished without extensive customizations.

A more suitable fit than LDAP might be *Universal Description, Discovery, and Integration* (UDDI), which is a web services standard for publication and discovery of web services and their providers. While some vendors have released UDDI-based products (such as HP's Systinet), it has never achieved significant adoption. This is perhaps due to several reasons: complexity of the standard and its jargoned and arcane nomenclature (tModels, for example); its initial emphasis on public-based registries; and the initial lack of any strong UDDI open source offering. At best, UDDI is limping along, and the now available open source UDDI projects show little activity or enthusiasm.

One trend that has begun to emerge is that proprietary registry offerings have started to appear in SOA governance products. They are usually integrated with policy management features that dictate what services can be called by which clients. This is a sensible marriage, as governance obviously is closely tied to asset and artifact lifecycle management. Until recently, there have been no real open source SOA governance projects. Thankfully, that's now changing. WSO2 has released their WSO2 Registry product, and MuleSource released Galaxy, a SOA Governance product that is predicated on a registry. Since both are an initial 1.0 release, they're obviously a bit green around the edges, but these are exciting developments. Let's now take a look at some of the criteria we'll use for evaluating registry products.

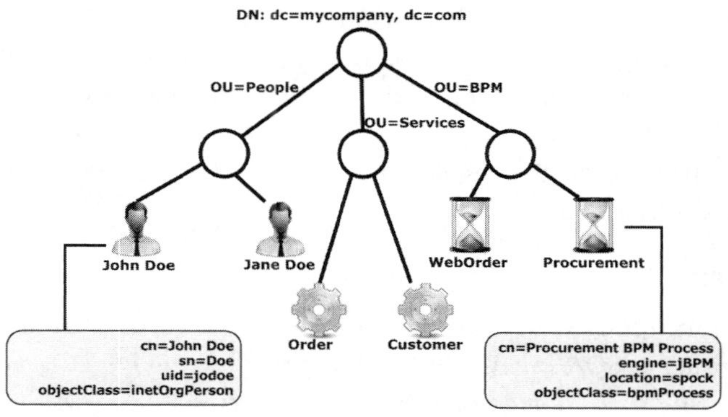

Figure 2.6 An example of an LDAP repository storing users, services, and BPM process metadata

2.6.1 Registry evaluation criteria

As you recall, in table 2.1 we identified some broad open source criteria that can be applied across all products we are evaluating. In addition, table 2.8 introduces some requirements specific to registries.

Table 2.8 Registry evaluation criteria

Criteria	Comments
Artifact and metadata repository	The ability to classify and store artifacts by type; for example, a WSDL or SCA configuration file. Should also allow for custom, searchable properties to be defined by artifact type.
Indexed searching	The ability to search metadata specific to the artifact type; for example, search operations within a WSDL, or components within a SCA composition.
Administration	Must include a graphical (preferably web) interface for managing and administering the repository. This would include the ability to add new artifacts, artifact types, search, and reporting.
Logging and activity monitoring	Should provide the ability to monitor activity within the system. This would include such things as new or modified artifacts and metadata modifications.
Role-based permissions	The ability to define users and user groups by roles.
API	The ability to interact with the repository through a programmatic API. Ideally, would be SOAP- or REST-based.

The next section identifies the possible open source products that can be used for the Open SOA Platform.

2.6.2 Open source registry products

The open source products that potentially can serve as the registry (see table 2.9) are broken into two main types: LDAP based and proprietary. For reasons we've already cited, the LDAP products have some disadvantages insofar as they're designed more as directory servers than artifact repositories. Nonetheless, it's worthwhile to consider them, since LDAP does provide extensibility features. The two open source UDDI implementations, Apache jUDDI and Novell's Nsure UDDI Server, weren't considered, for the reasons cited earlier regarding UDDI.

Table 2.9 Open source ESB product overview

Product	Type	Comments
OpenLDAP	LDAP	Proven, reliable, and has been around the longest. Now works with most popular backend databases. High performance and supports very large databases. Documentation is poor, which is surprising given its long heritage (though some LDAP books do cover OpenLDAP). Fairly complex to administer, and Windows platform support is sporadic (most run it on Linux or Unix).

Table 2.9 Open source ESB product overview *(continued)*

Product	Type	Comments
Fedora Directory Server (Red Hat)	LDAP	LDAPHeritage dates back to Netscape DS, and so it is mature. Excellent graphical administration console. Synchronizes with Active Directory. Good documentation. Intended to run on Red Hat or related Linux flavors (such as CentOS). No Windows capability.
ApacheDS	LDAP	100% Java-based solution. Excellent performance and support for many advanced features, such as triggers and stored procedures. Nice Eclipse-based plug-in (Studio) for browsing and editing repository. Lightweight and easy to administer.
OpenDS (Sun)	LDAP	100% Java-based solution that looks quite promising. Sun is positioning it as a possible replacement for their existing Sun ONE DS. At the time of this writing, version 1.2.0 has been released.
MuleSource Galaxy	Proprietary	Position as a SOA Governance product, it's based on a repository designed for managing SOA-based artifacts. This includes Mule configurations, WSDL, XML files, and Spring configurations.
WSO2 Registry	Proprietary	Designed to store, catalog, index, and manage enterprise metadata related to SOA artifacts. Includes versioning features and is lightweight enough to be embeddable.

As you can see, selecting the right product for the metadata repository service is difficult, as many high-quality open source products now exist (a good problem to have!).

2.6.3 Selecting a registry

We eliminated Sun's OpenDS from consideration, as it was still in beta during the early stages of writing this book. It is worth noting, however, that it has received excellent marks by those who have used it extensively. Some early benchmarks indicate that it's much faster than other Java-only based solutions (such as ApacheDS). It's being positioned as a complete, enterprise-ready solution, with advanced features such as "multi-master" replication and load balancing. The three principles touted in its development are ease-of-use, performance, and extensibility. The documentation is surprisingly strong for a fairly young open source project. Even though OpenDS's earlier beta status eliminated it from consideration, it's worth keeping a close eye on moving forward.

The Fedora Directory Server appears positioned primarily for Red Hat flavors of Linux—no Windows version exists. This fact limits its appeal and excludes it from our consideration. Even though it doesn't run natively on Windows, it's worth pointing out that it does have one of the best Active Directory synchronization features available.

This venerable OpenLDAP makes for an excellent choice. However, it too lacks strong Windows platform support (there are some Windows releases, but they're significantly behind the Linux versions). It can also be a challenge to administer and is fairly complex for those not well versed in Linux systems administration. ApacheDS, unlike OpenLDAP, is lightweight and simple to set up. It's also the only LDAP-certified open source product (Open Group certification). New releases appear to be bridging the performance gap between DS with OpenLDAP, and its Java codebase is appealing (assuming you're a Java developer).

While ApacheDS shows great promise as a directory server, it's still LDAP, which makes it rather challenging for supporting the storage and search of artifacts. The hierarchical nature of LDAP is also not ideally suited for our needs. Let's look at the two remaining proprietary products, Galaxy and WSO2 Registry, both of which were released in early 2008.

WSO2's Registry product appears to be a great fit for our registry needs. Positioned solely as a registry product, it's designed as a catalog for services and service descriptions. Artifacts can be structured data, such as XML-based files, or binary documents, such as Word or Excel. Metadata classification is supported, as are user-assigned tags, which can be useful for searching (think Flickr for the services). Versioning capabilities are supported, and the user experience is intuitive due to its Web 2.0 design (which is beautifully designed). User roles are also supported and configurable. Dependency and lifecycle management support is built in as well. One of the most attractive aspects of the product is the simple-to-use API. You can programmatically fetch objects from a remote repository in a few lines of code, and extending the registry to support custom object types by adding specific behaviors specific to them can be easily done.

The Galaxy product supports the same general feature set as WSO2's Registry, such as resource categorization, monitoring, and lifecycle and dependency management. In addition, the 1.5 release included some advanced features such as replication (available only in their pay version called Enterprise), scripting support, and an event API. That said, WSO2's Registry is easy to use, and trumps Galaxy with better Atom/RSS support and automatic versioning/rollback features. A good case could be made for selecting either product, but I remain a little leery of MuleSource's dual-licensing model, whereby some of Galaxy's most attractive features are only available for those who purchase the Enterprise license. WSO2, however, is 100 percent open source end to end, so no features are purposely excluded from their base product. For these reasons, we selected WS02's Registry product.

2.6.4 Introducing WSO2 Registry

WSO2's Registry product is officially positioned as a marriage of SOA registry with Web 2.0 collaboration features. The Web 2.0 features pertain to its ability for users to tag, comment on, and even rate registry entries/metadata. Figure 2.7 shows the essentials parts of Registry.

Beyond the core requirements of searching and managing artifacts and their metadata, the product supports the definition of artifact types. Using this feature, Registry can automatically introspect and index certain types of artifacts. Those supported out of the box include things such as WSO2's ESB (Synapse with added management capabilities) XML configuration files, WSDLs, and XML Schemas. You can easily define,

Figure 2.7 WSO2's Registry "marketecture" of features

through its extensible handler mechanism, your own custom behaviors related to filtered object types.

The lifecycle features of Registry enable larger enterprises to manage artifacts by their state within the development lifecycle. For example, you could search on artifacts that are in the QA state. Promotion of the objects throughout the defined lifecycle is also supported. The dependency management features pertain primarily to document types that support inclusions. For example, an XSD schema import within a WSDL can be automatically detected and then associated with the WSDL. Since schema documents play such a central role in a SOA environment for defining services, this is an important feature. The monitoring features provide excellent logging of all activity performed within the system, and nearly everything is exposed through a RESTful AtomPub API.

Bonus chapter

Coverage of WSO2's Registry product can be found in a bonus chapter found at Manning's website: http://www.manning.com/davis/. In part, we chose this approach since the Registry product is currently undergoing a major rewrite as part of WSO2's new Carbon platform, and we want to use that release as the focus for the chapter.

Let's now turn our attention to arguably the most critical artifacts of all: the services that constitute a SOA environment.

2.7 Choosing a service components and composites framework

Services are the catalyst behind a successful SOA environment. Exciting developments have occurred in this area over the past few years. The first salvo occurred with the release of Eclipse 3.0. The product was rewritten to include the OSGi framework for its runtime engine. OSGi uses a Java-based component model to dynamically manage the lifecycle of applications. With it, you can install, uninstall, start, and stop models within a runtime application. This technology represents the basis for Eclipse's plug-in architecture.

The OSGi framework, whose specification is managed by the OSGi Alliance, was initially formed with an emphasis on embedded devices and appliances. However, it rapidly has become adopted within regular and even enterprise, applications. There are currently three excellent implementations: Apache Felix, Knopflerfish, and Equinox (the basis for the Eclipse OSGi implementation). Many of the Apache-based projects are beginning to incorporate the OSGi framework.

Arriving a bit later was the *Service Component Architecture* (SCA) and its companion technology, *Service Data Objects* (SDO). The 1.0 specification was delivered in fall 2005 and included such notable sponsors as IBM, Oracle/BEA, and IONA. SCA positions itself as an architecture for building applications and systems using a SOA. It defines a declarative XML-based mechanism for creating components and for exposing those components as services that can be invoked through any number of different protocols. Components can be wired together in a fashion similar to Springs "inversion-of-control" feature, and are written in a way that is communication protocol neutral (that is, the components have no awareness as to which protocol will be used to invoke them, such as SOAP, JMS, or EJB). Given that a lot of folks are probably not yet familiar with SCA, let's examine some of its core concepts in more detail.

2.7.1 Examining the Service Component Architecture

In SCA parlance, a *composite* is a collection, or assembly, of components or services. A service can be thought of simply as a component that's exposed through an external protocol (for example, SOAP). A component, like a composite itself, can contain properties and references to other components or services. You can see the relationship between these items in figure 2.8 (which is a simplified view of SCA).

As figure 2.8 shows, a *binding* is how you define through what communications protocol to expose a given component as a service.

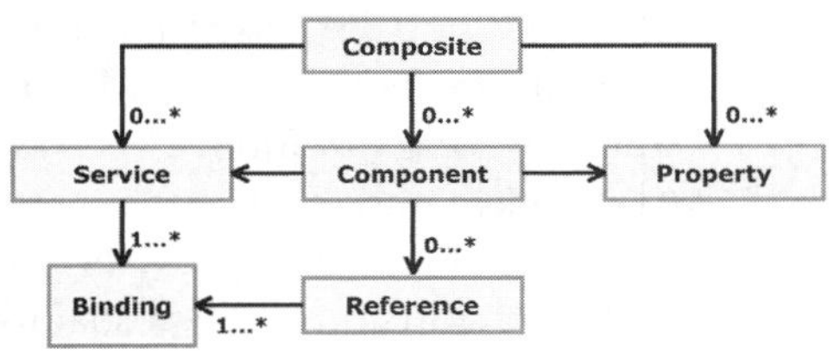

Figure 2.8 A simplified SCA class diagram

SDO is a companion specification that defines a standard for exchanging data graphs or sets. What's unique about the standard is that it supports the notion of *change logs*. This allows for offline modifications to be captured and recorded. The graphs themselves can be serialized into XML, and class-generation tools exist to create SDO objects from an XML Schema (alternatively, they can be created dynamically, and the metadata describing the structure can be gleaned dynamically as well).

What's the relationship between OSGi and SCA? In a sense, they're competing technologies, as they both define a component framework for creating services. However, OSGi primarily was designed for running within a single JVM and doesn't inherently support exposing of services through a wide range of protocols. SCA, on the other hand, was developed with the goal of supporting a multilanguage distributed environment. There's an initiative to bridge the two so that you can, for instance, easily deploy

OSGi services within SCA. In that respect, the technologies can nicely complement each other, and indeed, the next major release (2.0) of Tuscany is being internally rewritten to run within an OSGi container. For purposes of our SOA Platform, we won't specifically address OSGi, but we strongly encourage further research on the subject if you aren't already familiar with it. Apache Tuscany, an SCO and SDO open source implementation, will be addressed in great detail starting in chapter 3.

Upon first examination of SCA, many Java developers are led to believe that it's a substitute for Spring (as many of you are aware, Spring is a popular Java application framework). In part this confusion arises because SCA, like Spring, enables references (or other components) to be injected at runtime. Spring, like SCA, also supports the notion of properties, which can be declaratively defaulted in the XML configuration. Spring-WS even supports exposing Spring-based beans as web services, so that's another similarity. That said, important distinctions exist, such as SCA's aforementioned multiprotocol and multilanguage support. In addition, SCA more intuitively supports asynchronous and conversational programming models. Like OSGi, Spring integration is also available for SCA.

Because of the reasons cited, and SCA's integrated support for SDOs, it's the service and component framework technology of choice for the Open SOA Platform. Let's now further explore Apache Tuscany, the open source implementation for SCA and SDO.

2.7.2 Introducing Apache Tuscany

Apache Tuscany is a fairly new project, with its first beta releases in 2006 followed by the 1.0 release in fall 2007. The development team appears well staffed and is likely funded by the likes of IBM. The project recently was anointed as a top-level Apache Project from its prior incubator status, which corresponded with the 1.3 release in August 2008. Version 1.4 was released in January 2009, and is the basis for the code samples used in this book. The SCO and SDO standards have been transferred to the aegis of the OASIS organization. This is a significant development, as it lends great credibility to the project and removes the cloud that the combined specification was just a product of a few select vendors. OASIS has also set up a special website called Open Service Oriented Architecture (www.osoa.org) dedicated to advancing the standards.

The Tuscany and OASIS websites collectively contain extensive documentation. The specification documents for SCA and its related technologies are well written and comprehensive. There are also a burgeoning number of SCA-related articles and some upcoming books dedicated to the standard. The demo and code samples that come with the Tuscany distribution are also very solid and a wonderful source of information.

Commercial support for SCA and SDO has become realized by product releases by IBM (WebSphere), Oracle/BEA (WebLogic, AquaLogic, Workshop) and Oracle (SOA Suite 11g). Clearly, the momentum for SCA and SDO continues unabated.

The last remaining technology that helps form the basis for the Open SOA Platform is web service mediation.

2.8 Choosing a web services mediation solution

Web service mediation rounds up our Open SOA Platform. Web service mediation plays several key roles within a SOA environment. They include the following:

- *Runtime governance*—A service mediator can use security profiles to determine which clients can access what data. For example, you can modify an outbound data packet to restrict what data is presented. You can also monitor compliance with service-level agreements. Monitoring and logging can be used for compliance and auditing.
- *Version rationalization*—Often multiple versions of a company's API exist. A mediator can transform earlier versions into a format/specification consistent with the most recent version. This eliminates having to manage multiple versions of backend code.
- *Traffic management*—In certain circumstances, it may be desirable to discriminate traffic based on a client profile. For example, a SaaS provider may choose to charge extra for more than *x* number of requests per minute. For those clients not paying extra, inbound requests will be governed.
- *Protocol mediation*—This refers to the ability to easily translate messages from one protocol to another: for example, converting a REST-based XML-over-HTTP request into a SOAP format required for internal consumption. Or another scenario is to add or remove WS-Security headers from an inbound SOAP request.

Figure 2.9 illustrates the role a web service mediator plays in receiving inbound requests from a client.

Historically, some of these features were available through hardware devices, such as F5 Networks' BIG-IP family of products, Cisco's various content switches, or Intel's XML Content Router. As you might imagine, these generally require a fairly deep pocketbook. Until recently, pure-play open source mediation products didn't exist.

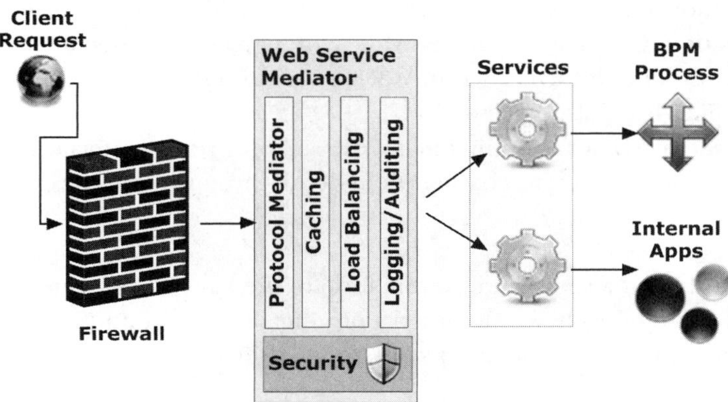

Figure 2.9 Web service mediation used as a proxy for inbound requests

> **Open source's hidden documentation**
>
> One of the most undervalued forms of documentation available in open source projects is the JUnit test cases that are usually available with the source. There are often a multitude of tests available for nearly every facet of behavior. What's most instructive is how the tests, or assertions, are defined, as they shed great light on the anticipated behavior of the application. Sometimes the test cases also provide insights into methods not documented within the regular documentation.

Granted, some of the features can be accomplished through an ESB, such as version rationalization. Some proxy and caching servers, such as Squid, also provided some of the requisite functionality.

The Apache Synapse project, which launched in 2005, became the first open source web service mediation designed solution. Because it does share some overlap in terms of functionality with an ESB, it can also do double duty as a lightweight ESB (you may recall from section 2.4 that it was, in fact, selected as the ESB for our Open SOA Platform). The Synapse feature set, which includes proxy, caching, load-balancing/fail-over capabilities and superb WS-Security support, clearly positions it as best suited for web service mediation. Let's examine the Synapse project in more detail.

According to the press release announcing Apache Synapse, it's "an open source implementation of a Web service mediation framework and components for use in developing and deploying SOA infrastructures" [Synapse]. Joining WSO2 in announcing Synapse was Blue Titan, IONA, and Sonic Software—all well-respected players in the SOA community. The first production release was in June 2007, and was followed by a 1.1 release in November of that year. Synapse is part of the Web Services Project at Apache (and is also a top-level Apache project), and the 1.2 release is the basis for our coverage of the product in this book.

The documentation, at first blush, seems rather inadequate. However, much of the best documentation resides within the write-up for the 50 or so samples that come with the distribution. Collectively, they provide a great deal of worthwhile information (you can find additional information on WSO2's website listed as their ESB product). The project mailing list is also fairly active.

WSO2's release of Synapse also includes a nice administrative interface to Synapse, and you'll learn more about it in chapter 9's in-depth dive into Synapse.

2.9 Summary

This chapter conducted a whirlwind examination of the key product categories of the Open SOA Platform. For each, we identified a product, usually among several excellent choices, as our selection. The categories and products selected are shown in table 2.10.

Table 2.10 Product categories and selections

Product category	Product selection	Home
Business process management	JBoss jBPM	http://labs.jboss.com/jbossjbpm/
Enterprise decision management	JBoss Rules (Drools)	http://labs.jboss.com/drools/
Enterprise service bus	Apache Synapse	http://synapse.apache.org/
Event stream processing	Esper	http://esper.codehaus.org/
Metadata repository	WSO2 Registry	http://wso2.org/projects/registry
Service components and composites	Apache Tuscany	http://tuscany.apache.org/
Web service mediation	Apache Synapse	http://ws.apache.org/synapse/

These products are well regarded and supported, and form the basis for the remainder of the book. The biggest challenge is how to integrate these products in a meaningful way so as to create a compelling open source SOA.

A note on the examples and source code

Throughout many of the chapters, example code is presented to assist the reader in understanding the concepts. To move the discussion along, we skirt past how to set up and run the examples. However, the downloadable source code contains a README.txt file for each chapter that walks through setting up your environment and running through each of the examples. If you encounter any issues, please use the Manning Author forum associated with this book at http://www.manning-sandbox.com/forum.jspa?forumID=416 to report any problems, and we'll attempt to resolve them as quickly as possible.

Part 2

Assembling components and services

Services are core to SOA. They represent functional, reusable units of code that can be combined to form applications or business processes. In chapter 1, we discussed what constitutes an ideal service, including its adherence to a well-defined service contract, as well as the fact that it's loosely coupled, abstractly designed, and stateless (among other traits). Building such services in a way that they can be exposed through multiple protocols and languages and then distributed and administered through a service cloud can be challenging. Fortunately, the emergence of two important frameworks has greatly simplified the creation of such services: OSGi and the Service Component Architecture (SCA). OSGi, squarely aimed at Java, provides a modular framework for constructing components along with a runtime container in which they run. By itself, it doesn't provide the features necessary for constructing SOA-ready services (that's not its intended purpose). But this is SCA's sweet spot.

Using SCA, you can build units of functionality, or components, supporting a variety of languages, and then expose them as services over protocols such as SOAP, JMS, RMI, REST, and others. Moreover, these components can be wired together internally to form higher-level services, or composites. The services can run in a distributed fashion and be managed as a virtual cloud. Since this book's focus is on SOA, we'll cover SCA through the open source Apache Tuscany implementation (for those interested in OSGi, *OSGi in Action* [Manning, 2008] is an excellent resource).

3 Creating services using Apache Tuscany

This chapter covers

- Introducing SCA
- Defining services using SCA
- Setting configuration options using SCA

In the previous two chapters, we dissected the technical underpinnings of what constitutes a service-oriented architecture, and selected a set of open source products that can be used to develop what we are calling the Open SOA Platform. Now, let's shift gears and focus, in considerable detail, on each of the selected products. As you make your way through this chapter, you'll notice that we place special emphasis on how to integrate the sometimes disparate technologies and how to best leverage the strengths of each. We'll begin this journey by looking at one of the foundational technologies behind SOA: services.

Services, as the *S* in SOA suggests, are instrumental in building a SOA environment. To recap, a *service* is a self-contained, reusable, and well-defined piece of business functionality encapsulated in code. To most people, a service is understood as simply something that's performed as part of their day-to-day job. A person at the checkout counter where you buy your milk is performing a service, after all. A software service is no different when you think about it. It's simply a routine that performs some unit of work. For example, when you encounter a problem when placing an order on some e-commerce website, the first thing that probably comes to mind is to locate the site's "Contact Us" link. This is an example of a service used to create a customer incident or problem ticket. Typically, there are multiple channels by which customers can report service problems that may include a web form, a customer service hotline, or direct contact with a sale representative. Regardless of the channel used, there ideally would be a single service that could be used to record such tickets. This would be an example of a discrete, reusable service that could be used by multiple applications (this scenario forms the basis for our examples later in the chapter).

Services are indeed the holy grail of SOA. If properly designed, publicized, and self-describing, services become assets that can be widely reused in a variety of applications. This maximizes the investment in these assets and enables creation of a more agile enterprise since every business process doesn't have to be re-created from scratch. Other tangible benefits include a reduction in maintenance costs and more bug-free applications. This chapter explores how such services can be created using the exciting new framework known as *Service Component Architecture* (SCA). You're probably thinking, "Not another framework!" There are already a multitude of frameworks that can be used for making web services, and a fair number oriented toward creating reusable components. The difference, as you'll soon discover, is that SCA takes a fresh approach and uses a protocol- and language-neutral design coupled with a clever way of assembling components for maximum reusability. More exciting still is the fact that this can be done entirely with an open source SCA implementation known as Apache Tuscany (http://tuscany.apache.org/)! Let's begin by taking a close look at what it means to be a service and how such services are created.

3.1 What are service components and compositions?

A service can run the gamut from a narrowly defined piece of functionality (fine-grained) to one that encapsulates a multitude of lower-level services and is thus considered more coarse-grained in scope (see the sidebar "Coarse- vs. fine-grained services"). Regardless of a service's scope, what underlies it are concrete implementations in code. Classes and methods are used to create the services that are made available to the consuming client. You can think of these classes as components, and the SCA framework provides a uniform and consistent way to develop and wire together such components, using a variety of languages.

Although the terms are sometimes used interchangeably in the literature, a distinction can be made between a component and a service, and this distinction is important for understanding SCA. A service, like a component, is a self-contained unit of functionality. However, unlike a service, a component isn't necessarily intended to be exposed for external consumption—its purpose may be limited to providing functionality within the context of the application for which it runs. A cash register at the store performs a service both for you and the attendant, but you could think of the routine used to calculate sales tax as more analogous to a component—in and of itself, its utility is limited,

> **Coarse- vs. fine-grained services**
>
> What is the distinction between a fine- and a coarse-grained service? As the name suggests, a *fine-grained* service has a narrow, specific set of functionality. For example, a service to activate a user in a CRM application may be considered fine-grained in nature. A *coarse-grained* service may encapsulate the functionality of many fine-grained ones. For example, creating users in a CRM would be considered a coarse-grained service if it could be invoked as a single, stand-alone call. In turn, that coarse-grained service may have to call numerous fine-grained ones, such as identifying the permission and organization IDs to associate with the new user; create the user; and then activate and send an email notification to the user. Obviously, from a client's perspective, the fewer calls and less knowledge of the target system, the better.

but when used by the register, it's a valuable part of the service offering. A "helper" class in Java, which provides static methods that are used by multiple other Java classes, could be considered a component. Enterprise JavaBeans (EJBs) in the Java EE world are often considered components if they're intended for use exclusively within the application in which they were written (that is, not exposed as an external API).

In the SCA world, they add a concept that they call a *composition*. A composition, which itself is a form of component, is made up of *one or more components*. You could think of it like a Pointillism painting [Pointillism], where many small distinct points (components) combine to make a larger image (composite). You could consider a composite analogous to a coarse-grained service, as it's the product of one or more fine-grained services. Compositions themselves may even be combined to form higher-level forms of compositions. Like a component, a composite becomes considered a "service" when it's wrapped for external consumption. The benefits of building software based on the reusable building blocks of components and composites have been espoused for several decades, as we discuss next.

The *Service Component Architecture* (SCA) initiative, and its companion, *Service Data Objects* (SDO), were advanced in 2005 by a consortium of companies, including IBM, BEA, and Oracle. SCA grew out of the need to create a framework exclusively designed for developing components supported by multiple protocols and languages—a key facet of SOA. No other existing framework appeared suitable to meet this requirement. Apache Tuscany was the first open source reference implementation of this technology. For the reasons cited in chapter 2, we selected Tuscany as the component framework for our Open SOA Platform. Recently, management of the SCA and SDO standards was moved to the OASIS group, a highly respected standards organization responsible for such notable standards as Electronic Business Using XML (ebXML), Security Assertions Markup Language (SAML), and OpenDocument, among others. Of course, you're probably a bit skeptical of yet another standard, along with the supporting vendors who have less than altruistic motives in offering their support. To dispel some of these concerns, a broad interest group was established to further the development of the SCA-related standards; it's known as the Open Service-Oriented

Architecture (OSOA) collaboration (this was the group initially established to promote SCA, and predates the move to OASIS—it remains unclear what impact this may have on OSOA).

Let's now explore SCA in greater detail and discover how its innovative assembly model advances the creation of services that are fundamental to a SOA architecture.

3.2 The SCA assembly model

To gain an understanding of SCA, it's useful to first take a high-level overview of what's called the SCA Assembly model. This model represents the core of the specification as it describes how services are constructed. The main ingredients of the model are shown in figure 3.1.

Figure 3.1 shows us that multiple *composites* can reside within a single SCA *domain*. What this means is that you can decompose an assembly into multiple composites, which can help you organize related functionality into logic groupings. A composite itself can contain one or more *services*, which are, in turn, constructed from *components*. A component has a concrete *implementation* and can *reference* other components or services. So, to keep the ball rolling, let's examine these concepts by looking at each part of the assembly as well as sample illustrations of how they're used. In our examples, we'll use Apache Tuscany, the open source SCA implementation that we selected for our Open SOA Platform (the README.txt file in this chapter's source code describes how to run the examples).

To demonstrate the concepts, let's partially construct a hypothetical problem ticket system using SCA. We'll start with simple constructs to illustrate the main concepts of building services and then progressively embellish the system to demonstrate advanced SCA features. Once the system is completed, you'll have a solid understanding of how to use SCA to create services—an essential ingredient for building a SOA environment.

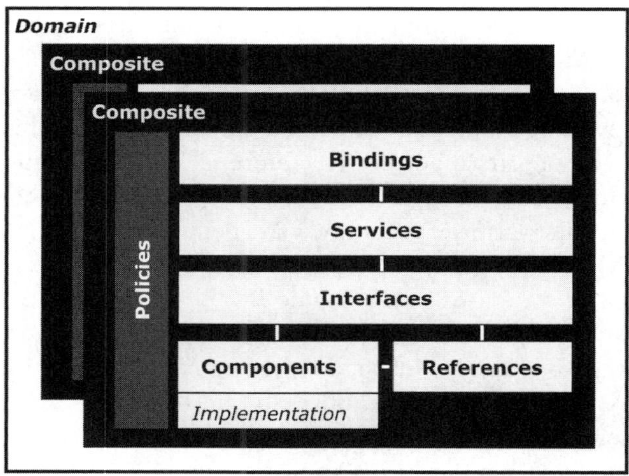

Figure 3.1 A high-level overview of the SCA Assembly model. Configuration options are highly flexible.

SCA tooling?

As is often the case with a new framework, the tooling and design tools often lag considerably behind the first implementations. SCA has been no exception to this rule (as of this writing, Apache Tuscany had released its 1.4 version). The good news is that there's an active Eclipse subproject working on an SCA editor (and related tools). The first feature-rich release appeared in August 2008, followed by several maintenance releases. Known as the SCA Tools subproject, the plug-in works with the Ganymede release of Eclipse. You can download it from the Eclipse update site: http://download.eclipse.org/stp/updates/ganymede. Using the tools, you can graphically build and manage your composite definitions.

We elected not to use the tools for this book since we believe they could have detracted from learning the underlying semantics of SCA. The README.txt instructions for setting up the source include instructions on setting up the SCA Tools plug-in.

Let's assume the following high-level requirements for our hypothetical ticket system:

- Must be exposed as one or more services so that it can be called by a variety of different communication protocols. This includes web, JMS, and SOAP. This ability will allow the system to be "embedded" within many different applications.
- Must accept a variety of ticket types or templates—for example, a web form for collecting issues directly from a user, or directly from application or systems monitoring solutions.
- Must provide support for a distributed architecture to support future scaling.
- Must provide the ability to generate real-time events on all activity. This is beneficial for integration with complex event processing (CEP) systems, the topic of chapter 8.

These obviously only skim the surface of possible requirements, but they do provide context for our examples as we move forward. If you were developing this application without SCA, you'd likely use a Spring-based framework for building it. In particular, Spring now provides excellent support for JMS and SOAP, as well as a distributed computing solution. Many other viable solutions exist as well. We suggest you think through how you'd tackle this challenge, using whatever frameworks you're accustomed to, and then contrast that approach with the SCA one we're building as this chapter progresses. We think you'll find that SCA dramatically simplifies many areas of development and, in particular, offers a refreshingly new approach for thinking about components and services.

With this use case in mind, let's start our examination of Tuscany with *composites*—the top-level building blocks of SCA.

3.2.1 *Introducing the composite file*

A *composite* is a container that's used for defining services, components, and their references. It's used to assemble SCA artifacts into logical groupings of components. For example, all operations that deal with a CRM system's customer management might be grouped together in a single composite.

NOTE For those familiar with Spring, the SCA composite would be considered roughly analogous to what Spring typically calls the application context XML file, where beans are defined. The `component` element, described in the next section, is similar in function to the `bean` element within Spring configurations.

Interestingly, a composite itself may be treated as a component, which is an example of what SCA calls a *recursive composition* (as you may recall from earlier, multiple composites may exist within a given *domain*). A composite defines the public services that are made available through one of the available SCA bindings (JMS, SOAP, etc.). Figure 3.2 is an abbreviated look at the XML Schema definition for composites. Many elements, such as `reference` and `service`, can also be defined within an individual component configuration.

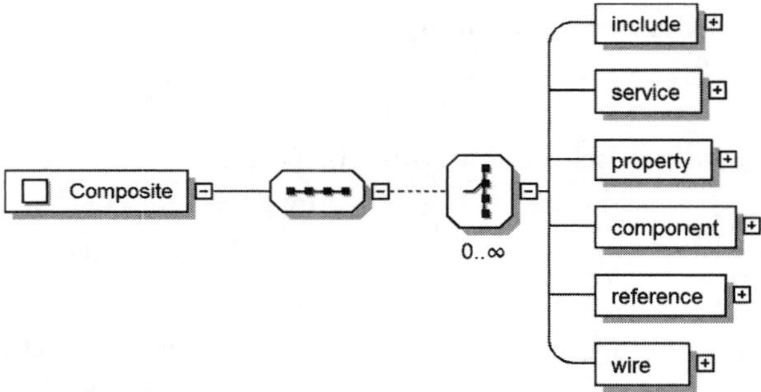

Figure 3.2 XML Schema definition overview for composites

Most composite files will likely contain one or more components, references, and often at least one service (the composite element is the root of the XML file, which is why it's sometimes referred to as a composite file). You'll learn later in this chapter and the next how to combine multiple composites within a domain to simplify maintenance or aid in classification. Figure 3.3 illustrates a distributed SCA environment setup using three virtual machines (VMs).

The top-level domain is defined using a composite that incorporates the node-specific compositions. The next chapter describes distributed SCA options and configurations.

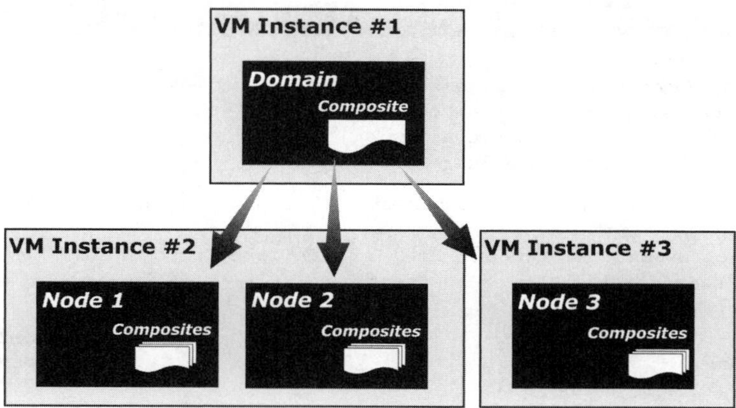

Figure 3.3 Relationships between domains, nodes, and composites

The SCA specification uses a graphical notation to visually illustrate how a given composition is defined. An example that we'll build on is shown in figure 3.4.

Figure 3.4's composite shows two defined components: `ProblemTicketComponent` and `CreateTicketComponent`. The `CreateTicketComponent` is responsible for creating the problem ticket, whereas the `ProblemTicketComponent` can be considered more of a "controller" component that merely delegates its work to a dependent component. This makes sense when you consider that additional components would then be added for deleting and updating tickets. For now, the service we'll be creating is very simple—a web service used for creating new problem tickets.

How is the composite illustrated in figure 3.4 defined within the XML? Listing 3.1 shows the assembly definition (all composites have a .composite extension, which makes them easily identifiable in the source code for this chapter).

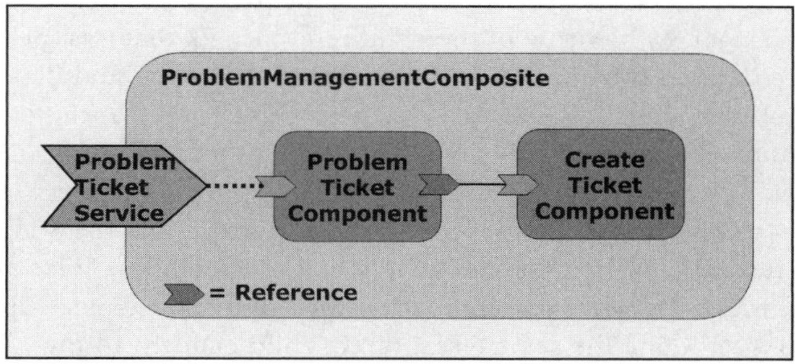

Figure 3.4 A simple composite example with two components

Listing 3.1 SCA composite assembly XML for figure 3.4

```
<composite
  xmlns="http://www.osoa.org/xmlns/sca/1.0"          <-- Specifies required namespace
  targetNamespace="http://opensoa.book.chapter3"
  xmlns:hw="http://opensoa.book.chapter3"
  name="ProblemManagementComposite">

  <component name="ProblemTicketComponent">          <-- ❶ Defines new component
    <implementation.java
     class="opensoa.book.chapter3.impl.ProblemTicketComponentImpl" />
    <service name="ProblemTicketComponent">          <-- ❷ Exposes as service
      <binding.ws uri=
      "http://localhost:8085/ProblemTicketService"/>       <-- ❸ Injects reference
    </service>
    <reference name="createTicket"
           target="CreateTicketComponent"/>          <-- ❹ References component
  </component>

<component name="CreateTicketComponent">             <-- ❺ Adds SOAP binding
    <implementation.java
     class="opensoa.book.chapter3.impl.CreateTicketComponentImpl"/>
  </component>
</composite>
```

Notice the two components elements that are defined ❶, ❺. The `ProblemTicket-Component` ❶ is exposed as a SOAP-based web service by way of the embedded service element ❷ that's included. A dynamic WSDL is generated for this service, since an actual WSDL wasn't specified (one of the features of SCA). The `binding.ws@uri` attribute ❸ defines WSDL endpoint as http://localhost:8085/ProblemTicketService?wsdl.

NOTE To differentiate attributes from elements, we preface attributes with the XPath convention of using the at-sign (@). So, when you see something like `binding.ws@uri`, we're referring to the `binding.ws` element's `uri` attribute.

Lastly, the `ProblemTicketComponent` defines a dependency or reference to the `CreateTicketComponent` ❺ by virtue of the child reference ❹ that was specified. So at this point we've defined two components, wired them together, and exposed one, the `ProblemTicketComponent`, as a SOAP-based web service with an autogenerated WSDL. We'll examine, in much greater detail, the definition of the components, services, and references in the sections that follow.

One thing that will become apparent as we move forward is that the SCA specification offers great flexibility in how to configure the SCA assemblies. For example, in listing 3.1, the `service` element was embedded with the `component` definition ❷. However, you can also define the service as a direct child element to the `composite`. This is illustrated in listing 3.2.

> **Using the code examples**
> The examples described in each of the sections are provided in the accompanying Eclipse project. Along with the project source is a document called "Steps for Setting Up Eclipse for Code Samples.pdf." It contains instructions on what prerequisites are required for each of the technologies, and details how to install the Eclipse project. Once installed, each chapter's code will contain one or more README.txt files that provide further instructions on running the samples.

Listing 3.2 Example of an SCA composite alternative configuration

```
<composite
  xmlns="http://www.osoa.org/xmlns/sca/1.0"
  targetNamespace="http://opensoa.book.chapter3"
  xmlns:hw="http://opensoa.book.chapter3"
  name="ProblemManagementComposite">          ❶ Service defined at root level

  <service
    name="ProblemTicketComponent"               ❷ Service promotes component
   promote="ProblemTicketComponent">
    <binding.ws uri="http://localhost:8085/ProblemTicketService" />
  </service>

  <component name="ProblemTicketComponent">
     <implementation.java
     class="opensoa.book.chapter3.impl.ProblemTicketComponentImpl" />
    <reference
      name="createTicket"                        No service defined
      target="CreateTicketComponent" />          in component
  </component>

  <component name="CreateTicketComponent">
    <implementation.java
      class="opensoa.book.chapter3.impl.CreateTicketComponentImpl" />
  </component>
</composite>
```

The functionality of the composites defined in listings 3.1 and 3.2 is identical, but in 3.2, the service is defined separately in a stand-alone fashion ❶, as a child of the document's root node. To associate the service to the component implementation, the `@promote` attribute of the `service` element is used—its value identifies which component to expose as the service ❷. Having multiple ways to configure an assembly adds flexibility when more complex scenarios are encountered.

NOTE Since services represent the key functionality offered by SCA, we generally prefer the greater visibility afforded them when they're defined as direct children of the root composite, as illustrated in listing 3.2.

How would you instantiate the assembly defined in listing 3.1 or 3.2? You can use different approaches, and we'll discuss them in greater detail as we move forward. The easiest way to start the assembly is to use what's referred to as an *embedded SCA domain*. This code fragment provides a brief illustration of how this can be done:

```
SCADomain scaDomain = SCADomain.newInstance("problemMgmt.composite");
```

In this case, assume the code in listing 3.1 was saved to a file called problemMgmt.composite. The `SCADomain.newInstance` method then receives that file as a single parameter and launches the domain using that assembly definition. Of course, we wouldn't get very far if we tried running this assembly—after all, we haven't actually developed the components yet! This is the topic of the next subject—components.

3.2.2 Configuring components

A *component* is a business function expressed within code. Components are, in a sense, the building blocks that constitute an application, somewhat akin to the ingredients in a recipe. Components can both provide and consume services. To be a functional unit, a component must provide an *implementation* that consists of the actual code used to perform the functionality. As we demonstrated in the previous section, a component can also directly specify a *service* by which it can be exposed for external consumption, as well as identify any *references* or dependencies of the component. The high-level definition of the component element is shown in figure 3.5.

As you recall from the previous section, we provided an example definition of a component. That fragment is shown here for convenience:

```
<component name="ProblemTicketComponent">
  <implementation.java
    class="opensoa.book.chapter3.impl.ProblemTicketComponentImpl"/>
  <service name="ProblemTicketComponent">
    <binding.ws uri="http://localhost:8085/ProblemTicketService"/>
  </service>
  <reference name="createTicket" target="CreateTicketComponent"/>
</component>
```

The concrete implementation for this component is performed by the class `ProblemTicketComponentImpl`. Let's create this class (listing 3.3) so we can illustrate what has to be done to provide the SCA component functionality (we've purposely kept our example simple to begin with).

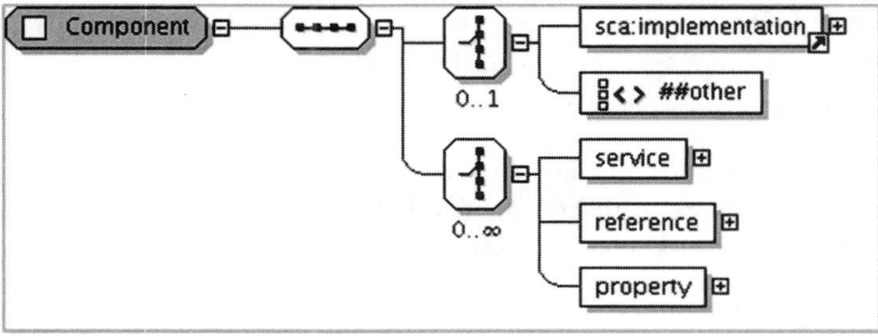

Figure 3.5 XML Schema definition overview for components

Listing 3.3 Java implementation for `ProblemTicketComponentImpl`

```
@Service(ProblemTicketComponent.class)                       ❶ Defines service implementation
public class ProblemTicketComponentImpl implements
  ProblemTicketComponent {
  private CreateTicketComponent createTicket;

  public int createTicket(TicketDO ticket) {
    System.out.println(ticket.toString());
    return createTicket.create(ticket);
  }

  @Reference                                                 ❷ Defines method for injected reference
  public void setCreateTicket(
      CreateTicketComponent createTicket) {
    this.createTicket = createTicket;
  }
}
```

As you can see, there are two SCA annotations specified in the class ❶, ❷. The `@Service` annotation ❶ is used to identify the service interface implemented by this component's implementation. In this case, the `ProblemTicketComponent` interface class provides this specification (see listing 3.4). The methods of this interface are what SCA will use when exposing the service's public operations (the next section covers services in detail). The `@Reference` ❷ annotation specifies the setter method used for injecting the `CreateTicketComponent` reference. This, as you recall, was specified in the component definition as

```
<reference name="createTicket" target="CreateTicketComponent"/>
```

Listing 3.4 contains the interface definition for the service operations implemented by `ProblemTicketComponentImpl`.

Listing 3.4 Interface used by `ProblemTicketComponentImpl`

```
@Remotable                                                   ❶ Defines interface as remotable service
public interface ProblemTicketComponent {
   public int createTicket(TicketDO ticket);
}
```

The only unique aspect to the interface class is the SCA `@Remotable` annotation ❶. This informs the container that the services provided by the interface should be made available for remote communications (such as a SOAP-based web service).

TIP SCA's Java implementation doesn't require the use of annotations, such as the ones we've used in the examples so far. Instead, you can use SCA's *component type* file. This is covered in more detail in the next chapter.

The service operation we're exposing is defined within the `createTicket` method. This method takes, as its single parameter, a `TicketDO` object. This data object class just contains the details of the problem ticket, along with corresponding accessor methods. The member variables for the `TicketDO` object are

```
private String customerEmail;
private String customerName;
private String subject;
private String problemDesc;
private int caseNumber;
```

The only thing that remains to be described is the referenced component class, `CreateTicketComponentImpl`, which is responsible for creating the problem ticket and returning an identifier (as we pointed out previously, other components such as those used for updating and deleting would eventually be added as service operations). For now, the `CreateTicketComponentImpl` class's `create` method is a placeholder and simply returns a random identifier regardless of what is submitted to it. The class is shown in listing 3.5.

Listing 3.5 `CreateTicketComponentImpl` reference class

```
public class CreateTicketComponentImpl implements
    CreateTicketComponent {

  public int create(TicketDO ticket) {
    System.out.println("createTicket: " + ticket.getCaseNumber());
    Random r = new Random();                    <-- Class used to generate random number

    return r.nextInt(300000);    <-- Returns random number
  }
}
```

Given that our sample involves several classes, let's recap the process of starting an SCA domain/server, receiving an inbound web service request for our exposed service, and creating a ticket. Figure 3.6 illustrates the steps, which are described in table 3.1.

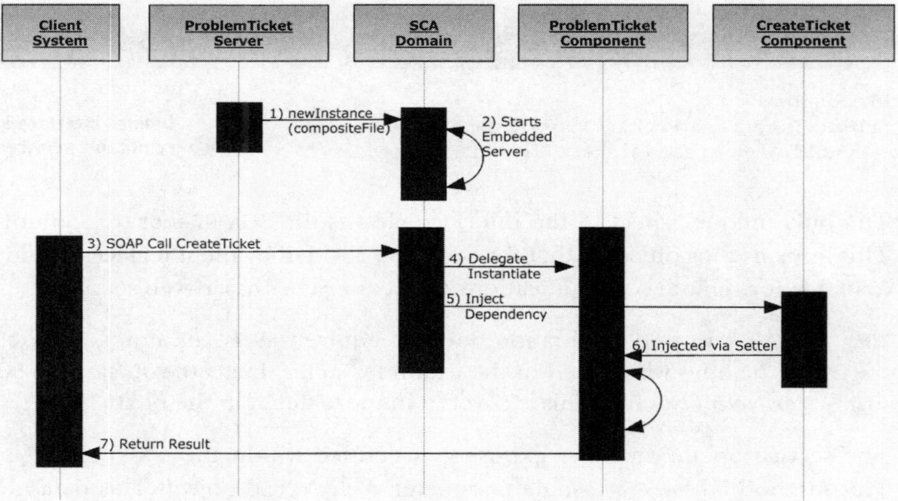

Figure 3.6 Overview of the sample assembly we've constructed

Table 3.1 Description of the steps shown in figure 3.6

<table>
<tr><th>Step</th><th>Description</th></tr>
<tr><td>1</td><td>The <code>ProblemTicketServer</code> class starts the SCA domain/container by using the “embedded” server. It instantiates the server by specifying the composite XML file used, which in this case is called <code>problemMgmt.composite</code>.</td></tr>
<tr><td>2</td><td>The <code>SCADomain</code> class, which is part of the Apache Tuscany implementation, is used to start the embedded Jetty server. In turn, this is used to host the web service that’s being exposed by the assembly’s <code>service</code> element.</td></tr>
<tr><td>3</td><td>A web services client initiates a <code>CreateTicket</code> request against the hosted web service using the dynamically generated WSDL created by the web service binding associated with the <code>service</code> element defined in the composite. The web service SOAP request might resemble the following:

```
<soapenv:Envelope
xmlns:soapenv="http://schemas.xmlsoap.org/soap/envelope/"
xmlns:chap="http://chapter32.book.opensoa/">
  <soapenv:Header/>
  <soapenv:Body>
    <chap:createTicket>
      <arg0>
        <caseNumber>10001</caseNumber>
        <customerEmail>jdoe@someplace.com</customerEmail>
        <customerName>John Doe</customerName>
        <problemDesc>This is a problem desc</problemDesc>
        <source>This is the source</source>
        <subject>This is the subject</subject>
      </arg0>
    </chap:createTicket>
  </soapenv:Body>
</soapenv:Envelope>
```

</td></tr>
<tr><td>4</td><td>The inbound request is received by the SCA embedded server, which then delegates the processing of the request to the component implementing the service, <code>ProblemTicketComponentImpl</code>.</td></tr>
<tr><td>5</td><td>The <code>ProblemTicketComponentImpl</code> has an associated dependency created through the <code>reference</code> element in the component’s definition XML: <code>CreateTicketComponent</code>.</td></tr>
<tr><td>6</td><td>The reference is injected into the <code>ProblemTicketComponentImpl</code> by way of setter injection. Now the <code>CreateTicketComponent</code> is instantiated. This class is responsible for processing the inbound problem ticket.</td></tr>
<tr><td>7</td><td>The request is processed and the results are returned to the client.</td></tr>
</table>

What we have demonstrated thus far is a fairly simple example of an SCA assembly. We’ve exposed a component as a web service and demonstrated how references to other components can be declaratively defined within the SCA assembly. Even though it’s a simple example, it’s worth noting that the components we’ve created have no awareness of what communications protocol will be used to interface with them.

There's no SOAP- or web service–specific code anywhere within the component implementation class, so the component itself isn't bound directly to a specific protocol. Instead, the binding of the protocol to the component is done declaratively through the service element definition. This form of loose coupling is very appealing, because as we'll see next, we can now expose services through any number of different protocols, or bindings, without having to change any implementation code. This is truly exciting stuff!

3.2.3 Defining services

We've already demonstrated some of the capabilities of the service element using the problem ticket example we've been building. To recap, the service element is used to expose a component's functionality for external consumption through any number of communication protocols, such as SOAP or JMS. The consumer of the service can be another component or an external client running outside the SCA framework. An example of such a client is one using a SOAP-based web service or perhaps instead interfacing through JMS queues. The service's binding method specifies the protocol by which it will be exposed. Figure 3.7 depicts the schema definition overview for services.

In our simple example from listing 3.1 (listing 3.2 is functionally equivalent, as you may recall, but defines the services at the root composite level), we specified the `service` as a nested element inside the component we're exposing. The `service` was defined as

```
<service name="ProblemTicketComponent" promote="ProblemTicketComponent">
  <binding.ws uri="http://localhost:8085/ProblemTicketService" />
</service>
```

In the preceding code, we *did not* specify an `@interface` attribute, as the service is supporting all the available business functions. However, by using the `@interface` attribute, you can selectively decide which methods to expose as public operations. For

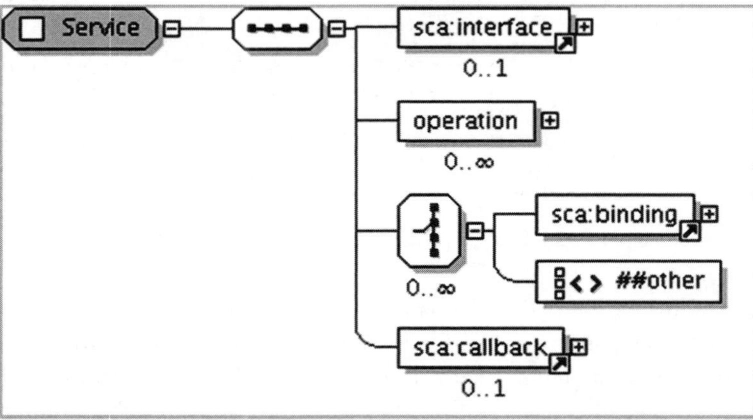

Figure 3.7 XML Schema definition overview for services

example, let's assume we've created another component called `ProblemTicket-Component2` (and its corresponding implementation, `ProblemTicketComponent-Impl2`) that's the same as `ProblemTicketComponent` with the exception that we've added another method to the `ProblemTicketComponent2` called `deleteTicket`. If we then add this method to the interface and run the assembly, we'll notice in the generated WSDL that two operations are exposed through this web service, `createTicket` and `deleteTicket`, as illustrated in this WSDL fragment:

```
<wsdl:binding name="ProblemTicketComponent2SOAP11Binding"
    type="ns0:ProblemTicketComponent2PortType">
   <soap:binding style="document"
     transport="http://schemas.xmlsoap.org/soap/http"/>
   <wsdl:operation name="createTicket">
     <soap:operation soapAction="urn:createTicket" style="document"/>
     … wsdl input and output
   </wsdl:operation>
   <wsdl:operation name="deleteTicket">
     <soap:operation soapAction="urn:deleteTicket" style="document"/>
     … wsdl input and output
   </wsdl:operation>
 </wsdl:binding>
```

If we then decide that only the `createTicket` operation should be exposed as a web service, we can specify an interface that only includes the `createTicket` method, even though the implementation class `ProblemTicketComponentImpl2` contains two methods. For example, we can specify the original `ProblemTicketComponent` as the interface, since it only contained the single `createTicket` method. This would result in the following component definition:

```
<service
  name="ProblemTicketComponent2"
  promote="ProblemTicketComponent2">
  <interface.java
    interface="opensoa.book.chapter3.ProblemTicketComponent" />
  <binding.ws uri="http://localhost:8085/ProblemTicketService" />
</service>
```

When the WSDL is automatically generated, it will only contain the single operation, `createTicket`. What's interesting to note is that the interface class used doesn't necessarily have to be the actual Java interface class that was implemented by the component. Instead, think of it as simply a definition for what services will be provided by the component. You can also use the `interface.wsdl` and specify a WSDL to define the full or subset of the method to expose. Enforcing which operations are permitted, as defined by the method signatures of the interface class, is performed at the container level, so it's secure. The alternative approach of simply creating a custom WSDL with only the operations specified that you want exposed isn't secure, since those operations could still be invoked by someone knowledgeable of the source (as pointed out previously, this custom WSDL could be referenced as the interface, in which case it's secure).

The `binding` child element associated with `service` described earlier is discussed in section 3.2.7. The callback functionality, which can be used for creating bi-directional services, is an advanced feature and will be discussed in chapter 4. Let's now focus on how property values can be set declaratively through the XML composition into component variables. Known as SCA properties, this capability allows runtime configurations to be easily made without having to recompile or modify code.

3.2.4 Working with properties

Up to this point we've covered the basics of creating components and services—the building blocks of SOA. The SCA standard also provides convenient runtime configuration capabilities through properties and references. Properties, the subject of this section, are much like their namesake in the Spring framework and are used for populating component variables in an injection-style fashion (references are the topic for section 3.2.6). This is obviously useful when you have to set environment-specific values without having to resort to using an external property file. More impressively, properties can be complex XML structures, which can be referenced via XPath locations by the components using it. This adds convenience and manageability to the assembly process. Figure 3.8 displays the schema fragment associated with the `Property` element.

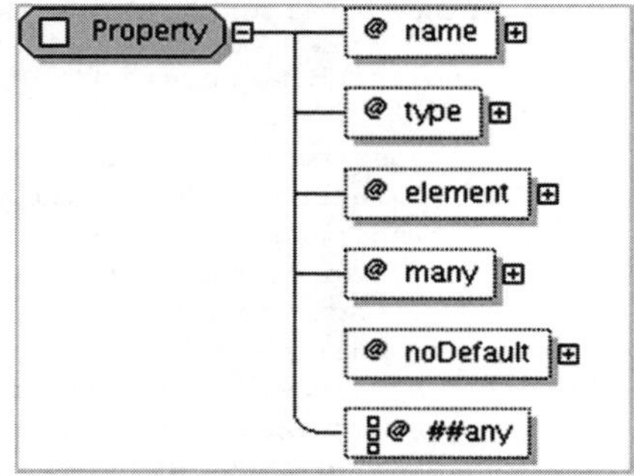

Figure 3.8 Figure 3.8 XML Schema definition overview for properties

We haven't previously illustrated any components that have utilized a property value, so we'll modify our `ProblemTicketComponent` to use some properties. In this case, let's assume that we want to pass a username and password to the component. In a real-life scenario, this may be necessary for establishing database connectivity or for accessing other types of resources (SMTP/POP3, File, etc.). In this instance, we'll create the username and password as "global" properties at the composite level (that is, created as a direct descendent of the document root element). They'll then be referenced from within the `ProblemTicketComponent` definition. This is illustrated in the updated composition definition shown in listing 3.6.

Listing 3.6 Example of using global properties

```
<composite xmlns="http://www.osoa.org/xmlns/sca/1.0"
  targetNamespace="http://opensoa.book.chapter3"
  name="ProblemManagementComposite">

  <property name="username">jdoe@my.com</property>
  <property name="password">mypassword1</property>
  <component name="ProblemTicketComponent">

    <implementation.java
      class="opensoa.book.chapter3_24.impl.ProblemTicketComponentImpl" />
    <service name="ProblemTicketComponent">
```

Defines properties

```
    <binding.ws uri="http://localhost:8085/ProblemTicketService"/>
  </service>
  <property name="username" source="$username"/>
  <property name="password" source="$password"/>
  <reference name="createTicket" target="CreateTicketComponent"/>
</component>

<component name="CreateTicketComponent">
  <implementation.java
   class="opensoa.book.chapter3_24.impl.CreateTicketComponentImpl"/>
</component>

</composite>
```

References to properties

Notice that, within the `component`, the global properties were referenced using the `@source` attribute of the embedded `property` element. The naming convention requires that you preface the referenced named variable using a `$` sign within the `@source` attribute, as is shown in the listing.

As an alternative to using global properties, you could have included the property settings directly within the component element, such as

```
<component name="ProblemTicketComponent">
  <implementation.java
   class="opensoa.book.chapter3_24.impl.ProblemTicketComponentImpl" />

  <service name="ProblemTicketComponent">
   <binding.ws uri="http://localhost:8085/ProblemTicketService"/>
  </service>

  <property name="username">jdoe@mycompany.com</property>
  <property name="password">mypassword1</property>
  <reference name="createTicket" target="CreateTicketComponent"/>
</component>
```

Regardless of the approach used, the `ProblemTicketComponentImpl` class must be modified to capture the injected properties. This can be done most easily by just adding two new member variables along with the SCA `@Property` annotation:

```
@Property
protected String username;
@Property
protected String password;
```

The `@Property` annotations spell out that these two class variables are set as properties. Note that there's no need to create setter methods to inject these values, although they must be specified with `public` or `protected` visibility in order for this approach to work. If specifying a nonprivate access level modifier is a concern, you can use the more traditional JavaBean-style approach and use setters to instruct the container to populate the properties in this fashion. Here's an example:

```
private String username;
private String password;

@Property(name="username")
 public void setMyUsername(String username) {
```

```
    this.username = username;
}

@Property
public void setPassword(String password) {
  this.password = password;
}
```

Notice that, for the username property, we created a method that didn't adhere to the standard "accessor" method style of set*Variable*—instead of setUsername, we used setMyUsername. Since the standard JavaBean accessor convention wasn't used, the optional @name attribute associated with the @Property reference had to be specified. Using the setter style injection can also be helpful if you want to perform additional processing after the value has been assigned (such as validation checks).

Using a Java Collection is also straightforward. For example, instead of using two properties to set the username and password, we can use a single property defined as

```
<property name="credentials" many="true">
  "jdoe@mycompany.com"
  "mypassword1"
</property>
```

Then, within the component class, it will be injected by using

```
@Property
protected Collection<String> credentials;
```

You can then access it like you would any other Collection class, such as

```
  credentials.iterator().next()
```

which will return the first item in the collection, or jdoe@mycompany.com.

More interestingly, properties can also be complex XML structures. You can then use XPath expressions to selectively identify which value you wish to populate into a given variable. For example, the following property called credentials is set to an embedded XML fragment as a global directly within the composite element:

```
<property name="credentials" type="hw:CredentialsType" >
  <Credentials>
    <username>jdoe@mycompany.com</username>
    <password>mypassword1</password>
  </Credentials>
</property>
```

To then pass the specific values associated with username and password, the following property reference can be used within the component definition:

```
<property name="username"
  source="$credentials/*[local-name()='Credentials']/
        *[local-name()='username']" />
<property name="password"
  source="$credentials/*[local-name()='Credentials']/
        *[local-name()='password']" />
```

The source attribute must be a valid XPath, as shown here; otherwise the injected reference will be set to `null`. The complete modified composition is shown in listing 3.7.

Listing 3.7 Modified composition illustrating use of embedded XML properties

```
<composite xmlns="http://www.osoa.org/xmlns/sca/1.0"
  targetNamespace="http://opensoa.book.chapter3"
  xmlns:hw="http://opensoa.book.chapter3"
  name="ProblemManagementComposite">

  <property name="credentials" type="hw:CredentialsType" >
    <Credentials>
      <username>jdoe@mycompany.com</username>
      <password>mypassword1</password>
    </Credentials>
  </property>

  <component name="ProblemTicketComponent">
    <implementation.java
      class="opensoa.book.chapter3_24.impl.ProblemTicketComponentImpl" />
    <service name="ProblemTicketComponent">
      <binding.ws uri="http://localhost:8085/ProblemTicketService"/>
    </service>
    <property name="username"
      source="$credentials/*[local-name()='Credentials']/
            *[local-name()='username']" />
    <property name="password"
      source="$credentials/*[local-name()='Credentials']/
            *[local-name()='password']" />
   <reference name="createTicket" target="CreateTicketComponent"/>
  </component>

  <component name="CreateTicketComponent">
   <implementation.java
     class="opensoa.book.chapter3_24.impl.CreateTicketComponentImpl"/>
  </component>
</composite>
```

As you can see, there's considerable flexibility in how static property values can be injected into component classes at runtime. The next "essential" SCA technology we'll address is *implementation*. Implementation is how SCA provides for multilanguage support and is the mechanism by which recursive compositions are created, which is the nesting of composites to create higher-level assemblies. As you may recall from our SOA discussion in chapter 1, the ability to easily create components that are themselves composed of one or more subcomponents greatly facilitates code reuse—a key objective behind SOA.

3.2.5 Implementation options

The `implementation` node, as we've seen in previous examples, is a child element of `component`. It's used to define the concrete implementation for the component. In the examples thus far, we've used the Java implementation, as specified by using `implementation.java`. However, SCA is designed to support multiple languages. Which languages are supported is driven by the SCA implementation. Apache Tuscany, the open source SCA offering we're using, supports the following types, shown in table 3.2.

Table 3.2 Apache Tuscany SCA implementation types

Type	Description
Java components	We've been using Java components in the examples so far.
Spring assemblies	You can invoke Java code exposed through Spring.
Scripting: JavaScript, Groovy, Ruby, Python, XSLT	Uses JSR 223 to support a wide variety of scripting languages.
BPEL	Integration with Apache ODE for BPEL support.
XQuery	Supports Saxon XQuery.
OSGi	Supports Apache Felix OSGi implementation.

One implementation that's anticipated to be supported by all SCA-compliant products is the composite implementation. Using `implementation.composite`, you can construct a hierarchy of services that are layered upon each other. At the lowest level, you would presumably have finer-grained components that perform specific, narrow functions. As you move up the hierarchy, you could construct coarser-grained services that incorporate or build upon the lower-level ones. You could also wrap components that are designed primarily for one purpose and repurpose them for other users. This strategy can best be illustrated through an example, which follows.

So far, we've created a service that can be used to submit a hypothetical problem ticket. The ticket data structure used resembles that of an inbound customer service email, and contains such fields as *subject*, *body/description*, and *to*. Let's assume now that someone in IT decided that it would be an outstanding idea to also generate cases/tickets for system events that occur, since they too need to be followed up on in a similar manner. Rather than build an entirely new service to perform this function, the development team decides to create a façade or wrapper service that, while using the nomenclature familiar with IT guys, really just leverages the existing problem ticket service. This new service will use a new component called `SystemErrorComponent`, which just calls `ProblemTicketComponent` under the covers. In fact, foresight would tell us that other organizations within the company will also likely be interested in similarly leveraging the problem ticket system. Figure 3.9 illustrates what is now more broadly called the Issue Management System (IMS) that supports receiving tickets from any number of sources.

To support this new capability, we'll create a new composite assembly called `IssueManagementComposite` that references the problem ticket assembly we created in listing 3.1. This new assembly will be constructed so that it will be the main service interface for the various interfaces, such as system IT tickets or customer service tickets. The `ProblemManagementComposite` will be used for the low-level create,

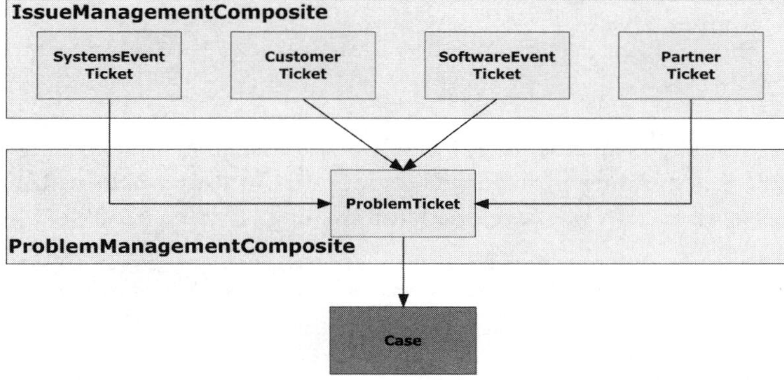

Figure 3.9 Overall plans for the Issue Management System

delete, and update ticket operations, which are in turn called by those components defined in the `IssueManagementComposite`. Why follow such an approach? It enables us to create customized service interfaces for each of the audiences interested in using the service. This approach will lower the barrier for widespread acceptance of the system, and marketing is an important part in improving the adoption rate of SOA. Listing 3.8 shows the `ProblemManagementComposite` assembly we created earlier.

Listing 3.8 ProblemManagementComposite

```
<composite
 xmlns="http://www.osoa.org/xmlns/sca/1.0"
 targetNamespace="http://opensoa.book.chapter325"
 xmlns:hw="http://opensoa.book.chapter325"
 name="ProblemManagementComposite3">

 <property name="username">jdoe@mycompany.com</property>
 <property name="password">mypassword1</property>

 <service
  name="ProblemTicketService"
  promote="ProblemTicketComponent">
  <interface.java
     interface="opensoa.book.chapter3_25.ProblemTicketComponent"/>
 </service>

 <component name="ProblemTicketComponent">
  <implementation.java
    class=
    "opensoa.book.chapter3_25.impl.ProblemTicketComponentImpl" />
  <property name="username" source="$username" />
  <property name="password" source="$password" />

  <reference
     name="createTicket" target="CreateTicketComponent" />
  </component>
```

```
  <component name="CreateTicketComponent">
    <implementation.java
      class="opensoa.book.chapter3_25.impl.CreateTicketComponentImpl" />
  </component>
</composite>
```

The new IssueManagementComposite, which is the assembly for exposing issue-specific services for generating problem tickets, appears in listing 3.9. In this example, only a single new interface was developed: for creating IT system trouble tickets.

Listing 3.9 IssueManagementComposite for creating issue-specific problem tickets

```
<composite xmlns="http://www.osoa.org/xmlns/sca/1.0"
  targetNamespace="http://opensoa.book.chapter325"
  xmlns:hw="http://opensoa.book.chapter325"
  name="IssueManagementComposite">

  <service                                            <-- 1 Defines new
    name="SystemErrorService"                              service using SOAP
    promote="SystemErrorComponent">
    <binding.ws uri="http://localhost:8085/SystemErrorService"/>
  </service>

  <component name="SystemErrorComponent">       <-- 2 Defines component
    <implementation.java class=
      "opensoa.book.chapter3_25.impl.SystemErrorComponentImpl" />
    <reference
        name="problemTicket"
        target="ProblemTicket"/>            <-- 3 Injects referenced component
  </component>

  <component name="ProblemTicket">
    <implementation.composite                        <-- 4 Defines composite
      name="hw:ProblemManagementComposite"/>               implementation
  </component>
</composite>
```

Before we examine the Java code associated with SystemErrorComponentImpl ❷, let's examine more carefully how the ProblemManagementComposite is used. The SystemErrorComponentImpl contains an injected dependency in the form of a ProblemTicketComponent that's assigned to the instance variable called problemTicket. This is accomplished through the ProblemTicket component ❹ that's defined as a reference ❸. This component defines an implementation that uses the composite named ProblemManagementComposite, which, as you may recall, is the name we assigned to our assembly used to create the problem tickets (listing 3.8 defines this composite). The single service provided by the composite is called SystemErrorService ❶, which is exposed using a SOAP binding.

Two questions might come to mind: how do you specify the file location containing the ProblemManagementComposite, and how does the container know which component within ProblemManagementComposite to use for injecting ProblemTicketComponent? The answer to both can be summed up, somewhat tongue-in-cheek, as "automagically." To answer the first question: the container automatically loads and parses all composite files that it finds on the classpath. Hence, it could identify where to find `ProblemManagementComposite` (in my example, it's in a file called `problemMgmt.composite`). As for the second question, a form of autowiring is performed—the `SystemErrorComponentImpl` is expecting a class of type `ProblemTicketComponent`, and through the container's parsing of the `ProblemManagementComposite`, it could identify a match since only a single component matched that class signature.

We can now take a closer look at the implementation of the `SystemErrorComponentImpl` class (listing 3.10), which is responsible for receiving an inbound system IT problem ticket request and then wraps and resubmits it to the `ProblemTicketComponent` service.

Listing 3.10 SystemErrorComponentImpl.java

```
@Service(SystemErrorComponent.class)                          <-- 1 Identifies service implementation
public class SystemErrorComponentImpl implements
    SystemErrorComponent {

  @Reference                                                  <-- 2 Identifies injected reference
  public ProblemTicketComponent problemTicket;

  public int systemProblem(String system, String title,
      String problem) {
    System.out.println("*** SystemErrorComponentImpl ***");
    int rval = 0;

    TicketDO ticket = new TicketDO();
    ticket.setSubject(title);
    ticket.setSubject(problem);
    ticket.setSource(system);

    rval = problemTicket.createTicket(ticket);                <-- 3 Returns from referenced component

    System.out.println("problemTicket:" + rval);

    return rval;
  }
}
```

The code represents a simple component implementation and identifies the SCA service interface ❶ and injected references ❷. As we pointed out earlier, the injected `ProblemTicketComponent` represents the service used for processing the request, as `SystemErrorComponentImpl` is a wrapper that simply takes the inbound request that is tailored for IT system event errors and resubmits the ticket using the more generic `ProblemTicketComponent` ❸. The service interface class, `SystemErrorComponent`, defines the method signature `systemProblem` as accepting three string parameters. This will be the service operation that's exposed.

Starting the SCA container can be done as you saw earlier by using the SCA embedded domain class, in which case you just specify the composite file used to initiate the desired assembly. In this case, the `IssueManagementComposite` was defined in a file called issueMgmt.composite, so the SCA embedded domain was started using the code shown in listing 3.11.

Listing 3.11 Starting the SCA embedded domain

```
public class ProblemTicketServer {

   public static void main(String[] args) {

      SCADomain scaDomain = SCADomain.newInstance("issueMgmt.composite");
      try {
         System.out.println("ProblemTicket server started" +
          " (press enter to shutdown)");
         System.in.read();
      } catch (IOException e) {
         e.printStackTrace();
      }

      scaDomain.close();
      System.out.println("ProblemTicket server stopped");
   }
}
```

What have we accomplished in this section? We've created a new higher-level composite assembly (`IssueManagementComposite`) that uses the services defined within another, different composite (`ProblemManagementComposite`). This demonstrates how you can truly create compositions of services, which is one of the foundational objectives behind SOA. We accomplished this using the `implementation.composite` implementation type, which is currently supported in Apache Tuscany (in chapter 4 I'll show how other languages can be used to create concrete implementations). You also saw how we can inject, by reference, a component service that was defined in a different composite assembly. In the next section, we further examine references that, similar to properties, allow runtime configurations to be made without requiring implementation code changes. Such flexibility contributes to the agility so often touted as a major benefit of moving to SOA.

3.2.6 Using references for dependency injection

The SCA reference, as we've demonstrated in a variety of ways, is used to insert dependent class instances in much the same way that properties can be used to insert static data into a class. This approach was first popularized by Spring's innovative inversion of control features, which defined a form of dependency injection. SCA builds on many of the best practices of Spring while introducing some additional capabilities. The definition of the reference node is illustrated in figure 3.10.

In the assembly examples we've created so far, we've specified references directly within the component definition, such as

```
<component name="SystemErrorComponent">
  <implementation.java
    class="opensoa.book.chapter3_26.impl.SystemErrorComponentImpl" />
  <reference name="problemTicket" target="ProblemTicket"/>
</component>
```

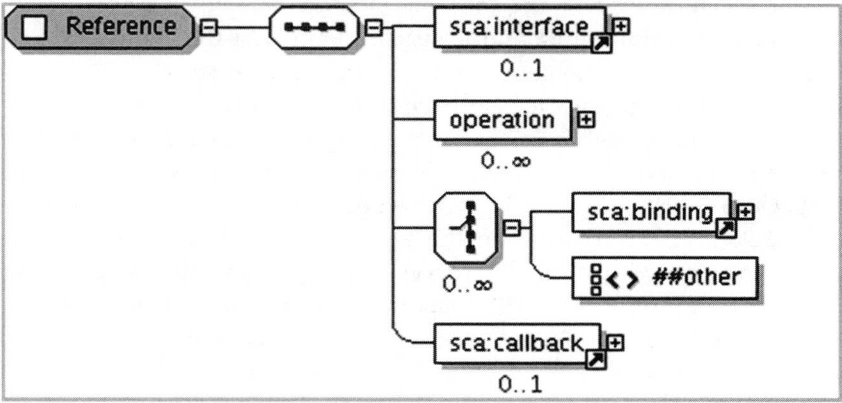

Figure 3.10 XML Schema definition overview for references

However, similar to the `service` and `property` elements, the `reference` element can also be specified at the composite level, with the `@promote` attribute used to indicate what component will use the reference. This approach is generally used when you're specifying an external service that will act as the referenced object. For example, in the previous section we referenced a component that consisted of an `implementation.composite` to invoke a service located in another assembly. You could also accomplish this by using a reference that had a web service binding. This approach is best illustrated through an example (see listing 3.12).

Listing 3.12 Using web service binding to specify a remote reference

```
<composite xmlns="http://www.osoa.org/xmlns/sca/1.0"
  targetNamespace="http://opensoa.book.chapter3"
  xmlns:hw="http://opensoa.book.chapter3"
  name="IssueManagementComposite">

  <service
    name="SystemErrorService"
    promote="SystemErrorComponent">
    <binding.ws uri="http://localhost:8085/SystemErrorService"/>
  </service>

  <component name="SystemErrorComponent">          ❶ Defines component
    <implementation.java
      class="opensoa.book.chapter3_26.impl.SystemErrorComponentImpl" />
  </component>

  <reference name="ProblemTicket"                  ❷ Defines using promotion
    promote="SystemErrorComponent/problemTicket">
    <binding.ws uri="http://localhost:8086/ProblemTicketService"/>   ❸ Uses remote service
  </reference>

</composite>
```

As you can see in listing 3.12, the `reference` element has been removed from the component element definition ❶ and is instead defined at the composite level ❷. The `@promote` attribute uses the convention of `<component-name>/<reference-name>`, so in this case, the source for the reference is `SystemErrorComponent`'s `problemTicket` object. Unlike in the previous section's example, this dependency isn't satisfied by specifying a target component within the same assembly. Rather, it uses a web service binding ❸ to specify a service located remotely (in both examples we're using the `ProblemTicketService` defined in the `ProblemManagementComposite)`. As you can see, we aren't limited to local references running within the same VM but can use remote references using any of the supported bindings. Regardless of whether you are using a local or a remote reference, the source class recipient of the injected reference is completely oblivious to how the container performs the injection.

Reference protocol transparency

We've frequently pointed out that one of the major benefits of using SCA is that you can create services in a protocol-neutral fashion, with the selected binding defined declaratively at runtime. The same benefits also apply to references, whereby the class receiving the referenced object is oblivious to what communications protocol is being used (the referenced object's interface must be defined, but not the implementation details). Thus, the recipient component couldn't care less whether the injected class arrives via SOAP, JMS, or EJB.

Listing 3.3 illustrated how a reference was associated with a setter method that followed standard JavaBean conventions. Similar to how properties are injected, references can also be injected either by specifying a public or protected instance variable designated with the `@Reference` annotation. Here's how we specified the `CreateTicketComponent` as a reference:

```
@Reference
protected CreateTicketComponent createTicket;
```

Using the setter approach is similar (note that we changed the instance variable to `private` using this approach, to be consistent with the JavaBean convention).

```
private CreateTicketComponent createTicket;

@Reference
public void setProblemTicket(ProblemTicketComponent problemTicket) {
  this.problemTicket = problemTicket;
}
```

Depending on your coding conventions, this approach may be preferred, and it does add some flexibility, as you can use the setter to perform other actions, if need be, during the time of injection.

References are one of the most powerful features of SCA, and they likely will play a central role in how you design assemblies. Let's now turn to the last of the core SCA technologies: bindings.

3.2.7 Defining available bindings

Bindings represent one of the most innovative and value-added aspects of SCA, for they allow you to create and reference services over a variety of communication protocols, and the underlying implementation classes are oblivious to them. Figure 3.11 shows a simplified definition for the binding element.

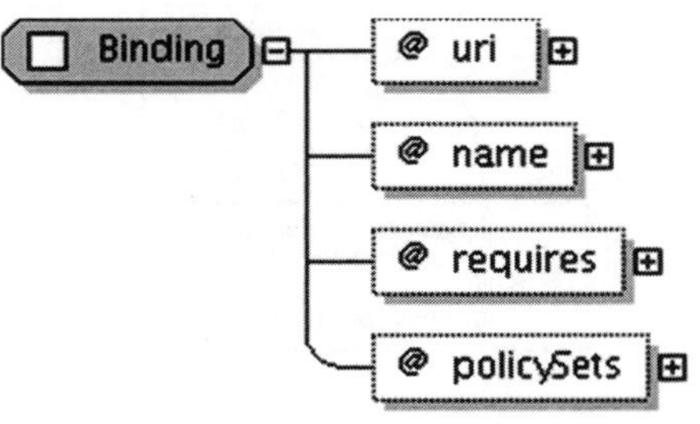

Figure 3.11 XML Schema definition overview for bindings

The supported SCA bindings, much as with implementation types, will likely vary from one SCA product to another. However, we anticipate that most SCA implementations will support a web service binding (`binding.ws`). The supported bindings within the Apache Tuscany project are shown in table 3.3.

Table 3.3 Apache Tuscany binding types

Type	Description
Webservice	Uses Apache Axis 2 as the underlying engine.
JMS	Default implementation uses ActiveMQ.
JSON-RPC	JavaScript JSON support for browser/server type connectivity.
EJB	Only stateless session beans are currently supported.
Feed	RSS feed.

We've already seen some of the capabilities of the web services binding (`binding.ws`), such as the ability to dynamically generate a WSDL if one isn't present. Often it's beneficial to create your own WSDL—for example, if you want to consolidate your web services into a single WSDL file instead of having a separate WSDL constructed for each exposed service. Let's consider how this can be done.

The sample application we've created has thus far involved creation of two web services. The first service was the `ProblemTicketService`. It's a "generic" service that eventually will be used to create cases. The second web service, `SystemErrorService`, is a wrapper service tailored specifically for inbound IT system tickets (as you recall, it repackages the request and resubmits it to the `ProblemTicketService`). Until now, we've used the WSDL autogeneration feature of Tuscany to create a WSDL for each of the two services. However, it would be preferable to create a single WSDL that incorporates both of these services. Figure 3.12 shows the custom-created WSDL.

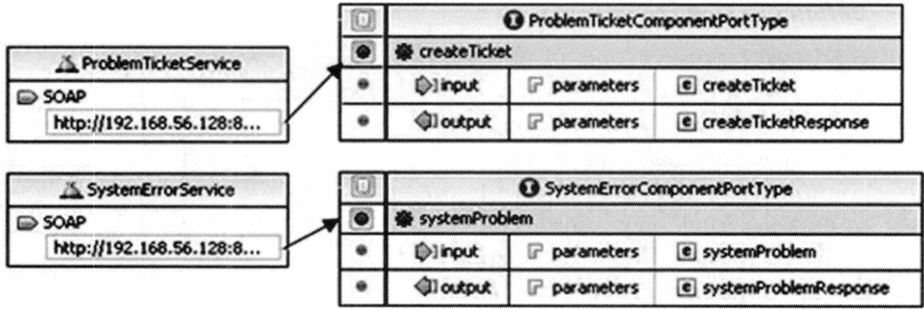

Figure 3.12 Graphical depiction of WSDL for combined services

As illustrated, two separate services are defined within the WSDL, one for each SCA service we've exposed. Combining definitions into a single WSDL is often convenient as there are less definition files to manage and everything is in one place. The service definitions within the WSDL are shown here:

```
<wsdl:service name="SystemErrorService">
  <wsdl:port name="SOAP" binding="ns0:SystemErrorServiceSOAPBinding">
    <soap:address
      location="http://localhost:8085/SystemErrorService"/>
  </wsdl:port>
</wsdl:service>

<wsdl:service name="ProblemTicketService">
  <wsdl:port name="SOAP" binding="ns0:ProblemTicketServiceSOAPBinding">
    <soap:address
      location="http://localhost:8085/ProblemTicketService"/>
  </wsdl:port>
  </wsdl:service>
```

To create the single WSDL, use the two generated WSDLs and merge them together. To make the WSDL more manageable in size, separate the XSD schemas into individual files and assign them their own namespaces. Then include them using the schema `include` element, which results in a much abbreviated `wsdl:types` section:

```
<wsdl:types>
  <xs:schema >
    <xs:import
      namespace="http://chapter3.book.opensoa/system"
      schemaLocation="systemTicket.xsd"/>
    <xs:import
      namespace=http://chapter3.book.opensoa/issue
      schemaLocation="issueTicket.xsd"/>
  </xs:schema>
</wsdl:types>
```

Now, for us to use this new WSDL, it must be referenced in the service definition of our assembly. Let's modify the `ProblemManagementComposite`, which defines the `ProblemTicketService`, so that the service entry reads

```
<service name="ProblemTicketService" promote="ProblemTicketComponent">
  <binding.ws wsdlElement=
    "http://chapter3.book.opensoa#wsdl.port(ProblemTicketService/SOAP)"/>
</service>
```

Two things will likely jump out at you when reviewing this code: the `wsdlElement` definition and the `#wsdl.port` syntax. The Web Service Binding Specification [SCAWS] defines several implementation patterns for how you can dynamically reference specific portions of the WSDL. The `#wsdl.port` pattern accepts as its parameter `<service-name>/<port-name>`. So in our example we're stating that the service we want to expose for this component can be found, as shown in figure 3.13.

The definition for `SystemErrorService` similarly references the WSDL location for the service being exposed:

```
<service name="SystemErrorService" promote="SystemErrorComponent">
  <binding.ws wsdlElement=
    "http://chapter3.book.opensoa#wsdl.port(SystemErrorService/SOAP)"/>
</service>
```

To recap what this has accomplished: (a) we now have a single WSDL that defines both services, and this simplifies management; and (b) a single port is used, whereas previously we used a port for each service exposed (multiple ports can cause network headaches, as firewall changes may be required to support each additional port used).

One of the main benefits of SCA is that it supports introducing different protocols without having to modify the underlying components to reflect any protocol-specific configurations. The `ProblemTicketComponentImpl` class we developed earlier (listing 3.3) had no SOAP-specific code present, such as Axis2 classes, and yet we exposed the service through SOAP. That said, many Java shops choose not to use SOAP over HTTP internally and instead prefer JMS. In part, this is due to the flexibility inherent in JMS to support asynchronous communications (something only recently becoming more widespread in SOAP over HTTP). JMS is arguably also stronger in the areas of guaranteed message delivery, and ActiveMQ's built-in support for Apache Camel [Camel] provides powerful support for many common enterprise integration patterns.

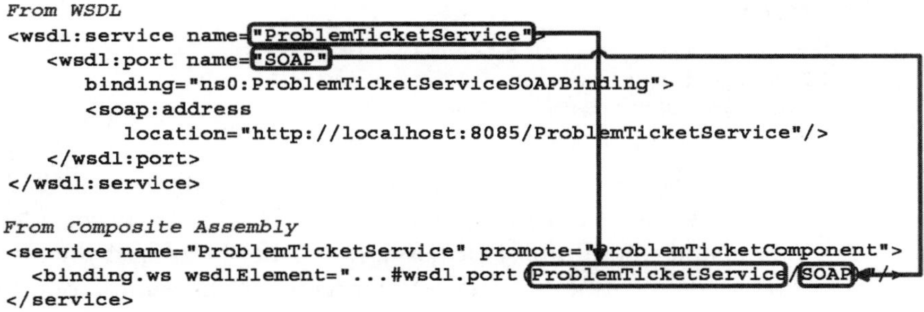

Figure 3.13 How the WS binding service and port definition maps to the WSDL file

Let's demonstrate how easy it is to change protocols using SCA. You may be skeptical that this works as advertised (we must confess to being dubious at first as well), so we'll add a JMS binding to the `SystemErrorService` service. We chose this service because it represents tickets that can be created internally through monitoring applications, and JMS is commonly used as the communications protocol for these types of event notifications.

Adding a JMS binding as an additional service entry point for `SystemErrorComponent` requires three steps: (1) adding a new binding element definition to the existing `SystemErrorService` service, (2) adding a JMS WSDL binding, and (3) creating a test JMS client. Let's take a look at the first task.

NOTE Apache Tuscany, which I'm using for examples, supports two methods of JMS binding. The first, which I'm demonstrating in this section, uses SOAP over JMS. The other uses the `binding.jms` type. The latter appears to be a more flexible solution insofar as configuration is concerned, but the former (which still uses `binding.ws`, since it uses SOAP) is easier to configure.

We can add an additional binding protocol by including another binding element within the service definition. In our example, we'll add another `binding.ws` element, but this one will specify a JMS queue and configuration as well as specify a WSDL `wsdl.binding` that has been added to support SOAP over JMS (more on this shortly). The code example in listing 3.13 demonstrates the changes.

Listing 3.13 Adding a JMS as an additional binding to a service

```
<service
  name="SystemErrorService"
  promote="SystemErrorComponent">
  <binding.ws                                        ❶ Defines SOAP over JMSbinding
   ➥wsdlElement="http://chapter3.book.opensoa/system#
   ➥wsdl.binding(SystemErrorServiceJMSBinding)"
   ➥uri="jms:/SystemErrorInQueue?transport.jms.ConnectionFactoryJNDIName=
   ➥QueueConnectionFactory&amp;java.naming.factory.initial=
   ➥org.apache.activemq.jndi.ActiveMQInitialContextFactory&amp;
   ➥java.naming.provider.url=tcp://localhost:61616?
   ➥wireFormat.maxInactivityDuration=0" />

  <binding.ws
    wsdlElement="http://chapter3.book.opensoa#➥
    wsdl.port(SystemErrorService/SOAP)" />
</service>
```

The first `binding.ws` was the one added to support the JMS protocol ❶. The lengthy `uri` string defines the ActiveMQ configuration. The `SystemErrorInQueue` is the inbound JMS queue where inbound messages will be lifted, and the `java.naming.provider.url` value identifies the ActiveMQ instance. A description of other settings, and instructions for setting up ActiveMQ, can be found in the ActiveMQ documentation [ActiveMQ].

Using SCA to rationalize your existing services

One of the big challenges encountered by most enterprises is that they may already have a scattershot of services exposed via JMS or SOAP. Rationalizing them to provide for a consistent interface or to enforce governance requirements can be challenging, especially when making wholesale modifications is out of the question. Historically, ESBs were useful in such scenarios, because you could create new services that simply call or wrap the existing ones. Because SCA is equally adept acting as a server or client, it could also perform a similar role. That is, you could use SCA to repackage or provide new binding protocol support for an existing set of services.

To test the JMS binding, let's develop a client assembly that posts messages to the designated JMS queue. This will be used to simulate a regular JMS client that interfaces with the service. Although we could do this without using SCA, the exercise is beneficial because it demonstrates how SCA can be used within a client capacity. To develop this assembly, we'll create a new component that remotely references the `SystemErrorService` via JMS. This reference will then be used to invoke the JMS call and return the results (the default SOAP over JMS binding supports synchronous JMS calls). The assembly for the JMS client is shown in listing 3.14.

Listing 3.14 Assembly for the JMS client used to submit remote requests

```
<composite
  xmlns="http://www.osoa.org/xmlns/sca/1.0"
  targetNamespace="http://opensoa.book.chapter3"
  name="jmsclient">

  <component name="JMSComponent">
    <implementation.java
      class="opensoa.book.chapter3_27.impl.JMSClientImpl" />
  </component>

  <reference
    name="JMSClientReference"
    promote="JMSComponent/jmsClient">                    ❶ Assigns reference to JMSComponent
    <interface.wsdl
      interface="http://chapter3.book.opensoa#
      ➥wsdl.interface(SystemErrorComponentPortType)" />   Uses interface defined by WSDL portType

    <binding.ws
     wsdlElement="http://chapter3.book.opensoa/system#
     ➥wsdl.binding(SystemErrorServiceJMSBinding)"        Uses SOAP over JMS binding

     uri="jms:/SystemErrorInQueue?
     ➥transport.jms.ConnectionFactoryJNDIName=
     ➥QueueConnectionFactory&amp;java.naming.factory.initial=
     ➥org.apache.activemq.jndi.ActiveMQInitialContextFactory&amp;
     ➥java.naming.provider.url=tcp://localhost:61616?
     ➥wireFormat.maxInactivityDuration=0" />
  </reference>
</composite>
```

The reference element injects an object into JMSComponent's jmsClient instance variable that adheres to the specification provided by interface.wsdl element ❶. Since we can't directly inject a WSDL interface into the Java component, we used the class JMSClientImpl for the concrete implementation, as it was created with the same method and parameters defined in the WSDL (indeed, interface.java could have been used in lieu of interface.wsdl). The JMSClient interface implemented by JMSClientImpl is shown here:

```
@Remotable
public interface JMSClient {
   public int systemProblem(SystemErrorDO ticket);
}
```

To simplify what's happening, consider the reference being injected as a remote "handle" that's provided to the local component, JMSClientImpl. The handle's interface can be defined either via a Java class or through a WSDL (in this case, we used the WSDL). If a WSDL is used, then an implementation class that adheres to the WSDL specification must be used for receiving the handle with the component class. In other words, the interface defines the contract or structure of the reference and it can be defined using either a Java class or WSDL. The implementation of that interface can be satisfied using any of the supported implementation types, such as implementation.java or implementation.spring. Listing 3.15 displays a Java component class implementation for our JMS client.

Listing 3.15 JMSClientImpl component class

```
public class JMSClientImpl implements JMSClient {

  @Reference
  public JMSClient jmsClient;                    ❶ Injects reference to JMS client

  public int systemProblem(SystemErrorDO ticket) {
    int rval = jmsClient.systemProblem(ticket);      ❷ Invokes method on JMS client
    System.out.println("rval: " + rval);
    return rval;
  }
}
```

When the systemProblem method is invoked, it uses the remote JMS handle represented by the jmsClient variable ❶ to invoke the remove service ❷. To invoke this component, a Main class is then used to instantiate the SCA domain and invoke the component:

```
SCADomain scaDomain = SCADomain.newInstance("jmsclient.composite");
JMSClient jmsClient = scaDomain.getService(JMSClient.class,
  "JMSComponent");

SystemErrorDO ticket = new SystemErrorDO();
ticket.setProblem("test problem");
ticket.setSystem("test system");
ticket.setTitle("test title");
```

```
jmsClient.systemProblem(ticket);
scaDomain.close();
```

As previously pointed out, you're obviously not limited to using SCA to populate the remote JMS message. You can also use the ActiveMQ administrative console to submit a test messages.

To recap: We added a new binding to the `SystemErrorService` that enabled it to receive SOAP over JMS in addition to the SOAP over HTTP we previously set up. Then we created a JMS client using an SCA assembly for purposes of creating test requests. Adding the new JMS binding didn't result in any changes to the underlying target components. This exemplifies some of the great power and flexibility afforded by SCA. We've now covered all of the core SCA technologies and illustrated their usage.

3.3 Summary

One of the biggest challenges software developers face today is selecting the right framework. As you know, we're awash in frameworks, ranging from those used to create web applications and web services to application assembly. So there's probably a healthy dose of skepticism about the Service Component Architecture (SCA), regarding both its ability to fulfill its promise of an easy-to-use component assembly model with protocol and language neutrality as well as its vendor commitment. After all, we've seen in the past standards like Java Business Integration (JBI), which was launched with great fanfare, only to die and whither on the vine as vendor support, once so promising, quickly evaporated. Will SCA suffer from the same grim future? While my crystal ball may not always be accurate, We do think the future is bright for SCA. Why? Because SCA is the product of SOA best practices that have been learned over the past several years, and it also recognizes the heterogeneous environment in which most enterprises operate.

The SCA assembly framework, centered on the notion of components and services, nurtures a SOA mind-set of creating discrete, reusable units of code that can easily be shared and distributed. To demonstrate SCA's capability, we created in this chapter a hypothetical problem ticket service constructed of SCA components. We used Apache Tuscany, an excellent open source SCA implementation. The services we created were then exposed as SOAP-based web service over both HTTP and JMS. The code used to build the components was completely oblivious to the underlying protocol used when exposing it as a service. This is very exciting stuff, and means that as an architect, you don't have to worry about locking yourself into having to select up-front a single protocol or language. The power and flexibility of SCA also became apparent as we created higher-level compositions that consisted of lower-level components. We used Spring-like "inversion of control" dependency injection to configure the classes at runtime with dependent classes or properties.

While this chapter has covered the core SCA functionality, there's much more to learn about SCA, and we'll dive into some of the more advanced features in the next chapter.

4 Advanced SCA

This chapter covers

- Advanced SCA features
- Scripting languages in SCA
- Service Data Objects

In the previous chapter, we covered many of the basics for getting up and running with SCA using Apache Tuscany. This included how to create compositions, components, and services. These are important ingredients for building a foundation for your SOA environment, as they directly address the *S* in SOA, which is about creating reusable and discrete services. However, a lot of additional considerations exist that go beyond what we've demonstrated, particularly within an enterprise setting. They include such SCA capabilities as conversational services, complex deployment scenarios, multilanguage support, and Service Data Objects (SDOs). Without such features, the appeal of SCA would be limited, and its attendant contribution to SOA marginal. In this chapter, we'll address these more advanced capabilities, and by the end of this chapter, you'll have the know-how to begin using SCA in your real-life scenarios. Let's begin our coverage by looking at *component types*, which are used in lieu of the SCA annotations we have relied on until now.

4.1 Configuration using component types

Component types, like the SCA Java annotations shown in this book's examples so far, are used to define the configurable aspects of an implementation. By this, we're referring to the ability to configure, at runtime, dependencies such as properties and references. The SCA Java annotations we've used so far were essentially metadata used to notify the SCA engine of the relationships that existed between the classes. When using non-Java languages (section 4.5), the option of using annotations isn't always available, and so component types must be used. In certain scenarios, you may not find it desirable to use annotations, even if they're available. For example, since annotations are defined within the code, they aren't suitable when runtime configuration flexibility is required. Or perhaps you're exposing existing Java classes as components, and can't or don't want to make any source modifications. Let's take a look at how the component type facility works.

NOTE You can mix and match using component types and annotations, if you so desire. For example, you can use a component type file to identify properties but annotations for references and services.

To use component types, you first create a component type file, which is an XML document that follows a naming convention of

```
<component-implementation-class>.componentType
```

where *component-implementation-class* is the name of the implementation class associated with the component. The file location is also important, and must be within the same relative classpath as the implementation object. What's inside the file? Let's create an example.

NOTE In the source code that accompanies this section, the component type files are located under the src/main/resources folder.

The `ProblemTicketComponentImpl` class, which we created in listing 3.2 in the previous chapter, used the `@Service`, `@Property`, and `@Reference` annotations to identify what services are being offered by the implementation class. Let's assume we've created a new class called `ProblemTicketComponentImplNA`, which is function-wise identical to the original but without the use of the Java annotations (the class is in the sample code for this section). The component type definition used in lieu of the annotations is shown in listing 4.1.

Listing 4.1 Component type file used in lieu of SCA implementation class annotations

```
<componentType
  xmlns="http://www.osoa.org/xmlns/sca/1.0"
  xmlns:xsd="http://www.w3.org/2001/XMLSchema">

  <service name="ProblemTicketComponent">          ❶ Defines new service
    <interface.java                               ❷ Defines service interface class
      interface="opensoa.book.chapter4_1.ProblemTicketComponent"/>
  </service>
```

```
  <reference name="createTicket">                    <-- 3 Identifies reference to be injected
    <interface.java
      interface="opensoa.book.chapter4_1.CreateTicketComponent"/>
  </reference>

  <property name="username" type="xsd:string"/>      <-- 4 Identifies properties
  <property name="password" type="xsd:string"/>          to be injected
</componentType>
```

The service element is used in lieu of the @Service annotation to describe the services being offered by the component ❶. In this case, the interface for the service is defined by the method signatures found in the ProblemTicketComponent interface class ❷. The reference element similarly identifies, by its @name attribute, which class member variable it's associated with, as well as the interface ❸ for the referenced object. The property entries ❹ are used instead of @Property annotations to indicate which member variables in the class will be receiving the injected property values at runtime.

NOTE It may seem a bit superfluous for the reference and property elements to require an interface or type to be specified. We believe this may be because the target component class associated with the type file isn't reflected (perhaps because of the multilanguage nature of SCA). Without reflection, the reference interface and property types must be manually identified.

As you can see, using a component type file allows you to declaratively define your configuration in a way that's more flexible, though less convenient, than using annotations. We'll touch on component types again in our coverage of scripting language support in section 4.3. Next up, we'll look at SCA interaction models, which provide the ability to make more complex, long-running interactions between a client application and the service.

4.2 SCA interaction models

The services we've defined so far have all followed the commonly used stateless request/response pattern. In chapter 1, we discussed how using stateless services represents SOA best practice. This is because stateless services are more stand-alone, self-contained, and amenable to clustering for high performance. However, in certain scenarios statelessness isn't always an option and, in fact, can sometimes cause its own performance-related problems. For example, if a request typically takes a while to respond, the calling service must "block-and-hold" while the service completes its work. This can cause unacceptable delays, particularly when real-time user interactions are required, such as within a web application. So in certain scenarios using stateful conversations and callbacks can be worthwhile.

4.2.1 Using conversations

What is an example where we might want a conversational stateful service? Many third-party APIs, such as the one offered by Salesforce, require that you first call a login operation with your provided credentials. If successful, you're returned a `sessionId` that must be used in subsequent calls. In the case of Salesforce, the `sessionId` will become invalid after some period of inactivity (two hours) and has to be refreshed. Retrieving a `sessionId` is an expensive operation and can be relatively slow, so fetching a new one for each and every operation called isn't advisable. Before we delve into how to address this in SCA, let's first take a look at the various conversation scope levels that are supported. There are currently four types:

- *COMPOSITE*—All requests are dispatched to the same class instance for the lifetime of the composite. A classic scenario for this is a counter, where you increment it for each call made to a given service.
- *CONVERSATION*—Uses correlation to create an ongoing conversation between a client and target service. The conversation starts when the first service is requested and terminates when an end operation is invoked. An intelligent client is needed to support this capability.
- *REQUEST*—Similar to a web servlet request scope, whereby a request on a remotable interface enters the SCA runtime and processes the request until the thread completes processing. Only supported by SCA clients.
- *STATELESS*—The default is that no session is maintained.

Let's build on the example of the `sessionId` by using COMPOSITE scope. We'll simulate the behavior of the Salesforce.com API. Listing 4.2 shows the interface class for what we're calling the `SessionManager`. To keep things simple, the implementation will simply return a random integer.

Listing 4.2 `SessionManager` interface class annotated for conversational scope

```
@Remotable
@Conversational                                    <-- (1) Identifies service as conversational
public interface SessionManager {
  public void initialize();                        | Service
  public int getSessionId();                       | operations
}
```

The only difference here from what we saw with previous interfaces is the addition of the `@Conversational` annotation ❶, which notifies the container that this service must support a conversational scope. The implementation class, shown in listing 4.3, is where the real action takes place.

Listing 4.3 `SessionManagerImpl` implementation annotated for conversation

```
@Service (SessionManager.class)
@Scope ("COMPOSITE")                                         <-- (1) Identifies scope of service
@EagerInit                                                   <--
public class SessionManagerImpl implements SessionManager {      (2) Initializes when
                                                                     SCA domain starts
  private int sessionId = 0;

  public int getSessionId() {
```

```
    return sessionId;
  }

  @Init                                    <-- ❸ Calls method when
  public void initialize() {                     class initialized
    Random r = new Random();
    sessionId = r.nextInt(300000);
  }
}
```

Listing 4.3 contains a number of new annotations that we haven't seen yet. The `@Scope` annotation ❶ is used to specify the scope type (COMPOSITE, CONVERSATIONAL, REQUEST, STATELESS), and `@EagerInit` ❷ instructs the container to instantiate this class immediately when the domain is started (it otherwise would only be instantiated the first time it was called, or "lazily"). The `@Init` annotation ❸ is used to specify that the method that follows is to be called immediately after class instantiation—this is required when using the `@EagerInit` annotation. Since this method is called on class instantiation, no method parameters are permitted. In the example from listing 4.3, the method returns a fake `sessionId`, and it will be retrieved automatically by the SCA engine when the class is first created (this is assuming that we want to preserve the same `sessionId` during each subsequent call, which is the case when using Salesforce.com's API).

With the new conversational-ready class now in hand, we can inject it into the `CreateTicketComponent` we originally created in listing 3.5. We made the following additions to that class so that it receives the injected reference to the new `SessionManager` class we created earlier:

```
@Reference
protected SessionManager sessionManager;
```

Lastly, we'll update the `ProblemManagementComposite` assembly to configure the new component to represent the `SessionManager`, and add the reference to that component from within the `CreateTicketComponent` definition:

```
<component name="CreateTicketComponent">
  <implementation.java
    class="opensoa.book.chapter4_21.impl.CreateTicketComponentImpl"/>
  <reference name="sessionManager"
      target="SessionManagerComponent"/>
</component>

<component name="SessionManagerComponent">
  <implementation.java
    class="opensoa.book.chapter4_21.impl.SessionManagerImpl"/>
</component>
```

We've now added the conversation component called `CreateTicketComponent` to the assembly. When the SCA domain is launched using this assembly, the `SessionManagerComponent` is instantiated and the `initialize` method invoked, populating the `sessionId` value. This component is subsequently injected into the `CreateTicketComponent` service, and because `SessionManagerComponent` is conversational using a COMPOSITE type, the `sessionId` acquired at startup will persist across multiple calls to the `CreateTicketComponent` service (the `getSessionId` returns the same value every time), regardless of the client.

In a real-world implementation, we'd obviously have to accommodate for the occurrence where the `sessionId` is no longer valid due to the inactivity timer, but including that logic would be straightforward. Another related but slightly different form of conversational support is *callbacks*. The distinction between them is that the conversational services described so far pertain to the server service retaining some ongoing session-related data that extends beyond a single client request. A callback, on the other hand, is intended more for asynchronous communications, where there's no expectation that the client will again call the service within a related session. When the server service has completed processing the request, it will "call back" the client and provide the completed results. Callbacks are typically used when there's no guaranteed service level. In other words, the service may not be able to provide an immediate, synchronous response to the request. Let's take a look at the callback support within SCA.

4.2.2 Understanding callbacks

Callbacks are a form of bidirectional communications whereby a client requests a service and the provider or server returns back the results by "calling back" the client through a given interface or operation. It's considered an asynchronous form of communication because the server doesn't return the results through its synchronous reply, as most commonly exemplified by web services or RFC-style communications. Figure 4.1 contrasts synchronous versus callback-based asynchronous operations.

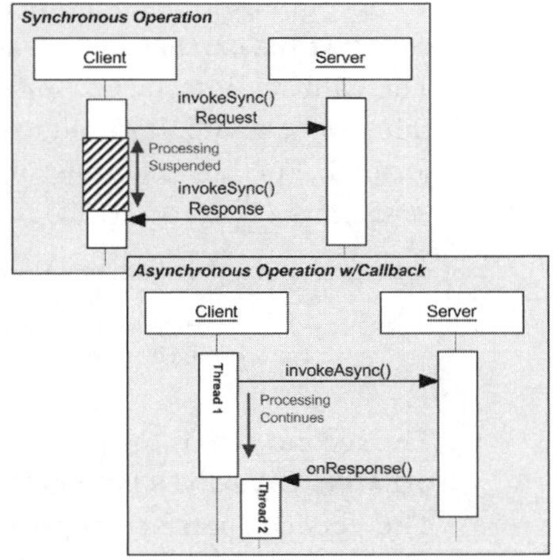

Figure 4.1 Differences between synchronous and asynchronous callback operations

As figure 4.1 shows, a client making a synchronous operation request will block and wait for a response from the server. On the other hand, with a callback the client makes the request and then continues processing. When the server has completed processing the request, it then calls back the client method on a separate thread to present the results.

Callbacks are often used when the processing time required to fulfill a request is unpredictable or slow. What's a scenario of how it might be used in the examples we've been building thus far? Let's say that we want to capture all create ticket events so that they can be fed into a business activity monitoring (BAM) dashboard that executives would monitor. For example, they might want to be apprised of any unusual spikes in ticket-creation activity. To illustrate this, let's create a new component that's called in an asynchronous fashion, with the component responsible for sending an event to the BAM or CEP system (we'll simulate this part). Since we want to ensure that the component was able to process the event successfully, a callback will be used to indicate the message was processed correctly. Because this is for event propagation and not directly related to the functioning of the service, we don't want to risk delaying a response to the client. Therefore, an asynchronous callback is sensible.

Creating a callback service does involve a few steps, and the SCA documentation can be a bit confusing as to how to accomplish this goal. The steps are as follow:

1. Create an interface class that defines the operation that will be called when the callback is performed.
2. Create the server interface and implementation class, and add the callback annotations.
3. Create or modify the client class to implement the callback interface defined in step 1 and add a reference to the server created in step 2. Modify the business logic to use the server component's functionality.
4. Modify the composite file to configure the assembly.

We'll begin by looking at the creation of the interface class.

CREATING THE CALLBACK INTERFACE

The callback interface is an SCA requirement for callback support, and it's the first thing we'll create. It's used to define the method to be called when the callback is performed. For our example of an event notifier, we developed the following simple `EventNotificationCallback` interface:

```
package opensoa.book.chapter4_22;

public interface EventNotificationCallback {
    void success(boolean status);
}
```

The second step is to create the server interface and implementation.

CREATING THE SERVER INTERFACE AND IMPLEMENTATION CLASSES

The service interface represents the business functionality being provided by the server, and in turn, will call back the results to the client. In our example, this is the component used for processing the event. To keep things simple, our server class doesn't do much—it just receives the inbound event and always returns a success. As we move forward into future chapters, this will be greatly expanded (specifically in chapter 8, which covers event stream processing). Listing 4.4 shows the interface class used for the new service.

Listing 4.4 `EventNotificationComponent` interface setup for callback support

```
package opensoa.book.chapter4_22;

import org.osoa.sca.annotations.*;
```

```
@Remotable
@Callback(EventNotificationCallback.class)        ❶ Specifies callback
public interface EventNotificationComponent {

  @OneWay                                         ❷ Identifies callback
  public void notify(TicketDO ticket);              method type
}
```

The @Callback annotation identifies this component as supporting a callback ❶, and it identifies EventNotificationCallback.class as the callback's interface. The @OneWay annotation ❷ flags the notify operation as nonblocking and instructs the client to continue processing immediately, without waiting for the service to execute. Now let's take a look at the corresponding implementation class (listing 4.5).

Listing 4.5 Implementation class for interface EventNotificationComponent

```
package opensoa.book.chapter4_22.impl;

import opensoa.book.chapter4_22.*;
import org.osoa.sca.annotations.*;

@Service(EventNotificationComponent.class)

public class EventNotificationComponentImpl
  implements EventNotificationComponent {

  @Callback                                       ❶ Injects callback class
  protected EventNotificationCallback callback;

  public void notify(TicketDO ticket) {

    try {
      Thread.sleep(40000);                        ❷ Sleeps 40 seconds
    } catch (InterruptedException e) {
      e.printStackTrace();
    }
    callback.success(true);                       ❸ Invokes callback
  }                                                 method
}
```

The @Callback annotation ❶ in the implementation class is used to identify the class that will be injected by the container at runtime. In this case, a class implementing the EventNotificationCallback will be injected, and this will represent the client that's invoking the service (consider it a handle to the calling client; the client must implement this interface). The Thread.sleep call ❷ is present to just simulate that it may take a while for the server function (notify) to complete its processing. But since this is an asynchronous operation, it doesn't matter how long the processing takes. Lastly, the callback itself is placed ❸, using the operation specified in the interface. This is calling the client class's callback method, as specified by the EventNotificationCallback interface, which the client must implement. Let's explore the modifications required to the client class next.

MODIFYING THE CLIENT CLASS TO IMPLEMENT THE CALLBACK INTERFACE

The client class in this example, `CreateTicketComponentImpl`, is injected with an implementation of `EventNotificationComponent`, whose `notify` method is subsequently invoked. The modified `CreateTicketComponentImpl` class is shown in listing 4.6.

Listing 4.6 Client implementation class

```
public class CreateTicketComponentImpl implements
    CreateTicketComponent, EventNotificationCallback {      ❶ Implements callback interface

  @Reference
  protected SessionManager sessionManager;

  @Reference
  protected EventNotificationComponent eventNotifier;

  public int create(TicketDO ticket) {
    Random r = new Random();
    int ticketId = r.nextInt(300000);
    eventNotifier.notify(ticket);

    return ticketId;
  }

  public void success(boolean status) {                    ❷ Invokes method
    System.out.println("Notify results: " + status);
  }
}
```

As you can see, only a few changes are necessary to support the callback functionality. First, the client must implement the callback interface ❶, and second, it must implement the required `success` method ❷. This method for now will simply print out to the console a boolean value returned through the callback parameter. The remaining step we must perform to enable the callback is to modify the composite assembly file.

MODIFYING THE COMPOSITION FILE TO INCORPORATE THE CALLBACK

The changes required in the composition file include adding the new `EventNotificationComponent`, which is the component that will perform the callback; creating a reference to that component from within the `CreateTicketComponent` component; and within the reference, identifying it as a callback. The updated assembly is shown in listing 4.7.

Listing 4.7 Updated composite assembly file for callback example

```
<composite
  xmlns="http://www.osoa.org/xmlns/sca/1.0"
  targetNamespace="http://opensoa.book.chapter4_22"
  xmlns:hw="http://opensoa.book.chapter4_22"
  name="ProblemManagementComposite">

  <property name="credentials" type="hw:CredentialsType">
    <hw:Credentials>
      <hw:username>jdoe@mycompany.com</hw:username>
      <hw:password>mypassword1</hw:password>
```

```
    </hw:Credentials>
  </property>

  <service
    name="ProblemTicketService"
    promote="ProblemTicketComponent">
    <binding.ws wsdlElement=
 "http://chapter4_22.book.opensoa#wsdl.port(ProblemTicketService/SOAP)"/>
  </service>

  <component name="ProblemTicketComponent">
    <implementation.java class=
      "opensoa.book.chapter4_22.impl.ProblemTicketComponentImpl" />
    <property name="username"
      source="$credentials//*[local-name()='username']" />
    <property name="password"
      source="$credentials//*[local-name()='password']" />

    <reference name="createTicket" target="CreateTicketComponent"/>
  </component>

  <component name="CreateTicketComponent">
    <implementation.java class=
      "opensoa.book.chapter4_22.impl.CreateTicketComponentImpl" />
    <reference name="sessionManager" target="SessionManagerComponent"/>

    <reference name="eventNotifier"
       target="EventNotificationComponent">           <-- 1 Defines reference to inject
       <interface.java interface=
         "opensoa.book.chapter4_22.EventNotificationComponent"
       callbackInterface=                               <-- 2 Identifies callback interface
       "opensoa.book.chapter4_22.EventNotificationCallback"/>
    </reference>
  </component>

  <component name="SessionManagerComponent">
    <implementation.java
      class="opensoa.book.chapter4_22.impl.SessionManagerImpl"/>
  </component>

  <component name="EventNotificationComponent">      <-- 3 Defines callback component
    <implementation.java class=
      "opensoa.book.chapter4_22.impl.EventNotificationComponentImpl"/>
  </component>
</composite>
```

The new `EventNotificationComponent` is defined in standard fashion consistent with the others ❸, and a reference to that component is included within the `CreateTicketComponent` definition ❶. The only distinction between this and the other references we've seen is the addition of the `@callbackInterface` attribute ❷—this signals that the reference includes callback functionality and also specifies the interface used.

NOTE You could also reference a callback that's running within a remote domain by specifying a binding element within the callback definition (in which case, you'd need a binding defined within the server component as well).

If you now launch this assembly using the source code for this section, you can submit a SOAP message to the `ProblemTicketService` and witness through the console that the callback is working successfully.

This discussion of how to use callbacks has demonstrated the use of asynchronous, bidirectional communications to create even more loosely bound services. Such services contribute to a more robust SOA environment. Although there are a few steps involved in setting this up, the results can pay big dividends, especially when you're calling remote services that can have unpredictable response times.

One of the most exciting parts of Tuscany we've yet to touch on is its support for scripting languages. Given the popularity of Ruby, along with the growing interest in Groovy, this support is an important value proposition. Let's look at scripting language support next.

4.3 Scripting language support

One of the main selling points of SCA is that it supports multiple languages (the particular SCA implementation, such as Apache Tuscany, determines which individual languages are supported). The days are likely past when an organization is entirely homogenous in their selection of which programming language to use. In particular, scripting languages such as Python, Perl, and Ruby have become increasingly popular. Their agile development cycles and, in some cases, simplified language structures have contributed to their success. Thus, support of multiple languages is fast becoming a requirement for enterprises adopting SOA.

NOTE Tuscany's SCA Java distribution, which is what we've been using, supports scripting languages through their Java implementations. For example, you're not really using native Ruby, per se, but instead, JRuby. In most cases, the Java implementations are excellent, but they may not be as feature rich in some areas nor offer complete support for external libraries that are available for the native versions. Also, dynamic modifications at runtime are not currently supported.

Tuscany's SCA implementation supports the following scripting languages: JavaScript, Groovy, Ruby, Python, XSLT, and XQuery. Space won't permit me to demonstrate each of these languages, so let's select Ruby for the example that we'll build (this seems like a good choice, given Ruby's widespread popularity). This example will create an email component in Ruby that will send out a confirmation email when a problem ticket has been reported. This can be accomplished by following these steps:

1. Create the Ruby component code/implementation.
2. Create a Java interface that mirrors the Ruby class signature.
3. Modify the `ProblemTicketComponentImpl` class to inject the component.
4. Add the Ruby component to the composite assembly.

The first step is to create the Ruby implementation class.

4.3.1 Creating a Ruby component

The Ruby class that we'll create, called `Email.rb`, is responsible for receiving a problem ticket and sending a reply email that contains the case number that was generated by way of the `CreateTicketComponentImpl` class. Thanks to Ruby's powerful string interpolation features, you can construct strings with placeholder variables that are injected at runtime. Listing 4.8 shows the very simple and terse code.

Listing 4.8 Ruby class `Email.rb` for defined component `EmailServiceComponent`

```
require 'net/smtp'                                    <-- 1 Imports required library

def email(from, to, subject, body, caseNo)            <-- 2 Defines method
   puts "Inside Ruby Email.rb Component"

   myMessage = <<END_OF_MESSAGE                       <-- 3 Creates string using tokens
From: #{from}
To: #{to}
Subject: Case: #{caseNo} - #{subject}

#{body}
END_OF_MESSAGE

  Net::SMTP.start('localhost', 25, 'localhost.localdomain',   <-- 4 Sends email using injected properties
   'uname', 'password', :login) do |smtp|
    smtp.send_message myMessage, from, to
  end
   return "true"
end
```

The first line imports the Ruby library required for email support ❶, followed by the definition of the `email` method ❷ that will be exposed as the component service to be called by the Java program. The `myMessage` string variable is then defined as a text template, delimited between the two `END_OF_MESSAGE` markers (this can be any arbitrary string value pair to delineate the start and end of the message). Within the message you'll notice the interpolation variables we alluded to a moment ago, which are identified by the format `#{variable}` ❸. These placeholders will be replaced by the actual value associated by the variable at runtime. Lastly, we use a Ruby closure ❹ to initiate the SMTP communication using the login parameters provided. The message is then sent by invoking the `send_message` method (see [Cooper] if you're a Ruby novice).

The Email.rb file is stored under the resources directory, using the same path convention as used for the Java implementation code (opensoa/book/chapter4_3/impl). Now, you might be wondering, how do we integrate this Ruby code with our Java classes? Good question. The first step is to create a Java interface that mirrors the Ruby method signature.

4.3.2 Creating a Java interface using the Ruby method signature

Obviously, we can't inject a Ruby dependency directly into a Java class, but SCA, through its magic, does essentially that. This is accomplished by creating a Java interface class that has the identical method signature that we defined within the Ruby class, `Email.rb`. As shown in the Ruby code in listing 4.8, this was defined as

```
def email(from, to, subject, body, caseNo)
```

A Java interface that mirrors this was created as `EmailServiceComponent.java`:

```
package opensoa.book.chapter4_3;

public interface EmailServiceComponent {
  public String email(String from, String to,
       String subject, String body, String caseNo);
}
```

This interface class is then used when injecting the reference to the Ruby class into Java, which takes us to the next step.

NOTE The two steps that follow are no different whether we're using a scripting language or a native Java class.

4.3.3 Modifying the service implementation class

Let's now modify the `ProblemTicketComponentImpl` class we worked with in previous examples to receive the injected reference. The following code illustrates how the component will be injected, in this case using "setter"-style injection:

```
private EmailServiceComponent emailService;

@Reference
public void setEmailService(
  EmailServiceComponent emailService) {
    this.emailService = emailService;
}
```

The `emailService` variable now contains an indirect handle to the Ruby code (we say indirect because it's proxied through the Java interface `EmailServiceComponent`). Calling the new service method is done using

```
System.out.println("email: " + emailService.email("doNotReply@none.com",
  ticket.getCustomerEmail(),
  ticket.getSubject(),
  ticket.getProblemDesc(),
  String.valueOf(ticket.getCaseNumber())));
```

As you can see, we're invoking the `email` method associated with the `EmailService-Component` interface but whose concrete implementation is being performed by the Ruby `Email.rb` class. This is pretty clever stuff from SCA. Our last step is to wire everything together in the assembly.

4.3.4 Modifying the composition assembly

The changes to the assembly composite file are minimal. The first thing we have to do is define the Ruby component corresponding to the `Email.rb` class we created:

```
<component name="EmailServiceComponent">
  <tuscany:implementation.script script=
   "opensoa/book/chapter4_3/impl/Email.rb"/>
</component>
```

Notice that the implementation is done using a Tuscany namespace; this is because Ruby support is a Tuscany feature and not defined explicitly in the SCA specification. That namespace, coincidentally, must be defined at the root element as `xmlns:tuscany="http://tuscany.apache.org/xmlns/sca/1.0"` (other SCA implementations may handle this differently). Now that the component is defined, the last thing we need to do is wire the reference to that component into our existing `ProblemServiceComponent`. Here's the new definition for that component, with the new reference shown in italics for emphasis:

```
<component name="ProblemTicketComponent">
  <implementation.java
    class="opensoa.book.chapter4_3.impl.ProblemTicketComponentImpl"/>
  <property
    name="username"
    source="$credentials//*[local-name()='username']"/>
  <property
    name="password"
    source="$credentials//*[local-name()='password']"/>

  <reference name="createTicket" target="CreateTicketComponent"/>
  <reference name="emailService" target="EmailServiceComponent"/>
</component>
```

Now this is a fairly simple example of using scripting, so you may be skeptical whether scripting languages are truly treated like first-class objects in SCA. For example, how would you inject properties into a Ruby script/class? Surely Java annotations can't be used? That's true, but you can use component types, as we discussed in section 4.1. For example, let's modify the `Email.rb` class so that we pass the SMTP settings as SCA properties. Here's the `Email.componentType` file:

```
<componentType xmlns="http://www.osoa.org/xmlns/sca/1.0"
      xmlns:wsdli="http://www.w3.org/2006/01/wsdl-instance"
      xmlns:xsi="http://www.w3.org/2001/XMLSchema-instance"
      xmlns:xsd="http://www.w3.org/2001/XMLSchema">

  <property name="smtp_username" type="xsd:string">uname</property>
  <property name="smtp_password" type="xsd:string">pass</property>
  <property name="smtp_host" type="xsd:string">localhost</property>
</componentType>
```

We have now defined three properties that we can reference within the `Email.rb` Ruby script by prefacing each property with a $ sign, as shown here:

```
Net::SMTP.start($smtp_host, 25, $smtp_domain, $smtp_username,
$smtp_password, :login) do |smtp|
    smtp.send_message myMessage, from, to
  end
```

You can similarly inject properties and define services using the component type file for any of the supported scripting languages.

NOTE In the previous example, the property values were assigned within the component type file, and not just used to define the name and type, as demonstrated in listing 4.1. You could follow this approach and define the actual property values in the composite definition—the approach we used earlier.

At this point, we've covered many of the key capabilities provided by Tuscany. However, there are two important subjects we have left off: deploying Tuscany in a production environment, and using its sister technology, *Service Data Objects* (SDOs).

4.4 Advanced Tuscany/SCA

The next section offers some tips on leveraging the distributed capabilities of SCA to make your services more scalable. The ability to create a distributed SCA environment, or service cloud, is an essential part of SOA, as it enables you to expand and grow your infrastructure with confidence.

4.4.1 Production deployment

Until this point, we've only discussed using the SCA embedded domain container. That includes a built-in Jetty engine for surfacing the bindings that we've been using (such as web services). In most production scenarios, however, you'll likely use a servlet container such as Apache Tomcat, at least for exposing HTTP-based services like SOAP. In part, this is because, when you're using the embedded container, each domain will require its own dedicated IP port. By contrast, when using a servlet container you can run multiple domains within a single instance.

Continuing with our example, let's configure the `ProblemTicketComposite` assembly to run under Tomcat 5.5 as a deployable web archive (WAR). Figure 4.2 depicts the new configuration.

This exercise is a good example of how to set up a distributed architecture using SCA, as one domain will run within the embeddable engine (Domain 1) and the other under Tomcat (Domain 2). You can add as many domains as needed, each running

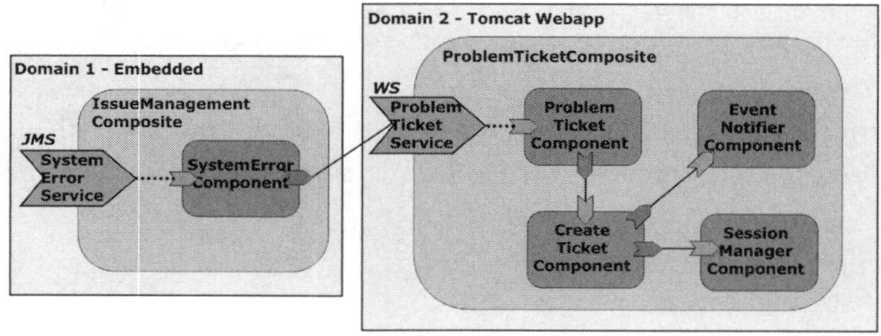

Figure 4.2 Domain configuration with `ProblemTicketComposite` set up to run under Tomcat 5.5

within its own JVM instance. The steps in setting up the second domain (Domain 2 in the illustration) to run within the servlet container are as follows:

1. Create a directory structure to reflect a WAR files requirement (META-INF, WEB-INF).
2. Create an sca-contribution.xml file that defines which domain and composite to use.
3. Create a web.xml file that configures Tuscany as a servlet filter to intercept requests targeted to the SCA domain.
4. Create an Ant task to assemble the WAR file.

The first step is to create a subdirectory structure that mirrors a WAR file's requirements.

CREATING A WAR-READY DIRECTORY STRUCTURE

Creating a directory structure that mirrors the layout of a WAR file simplifies the Ant script needed to assemble the WAR file. This entails creating a webapp folder under the src/main location. Then, under webapp, add a META-INF and a WEB-INF folder. The end result will resemble the image shown in figure 4.3.

Once this directory structure is in place, we can move forward to populate it with the required files, starting with the sca-contribution.xml file.

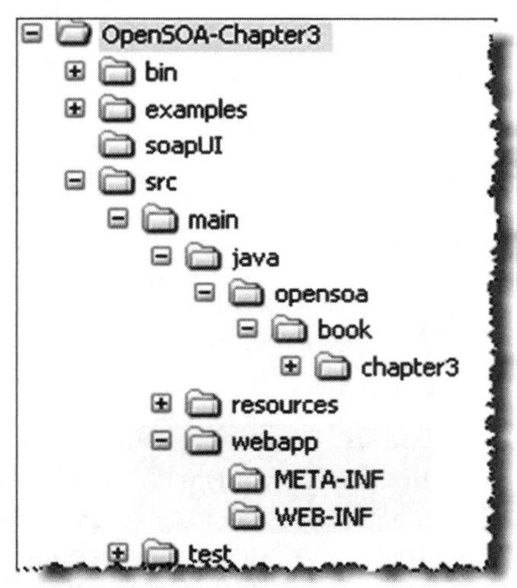

Figure 4.3 The webapp subdirectories are used for building the WAR file

CREATING AN SCA-CONTRIBUTION.XML FILE

Create a new file called sca-contribution.xml and place it under the META-INF directory. We use this file to define which composite will be deployed within the WAR application. Populate the sca-contribution.xml file with the XML shown in listing 4.9 (like all of this book's listings, it's available in the source code that comes with the book).

Listing 4.9 The sca-contribution.xml file, which belongs under the META-INF directory

```
<contribution xmlns="http://www.osoa.org/xmlns/sca/1.0"
         xmlns:hw="http://opensoa.book.chapter4_41">
  <deployable composite="hw:ProblemManagementComposite"/>
</contribution>
```

❶ Defines namespace

❷ Identifies composite being deployed

As you can see, the contribution file in this instance is very terse. The `deployable` element identifies the composite being deployed by referencing the composite name ❷, which is defined in the composite assembly file (see listing 4.7 for the full file). Notice that the composite name is namespace aware, so the namespace alias `hw` must first be declared ❶. The namespace provided must match the one used in the composite file (listing 4.7).

The third step in setting up the domain for running within a web application is to create a customized web.xml file.

CREATING A WEB.XML FILE

All WAR files require a web.xml file. Tuscany's SCA implementation requires a servlet to be configured in order to field the inbound requests and route them properly to their endpoint destination. The entries required in the web.xml are displayed in listing 4.10.

Listing 4.10 A web.xml file configuration that specifies the servlet filter

```
<web-app>

  <display-name>OpenSOA Chapter 4</display-name>

  <filter>
    <filter-name>tuscany</filter-name>
    <filter-class>
   org.apache.tuscany.sca.host.webapp.TuscanyServletFilter     <-- ❶ Specifies matching URL pattern
    </filter-class>
  </filter>

  <filter-mapping>
    <filter-name>tuscany</filter-name>
    <url-pattern>/*</url-pattern>          <-- ❷ Invokes servlet
  </filter-mapping>

</web-app>
```

The `url-pattern` associated with the `filter-mapping` element identifies, by way of the asterisk wildcard character ❷, that all inbound requests will be sent through the `TuscanyServletFilter` ❶. This servlet is responsible for processing any requests associated with the services identified within the assembly. Note that we've made no changes to the composite assembly file (problemMgmt441.composite).

Now that we've populated the new directories and files, let's move on to generating the WAR file. For this, we'll use Ant, as it's the most widely used tool for managing the Java build process. An Ant target will compile the Java code and create the WAR using these artifacts (for those unfamiliar with Ant, you can read more about it at http://ant.apache.org/). The relevant fragment from the Ant script is shown in listing 4.11 (you can find the entire Ant script, which is rather verbose, in the code samples as build.xml). There's nothing SCA-specific about the target's tasks—they use standard Ant commands to generate the WAR file.

Listing 4.11 Ant file fragment used to generate the SCA domain WAR file

```
<target name="compile">
  <mkdir dir="target/classes"/>

  <javac destdir="target/classes" debug="on" source="1.5" target="1.5">
    <src path="src\main\java"/>
    <classpath>                    <-- ❶ Includes Tuscany JARs
```

```
      <fileset refid="tuscany.jars"/>
      <fileset refid="3rdparty.jars"/>
    </classpath>
  </javac>

  <copy todir="target/classes">
    <fileset dir="src\main\resources"/>          ❷ Compiles classes
  </copy>

  <WAR destfile="target/opensoa-chapter4.WAR"     ❸ Creates WAR file
    webxml="src/main/webapp/WEB-INF/web.xml">
    <fileset dir="src/main/webapp"/>
    <lib refid="tuscany.jars"/>
    <lib refid="3rdparty.jars"/>
    <classes dir="target/classes"/>
  </WAR>

</target>
```

Three basic activities are taking place in the Ant target: compiling all of the Java code ❶ in a staging location; copying the required resource files, such as the composite files, into the staging/target directory ❷; and then creating the WAR file ❸. Once the WAR file is generated, you can copy it over to the webapps directory of your Tomcat 5.5 installation (we presume it would also work on more recent or slightly older versions of Tomcat or other containers, but we haven't tested it on those versions). The URL for the `ProblemTicketService` web service can be found at http://localhost:8080/opensoa-chapter4/ProblemTicketService; the WSDL is located at http://localhost:8080/opensoa-chapter4/ProblemTicketService?wsdl.

Using soapUI to interactively test SOAP-based web services

soapUI (www.soapui.org), an excellent tool for testing SOAP-based web services, is the primary tool we use for interactively testing SCA-derived web services. Two editions of the product are available: an open source, "free" version, and a more advanced, commercial version. While the commercial product does offer some nice-to-have advanced features, the open source release is very capable and sufficient for most needs. To use it, simply download, install, and run the product (to simplify things, in the source code we also include the soapUI jars so that it can be run without any separate download through Ant targets—see the project README.txt files for more details). Once soapUI is running, you can then select File > New WSDL Project, and enter the WSDL URL or file location. The new project will contain sample requests for each of the operations, and you can then tinker with the XML to submit various requests. soapUI has some advanced QA test automation features that can be handy for regression testing following new releases. We highly recommend the product and find it indispensable for my testing.

You should now be able to submit SOAP requests to the `ProblemTicketService` and see the results appear without error (see the sidebar "Using soapUI to interactively test SOAP-based web services"). This means that you have the Tomcat domain running successfully (shown in figure 4.2 as Domain 2). Now let's look at the embedded domain (shown as Domain 1 in figure 4.2), which is the `IssueManagementComposite` assembly. This assembly, as you may recall, interacts with the `ProblemManagement-Composite` (used by Domain 2) by way of a reference injected into the `SystemError-Component`. We've demonstrated two ways for this reference to occur:

- Using a composite as a reference (listing 3.9)
- As a remote binding using a web service (listing 3.12)

We'll again use the remote style binding, since we're discussing a distributed SCA architecture.

To demonstrate this approach, let's create a new composite file called issueMgmt-distributed.composite, which will replace our previous `IssueManagementComposite` (we could have just modified the existing issueMgmt.composite file we used earlier). The only difference in this file is that the reference now specifies the remote URL to the service running within Tomcat for the `binding.ws` element. The relevant fragment for this assembly is shown in listing 4.12 (in this case, for simplicity of presentation, I'm only showing the `SystemErrorService` using the `binding.ws` for web services).

Listing 4.12 Composite assembly file issueMgmt-distributed.composite

```
<composite
  xmlns="http://www.osoa.org/xmlns/sca/1.0"
  targetNamespace="http://opensoa.book.chapter3"
  xmlns:hw="http://opensoa.book.chapter3"
  name="IssueManagementComposite">

  <service
    name="SystemErrorService"
    promote="SystemErrorComponent">
    <binding.ws
      wsdlElement=
    "http://chapter44.book.opensoa#wsdl.port(SystemErrorService/SOAP)" />
  </service>

  <component name="SystemErrorComponent">
    <implementation.java
      class="opensoa.book.chapter44.impl.SystemErrorComponentImpl" />
  </component>
  <reference name="ProblemTicket"

    promote="SystemErrorComponent/problemTicket">
    <binding.ws uri=
     "http://localhost:8080/opensoa-chapter4/ProblemTicketService"/>
  </reference>
</composite>
```

Defines SOAP service using WSDL details

❶ Injects reference using remote service

As you can see, the assembly is straightforward, with the interface to the remote SCA service defined in the reference ❶. This composite's service, `SystemErrorService`, will continue to be accessible as a web service running within the embedded Jetty domain. When invoked, however, it will in turn call the `ProblemTicketService` running in the Tomcat domain to process the request. To run this domain locally, you'd simply start it using the following:

```
public class ProblemTicketServer {

  public static void main(String[] args) {

    SCADomain scaDomain =
      SCADomain.newInstance("issueMgmt-distributed.composite");

      try {
         System.out.println("IssueManagement server started");
         System.in.read();
      } catch (IOException e) {
         e.printStackTrace();
      }
      scaDomain.close();
  }
}
```

Now you know how to configure an SCA domain to run within a servlet container (for the examples, Tomcat was used). We also demonstrated a distributed architecture by interfacing between an embedded SCA domain and a remote domain running within that web server. As you can see, creating a distributed SCA environment is straightforward and offers exciting scalability options.

Alternative approaches for distributed SCA

Another approach to building a distributed SCA architecture is to use the strategy found in Tuscany's calculator-distributed sample (in the samples folder associated with a Tuscany binary installation). It demonstrates how Tuscany's `DomainManagerLauncher` can be used to start a domain in one VM, which acts as the master. Within other VM instances, assemblies can be added to that domain, using the `NodeLauncher`, which register themselves as nodes within the master domain. Prior to the 1.2 release of Tuscany, this approach was somewhat of a work in progress, but after some refactoring since the 1.1 release, a solid solution now appears to be in place.

If we concluded our discussion of SCA now, we think you'd walk away impressed by Tuscany's implementation of the standard, and perhaps even eager to begin using it in your environment. But we have omitted one important topic: SCA's complementary "sister" technology, *Service Data Objects* (SDOs). You will find that SDOs greatly simplify working with more complex, real-life type data structures, such as a purchase order or invoice. Without the ability to support complex nested data, the use of SCA would be limited and its contribution to a SOA environment minimal.

4.4.2 Introducing Service Data Objects (SDOs)

When examining SDOs, an inevitable question often arises: how is this binding technology different from the multitude of others that exist, such as Castor, JiBX,

XMLBeans, or Java Architecture for XML Binding (JAXB)? To be honest, the SDO does share many characteristics with these technologies, but it offers extended functionality that doesn't exist in those binding solutions. Specifically, the SDO was designed to support "offline" processing, where changes to the dataset are automatically captured into change summaries that indicate any new, modified, or deleted data. What's an example of where this functionality could be relevant? Consider data validation, where perhaps an outside organization is contracted to verify certain results, such as the accuracy of the information provided in someone's resume (such as education and employment history). The outside company could update the SDO dataset provided, and when returned, the API could be used to identify all data modified by the verifier. In the absence of SDOs, establishing a system to identify modified data can be surprisingly tricky (if you want to detect any changes made between the source and update results). This is a fairly advanced feature that's outside the scope of this chapter, but if you're interested, the SDO specification describes how this is accomplished.

SDOs also support a rich set of metadata that allows the client to retrospectively examine the "data graphs" for their structure and form. Last but not least, SCA was designed to work seamlessly with SDOs. This becomes apparent when working with more complex XML structures, such as the ones we'll be exploring in this section.

Until now, we have let SCA perform automatic, on-the-fly, dynamic binding between the inbound XML that's incoming via a service call into the internal Java data structures. For example, the `TicketDO` class (described in the previous chapter) defines a flat data structure that represents an inbound problem ticket (such as `customerEmail` or `customerName`). For simple structures such as that one, the dynamic binding approach provided by SCA has worked fine. However, when we're dealing with complex XML data structures more reflective of real-life scenarios, the automatic binding approach doesn't cut it. Also, there may be times when you already have a specified XSD schema and would prefer to use that.

To demonstrate using SDOs with SCA services, let's create a more complex XML structure to represent inbound issue/problem tickets (this replaces `TicketDO` used earlier). Figure 4.4 shows the XML Schema.

Here's an XML example using the schema in figure 4.4:

```
<problem category="software" severity="medium"
  xmlns="http://opensoa.chapter4/xsd">
  <header>
    <from>jsmith@test.com</from>
    <subject>This is a test</subject>
    <to>jdoe@test.com</to>
    <ccs>
      <cc>jndoe@test.com</cc>
      <cc>joeschmoe@test.com</cc>
    </ccs>
    <creationDate>2008-01-30T01:23:00</creationDate>
  </header>
  <description>This is a test </description>
</problem>
```

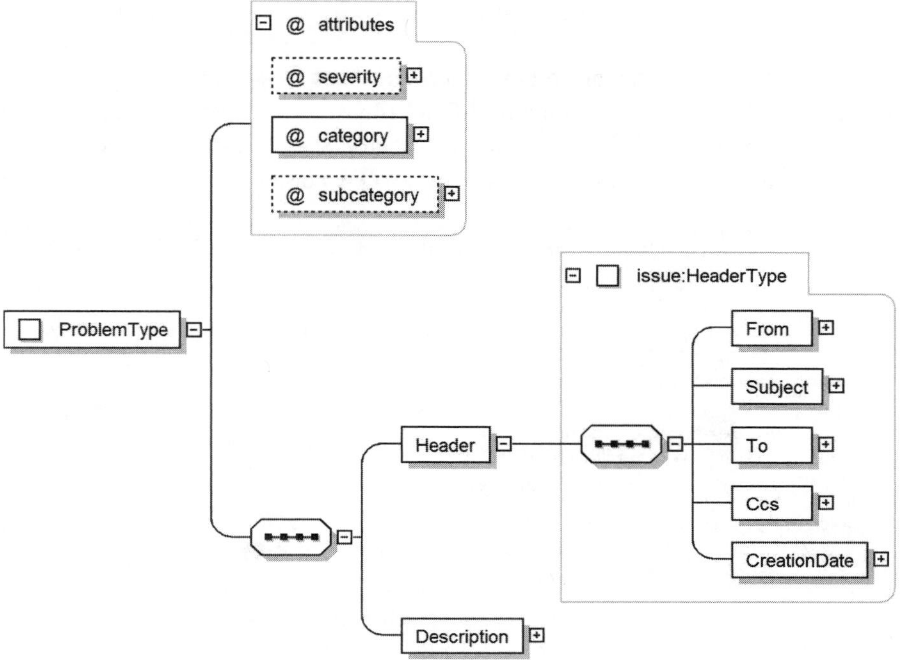

Figure 4.4 Our new problem ticket XML Schema using a complex XML structure

As you can see, this structure is a bit more complex than ones we've previously used. It includes some repeating elements, such as the ones used for the CC lines. To support this XML, the schema depicted in figure 4.4 was incorporated into a new WSDL for the web service called `ProblemServiceSDO.wsdl` (the WSDL used for the previous examples was `ProblemService.wsdl`).

NOTE Because XML Schemas are pretty verbose, ours won't be reproduced here, but you can find it in the sample code for this chapter.

The schema is necessary for two reasons: (1) the WSDL requires it for defining the structure of the web service, and (2) it's used to generate, using SDO utilities, corresponding class files that can programmatically marshal/unmarshal the data to and from XML. This sort of binding was taking placing behind the scenes by SCA when we were working with our simpler `TicketDO` class. The steps to explicitly use SDO are as follow:

1. Run an Ant target using `XSD2JavaGenerator` to generate Java classes from the WSDL XMLSschema definition.
2. Create a new service interface and implementation that uses the new SDO-generated classes.
3. Create a client composition and components so that we can submit test SOAP requests.

The first step is to generate the Java classes from the XSD that's embedded within the WSDL.

RUNNING XSD2JAVAGENERATOR TO CREATE JAVA CLASSES FROM XSD

Listing 4.13 is a fragment from a build.xml file that shows an Ant target used to generate the Java SDO classes. Notice that no specific SDO Java task has been developed to perform this generation, so we use a standard Java task to run the XSD2JavaGenerator.

Listing 4.13 Ant target used to generate Java SDO classes

```
<target depends="init" name="generate.class.from.wsdl">

  <java classname="org.apache.tuscany.sdo.generate.XSD2JavaGenerator"
      fork="true">
    <arg value="-targetDirectory"/>
    <arg value="src/main/generated/wsdl2javasource"/>          ❶
    <arg value="-noContainment"/>
    <arg value="-noUnsettable"/>
    <arg value="src/main/resources/ProblemServiceSDO.wsdl"/>    ❷

    <classpath>
      <fileset dir="${tuscany.lib}">          ❸
        <include name="*.jar"/>
      </fileset>
    </classpath>
  </java>

</target>
```

The arguments provided for running the Java class XSD2JavaGenerator are used to specify where the Java files are to be generated ❶, along with the location of the WSDL file ❷ that contains the embedded XSD Schema (you can also run it directly against an XSD file if it's not included in the WSDL). A number of JAR library files must be included in the classpath, and they're specified by reference ❸ and can be seen in the build.xml file in the example code.

Now, you may be wondering where exactly we're going with this. Well, we're going to use these generated classes as a replacement for the TicketDO class we created earlier. This takes us to our next step: plugging these generated classes into our method that will be exposed as a service.

CREATING A SERVICE TO USE SDO-GENERATED CLASSES

Rather than modify the existing ProblemTicketComponent and related classes, let's create new ones with SDOs appended to them. For example, the ProblemTicketComponentSDO interface class looks like this:

```
@Remotable
public interface ProblemTicketComponentSDO {
   public int createTicket(createTicket ticket);
}
```

Notice that the createTicket class, which is a generated SDO class, doesn't follow the normal CamelCase class convention of uppercase first letter and each additional word starting in an uppercase letter. This is because this class was automatically generated by XSD2JavaGenerator (you could modify all complex types and elements within the schema to uppercase to avoid this problem). The SDO classes found in the example code for this section were all modified to support the generated createTicket class instead of our older TicketDO class. Similarly, a new composite file was created, problemMgmtSDO.composite, which is identical to the previous problemMgmt.composite file displayed in listing 3.7, with the exception that it uses our new SDO classes.

At this point, the changes made to support SDO are completed. We can now start up an embedded SDO domain and test the new functionality by submitting a SOAP message via soapUI or a similar tool that uses the new ProblemServiceSDO.wsdl. Thus, the calling clients using the SOAP message are oblivious to whether SDO or automatic binding is being used by the Tuscany backend—a requirement for ensuring WS-I compatibility [WS-I].

This brings us to our last step: creating an SCA client that we can use to submit SOAP requests to the service.

CREATING A CLIENT TO TEST THE SERVICE

This step illustrates how you can use the SDO classes to populate the Java objects that are eventually transmitted over the wire as an XML SOAP request (in other words, you don't write the XML document manually). To create the client, let's first start by creating a composite file that will define our client components (see listing 4.14).

Listing 4.14 Composite file used by the client to submit create ticket requests

```
<composite
  xmlns="http://www.osoa.org/xmlns/sca/1.0"
  targetNamespace="http://opensoa.book.chapter4"
  xmlns:hw="http://opensoa.book.chapter4"
  name="jmsclient">

  <component name="SDOComponent">
    <implementation.java class=
     "opensoa.book.chapter4_42.impl.SDOClientImpl" />     <-- 1 Identifies implementation
  </component>

  <reference                                               2 Defines reference to inject
    name="SDOClientReference"
    promote="SDOComponent/sdoClient">                      <--
    <interface.java interface="opensoa.book.chapter4_42.SDOClient"/>
    <binding.ws wsdlElement=                                       <--
 "http://chapter4.book.opensoaSDO#wsdl.port(ProblemTicketService/SOAP)" />
  </reference>
</composite>                               References service through SOAP 3
```

The new client class we'll create is SDOClientImpl ❶, which represents the implementation for the client component named SDOComponent. The class contains an injected reference to the service that's used to perform the web service call ❷. The reference definition, via its promote attribute, is injected into the SDOClientImpl member variable defined as sdoClient. The service associated with the reference is identified by the web service binding that's specified through the binding.ws element ❸. The SDOClientImpl class is shown in listing 4.15.

Listing 4.15 SDOClientImpl client class responsible for placing SOAP call

```
public class SDOClientImpl implements ProblemTicketComponentSDO {

  @Reference
  public SDOClient sdoClient;                         <-- 1 Injects SDO reference class

  public int createTicket(createTicket ticket) {
    int rval = sdoClient.createTicket(ticket);        <-- 2 Calls method on referenced SDO

    System.out.println("rval: " + rval);
    return rval;
  }
}
```

The injected reference ❶ represents a handle to the remote web service, defined by the interface of `SDOClient`. The `createTicket` method requires the populated class `createTicket`, which is the autogenerated SDO object representing the problem ticket. A Java main class, called `SDOClientMain`, is responsible for initiating the `SDOComponent` (which is mapped to `SDOClientImpl` in the composite file, as you recall) and invoking its `createTicket` method used to perform the web service call ❷. Listing 4.16 shows the main method fragment from `SDOClientMain`.

Listing 4.16 Main client class used to initiate the web service test request

```
public final static void main(String[] args) throws Exception {
  SCADomain scaDomain =
SCADomain.newInstance("SDOclient.composite");                      1
  SDOClient sdoClient = scaDomain.getService(SDOClient.class,
                    "SDOComponent");

  IssueFactory factory = IssueFactory.INSTANCE;        <-- 2

  HeaderType header = factory.createHeaderType();
  ProblemType problem = factory.createProblemType();
  createTicket ticket = factory.createcreateTicket();      <-- 3

  problem.setHeader(header);
  ticket.setProblem(problem);

  header.setFrom("jeff");              <-- 4
  header.setSubject("test subject");
  header.setTo("jeff");
  problem.setDescription("test description");
  problem.setCategory("customer");
  problem.setSeverity("low");

  System.out.println("Case #: " +
     sdoClient.createTicket(ticket));          <-- 5

  scaDomain.close();
}
```

The `SDOClientMain`, in the first lines within the main method ❶, creates an embedded SCA domain and receives a handle to the `SDOComponent` implementation class. From there, it uses the SDO factory ❷ that was created along with the other SDO classes to create the SDO data classes ❸. The factory should always be used when creating SDO objects. The SDO data classes are then populated with a sample request ❹, and ultimately the service method is called to place the SOAP call ❺.

The generated SDO classes should be fairly straightforward to navigate, as they correspond closely to the defined XSD Schema. You'll find that XSD complex types are usually generated as separate Java classes, as is the case in the example with the `HeaderType` and `ProblemType` generated classes. The `createTicket` class, as we mentioned earlier, is the top level or root of the XML. When this main class is run, you should see console output showing the new case number that was generated, which indicates that it successfully placed the web service call to `ProblemTicketService` (obviously, that domain must be running for this test to work).

The SDO specification contains many additional features that we haven't touched on, such as its ability to track offline changes to the SDO data graphs. While time won't permit an examination of this feature, we can discuss some of the other capabilities that SDO provides for working with XML data.

4.4.3 Advanced SDO features

When you have an SDO object, you can easily transform it into its corresponding XML representation. For example, listing 4.17 shows a method that I've added to the `ProblemTicketComponentImpl` so that it can be used to output the XML using Apache log4j. Why would you want such a thing? One use case that comes to mind is for logging the results for archival (or compliance) purposes, or for generating events for a complex event processor (the topic of chapter 8). Depending on your needs, working with raw XML can be preferable compared to serialized Java classes (which can be problematic if the structure changes over time). Listing 4.17 illustrates how marshalling can be accomplished for outputting to log4j.

Listing 4.17 Marshalling SDO objects to XML for logging

```
private static Logger logger = Logger                          ❶ Creates new logger
  .getLogger(ProblemTicketComponentSDO.class
  .getPackage().getName());

private String getXML(ProblemType problem) {                   ❷ Creates XML helper

  HelperContext scope = SDOUtil.createHelperContext();
  XMLHelper helper = scope.getXMLHelper();

  String xml = helper.save((DataObject) problem,               ❸ Outputs SDO to XML string
    "http://chapter4.book.opensoa/issue", "ProblemType");

  return xml;
}
```

The first step is to create the log4j logger that's used to generate the output ❶, which is customary log4j logic. Then the `SDOUtil` class, which is part of Tuscany SDO, is used to create a `HelperContext` ❷. This, in turn, is used to create an SDO `XMLHelper`, which likewise is included in the standard SDO library. The `save` method of the

XMLHelper class, represented by the variable helper, is then called ❸. It outputs a String XML representation of the SDO data object that was passed to it. To output the XML to log4j, we could then use the getXML method we created in listing 4.17

```
logger.info(getXML(problem));
```

where problem is a createTicket class object. The configuration of your log4j.properties will determine where or if the output is generated (learn more about log4j at http://logging.apache.org/log4j/1.2/index.html).

Finally, let's address the scenario where we already have an XML message within a String and want to use the SCA client to submit it through a remote web service. Listing 4.18 demonstrates how this can be done using a code fragment from the SDOClientMain class.

Listing 4.18 Raw XML used to populate SDO classes

```
HelperContext scope = SDOUtil.createHelperContext();        ❶
XMLHelper helper = scope.getXMLHelper();
IssueFactory.INSTANCE.register(scope);             ❷

String xml =
  "<iss:createTicket xmlns:iss=\"http://chapter4.book.opensoa/issue\">" +
    "<iss:Problem severity=\"low\" category=\"systems\">" +
      "<iss:Header>" +
        "<iss:From>jdavis</iss:From>" +
        "<iss:Subject>test subject</iss:Subject>" +        ❸
        "<iss:To>jdavis</iss:To>" +
      "</iss:Header>" +
      "<iss:Description>test description</iss:Description>" +
    "</iss:Problem>" +
  "</iss:createTicket>";

XMLDocument doc = helper.load(xml);             ❹
createTicket newTicket =
  (createTicket) doc.getRootObject();           ❺
System.out.println("newTicket: " + newTicket.getProblem().getDescription());

System.out.println("New Case #: " + sdoClient.createTicket(newTicket));
scaDomain.close();
```

The process for populating SDO classes from raw XML has some steps similar to what we saw in converting SDO objects into XML (listing 4.17). First, you create the SDO helper objects ❶, and then register your generated factory class ❷. This registers the data types associated with that factory, which in this case are the SDO data objects. Then, an XML String is constructed representing the data we want to populate into SDOs ❸. With the String in hand, represented by the variable xml, we pass it as a parameter to the XMLHelper object's load method ❹. This generates an XMLDocument. This is a "generic" XML object, which is then cast directly into the SDO root object you wish to populate ❺. At this point, we have our populated createTicket SDO object, represented by newTicket. Obviously, a few steps are involved in the process, but you can always create helper classes to perform the heavy lifting if there's a frequent requirement to convert raw XML into SDOs.

Our coverage of SDO was obviously pretty brief, and we didn't specifically address all of its advanced functionality. The Tuscany SDO project has more comprehensive examples on these topics. Hopefully you've developed a good understanding of how SDOs can be used as a binding technology for more complex XML structures, which are likely prevalent throughout the organization in which you work. Like many of the advanced features we discussed, the SDO is an enabling technology that allows SCA to be used for more than just trivial purposes, and thus helps SCA play a central role in our Open SOA Platform.

Now you're probably disappointed to hear that we've completed our coverage of SCA features. Although we haven't touched on some aspects such as policies, intents, and contributions, you'll likely find that you may not need them, at least initially. The SCA documentation covers these subjects fairly well, so we encourage you to reference those materials if you're interested in learning more.

4.5 Summary

This chapter built on what you learned in chapter 3 and demonstrated some of the advanced capabilities and features of SCA. You learned how to create conversational services that had different scoping levels, not unlike what's found in the Java Servlet API (such as request, application level, and so on). We also discussed more advanced conversations through callbacks. While some of these features may not be immediately used by newcomers to SCA, any widespread rollout will likely involve them to some degree.

Other exciting capabilities we explored were how to use languages other than Java to create and consume services. The ability to use increasingly popular languages such as Ruby is a major selling point of SCA. Lastly, we described how SDO can be used in tandem with SCA. This enables the creation of more complex web services that go beyond the trivial "hello-world" or simple RPC-style services. Complex data structures can be created programmatically using SDOs, and configuring SDOs to work with SCA is straightforward.

Let's now turn our focus to *business process management* (BPM), which enables us to create complex business processes that leverage the services exposed by SCA. This is where we begin to see the synergies that exist among the various technologies we're covering.

Part 3

Business process management

Business process management (BPM) is one of those technologies that arrived with great fanfare and high expectations. Vendors who peddled their proprietary solutions evangelized it as a revolutionary advancement in how business applications would be developed. Sadly, like many promising technologies, it followed a hype cycle of inflated expectations that quickly gave way to a trough of disillusionment. However, as we'll see in the next two chapters, when BPM is married with SOA, the benefits can be real and tangible. With this combination in place, business processes can be continually optimized and new ones quickly introduced to support new product offerings. BPM enables business and IT to become more closely aligned, leading to greater efficiencies and less frustration.

The open source community is fortunate to have a BPM solution as rich in functionality and as stable as JBoss jBPM. In part 3, we'll cover the basics of how to use jBPM, and then tackle some of its advanced functionality and extensibility. We'll conclude this part by examining how it can be used in tandem with Apache Tuscany so that it can be integrated nicely within your SOA environment.

5 Introducing jBPM

This chapter covers

- Introducing JBoss jBPM
- Understanding jBPM nodes and transitions
- Extending jBPM with actions

We've spent the last two chapters talking about the Service Component Architecture (SCA) and its implementation using Apache Tuscany. You've learned how to use this framework to create reusable services that can be exposed through a variety of protocols, such as SOAP-based web services, JMS, and RMI. The ability to create and propagate such component-based services is one of the central principles of SOA. Now, in the next three chapters we'll address *business process management* (BPM), which, at its core, is about leveraging these services to create business processes. In other words, we're transitioning from how to create the services to how they can be consumed and used. As you'll learn, BPM represents a new paradigm for software application development where services can be woven together into visual models that reflect actual business processes.

There's reason to believe that BPM won't suffer the same ignominious fate as other business and technology initiatives such as total quality management and process reengineering. This is because it's grounded in the notion of the process, which, after all, is what defines a business. What exactly constitutes a business process? Prahalad and Krishnan define it as "the link between the business strategy, business models, and day-to-day operations" [Prahalad]. Or, as Smith and Fingar put it, "Processes are the business" [Fingar]. BPM, unlike reengineering, strives to leverage the information systems already in place. BPM's aim is multifold, but its main objectives are to

- Streamline business processes
- Improve/maximize automation
- Improve visibility/control of ongoing processes
- Rapidly orient processes to support new or changed business initiatives

The last point is particularly noteworthy—improving business agility is a central objective of nearly any organization today. When process and workflow are codified into business systems such as ERP or CRM, changing them can be an enormous and disruptive undertaking. Moreover, such systems often only span a portion of the entire value chain used for supporting a product or service. BPM, on the other hand, is intended to encompass the entire value chain process, including interactions with external partners or customers.

An often-overlooked benefit of BPM is how it accelerates the rollout of new business processes within the enterprise. Back in the day, modifying or rolling out a new business process usually relied on manual training to implement. That entailed new procedure guidelines, training materials, and some wishful thinking that the process would be followed. With BPM, automation eliminates the human interpretation factor. In a recent article in *Harvard Business Review* titled "Investing in the IT That Makes a Competitive Difference," the authors cite this ability as a key differentiator, noting that "a company's unique business processes can now be propagated with much higher fidelity across the organization by embedding it in enterprise information technology. As a result, an innovator with a better way of doing things can scale up with unprecedented speed to dominate the industry" [McAfeeBrynjolfsson].

Another unique concept introduced by BPM is that of visualization. A BPM system is designed to enable business users to craft and design business processes in a visual fashion, resembling a flowchart. While Visio and other modeling tools have been used for years by subject matter experts for conveying requirements, they were static in nature, and the resulting codification by developers often bore little or no resemblance to what was modeled. Ultimately, developers, who lacked the deep understanding of the business processes, were left to interpret their meaning, often with disastrous results. BPM models, however, are intended to be executable manifestations of actual business processes. Thus, they can be interrogated at runtime to determine status as well as optimized for efficiency and for service-level monitoring.

NOTE It's not practical to assume that a business model developed by an analyst is going to be "execution-ready" without some technical embellishment by developers. At least both the developer and analyst are working with a common visual notation.

The benefits of BPM may now seem obvious, but what's the relationship between BPM and SOA? Quite simply, a service-oriented architecture is a critical enabler for BPM. Workflow systems in the past have failed because there was often no easy way to integrate the steps within the workflow to the functions within the business applications (this is also what doomed early proponents of rule-based systems). For example, a purchasing workflow application of yesteryear might have had convenient ways to collect the details of a purchase order (PO) and offer routing and approval capabilities, but there was often no easy way to tie the approved PO into the system used by accounts payable or inventory management. Thus, "swivel" chair integration resulted, with someone rekeying the data from the workflow app into the other systems. More complex workflow scenarios had even more challenging integration requirements that often went unmet due to the historically stovepipe nature of IT systems. Now, since SOA is all about exposing discrete business services in an easily accessible fashion, BPM can easily tap into and exploit these capabilities.

Now that we've covered some of the background of BPM and its benefits, we can examine more closely its role within SOA. After that, we'll explore the basics of our Open SOA Platform's BPM product of choice: JBoss jBPM. In the next chapter we'll more closely dive into human interface tasks, which constitute an important part of any BPM solution. We'll conclude with a final chapter on advanced jBPM concepts and also describe how jBPM can be integrated with Apache Tuscany SCA to create a truly compelling service and orchestration solution. Let's get started!

5.1 BPM: the "secret sauce" of SOA

Bear in mind that SOA, by itself, is not the endgame. Instead, it's intended to help forge a more flexible, easy-to-manage, and ultimately higher-quality software infrastructure. The promises of BPM can be realized when surrounded by a SOA-based environment. Figure 5.1 depicts the relationship among the components, services (which were the topic of the last two chapters on SCA), and BPM.

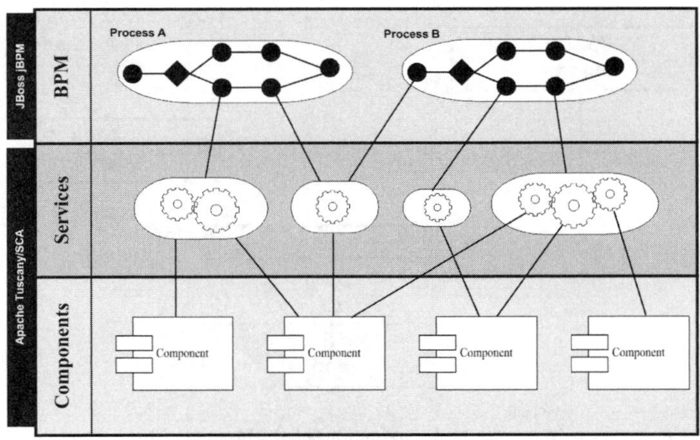

Figure 5.1 The relationship among BPM, services, and components

As figure 5.1 illustrates, the services exposed through SCA, which themselves consist of one or more components, can then be consumed by BPM, for which we're using jBPM. Of course, business processes may also invoke externally accessible services and include human interface tasks.

In addition to being a benefactor of SOA, BPM also nicely complements other SOA-related technologies such as complex event processing (CEP). This is because, by decomposing a process into individual steps within a workflow, you can transmit events at each node throughout the lifecycle of the process. This can be most easily illustrated through a sample BPM process, as shown in figure 5.2.

In figure 5.2, the event notifications are illustrated by the little bell icon. Where shown, each transition would fire an event that could be consumed by a CEP (covered in chapter 8) or business activity monitoring (BAM) dashboard. Additionally, the highlighted nodes (`ship item`, `update books`) represent callouts to external services, such as those that can be created through SCA (chapters 3 and 4).

While figure 5.2 illustrates the complementary nature of many of the technologies used in building our Open SOA Platform, there's enough overlap between some of the technologies to cause confusion. One area in particular that comes to mind is how

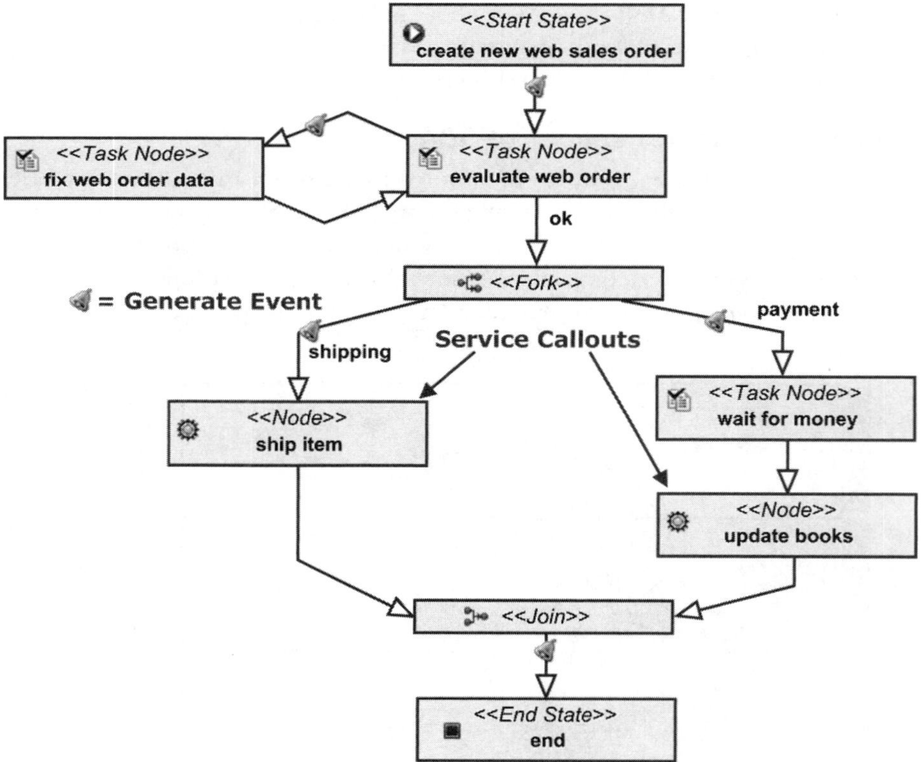

Figure 5.2 The BPM process, with events and services highlighted using JBoss jBPM

to distinguish between an ESB's flow control capabilities versus the process flows inherent in a BPM. Understanding this distinction will help you better frame where the technology boundaries lie between these technologies, and thereby become a more effective advocate of BPM within your organization.

As we'll discuss in chapters 9 and 10 in our coverage of Apache Synapse, our open source ESB component of our Open SOA Platform, an ESB is most effectively positioned as a messaging broker between various systems and protocols. In other words, it's most effective when used to bridge between different communication protocols and/or transforming messages from one format or vocabulary to another.

BPMs, on the other hand, are designed to model and execute complex business processes. As such, they are frequently long-running in nature and often involve a "human-in-the-loop" at various points along the way. The notion of *wait states* is a central concept to a BPM solution. On the other hand, an ESB's routing capabilities are intended for real-time processing. Best practices thus suggest that BPM be used for modeling business processes, with ESB's routing limited to real-time data flows required for brokering and transforming messages between systems and protocols.

Wait states and BPM

A BPM process is intended to reflect an actual business process. More often than not, business processes includes steps that involve either a human activity task or some pending work that needs to be done elsewhere, perhaps by a business partner. In either case, the process execution is temporarily waiting for an external entity to signal completion of work. This ability is core to a BPM and not easily managed through traditional programming languages, which don't support the concept of persisting wait states [Baeyens].

Now that we've established the benefits of BPM and you understand its role in relation to SOA and its place within the enterprise, we can proceed with exploring JBoss jBPM, which is our Open SOA Platform's BPM selection. Let's begin by looking at a bit of its history as a product, and then we can examine key concepts and features. For those anxious to dive into some actual examples, rest assured that will be happening shortly.

5.2 History and overview of JBoss jBPM

The first significant release of jBPM occurred with the 2.0 edition that was introduced in 2004. It represented a major milestone, as many of the core features that represent today's product (release 3.2.6 as of this writing) were first introduced in that version. jBPM includes the features required of any BPM system, and commercial alternatives often start with a price tag in the six-figure range. The product's popularity has steadily grown, according to the download statistics on SourceForge.net. There have been over 150,000 downloads of the most recent release, contrasting with about 15,000 for the 3.0 product that was released in 2005. The jBPM user forms hosted on the JBoss community site also testify to the increasing popularity of the solution. One of the most significant features released in the 3.2 edition was the jBPM Console, which provided an easy-to-use graphical interface for managing processes and instances.

Besides its rich set of functionality, one of the main selling points for jBPM is the proven and fast process execution engine that represents the core foundation of the product. Further, the engine itself is lightweight and represents just a handful of JAR files. The persistence engine, where the processes, process instances, and state metadata reside, supports nearly all popular databases, both commercial and open source. Since the product is open source and designed for adding new functionality extensions, it's also highly flexible.

Before we get into the features and capabilities, let's first examine the lifecycle of how a jBPM process is typically developed and deployed, as this will provide context for our technical discussion later.

5.2.1 Development lifecycle of a jBPM process

There are six major phases in developing a jBPM process (and indeed, likely any BPM product). They're illustrated in figure 5.3.

Some of the steps resemble those in a typical software development project, but others are unique to developing a BPM process. Let's take a look at each step in the process in more detail.

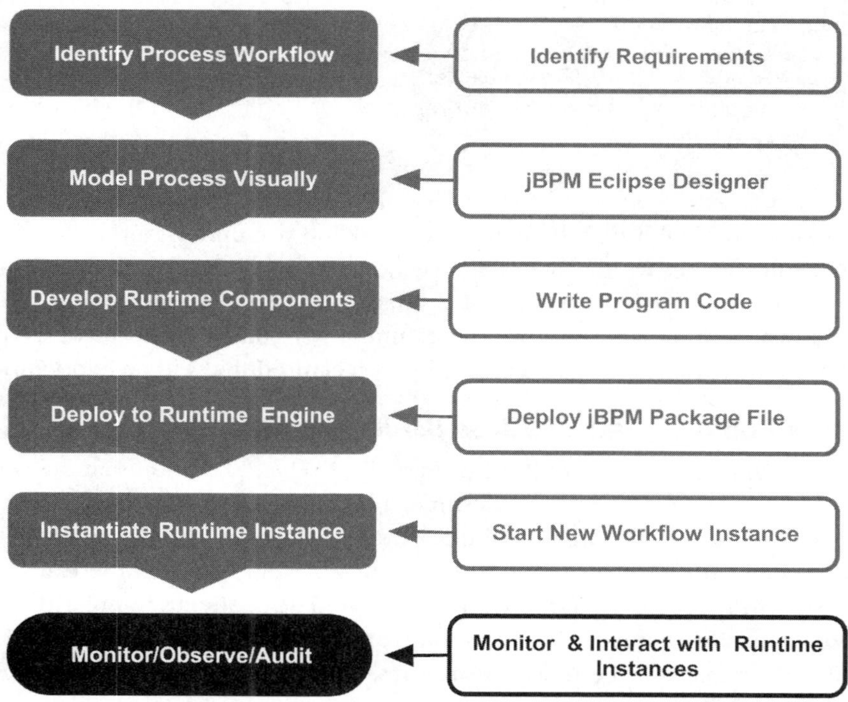

Figure 5.3 BPM process lifecycle steps using JBoss jBPM

IDENTIFYING PROCESS WORKFLOW

As we pointed out earlier, BPM is suited for modeling, automating, and executing business processes. A business process, by definition, is a sequence of steps (or collection of activities) necessary to perform a business function. Examples abound in any organization, from on-boarding of new employees or customers to order processing, and invoice and purchase order approval. Other processes are specific to a given industry, such as a patient registration process for a hospital, or the setup of clinical trials for a pharmaceutical company. Identifying a candidate process in which to use BPM can be challenging, since the complexity of some processes make them more difficult than others to implement. The biggest benefit can likely be achieved where there is a clearly defined existing, high-volume process that involves integration with one or more systems and perhaps includes human interface tasks. An example is the web-based sales order process shown earlier in figure 5.2 (which admittedly is simplified).

MODELING THE PROCESS VISUALLY

Once an appropriate business process is identified, the next step is to model it using the visual process editor. The jBPM Graphical Process Designer (GPD) editor, which is an Eclipse IDE plug-in (and like the rest of jBPM, fully open source), is shown in figure 5.4 and is included in what's known as the jBPM Suite.

As you can see, the editor likely resembles other modeling or illustration tools you have previously used. There is a tools palette you can click on to select any of the available nodes or controls, and then click again within the design palette to paint the

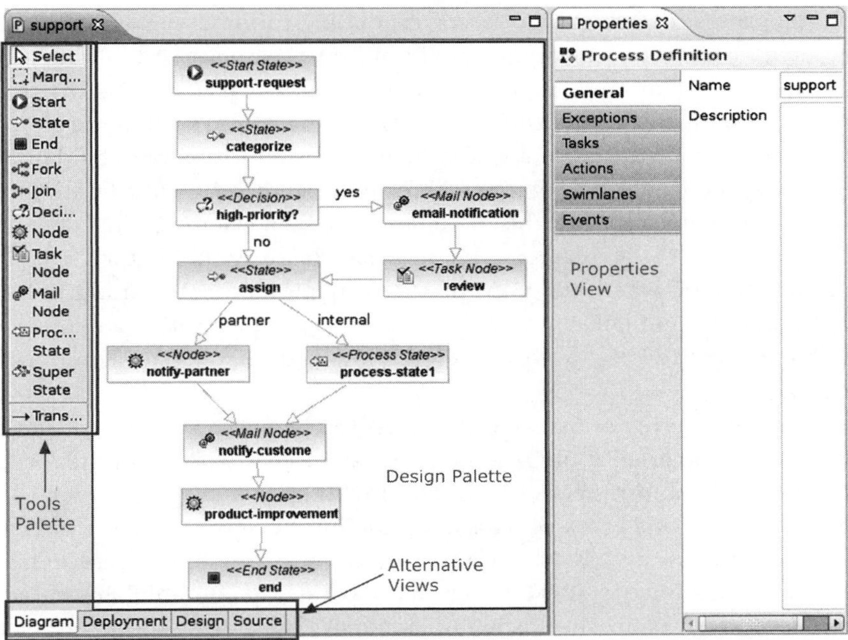

Figure 5.4 jBPM Graphical Process Designer

object. In the next section we'll describe what each of the objects represented by the various icons means in figure 5.4.

The process design tools are kept purposely at a fairly abstract level so that an analyst can model processes without being overly concerned with the underlying implementation. It's not realistic to assume that an analyst can develop completely production-ready models, because executable business processes usually contain some amount of programming code, which is addressed next.

DEVELOPING THE RUNTIME COMPONENTS

In figure 5.4, you'll notice the diagram items identified as `<<state>>` (`categorize`, `assign`) and `<<node>>` (`notify-partner`, `product-improvement`). These represent examples where underlying code is required for implementation. For example, let's assume that the `notify-partner` node is used to send the support request to a business partner via XML over HTTP. Obviously, this will entail a programmatic exercise (even assuming you developed custom components for such things, it would still entail configuration that likely must be done by a developer). While the analyst can develop the overall workflow, a developer is needed to "fill in the holes" and provide the implementation logic. This can be done within jBPM without having to complicate the visual model by implementing action handlers, or classes, that perform the actual work. So the visual process model created in the previous step is then followed by development of the runtime implementation. Examples of such implementation code will follow shortly.

DEPLOYING TO THE RUNTIME ENGINE

Once the process definition and its corresponding runtime implementation code are completed, it can then be deployed. Within jBPM, there are several different deployment scenarios. The most common one, which we'll focus on, is where the jBPM engine is running within the context of a web application, such as the jBPM Console. However, the engine instance can also be instantiated within any standard Java class. This is most applicable in scenarios where you're embedding jBPM entirely within an application (an illustration of this method can be seen when creating a new jBPM project within the GDP, as it creates a JUnit test class that uses this method).

In the scenario where the jBPM process is deployed to run within the jBPM Console, the Deployment tab shown in figure 5.4 is used for creating a deployment package. When selected, it provides configuration options for packaging, as shown in figure 5.5.

As illustrated in figure 5.5, a jBPM process can be packaged for deployment in one of two ways. (The archive file is sometimes called Process Archive file, or PAR). The first option is to export the archive file to the file system as a PAR, which can then be manually uploaded as a new process using the jBPM Console. The second option is to deploy the process directly to a running instance of the jBPM Console. Each time a process is loaded into the jBPM, it's given a separate version number—this is the only practical approach, since an existing version may have active process instances, or historical instances that must be preserved for auditing purposes.

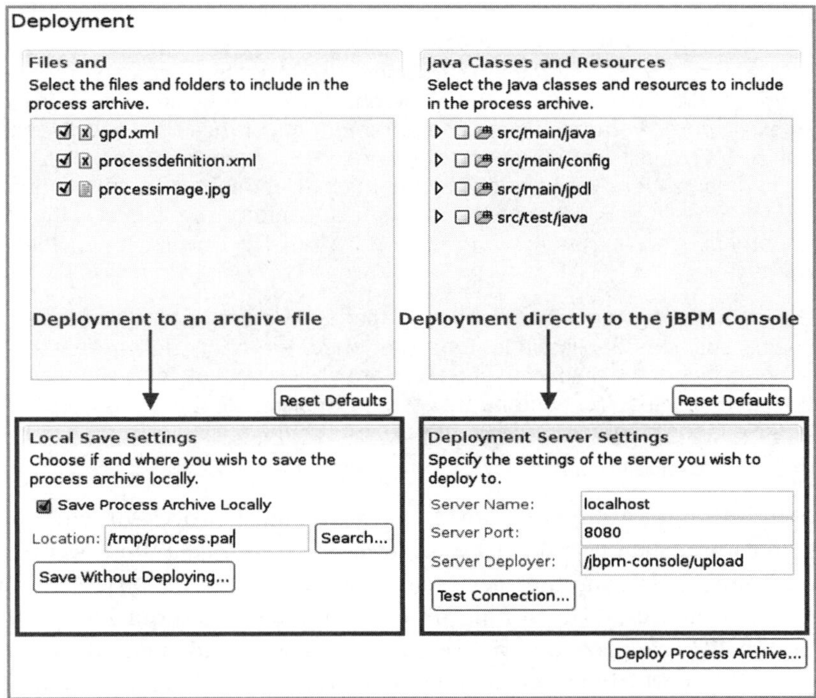

Figure 5.5 Deployment options for the jBPM process

NOTE In actuality, a PAR file is really just a zip file that contains all the necessary artifacts required for deployment, such as the process diagram. In the sample code for chapter 6, Ant targets can be found that will (a) prepare the PAR files, and (b) deploy them automatically to the jBPM Console.

INSTANTIATING THE RUNTIME INSTANCE

Once a process is deployed, a new instance of it can be instantiated. How this is done, in part, depends on the nature of the business process. In our example from figure 5.4, it would begin once a new customer service request has arrived. What exactly does that mean? If you recall from chapters 3 and 4, we developed a SOAP web service that could receive inbound problem tickets. The web service implementation, written in Java using SCA, could act as a jBPM client and initiate a new process instance directly. You'll learn how to do this in chapter 7. Another approach is to use the jBPM Console to start a new process instance manually.

Keep in mind that, like BPEL-based orchestrations, an *instance represents a single execution of a given process/definition.* So in our example of a customer service request, each request would instantiate a new process instance. That process instance, in turn, is persisted to the database when it's not active (that is, it's in a wait state, such as waiting for a human interface task to be completed) and then reactivated when some activity

> **If BPM is so great, why is nobody using it?**
>
> This is a question we hear frequently. Obviously, BPM adoption has been slow to take hold (though that trend does appear to be changing). We believe two major impediments exist: *perceived complexity* and *paradigm resistance*. Historically, only commercial BPM products existed, and they were expensive and complex. Only the largest of organizations could justify the return on investment. As a consequence, the impression arose that BPM was overkill for smaller enterprises. It is true the first-generation products were complex and required extensive training, often resulting in shelfware.
>
> The other reason for the slow adoption is that BPM represents a new paradigm for developing business applications. Paradigm shifts are often slow to materialize because of the risk of the unknown, and there are always pockets of resistance in learning new technologies. We contend that to not embrace BPM is far riskier, since the competitive landscape only rewards the agile.

is triggered within it. In the BPEL world, they refer to the process of persisting an idle process's data and state to a database as *dehydration*. *Hydration* then occurs when the process becomes active, and the data and state are placed in memory. Without such an approach, a proliferation of running process instances could quickly consume available memory. (This approach is one reason why BPM is fundamentally different from ESB-based routing, which takes a queue-based approach when it passes messages from one state to another.)

Once processes are running, it's obviously essential that they be able to be monitored for ongoing progress. Although monitoring isn't a particularly glamorous topic, widespread BPM deployment depends on this capability.

MONITORING, OBSERVING, AND AUDITING

This is a fairly broad topic, and we devote considerable coverage to it in chapter 8, which focuses on event stream processing. One of the big benefits of BPM is that, because it's intended to encapsulate and execute business processes in a manner that reflects the "real-life" process, the metrics that can be captured throughout the process should be business relevant. For example, in figure 5.4 each step in the process can emit events that can be presented and analyzed in real time. In this case, it may include monitoring whether the number of high-priority problems has exceeded certain thresholds or exhibits greater variance than normal. These metrics can form what is sometimes called a *sense and respond* solution. This involves

- *Event monitoring*—Each step, or "hop," in the process should publish events.
- *Determining what matters to customers and partners, and focus monitoring efforts on these critical areas (the "sense")*—For example, verifying that service-level agreements are being satisfied by monitoring response or completion time.
- *Alerting people and systems when unanticipated trends or anomalies occur*—This is the "response."

Process Instances for "Problem Ticket Process" v3 — Page 1 of 1 -

Instance ID	Key	Status	Start Date	End Date	Actions			
		☑ R ☑ S ☑ E			Apply Filter	Clear Filter		
146	Received the wrong item	Running	Mar 16, 2008 6:00:18 PM		Examine	Delete	End	Suspend
145	I still haven't received my item!!!!	Running	Mar 16, 2008 5:53:43 PM		Examine	Delete	End	Suspend
144	Billing question	Running	Mar 16, 2008 5:53:29 PM		Examine	Delete	End	Suspend
143	Item shipped broken	Suspended	Mar 16, 2008 5:53:12 PM		Examine	Delete	End	Resume
142	Website error occurred	Ended	Mar 16, 2008 5:52:05 PM	Mar 16, 2008 6:00:29 PM	Examine	Delete		

Allows you to filter by instance status

Figure 5.6 jBPM Console Process Instances view

jBPM, like most BPM solutions, addresses some of these requirements through built-in functionality. For example, tasks within jBPM can be assigned timers, so that if items aren't completed in the appropriate period, an escalation path can be triggered. Also, jBPM Console provides a convenient way to monitor process instances, as you can see in figure 5.6.

As highlighted in figure 5.6, you can filter by process instance status (R=Running, S=Suspended, E=Ended). Additional filtering can be done by searching on the instance key (the field to the left of the status flags), which in this example represents the subject line of the problem report. If you select the Examine link associated with each process instance, you can see the particulars about the process instance. This includes process variables, tasks, instance comments, tokens (which represent execution paths, discussed in the next section), and a visual depiction of the current state of the instance, as shown in figure 5.7.

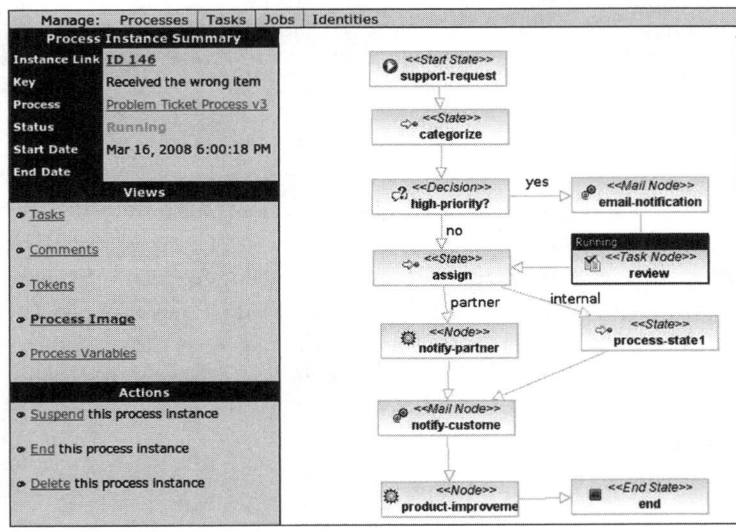

Figure 5.7 jBPM process instance detail view displaying the process instance image

The jBPM Console view thus provides considerable details about running process instances, and enables the administrator to perform actions such as stopping, starting, and suspending instances. (Note that within the instance image graph, you can click on the highlighted node text to drill down into the details of the node, such as the `review` node shown in figure 5.7). The jBPM API can be used to retrieve additional information and allows for querying the database that houses all instance data. We'll cover this topic in detail in the next chapter.

Although the overview of the product and its development lifecycle may have had you reaching for your coffee, we'll now switch gears and lift up the hood (where all the exciting stuff happens). We'll begin by looking at the jBPM process language and touch on the integration points where runtime code can be introduced.

5.2.2 Graph-oriented programming and jBPM

The authors of jBPM like to refer to jBPM as a form of *graph-oriented programming*. By this, they refer to the use of visual graphs that can be used to describe and execute application logic. The graphical nature obviously deviates from conventional programming, as does its inherent support for wait states and long-running transactions. How a process is defined is determined by the process language that's used. In jBPM's case, you have two choices: jPDL (jBPM Process Definition Language) and BPEL. So, at its core, jBPM can be considered a platform or engine that can support multiple process languages. For the reasons cited earlier, our focus is on jPDL, which is better suited for BPM than BPEL (jPDL was initially the only language supported by jBPM).

Understanding jBPM release editions

A common source of confusion is the various jBPM editions that are available. We categorize them by three types: *Embedded*, *Web Application*, and *Enterprise* editions. The Embedded edition is comprised of the jbpm-jpdl.jar file, which allows you to run the process engine within any Java class in an embedded fashion. The Web Application edition adds the jBPM Console and can be run in any standard Java web server, such as Tomcat or Resin. The Enterprise edition includes the jBPM Console but adds support for the scheduler/timer, asynchronous continuations, and mail. For this book, we're using the Enterprise edition.

While jPDL isn't a standard per se—it hasn't been formally submitted to any standards body—it's well documented and licensed as open source. Compared with competing process languages such as XML process definition language (XPDL), business process definition metamodel (BPDM), or BPEL, it's very elegant in its simplicity and is easily extendable. For example, the source jPDL used for the process illustrated in figure 5.7 is about one page of XML code, which is easily understandable by those not even well versed in jPDL (numerous examples can be found in the sample source code, and are usually named processdefinition.xml).

NOTE Those familiar with BPEL can attest to what a contrast jPDL represents compared with that standard. Further, the semantics of BPEL can be confusing to those first trying to learn it—jPDL's XML Schema is refreshingly concise and easy to follow.

Let's now examine the constructs that constitute the language, which at its core is composed of *nodes* and *transitions*. These form the basis for how processes are constructed.

5.3 Understanding nodes

In the process diagrams you have seen so far, the steps (or blocks) in the process flow represent *nodes* and the lines between them *transitions*. As you may recall from figure 5.4, different types of nodes are available, including task, node, state, mail, and decision (the types were specified by the text surrounded by << and >>). Regardless of the type, nodes serve two purposes: (a) they can execute Java code, and (b) they're responsible for moving forward or pausing the process execution. When a node is entered, it begins executing any code associated with it. This may entail entering a *wait state* pending some outside action, or it may *propagate* the execution, which simply means that it advances the execution forward. Since there can be more than one transition path leaving the node, the node is responsible for telling the process engine which transition to follow.

Let's examine the built-in nodetypes that come included in the jPDL language: node, task-node, state, mail, decision, and fork/join.

5.3.1 Node nodetype

The node nodetype is the basis from which the other nodetypes are derived (or custom ones you might create), but it can be used by itself in situations where you want to code the runtime behavior. You can think of the node nodetype as a *generic* style node, with no specific behaviors associated with it. For example, a node nodetype could be used by an analyst to graphically depict that a call to an external system must be made. However, the implementation logic to perform this action will be left for development. In figure 5.7, a node was used to identify that the problem ticket should be sent to a partner for resolution. The developer would then write the implementation action handler, which is discussed in section 5.5. What's important to recognize, however, is that the implementation code for this type of node must identify and trigger the transition path to be followed when the execution exits the node. Here's an example of how a node is defined within jPDL:

```
<node name="notify-partner">
  <action
    name="partnerNotification"
    class="info.open-soa.actions.NotifyPartnerAction">
  </action>
  <description>
Notify partner of problem ticket for them resolve.
```

```
  </description>
  <transition to="notify-customer"/>
</node>
```

Notice in this example that an `action` element is defined, and the `@class` attribute specifies the name of the Java class used to implement the logic. The `description` element is used to enrich the node definition, and the `transition` element identifies the possible transition paths that can be followed; in this example there's just one transition called `notify-customer`. The action handler assigned to the node, as we pointed out earlier, must propagate the execution—in other words, move it along.

> **Handler classes and scripts**
>
> In jBPM, you can define handlers using a Java class either by identifying its full path location or by embedding a script in the form of a BeanShell within the body of the process definition. When we specify "class," we mean it to be synonymous with either a Java class or BeanShell script (which, after all, is interpreted into a Java class at runtime).

A standard set of possible elements and attributes is available that can be used when defining any of the nodetypes. Table 5.1 lists them (attributes are prefixed with an @), and the description of the subsequent nodetypes will identify any deviations from this standard set (some of the others will add configuration options).

Table 5.1 Standard nodetype attributes and elements

Element/Attribute Name	Description
`@name`	Specifies the name of the node. *Required.*
`description`	Describes the node for documentation purposes. *Optional.*
`event`	Describes actions to be performed when events are triggered at various moments in the execution of the node. Common events include `transition`, `node-enter`, and `node-leave`. The actions defined as part of an event *cannot influence the flow control of the process*. This contrasts with the `action` element defined as a descendant of the node nodetype, which *must* do so. Section 5.8 will discuss events in more detail. *Optional.*
`exception-handler`	Allows the developer to define a list of actions to take based on the type of error being caught. However, like event actions, they can't modify the graphs event flows. Exception handling is a relatively advanced topic and will be discussed in more detail in chapter 7. *Optional.*
`timer`	A timer can be assigned to a node with the clock starting when the node is entered. Actions can be triggered based on timer expiration. Since timers are most often used in conjunction with tasks, they're covered in more detail in chapter 6. *Optional.*

Table 5.1 Standard nodetype attributes and elements ***(continued)***

Element/Attribute Name	Description
`transition`	Defines the destination node for the execution path. Transition names should generally be unique to avoid unexpected problems. A transition path can be explicitly invoked by name, but if no name is specified and multiple transitions are available, the first one will be selected. Transitions can also define an action class or script that's invoked when it's entered. *Optional.*

The only thing unique to the node nodetype is the `action` element, which is required. As we pointed out earlier, for the node nodetype, the action handler specified in the `action` element is responsible for signaling the advance of the process and for identifying the transition path.

5.3.2 *Task-node nodetype*

The task-node nodetype is used to specify one or more tasks that are to be performed by a human (but they can be processed programmatically through the API as well). The individual performing the task then signals what transition path to following moving forward. Unlike the other nodetypes described thus far, tasks involve human interaction with the business process.

NOTE Although tasks are usually associated with human interface activities, using the API you can interact with them in any fashion you want. The next chapter focuses on using tasks.

As you might imagine, there's a significant amount of functionality that necessarily accompanies the task nodetype. This includes how the task information is conveyed to the user, how an actor or user is assigned a task, and how it can be monitored for timely completion. Because of the broad scope that tasks involve, the next chapter is dedicated to covering this subject.

5.3.3 *State nodetype*

Described in the jBPM documentation as a "bare-bones" node, the state nodetype is somewhat of a hybrid between a node nodetype and a task-node nodetype. It's similar to the latter in that it introduces a wait state not unlike a task pending completion. However, a state nodetype is waiting for what presumably is another system to complete, not a human. The external system could be notified via an event action, such as `node-enter`, and then waits for a stimulus to signal advancement of the token. The only real distinction between a state nodetype and a node nodetype is that a state doesn't allow a direct action handler to be defined. Additionally, the node nodetype doesn't introduce a wait state and is expected to be processed immediately.

What's an example of where a state nodetype would be useful? One scenario is where some additional information is required from a third-party system. In such a case, the original system must wait for a response from the third-party system before

> **Tokens and signals—what are they?**
> You'll see in the jBPM literature, and even in the jBPM Console application, frequent references to *tokens*. Basically, a token is just a *path of execution*; it's a pointer to a node in the graph that's currently accessible within the process instance. A signal is just an instruction to a token to *advance forward* in the execution. So, if a token is currently waiting in a state nodetype, a signal would move it forward using a specified (or default) transition.

proceeding. For example, a quote request that's part of a process might forward the information to a CRM system, and a user of that system would receive and process it. Once the quote is completed, a notification would be sent from the CRM to a service, which would receive it and interact with the jBPM API to advance the process.

5.3.4 Mail-node nodetype

As the name suggests, the mail-node nodetype is used to send outgoing email, which is triggered when the node is entered. Here's an example of how you can use it:

```
<mail-node
  name="notify-customer"
  actors="jdoe"
  subject="Urgent customer email received: #{problem_subj}"
  text="#{problem_desc}">
  <transition to="product-improvement"/>
</mail-node>
```

In the example, you'll notice the use of tokenized variables, which take the form of `#{varname}`. These allow you to dynamically assign variable values at runtime (section 5.7 will discuss how variables are created). In the preceding code fragment, the mailing address will be resolved by using the `@actors` attribute (actors are described in more detail in the next chapter, in our coverage of tasks). In lieu of the `@actors` attribute, the `@to` attribute can be used to explicitly set the destination email address. See table 5.2 for a full description of the mail-node nodetype elements and attributes.

Table 5.2 Mail-node nodetype elements and attributes

Element/Attribute name	Description
`subject`	Subject of the outbound email. *Optional*.
`@subject`	A convenience alternative to using the `subject` element. *Optional*.
`text`	Text/body of the outbound email. *Optional*.
`@text`	A convenience alternative to using the `text` element. *Optional*.
`@async`	A boolean used to indicate whether to use an asynchronous continuation to send the email (asynchronous continuations are covered in chapter 7). Defaults to `false` and is *optional*.

Table 5.2 Mail-node nodetype elements and attributes *(continued)*

Element/Attribute name	Description
`@template`	Enables you to specify a different template to use. This allows you to tailor the format and content of the outbound message. *Optional*.
`@actors`	Specifies one or more actors to send the outbound message. Uses the `actorId` to resolve the email address associated with that individual. The @actors attribute, or @to is *required*.
`@to`	Specifies an actual email address to which the mail will be sent. Either it or the `@actors` attribute is *required*.

Within the task-node nodetype, you can also specify that an email be created when the task is assigned, followed by reminder emails that adhere to a timer-style configuration. Thus, in the case of emails associated with a task, there may not be the need to use the mail nodetype.

As briefly mentioned in table 5.2, you can use a mail template file called jbpm.mail.templates.xml to define customized messages (if a different name is used, it must be defined within the `jbpm.cfg.xml` file in the format of `<string name="resource.mail.templates" value="jbpm.mail.myfile.xml" />`, for example). Within this file, you specify one or more `mail-templates` and then reference a given template name when configuring your mail node. Here's an example of a mail template definition:

```
<mail-templates>
  <variable name="BaseTaskListURL"
    value="http://yourhost:8080/jbpm-console/sa/task.jsf?id=" />

  <mail-template name='task-assign'>
    <actors>
      #{taskInstance.actorId}
    </actors>
    <subject>
      Task '#{taskInstance.name}' has been assigned to you!
    </subject>
    <text><![CDATA[Hello,

Task '#{taskInstance.name}' has been assigned to you by
your friendly Business Process Manager application.

Please visit #{BaseTaskListURL}#{taskInstance.id} to complete

Thanks.]]></text>
  </mail-template>
</mail-templates>
```

Notice the use of the variable substitutions, which are delimited by #{}. The variables that can be exposed in this fashion are the properties associated with these objects: `TaskInstance`, `ProcessInstance`, `ProcessDefinition`, `Token`, `TaskMgmtInstance`, `ContextInstance`, and any process variable. You can also create your own variables within the template itself, as demonstrated earlier when we created the variable

BaseTaskListURL. To reference this template in your mail node definition, you'd specify the template name task-assign in the @template attribute.

5.3.5 Decision nodetype

Within jBPM you have multiple ways in which decisions can be made as to which transition or path to follow. One method is to specify a condition within the definition of the transition itself (discussed in the next section). Another method, which can be used in node, state and task-node nodetypes, is for an action handler or individual (in the case of a task) to elect a transition path to take. The last approach is to use a decision nodetype; this is appropriate when you want the process to make the decision based on a BeanShell expression result. Here's an example of a decision nodetype definition:

```
<decision name="high-priority?"
  expression='#{ ( priority == "HIGH" ? "yes" : "no") }'>
  <transition to="email-notification" name="yes"/>
  <transition to="assign" name="no"/>
</decision>
```

In this example, priority is a process variable that contains values such as HIGH, MEDIUM, or LOW. This decision rule will direct HIGH priority messages to the transition named yes. The same effect can be achieved using the following variation:

```
<decision name="high-priority?" >
  <transition to="email-notification" name="yes">
    <condition>#{priority == "HIGH"}</condition>
  </transition>
  <transition to="assign" name="no">
    <condition>#{priority != "HIGH"}</condition>
  </transition>
</decision>
```

Lastly, you can also use a handler class to determine which transition path to follow. Simply specify the class in the handler child element, for example:

```
<decision name="high-priority?" >
  <handler class="com.sample.MyDecisionHandler"/>
</decision>
```

In this case MyDecisionHandler must implement DecisionHandler and its required method decision. This method must return a string value to indicate which transition path to follow (we'll demonstrate several handler examples beginning in section 5.5, and all handlers follow a similar usage convention and are simple to implement). Unlike in many other cases, there doesn't appear to be support for using an embedded BeanShell script to function as a handler in the case of a decision node.

5.3.6 Fork and join nodetypes

In many business processes, there can be concurrent paths of execution. For example, the on-boarding process for a new hire may involve several tasks that can be done in parallel, such as issuance of security credentials, I-9 form processing (used for

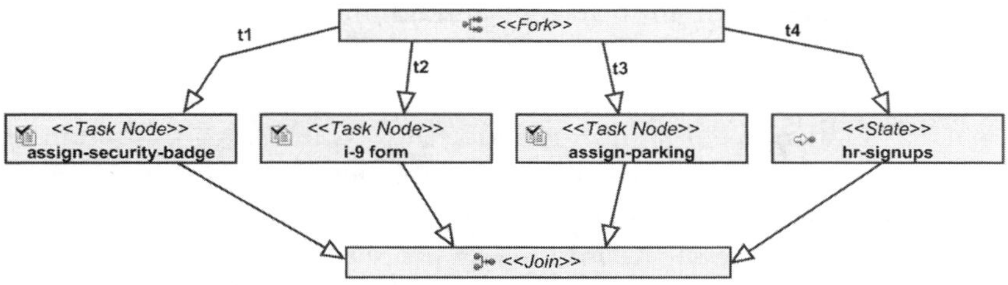

Figure 5.8 An example of jBPM fork and join

employment eligibility in the United States), parking pass assignment, and HR systems registration. While they can be done concurrently, they must all be completed and closed for the process instance to conclude. This is where the fork and join nodetypes can be used (see figure 5.8 for an example).

While conceptually the fork and join construct is rather straightforward and intuitive, it's considerably more complicated from a process engine standpoint. In particular, each forked path necessarily results in a new token being created. These represent *child* tokens of the parent *root* token. This behavior can be best witnessed through the jBPM Console when viewing the tokens for an active process instance that includes a fork, as shown in figure 5.9.

In the example shown in figure 5.9, the parent token is `565` as it has no parent and resides at the forked node. The remaining tokens are child tokens and will be merged back when all of them enter the join node. When a token execution arrives at the join, the join will determine whether any active siblings of the parent remain. If not, the parent execution token is reactivated. Otherwise, it will wait for the remaining tokens to complete.

We've done a whirlwind tour of the nodetypes, and you're probably a bit fatigued at this point. The next section on transitions will conclude our coverage of how

Tokens — First Prev - Page 1 of 1 - Next Last

Token ID	Parent	Node	Status	Start Date	End Date	Actions			
565	*(no parent)*	fork1	Running	Mar 18, 2008 2:51:49 AM		Examine	End	Suspend	Signal: **t1** Signal: **t2** Signal: **t3** Signal: **t4**
566	ID 565	assign-security-badge	Running	Mar 18, 2008 3:49:54 AM		Examine	End	Suspend	Signal
567	ID 565	assign-parking	Running	Mar 18, 2008 3:49:54 AM		Examine	End	Suspend	Signal
568	ID 565	hr-signups	Running	Mar 18, 2008 3:49:54 AM		Examine	End	Suspend	Signal
569	ID 565	i-9 form	Running	Mar 18, 2008 3:49:54 AM		Examine	End	Suspend	Signal

Child Tokens

Figure 5.9 BPM Console illustrations of forked tokens in a process instance

processes are diagrammed. After that, we'll move on to how you can incorporate your own custom implementation code.

5.4 Using transitions

We've already demonstrated some of the capabilities associated with transitions, particularly in the coverage of the decision nodetype in the previous section. Transitions represent a central role in the definition of a process, as they link the various nodes to create a directed graph. In other words, transitions can be thought of as the glue that holds together the nodetypes that we just described into a complete business process. The configurable elements and attributes available to transitions are displayed in table 5.3.

Table 5.3 Transition elements and attributes

Element/Attribute name	Description
description	Description of the transition; beneficial for documentation purposes. *Optional*.
condition	Optional expression that acts as a guard to determine whether or not the transition should be followed. The expression can either exist as element text (i.e., <condition>#{a > 5}</condition>) or as empty element when the @expression attribute is used (i.e., <condition expression="#{a > 5}"/>). *Optional*.
action	Allows for a Java action class or BeanShell script to be used for custom logic. See the next section. *Optional*.
exception-handler	Allows the developer to define a list of actions to take based on the type of error being caught. However, like event actions, they can't modify the graph's event flows. Exception handling is discussed in chapter 7. *Optional*.
@name	The name of the transition. Each transition leaving a specific node must have a unique name. *Optional*.
@to	The name of the destination node. *Required*.

Deciding which transition to follow when multiple transitions exist depends in part on the nodetype being exited. For example, in a task node, the decision on which transition to follow is usually made by the user. A web-based task form, for instance, might include buttons for each of the available transitions (such as send-back, approve, reject, etc.). For node and state nodetypes, a custom Java class or script can dictate the transition path through explicit signaling.

We've now covered the basics of diagramming within the process model. We've identified the available nodetypes, and you learned how they can be wired together via transitions. Of course, using the nodes as is doesn't provide all that much capability. The real power behind jBPM lies in *actions*, which are hooks where developers add their own programming logic.

5.5 Extending using actions

Actions and events allow programming logic to be inserted within a process model in a way transparent to the analyst or subject matter expert who designed the model. In most circumstances, the business modeler won't have the requisite skills or inclination to deal with the underlying plumbing necessary to create a truly runtime execution process. Indeed, if the model becomes complicated by visual representation of such technical details, the utility of the model in conveying the flow of the business process will quickly become lost. Instead, Visio and other static modeling tools will again become prevalent, with the models developed by them entirely abstract in nature. jBPM attempts to balance between creating a descriptive model and producing an executable process. This balance is achieved through the use of *actions*.

Actions are the integration points for interfacing with other applications or services. It's through actions that the services designed using SCA (chapters 3 and 4) can be readily used and consumed (you'll learn more about this in chapter 7). Depending on how it's configured, an action can be used to asynchronously send out a message to another system; used synchronously, such as when calling an external web services; or even used in a callback scenario where a request to a remote system is made and initiates a method call when it's completed.

The `action` element within jPDL defines the locations where actions can be used. They are as follows:

- *Node nodetype*—An action handler is used to implement the custom functionality associated with the node and to advance its token to the proper transition. An action is required when using a node, as no other inherent functionality is provided by this nodetype.
- *Transitions*—As a child of the `transition` element, an action can be invoked when the transition is triggered. This is often useful for setting process instance variables.
- *Events*—Discussed in more detail in section 5.6, actions are used within events to invoke programming logic based on various triggers, such as when a node is entered or exited. Actions, when used as part of events, can't directly influence the flow of the process but instead should be used for notification purposes, such as setting or updating process instance variables.
- *Exceptions*—We dive into exception handling in chapter 7, but suffice it to say that actions can be triggered when an exception occurs. Similar to event actions, they can't (or shouldn't) affect the flow of the process, but can indirectly do so by setting process variables (which downstream may use the variables in decision nodes, etc). Also, actions in this context are useful for sending error notifications.
- *Timers*—Actions can be triggered when a timer expires.

Creating a Java action class is straightforward—it's just a plain old Java object (POJO) that simply implements `ActionHandler`. The only method required to be implemented

> **Handler classes and jBPM**
>
> As we move deeper into exploring the ways in which custom logic can be introduced into jBPM, a recurring concept is one of handlers. As the name suggests, a handler assumes responsibility for performing a particular function. In the case of a `DecisionHandler`, that means implementing a method called `decision`. There are many different types of handler classes within jBPM. Commonly used ones are `ActionHandler`, `AssignmentHandler`, `ExceptionHandler`, and `TaskController-Handler`. Fortunately, the developers of jBPM make implementing such handlers typically easy (usually just one method must be implemented). Handlers in jBPM represent powerful extension points for introducing your customer code!

by `ActionHandler` is `execute`. The `execute` method, which returns `void`, takes a single parameter of type `ExecutionContext`, which is passed to it by the jBPM engine at runtime. The simplest way to get started with creating an action class is to create a new *process project* using the jBPM Eclipse-based Graphical Process Designer. This creates a skeleton project that includes a sample process with an example of an action class. The sample process's jPDL code and image are depicted in figure 5.10.

As shown in figure 5.10, the jPDL XML code contains a reference to the generated sample action class called `MessageActionHandler`. This sample class, shown in listing 5.1, illustrates how property values can be injected into the action class, and in turn, stored within a process variable.

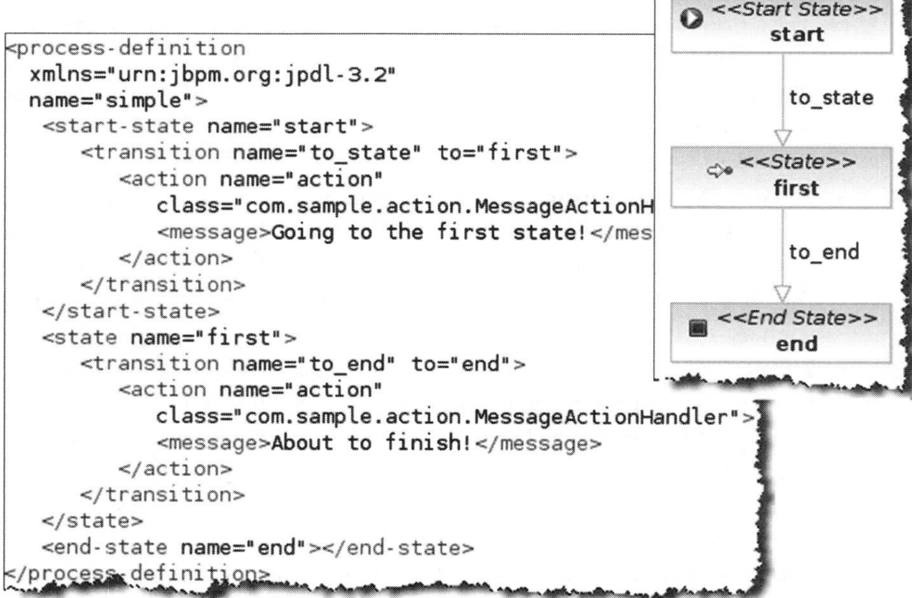
<process-definition
xmlns="urn:jbpm.org:jpdl-3.2"
name="simple">
<start-state name="start">
<transition name="to_state" to="first">
<action name="action"
class="com.sample.action.MessageActionH
<message>Going to the first state!</mes
</action>
</transition>
</start-state>
<state name="first">
<transition name="to_end" to="end">
<action name="action"
class="com.sample.action.MessageActionHandler">
<message>About to finish!</message>
</action>
</transition>
</state>
<end-state name="end"></end-state>
</process-definition>
<<Start State>>
start
to_state
<<State>>
first
to_end
<<End State>>
end

Figure 5.10 A jBPM sample process created automatically when a new process project is created

Listing 5.1 Sample action class generated when new a process project is created

```
public class MessageActionHandler
  implements ActionHandler {                    <-- ❶ Requires implementation

  private static final long serialVersionUID = 1L;

  String message;                               <-- ❷ Populates from injection

  public void execute(ExecutionContext context) <-- ❸ Executes this method
    throws Exception {
    context.getContextInstance()
        .setVariable("message", message);       <-- ❹ Sets jBPM variable
  }
}
```

Since this class is defined as the implementation for an action (shown in figure 5.10), it must implement the `ActionHandler` ❶ interface and its required `execute` method ❸. Notice as well that, in figure 5.10, the `action` element contains a child element called `message`. This is a property value that, when the corresponding action class is instantiated, will automatically look for a member variable with the same name ❷. If found, it will populate that Java field with the value specified in the jPDL. So, in this case, the Java variable `message` is populated with the value "Going to the First State!" The `execute` method then takes the value that was populated into the `message` variable and assigns it to a process variable that's created with the same name ❹. This process variable, in turn, will then be available to downstream nodes, as it's saved in the context of the process instance. This demonstrates how properties and configuration data can be populated at runtime using Spring-style injection.

In some cases, you may find that you're repeating the same action class in multiple locations within your jPDL. For example, you may have an event that triggers an action class for event stream processing or BAM purposes. Rather than repeating that action definition, you can define it at the root level of the jPDL, and then reference it where needed by using the `@ref-name` attribute of the `action` element (in fact, you can reference it anywhere, even if it's within a child element elsewhere). Here's an example:

```
<action ref-name='shared-action'/>
```

`shared-action` is the assigned name of an action located elsewhere (or at the top level) of the jPDL. This points out the importance of using unique names for your actions.

When creating the new process project, the generated code will also contain a JUnit test class called `SimpleProcessTest`. This test class illustrates how to locally instantiate a jBPM instance, install a process, run the process, and step through it programmatically. Although limited in what it achieves, the sample process and code provide a useful template or starting point for developing your process. The generated action class created in listing 5.1 when the project was created only demonstrates one way to populate property values. As it turns out, there are four methods for populating property values from within the jPDL—let's take a look.

5.5.1 Action class property instantiation

An optional attribute of the action element not shown in figure 5.10 is called @config-type. This attribute is used to specify the method by which property values can be injected into an action class upon instantiation. If omitted, it defaults to a value of field, which is the method used in figure 5.10 and the corresponding action class shown in listing 5.1. Other @config-type values include bean, constructor, and configuration-property. In general, we don't see any real advantage to using anything other than the default field type, so we won't bother explaining the others (they're covered in the official documentation, if you're interested).

When specifying the field-style method of class instantiation, jBPM will attempt to automatically populate class member variables that match the XML element name passed as a child to the action element. We witnessed this earlier when we used a message element to pass a string that was populated into a similarly named class variable. When more complex data must be passed, choose one of two other approaches: use arbitrarily complex XML data that will then be converted into a dom4j Element, or use a <map><entry><key> XML format to pass the data as a Java Map object. All three approaches are shown here using a jPDL snippet, with message passed as a string, xml as a dom4j Element, and map as a Java Map object:

```
<action class="com.sample.action.MessageActionHandlerField"
 config-type="field" name="action">
<message>Going to the field state!</message>
<xml>
  <value1>Value 1</value1>
  <value2>Value 2</value2>
  <value3 value="Value 3"/>
</xml>
<map>
  <entry><key>key1</key> <value>Value 1</value></entry>
  <entry><key>key2</key> <value>Value 2</value></entry>
</map>
</action>
```

As we pointed out, the field style will attempt to match each top-level XML element with a corresponding Java member class. Here's a fragment of the MessageActionHandlerField class used to receive the injected data (the complete class is in the example code):

```
public class MessageActionHandlerField implements ActionHandler {

  String message;
  Element xml; //org.dom4j.Element;
  Map<String, String> map;
  public void execute(ExecutionContext context) throws Exception {

    context.getContextInstance().setVariable("message", message);

    System.out.println("map is: " + map.size());
    System.out.println("xml is: " + xml.asXML());
  }
}
```

When the process is run and the node encountered, the three member variables are automatically populated with the corresponding data from the jPDL (`map.size()` is 2, `xml.asXML()` shows the XML `nodeset`). As you can see, this provides considerable flexibility for populating data on invocation. Let's now switch gears a bit and examine action expressions.

5.5.2 Using action expressions

One of the most interesting, but we believe underused, capabilities of the `action` element is the `@expression` attribute. This option enables you to invoke a method on a process variable (variables will be discussed in more detail in the next section). Thus, a process variable can not only be used to store process-related data, but can also be a complex Java object whose method is invoked with the `@expression` attribute specified. In that sense, process variables can encapsulate both data and function. This concept is most easily illustrated with an example. In listing 5.2 is a class that will be stored as a process variable within jBPM (notice that it's serializable for this reason).

Listing 5.2 Java class used as a process variable object

```
public class SalaryObject implements Serializable {

  private static final long serialVersionUID = 1L;

  // public used minimize code, not recommended
  public String fname;
  public String lname;
  public String approvedBy;
  public int currentSalary;
  public int proposedSalary;

  public void populateVars() {                       <-- 1 Initializes variables
    System.out.println("in populateVars()");
    fname = "John";
    lname = "Doe";
    currentSalary = 50000;
    proposedSalary = 55000;
  }
                                                  2 Is invoked by
  public void logApprovedSalary() {             <--  process
    System.out.println("in logApprovedSalary()");          3 Acquires
    ContextInstance contextInstance = ExecutionContext  <-- jBPM context
      .currentExecutionContext().getContextInstance();

    approvedBy = (String) contextInstance.getVariable("approver");

   if ( (float) proposedSalary / currentSalary > 1.0) {
    System.out.println("That's a nice increase");
   } else
    System.out.println("Maybe next year :-(");
  }
}
```

Let's assume that a start task action is responsible for instantiating the `SalaryObject` as a process variable identified with a name of `salary`. Then, during the lifecycle of the process instance, the two methods will be called. The `populateVars` method ❶ will simply assign values to four of the member variables. When called, the `logApprovedSalary` method ❷ will output a message to the console. Notice as well how a `ContextInstance` ❸ is used to enable the retrieval of the process variable called `approver`, which is then stored in a `String` variable called `approvedBy`.

How will the two methods in listing 5.2 be invoked? Let's take a look at a sample process diagram (jPDL) that uses this object (see listing 5.3).

Listing 5.3 jPDL demonstrating the `action` element's `expression` attribute

```
<process-definition xmlns="" name="salary">
  <start-state name="start">
    <event type='node-leave'>
     <action expression='#{salary.populateVars}'/>
    </event>
 <transition to="approve"/>
  </start-state>

  <state name="approve">
   <transition to="end">
    <action expression='#{salary.logApprovedSalary}'/>
   </transition>
  </state>

  <end-state name="end"/>
</process-definition>
```

❶ Invokes when node entered

❷ Invokes when approved

The highlighted code in listing 5.3 shows how the two methods are invoked using the `@expression` attribute. In the `start-state` node, the method `populateVars` is invoked on the object represented by `salary` in a process variable during the `node-leave` event ❶. In the `approve` state node, the `logApprovedSalary` method is invoked on the same object during the transition to the `end` node ❷. Thus, through the use of the `@expression` attribute, methods within a process variable or object can be invoked.

What's the implication of this capability? One clear benefit of this approach is that the process instance now has the encapsulated functionality within its unique context. By that, it becomes more immune to changes that may otherwise occur through the use of normal action classes. For example, if a regular action class is used but its functionality has changed through a new version, this would impact all in-progress instances that subsequently make calls to it. That may or may not be desirable. By using methods within a serialized Java class, this becomes less of a concern (though change management challenges always exist). It's also more consistent with the principles behind object-oriented programming, which is based on the notion of behavior and data being stored logically together.

What you may be left wondering in this example is how the `salary` process variable is initialized. Since it's a complex Java object (`SalaryObject` in listing 5.2), it can't be set via the standard property approach we discussed in section 5.5.1. We'll cover that shortly in section 5.7, but for now, suffice it to say that it's through the `ContextInstance`, which is used in listing 5.2 to retrieve a process variable.

The other remaining attributes that can be defined for an `action` element are `@accept-propagated-events` and `@async`. You'll learn more about both in the next chapter, which covers advanced features.

One of the main ways in which actions are used is in conjunction with events. Events, as the name implies, are triggered at various points in the process and reflect state changes that are occurring. The ability to invoke action code based on these events provides many interesting opportunities, ranging from activity monitoring and logging to asynchronous messaging. Let's investigate events further.

5.6 Using events for capturing lifecycle changes in a process

Events, as the name suggests, are triggers that are fired throughout the course of the lifecycle of a process instance. For example, when a token execution arrives in a given node, the `node-enter` event is fired. For each event that can occur, you can inject code via actions. This enables great flexibility for instituting custom behaviors within your process. Also, events represent a wonderful way to monitor the ongoing activity within a process. They can be used to monitor for any abnormalities or unusual trends that may be occurring, which we identified in chapter 1 as an important part of a SOA environment.

Table 5.4 categorizes the types of events that occur for the various objects (events aren't limited to nodes, but also affect transitions and the overall process).

Table 5.4 Object events

Event	Literal value	Object supported
EVENTTYPE_TRANSITION	transition	Transition, SuperState, Process
EVENTTYPE_BEFORE_SIGNAL	before-signal	Node *
EVENTTYPE_AFTER_SIGNAL	after-signal	Node
EVENTTYPE_PROCESS_START	process-start	Process
EVENTTYPE_PROCESS_END	process-end	Process
EVENTTYPE_NODE_ENTER	node-enter	Node, SuperState, Process
EVENTTYPE_NODE_LEAVE	node-leave	Node, SuperState, Process
EVENTTYPE_SUPERSTATE_ENTER	superstate-enter	SuperState, Transition, Process

* The Node nodetype in this table refers to it and all implementing types, such as State, Decision, Join, Fork, Task, and Mail.

Table 5.4 Object events *(continued)*

Event	Literal value	Object supported
EVENTTYPE_SUPERSTATE_LEAVE	superstate-leave	SuperState, Transition, Process
EVENTTYPE_SUBPROCESS_CREATED	subprocess-created	SuperState, Process
EVENTTYPE_SUBPROCESS_END	subprocess-end	SuperState, Process
EVENTTYPE_TASK_CREATE	task-create	SuperState, Process, Task
EVENTTYPE_TASK_ASSIGN	task-assign	SuperState, Process, Task
EVENTTYPE_TASK_START	task-start	SuperState, Process, Task
EVENTTYPE_TASK_END	task-end	SuperState, Process, Task
EVENTTYPE_TIMER	timer	SuperState, Process

In listing 5.3, you may recall that we showed how an event is defined. Besides the action element, the only other configurable option is the required @type attribute, which specifies one of the literal values shown in table 5.4 (node-leave in this case). While the use of events is fairly self-explanatory, one noteworthy and perhaps not obvious feature is that you can assign events at the process definition level. For example, consider the jPDL shown in figure 5.11.

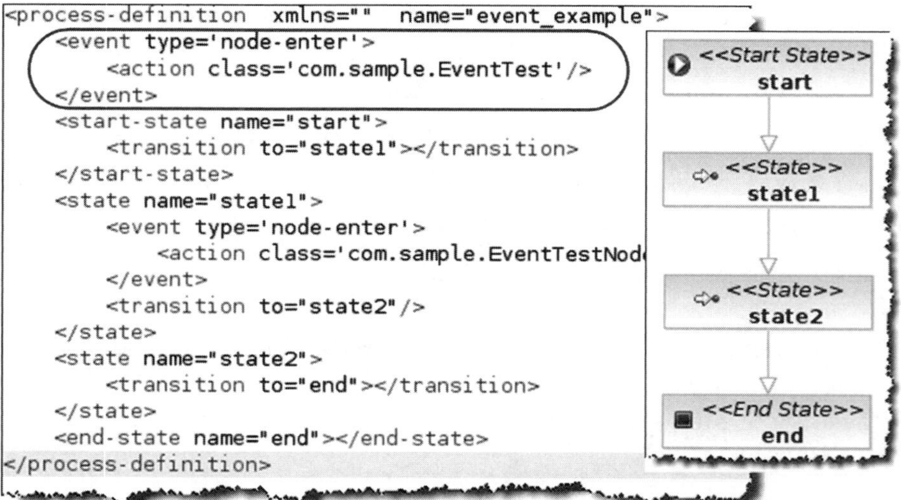

Figure 5.11 An example of a root-level event definition

Notice the event element is defined directly as a child element of the top-level process-definition root node. The event's action class is triggered for every node-enter event that occurs within the process. In this example, that means the EventTest class is instantiated and its execute method called when both state1 and state2 are entered. Notice as well that an additional node-enter trigger was defined within the definition of the state1 node. Hence, they aren't mutually exclusive—both EventTest and EventTestNode are fired when state1 is entered. Using root-level events can be beneficial for scenarios such as BAM, where you want events fired for certain event types across the board (this obviously simplifies configuration, because otherwise you'd have to configure each node individually).

As we pointed out earlier, it's important to remember that events can't directly influence the execution of the process. For instance, an action defined within an event can't dictate which transition to follow. Events are best used for triggering notifications to external services, and they can indirectly influence execution through the setting of process variables (for example, a decision node may use a process variable to determine which transition path to follow).

5.7 Managing context using variables

In several of the examples so far, we've demonstrated how variables can be used within a process instance. Variable value types supported include String, Boolean, Float, Double, or Long. In addition, most serializable Java objects can be stored, and any classes that are persisted with Hibernate. If a class instance can't be persisted, an error will occur when you attempt to retrieve it (not when you attempt to persist it). The types we've used so far have been *process variables*, but there are two other types: *local* and *transient*. Let's take a look at each type.

PROCESS VARIABLES

In the logApprovedSalary method in listing 5.2, we used the ContextInstance to retrieve a process variable called approver:

```
ContextInstance contextInstance =
ExecutionContext.currentExecutionContext().getContextInstance();
approvedBy = (String) contextInstance.getVariable("approver");
```

Setting a process variable can be done in a similar fashion using the setVariable method. Here's how we might set the approver variable that we retrieved earlier:

```
ContextInstance contextInstance =
  ExecutionContext.currentExecutionContext().getContextInstance();
contextInstance.setVariable("approver", "john_doe_approver");
```

In this example, since we're using one of the supported simple Java types (String, Boolean, etc.), nothing additional had to be done to store the string john_doe_approver using the variable key approver. If you want to store a more complex Java object, the class must implement Serializable (the class in listing 5.2 was stored as a process variable, you may recall).

Note that, although we're calling this type of variable a *process* variable, that definition varies slightly from the official jBPM documentation. My definition of a process variable is one that's *available throughout any node in the process instance.* This is accomplished by using the `setVariable` and `getVariable` methods. `setVariable` accepts as its signature a supported data type or a serializable `Object`. The variable is automatically available within the *root* token of the process instance. Because it's at the root token level, it's visible to all child tokens that may be created throughout the life of the process instance (for example, in a fork scenario, the child tokens created would have visibility to that variable). You can, alternatively, make a variable *local* within a token execution, which is described next.

LOCAL VARIABLES

A local variable is one in which the variable is only accessible within the scope of a token. This can be accomplished by use of the `ContextInstance`'s `setVariableLocally` method. As you may recall, a token represents a given *path of execution.* Using a local variable, you can define a variable that will be visible only within a specific token. Multiple tokens are most typically found in processes that include fork/join nodes, as shown in figure 5.12.

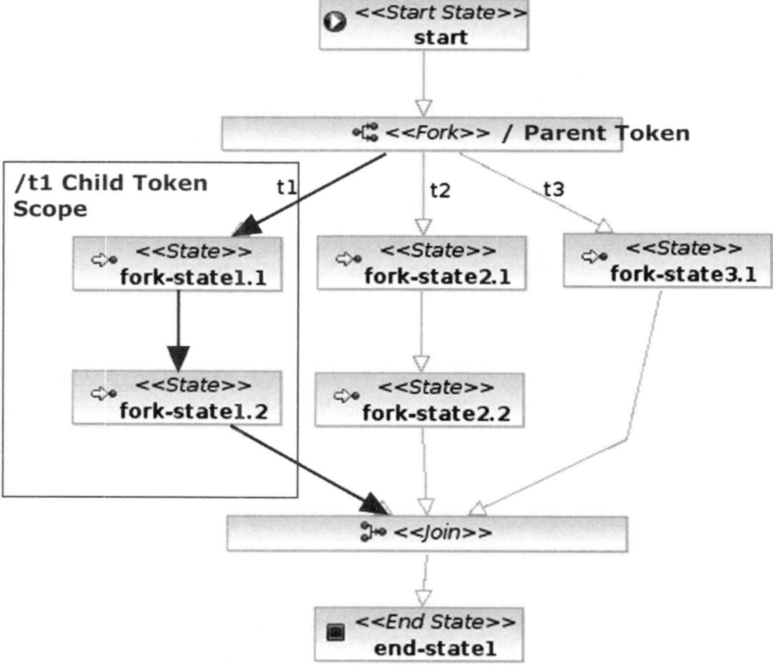

Figure 5.12 A token scope example when using fork and join nodes

In figure 5.12, you can assign a local variable to the /t1 path by using code such as

```
Token t1 = instance.findToken("/t1");
t1.instance.getContextInstance()
  .setVariableLocally("t1TokenVar", "true", t1);
```

In this example, the t1 child token that's created from the fork node is assigned to a variable called t1 (notice the token name is assigned, by default, to the transition name). Then the ContextInstance is used to set a local variable key called t1TokenVar to true for the token t1. Once it's assigned, you can retrieve the local variable by using the getVariableLocally method, which receives two parameters: variable key and token. If you attempt to fetch the value using the getVariable method that only accepts as its signature the variable key, null will be returned, because this is used for accessing process variables only. However, you can add the additional token parameter to the getVariable method to achieve the same result (that is, getVariable("t1TokenVar", t1)).

On what occasion would you want to use local variables? For highly complex processes, it might be beneficial to limit visibility and scope. In other circumstances, local variables might be used to initially populate task nodes, since it may not be necessary to expose them to the entire process. A close cousin of local variables are transient variables, which, as the name suggests, are limited to runtime actions and aren't persisted to the database with the process instance. For example, you could use them to populate static values that are required by downstream classes but that aren't relevant for keeping as part of the historical record.

The last topic we'll briefly touch on is *converters*. You may recall that many standard Java types can be stored automatically in jBPM. These include the types String, Date, Double, and Long. They can be saved as-is because converters have been defined that manage how these types can be converted into a jBPM VariableInstance class. You can provide your own converters to augment those that come out of the box. For example, you could create a converter that takes a Tuscany SDO object, marshals it into XML, and then stores the XML as a String when it's persisted. A reverse process could extract the XML and unmarshal it into an SDO object upon retrieval. The jBPM User Guide describes the process of creating converters in more detail.

5.8 Summary

One of the fundamental selling points of SOA is the promise that new solutions and processes can be developed quickly. By exposing reusable services through frameworks like SCA (covered in chapters 3 and 4), functionality that was locked into standalone applications or systems can be creatively and quickly leveraged and meshed into new business processes. BPM solutions are designed for creating such processes, and they represent a revolutionary alternative to conventional software development. Using BPM, subject matter experts can graphically craft new business processes and, when augmented by development, create executable models that can be deployed and managed. The upshot? Dramatically reduced development costs; better alignment between analysts and developers; and improved business agility.

JBoss jBPM is a mature BPM solution that offers many of the advanced features that have historically only been found in expensive commercial solutions. Capabilities include a graphical process designer, extensive task management features, a capable administrative console, and a powerful API. Perhaps more importantly, jBPM is highly extensible. You learned how custom functionality and code can be injected at nearly every point in the business process. What's more, this can be done in a transparent fashion that doesn't needlessly obfuscate the visual executable model.

One important feature of any BPM solution that we haven't covered in any great detail yet is tasks. I've reserved that subject for the next chapter, so turn the page.

6 jBPM tasks

This chapter covers

- Understanding the role of tasks in jBPM
- Assigning actors to tasks
- Using the task API

In the previous chapter, we covered many of the basics of what constitutes a BPM solution and then looked at a specific BPM implementation using JBoss jBPM, which we selected for our Open SOA Platform. Omitted from our coverage of core jBPM features were tasks—a broad and important topic. This chapter's focus will address this very subject.

Many of the greatest improvements in productivity that have resulted from IT systems involve automation. When systems, instead of humans, make decisions by way of business rules, immediate benefits are achieved through dramatically reduced processing time. Other payoffs include improved consistency, error reduction, more demonstrable compliance, and operational reporting. The fact remains, though, that humans, not computers, are still necessary for many process-related decisions or tasks. Despite our best efforts, the nuances of human judgment are often necessary (after all, how can we forget what happened in the movie *2001: A Space Odyssey*?). Such tasks and decisions that must be performed by humans are now even given a fancy name—*human intelligence tasks* (HITs).

> **Amazon's Mechanical Turk**
>
> Amazon's Mechanical Turk, named after the phony chess-playing "computer" from the 18th century later discovered to be a chess master hidden in a special compartment, is a web services–based product for assigning and managing human intelligence tasks (HITs). What is unique about this service is that it's intended for distributing work to an unlimited number of "workers" across the world, who can sign up to participate in the program. It initially was created for internal uses by Amazon for things such as product language translation, QA of product descriptions, and image processing. There are now reportedly over 100,000 workers signed up to use the system, though the number of available HITs has only now started to experience appreciable increases. This interesting service is worth monitoring as a potential outsourcing opportunity for your HITs.

Business process management (BPM) systems, from their earliest days harking back to when they were commonly known as workflow management, have built-in support for human-in-the-loop interface tasks. Most often, as is the case with jBPM, this is done by way of a forms framework that can be used to develop interfaces, along with built-in capabilities for assigning tasks, monitoring task completion, and issuing notifications. How do tasks relate to SOA? As we discussed in the previous chapter, BPM systems are uniquely suited at leveraging the services that result from SOA, enabling the rapid creation of new business processes. As you learned, many (if not most) business processes contain orchestrations that involve a combination of automated services and human tasks. Failure to cover this important topic would limit the full scope of jBPM solutions. Because of the human interface considerations that typically surround tasks, unlike the other nodes we've covered, tasks can involve more by way of setup and configuration. For these reasons, we decided to devote this entire chapter to tasks. We'll also explore how to use the task API to provide additional flexibility beyond what comes out of the box with jBPM. By the conclusion of this chapter, you'll have a solid understanding of what tasks are used for, their implementation, and how they can be integrated within your environment. Let's begin by taking a look at how tasks are managed using jBPM's Console application.

6.1 What are tasks?

As you may recall, we spent a fair amount of time in chapter 5 on the various nodetypes that are supported within jBPM. Nodetypes represent the prebuilt components that can be invoked at the various states (that is, nodes) within a process. Examples included nodetypes used for forking a process flow, for emailing, and as a placeholder for calling out to another service. A task nodetype is unique in that it's used to represent work that's to be completed by humans. Within jBPM's Process Definition Language, jPDL, it's represented by the `task-node` element. Options exist to manage who the task is assigned to, to specify who receives automatic notifications when a task assignment occurs, and to set up timers to ensure it's completed within the appropriate period (escalations can be defined). Multiple individual tasks can be assigned to a specific task node. By their nature, tasks usually involve an individual analyzing some information and then acting on it. A classic example is the purchase order (PO) approval process, where a director or VP-level individual must approve POs that are in excess of a certain amount. The approver must be supplied with the details of the PO, including the line items, supplier(s), shipping costs, warranty data, and so forth. Such a scenario is well tailored for a web form interface, where the approver can receive an email with a link to a web page displaying the PO details, with options for approving, rejecting, or sending back the PO.

6.1.1 Task management using the jBPM Console

Recognizing this as a common scenario, jBPM comes with a built-in capability for creating web forms that can be used for task processing. Figure 6.1 illustrates a jBPM task form.

In the example shown in figure 6.1, the depicted form is used by an approver for a hypothetical PO process. It demonstrates how the action buttons of `Approve`, `Reject`,

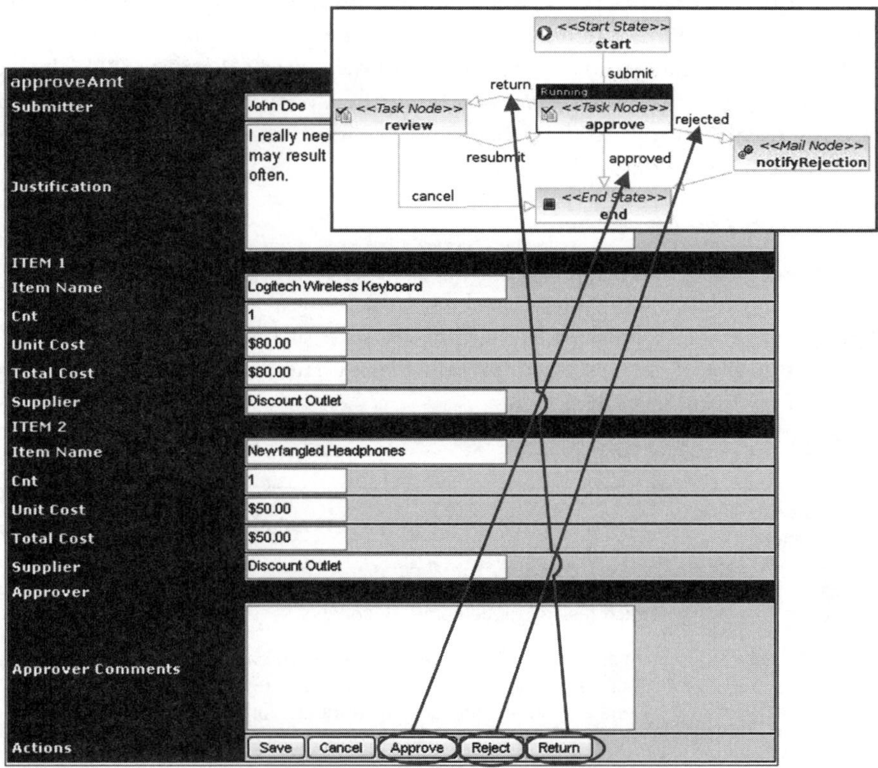

Figure 6.1 jBPM task form and its relation to the business process flow

and Return correspond to the transitions available from the task. The task-node element definition in jPDL is similar to the others we looked at in the previous chapter:

```
<task-node name="approve">
  <task name="approveAmt"/>
  <transition to="end" name="approved"/>
  <transition to="notifyRejection" name="rejected"/>
  <transition to="review" name="return"/>
</task-node>
```

The form itself was created using the jBPM Graphical Process Designer (for an excellent tutorial on how to create task forms, see the *Getting Started Guide* in the jBPM Wiki [jBPMGettingStarted]). As you've likely concluded, the layout of this particular example is found wanting. Unfortunately, the task form layout options when using the jBPM Console are rather limited. Repeating data sets, as would be the case in this example where multiple line items may exist per PO, can't be easily managed. My experience with the task form capabilities is that, while they may be sufficient for simple processes with simple form collection requirements, they are more often than not inadequate. Fortunately, since everything in jBPM is accessible via the Java API, it's not difficult to create your own forms using whatever web framework you're most accustomed to (we'll cover the API in much greater detail in the next chapter).

Now that you have some general idea of how tasks work within jBPM, let's peel back the layers of the onion and examine what the various configuration options are for creating tasks within jBPM. Let's begin by looking at the task element, which is where individual tasks are defined.

6.1.2 *task element configuration*

A common source of confusion when working with tasks is distinguishing between the task-node, which is a nodetype, and its child element task. The task-node nodetype shares most of the characteristics with the *node* or *state* nodetypes, but what distinguishes it is that it can have one or more tasks. The task element has the configuration options listed in table 6.1.

Table 6.1 task element configuration

Element/Attribute name	Description
@name	Specifies the name of the task. While not specifically required, I'd suggest giving each task a unique name. *Optional*.
@blocking	If set to true, the node can't be exited unless the task is completed. If set to false, the default, signaling the token to proceed past the node is permitted. Generally, setting this *optional* attribute isn't necessary, as the GUI controls this behavior.

Table 6.1 task element configuration *(continued)*

Element/Attribute name	Description
`@duedate`	Used to specify when the task must be completed. Can be expressed using actual or business hours. Examples are `2 business hours`, `3 days and 30 minutes and 20 seconds`, `5 minutes and 30 seconds`, `1 day`, `2 business hours`, and `30 business minutes`. Business calendar settings are specified in the jbpm.business.calender.properties file (see the User Guide for more details). *Optional*.
`@description`	Contains a description of the task. *Optional*.
`@signaling`	Indicates whether the task can signal the token to proceed forward beyond the parent `task-node`. For example, there may be more than one task associated with the `task-node`, and you don't wish to permit one or more of the individual tasks to forward the process execution. This option is *optional*; the default is `true`, which permits signaling.
`@priority`	Defines the priority of the task. Can be set to `highest`, `high`, `normal`, `low`, `lowest`, or any integer value. *Optional*.
`@notify`	Indicates whether to notify the actor, via email, that the task has been assigned to them. Default is `false`. *Optional* (and requires Enterprise edition).
`description`	An alternative to the `@description` attribute. *Optional*.
`assignment`	Describes who is assigned to complete the task. Discussed in the next section, on actors. *Optional*.
`controller`	Manages how process variables are transformed into and from task form parameters when using the jBPM Console forms framework. Discussed in section 6.4. *Optional*.
`event`	Supported event types are `task-create`, `task-start`, `task-assign`, and `task-end`. Events were described previously in chapter 5. *Optional*.
`timer`	Creates a timer that monitors the time duration of the task. Discussed in section 6.3. *Optional*.
`reminder`	Similar in functionality to `timer`, but is limited to sending out reminder emails (you can create actions with timers). Discussed in section 6.3 along with timers. *Optional*.

As you can see, a fair number of options are available when you're configuring a task. One child element that you'll likely use frequently is `assignment`. It represents how you assign users, known in jBPM as actors, to a particular task. You can also define how assignments occur downstream in the process through a method known as *swimlanes*. We'll take a closer look at this subject next.

6.2 Task user management

Tasks are fundamental to any BPM solution, and they represent work items that must be performed by individuals. So BPM systems must provide a means for assigning an individual or group the responsibility for completing a given task when it arises. As we pointed out, in jBPM this is accomplished using the assignment definition, which can optionally be configured for each task that is created. Let's take a deeper look.

6.2.1 Actors and assignments

In jBPM, a task is completed by an *actor*. An actor is identified through an `actorId`, which uniquely identifies that user. Within the jBPM Console, the `actorId` is assigned when the user logs in and is assigned as the individual's username. An `actorId` can be any unique string value, so it's a fairly flexible construct. Interestingly, you can assign a task to an `actorId` that hasn't previously been defined in the process. Closely related to an actor is a *pooled actor*, which is just a grouping construct.

A task can be assigned to an individual actor or to a pool of actors. When assigned to a pool, any individual actor within that pool can choose to take possession, or process the task. How do you specify which actors or pool of actors are associated with a given task? That's done in the process definition, or jPDL, through the `assignment` child node.

NOTE Like everything in jBPM, assignments can also be done using the API.

For example, for the task shown in figure 6.1, an assignment could be made to a specific individual, `jdoe`, by using the following:

```
<task-node name="approve">
  <task name="approveAmt">
    <assignment actor-id="jdoe"/>
  </task>
  <transition to="end" name="approved"/>
  <transition to="notifyRejection" name="rejected"/>
  <transition to="review" name="return"/>
</task-node>
```

Alternatively, if you wanted to assign a task to a group of actors, you could use the `@pooled-actors` attribute by including this assignment definition:

```
<assignment pooled-actors="dgenkin,jdavis"/>
```

Now, if `dgenkin` or `jdavis` log in via the jBPM Console with that `approve` task active, either will have the option of assigning it to themselves or the other, as shown in figure 6.2.

You can also use both the `@actor-id` and `@pooled-actors` together, in which case the task would be assigned to a specific individual by `@actor-id` but could then be reassigned by anyone included in the `@pooled-actors` list.

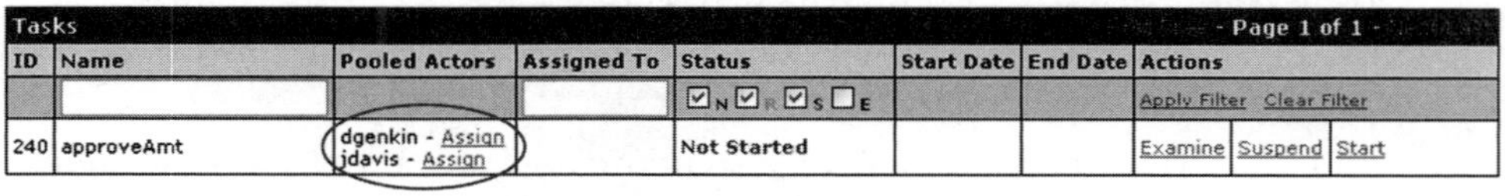

Tasks - Page 1 of 1 -

ID	Name	Pooled Actors	Assigned To	Status	Start Date	End Date	Actions
				N R S E			Apply Filter Clear Filter
240	approveAmt	dgenkin - Assign jdavis - Assign		Not Started			Examine Suspend Start

Figure 6.2 The tasks view in the jBPM Console where pooled actors are being used

> **jBPM Console identity component**
>
> One source of confusion that often arises is the interplay between the jBPM *identity component* that's used by the jBPM Console and the actors within a process. The identity component that comes with jBPM Console is used only for purposes of managing the login process and for controlling the permission-based menu options that are used within jBPM Console. It's not referenced, directly or otherwise, by the process engine itself (with one apparent caveat: email resolution requires it). For example, when you log in to jBPM Console, the identity component is used to validate your credentials. Then, once completed, your username acts as your `actorId` for determining which tasks you've been assigned. The identity component also uses *groups* to determine which menu options exist through jBPM Console, such as `user`, `manager`, and `admin`. A user is associated with one or more of these groups through a *membership*. Thus, the identity component is used by the jBPM Console to determine which menu options and privileges the user has, and effectively associates the user's login username with an `actorId` when interacting with the jBPM engine. The jBPM User Guide and some community forum entries describe, in some detail, how you can replace the default identity component with a custom alternative.

While assigning the actors within a jPDL is simple, in many cases a dynamic assignment may be required. To further expand on our example of the PO process, the individual assigned to the task would likely depend on whom the requestor is reporting, from an organizational perspective. Perhaps `jdoe` would require `djohnson`'s approval, but `msmith` would need `ltaylor`. While you could attempt to create separate process flows to accommodate this, a far easier solution would be to use a custom assignment class or script. This is referred to as creating a custom *assignment handler*. An assignment handler class must implement the `AssignmentHandler` interface, and with it the required method `assign`. Listing 6.1 shows a simple assignment handler that implements the rules we defined earlier (this class can also found in the sample code).

Listing 6.1 An example of a jBPM `AssignmentHandler` class

```
public class AssignmentExample implements AssignmentHandler {

  public void assign(Assignable assignable,
    ExecutionContext context) throws Exception {      <-- Implements required method

  String submitter = (String) context.getContextInstance()
     .getVariable("submitter");

  if (submitter.equalsIgnoreCase("jdoe"))
    assignable.setActorId("djohnson");
  else if (submitter.equalsIgnoreCase("msmith"))        Specifies assignment logic
    assignable.setActorId("ltaylor");
  else
    assignable.setActorId("rharris");
  }
}
```

In the highlighted code, you see how we are just hard-coding (for demonstration purposes) some logic for how to perform an assignment. In the first case, we're simply checking to see whether the `submitter`'s name (`submitter` was retrieved as a process variable) is `jdoe`, and if so, we assign the task to `djohnson` (using the `setActorId` method). In a real-life scenario, a lookup to an LDAP directory server might be used to retrieve the organizational approvals that are required. Also, instead of using `Assignable.setActorId()`, you could just as easily assign a pooled group of actors using `Assignable.setPooledActors()`, which takes an array of `actorId` Strings.

NOTE The same configuration options available for the `AssignmentHandler` class are available for the `ActionHandler` class. See chapter 5.

You've probably encountered scenarios where, once a given task is assigned to an individual or group, it makes sense for any follow-up tasks related to the same work order or process to also be assigned to that same individual or group. After all, they're already familiar with the issue. This can be accomplished with jBPM using a concept called *swimlanes*. Let's explore this further so that you may consider using this functionality in the processes you develop.

6.2.2 Understanding swimlanes

Swimlanes, whose terminology is derived from UML activity diagrams and/or cross-functional flowcharts, represent roles that can be assigned to an individual actor or pooled group. Swimlanes are used when multiple tasks within a process should be performed by the same actor. For example, if tasks A and B are sequential and both are assigned the same swimlane, then when task A is completed, task B will automatically be assigned to the same actor as was assigned to task A. When do swimlanes make sense? When several tasks within a process exist within a given organization, say Human Resources, it often makes sense to have the same individual perform all of the given tasks as it relates to a given process instance. Also, because of the sensitivity of many HR-related tasks, it's sometimes better to limit exposure beyond what is necessary—spreading out the work to multiple people for a given process instance may be undesired.

Thus, when using a swimlane within a task, you don't specify an assignment to an individual actor or pooled group of actors, since the assignment is done within the definition of the swimlane itself. This can best be illustrated through a simple example, so consider the process shown in figure 6.3.

In the example shown in figure 6.3, the swimlane called `approver` was created at the root level of the jPDL definition. The two tasks that follow, `approveAmt` and `assign-charge-codes`, both use the `@swimlane` attribute to associate the task with that previously defined swimlane. Notice that the swimlane was defined using the `@pooled-actors` attribute, but a single assignment using `@actor-id` is permitted as well (or even a combination of the two).

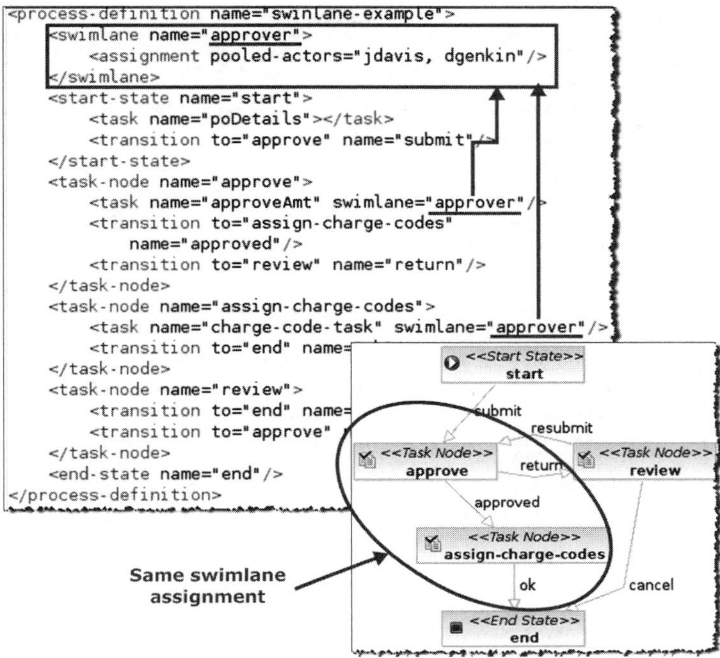

<process-definition name="swinlane-example">
<swimlane name="approver">
<assignment pooled-actors="jdavis, dgenkin"/>
</swimlane>
<start-state name="start">
<task name="poDetails"></task>
<transition to="approve" name="submit"/>
</start-state>
<task-node name="approve">
<task name="approveAmt" swimlane="approver"/>
<transition to="assign-charge-codes"
name="approved"/>
<transition to="review" name="return"/>
</task-node>
<task-node name="assign-charge-codes">
<task name="charge-code-task" swimlane="approver"/>
<transition to="end" name=
</task-node>
<task-node name="review">
<transition to="end" name=
<transition to="approve"
</task-node>
<end-state name="end"/>
</process-definition>
<<Start State>>
start
submit
resubmit
<<Task Node>>
approve
return
<<Task Node>>
review
approved
<<Task Node>>
assign-charge-codes
ok
cancel
<<End State>>
end
Same swimlane assignment

Figure 6.3 An example of a swimlane definition and use

The swimlane's `assignment` child element is the same definition as we saw in the previous section. Thus, you can use an `AssignmentHandler` class to dynamically define how the assignment occurs. Regardless of how the assignment is made, humans, being humans, may not always complete the work or task within the required time frame. This is where timers come into play.

6.3 Using timers

Timers are used to monitor the duration of an execution of a node, and they expire when the execution token has exited the node. Timers are only supported in jBPM Enterprise since they require the presence of an application server to function properly. While timers aren't actually unique to tasks and can be used by any node, they're most frequently used in combination with tasks. Timers can also be created and cancelled within `action` and `event` elements using the `create-timer` and `cancel-timer` elements. The easiest way to create a timer is to specify the `timer` element directly as a child element of the node that you want to monitor. The `timer` element's configurable options are shown in table 6.2.

Table 6.2 Timer configuration

Element/Attribute name	Description
`@duedate`	Used to specify when the node's execution must be completed. Can be expressed using actual or business hours. Examples are `2 business hours`, `3 days and 30 minutes and 20 seconds`, `5 minutes and 30 seconds`, `1 day`, `2 business hours`, and `30 business minutes`. Business calendar settings are specified in the jbpm.business.calender.properties file (see the User Guide for more details). *Required*.
`@name`	Specifies the name of the timer. *Required*.
`@repeat`	After a timer has expired based on the `@duedate`, this can be used to specify repeating timer executions (follows the same usage conventions as `@duedate`). The value can also be specified as `yes` or `true`, in which case the timer settings from `@duedate` will be used. *Optional*.
`@transition`	Specifies the name of a transition to follow when the timer executes. Note that if a transition is specified, then any value provided in `@repeat` will be ignored, as the transition will be acted upon when the `@duedate` timer is fired. *Optional*.
`Action`	An `ActionHandler` implementation class that will be triggered when the timer fires (see chapter 5). *Optional*.
`Script`	A BeanShell script that will be triggered when the timer fires. *Optional*.

As you can see, there's considerable flexibility in how a timer can be configured. Here's a simple illustration of how it can be done within a process definition:

```
<task node name="approve">
  <task name="approveAmt" swimlane="approver"/>
  <timer duedate="5 minutes" name="past-due-timer" transition="past-due"/>
  <transition to="assign-charge-codes" name="approved"/>
  <transition to="review" name="return"/>
  <transition to="pastdue" name="past-due"/>
</task node>
```

In this example, a timer called `past-due-timer` was created that will trigger the transition to `past-due`, which is a transition to the `pastdue` node, if the task node isn't completed within 5 minutes. Within the jBPM Console, you can see the running timers by logging in as an administrative user, selecting Manage > Jobs from the top-level menu, and choosing Timers. This will display the running timers, as shown in figure 6.4.

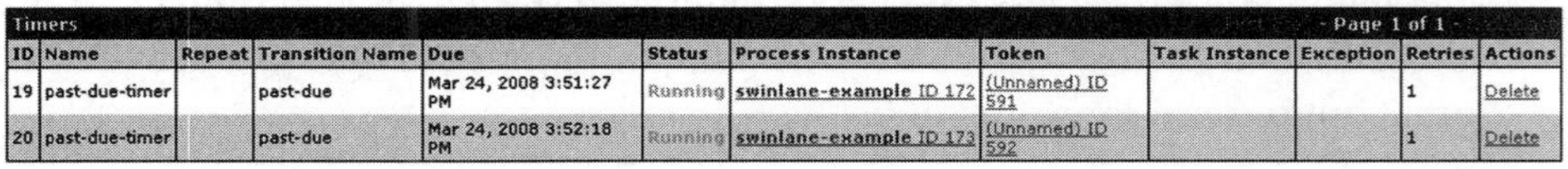

Timers — Page 1 of 1

ID	Name	Repeat	Transition Name	Due	Status	Process Instance	Token	Task Instance	Exception	Retries	Actions
19	past-due-timer		past-due	Mar 24, 2008 3:51:27 PM	Running	swinlane-example ID 172	(Unnamed) ID 591			1	Delete
20	past-due-timer		past-due	Mar 24, 2008 3:52:18 PM	Running	swinlane-example ID 173	(Unnamed) ID 592			1	Delete

Figure 6.4 Timer view in jBPM Console

While the ability to trigger a transition is obviously a nice feature, the limitation is that you can't use the repeat timer in this scenario, as the transition will occur once the initial `duedate` trigger is fired. Fortunately, the `task` element (which is a child element of the `task node`) has a unique element called `reminder` that can be use to achieve the desired effect.

> **Timers are critical to BPM**
>
> Once you begin using jBPM, you'll increasingly find that timers play an essential role, especially where human interface tasks are required. Most commonly, they're used for escalating or reassigning a task to someone else if it hasn't been completed within a certain period. This is especially important if compliance or regulatory implications exist for not performing a given process within the allocated time frame (in the pharmaceutical world, one can think of adverse reaction reporting). Financial implications may also exist for not performing a process within a given time frame, such as when penalties are crafted into service-level agreements. Using the API, you could also do some creative things, such as varying the timer settings based on some identifier associated with the process instance. For example, if a customer is a "gold" customer, the timer settings might be shorter for a sales order process.

The `reminder` element has only two settings: a `@duedate` and a `@repeat` attribute that function the same as when used with the `timer` element. Here's an example of using the `reminder` element to send out a reminder email every 15 minutes until the task is completed:

```
<task name="approveAmt" swimlane="approver">
  <reminder duedate="0 seconds" repeat="15 minutes"/>
</task>
```

The only downside in just using the reminder capability is that there's no way to specify a transition path to another node in the event of repeated failures to respond. For example, you cannot simply incorporate logic such as "If X actor doesn't respond after 4 notices, then escalate to a Y." All is not lost, however. By using a reminder with a timer, you can achieve this:

```
<task node name="approve">
  <task name="approveAmt" swimlane="approver">
     <reminder duedate="0 seconds" repeat="10 minutes"/>
  </task>
  <timer duedate="30 minutes" name="past-due-timer"
       transition="past-due"/>
   <transition to="assign-charge-codes" name="approved"/>
   <transition to="review" name="return"/>
   <transition to="pastdue" name="past-due">
     <cancel-timer name="past-due-timer"/>
   </transition>
</task node>
```

In pseudo-code, you could interpret the previous code as

When the task node approve is activated, send an immediate notice to the assignee (reminder duedate="0 seconds").
Follow this with a reminder every 10 minutes (repeat="10 minutes") until 30 minutes has transpired (timer duedate="30 minutes").
If 30 minutes has passed, then move the execution to the pastdue node (timer transition="past-due", which initiates the transition to the node pastdue).

You likely noticed in the jPDL example the cancel-timer element, which is triggered when the transition named past-due is invoked. This is required because the timer associated with the reminder element doesn't expire automatically if the transition is triggered through the timer element (it does expire, or get cancelled, if the actor processes the task). I suspect this is a bug, but this solution is an acceptable work-around. If you aren't interested in using a timer but just want to send a reminder email, you can do so by just using the task element's @notify attribute, setting it to yes (that is, <task name="approveAmt" swimlane="approver" notify="yes"/>).

NOTE The action child element available to create-timer and cancel-timer enables you to instantiate Java code when the timer due date is activated (you can also use a BeanShell script in lieu of a Java class). In the case of the cancel-timer, the code would be invoked when the cancel-timer is triggered.

Let's take a look next at task controllers, which provide considerable flexibility when you're working with task forms.

6.4 Task controllers

Task controllers provide a means to bridge between data that's stored within process variables and data required by the task form presentation or UI. In figure 6.1, we illustrated how the jBPM Console can be used to render task forms. In this simple example, the task directly interfaced with the process variables. However, instead of working with process variables directly, a task controller can convert them into and out of *task variables*. A task controller can also be used to control read/write access permissions. The default task controller can only perform fairly simple mapping, as shown here:

```
<task node name="approve">
  <task name="approveAmt">
    <controller>
      <variable name="fname" access="read,write"
        mapped-name="firstName"/>
      <variable name="lname" access="read,write,required"
        mapped-name="lastName"/>
      <variable name="middle" />
    </controller>
  </task>
  <transitions…/>
</task node>
```

The `@name` attribute of the `variable` element is required and refers to a process or local variable that's accessible in the context that the task is running within. The `@mapped-name` attribute is the task variable name that's assigned, and if omitted, it would assume the same name as the process variable. The `@access` attribute controls the behavior of how the task variable is written back to the process variable at the completion of the task. The three possible values are `read`, `write`, and `required`. A `read` value indicates the task can only read the process variable. A `write` value indicates the task variable will be written back to the corresponding process variable by the task. A value of `required` indicates the task variable must be populated when attempting to convert the value to the process variable.

As you can see, the built-in task controller has fairly limited capabilities. However, as with most things in jBPM, you're free to create your own task controller by implementing the `TaskControllerHandler`. Depending on your requirements, this could be a fairly complex undertaking, so we won't cover it here (the User Guide provides some guidance on this, and I suggest looking at the source code). However, you can easily see how this approach could greatly simplify the form and process variables we created in figure 6.1. In that example, each field in the form represented a process variable. A far better solution would be to create a complex Java class that houses the data as a single process variable, and then use a controller to carve it into task variables more suitable for use within the form framework you're using. Another intriguing idea would be to store the complex objects as service data objects (SDOs are discussed in chapter 4), and then use the metadata features of SDO to dynamically build your form.

In the next section, we're going to change the pace a bit and begin to tap into the abilities that the jBPM API provides. It is through the API that you really start to appreciate the capabilities of jBPM, because it unlocks so many fascinating integration opportunities. My interest in jBPM began to flourish as I learned how to fully leverage this capability. Indeed, this is what distinguishes open source from proprietary solutions. When using a closed source, commercial application, you're usually beholden to a limited number of public APIs that they deem worthy of sharing. The good stuff is kept private. With open source, you have access to everything, and you can look at the code to understand exactly how it's being used. I chose to begin talking about the API in conjunction with tasks because this is likely one of the first places you'll want to use it. I pointed out earlier that the task form capabilities of jBPM are fairly restricted, but with the API, you can easily augment it with your own code. Let's begin.

6.5 Developing with the task API

As we discussed in section 6.1, while the form framework that comes with building task forms for the jBPM Console is simple to use, it also is fairly limited. Specifically, it's limited in its ability to display and work with complex data, such as repeating rows and complex table layouts. Most enterprise users of jBPM will quickly determine that they must create their own forms using their framework of choice, be it Google's GWT, Adobe Flex, or TIBCO's GI, among others. Fortunately, using the jBPM API makes doing this far less daunting than you might imagine. Let's illustrate some of the more common API calls that you might find beneficial.

6.5.1 Identifying processes within a jBPM instance

Although not directly related to tasks, finding all process definitions with a jBPM instance is likely one of the first places you'll begin when using the API and working with tasks. As a refresher, a *process* is simply a unique process definition, whereas a *process instance* is an instantiated instance of a given process.

> **Using hibernate.properties to specify which jBPM instance to connect**
>
> When you create a jBPM process project within the Eclipse Graphical Process Designer, it will automatically create a hibernate.cfg.properties file in the src/main/config directory. By default, this is set up to connect to a hypersonic in-memory database. To connect to a remote database, you have two options: (1) specify the connection settings in the hibernate.cfg.xml file (search for "JDBC connection properties (begin)"), or (2) comment out the connection properties in hibernate.properties and instead create a hibernate.properties file in the same config directory. Configure this file to resemble this:
>
> ```
> hibernate.connection.driver_class=org.hsqldb.jdbcDriver
> hibernate.connection.url=jdbc:hsqldb:hsql://localhost/
> hibernate.connection.username=sa
> hibernate.connection.password=
> hibernate.dialect=org.hibernate.dialect.HSQLDialect
> ```
>
> Obviously, change the property values to reflect your environment. Although there is no single correct choice for specifying connection settings, my preference is the hibernate.properties file, since you isolate your changes and don't risk inadvertently modifying other nonrelated settings.

The first step in using the API, regardless of which operation you wish to perform, is to acquire a `JbpmContext` instance. In conjunction with the `hibernate.cfg.xml` (and/or `hibernate.properties`; see the sidebar "Using hibernate.properties to specify which jBPM instance to connect"), the `JbpmContext` instance is used to establish which jBPM database or instance to connect. Once a `JbpmContext` is acquired, you can then perform a variety of operations, as listing 6.2 shows. In this listing, we retrieve a list of process definitions within a given jBPM instance. In this case, we're creating a helper class called `JBPMHelper`, to which we'll gradually add additional static methods, starting with `listProcesses` (I settled on static in order to simplify calling these helper methods without having to first instantiate the class).

Listing 6.2 Helper class method to retrieve a process from a jBPM instance

```
public class JBPMHelper {

  public static List<ProcessDefinition>
```

```
    listProcesses(JbpmContext jbpmContext) {          ❶

    List<ProcessDefinition> processDefinitionList =                ❷
      jbpmContext.getGraphSession().findAllProcessDefinitions();

    return processDefinitionList;
  }

  public static JbpmConfiguration getConfiguration() {     ❸
    return JbpmConfiguration.getInstance();
  }
}
```

As you can see, the class currently has one static method, `listProcesses` ❶. Within it, a single call is made to retrieve the list of process definitions using `GraphSession`'s `findAllProcessDefinitions` method ❷. This returns a `java.util.List` of `ProcessDefinition` objects, which in turn represents the return value for our helper method.

The `JbpmContext` that's given as a sole parameter to the `listProcesses` method must be provided for all of the helper methods we'll be creating. Creating the context within the helper method isn't advisable, as any transactions that result from using the returned `List` could result in Hibernate transactional errors. Instead, the `JbpmContext` should be created by the calling routine and then closed by it when finished. The `getConfiguration` helper method shown in listing 6.2 can be used by the caller or client as a convenience to retrieve the context ❸.

Let's now see how to use the `listProcesses` method by creating a Java static `main()` class that invokes it and simply prints back information about the process definitions returned. Listing 6.3 calls the static helper method we created in listing 6.2, and then iterates through the `List` and prints out the `processId`, `name` and `version` associated with each process.

Listing 6.3 Main class utilizing `listProcesses` helper method

```
public class MainProcessDefinitions {

  public static void main(String[] args) {
                                                         Retrieves JbpmContext
  JbpmContext jbpmContext =                              from helper
    JBPMHelper.getConfiguration().createJbpmContext();
                                                         Calls helper method to
  List<ProcessDefinition> processDefinitionList =        retrieve processes
    JBPMHelper.listProcesses(jbpmContext);
  ProcessDefinition process;
  for (Iterator<ProcessDefinition> i =                      Iterates through list
      processDefinitionList.iterator(); i.hasNext();) {     of processes
      process = i.next();
      System.out.println("ProcessId: " + process.getId() + " ProcessName: "
        + process.getName() + " Version: " + process.getVersion());

  }
  jbpmContext.close();      Closes context
  }
}
```

What have we accomplished here? With very few lines of code, we've demonstrated how you can use the jBPM API to retrieve a list of processes associated with a given jBPM instance. As part of our approach, we created a helper class in listing 6.2 to which we'll add functionality as we proceed. This helper class will be useful for performing some of the heavy lifting in using the API as well as facilitate reuse. Let's now add another method to the helper that will return a list of process instances associated with a given process.

6.5.2 *Identifying running process instances for a given process*

The method we'll create to retrieve a list of process instances will be a tad more involved. Instead of just bringing back all process instances, a far more valuable use case involves the ability to filter by status. For example, you may want to retrieve a list of all *running* instances that are associated with a given process. Other statuses would include those that have been *suspended*, *ended*, or just simply *all*. However, there is no specific API method to retrieve filtered process instances. Fortunately, you can use the built-in Hibernate functionality to achieve the desired effect. To accomplish this, we'll construct and run a Hibernate query that returns a `List` of `ProcessInstances` (learn more about Hibernate at the official website, www.hibernate.org). Listing 6.4's code fragment demonstrates how this can be accomplished.

Listing 6.4 Helper method used to retrieve process instances

```
public final static String RUNNING = "RUNNING";
public final static String SUSPENDED = "SUSPENDED";
public final static String ENDED = "ENDED";

public static List<ProcessInstance>
listProcessInstances(JbpmContext jbpmContext, long processId,
String filter) {

Query query;                          <-- 1

StringBuffer queryText =
  new StringBuffer("select pi from"                <-- 2
  + " org.jbpm.graph.exe.ProcessInstance as pi ");

if (processId != 0)
   queryText.append(" where pi.processDefinition = "      3
     + String.valueOf(processId));

if (filter.equalsIgnoreCase(ENDED)) {
  queryText.append(" and pi.end != null");
}
if (filter.equalsIgnoreCase(RUNNING)) {
  queryText.append(" and pi.end = null");              4
}
if (filter.equalsIgnoreCase(SUSPENDED)) {
  queryText.append(" and pi.isSuspended = true");
}

queryText.append(" order by pi.start desc");
```

```
query = jbpmContext.getSession()
  .createQuery(queryText.toString());          ⑤

List<ProcessInstance> processInstanceList =
  (List<ProcessInstance>) query.list();        ⑥

return processInstanceList;      ⑦
}
```

This new method, `listProcessInstances`, requires three parameters. The first is `JbpmContext`, which as you saw in the previous example, represents a connection to the jBPM instance being used. The second parameter is `processId`, which is the unique process identifier associated with all jBPM processes (the `listProcesses` method in listing 6.2 returns such an ID for each process). The third value is the filter criteria, which can be either `ENDED`, `RUNNING`, or `SUSPENDED`. The second and third parameters will be used to construct the Hibernate query.

NOTE For those unfamiliar with Hibernate, it uses its own query language, which is similar but not identical to SQL.

The method logic begins by defining a Hibernate `Query` object ❶. This will be used for creating and executing the Hibernate query. The query statement is defined by building a `StringBuffer` called `queryText` that will contain the generated query statement ❷. The statement is built dynamically ❸ and ❹. Once completed, the `Query` object (`query`) is populated with the generated SQL statement ❺, and then its `list` method called to return a `List` of results ❻. The resulting `List`, which is cast to `ProcessInstance`'s, is returned by the method ❼.

Listing 6.5 shows a fragment of a Java `main()` class (in the code samples, the class name is `MainProcessInstances`) that utilizes this new helper method.

Listing 6.5 Example code for running the `listProcessInstance` method

```
public static void main(String[] args) {

  if (args.length != 2) {
    System.out.println("Syntax is: MainProcessInstances <processId>" +
      "<one of RUNNING | ENDED | SUSPENDED>");
    System.exit(1);
  }

  JbpmContext jbpmContext =            Acquires jBPM Context
    JBPMHelper.getConfiguration().createJbpmContext();

  List<ProcessInstance> processInstanceList;

  processInstanceList =
   JBPMHelper.listProcessInstances
     (Integer.parseInt(args[0]), args[1]);     Call to fetch process instances

   if (processInstanceList != null) {
    for (ProcessInstance instance :            Iterates through list, prints details
      processInstanceList) {
      System.out.println("  >> Instance: "
```

```
            + instance.getId()
            + " Started:"
            + new SimpleDateFormat("yyyy-MM-dd:HH:mm:ss z")
            .format(instance.getStart()));
      }
    }
    jbpmContext.close();
  }
}
```

In the example from listing 6.5 (included in the book's source code), the `Main` class accepts two parameters: a `processId` and a search filter. Those values, in turn, are passed to the `listProcessInstances` method we created in listing 6.4. If any matching results are found, it simply prints some information about the process instance to the console. What has this exercise accomplished? We've demonstrated how, through the use of the API, we can return a filtered list of process instances associated with a given jBPM process. This could be useful apart from any task-related functions, such as for populating a desktop gadget or dashboard for executives.

Next, let's build on this and use the API to return a list of all open tasks associated with a given process instance.

6.5.3 *Finding open tasks within a process instance*

Now that we've established what process instances are running, we are in a position to interrogate a given instance to determine what open tasks might exist. This API call is particularly relevant if you're developing your own forms front-end to jBPM tasks. For example, you could create your task collection and approval forms in Flex (AIR), GWT, or another framework.

The operation for fetching a list of one or more tasks within a process instance is similar to the one we used in listing 6.4 to retrieve the process instances. We'll again use Hibernate's `Query` object to dynamically build an SQL statement `String` based on filter criteria provided as method parameters. Once a given task is returned, further API operations can be performed to return the details of a task, such as assignment details, task variables, and associated timers. First, listing 6.6 will return a `List` of `TaskInstances` based on the parameters passed to the `listTaskForProcessInstance`.

Listing 6.6 Retrieves list of tasks for a given process ID

```
public static List<TaskInstance>

    listTasksForProcessInstance(JbpmContext jbpmContext , long
    processInstanceId, String filter) {

  Query query;          <— Defines Hibernate Query

  StringBuffer queryText =
    new StringBuffer("select ti from"     <— Builds SQL statement
    + " org.jbpm.taskmgmt.exe.TaskInstance as ti ");

  if (processInstanceId != 0)
    queryText.append(" where ti.processInstance = "
```

```
    + String.valueOf(processInstanceId));

  if (filter.equalsIgnoreCase(ENDED)) {
    queryText.append(" and ti.isOpen = false");
  }
  if (filter.equalsIgnoreCase(SUSPENDED)) {
    queryText.append(" and ti.isSuspended = true");
  }
  if (filter.equalsIgnoreCase(CANCELLED)) {
    queryText.append(" and ti.isCancelled = true");
  }
  if (filter.equalsIgnoreCase(OPEN)) {
    queryText.append(" and ti.isOpen = true");
  }

  queryText.append(" order by ti.priority asc");      <-- Adds order by for sorting
  query = jbpmContext.getSession().createQuery(queryText.toString());

  List<TaskInstance> taskInstanceList = (List<TaskInstance>) query.list();

  return taskInstanceList;         <-- Returns result List
}
```

In the case of tasks, the four most common statuses are `ENDED`, `SUSPENDED`, `CANCELLED`, and `OPEN` (additional criteria could be added, such as filtering by actor or whether it's past due). For a client class using this `listTasksForProcessInstance` method, the `TaskInstance` objects returned within the `List` provide a wealth of information about a given task. Listing 6.7 is a code fragment that shows details being printed about a given task, picking up at the point where you've received a `TaskInstance` (referred to as the variable `taskInstance`).

Listing 6.7 Using a `TaskInstance` to retrieve information about a given task

```
System.out.println(">> Task: " + taskInstance.getId()
  + " Created: "
  + new SimpleDateFormat("yyyy-MM-dd:HH:mm:ss z")
   .format(taskInstance.getCreate())
  + " Task Name: " + taskInstance.getName());          Outputs details about task

System.out.println("    >> assigned actor is: " +     <-- Outputs actor assigned task
  taskInstance.getActorId());

Set pooledActors = taskInstance.getPooledActors();     <-- Retrieves assigned pooled actors
PooledActor actor;

Iterator it;

for (it=pooledActors.iterator();it.hasNext();) {
  actor = (PooledActor) it.next();
  System.out.println("    >> pooled actor is: "
  + actor.getActorId());                               Iterates actors, prints details
}
```

In listing 6.7, we're simply printing details about a given task, such as when it was created, its ID, name, and assigned actor. Then, using the `TaskInstance.getPooledActors` method, a list of pooled actors, if any, are iterated, with the details output to the console.

Next, let's look at how we can find all tasks that are assigned to a particular user, regardless of the process instance.

6.5.4 Finding all tasks assigned to a user

The ability to locate all open tasks for a user or actor would be a common requirement of anyone building a custom front end to jBPM. As it turns out, this is easy to do because jBPM provides a `TaskMgmtSession` object, available through the `JbpmContext`. `TaskMgmtSession` provides a method, `findTaskInstances`, that allows you to find all tasks assigned to a given `actorId` (as you recall, `actorId` is just a string value that can be any arbitrary value). Thus, our `listAssignedActorTasks` helper method is terse:

```
public static List<TaskInstance>
  listAssignedActorTasks (JbpmContext jbpmContext,String actorId) {

  List<TaskInstance> taskList =
    jbpmContext.getTaskMgmtSession().findTaskInstances(actorId);

  return taskList;
}
```

The `listAssignedActorTasks` receives, as its sole parameter, an `actorId`. Then the `TaskMgmtSession`'s `findTaskInstances` method is used to return a `List` of `TaskInstance` objects. Once received, a client can process the `TaskInstance` in the same way as in the previous example (listing 6.7). Let's consider next how to determine what pooled tasks are assigned a given actor.

6.5.5 Finding all pooled tasks for an actor

As you may recall from section 6.2, a *pool* of actors can be identified for a given task. Once the task is initiated, any of the pooled actors can assign themselves (or be assigned, in certain circumstances) the task. Obviously, this is useful in circumstances where multiple individuals can perform a certain task. You can also, by default, assign a task to a given actor, but any pooled actor can then reassign the task to themselves. The helper method we'll create for this task is called `listPooledActorTasks`, and it's nearly identical to the one described earlier for identifying assigned tasks. The one exception is that we're using a different `TaskMgmtSession` method, `findPooledTaskInstances`, instead of `findTaskInstances`. Beyond that, this method is identical to `listAssignedActorTasks`, so I won't show the code.

NOTE The `TaskMgmtSession.findPooledTaskInstances` method won't return a task result if the task has already been assigned from the pool of users to a single actor. The purpose of this call is to identify unassigned tasks where an actor is a principal.

An unassigned task can be assigned to one of the pooled users by using the method `TaskInstance.setActorId`, which takes the `String actorId` as its parameter. Let's conclude our Task API coverage by looking at how you can complete a task.

6.5.6 Completing a task

The first step toward ending a task through the API is to identify the task within the process instance. If you want to complete a task programmatically, you're obviously only interested in those tasks that are unfinished or open. To accomplish this, we'll tackle it in two steps: (1) we'll get a list of all tokens in the process instance (as you remember, a token can be thought of as an execution path); and (2) within each token, we'll identify all unfinished tasks. The method we'll create, `listUnfinishedTasksByInstance`, is used to identify the unfinished tasks (see listing 6.8). Like the other methods we've demonstrated, it will be incorporated into our helper class, `JBPMHelper`, created in listing 6.2.

Listing 6.8 Method to determine unfinished tasks within a process instance

```
public static List<TaskInstance>
  listUnfinishedTasksByInstance(JbpmContext jbpmContext,long processId) {

  TaskMgmtInstance taskMgmtInstance = (TaskMgmtInstance) jbpmContext    // 1 Acquires jBPM task instance
    .getProcessInstance(processId).getInstance(TaskMgmtInstance.class);

  List<Token> tokens = jbpmContext.getProcessInstance(processId)        // 2 Retrieves list of tokens
    .findAllTokens();

  Token token;
  List<TaskInstance> returnInstances =
   new ArrayList<TaskInstance>();

  for (Token token : tokens) {                  // 3 Iterates through tokens

   List<TaskInstance> instances =               // 4 Fetches task instances
    (List<TaskInstance>) taskMgmtInstance
     .getUnfinishedTasks(token);

   for (TaskInstance ti : instances)            // 5 Iterates task instances
     returnInstances.add(ti);
  }

  return returnInstances;}
```

Unlike the methods we've used so far, this listing uses the `TaskMgmtInstance` ❶ and `Token` ❷ classes. An instance of `TaskMgmtInstance` is retrieved by casting the results of the `ProcessInstance.getInstance` method ❶. This class is necessary because it's used to retrieve all the unfinished tasks in a given token. A `List` of tokens for a given instance is retrieved by the `ProcessInstance.findAllTokens` method ❷. This `List`, stored in the `tokens` variable, is then iterated one by one ❸. A `List` of unfinished `TaskInstances` spanning across all tokens is then retrieved ❹. Then the individual `TaskInstance` members are retrieved and stored in the `returnInstances` variable ❺, which is returned to the calling routine. Now that we have a `List` of unfinished tasks, let's pursue the next step: closing a given task.

Closing a task is straightforward once you have a handle to the `TaskInstance`. You can do this simply by using the `TaskInstance.end` method. There are a few different signature variants for the `end` method. The simplest is to use no parameter, in which case the first transition path will be followed. More often than not, this is not the desired behavior. Instead, you probably want to specify a specific transition path, depending on the outcome of the task. At the beginning of this chapter in figure 6.1, you saw how jBPM Console's forms framework uses submit buttons to determine which transition path to follow. This is the question we're facing here: if multiple transitions occur, how do you specify which one to use? If we want to use a specific transition, we obciously must know which one to use. The following is a new method added to the `JBPMHelper` that returns a list of transitions for a given task ID, passed as the second argument to the `listTransitionsForTasks` method.

```
public static List<Transition>
  listTransitionsForTasks(JbpmContext jbpmContext,long taskInstanceId) {

  JbpmContext jbpmContext = getConfiguration().createJbpmContext();

  TaskInstance taskInstance =
   jbpmContext.getTaskMgmtSession().getTaskInstance(taskInstanceId);
  List<Transition> transitions = taskInstance.getAvailableTransitions();

  return transitions;
}
```

As you can see, after acquiring the `JbpmContext`, we're simply retrieving the specific `TaskInstance` associated with the task ID that was passed as the second method parameter. The `TaskInstance.getAvailableTransitions` method is then used to populate a `List` of `Transition` objects, which is returned as the method response. The `List` of `Transitions` can then be iterated to identify all available transitions, such as

```
List<Transition> transitions =
  JBPMHelper.listTransitionsForTasks(taskInstance.getId());
for (Transition transition : transitions) {
  System.out.println("  >> Transition: " + transition.getName());
}
```

You can now end the task and use the appropriate transition by using the `Task-Instance.end(Transition)` method (before working on a task, be sure to start it using the `TaskInstance.start` method).

What have we accomplished here? For a given task ID, we're able to identify all unfinished tasks, regardless of the token in which they reside within the process instance. We then established how you can close the task and optionally specify what transition path to follow as the process moves forward. To do this, we had to identify the available transitions for a given task.

This concludes our coverage of using the task API. Obviously, there's a lot more we could demonstrate, but you should have a good idea of what you can accomplish, and be armed with sufficient knowledge of how to develop your own implementations.

6.6 Summary

In this chapter and the last, we covered most of the fundamental capabilities of jBPM. In chapter 5 we provided an overview of how jBPM works, and we discussed the various nodes, transitions, and events that you can use. This chapter's focus was on tasks, which are central to any BPM solution.

Despite our best efforts at automation, there will likely always be a need for a "human-in-the-loop" when it comes to complex business processes. Since tasks involve humans, jBPM provides a means for assigning actors (users), or groups of actors, to tasks, and through timers, provides for notifications and escalation paths. While jBPM comes with a forms framework for developing task GUIs, you may find that it isn't powerful enough to suit your needs. So we demonstrated how the jBPM API can be used to access nearly every aspect of how tasks are managed within the jBPM process engine. Armed with this information, you can build task GUIs, widgets, or dashboards using whatever framework you prefer—you are by no means locked into using the jBPM Console (indeed, this applies to any aspect of jBPM).

You should now have sufficient knowledge to begin building nontrivial jBPM applications. In the next chapter, we'll focus on advanced capabilities of jBPM and provide patterns for integrating with our other Open SOA Platform products.

7 Advanced jBPM capabilities

This chapter covers

- Managing complex jBPM processes
- Scripting and logging in jBPM
- Service enabling jBPM using SCA

The previous two chapters on jBPM covered most of the fundamental features of this very capable BPM solution. You saw descriptions, with examples, of most of the constructs used in jBPM, such as nodes, transitions, and in chapter 6, tasks. In addition to describing how to build business processes, we also discussed how its API can be leveraged to build powerful, customized applications. Clearly, this is a very capable horse—but is it a thoroughbred? Does it possess the advanced features to warrant being considered "enterprise ready"? What characteristics must it possess to fulfill this role? We'll address some of these questions in this chapter.

This chapter covers how to handle highly complex processes by breaking them into more manageable subprocesses. These subprocesses, in turn, can be reused by other processes. Exception handling and audit logging, both essential for production deployment, are addressed through implementation examples and best practices. In addition, you'll learn how jBPM can be integrated with Apache Tuscany's *Service Component Architecture* (SCA) and *Service Data Objects* (SDOs). As you recall,

SCA and SDO were the focus of chapters 3 and 4, and they provide a framework for building reusable, multilanguage components that can be easily exposed as services through a variety of communication protocols. We demonstrate how the SCA/SDO can be used to service enable jBPM, thereby making it a first-class citizen in your SOA environment. When you finish reading this chapter, you'll have all the tools you need to design, deploy, and monitor jBPM business processes. The savings that will result from your evangelism of BPM will pay off handsomely!

7.1 Important enterprise features of jBPM

The jBPM business process examples we've developed so far have all, by design, been fairly simple in nature. My goal was to ease the learning process and focus on the specific topic at hand. In a real-world scenario, you'll often find that you're creating processes that can contain dozens, or even hundreds of steps, in an orchestration. In such a scenario, it's useful to be able to break down, or group, the process into more manageable pieces. We'll discuss two means of accomplishing this in jBPM: *superstates* and *subprocesses*. Later, we'll provide solutions for managing exceptions that may occur as a result of any custom code you've introduced as part of a process definition.

While not an "advanced" feature per se, our focus will then turn to describing how you can use inline code in the form of BeanShell scripts. I'll offer solutions for monitoring a process instance through the extensive logging features available in jBPM. I'll conclude this section by looking into a concept called *asynchronous continuations*, which enable you to distribute processing to the jBPM server in which jBPM enterprise is running. Let's begin by looking at jBPM superstates.

7.1.1 Superstates for grouping

Superstates in jBPM are simply a grouping of nodes. They're useful, for example, when you want to logically associate a group of nodes. You might want to do this to delineate phases of a process or to group node activity by organizational responsibilities. For example, an employee termination process is typically cross-departmental, with various responsibilities falling in several departments. This is illustrated in the hypothetical employee termination process shown in figure 7.1.

In figure 7.1, superstates are used to group the nodes related to HR, Finance, and Security. In the jBPM Graphical Process Designer (GPD), when you deposit a superstate node into the jBPM working area or canvas, a bordered region is created where you can then place nodes and transitions. As you can see, these border areas can be resized and will sprout scroll bars where necessary. With the jPDL XML, how is a superstate defined? It's pretty simple, as this example illustrates:

```
<super-state name="security">
  <node name="disable ldap">
    <transition to="security-fork" name="t"></transition>
  </node>
  <!-- other nodes here -->
</super-state>
```

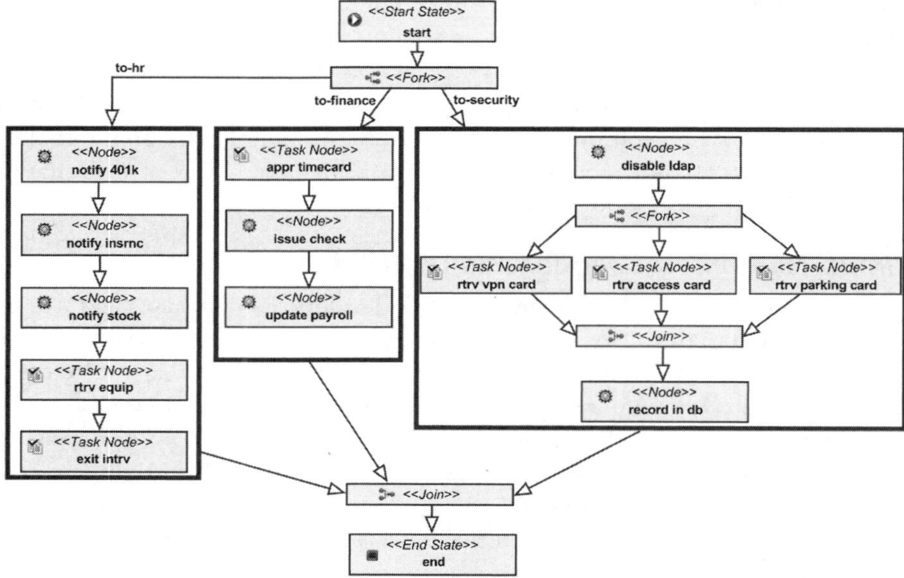

Figure 7.1 A hypothetical employee termination process illustrating superstates in use

The available options for the `super-state` element are fairly minimal. Attribute values include `@name` and `@async` (covered in more detail in section 7.1.6) and, similar to all jBPM nodes, support the standard node elements (see chapter 5).

Superstates provide some additional functionality beyond just diagrammatic grouping. As you learned in chapter 5, superstate-specific events are also available (`superstate-enter` and `superstate-leave`). You can associate action handlers with these events, so with this ability, you can call custom code when the superstate has been entered or exited. When would you consider using this? One use case that comes to mind is business activity monitoring, where you want to highlight when certain milestones or activities take place in a process.

NOTE The code examples that accompany this section of the book demonstrate superstate events in use. Notice in particular the `SuperStateTest` JUnit test class, which demonstrates how you can reference nodes in the superstate.

Perhaps more importantly, you can also associate timers with the superstate (this does require the Enterprise edition of jBPM—in other words, the app server edition). In the scenario shown in figure 7.1, you could, for instance, notify a manager of the HR department that their team's work hasn't been completed in a timely fashion. Thus, when using events and timers in tandem with superstates, there's a benefit beyond the obvious achieved by providing visual hierarchy and grouping. Related in concept to superstates are subprocesses, which are intended to provide greater process composition flexibility.

7.1.2 Using subprocesses to manage complexity

Whereas a superstate in jBPM is used to logically group nodes, a *subprocess* could be used to split those grouped nodes into entirely separate processes. Thus, subprocesses provide a means to create decomposed processes. You can define a master process, which in turn calls subprocesses. The subprocess can be thought of as simply another individual node in the parent process. When the subprocess is completed, execution will resume in the parent process which had invoked the subprocess. In that respect, it behaves much like a state nodetype in jBPM. Using subprocesses enables you to create more complex processes without overly complicating the visual layout. Additional benefits include the ability to create reusable process modules that can be incorporated by other process definitions. In chapter 1 you learned that an important aspect of SOA is the ability to create composite services. Using subprocesses, you can achieve this same objective. The subprocesses can be run in a stand-alone fashion, or as subprocesses to a larger orchestration.

In figure 7.1, I showed a modestly complex business process used for employee termination. In that case, superstates are used to provide logical structure to the diagram. Since the security-related nodes are the most involved, let's instead break that out into a separate subprocess rather than using a superstate (see figure 7.2).

In figure 7.2, the node named `security` represents the new subprocess (identified in the node icon as `<<Process State>>`). When this node is encountered, a new process instance for the `security` process is instantiated. This can be illustrated most effectively through the jBPM Console, which will clearly show a new process instance

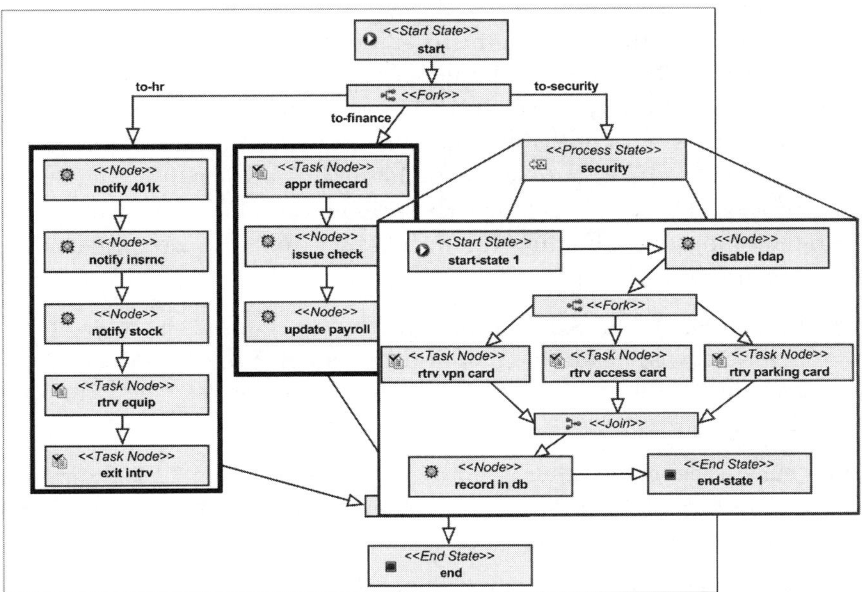

Figure 7.2 The relationship between a main process and a subprocess

for the subprocess being created. Of course, you can also use the API, as we described in chapter 6, to identify the new process instance. In the parent process jPDL XML definition, you can see how this subprocess is defined (see listing 7.1).

Listing 7.1 jPDL subprocess definition example

```
<process-state name="security">
  <sub-process name="security" binding="late"/>
  <variable access="read" name="name"></variable>
  <variable access="read" name="employeeId"></variable>
  <variable access="read,write" name="securityComplete"></variable>
  <transition to="join1"/>
</process-state>
```

The `process-state` element, in addition to accepting the `@name` attribute, also supports asynchronous continuations, covered in section 7.1.6, through the `@async` attribute (by default, this is off, or `false`). The standard set of node elements are also supported, such as timers, events, descriptions, and exception handlers.

NOTE One neat feature not currently available in jBPM would be the ability to use a subprocess that resides on a different jBPM instance. Such a distributed feature would make jBPM more scalable for large implementations.

In the example from listing 7.1, the `sub-process` child element of `process-state` is where the subprocess is defined. The `@name` attribute of the `sub-process` element must equate to the name assigned to the subprocess. This corresponds to the value provided to the `@name` attribute of the `process-definition` root element of the subprocess being invoked. Additionally, the `@binding` attribute (which is set to `late` in listing 7.1) instructs the jBPM engine to wait until runtime to identify the subprocess version to invoke. Otherwise, the binding will occur when the process (*not a particular process instance*) is created, at which time it will attempt to identify the subprocess to use when a process instance is subsequently created. Thus, if you opt to not use late binding, you must also be sure to create the subprocess first, followed by the main or calling process. The optional `@version` attribute can also be used to specify the version of the subprocess definition you wish to use—in its absence, the most recent version will be used.

NOTE I recommend always using the `@binding` attribute set to `late`. This will help you avoid headaches that result from trying to determine which process must be installed first. The resulting errors can be confusing to debug.

Besides `sub-process`, the other important element in listing 7.1 is the `variable` child element. This variable is used to manage how process variables are propagated to the subprocess. It accepts three attributes:

- *`@name`*—The name of the process variable to be passed to the subprocess.
- *`@access`*—A comma-delimited set of values used to define the access rights permitted by the subprocess when working with the variable. Permissible values

are `read`, which indicates the subprocess will have read-only access, and `write`, which indicates the value can be modified by the subprocess.

- *@mapped-name*—When present, this variable allows you to specify a different name for the variable that's passed when it's received by the subprocess. This is a helpful feature if a subprocess is reused elsewhere and has different process variable name expectations.

We've now covered two approaches for helping you organize or decompose complex business processes—essential tools for building enterprise orchestrations. You may be thinking that you've learned enough about jBPM, and you're perhaps tempted to skip to the next chapter. At this point, you're like a doctor trained in the art of surgery but not well versed in the art of recuperation. As we all know, despite our best intentions, things don't always work out the way we anticipate. This is where exception handling comes into play.

7.1.3 Managing exceptions

Exception handling in jBPM is a bit different than you might imagine. When managing exceptions in jBPM, you're only dealing with those that result from any handler classes that you've created. They aren't used for any sort of internal jBPM error that may have resulted from processing within the engine itself. So, for example, if you're extending functionality with an action or assignment handler, you can trap and manage those errors using the exception-handling techniques we'll discuss.

A source of common misunderstanding about exception handling in jBPM is whether you can use this mechanism to directly alter the flow of the process. The official documentation is rather contradictory on this matter. The upshot is this: while technically you can redirect the flow using a `Token.setNode(Node node)` call, this approach is strongly discouraged. Instead, the proper strategy is to set a process instance variable, which can then direct subsequent flows by way of a decision node. In addition, you can use the exception mechanism to issue an alert or notification through JMS, email, and so forth so that someone can perform remedial actions.

Let's create a simple example to illustrate exception handling at work. Figure 7.3 shows a process that uses a transition action handler to purposely throw an exception (it occurs at the `to-state` transition). An exception handler action then creates a process instance variable called `errorMsg` and sets it to a `String` value. The downstream decision node (`err-check`) checks for the presence of the `errorMsg` process variable. If the variable is present, the decision node redirects the flow to the `notify-of-error` node.

In the jPDL used to define figure 7.3 (the full code is available in the source code for this chapter), the transition is expressed in XML as

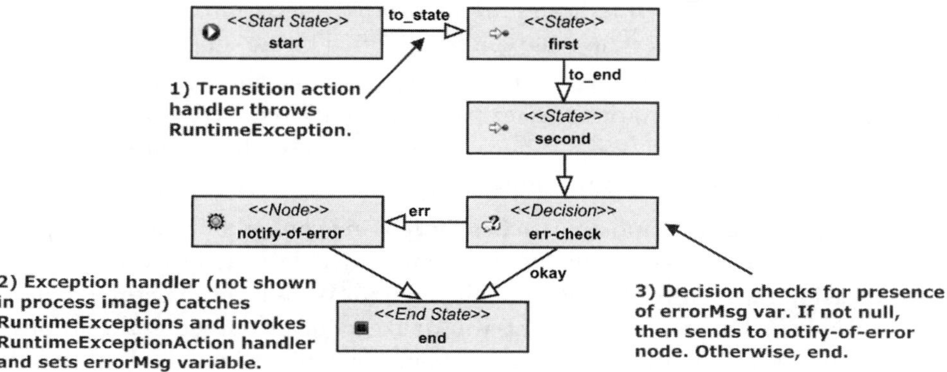

Figure 7.3 An example process that illustrates exception-handling features

```
<transition name="to_state" to="first">
  <action name="action" class="com.sample.action.MessageActionHandlerExc2">
    <message>Going to the first state!</message>
  </action>
  <exception-handler exception-class="java.lang.RuntimeException">
    <action name="RuntimeExceptionAction"
      class="com.sample.action.RuntimeExceptionAction">
    </action>
  </exception-handler>
</transition>
```

As you can see, the `exception-handler` element is defined as a child along with the action handler used to generate the exception. The `exception-handler`'s `@exception-class` attribute defines the type of exception it will catch, which in this case is a `java.lang.RuntimeException`. When this exception is caught, the handler class defined by the `@class` attribute will be invoked, which in this case is `RuntimeExceptionAction`. This is a standard action handler that implements the `ActionHandler`'s `execute` method. In this example, it simply creates a process instance variable `errorMsg` using

```
executionContext.setVariable("errorMsg",
  "A runtime error has occurred in node");
```

Later on in the process, the decision node called `error-check` in figure 7.3 checks to see if `errorMsg` is defined as a process variable. If it is, `error-check` transitions the token to the node responsible for alerting or otherwise taking corrective action (`notify-of-error`). The decision node's jPDL definition is shown here:

```
<decision name="err-check"
  expression='#{errorMsg != null ? "err" : "okay"}'>
  <transition to="notify-of-error" name="err" />
  <transition to="end" name="okay"></transition>
</decision>
```

I used the `@expression` attribute in this case to identify what transition path to follow. The value returned by the expression is the transition name to follow. Using Java's ternary operator, the statement checks to see if the `errorMsg` variable isn't null. If the variable is null, the statement returns the string `err`, which contains the name of one of the defined transitions. Otherwise, it returns the string `okay`, which corresponds to the transition name used to go to the end node.

In the source code for this section, you'll see how exception handlers can be defined at the root process level. Such handlers can be useful as a catchall, since exceptions will bubble up from the node and transition level if no corresponding exception handler catches the exception. In our example, `java.lang.Exception` was provided as the `@exception-class`, since many of the standard Java exceptions are subclasses of that and will thus be caught. Much like with standard Java, you can be as explicit as necessary in identifying what types of exceptions you want to trap.

Let's recap what we've learned. This section described how exception handling is managed in a jBPM process. This facility is only used for managing exceptions that occur as part of any custom code you introduce, such as handlers. A common source of confusion is knowing what to do when an error is encountered. I strongly recommended that you not alter the execution flow directly in your action handler class defined in your `exception-handler` element in jPDL. Instead, use exceptions for notification purposes or indirectly affect the process flow by setting process variables that can be interpreted downstream.

Up to this point, we've used Java handler classes to provide custom functionality. A more convenient approach is to use BeanShell scripts.

7.1.4 Scripting with BeanShell

At times it may seem like overkill to resort to writing Java code when only simple or trivial functionality needs to be introduced into your business process. Maybe you just need to introduce a few lines of programming logic. In these situations, you can use BeanShell scripts inline within your jPDL code. This approach is very convenient and allows for more rapid application development. In addition, BeanShell expressions are also used in a variety of capacities in jBPM, such as in decision node logic.

BeanShell was one of the earliest Java scripting implementations and recently has initiated the Java Community Process to become JSR-standards compliant. Having enjoyed fairly wide support, BeanShell is included in a variety of applications as a lightweight scripting alternative to Java (visit the official web site, http://www.beanshell.org/, for more details). The syntax and usage closely mirror that of standard Java, so Java developers can generally pick it up quickly. Table 7.1 identifies the various places in jBPM's jPDL where BeanShell scripts can be used.

Table 7.1 jPDL BeanShell scripting usage

Element name	Description
create-timer/ cancel-timer	When used in a create-timer element, the script will be called when the timer is first created. For cancel-timer, the script is invoked when the timer is called.
exception-handler	In the previous section, we demonstrated how a Java action handler can be invoked when an exception handler traps an exception. Instead of invoking a Java action handler, you could instead call a BeanShell script.
action	Anywhere you can specify an action element you can use a BeanShell script. So, for example, scripts can be specified in the actions associated with transitions, the process definition root, nodes, and events.

A BeanShell script would be of limited utility if you couldn't access the jBPM process instance context. Fortunately, jBPM provides exposure to instance variables such as executionContext, token, node and a variety of task-related objects. Obviously, the context by which the script is called determines whether these script variables will be populated. Here's an example of using a BeanShell script in a start-state node:

```
<start-state name="start">
  <transition name="to_state" to="first">
    <script name="beanshell-example">
      System.out.println("Event type is: " +
        executionContext.getEvent().getEventType());
      System.out.println("Token is: " + token);
      System.out.println("Task is: " + task);
    </script>
  </transition>
</start-state>
```

The first println statement reports the event type as transition. The second println displays a root token ("/"), and the last println shows the task is null, since no task is associated with that node. The source code for this section contains the process shown in figure 7.4.

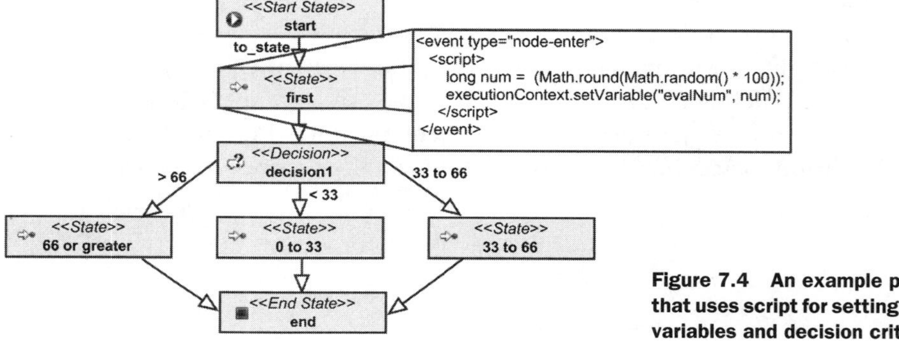

Figure 7.4 An example process that uses script for setting instance variables and decision criteria

In this simple demonstration, a random value is assigned to a process variable called `evalNum`. The event callout BeanShell script shown in figure 7.4 shows how this variable is set. After that event occurs with its BeanShell script in the node named `first`, the decision node, `decision1`, is encountered. This decision node is configured so that the transition path taken will depend on the random value assigned to `evalNum` in the BeanShell script. To accomplish this, the `decision1` decision node uses a BeanShell expression, a one-line statement that must evaluate to `true` or `false` (this is true whenever an expression attribute is used). Here's the jPDL implementation for this decision node:

```
<decision name="decision1">
  <transition to="0 to 33" name="&lt; 33">
    <condition>
       #{evalNum &lt; 33}
    </condition>
  </transition>
  <transition to="33 to 66" name="33 to 66">
    <condition>
       #{evalNum &gt;= 33 &amp;&amp; evalNum &lt; 66}
    </condition>
  </transition>
  <transition to="66 or greater" name="&gt; 66">
    <condition>
       #{evalNum &gt;= 66}
    </condition>
  </transition>
</decision>
```

The `condition` element contains the BeanShell expression used to determine whether a given transition should be followed. If the expression evaluates to `true`, then the transition is selected (if multiple transitions evaluate to `true`, the first one present will be used). As you can see, when used in combination with decision nodes BeanShell expressions are a convenient choice, and are easier than resorting to a Java class decision handler. I anticipate that future releases of jBPM will add scripting support, such as Groovy, JRuby, or Jython (perhaps by embracing the Apache Bean Scripting Framework [BSF] or the Scripting API in Java 6 [JSR-223]).

NOTE You can pretty much do anything in BeanShell scripts that you can in Java. For example, you can use import statements to provide access to external libraries. This approach is convenient since you can easily reuse your existing libraries without having to wrap them specifically within jBPM handlers.

Regardless of whether you extend jBPM functionality with BeanShell or Java, you inevitably will want the ability to log and monitor the activity that occurs in your process instance. This is where jBPM audit logging comes in handy, as you'll see in the next section. (You'll also learn in the next chapter how this capability can be used to generate events that can be consumed by an event stream processor, thus providing real-time metrics and monitoring of your jBPM processes.)

7.1.5 *Audit logging*

By default, a variety of audit logs are produced as a result of process instance execution. Collectively, these logs will provide you with complete insight into every activity that has occurred in a process instance. How can this information be beneficial? For example, you could load it into a data warehouse for reporting and analytics. Or perhaps you could monitor the data in real time for business activity–monitoring dashboards. As with most aspects of jBPM, you can also extend the logging features to add your own capabilities. For example, perhaps you want to dynamically filter log output for only content you deem relevant. To do so, you just implement your own `LoggingService` class—you'll see an example in our next chapter where we cover Esper, the open source event stream processing (ESP) engine.

NOTE You can disable logging by commenting out the XML line beginning with `<service name="logging…>` in the `jbpm.cfg.xml` file. When you use the Eclipse Graphic Process Designer plug-in and specify New > Process Project, it will, by default, create a blank `jpdl.cfg.xml` file. If you want to selectively add entries to this file, locate the `default.jbpm.cfg.xml` file in the `jbpm-console.war` and copy the desired entries from there. Also, depending on your Eclipse configuration, it may not find your `jbpm.cfg.xml` file in your classpath, so be sure to specify the directory where it resides if running your samples directly through Eclipse (using the Open Run Dialog options).

Before we look at how to access the logs via the jBPM API, let's identify the types of logging classes (see table 7.2).

There are two ways in which you can acquire logs: via a `LoggingInstance` and via a `LoggingSession`. Let's begin by looking at the `LoggingInstance`.

Table 7.2 jBPM logfile types

Logfile class	Description
`org.jbpm.graph.log.*`	Likely the most useful set of logs, classes such as `ActionLog`, `TransitionLog` and `NodeLog` can be used to track any activity related to these objects.
`org.jbpm.context.log.*`	Includes classes such as `VariableCreateLog` and `VariableDeleteLog`, which can be used to track variables that were created and deleted throughout the lifecycle of a process instance.
`org.jbpm.context.log.variableinstance.*`	These classes, such as `StringUpdateLog`, are used for tracking individual changes to supported variable types (`Byte`, `Date`, `Double`, `String`). For complex, serializable Java types, logging of individual changes isn't directly supported (chapter 5 did address how you can create *converters* for other object types, and then you could create new associated logging classes).

A LoggingInstance can be retrieved by using the ProcessInstance.getLoggingInstance() method. For example, if you're running jBPM in an embedded style manner (such as used for the JUnit tests that are generated when you create a new process definition project in GPD), this could be done using a fragment such as

```
ProcessDefinition processDefinition =
   ProcessDefinition.parseXmlResource("logging/processdefinition.xml");
ProcessInstance instance = new ProcessInstance(processDefinition);
LoggingInstance loggingInstance = instance.getLoggingInstance();
```

Once you have an instance of the LoggingInstance class (shown here as loggingInstance), you can use it to retrieve the set of logs associated with that process instance. The number and type of logs that appear will vary based on where the execution cycle is in the process instance(s), as well as the type of nodes being used. The following is an example of how you can retrieve all of the available logs via the loggingInstance we acquired earlier:

```
List<Object> logs = loggingInstance.getLogs();

for (Object obj : logs) {
    println("Logtype is: " + obj.getClass().getName());
}
```

As you can see, we're simply fetching a List of the logs through the getLogs method, iterating through them, assigning each to a Java Object (since they can be of different types), and then printing out the object's name to the console. Depending on the log class, various methods can then be interrogated to retrieve the details of the log. For example, the VariableCreateLog log class can return a VariableInstance, from which you can get the name and value of the variable that was created.

NOTE Although LoggingInstances can be used to access logs, they're only *transitory* in nature, and thus may be of limited value. Once a process instance is flushed to the database or persisted, all logs in the LoggingInstance will be cleared. Instead, use LoggingSession to retrieve historical logs. You can flush the logs by issuing a JbpmContext.save(ProcessInstance) method call.

As pointed out in the callout, the logs obtained through LoggingInstance are only available while you're working in an existing process instance context. To retrieve the logs after a process instance has been persisted to the database, use LoggingSession, which is the second method we mentioned in the section introduction.

To obtain an instance of LoggingSession, you can use the method JbpmContext.getLoggingSession(). From there, you can retrieve all logs using the LoggingSession method findLogsByProcessInstance, which takes as a parameter a ProcessInstanceId. This will return a Map, with a key representing each token in the given process instance. The following is an example that prints out the logs available for a given process instance where we're assuming only one token execution path is used (for example, no forks exist in the process). In this example, jbpmContext represents a JbpmContext and instance is of type ProcessInstance:

```
LoggingSession loggingSession = jbpmContext.getLoggingSession();
Map logMap = loggingSession.findLogsByProcessInstance(instance.getId());
Map.Entry entry = (Entry) logMap.entrySet().iterator().next();
ArrayList<Object> sessionLogs = ((ArrayList) entry.getValue());

for (Object log : sessionLogs) {
  println("Log is: " + log.getClass().getName());
}
```

When run, this will result in output that resembles the following:

```
Log is: org.jbpm.graph.log.NodeLog
Log is: org.jbpm.graph.log.TransitionLog
Log is: org.jbpm.graph.log.ActionLog
Log is: org.jbpm.context.log.variableinstance.StringUpdateLog
Log is: org.jbpm.graph.log.ProcessInstanceEndLog
```

If multiple tokens can be present in the process, you'd obviously want to also iterate through the `Map.Entry` keys. Lastly, if you already have a handle to process instance's token, you can also use the method `LoggingSession.findLogsByToken(long tokenId)`, which also brings back the `List` of logs associated with that token execution.

NOTE In the previous chapter's coverage of APIs, you may recall we demonstrated how to return the number of execution tokens for a given process instance. See listing 6.8.

In wrapping up our coverage of jBPM audit logs, I want to warn you that you shouldn't confuse jBPM audit logs with standard Java logging, like that provided by Apache log4j. Instead, jBPM audit logs are used for auditing purposes, where you want to keep a historical record of the execution steps that occurred in a given process instance. The logging capabilities, which are extensive, are exposed through a set of logging classes that are specific to the type of activity being logged. For instance, the `TransitionLog` captures the details about transitions that have taken place in the process instance. Earlier I pointed out that the `LoggingSession` is probably how you want to acquire the logs, and not the transitory `LoggingInstance`. I also demonstrated how you can retrieve the logs for an instance and put them to use.

We're nearing our completion of advanced jBPM features, but we have one last topic to examine: *asynchronous continuations*. Perhaps because of its fancy name, you might be confused about its meaning and purpose. However, it's not as complex as it sounds; it simply enables process execution to be asynchronously performed by a server process. The benefits, as I'll show next, can be substantial.

7.1.6 Understanding asynchronous continuations

You've likely noticed that when you signal the execution of a process instance, it will continue to execute within the thread you're running until it encounters a wait state, such as a state or task node. At that point, you could consider the transaction to be completed. While generally this doesn't cause any problems—most transactions complete within milliseconds—there are times when that may not be the case. Do any scenarios come to mind? How about when you have a node nodetype that performs a web service call to a remote system using a traditional request/reply message exchange. In that scenario, the node (and your thread) will block and wait until the reply is received (or it times out). This could have highly undesirable consequences for your process if, for example, an immediate response is anticipated (maybe it's a web order being kicked off through the BPM process, and the user is awaiting a response with an order identifier).

You might be thinking whether it would be better to asynchronously manage this by creating a separate service apart from jBPM and using a state nodetype to call it via a JMS message. By using a state and not a node nodetype, execution would be returned immediately to your thread as the process instance was persisted and put on hold until it was instructed to proceed. That approach is sound, but bear in mind one complexity: some Java process must be running to receive the results from JMS, and to then interact with jBPM to access the process instance and signal the state's token to advance. While certainly not that complicated, it's not trivial either, especially when you factor in exception management.

Fortunately, there's already a built-in approach for managing this scenario directly within jBPM. It is called *asynchronous continuations.* How this works is best illustrated through a simple example. Figure 7.5 shows a simple process model.

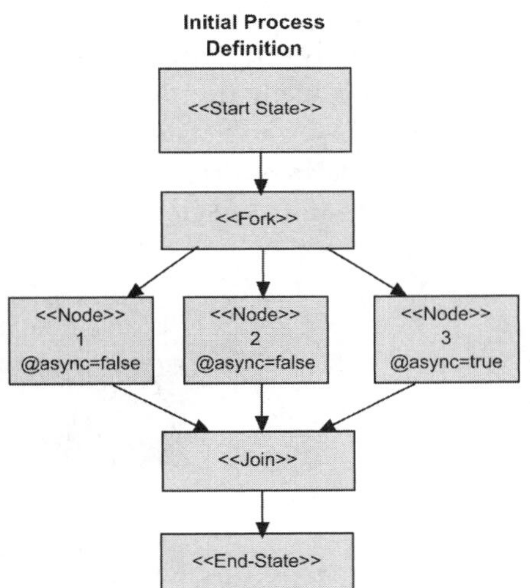

Figure 7.5 Process definition that uses one asynchronous node

In the process shown in figure 7.5, let's assume `<<Node>>`s 1, 2, and 3 include Java action handlers that perform some external action. In `<<Node>>`s 1 and 2, those action handlers perform their work synchronously in the same transaction in which the process is initiated (this is the default behavior). However, the third `<<Node>>` is specified using `@async=true`. What this means is that the node, and within it any Java action handlers, will be processed by an external command executor. Since `<<Node>>` 3 is processed asynchronously, the transaction is completed and placed in a wait state (that is, persisted) until the `<<Join>>` node depicted receives `<<Node>>` 3's signal.

The jBPM Enterprise edition, which runs within the context of an application server, is by default configured to support asynchronous continuations using its built-in *Job Executor.* The Job Executor receives its command message through a JMS queue that's automatically configured when jBPM Enterprise is run. In our example, this means that the jBPM Job Executor will asynchronously process `<<Node>>` 3 in figure 7.5. Once completed, `<<Node>>` 3's action handler instruction to signal continuance of the execution will be performed. Figure 7.6 shows the process instance just after initiation, where <<Node>>s 1 and 2 have been completed and now wait in the join node for the conclusion of <<Node>> 3.

As figure 7.6 illustrates, the asynchronous processing of <<Node>> 3 occurs in three steps: (1) a JMS message that includes the action handler to be executed is sent to a JMS queue, (2) the jBPM Enterprise server's command listener is listening for new messages submitted to the queue, and (3) once a message is received, it's sent to the Job Executor for processing. The Job Executor will initiate a new transaction from which the action handler is run, and will forward the execution. Although not shown, all three <<Node>>s will then have completed, the <<Join>> consummated, and execution moved to the end to complete the process instance (<<End-State>>).

Asynchronous continuations can be specified for all nodetypes as well as within action handlers. This approach provides a great deal of flexibility, and can be used as an effective way to distribute load, since the server in which jBPM Enterprise edition is running may be more suitable for CPU-intensive processing. When you're contemplating interacting with external services via a node nodetype, you'll definitely want to consider using asynchronous continuations.

This wraps up our coverage of some of the most important advanced jBPM features you'll likely use. Now let's turn our focus to a very exciting topic: integrating jBPM with SCA and SDO (the topic of chapters 3 and 4). You'll find that combining these technologies will unlock jBPM's role within the enterprise and become a key cornerstone in your SOA environment.

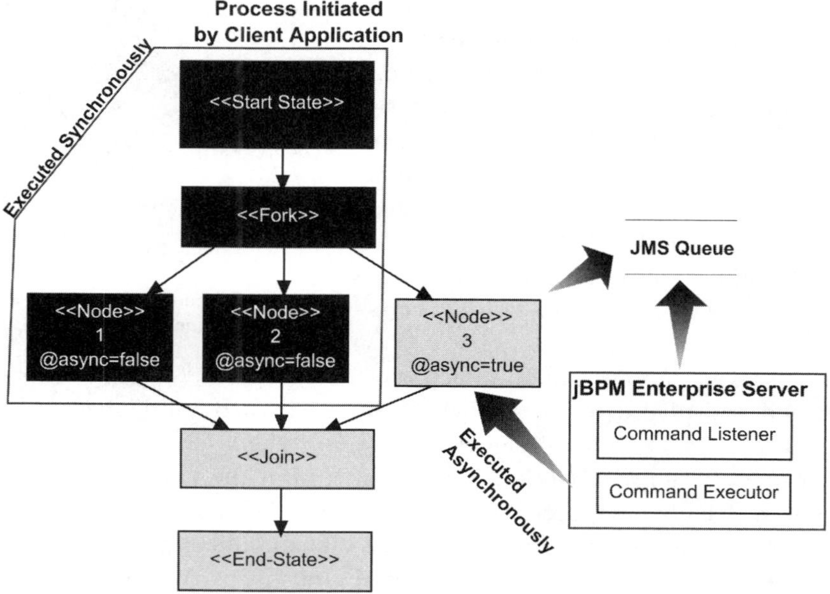

Figure 7.6 The process once the instance is initiated—node 3 is executed asynchronously

NOTE Some topics, such as how to create your own nodetypes and integration of jBPM Console security, have not been addressed. The jBPM User Guide provides guidance on these matters, and the forum and source code can be indispensable as well.

7.2 Integration with SCA/SDO

The *Service Component Architecture* (SCA), and its sister technology, *Service Data Objects* (SDO), are an emerging standard for creating multiprotocol, multilanguage services based on the concept of reusable components. Apache Tuscany, a reference implementation of SCA/SDO, has recently achieved its 1.4 release. Chapters 3 and 4 covered Tuscany in some detail, and we'll build on the examples presented in those chapters to demonstrate how we can integrate jBPM with SCA/SDO to make a powerful SOA combination.

Nearly any nontrivial business process that's being modeled and executed using jBPM will contain requirements to call out or access external systems or services. Web services, in particular those that are based on SOAP, REST, or even plain old XML (POX) over HTTP, are becoming increasingly ubiquitous. This trend has become even more pronounced as companies scramble to adopt a SOA environment, which is predicated on the notion that reusable services can be exposed through a variety of communication protocols. While there is no lack of tools and libraries available for creating web service clients and servers, they're often tied to one of the specific communication protocols, such as SOAP. As we discussed in chapter 3, the beauty of SCA is that you can expose clients through a number of protocols, all the while keeping your code completely neutral and protocol free (in other words, plain Java classes with no dependency on a given protocol). Section 7.2.1 will demonstrate how to use an SCA client in a jBPM node to access third-party web services and SCA services directly.

One of the most frequent themes in the jBPM forums hosted by JBoss are questions about how to expose jBPM through web services. We've demonstrated many examples of using the jBPM API, and explored the capabilities and flexibility it offers. However, it is Java specific, and clients wishing to access jBPM must embed jBPM libraries and calls in their code. This runs contrary to one of the main premises behind SOA: loose coupling. By embedding jBPM API calls in your clients, you have effectively limited flexibility, as you are tightly integrated with jBPM. If at some point you migrate to a different BPM engine, wholesale client code changes will be necessary. Further, it puts the onus on developers of client applications using jBPM to become jBPM experts. While I hope my book helps lower that learning barrier, jBPM is still a fairly complex product, and becoming conversant with the API is not child's play.

NOTE The most recent release of jBPM, 3.2.6, offers an experimental web services interface. However, the interface is extremely limited and is intended as an example the developer can build on.

A far better approach is to abstract some of the complexities of the API into a web service façade. This strategy simplifies client development, promotes loose coupling, and exposes jBPM as a cross-platform and cross-protocol solution. You'll learn how this can be accomplished in section 7.2.2. In the meantime, let's begin by figuring out how to use SCA as a client acting on behalf of a jBPM node.

7.2.1 Using SCA client components for service integration

Although SCA is primarily thought of as a technology for developing components and exposing them as services, it can also effectively be used in a client capacity for integration with any existing services, whether or not they originate from SCA (assuming the service supports one of the SCA protocols). In fact, you achieve the same benefit when using SCA as a client or server: the ability to interact in a protocol- and language-neutral capacity through a flexible component framework. The upshot is that when you need to integrate with a service from within jBPM, SCA makes an outstanding choice.

To illustrate, we'll provide a brief example that demonstrates how using SCA as a client can be achieved using one of the web services we developed in chapter 3. As you'll recall, we created an SCA SOAP-based web service for a hypothetical problem ticket service. Intended to demonstrate how easily a component can be exposed as a web service, our example didn't provide any real functionality beyond returning a fictitious, random case number. However, this simple service will serve our purposes for this example (in the sample code for this section, everything is included). First, let's look at the jBPM process that will use this web service, shown in figure 7.7.

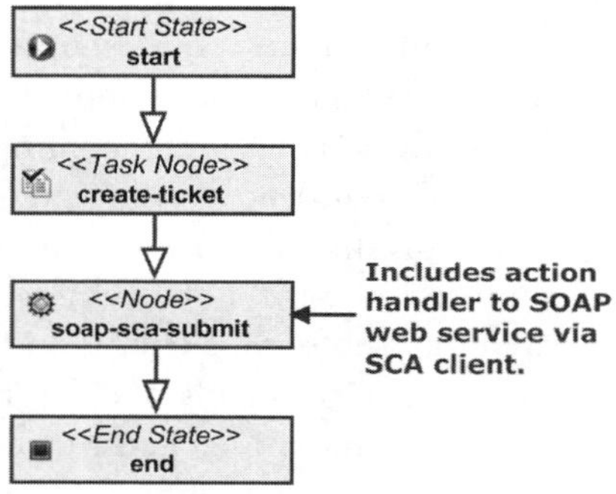

Figure 7.7 An example business process that invokes an SCA web service through a node

In our example, a human interface task is used to capture the details of the hypothetical problem ticket/issue using the `create-ticket` task. When the task is completed, the `soap-sca-submit` node's action handler will submit the details collected from the prior task to the web service. The WSDL for the web service is included in the sample code; it's very simple and includes a single operation called `createTicket`. Here are the steps to establish the web service client:

1. Create the Java interface and implementation classes.
2. Construct the SCA composite XML file that identifies how to interact with the web service.
3. Create the jBPM action handler class that invokes the service through the node.

Let's look at each step.

CREATING A JAVA INTERFACE AND IMPLEMENTATION CLASSES

This step involves creating a Java interface and an implementation class that correspond to the interface of the web service we'll be calling. If you're working with a third-party web service, here's the most straightforward way to accomplish this:

1. Download the WSDL locally for the remote service.
2. Generate Java SDO classes for the XML binding required to interact with the web service (using `XSD2JavaGenerator`, which is described in chapter 4).
3. Create Java methods to reflect the web services you'll be integrating with.

In our example, since the web service itself was designed using SCA and sports a simple data structure, there's no need to use SDO. We can instead use the autobinding facility that comes with SCA along with the same data object class that we used to dynamically construct the WSDL (chapter 3 describes these concepts in detail, so it may be worth reviewing). Figure 7.8 illustrates the link between the WSDL artifacts and the Java classes created to interface with the remove service.

In figure 7.8, the `SOAPClient` interface class contains one method, `createTicket`, that mirrors the operation of the same name identified in the WSDL. Within the WSDL, the `createTicket` accepts, as an input, the `TicketDO complexType`, which is shown on the top left of the figure. As you can see, the `TicketDO` Java class used as a parameter for the `SOAPClient.createTicket` method also mirrors the `complexType` definition in the WSDL schema. If you did use SDO to generate the Java classes from the WSDL schema using `XSD2JavaGenerator`, the classes generated would be used in lieu of the `TicketDO` Java class shown here.

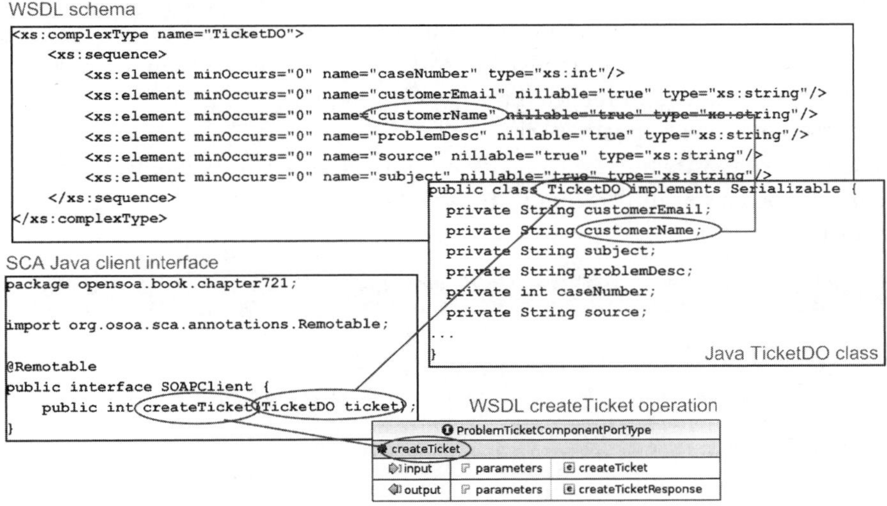

Figure 7.8 The relationship between the WSDL schema and Java SCA classes

NOTE Using SDO isn't a requirement when you're working with SCA. It's appropriate if you (a) are working with complex XML structures or (b) require some of the advanced SDO capabilities such as disconnected data sets. We'll use SDO in the next section when we talk about exposing jBPM as a service.

So far, we've depicted two Java classes: the `SOAPClient` interface and the `TicketDO` data object class. The last class we need is the actual implementation class for `SOAPClient`, which is shown in listing 7.2.

Listing 7.2 `SOAPClientImpl` implementation class

```
package opensoa.book.chapter721.impl;

import opensoa.book.chapter721.*;
import org.osoa.sca.annotations.Reference;

public class SOAPClientImpl implements SOAPClient {
  @Reference                                          ❶ Injects component reference

  public SOAPClient soapClient;

  public int createTicket(TicketDO ticket) {
    return soapClient.createTicket(ticket);          ❷ Invokes method on injected class
  }
}
```

The real heavy lifting in the `SOAPClientImpl` class is performed by `SOAPClient`, which is acting as a proxy to the remote web service, injected through an SCA reference ❶. You can think of `SOAPClientImpl` as somewhat analogous to a local EJB bean class. This class and the `createTicket` method will be called by the jBPM's node action handler. The `createTicket` method then simply uses the injected `SOAPClient` to call the remove service ❷. This will make considerably more sense when we look at the declarative XML composition file used by our SCA client.

CREATING THE SCA COMPOSITE FILE

The SCA composite file is the glue that holds together the assembly of components for either exposing or interfacing with services. Listing 7.3 shows the composite file used for this example.

Listing 7.3 problemTicket.composite file used by the SCA client

```
<composite
  xmlns="http://www.osoa.org/xmlns/sca/1.0"
  targetNamespace="http://opensoa.book.chapter721"
  xmlns:hw="http://opensoa.book.chapter721"
  name="soapclient">

  <component name="SOAPComponent">                ❶ Identifies component implementation
    <implementation.java
      class="opensoa.book.chapter721.impl.SOAPClientImpl" />
  </component>
```

```
  <reference
    name="SOAPClientReference"
    promote="SOAPComponent/soapClient">          <-  ❷ Defines reference to be injected
    <interface.wsdl
   ➥interface="http://chapter721.book.opensoa#wsdl.interface
      ➥(ProblemTicketComponentSOAP11port_http)" />

    <binding.ws                                   <-  ❸ Uses SOAP binding
      ➥wsdlElement="http://chapter721.book.opensoa#
      ➥wsdl.port(ProblemTicketComponent/
  ProblemTicketComponentSOAP11port_http)"/>
  </reference>
</composite>
```

The only component defined in this composite is `SOAPComponent` ❶ (the name is how we reference the component when we access it), and its implementation is performed by `SOAPClientImpl`, which we defined in listing 7.2. As you recall, this class was injected with the reference `soapClient`, and how this is accomplished is defined in ❷. The `@promote` value of `SOAPComponent/soapClient` states that this reference must be injected into the component called `SOAPComponent` using the variable `soapClient` (there are multiple ways to configure such things, and the reference could've been defined within the `component` element). The reference is then identified as a web service binding through the `binding.ws` element ❸. The `@wsdlElement` attribute identifies the specific WSDL service and port to use when placing the call. The WSDL itself, as you may recall from chapter 3, is automatically located because it ends with `.wsdl`, resides in the classpath, and has the same matching namespace (`chapter721.book.opensoa`). In a nutshell, what we're doing here is defining a reference to a remote web service, and that reference is being injected into an SCA component called `SOAPComponent`, whose implementation is provided by the class `SOAPClientImpl`.

In the sample code that accompanies this section, you'll also find a class called `opensoa.book.chapter721.SOAPClientMain`, which is a Java class whose static `main()` method simply invokes a test request to the web service (the README.txt file in the root directory for the section details how to run the web service so that you can test against it). This class, shown in listing 7.4, creates a handle to the `SOAPComponent`, instantiates a `TicketDO` object, populates it with some dummy data, and invokes the web service by calling the `SOAPClient`'s `createTicket` method.

Listing 7.4 Example `Main` class used for simple testing of a remote web service

```
public class SOAPClientMain {

  public final static void main(String[] args) throws Exception {
    SCADomain scaDomain = SCADomain.newInstance("soapclient.composite");
    SOAPClient soapClient =                                    <-  Instantiates
      scaDomain.getService(SOAPClient.class,"SOAPComponent");      component

    TicketDO ticket = new TicketDO();                   <-  Creates then
    ticket.setCustomerEmail("jdoe@someplace.com");          populates ticket
    ticket.setCustomerName("John Doe");
```

```
    ticket.setProblemDesc("This is a sample problem desc");
    ticket.setSource("customer");
    ticket.setSubject("test subject");

    System.out.println("Case number created is: "
       + soapClient.createTicket(ticket));              <— Calls web service via proxy

    scaDomain.close();

  }
}
```

You can run this test using the Ant build file's `soap.client` target at the root directory for this section's sample code. So what we've completed thus far is an SCA client that can be used to access the remote SOAP-based web service. The `SOAPClientMain` class can be used for testing the client from the command line.

Now that our SCA client component has been configured, we can create the jBPM node's action handler.

THE NODE ACTION HANDLE CLASS

Figure 7.7 showed that the node `soap-sca-submit` is called immediately following the task node, which is used to capture the problem ticket specifics. Before we move into the action handler code, let's briefly look at the definition of the node within the jPDL:

```
<node name="soap-sca-submit">
  <action name="SOAPNodeAction"
       class="opensoa.book.chapter721.impl.SOAPNodeActionHandler"/>
  <transition to="end"/>
</node>
```

As it turns out, this step involves little more than what we've already covered. Listing 7.5 displays the complete action handler code.

Listing 7.5 `SOAPNodeActionHandle` implementation class

```
public class SOAPNodeActionHandler implements ActionHandler{

  private static final long serialVersionUID = 1L;

  public void execute(ExecutionContext executionContext)        <— 1
      throws Exception {

    SCADomain scaDomain = SCADomain.newInstance("soapclient.composite"); <— 2
    SOAPClient soapClient =                                       <— 3
      scaDomain.getService(SOAPClient.class, "SOAPComponent");

    Map<String, String> varMap =                                 <— 4
      executionContext.getContextInstance().getVariables();

    int caseNum =                                               <— 5
      soapClient.createTicket(populateTicketDO(varMap));

    executionContext.setVariable("caseNum", caseNum);         <— 6
    executionContext.getToken().signal();       <— 7
  }

  private TicketDO populateTicketDO(HashMap<String, String> mapVals) { <— 8
```

```
    TicketDO ticket = new TicketDO();
    ticket.setCustomerEmail(mapVals.get("emailAddress"));
    ticket.setCustomerName(mapVals.get("name"));
    ticket.setSubject(mapVals.get("title"));
    ticket.setProblemDesc(mapVals.get("details"));
    ticket.setSource(mapVals.get("source"));

    return ticket;
  }
}
```

Since this class is performing as an action handler, it implements `ActionHandler` and the required `execute` method ❶. From there, we create an SCA domain instance ❷ so that we can initiate the SCA client we'll use to instantiate our web service request ❸. In step ❹, we retrieve the process instance variables that were gathered by way of the previous task node. These variables, stored in a `Map`, contain the details of the problem ticket captured from the user. The `Map` values must be converted into the `TicketDO` object (the parameter object used in the method call), which is achieved through the `populateTicketDO` method ❽. The populated `TicketDO` is then passed to the SCA component's (`soapClient`) `createTicket` method ❺. The component will perform the remote web services call and return a random number that represents the case number (`caseNum`). The last steps simply take the `caseNum` value returned and store it as a process variable ❻, and then complete the action handler by signaling the token to continue its execution ❼. The class is now complete, and when the `execute` method is called, it will invoke the destination web service.

The purpose of this example was to demonstrate how SCA components can be used in a client capacity to initiate web service calls from within jBPM. Using SCA provides considerable flexibility, because it supports multiple protocols and allows non-Java languages such as Ruby to be used. For companies aggressively service enabling their enterprise, which is a prerequisite for SOA, SCA helps unleash the power of jBPM. Let's now reverse the roles—that is, let's service enable jBPM so that clients can interface with it through protocols such as SOAP or JMS.

7.2.2 Service enabling jBPM

In the introduction to section 7.2, we explored some of the reasons why you might want to service enable jBPM so that client applications can interact through a variety of protocols, including SOAP, JMS, and EJB. Obviously, the ability to use multiple protocols is beneficial in heterogeneous environments, such as when mixing Java and non-Java languages. In particular, the .NET environment has outstanding web services support, so applications based on that platform can integrate rather easily with jBPM using SOAP. You might be thinking that service enabling jBPM must be a very tall order or it would have been done before. Well, it's not entirely trivial, but you may be surprised how easy it is to selectively expose key jBPM features as services while providing a foundation for extending it, as needed, in your organization.

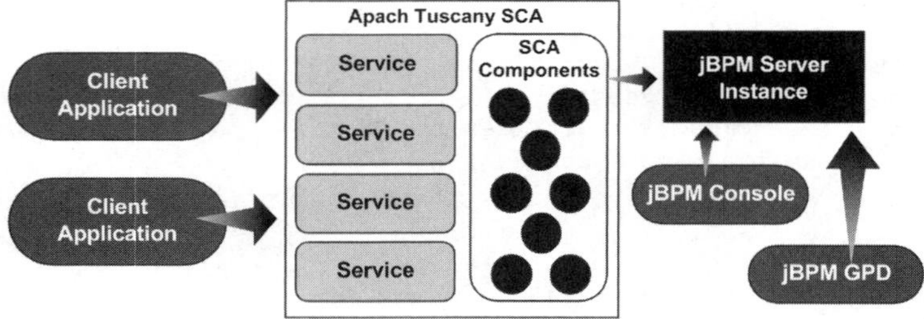

Figure 7.9 Service enabling jBPM using SCA/SDO

Figure 7.9 shows how we'll achieve this goal by marrying the capabilities of jBPM with SCA/SDO using Apache Tuscany. Client applications wishing to connect to jBPM can do so using any of the supported SCA binding protocols (SOAP, JMS, JSON-RPC, EJB). Internally, jBPM functions will be wrapped as SCA components, where they can be exposed as services individually or grouped together to form composite services (that is, those that combine several lower-level components into a more coarse-grained service). These SCA components will interface with jBPM using its rich and powerful API.

Attempting to expose the entire jBPM API through SCA-based services would be overly ambitious. However, like most things, I believe the 80-20 rule (Pareto principle) applies: 80 percent of what is really used can be derived from 20 percent of the functions. Further, what I hope to demonstrate is a framework for how you can build your own services as you need them (alternatively, if sufficient demand exists, we may create a SourceForge project to build the entire catalog). Table 7.3 lists a number of API calls that have been exposed through SCA that are included in this book's sample code. Although the operations represent only a small subset of what's possible, you may find it sufficient for integration with jBPM from external systems.

Table 7.3 Exposed jBPM services using SCA

Operation	Description
`createProcessInstance`	Creates a new process instance. Requires a process name as an input, along with optional instance-specific data.
`getObject`	Use in conjunction with db4objects to store Java instance objects.
`listActorTasks`	Given an `actorId`, this operation will bring back all tasks that are assigned to a given actor or user.
`listInstanceTasks`	Given a `processInstanceId`, this operation will list all tasks associated with that process instance. An optional filter attribute allows you to refine which tasks are returned.
`listInstanceTokens`	Given a `processInstanceId`, this operation will return all tokens for a given process instance.

Table 7.3 Exposed jBPM services using SCA *(continued)*

Operation	Description
`listProcessInstances`	Given a `processId`, this call will return all process instances associated with a process. You can filter results through the optional filter attribute.
`listProcesses`	This operation will list all processes available in the jBPM server instance.
`updateToken`	Given a `tokenId`, this service enables various token-related operations to be performed, such as signaling.

Rather than go through each operation one by one, we'll select a couple of these operations and dissect how they were created. The two we'll select are `listProcesses` and `createProcessInstance;` the former is very simple, and the latter is a bit more complex.

NOTE Bear in mind that, to run any of these examples, you'll need to connect to a jBPM instance that has some existing business processes deployed and running.

7.2.3 *Developing the ListProcesses service operation*

The objective behind this web service operation is to return a list of all processes that reside in a given jBPM server instance. The request itself doesn't contain any expected parameters. The output will return the list of processes in a format that resembles that shown in figure 7.10.

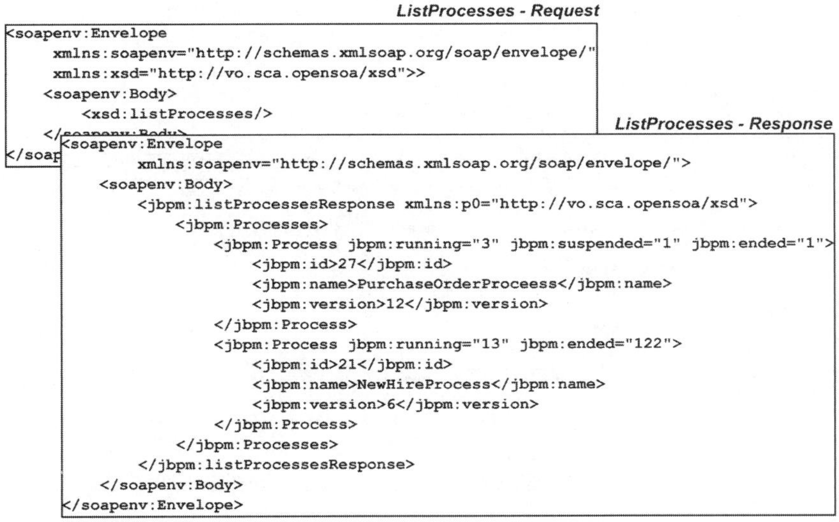

ListProcesses - Request

```
<soapenv:Envelope
    xmlns:soapenv="http://schemas.xmlsoap.org/soap/envelope/"
    xmlns:xsd="http://vo.sca.opensoa/xsd">>
   <soapenv:Body>
       <xsd:listProcesses/>
   </
</soap
```

ListProcesses - Response

```
<soapenv:Envelope
      xmlns:soapenv="http://schemas.xmlsoap.org/soap/envelope/">
   <soapenv:Body>
      <jbpm:listProcessesResponse xmlns:p0="http://vo.sca.opensoa/xsd">
          <jbpm:Processes>
              <jbpm:Process jbpm:running="3" jbpm:suspended="1" jbpm:ended="1">
                  <jbpm:id>27</jbpm:id>
                  <jbpm:name>PurchaseOrderProceess</jbpm:name>
                  <jbpm:version>12</jbpm:version>
              </jbpm:Process>
              <jbpm:Process jbpm:running="13" jbpm:ended="122">
                  <jbpm:id>21</jbpm:id>
                  <jbpm:name>NewHireProcess</jbpm:name>
                  <jbpm:version>6</jbpm:version>
              </jbpm:Process>
          </jbpm:Processes>
      </jbpm:listProcessesResponse>
   </soapenv:Body>
</soapenv:Envelope>
```

Figure 7.10 A sample of a request and response for the `ListProcesses` SOAP operation

NOTE The sample code for this section contains a hibernate.properties file that you can use to specify the database instance you want to connect to. You'll obviously want to change the properties to reflect your own environment.

Notice in figure 7.10 that the response returns a list of processes currently installed in your jBPM server instance. For each process, it provides the assigned `name`; a count of the process instances that are running, ended or suspended; the internal `processId`; and finally, the unique process `version` number. To create this operation (and the others), four main steps are involved: (1) create (or modify) WSDL entries, (2) autogenerate the SDO classes used for the request/response XML, (3) create the Java SCA implementation classes, and (4) create the SCA composite XML. Let's examine each step.

CREATING WSDL ENTRIES

Manually creating or modifying a WSDL is a tedious undertaking, even with the WSDL editors available in Eclipse and in tools such as Stylus Studio. While SCA can automatically generate a WSDL(s), the downside to this approach is that it can result in a proliferation of WSDLs, since each service will result in a separate WSDL. Furthermore, the generated WSDLs may not adhere to the desired format and structure. A better approach is to manually create a WSDL, which in the sample code for this section is called jbpm.wsdl. Obviously, it's outside the scope of this book to address the specifics of WSDL design, but I can highlight the entries necessary to construct our `ListProcesses` operation.

When modifying a WSDL, I find it easiest to work backward, if you will, from the service creation. Let's start by creating the `service`, `binding`, and `portType` definitions (using WSDL 1.1). Figure 7.11 shows the relationships between the entities.

As you may be aware, a WSDL can define multiple protocols for accessing a service. In our example, we're just using a SOAP binding, which is defined through the

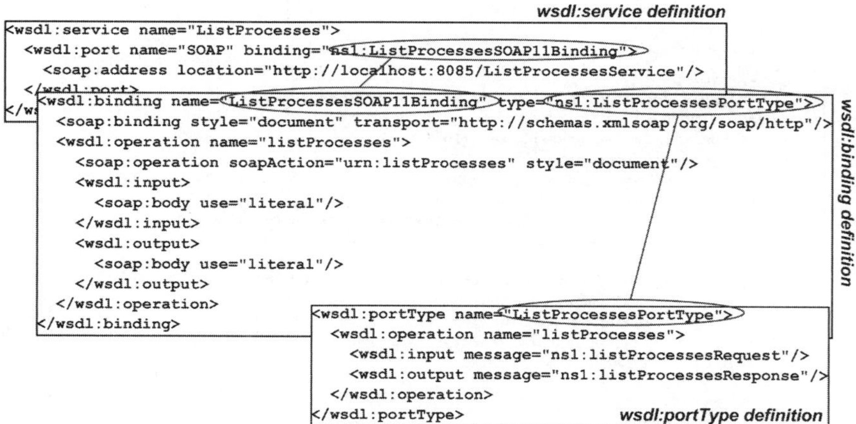

Figure 7.11 The `service`, `binding`, and `portType` definitions for the `ListProcesses` operation

`wsdl:binding` element. The `wsdl:service` definition for `ListProcesses` ties this binding to a specific URL and port. The `wsdl:portType` defines the inputs and outputs required for the operations. The `wsdl:portType` name is referenced by the `@type` attribute in the `wsdl:binding`, as illustrated in figure 7.11. What remains is the XML Schema definition used for the request and response. This relationship is shown in figure 7.12.

Figure 7.12 `ListProcesses` WSDL XML Schema definition

The `wsdl:portType`'s child `wsdl:input` and `wsdl:output` elements (see figure 7.11), via their `@message` attribute, associate to `wsdl:message`, which is shown in figure 7.12. The message parts identified in `wsdl:message`, through the `wsdl:part`'s `@element` attribute, finally tie it to the XML Schema. Obviously, keeping this all straight can be a challenge, but once you set up a few operations, it's fairly easy to clone your entries. Crafting the WSDL is the most difficult, or at least most tedious, part of this whole process. Next, we'll generate our Java data objects that correspond to the XML Schema elements shown in figure 7.12.

AUTOGENERATING SDO BINDING CLASSES

For a simple XML Schema like the one we're using with `ListProcesses`, we could clearly create our own Java objects that represent the request and response XML (as you recall, in section 7.2.1 we did just that in our example). However, once you begin to work with more complex types, doing so manually becomes untenable. Fortunately, you can easily generate Java binding classes using the SDO utility `XSD2JavaGenerator`. The suggested means for running this is within an Ant script, using a target, as shown in listing 7.6.

Listing 7.6 Example of an Ant target used to generate SDO classes

```
<property name="tuscany.lib.10"
value="..\..\..\tuscany\tuscany10\3rdparty"/>          <-- (1) Defines Ant property

<target depends="init" name="generate.classes.from.wsdl">
```

```
    <java classname="org.apache.tuscany.sdo.generate.XSD2JavaGenerator"
        fork="true">
      <arg value="-targetDirectory"/>
      <arg value="src/main/generated/wsdl2javasource"/>      <- 2 Specifies output location
      <arg value="-noContainment"/>
      <arg value="-noUnsettable"/>
      <arg value="src/main/resources/jbpm.wsdl"/>      <- 3 Specifies WSDL to use
      <classpath>
        <fileset dir="${tuscany.lib.10}">      <- 4 Sets classpath
          <include name="*.jar"/>
        </fileset>
      </classpath>
    </java>
</target>
```

The Ant target shown in listing 7.6 (also included in the build.xml file you'll find in this section's sample code) uses the Ant Java task to call the `XSD2JavaGenerator`, and it accepts a variety of parameters, such as the `targetDirectory` where the generated class files should be created ❷ and the WSDL (or XML Schema) file used as the source input ❸. A `classpath` must also be defined that includes the SDO-related libraries ❶, ❹. When run, a significant number of class files may be generated; generally, a class is created for each `complexType` or element defined in the input schema. In our example, there was no input XML for the request, but the response XML is defined as

```
<xs:complexType name="ProcessVO">
  <xs:sequence>
    <xs:element minOccurs="0" name="description" nillable="true"
       type="xs:string"/>
    <xs:element minOccurs="0" name="hasActions" type="xs:boolean"/>
    <xs:element minOccurs="0" name="hasEvents" type="xs:boolean"/>
    <xs:element minOccurs="0" name="id" type="xs:long"/>
    <xs:element minOccurs="0" name="name" nillable="true"
       type="xs:string"/>
    <xs:element minOccurs="0" name="version" type="xs:int"/>
  </xs:sequence>
  <xs:attribute name="running" type="xs:int"/>
  <xs:attribute name="suspended" type="xs:int"/>
  <xs:attribute name="ended" type="xs:int"/>
</xs:complexType>
```

When `XSD2JavaGenerator` is run on the WSDL, it generates a class called `opensoa.sca.vo.xsd.ProcessVOType` that corresponds to the `ProcessVO complexType` shown earlier. As a result, we know that this class represents the return value associated with the Java method used to process the service operation. In this case, the operation is `ListProcesses` (see figure 7.11). Let's examine how we implement this method and its corresponding implementation class.

CREATING JAVA SCA IMPLEMENTATION CLASSES

By now you're probably familiar with the standard approach for creating SCA components and exposing them as services. The first step is to create an interface class that defines the service signature. In this example, we call this class, appropriately enough, `ListProcesses`:

```
@Remotable
public interface ListProcesses {
  public ProcessVOType listProcesses ();
}
```

The `@Remotable` annotation indicates that this interface can be exposed externally outside of the SCA JVM runtime. The method `listProcesses`, as we expect, will receive no request parameters and will return an instance of type `ProcessVOType`. The next step is to implement this interface, which is where the logic resides for working with the jBPM service. Listing 7.7 shows the implementation class.

Listing 7.7 `ListProcesses` implementation class interfacing with the jBPM service

```
@Service(ListProcesses.class)
public class ListProcessesImpl implements ListProcesses {

  @Reference
  protected JBPMHelper jbpmContextHelper;                          1
  JbpmContext jbpmContext;

  private final static String RUNNING =
    "select count(*) from org.jbpm.graph.exe.ProcessInstance pi where " +
    "pi.processDefinition = ? and pi.end = null";             2
  /* other static definitions excluded */

  public ProcessVOType listProcesses() {

    jbpmContext = jbpmContextHelper.getConfiguration().createJbpmContext();

    List<ProcessDefinition> processDefinitionList =                3
    jbpmContext.getGraphSession().findAllProcessDefinitions();

    XsdFactory factory = XsdFactory.INSTANCE;
    HelperContext scope = SDOUtil.createHelperContext();                4
    XsdFactory.INSTANCE.register(scope);

    ProcessVOTypeImpl processList = (ProcessVOTypeImpl)
      factory.createProcessVOType();

    for (ProcessDefinition processDef :                     5
      processDefinitionList) {

      long pid = processDef.getId();
      ProcessVO process = factory.createProcessVO();
      process.setDescription(processDef.getDescription());               6
      process.setName(processDef.getName());
      process.setId(pid);
      /* other setters not shown */
      processList.getProcess().add(process);              7
    }

    jbpmContext.close();
    return processList;
  }                                                                  8

  private int queryCount(String querystring, long pid) {
    Query query = jbpmContext.getSession().createQuery(querystring);
    query.setLong(0, pid);
```

```
        Long i = (Long) query.list().iterator().next();
        return i.intValue();
    }
}
```

In the previous chapters on SCA and jBPM, we covered each of the steps that are occurring in listing 7.7. We're acquiring a jBPM session connection ❶, and then using the jBPM API to retrieve a list of processes ❸. Since we're using SDO for the XML binding, SDO classes are instantiated using the generated SDO factory classes ❹. At that point, we iterate through the `List` of the processes represented by the jBPM `ProcessDefinition` class, which was returned from the jBPM API method `findAllProcessDefinitions` ❺. For each process, we populate the SDO `ProcessVO` object ❻. That object is then added to the `List` of `ProcessVOTypeImpl` in ❼ (the implementation for `ProcessVOType`), which ultimately gets marshaled into the XML by SDO and returned as the `listProcesses` operation's response. The `queryCount` method ❽ uses a constructed Hibernate query ❷ to return the number of running process instances for a given process ID. The next step is to wire the SCA assembly together using the composite XML file definition.

CREATING SCA COMPOSITE XML FILES

The last step on our journey is to create SCA composite files, which declaratively define our services and how they're published. Because we ultimately want to create many such services and not just the one we're creating now, the composite files are deconstructed into several composite files. The parent composite file we'll call `jbpm.composite`, and it includes the child composites. This relationship is illustrated in figure 7.13.

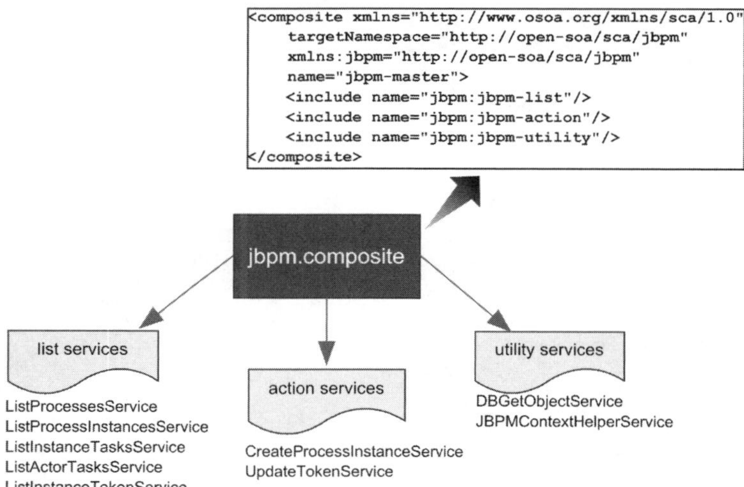

Figure 7.13 Decomposed construction of the `jbpm.composite` SCA file

The service we're defining, `ListProcessesService`, resides in the file listservices.composite:

```
<composite xmlns="http://www.osoa.org/xmlns/sca/1.0"
   targetNamespace="http://open-soa/sca/jbpm"
   xmlns:hw="http://open-soa/sca/jbpm"
   name="jbpm-list">

   <service name="ListProcessesService" promote="ListProcessesComponent">
     <binding.ws
      wsdlElement="http://sca.opensoa#wsdl.port(ListProcesses/SOAP)"/>
   </service>

   <component name="ListProcessesComponent">
     <implementation.java class="opensoa.sca.impl.ListProcessesImpl"/>
     <reference name="jbpmContextHelper"
       target="JBPMContextHelperComponent"/>
   </component>
</composite>
```

The service definition for `ListProcessesService` promotes the component `ListProcessesComponent`. This component uses as its implementation `ListProcessesImpl`, which we developed in listing 7.7. The `ListProcessesService` service definition includes the `binding.ws` child element, which indicates that the service is to be exposed as a SOAP-based web service. The `@wsdlElement` instructs the binding to use the WSDL we manually developed in the first step of this process.

You may have also noticed that the component definition for `ListProcessesComponent` includes the reference injection for `jbpmContextHelper`. This component is defined in `utility.composite` and provides services to the component for connecting to the jBPM session or instance (see listing 7.7).

NOTE You can find the utility.composite file in the sample code for this chapter.

The only remaining task is to create a class with a static `main()` method to host and run the assembly within an SCA domain. We'll use the embedded server for simplicity's sake, and the web service will be served by it. This class, appropriately called `Server` (Ant target `run.server`), just launches the SCA server:

```
public class Server {
  public static void main(String[] args) {
    Server server = new Server();
      server.run();
  }
  public void run() {
    System.out.println("Running");
    SCADomain scaDomain = SCADomain.newInstance("jbpm.composite");
  }
}
```

What have we accomplished by this exercise? Our objective was to create a web service that interacted with the jBPM API to return a list of all processes running within that jBPM instance. Toward this end, we constructed a WSDL that defined the web service.

That WSDL, in turn, was used to automatically generate SDO binding classes for each of the XML Schema elements and types included within the WSDL. A Java class was then developed to implement the service. It used the jBPM API to retrieve the list of processes, and populated the return response using generated SDO classes. An SCA assembly was then created with the Java class as the implementation for a component that was exposed as a web service. While there was some setup work involved in this solution, adding new services will be much more straightforward. Further, you can also expose the service through JMS or any of the other available Tuscany SCA protocols. Let's add one more example to reinforce the steps. This service will be used to instantiate a new jBPM process instance.

7.2.4 Developing the CreateProcessInstance service operation

Creating the `CreateProcessInstance` service mostly mirrors what we've already described in the previous example. Rather than going through each step, let's focus on the unique aspects of this service's implementation. In particular, when you create a process instance, such as instantiating a new employee hire process, you'll often have a significant amount of information already collected. While the data could possibly be passed via a web service as an unlimited map-type array (i.e., key/value pairs), doing so isn't always sensible or practical. Instead, a more intuitive approach is to create an XML Schema that fully expresses the complexity of the data you're passing. What's the downside to this approach? Your web service WSDL must potentially be modified for each process where you wish to incorporate complex data types.

Let's examine the approach of using a separate XML Schema for each process. Let's assume that you have an existing jBPM process that's used for hiring new people. We'll call this process `NewHireProcess`. Let's assume that some data is already available on the new employee, perhaps originating from an *Applicant Tracking System* (ATS), and we want to pass this information to the process when it's initiated. To facilitate this, we'll create an employee entity and define it within an XML Schema. Thus, when the `CreateProcessInstance` service is called, the employee XML data will be populated and passed when the service is invoked. Listing 7.8 shows an example of the `CreateProcessInstance` operation using the `Employee` XML Schema complex type.

Listing 7.8 XML example of a `CreateProcessInstance` operation

```
<ns:createProcessInstance xmlns:ns="http://vo.sca.opensoa/xsd">
   <ns:Process ns:processName="NewHireProcess">                    ❶
      <ns:key>John Doe</ns:key>                          ❷
      <ns:ProcessVars>
         <ns:var ns:name="emplName">John Doe</ns:var>          ❸
      </ns:ProcessVars>
      <ns:Employee objectId="232363">                      ❹
         <ns:indicative>
            <ns:familyName>Doe</ns:familyName>
            <ns:givenName>John</ns:givenName>
            <ns:dob>01/01/1901</ns:dob>
         </ns:indicative>
```

```
        <ns:contactInfo>
           <ns:emailAddress>jdoe@yahoo.com</ns:emailAddress>
           <ns:phones>
              <ns:phone ns:type="home">111-111-1111</ns:phone>
           </ns:phones>
           <ns:address>
              <ns:addressline1>Some Address</ns:addressline1>
              <ns:municipality>Some city</ns:municipality>
              <ns:region>Some state</ns:region>
              <ns:country>Some country</ns:country>
              <ns:postalCode>939221</ns:postalCode>
           </ns:address>
        </ns:contactInfo>
        <ns:employeeData>
           <ns:employeeId>A32-232221</ns:employeeId>
           <ns:title>VP of Planning</ns:title>
           <ns:department>Finance</ns:department>
           <ns:location>Central</ns:location>
        </ns:employeeData>
     </ns:Employee>
  </ns:Process>
</ns:createProcessInstance>
```

The `Process` element's `@processName` attribute identifies the process to use when creating the instance ❶. The `key` child element is for purposes of convenience, and is displayed when viewing the process instance through the jBPM Console ❷. The `ProcessVars` child `var` elements (one or more) are used to populate process instance variables, and are defined as always being string values ❸. The `Employee` element is obviously process specific ❹. If you look in the jbpm.wsdl in the sample code for this chapter, you'll see that the `ProcessType` schema declaration, which is the root for this operation, is defined like this:

```
<xs:complexType name="ProcessType">
   <xs:sequence>
      <xs:element name="key" type="xs:string" minOccurs="0"/>
      <xs:element name="ProcessVars" minOccurs="0"
        type="jbpm:ProcessVarsType"/>
      <xs:choice>
        <xs:element name="Applicant" type="jbpm:ApplicantType"/>
        <xs:element name="Employee" type="jbpm:EmployeeType"/>
        <xs:element name="Other"/>
      </xs:choice>
   </xs:sequence>
   <xs:attribute name="actorId" type="xs:string"/>
   <xs:attribute name="processName" type="xs:string" use="required"/>
</xs:complexType>
```

Notice the `choice` declaration, which accepts one of the three element types: `ApplicantType`, `EmployeeType`, or `Other`. You'd obviously modify this to reflect any complex types you require, and add them to the appropriate location within the XML Schema located within the WSDL (in the example for listing 7.8, the `EmployeeType` is being used).

The `CreateProcessInstanceImpl` class, which is the SCA implementation class, is analogous to the `ListProcessesImpl` class we created in listing 7.7. Therefore, it's the implementation for the `CreateProcessInstance` web service. One challenge that exists is that, depending on the process instance created, different inbound XML will be provided to the service request. This was illustrated in listing 7.8, where the `Employee` node information was sent since the process instance to be created was specified as `NewHireProcess`. This can be addressed by triaging the inbound requests based upon the process name provided (found in the `@processName` attribute of the `Process` element). For example:

```
if (process.getProcessName().equalsIgnoreCase("NewHireProcess")) {
  // process specific logic
}
```

Within the body of the `if` statement, you could then perform process-specific functions, such as adding process variables to the instance. This is illustrated in the sample code for this section.

NOTE In the code examples for this section, db4objects is used to store the inbound complex SDO data objects that represent an employee or applicant. There are a couple of reasons for this: (a) SDO objects can't be stored natively within the jBPM instance (or, at a minimum, it will cause errors when displaying process instance details within the jBPM Console); (b) storing them externally in a database makes them more readily accessible for reporting and other purposes; and (c) an object database such as db4objects is likely far more efficient at indexing and retrieval of native Java objects than jBPM. The index used to store them in these examples is the `@objectId` attribute associated with the object's root element (such as `Employee`).

There are undoubtedly other approaches, probably many superior, to handling the variability that surrounds an operation such as `CreateProcessInstance`. For example, Spring would likely be a great choice for declaratively managing which classes are used for different process instances. I tried to avoid introducing too many additional technologies beyond the core we're focusing on in an effort to keep things simple. jBPM is a wonderful and powerful BPM solution, and when coupled with SCA/SDO, can open a world of possibilities for integration within a SOA environment.

7.3 Summary

This chapter has been quite a journey. We've covered a lot of material! Hopefully your perseverance has paid handsome dividends. This chapter was split into two main sections: advanced features of jBPM and integration of jBPM with SCA/SDO through its Apache Tuscany implementation. The advanced features focused on some of the enterprise capabilities of jBPM, such as the ability to create superstates and subprocesses, both of which help bring greater order and management to defining complex business processes. We also touched on the use of asynchronous continuations, which can be used in circumstances where you're integrating with services that may not have predicable or timely responses. Asynchronous continuations can also help you create more distributed solutions.

The second main section focused on how you can integrate jBPM with SCA and its related technology, SDO. This marriage addresses some of the recurring concerns with jBPM, such as how you call external services within the context of a reusable and consistent framework. We demonstrated how you can easily integrate with web services using SCA components in a client-style capacity. We then reversed the requirement and provided a means by which the jBPM API can be exposed through SCA. The implication is that jBPM can now be integrated through any number of protocols, including SOAP and JMS. The ability to call out as a service consumer and perform as a service provider is equally important from a SOA standpoint. You may recall from our initial discussion in chapter 2 that services can be construed as high-level business processes or as more granular, component-level type services. Through the combination of SCA/SDO and jBPM, we have the full spectrum of services addressed, from fine to coarse-grained, layered upon a compelling technology stack.

The next chapter will describe how we can leverage the events derived from our services to provide complete operational insight and monitoring—an important value-added feature of a SOA environment.

Part 4

Event stream processing, integration, and mediation

In the previous five chapters we focused on the services aspect of SOA. We described how services can be easily developed using the Service Component Architecture and its implementation using Apache Tuscany. Then, using JBoss jBPM, we illustrated how such services can be combined to create entire business processes that can be modeled and executed, representing a new form of application development. In part 4, we'll switch gears a bit and discuss the role of the enterprise service bus (ESB), an important enabling technology for SOA. An ESB can act as middleware "glue" for integrating with systems, applications, and protocols that weren't necessarily designed with the precepts of SOA in mind. An ESB can act as a mediator for bridging differences in protocols, provide service transparency, and perform data transformations. In addition, it can be used to advance the cause of governance by enforcing service and security usage profiles. Related to this is event stream processing (ESP), which can be used to detect any unusual patterns of activity and provide real-time notification to the appropriate business users. We'll begin part 4 by examining the role of ESP in chapter 8, and you'll learn how to analyze complex business events using Esper, an outstanding open source ESP product.

8 Complex events using Esper

This chapter covers

- Defining event stream processing
- Introducing Esper
- Implementing Esper

The technologies we've covered so far have dealt with the topics of creating reusable services (SCA), and in turn, how they can be woven together to create complex business processes (BPM). In this chapter, we'll shift gears a bit and look at how we can tap into these services and orchestrations to provide deep insights into the operational aspects of your enterprise. This is accomplished through *event stream processing* (ESP), sometimes also known as *complex event processing* (CEP). According to the CEP Interest web site (a site devoted to covering this technology), CEP is defined as

> *...software technology that enables applications to monitor multiple streams of event data, analyze them in terms of key performance indicators that are expressed in event rules, and act upon opportunities and threats in real time, potentially by creating derived events, or forwarding raw events. [CEPInterest]*

Simply put, CEP technology enables you to monitor the vital signs of your organization.

Monitoring business events is critical for most enterprises, especially given the focus on metrics and accountability. In our hyper-competitive and compliance-crazy environment, monitoring must be done in real time (or perhaps near-time). In yesteryear, companies would monitor their performance once every few weeks, or even once a quarter; a company adhering to such a philosophy today would have a short shelf life. As Prahalad and Krishnan point out, "Competitiveness favors those who spot new trends and act on them expeditiously," and the "new competitive landscape requires *continuous analysis* of data for insight" [Prahalad].

SOA's emphasis on the propagation of discrete, largely stand-alone services brings with it some attendant difficulties not present in more monolithic application environments. The main question is how you manage or monitor a highly distributed environment. In the monolithic world, the entire app usually runs on a single or clustered set of machines and monitoring is fairly straightforward. In the SOA world, an application may be using service components from a multitude of machines (perhaps many of them virtual). If any single component goes down, it could wreak havoc. In other words, in a SOA environment the possible points of failure are much greater (an often-overlooked downside to SOA).

ESP can play a significant role in risk mitigation through its ability to monitor, in real time, any deviations from the norm. Further, the operational insights provided by ESP can help organizations rapidly detect new opportunities or trends, thereby improving their competitive position.

In this chapter, we'll first review why events are important to the enterprise, and how they're constructed and consumed by an event stream processor. We'll then explore how to use Esper, the open source ESP solution selected for our Open SOA Platform. Finally, you'll see a framework for exposing the Esper engine through web services—an important requirement for integration within our SOA environment. Let's begin by examining the importance of ESP for monitoring the ongoing pulse of your enterprise.

8.1 Business events in the enterprise

The ability to derive *instant insights* into the operations of your enterprise is essential. Businesses must engage in continuous evolution to remain competitive. Events are an important ingredient in this process. How? Let's examine a few possible scenarios:

- *Purchasing patterns*—Many companies, especially those in retail, must quickly identify changes in customer behavior. Buying trends, particularly those in the finicky youth and young adult markets, can change dramatically within a matter of weeks or even days. It's essential to identify any changes in purchasing habits quickly, as they drive product placement decisions, stocking requirements, and pricing. A sudden drop-off in a particular product line could also point to fulfillment issues or negative publicity arising from the dynamic communication channels now afforded by the web (blogs, emails, social networking sites, etc.).

- *Compliance*—Many companies, particularly those in the public realm, must abide by onerous compliance regulations. Some, like the Sarbanes-Oxley Act of 2002, touch nearly all public companies, but other domain-specific regulations—such as liquidity requirements for financial firms or adverse action reporting for pharmaceutical companies—are also common. Failure to abide and demonstrate ongoing controls can result in significant fines, or possibly even criminal prosecution.
- *Fraud detection*—The press is replete with stories of fraud and loss of data containing sensitive personal information (SPI). Although some of these incidents couldn't be detected by ESP (such as theft of backup tapes), in other scenarios comprehensive use of ESP could have more quickly identified possible breaches [Choicepoint]. Unusual activity that falls outside normal business patterns can help identify possible fraudulent behavior (you've probably encountered such controls firsthand if you've ever started buying unusual items on your credit card from a remote location only to find your account frozen until a call to your provider is placed).

These brief examples only scratch the surface of what's possible using ESP, and undoubtedly your organization has many other event-related activities that require close supervision. Before we progress further, let's dissect what constitutes events and ESP.

8.2 Understanding events

Up until now, we've discussed events at an abstract level within the context of the business or enterprise. Let's step back for a moment and consider, at its most basic level, what constitutes an event. Most agree, *an event is really just a fact of something occurring.* An *event object*, then, is a record of the activity expressed in a manner that allows it to be digested by an event processor. An *event processor* is an application that performs operations on event objects, including creating, reading, transforming, aggregating, or removing them. Finally, an *event stream* is a sequence of event objects, which typically arrive in the order in which they were generated.

One of the main responsibilities of an event processor is to analyze incoming event streams, discard events that are of no importance, and flag the relevant ones. Figure 8.1 depicts how applications or systems generate outbound events using objects or containers to represent the event data. Each event object is then streamed to the processor, which performs a variety of functions on the inbound stream.

Historically, two major impediments exist to embracing the "*Power of Events*" (to quote the namesake book written by David Luckham [Luckham2002]):

- The publishing of events
- The consumption of a vast array of event data

Unless you've coded for it up front, creating events throughout the workflow of your application can present a major refactoring effort. Often, event publishing is an

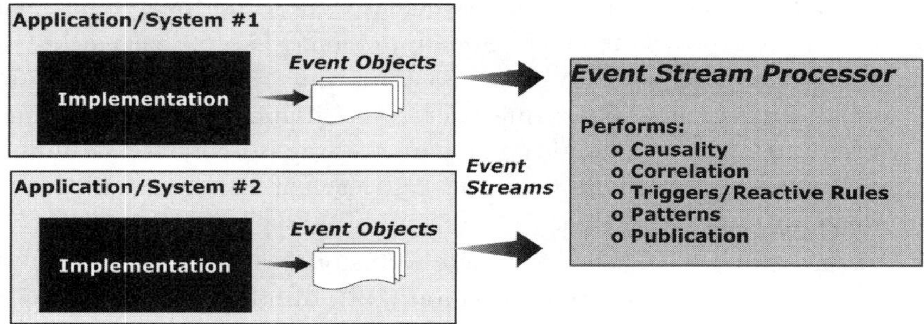

Figure 8.1 The relationship between event objects, streams, and the processor

afterthought, and thus difficult to bolt on after the initial development (since it touches so much of the code).

Assuming that you do begin publishing events, another challenge quickly comes to mind: how do you manage the processing and consumption of such events? Even a modestly sized enterprise may find that it's producing thousands of event messages per minute. Storing them all as they're received in a database isn't prudent, both because of the storage demands and the attendant CPU cycles necessary to process the information after it's arrived. An ESP engine can address the latter, but the former challenge of producing the events remains.

Fortunately, embracing SOA, and its notion of discrete services, does make the task of event production much more tenable. Further, adoption of BPM can dramatically advance this goal. How, you might ask? Let's consider a jBPM business process (the topic of chapters 5, 6, and 7). As you may recall, a jBPM process consists of nodes and transitions, with nodes representing states where actions usually occur (a task, a call-out to another system, etc.). Events can be generated as transitions occur from one node to another (indeed, there's the concept of events built into the fabric of jBPM). More importantly, events can indicate when a new process instance has been initiated, suspended, or completed. Extending jBPM to automatically generate such events is trivial, and I'll explain how that can be done.

Before we dive headfirst into ESP, let's briefly discuss its role with two related technologies: business activity monitoring (BAM) and Event-Driven Architecture (EDA).

8.2.1 BAM and ESP—what's the difference?

There is no doubt some confusion as to what are essentially two complementary technologies. BAM is often considered, in broad terms, to encompass all aspects of monitoring, from data collection, to transformation/analysis, to presentation. I prefer a more narrow interpretation, where BAM is thought of as the presentation layer but data collection is the purview of systems such as ESP. In other words, ESP is a delivery channel for BAM. Why this distinction? In part, as with web development, it's prudent to isolate or partition the various tiers involved in the monitoring process. Event publishing, collection, rule processing and interpretation, and presentation should each be considered separate tiers that are only loosely bound. This allows changes, for instance, to be made to the presentation layer without impacting the collection and interpretation layers. Indeed, a multitude of presentations may be necessary, from iPhone or Blackberry, to conventional web clients, to RSS feeds. Thus we refer to BAM, moving forward, as limited in scope to the display and presentation of information collected and analyzed via ESP.

Now let's conclude our theoretical discussion by briefly examining ESP's role within the context of an EDA. Some believe that CEP requires EDA, but as we'll see, this need not be the case.

8.2.2 Event-Driven Architecture and SOA

According to Wikipedia, EDA is defined as "a software architecture pattern promoting the production, detection, consumption of, and reaction to events" [WIKI]. EDA certainly shares a lot with CEP but is much broader in scope. In an EDA environment, communications between services are conducted asynchronously. Services are defined as being event producers, consumers, or both. The result is a loosely coupled system or environment. Some have suggested EDA is a competing architecture to SOA, but really it's just a particular manifestation of SOA. Within SOA, asynchronous forms of communications consistent with EDA are encouraged but, practically speaking, not always possible.

How does CEP fit with EDA? Events can be used exclusively in CEP for monitoring and analytics, quite apart from whether your services communicate exclusively using an asynchronous, event-driven fashion.

Now that we've developed a clear understanding of ESP—what it is, what it's used for, and its place in SOA—let's move into implementation using Esper, the open source ESP solution that's our ESP selection of choice for the Open SOA Platform.

8.3 What is Esper?

Esper is the first, and to my knowledge, the only open source event stream processing application available. Fortunately, hubris hasn't taken hold, and it continues to evolve at a rapid clip and offers exceptional functionality for such a fairly young product. The Esper project was founded by Thomas Bernhardt while he was consulting for a large financial institution. Asked to evaluate rule engines to be used in conjunction with monitoring a trading system, he discovered that what was needed was a high-performance event correlation engine—and Esper was born. The basic components of Esper are shown in figure 8.2.

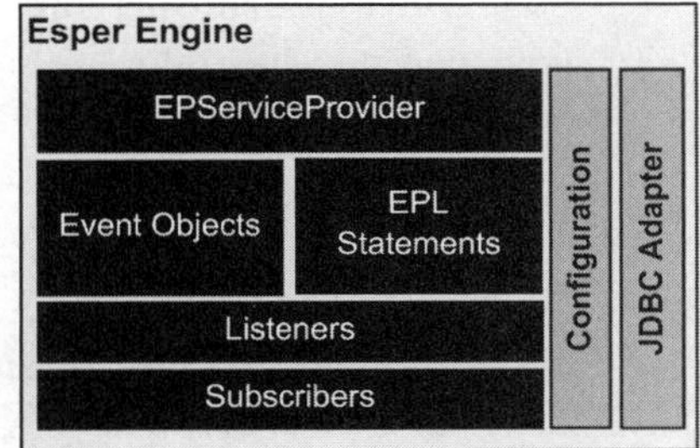

Figure 8.2 Core Esper components

Think of the `EPServiceProvider` as the *engine instance*, by which statements, events, and outputs (listeners or subscribers) are registered. You configure the engine programmatically or through an external XML file. Using the JDBC adapter, you can connect with an external database and cull information from it (with some restrictions, as we'll discuss later).

Recently, Esper graduated to a 3.0 release. This release produced several new features, and improved the performance and reliability of the system. While EsperTech was founded by Bernhardt to commercialize a business based around Esper, the core product remains open source under a favorable GNU license. Esper also now has a .NET version (NEsper for .NET) that parallels the feature set in the Java release. EsperTech monetizes Esper by offering support and an enterprise high-availability version of Esper called EsperHA (we don't cover that product in this book).

Unlike many open source products, Esper has superb documentation. Therefore, we'll just focus on using Esper in the context of our Open SOA Platform. This means that we'll only lightly cover all of the extensive features of Esper and show you how Esper can be used in tandem with our other Open SOA Platform products. Since we've only covered jBPM and SCA, we'll focus on integrating with those products, and in future chapters extend the discussion to include how Esper can be used in tandem with enterprise decision management using Drools.

Let's first look at integrating Esper with jBPM, which will provide real-time monitoring of business processes built using jBPM. You'll find that this greatly enhances the value proposition of jBPM.

As you recall, in chapter 7, we discussed the jBPM logging capabilities, focusing on the built-in capabilities jBPM provides for logging virtually all activities that pertain to the execution of a given process instance. This includes obvious things such as when the process started and stopped, but also includes abilities such as

- Logging the transitions that occur between the nodes
- Assigning process instance variables and their values
- Obtaining action and actor-related information

...in other words, basically everything. I'll show you how to create your own custom logger to automatically transmit these events to an exposed Esper web service. No specific coding within the business process itself will be required, as the event generation will take place in a completely transparent fashion (see figure 8.3).

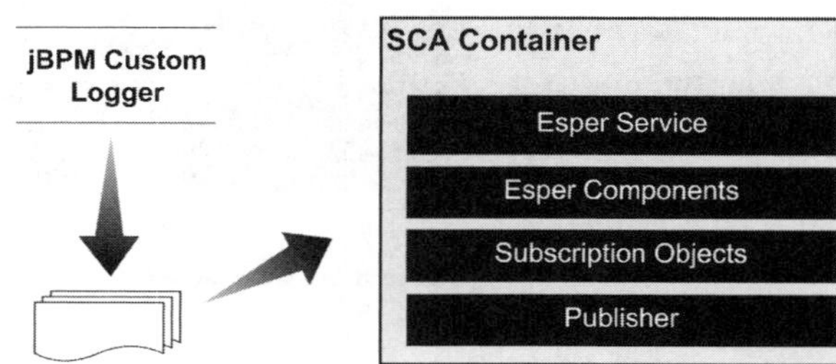

Figure 8.3 Emitting events from jBPM custom logger to Esper SCA service

In figure 8.3, you can see that jBPM emits the events from the jBPM custom logger. They are then sent to an Esper service running in an SCA container, which exposes Esper as an externally accessible service (through any of the available SCA bindings such as JMS or SOAP). In the SCA container, various Esper-related components are wired together to provide the underlying functionality. This includes the subscription objects used to receive the event notifications published by the Esper engine, which are based on the registered query statements. These notification and subscription objects, in turn, can publish their findings to a BAM solution, for example.

We'll use this case study throughout the chapter. In the sample code for this chapter, you'll see how the custom jBPM logger was implemented, but for now, it's sufficient to show you the event object on which we'll base many of our examples (I have kept it simple to keep the focus on Esper). Listing 8.1 shows the `ProcessEvent` event object.

Listing 8.1 `ProcessEvent` event data transfer object

```
public class ProcessEvent {

  private String processName;
  long processVersion;
  long processInstanceId;
  int state;

  public ProcessEvent() {
    super();
  }

  public ProcessEvent(String processName, long processVersion,
      long processInstanceId, int state) {
    super();
    this.processName = processName;
    this.processVersion = processVersion;
    this.processInstanceId = processInstanceId;
    this.state = state;
  }

  public String getProcessName() {
    return processName;
  }
/* Other getters and setters not shown */
}
```

Specifies event properties

Contains JavaBean style accessor methods

The `ProcessEvent` class in listing 8.1 can be used to capture when a jBPM process instance is initiated, suspended, or ended, as determined by the `state` property (`1=Started, 2=Ended, 3=Suspended`). As you can see, it's just a standard Java class, with no Esper-specific libraries. The case study we'll build on will use Esper to monitor a hypothetical process to capture metrics such as unusual delays in the time it takes to complete the process, the number of recently completed process instances, and the average number of running processes in a given time window. Let's begin by looking at the basics for setting up Esper.

8.4 Getting started with Esper

Esper is a lightweight application. The project is housed at Codehaus (http://esper.codehaus.org/), and the 3.0 version, released in February 2009, provides the basis for the examples we'll cover. The total size of the download is a testimony to its lightweight nature—it's just around 15 MB. When installed, the core Esper JAR files reside in the main project directory, with a handful of additional third-party JARs located in the esper/lib subdirectory.

NOTE An Ant target within the book's source code will automatically download the proper Esper libraries, so there is no need to separately install Esper to run the examples. See the README.txt file associated with this chapter's source.

Esper itself doesn't come with any application server, and instead can be considered more of an engine that can be embedded in other solutions. There's also no administrative interface and no built-in provisions for accessing Esper via web services (something we'll address in section 8.7).

There are four main aspects to setting up Esper to receive inbound events:

- Creating event objects
- Defining and registering query statements
- Specifying listeners or subscriber objects to receive Esper results
- Defining configuration options

Let's take a fairly high-level peek into each of these steps before proceeding to specific implementation details in section 8.5.

8.4.1 What are event objects?

In listing 8.1, we provided a simple illustration of a Java event object that can be used as a container for sending events to Esper. One caveat is that event classes have to adhere to standard JavaBean-style getter methods for accessing class member variables (we'll discuss some alternatives in a moment). In fact, it's through reflection of the public methods that Esper determines how to interface with the object (the member variables in the Java class may be private for this reason). The Esper event properties represent the member variables or fields within the `ProcessEvent` class, such as `processName` and `processInstanceId`, which are exposed using JavaBean standard getters. As an alternative to the JavaBean style classes, you can also optionally use `java.util.Map` or `org.w3c.dom.Node` objects, although we won't provide illustrations of these methods in this chapter (see the Esper reference documentation for more details).

Support also exists for creating far more complicated properties than illustrated in listing 8.1. This includes using nested properties that contain references to other objects, or mapped event properties, using a key value lookup This map, which refers to a getter method with a key value lookup such as `property('key')`, isn't to be confused with Java Map objects, although they can be implemented using Java Map objects, as we'll illustrate in a moment.

Let's assume that we want to enrich the ProcessEvent object with a list of jBPM process variables and their associated values. You may recall that standard jBPM variables support many standard Java types such as String, Boolean, Double, and Integer. Since Esper interrogates the class methods to determine how to work with a given property, returning a generic Object type wouldn't be as convenient for Esper to work with as type-specific properties would. For example, since jBPM variables can be of any of those types, using getProperty('propertyName') would have to return an Object, and then we'd have to cast it within our Esper statements to the proper type. Instead, we can create separate methods for each of the property types. These methods would manage the casting. The following snippet shows how this can be implemented:

```
// member variable properties defined
HashMap<String, Object> properties;
...
public String getStringProperty(String key) {
  return (String) this.properties.get(key);
}
public Long getLongProperty(String key) {
  return (Long) this.properties.get(key);
}
```

This will make more sense as we move into further examining the *Esper Processing Language* (EPL), which begins in earnest in section 8.5. Let's first develop an understanding of how you create and register EPL statements.

8.4.2 Defining and registering query statements

EPL is an SQL-like language used for querying the inbound event streams. The founder of Esper likes to state that using EPL is almost like working with a database turned upside-down—instead of using the query language to search against existing records in a database, with Esper you register the queries within the Esper engine, and inbound streams of data are then applied against the defined queries [Bernhardt].

NOTE While we'll explore the language in some detail in section 8.5, a comprehensive look is beyond the scope of this book. In addition, I'll assume you have some familiarity with SQL, which, like XML, seems to be a fairly ubiquitous skill for most Java developers and architects.

At a general level, you use EPL to define patterns on which to analyze the incoming streams. Unlike SQL, however, some unique time- and aggregation-specific extensions are available to help you perform queries such as, "Return the average total price of all orders received within the last 30 minutes continuously updated as orders appear" or "Return a list of orders where a shipment confirmation by the shipping vendor has not been provided within 12 hours." You can get specific in the types of notifications you'd like to receive. When matching results are found, they can be published to a registered listener, to a subscriber class, or "pulled" from the Esper engine, as we discuss next.

8.4.3 Specifying listeners or subscribers

In conventional database programming, the initiation of a query is performed on demand, or in a pull-style fashion, triggered by some application rules or logic. In Esper, the model is quite different: data is streamed in a continuous fashion. In this respect, it has more characteristics of conventional GUI-style development, where listeners are defined for the various window widgets, such as a button. When an action is detected, the associated listener will perform some function. In Esper, a listener can be defined in a similar fashion and will receive notification when an event of interest arrives. In Esper, the `addListener` or `removeListener` method of the `EPStatement` object is used to associate a listener with a specific EPL statement. The results are then delivered to an Esper `EventBean`, which contains methods for accessing the details of the notification.

As an alternative approach, a subscriber object can be used. It works in a somewhat similar fashion: using the `EPStatement.setSubscriber` method, you specify a class with an update method whose signature matches the results expected. For example, if your query returned a count, an `update` method with a `long` type parameter signature would be used. In this chapter's examples, this will be the style we use primarily. Why? One advantage to the subscriber approach is that, because you're specifically creating an `update` method with a signature that matches the query output, it's more efficient than using the listener-style approach, which must marshal the results into the more generic `EventBean` object. Because of this performance benefit, the recommended approach by the Esper team is to use subscribers. The only drawback to using subscribers is that only a single one can be registered per statement, whereas multiple listeners can be set up.

Esper also provides what it refers to as a "pull-API." This method enables you to retrieve query results in an on-demand fashion rather than having the results pushed to a listener or subscriber. Using this approach, an `iterator` is returned that allows you to scroll through any queued results. This solution may be appealing in circumstances where you only infrequently need to receive the information returned by Esper (both thread- and non-thread-safe methods are available).

8.4.4 Configuration options

In general, Esper requires few (technically none) configuration options. As a matter of practice, you'll find that, at a minimum, you'll want to use the event alias feature to simplify your EPL statements. For example, if you have an event object class of `com.mycompany.esper.MyEventClass`, by setting up an alias you can avoid having to specify the full package name when referring to the object in EPL statements. For example, instead of

```
select * from com.mycompany.esper.MyEventClass
```

you can use the shortcut

```
select * from MyEvent
```

The alias can be defined either programmatically, in the form of

```
Configuration configuration = new Configuration();
configuration.addEventTypeAlias("MyEvent",
  "com.mycompany.esper.MyEventClass");
```

or, you can define the alias in an XML file as

```
<esper-configuration
  xmlns:xsi="http://www.w3.org/2001/XMLSchema-instance"
  xmlns="http://www.espertech.com/schema/esper">
  <event-type alias="MyEvent" class="com.mycompany.esper.MyEventClass" >
</esper-configuration>
```

You can load the XML file using the `Configuration.configure` method, which accepts a `URL`, `File`, or `String` parameter. A variety of other configuration options pertain to implementing caching behavior, declaring variables automatically, and configuring JDBC settings for pulling data from a remote database. We'll delve deeper into several of these as we work through our examples.

Now let's drill down into the details of the Esper Processing Language (EPL). Using EPL, you define the rules for how to process the inbound streams, thus constituting the most important aspect in using the product.

8.5 EPL basics

I've briefly alluded to the fact that the EPL language shares many of the same constructs as the SQL used in popular relational databases like Oracle or MySQL. The decision to pattern EPL on SQL has obviously helped lessen the learning curve for users of Esper. The beauty of this approach is even more obvious when you consider that you can then mix native EPL statements with normal SQL via JDBC. This means you can pull information from event stream objects, which can be just standard Java-Bean-compliant classes (with a few exceptions). You can also retrieve information directly from a relational database. Rather than attempt to cover all of the language constructs, we'll instead focus on the most commonly used statements and highlight areas where EPL differs significantly from standard SQL. We'll begin by looking at the EPL constructs related to querying.

8.5.1 Querying events

The `select` clause in Esper closely mirrors that of standard SQL. However, instead of specifying tables in which to pull data, Esper event objects are used. Esper will determine, via reflection (or a similar means for `Map` or XML-based events), the properties or "columns" that can be derived. In listing 8.1 we presented a simple JavaBean, `ProcessEvent`, that will be used to capture process instance events from jBPM. As you recall, it had four properties: `processName`, `processVersion`, `processInstanceId`, and `state` (we subsequently added some properties, which we'll leave off for now to keep things simple). As with standard SQL, you can specify a wildcard character (*) in lieu of providing a list of all of the event properties. So the following two phrases are equivalent:

```
a) select s.processName, s.processVersion,
    s.processInstanceId, s.state
   from ProcessEvent as s
   // comment example
b) select * from ProcessEvent
```

Notice in the first example we created an alias for the ProcessEvent object in the from clause as s, and subsequently prefixed the properties with that alias (the as could have been dropped as well, as is customary with many SQL dialects). The alias becomes necessary when joining two or more tables that share the same property name in order to avoid column ambiguity. Comments follow normal Java coding conventions when used inline with EPL statements.

One interesting deviation from standard SQL is EPL's ability to filter event streams in the from clause of the SQL statement. For example, the state property for ProcessEvent has a value of 1 to indicate a new process instance was created, or 2 to indicate it has ended. If we're just interested in start process instance events, we could use this:

```
select * from ProcessEvent(start=1)
```

Indexed or mapped properties can be referenced as well, using a dot notation or key lookup. For instance, in section 8.4.1 we discussed introducing a properties variable to capture the process variables associated with a given jBPM process instance. I recommended using specific JavaBean methods such as getStringProperty since different property types are possible. So let's assume a String property of customerType is used within a jBPM process to indicate whether a customer is premium or regular. The following EPL select would filter only those events where customerType is premium:

```
select * from ProcessEvent(stringProperty('customerType') = 'premium')
```

You can also combine multiple and/or type statements by including those operators (i.e., stringProperty('customerType') = 'premium' and state=2). In addition, you can also use filter ranges, such as

```
select *
 from ProcessEvent(doubleProperty('totalPrice') in [1000:5000])
```

This code would capture events where the jBPM process variable totalPrice is between 1000 and 5000 (complete examples are provided in the JUnit Esper tests that accompany this chapter). Using filters is just a shortcut for adding a conventional where clause to your EPL statement. For example, the following two are equivalent:

```
a) select * from ProcessEvent(start=1)
// is equivalent to
b) select * from ProcessEvent where start = 1
```

Since we've been moving through these examples at a fairly brisk pace, let's create a complete example so that you get an idea of what's involved in using Esper. In this example, we'll use a subscriber object to receive the result output from Esper, and demonstrate the functionality using a simple JUnit test case. The steps involved in this example are

1. Create the event object.
2. Create a statement registration and subscription receiver class.
3. Create a JUnit test class.

We've already demonstrated an event object class called `ProcessEvent` (shown in listing 8.1), which represents jBPM create, suspend, and end process instance events. We'll use that for this example, so we can move on to discussing the remaining two steps.

CREATING A STATEMENT REGISTRATION AND SUBSCRIPTION RECEIVER CLASS

To keep things simple, we'll create a single class for registering our EPL statements used by the Esper engine. We'll use an inner class to capture the subscription events that result from any matching hits. Listing 8.2 contains the code for this class, called `ProcessStartEnd` (the code is included in the source code accompanying the book).

Listing 8.2 `ProcessStartEnd` statement registration and subscriber class

```
// imports and package not shown
public class ProcessStartEnd  {

  EPServiceProvider epService = null;                          ❶
  private EPStatement eps;

  private final static String EXAMPLE_SELECTED=                ❷
    "select * from ProcessEvent(state=2)";

  public void register(EPServiceProvider service) {            ❸
    this.epService = service;
    init();
  }

  private void init() {
    eps = epService.getEPAdministrator().createEPL(EXAMPLE_SELECTED);   ❹
    ExampleSelect exampleSelect = new ExampleSelect();
    eps.setSubscriber(exampleSelect);                          ❺
  }

  protected class ExampleSelect {                              ❻
    public void update(ProcessEvent event) {
      System.out.println("\n*** New Event Arrived ***");
      System.out.println("  processName: " + event.getProcessName());
      System.out.println("  procInstId: " + event.getProcessInstanceId());
    }
  }
}
```

The `EPServiceProvider` class ❶, an instance of which is passed as a parameter to the `register` method ❸, registers, via the `createEPL` method ❹, the EPL statement that has been defined in ❷. The inner class, `ExampleSelect` ❺, is then specified as a subscriber ❻ to receive any query results returned by the Esper engine. Thus, what we've created is a single class that's used to both register the EPL statements into the Esper engine and receive, via the inner class, any corresponding results. This is a convenient solution, since only a single subscriber can be configured for a given EPL statement. If we wanted, we could add statements and inner-class subscribers.

The next step is to create the JUnit test that will invoke the register method of `ProcessStartEnd` and populate and simulate some inbound events.

CREATING A JUNIT TEST CLASS

Our JUnit test class (listing 8.3) will instantiate an instance of `ProcessStartEnd`, invoke its `register` method to set up the query statement, and then publish some events to the Esper engine to simulate those arriving from a jBPM instance.

Listing 8.3 JUnit test case which simulates inbound events

```
// imports and package not shown
public class EsperTest841 extends TestCase {
  private EPServiceProvider epService;
  ProcessStartEnd statements = new ProcessStartEnd();

  public void setUp() {
    Configuration configuration = new Configuration();        // Instantiates Esper engine
    configuration.addEventTypeAlias("ProcessEvent",
    ProcessEvent.class.getName());
    epService = EPServiceProviderManager.getProvider("EsperTest",
       configuration);
    statements.register(epService);          // Registers EPL statements
  }

  public void testBasic() throws InterruptedException {

    epService.getEPRuntime().sendEvent(                           // Generates process events
       new ProcessEvent("PurchaseOrder", (long) 1.0, 1, 1, null));
    epService.getEPRuntime().sendEvent(
       new ProcessEvent("PurchaseOrder", (long) 1.0, 2, 1, null));
    epService.getEPRuntime().sendEvent(
       new ProcessEvent("PurchaseOrder", (long) 1.0, 3, 1, null));
    Thread.sleep(3000);

    epService.getEPRuntime().sendEvent(
       new ProcessEvent("PurchaseOrder", (long) 1.0, 1, 2, null));
    epService.getEPRuntime().sendEvent(
       new ProcessEvent("SalesOrder", (long) 1.0, 2, 2, null));
    Thread.sleep(10000);
    epService.getEPRuntime().sendEvent(
       new ProcessEvent("PurchaseOrder", (long) 1.0, 3, 2, null));

    assertEquals("Total events should be 6",                     // 1
      epService.getEPRuntime().getNumEventsReceived(), 6);
  }
}
```

When run, the JUnit class will publish a total of six events to the Esper engine ❶. What this test doesn't confirm is whether the defined query and select statement was actually fired. The output to the console, however, will display output such as

```
*** New Event Arrived ***
  processName: SalesOrder
  processInstanceId: 2

*** New Event Arrived ***
```

```
processName: PurchaseOrder
processInstanceId: 3
```

Confirming that these notification results were fired requires a bit more effort, as the Esper runtime itself (`EPRuntime`) doesn't provide such metrics. Retrieving a direct handle to the subscriber class is also not easily possible from within the JUnit test class (it would require some significant refactoring). One straightforward way of achieving this is to create an Esper variable and use it to capture the count of the results produced by Esper. This is the topic of our next section.

This exercise demonstrated how to register EPL statements in Esper, how to set up a subscriber class (in our example, an inner class) to receive output for events that match the EPL criteria, and how to initiate the Esper engine and test using JUnit.

NOTE Esper supports many of the standard query-related SQL keywords and features such as `group by`, `having`, `order by`, and subqueries. You can see the official reference documentation for more thorough coverage of these topics.

8.5.2 Using variables

An Esper variable is a single runtime value that can be referenced using the `EPRuntime`. Why would you consider using one? Well, one reason is for what we have cited already—we want to capture some information returned from a subscriber or listener objects to the `EPRuntime` to make it accessible to other classes. Perhaps a more common use is that a variable itself can be referenced directly in an EPL statement. Using this approach gives you greater runtime flexibility without requiring any code changes. We'll illustrate both uses.

VARIABLE EXAMPLE FOR A RUNNING COUNT OF SUBSCRIBER CALLS

You can create variables in one of four ways:

- Using EPL statements such as
  `create variable string varname = <somevalue or null>`
- Using an `on…set` clause such as
  `on ProcessEvent set varname = <somevalue>`
- Through the API using `EPStatementObjectModel`'s `setCreateVariable`
- Through configuration using the `Configuration.addVariable` method

Picking up from the example in the previous section, we'll use the `Configuration` method for creating our `counter` variable, which we'll then use to enhance our JUnit test created in listing 8.3.

To create the `counter` variable and increment it for each call made, a handle to the `EPServiceProvider` is necessary from within the subscriber inner class, `ExampleSelect` (listing 8.2). This is because we're using `EPServiceProvider` to retrieve the `EPAdministrator` by which the `Configuration.addVariable` method can be called. Thus, we modified the inner class to include a constructor that receives an `EPService` instance (you may recall the JUnit test class instantiated this upon startup, and passed it to the ExampleSelect's parent object, ProcessStartEnd). Listing 8.4 shows the updated inner class from the original ProcessStartEnd shown in listing 8.2.

Listing 8.4 Updated inner class with update that increments variable counter

```
protected class ExampleSelect {
  private int counter = 0;
  private EPServiceProvider epService;

  public ExampleSelect (EPServiceProvider epService) {        // 1 Contains constructor
    this.epService = epService;
    epService.getEPAdministrator().getConfiguration().        // 2 Adds counter variable to instance
     addVariable("counter", Integer.class, 0);
  }

  public void update(ProcessEvent event) {
    System.out.println("\n*** New Event Arrived ***");
    System.out.println("   processName: " + event.getProcessName());
    System.out.println("   processInstanceId: "
      + event.getProcessInstanceId());
    epService.getEPRuntime().                                 // 3 Sets counter variable
      setVariableValue("counter", Integer.valueOf(++counter));
    }
  }
```

The ExampleSelect constructor receives the EPServiceProvider ❶, and the getEPAdministrator method is then used to retrieve the Configuration instance associated with this Esper instance. The Configuration.addVariable method then adds the new variable counter into the existing Esper runtime configuration ❷. When the update method is invoked and Esper returns a query result, the variable is incremented by 1. The only change required by the parent class ProcessStartEnd (listing 8.2) is to include the EPServiceProvider when creating the inner class:

```
ExampleSelect exampleSelect = this.new ExampleSelect(epService);
```

We can now enhance the JUnit test class (listing 8.3) by using the counter variable ❸ in a new assertion test to verify that the subscriber inner class ExampleSelect was called the anticipated number of times:

```
assertEquals("Counter should be 3",
  epService.getEPRuntime().getVariableValue("counter"), 3);
```

In this brief example, we demonstrated how to create a variable, set it, and then use the value within a JUnit test to verify the anticipated result was achieved. This greatly improved the preciseness of the JUnit test we first created in listing 8.3. Let's now look at how a variable can be used within EPL statements.

USING A VARIABLE IN EPL STATEMENT(S)

In this example, instead of hard-coding the ProcessEvent(state=2) as we did in the example shown in listing 8.2, we'll reference a variable as the expression value. The variable created will be called EVENT_STARTED; we're using uppercase to follow the naming convention typically used in Java for static final (i.e., constant) fields. The following is a modified setUp method from the JUnit test where the Esper configuration values are defined. It now includes the Configuration.addVariable method to create this new variable:

```
public void setUp() {
  Configuration configuration = new Configuration();
  configuration.addEventTypeAlias("ProcessEvent",
     ProcessEvent.class.getName());
  configuration.addVariable("EVENT_STARTED", Integer.class, 1);
  epService = EPServiceProviderManager.getProvider("EsperTest",
     configuration);
  statements.register(epService);
}
```

The addVariable statement highlighted creates the EVENT_STARTED variable, identifies it as of type Integer, and assigns it a value of 1. Using the variable with an EPL statement is just a matter of referencing it:

```
select * from ProcessEvent where state=EVENT_ENDED
```

As you can see, using variables is a straightforward process and provides flexibility you may find beneficial in your Esper usage. We've demonstrated how variables can be used to store and retrieve values within the Esper engine context, and also how they can be used directly in EPL statements to provide for more dynamic statement definitions.

Up until now, we've created and registered some simple EPL statements that apply filtering to inbound events. You might be thinking, "This is great, but can I do the same thing using my own Java logic?" It's true—we haven't yet touched on the correlation and analytical capabilities that are essential for an ESP engine (such as the ability to detect unusual event patterns that have occurred within a certain period of time). This is where the true power of Esper is apparent, and the ability is provided through what Esper calls *views*.

8.5.3 Understanding views

Views represent one of the most powerful, and most used, features of Esper. Typically, they take the form of a *time window*, which essentially is a time interval that extends into the past. A view can also be non-time related, and instead be tied to the last number of events generated. The concept can best be illustrated by some examples. Let's first consider the scenario in which you're capturing jBPM events from a sales order process and you want to calculate the average price for the last x number of orders placed. In this case, a length window would be used, resulting in a query such as this:

```
select avg(doubleProperty('totalPrice'))
  from ProcessEvent(state=2 and processName='SalesOrder').win:length(3)
  output snapshot every 3 seconds
```

In this example, the average price is computed based on the last three orders placed. Views are defined using a specific namespace, which prefaces the view function requested (that is, win:length(3)). Notice also the use of the output snapshot every

3 seconds clause. This allows you to stabilize the rate at which results are returned, thus streaming them back in a continuous fashion. In this case, an output result is generated every 3 seconds. In the absence of the output clause, the results would only be returned when a new qualifying event arrives (if no qualifying event arrives, no output would be generated).

Let's consider another example. We want to retrieve the total number of orders placed within the last 10 seconds. This query can be defined as

```
private static final String EXAMPLE_VIEW2 = "select size " +
  "from ProcessEvent(state=2 and processName='SalesOrder') " +
.win:time(10 sec).std:size() output snapshot every 3 seconds";
```

Notice how we combine different view types through chaining. In this case, win:time(10 sec).std:size() is chained together to indicate that we want a count of all events within the last 10 seconds. Quite a number of view functions are available, so I encourage you to consult the reference documentation for more details. This ability to provide analytics based on snapshots in time or on the volume of events is a powerful feature.

One final thought before we move on to named windows: you can use an anonymous inner class as well for specifying the subscriber class. This makes your code a bit more concise at the cost of reusability. Here's an example of this approach, which uses an anonymous inner class for the subscriber of the EXAMPLE_VIEW2 statement we discussed a moment ago:

```
eps = epService.getEPAdministrator().createEPL(EXAMPLE_VIEW2);
Object exampleView2 = new Object() {
  public void update(Long avgPrice) {
    System.out.println("Average orders for last 2 seconds: " + avgPrice);
  }
};
eps.setSubscriber(exampleView2);
```

A generic Java object is used as the basis for the inner class, and specifies the single update method whose parameters must match the select criteria of the EPL statement it's associated with. You can also specify an updateRStream method to capture events being removed from a stream, as well as start and end methods to capture the beginning and ending of an event delivery.

When working with select statements as we did in these view examples, the generated output is consumed by a listener or subscriber object. However, there will be times when you want to use the output to act as another input stream, or aggregate results for consumption by other queries. This can be accomplished by using the insert clause to create an altogether new stream, or populate the results into a holding area (what Esper refers to as a *named window*).

Imagine, for example, that you have many different jBPM processes that are firing off events to Esper. Maybe a group of the jBPM processes pertain to HR-related activities, such as a new hire or termination process. Ideally, you'd like to keep a running total of all HR-related process instance activity within a certain period of time, in addition to the normal event processing you're performing. As events arrive for each process instance event, a summary entry could be temporarily stored for use by other `select` statements. This is an example of where inserts—our next topic—come in handy.

8.5.4 Creating new event streams with named windows

EPL has an `insert into` clause that's analogous to SQL, with the exception that in Esper, you're actually creating a new derived event stream and not inserting data into a relational database table. Building on our sales order jBPM process example, let's assume we want to create a new derived stream that contains orders from only `premium` customers (obviously, this is a bit contrived, as we could easily modify any `select` statement to include any `where` filter). The designation of a `premium` or `regular` customer will arrive in the `ProcessEvent` event as a jBPM property called `custType`. Given that, we can create our new event stream by using an EPL such as

```
insert into PremiumOrders
  select * from ProcessEvent(state=2 and
  processName='SalesOrder' and stringProperty('custType') = 'premium')
```

This creates the new stream `PremiumOrders`, which is derived using the same event object structure as `ProcessEvent`, because the wildcard (*) was used for the column definition. This new stream can now be treated like any other event stream, and queried upon using statements such as `select * from PremiumOrders`.

Why would you want to dynamically create new streams using this approach? One possible reason is that it can help simplify creating downstream SQL statements, as you saw when we created `PremiumOrders` (that is, it doesn't have all the baggage associated with the filter clauses). For instance, if our jBPM engine has a multitude of different business processes running in it and they're all generating `ProcessEvents` (listing 8.1), creating the right filters can result in rather long EPL statements. Instead, carving those event streams into more specific ones tailored to the process in which you're interested can help avoid mistakes arising from highly complex EPL statements. Decomposing complex things into more manageable pieces is always beneficial (at least when there's no penalty for doing so).

One of the more intriguing capabilities introduced in the 2.0 release of Esper is the concept of *named windows*. Essentially, a named window represents a shared view on a stream that you can insert, delete, or query against. The process for creating it is straightforward: you use a `create window` clause and specify the column and property structure to be associated with it. When creating a named window, you use view functions to manage the retention policy of the events inserted into the window (with some notable exceptions, which we'll discuss in a moment). Then you can issue inserts against the named window or delete events contained within it. You can also query against it (the primary reason for creating it, after all). So, to recap, you first define your named window using the `create window` clause, and then use `insert` clauses to populate it with data.

To demonstrate the capabilities of named windows, let's create one that captures orders over $100. You may recall that retrieving the price of an order was somewhat tedious, as the value was stored in a jBPM process instance property. When creating this window, we'll simplify the query so that the named window contains only the columns we're interested in sharing. Later, we'll create a statement for querying against this window. The first step is to create the named window:

```
create window HighPricedOrders.win:time(1 hour) as
 select processName, processInstanceId, doubleProperty('totalPrice') as
 price from ProcessEvent
```

This statement creates the named window called `HighPricedOrders`, as well as three property columns: `processName`, `processInstanceId`, and `price` (an alias was used to create this property). The view specification `win:time(1 hour)` instructs the window to actively remove any events that are older than one hour. The ability for multiple statements to then access the events stored in this window is what distinguishes a named window from a normal event stream.

NOTE These examples can all be run using the JUnit test cases provided with the source code for this chapter.

Now that the named window has been created, you can add events to it with an `insert` statement. In our scenario, we use this:

```
insert into HighPricedOrders(processName, processInstanceId, price)
  select processName, processInstanceId, doubleProperty('totalPrice')
  from ProcessEvent(state=2 and processName='SalesOrder' and
   doubleProperty('totalPrice') > 100)
```

As you can see, this statement will insert events when a process instance is completed (`state=2`). The statement has a conditional that matches only events where the process name is `SalesOrder` and where the `totalPrice` process variable is greater than `100`. Notice that we specified the specific columns in which to insert the data—this is consistent with SQL standards. Any matching events will be preserved in the named window for a one-hour period. Lastly, we can query against the named window just as we would against any standard event stream:

```
select processName, processInstanceId, price from HighPricedOrders
```

Since this is a named window, we can also create multiple queries against it. For instance, to get an overall average order amount, we could add this query:

```
select avg(price) from HighPricedOrders
```

This query will generate a notification event with the average price returned every time a new event is entered into the `HighPricedOrders` named window. Using named windows, you can create buckets of events that can be used by multiple other event streams. These buckets will retain their event entries until they fall outside the view's retention criteria. In your own organization, can you envision scenarios where this capability would be useful?

As a final note on this topic, you can optionally create your named window to never expire any events using the view `win:keepall()`. You should then periodically purge the events through an `on event` or `on pattern` statement that includes a `delete from` clause. We'll discuss the use of `on pattern` statements in the next section.

8.6 Advanced Esper

The capabilities of Esper we've discussed so far give you a good taste of using the product and how it can be used in conjunction with products like jBPM to analyze events that are emitted from services such as BPM. Up to this point, however, we've kept things simple, and we've used only basic SQL-style constructs for creating EPL statements. Although we've covered concepts such as views and named windows, we haven't used advanced correlation capabilities, such as how to analyze whether event B was first followed by event A, or how to detect any unexpected latency between receiving those events. By the time you've finished reading this section, you'll know the answers to such questions and be fully prepared to roll out Esper in your enterprise. You'll also learn how to retrieve data from a relational database via JDBC and create custom functions to add new EPL extensions. Let's begin by looking at EPL functions.

8.6.1 Extending with functions

We've already used one of the built-in EPL functions, `avg`, which returns the average of the values provided in the expression enclosed within parentheses. There are several such built-in functions, with many similar to those available in SQL, such as `sum`, `count`, `min`, and `max`. There are also several evaluation-based functions, such as `case`, `cast`, and `coalesce`. Rather than cover all of these, many of which you may be already familiar with (or can learn more about in the reference documentation), I'll cover some that are unique to Esper as it relates to ESP—namely, `prev`, `instanceof`, and Java static methods (standard Java libraries or user-defined functions).

THE PREV FUNCTION

The previous function (`prev`) returns the value of a previous event. It accepts two parameters:

- The n*th* previous event in the order defined in the time window
- The property name or column whose value you're evaluating

At first, it may have been unclear why or how to use this function. One of the most interesting ways of using `prev` is in conjunction with a sorted window. The sorted window is one of the available view functions (see an overview in section 8.5.3). The `sort` function will preserve a specified number of events (parameter 3), sorted by a specific property (parameter 1), in ascending or descending order (parameter 2). The event window will therefore not exceed the size specified as the third parameter. By using the `prev` function with a sorted window, you can selectively return, for example, the last two highest-priced orders out of the previous ten for the `ProcessEvents` associated with a SalesOrder process (continuing our jBPM sales order example). We could achieve this using the EPL

```
select max(doubleProperty('totalPrice')) as price1,
prev(1,doubleProperty('totalPrice')) as price2
  from ProcessEvent(state=2 and processName='SalesOrder')
  .ext:sort(doubleProperty('totalPrice'), true, 10)
```

The first column property value, assigned an alias of price1, uses the max function to return the maximum totalPrice for the up to ten events that may exist in this view (the ext:sort window view specification, as its third parameter, specifies the maximum of events preserved at any given time). The second column property, given an alias of price2, uses the prev function to return the next highest price value (which is the first previous event to the max function). Table 8.1 shows a series of orders as they arrive, and the corresponding max and prev function values given the preceding EPL.

Table 8.1 Example of the prev function

ProcessEvent OrderPrice	Property price1 value	Property price2 value
$125.12	$125.12	Null
$50.45	$125.12	$50.45
$1200.87	$1200.87	$125.12
$73.34	$1200.87	$125.12
$250.23	$1200.87	$250.23
$12.05	$1200.87	$250.23

As you can see, the price1 property, which represents the max value, always produces the highest sale price. In addition, the prev function works as anticipated for the price2 property and returns the next highest sale price. Next, let's look at the EPL's instanceOf function.

THE INSTANCEOF FUNCTION

Much like the Java method of a similar name, the instanceof function evaluates a given property (parameter #1) and returns a boolean value to indicate whether the property type belongs to the Java class provided (parameter #2). This function is often used with a case or cast function. In section 8.3, we discussed managing jBPM process variables passed as part of ProcessEvent by creating special type-specific methods such as getStringProperty(String key). Instead of creating these getter methods for each of the possible jBPM variable types, we could create a single method called getProperty(Object obj) that's used in the EPL, and then use the instanceof function with a cast to publish the data to the appropriate subscriber object method. Let me illustrate. First, the ProcessEvent class (listing 8.1), which is the event object, was modified to include a generic getProperty method:

```
public Object getProperty(String key) {
  return (Object) this.properties.get(key);
}
```

Then, in the ProcessStartEnd class (listing 8.2), which is used to define and invoke the EPL statements and their associated subscribe objects, we add the following EPL definition:

```
private static final String EXAMPLE_FUNC4 =
  "select case " +
  "when instanceof(property('totalPrice'), java.lang.Double) " +
    "then cast(property('totalPrice'), double) " +
  "end " +
  "from ProcessEvent(state=2 and processName='SalesOrder')";
```

In this example, we're using the instanceof function to evaluate the object returned from the ProcessEvent.getProperty method call (property('totalPrice')) to determine whether it's of type Double. This, in turn, is wrapped within a case statement, so that if it evaluates to true, the cast function expression is performed. In this case, the cast simply converts the Double to a primitive double type. The sole property returned from this EPL is the total price returned as a double. So a new inner class used to subscribe to this EPL is defined as

```
EPStatement eps = epService.getEPAdministrator().createEPL(EXAMPLE_FUNC4);
Object exampleView4 = new Object() {
  public void update(double price) {
    System.out.println("Example 4 - Price is: " + price);
  }
 };
 eps.setSubscriber(exampleView4);
```

When a matching event occurs, the inner class should then print out the message found in the update method of that class. Notice that the update method accepts a double; we'd cast the output to that type in the EPL statement. The ability to use the instanceof function to cast column property types can be useful in cases where Esper is receiving generic event objects. Such might be the case where you have set up a web service to receive the inbound events, and for simplicity or compatibility reasons, you make all of the inbound event properties simple String values.

In addition to using the 20 or so single-row or aggregate functions, you can use any Java class that has a public static method. Let's explore further this capability.

USER-DEFINED FUNCTIONS

The ability to use any Java class that has a public static method as a user-defined function (UDF) opens up all sort of possibilities. Immediately coming to mind are functions that perform transformations or lookups, but you're obviously not limited to these areas. Continuing the example from the previous section, say we want to round the total price amount associated with ProcessEvent. Since the price arrives as a Java Double, the java.lang.Math round function can be used as a UDF, since it's a static method that accepts as a parameter a Double. Here's a simple EPL illustration of this in practice:

```
select Math.round(doubleProperty('totalPrice'))
  from ProcessEvent(state=2 and processName='SalesOrder')
```

As you can see, the full package specification wasn't necessary, as Esper automatically imports the following: `java.lang.*, java.math.*, java.text.*, java.util.*`.

Let's see how easy it is to create our own UDF. Assume for this example that we're receiving in our `ProcessEvent` event object a jBPM parameter value that identifies the customer who placed an order. The jBPM process variable is called `custId`. We can then create a UDF that simulates a lookup that will take the `custId` integer as its single parameter and return the actual customer name (in this case, Acme Corporation). Here's our simple lookup class:

```
package opensoa851.esper.jbpm.functions;
public class HelperFunctions {
 public static String lookupCustomer(Integer custId) {
   switch(custId) {
     case 100: return "Acme";
     case 101: return "Umbrella Corporation";
     case 102: return "Cybergen Inc";
     case 103: return "BioObjects, Inc";
     case 104: return "Idalica, Corp";
     case 105: return "Trilogy Corp";
   }
   return "Mysale.com";
 }
}
```

UDF method that returns String

As you can see, the class has one declared public static method, `lookupCustomer`. Using this UDF in an EPL is equally straightforward:

```
select integerProperty('custId'),
  opensoa851.esper.jbpm.functions.HelperFunctions.lookupCustomer
  (integerProperty('custId')) from ProcessEvent(state=2 and
    processName='SalesOrder')
```

As you can see, having to specify the full package is a bit tedious. You can avoid having to do this by automatically importing the package using the Esper configuration. For example, if using an XML configuration, you could use this:

```
<auto-import import-name="opensoa851.esper.jbpm.functions.*"/>
```

Or you could use the `Configuration` class (you may recall this class from section 8.4.4) via the API:

```
Configuration configuration = new Configuration();
configuration.addImport("opensoa851.esper.jbpm.functions.*");
```

Once imported, you can then remove the package from your EPL statement:

```
select integerProperty('custId'),
 HelperFunctions.lookupCustomer(integerProperty('custId')) from
 ProcessEvent(state=2 and processName='SalesOrder')
```

NOTE I stated earlier that, when using standard Java static methods that belong to `java.lang.Math` and similar classes, these are automatically imported. While this is true, when you do specifically import your own classes, it apparently overrides this standard behavior, and you must then import them when needed as well. I presume this is a bug in the 2.0 release.

As you can see, incorporating your own custom functions in your EPL is straightforward and unlocks a world of possibilities.

In the beginning of this section, we alluded to Esper's advanced correlation capabilities, which can be used to analyze the sequence and time of incoming event streams and determine whether they arrive in the anticipated order and duration. I'm referring to a type of advanced view known as *patterns*, which we explore next.

8.6.2 Applying event patterns

Event patterns, as the name suggests, allow you to define, via expressions, various matching rules that can be applied to incoming events. For example, you can use what are referred to as temporal operators that compare inbound events to see whether they arrive in the anticipated order. Patterns enable you to have very fine-grained control over how events are evaluated. Interestingly, patterns can be used in an EPL select or in a stand-alone fashion, whereby a listener can be registered to receive the event output.

In its most basic form, a pattern can be defined as just a single event. Consider this EPL, which creates a simple pattern definition specifying only jBPM process events that have ended (`state=2`) and whose process name is equal to `SalesOrder`:

```
String EXAMPLE_PATTERN1 = "process=ProcessEvent(state=2 and
  processName='SalesOrder')";
```

What distinguishes this from a normal EPL select is that this pattern will fire only once, regardless of how many inbound events match the specified filter criteria. Also, when registering a pattern, we use the `createPattern` method of `EPAdministrator` instead of `createEPL`. This is illustrated in the following fragment, which also uses an anonymous inner class that implements the `UpdateListener` interface (that is, we're using the listener instead of a subscriber class, unlike previous examples):

```
EPStatement  eps =
  epService.getEPAdministrator().createPattern(EXAMPLE_PATTERN1);
eps.addListener(new UpdateListener () {
  public void update(EventBean[] newEvents, EventBean[] oldEvents) {
     System.out.println("Listener for Single Pattern: " +
      ((ProcessEvent)newEvents[0].get("process")).getProcessInstanceId());
     }
   });
}
```

When run, if one or more qualifying events are matched, a single `println` message will be displayed to the console. Since a listener was used in this example, a tag called `process` was used to assign the pattern output (this was defined when the EPL assigned `EXAMPLE_PATTERN1` was created). In turn, this tag was used to extract the event from the EventBean using its get method, which accepts as its parameter a String value representing the tag name. The every operation loosely mimics the standard EPL select statement, and is used to manage repetition. The previous EPL statement, now modified to include every, will produce an output for each qualifying event:

```
every(process=ProcessEvent(state=2, processName='SalesOrder'))
```

Notice here that the and was removed from the filter expression and replaced by a comma— this is a convenience shortcut. The every clause causes the start of a new pattern expression and listens for new events that match the filter. One of the most useful aspects of this is that you can create an expression that checks for the occurrence and order of multiple events, which may be of different event object types. For example, if event B is always supposed to follow event A, you can define a pattern such as every (A -> B) that will fire once B arrives in order after A. In addition, you can devise fairly elaborate combinations when you use the every statement in conjunction with pattern timers. In our example, we could use it to flag any occurrences where the instance end event wasn't completed within a certain period of time in relation to when the process was started. Such a check would undoubtedly be useful for managing compliance with service-level agreements or in proactive detection of problems.

Before we delve into an example of this capability, let's first take a closer look at what Esper calls *pattern guards.* A pattern guard is a where condition applied through a custom function. Esper comes with three timer-based guards: timer:within, timer:interval, and timer:at (as with regular functions, you can also create your own). Let's look at the three timer-based guards provided by Esper in more detail.

TIMER:WITHIN GUARD

The timer:within guard is similar to a stopwatch in function. If the event associated with the timer fires within the timer period provided, true is returned, and false otherwise. What's an example of where this might be useful? Building on the scenario we've used so far, consider a situation where, as part of a fraud-detection initiative, you want to flag any orders placed by the same customer that arrive within a few minutes of each other. Perhaps such an occurrence would be unusual, and indicate that someone has possibly compromised the customer account. Using our ProcessEvent event object, the following EPL pattern will determine whether consecutive orders were placed by the same customer within 5 seconds of each other (I chose 5 seconds since it's more convenient for testing):

```
(
  every
(oldOrder=ProcessEvent(state=1, processName='SalesOrder'))
->
  every
   (newOrder=ProcessEvent(state=1, processName='SalesOrder',
   newOrder.integerProperty('custId')=
   oldOrder.integerProperty('custId')))
  where timer:within(5 sec)
)
```

Using the parentheses is critical for determining how the clause is evaluated. In pseudo-code, the pattern states, "For every new order placed, check every subsequent order with the same `custId` that occurs within 5 seconds of the previous order." Figure 8.4 demonstrates a scenario of how you'd apply this.

CUST ID	TOTAL PRICE	TIME
100	$25.25	00:00
101	$10.15	00:01
102	$9.54	00:03
100	$75.19	00:04
103	$29.83	00:07
101	$19.62	00:09
104	$38.87	00:10

CustId 101 places 2 orders but are more than 5 secs apart -- no flag.

CustId 100 places 2 orders within 5 seconds. Transaction flagged.

Figure 8.4 Example of `timer:within` guard rule being applied

You can craft many possible combinations of this type of time-based temporal matching, but exercise care to ensure the proper precedence of your phrases.

TIMER:INTERVAL GUARD

The `timer:interval` function will wait the specified period of time and then return `true`. While at first glance this function may appear to have limited utility, it can be useful for helping identify time gaps outside a given boundary. How would this be beneficial? One example related to our jBPM scenario would be to use this ability to identify any process instance that wasn't completed within a certain period of time. For example, continuing with the `SalesOrder` business process, here's how you could identify any instances that hadn't completed within 25 seconds:

```
every ord=ProcessEvent(state=1, processName='SalesOrder')
->
timer:interval(25 sec) and not
  ProcessEvent(state=2, processInstanceId = ord.processInstanceId))
```

In this case, the `timer:interval` clause will trigger an observer at 25 seconds, and if there's no corresponding `ProcessEvent` that has ended `(state=2)` with the matching `processInstanceId`, then an event notification will be triggered. The ability to identify when an event hasn't occurred is in many cases more important than whether an event has occurred. This capability has wide-ranging implications in helping organizations ensure that activities have occurred within a prescribed period.

TIMER:AT GUARD

The `timer:at` function resembles the functionality of the Unix/Linux crontab command. Using it, you can set up specific times for when the statement execution should be invoked. This could be used, for instance, to periodically purge events that have accumulated in a named window (section 8.5.4), or to periodically pull data from a relational database using the JDBC remote connectivity feature, described next.

8.6.3 Using JDBC for remote connectivity

Esper has the ability to query a remote database via JDBC and enables regular SQL statements to be embedded into EPL statements. This can be useful for gleaning reference or historical data that may be present based on some key value in the inbound event. While configuration for simple remote connectivity is straightforward, there are numerous, optional configuration settings that go beyond the scope of this chapter; find out more by checking out the official documentation. Many of these settings pertain to establishing the remote connection or cache settings.

We'll demonstrate a simple example that builds on section 8.6.1's discussion of UDFs. You may recall that we used a UDF to return a customer name based on a `custId` value that was passed to the function—it was a lookup-style routine. Let's see how this can be done using a relational database join, which is probably a more intuitive method for achieving this result. There are two main steps in accomplishing this:

1. Adding a data source reference in Esper's configuration
2. Adding the embedded SQL into your EPL statements

ADDING A DATASOURCE REFERENCE TO THE ESPER CONFIGURATION

Since you are connecting with a remote JDBC database, you must tell Esper how to connect to it. Esper provides a few options for doing this, which are documented in the official documentation. I'll demonstrate one approach using `java.sql.DriverManager`. Given the number of possible property settings, I suggest using the Esper XML-based configuration instead of the Java API approach. In the sample code for this section, I've shown how to configure a connection to an in-memory Hyperthreaded Structured Query Language Database (HSQLDB) instance. The Esper XML configuration looks like this:

```
<esper-configuration
  xmlns:xsi="http://www.w3.org/2001/XMLSchema-instance"
  xmlns="http://www.espertech.com/schema/esper">

  <database-reference name="mydb">                    <-- Esper database alias
    <drivermanager-connection
        class-name="org.hsqldb.jdbcDriver"            | HSQLDB
        url="jdbc:hsqldb:mem:aname"                   | connection
        user="sa" password=""/>                       |
    <connection-lifecycle value="retain" />           |
    <expiry-time-cache                                | Configuration
        max-age-seconds="60"                          | options
        purge-interval-seconds="120" ref-type="weak" />
  </database-reference>
</esper-configuration>
```

The `@name` attribute of the `database-reference` element defines the alias assigned when referencing this connection from within EPL. The child elements define connectivity parameters and various lifecycle and cache settings. In this case, our in-memory database uses a single table called CUSTOMER, which is created with the following line during the JUnit test code initialization:

```
create table CUSTOMER  (CUST_ID int, CUST_NAME varchar(30));
```

It's then populated with some initial sample records used for purposes of the test. Once the connection configuration is complete, the next step is to use it in an EPL statement.

USING SQL CALLS IN EPL

To combine an event stream with data from a relational source, you must specify the `sql` keyword followed by the database alias you defined, and then include the SQL phase within double brackets. In our example, let's assume we want to look up the customer name based on a `custId` that was provided. We could do this using

```
select integerProperty('custId') as custId, CUST_NAME
  from ProcessEvent(state=1 and processName='SalesOrder'),
  sql:mydb[\" select CUST_NAME from CUSTOMER where
          CUST_ID=${integerProperty('custId') \"]
```

In most respects, this code works like a normal join statement, with the exception that, rather than specifying an event object in which to join, you use the Esper `sql` keyword clause. Notice that in the `sql` clause you can reference properties from the joined event stream using the `${<variable>}` notation—in this case, we're resolving the value returned by `integerProperty('custId')`. The `select` statement then outputs the `custId` derived from the `ProcessEvent` event stream along with the joined `CUST_NAME` value that came from the HSQLDB CUSTOMER table. Obviously, this capability is useful for performing reference lookups.

Other interesting possibilities exist when using the SQL integration. Support for stored procedures is also available, so you can use it in conjunction with an EPL pattern to automatically pull data periodically from a relational database. The stored procedure would identify all new records that have accumulated since the previous call and return them as output, while flagging them so as to not be included in subsequent calls. The output of the EPL with the SQL join can be inserted into a new event stream or into a named window. In this fashion, you're using an existing relational database as an event publisher (albeit not real time, but probably sufficient for many situations).

The next topic we'll focus on is how to service enable Esper using SOAP-based web services.

8.7 Service enabling Esper

Earlier in this chapter I pointed out that Esper is more akin to an ESP "engine" as opposed to a full-fledged end-to-end solution. In a way this is a blessing, because the lightweight nature of it allows you to easily embed the solution into a variety of scenarios. Further, Esper's main attraction is its correlation engine and rule-processing language—peripheral enhancements may detract from this focus. Given that, the user community clamored for a more straightforward way for publishing to the Esper engine, so the folks behind Esper created a companion product called EsperIO that was released along with the 1.4 version. EsperIO provides a prebuilt configuration for receiving events via an input adapter to JMS along with the ability to optionally publish results to JMS using an output adapter.

If you're a pure Java show and don't anticipate receiving events from non-Java systems or applications, this could be an attractive and easy-to-configure option. For enterprise users, the Java-only nature of JMS is likely going to be an impediment (granted, there are some bridges available from .NET to JMS, for example). A more platform- and protocol-neutral approach based on SOAP-based web services would probably be more appealing. Fortunately, as you saw in chapters 3 and 4, SCA-based Apache Tuscany enables you to readily expose multilanguage components through a variety of protocols, including SOAP and JMS. As it turns out, exposing Esper through SCA is easy to do, and once you accomplish that, you'll have a reusable framework for supporting any multitude of inbound events. The steps involved are

1. Creating a framework and components
2. Creating the Esper service and session manager
3. Developing the SCA composition
4. Testing the web service using the soapUI testing tool

8.7.1 Creating a framework and components

Given the diversity of events that Esper will likely need to consume in most environments, it's obvious that attempting to define a single event schema or canonical representation would be challenging. More importantly, trying to generalize the events strips them of their ability to be easily self-describing. Thus, the approach I recommend is to recognize that each domain may have its own set of event objects (and related schemas). We've already been using this approach in our examples, where our `ProcessEvent` event object is tailored to jBPM process instances. Continuing with this approach, let's devise a framework that allows a single instance of Esper to be used and exposed through SOAP-based web services that are semantically tailored as needed. An overview of the framework can be seen in figure 8.5.

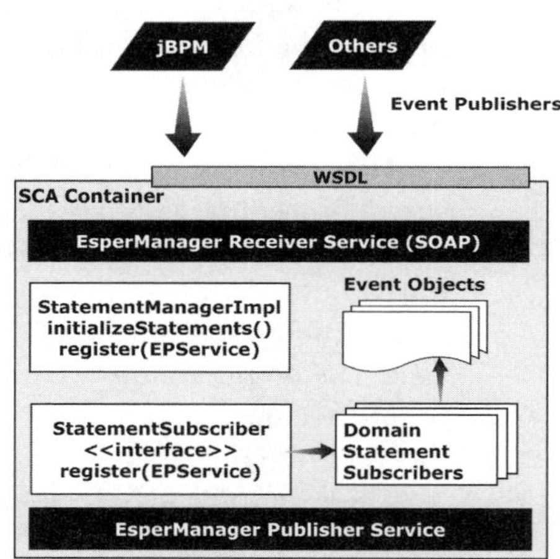

Figure 8.5 The Esper web service framework

The framework is simple in design. When you determine that a new event type needs to be sent to Esper, you create a specific `StatementSubscriber`. This implementation class must implement the `register` method, which takes as its only parameter `EPServiceProvider`. The `register` method is then responsible for registering the EPL statements specific to that domain and for creating the appropriate subscriber objects. We've already seen an example of this class with the `ProcessStartEnd` object we displayed in listing 8.2 (the only change to this class is to implement `StatementSubscriber`).

NOTE The framework I'm describing is found in its entirety in the source code available for this section.

The `StatementManagerImpl` class is where we register individual `StatementSubscriber` implementations. Listing 8.5 contains an example captured from the sample code for this section (the imports and package definition has been omitted for brevity).

Listing 8.5 `StatementManagerImpl.java`, which registers statement subscribers

```
@Service(StatementManager.class)                    SCA annotations
@Scope("REQUEST")
public class StatementManagerImpl implements StatementManager {

 ArrayList<StatementSubscriber> statements = new
  ArrayList<StatementSubscriber>();
 StatementSubscriber statement;

 public void initializeStatements() {           ❶ Registers statements
  statements.add(new ProcessStartEnd());
 }
                                                     ❷ Invokes register methods
 public void register(EPServiceProvider service) {
  for (Iterator<StatementSubscriber> i = statements.iterator();
     i.hasNext();) {
   statement = i.next();
   System.out.println("*** Registering: " + statement + " ***");
   statement.register(service);
  }
 }
}
```

The purpose of this class is to register all of the EPL statements and associated subscriber objects into the Esper engine. In this case, there's a single registration object called `ProcessStartEnd` ❶. This is where you would add event objects (`StatementSubscriber`) for new domains. Once the `initializeStatements` method is called, it must be followed by a call to the `register` method ❷, which in turn invokes the `register` method associated with each `StatementSubscriber` class that was initialized.

A nice enhancement would be to add JMX tooling to the class so that the registration process could be done on-demand, whereas currently, as you'll see, a restart of the Esper SCA container is necessary. The class currently is invoked only once upon Esper SCA startup.

8.7.2 Esper service and session manager

The `SessionManagerImpl` class, which can be viewed in the sample code, is responsible for calling the `initializeStatements` and `register` methods of `StatementManagerImpl` from listing 8.5. The `SessionManagerImpl` retains a handle to the currently running instance of Esper by way of `EPServiceProvider`. This is accomplished by using SCA's conversational features (see chapter 4 for a refresher). In other words, the `SessionManagerImpl` is responsible for keeping the Esper engine session active.

The main service class, which exposes Esper through SOAP, is called `EsperManagerImpl`. The public methods defined by its interface, `EsperManager`, identify the service operation being exposed by SCA. In this case, we're using SOAP, and the interface will be used to autogenerate the WSDL (of course, you can manually create your WSDL as well, as discussed in chapters 3 and 4). Here's an interface class signature:

```
@Remotable
public interface EsperManager {
  public void sendProcessStartEndEvent(ProcessEvent event);
}
```

As you can see, the `sendProcessStartEndEvent` method, by way of its `ProcessEvent` parameter, is tailored specifically for the event object it's consuming. Each new domain event sent to Esper would require a new service method to be created.

The last main development effort is to create the SCA composite file. This is really a onetime exercise given the nature of this framework.

8.7.3 SCA composite file

The SCA composite file, as discussed in chapter 3, is used to define the components and identify the services that are being made available. Listing 8.6 shows the composite file used for our Esper services.

Listing 8.6 esper.composite SCA composite file

```
<composite
   xmlns="http://www.osoa.org/xmlns/sca/1.0"
   targetNamespace="http://opensoa.book.chapter8"
   xmlns:hw="http://opensoa.book.chapter8"
   name="esper">

   <service name="EsperManagerService" promote="EsperManager">
     <binding.ws uri="http://localhost:8085/EsperManagerService"/>      ❶
   </service>

   <component name="EsperManager">
     <implementation.java class="opensoa.esper.impl.EsperManagerImpl"/>
     <reference name="sessionManager" target="SessionManager"/>         ❷
   </component>

   <component name="SessionManager">
     <implementation.java class="opensoa.esper.impl.SessionManagerImpl"/>
     <property name="configurationFile">esperconf.xml</property>        ❸
     <property name="providerName">EsperManager</property>
     <reference name="statementMgr" target="StatementManager"/>         ❹
   </component>

   <component name="StatementManager">
     <implementation.java
       class="opensoa.esper.impl.StatementManagerImpl"/>
   </component>
</composite>
```

The composite file is fairly minimal in scope. A single service is defined ❶ and made accessible via a web service binding with a WSDL URL of http://localhost:8085/EsperManagerService?wsdl (this was simply derived by adding `?wsdl` to the `binding.ws @uri` attribute). The `EsperManagerService` is defined by promoting the `EsperManager` component. This component in turn contains a reference to `SessionManager` ❷. The `SessionManager` component is responsible for instantiating the Esper engine, and is thus passed, as a property, the location of the Esper XML configuration file to use ❸. It also is responsible for registering the EPL statements and their associated subscription objects ❹ by way of the `StatementManager` component.

The SCA container is started by way of a Java main class called `EsperManagerMain`:

```
public class EsperManagerMain {

  public static void main(String[] args) {
    EsperManagerMain server = new EsperManagerMain();
    server.run();
  }
  public void run() {
    System.out.println("Running");
    SCADomain scaDomain = SCADomain.newInstance("esper.composite");
  }
}
```

The class simply instantiates a new `SCADomain` using the SCA composite file shown in listing 8.6 and, when running, will be listening for incoming service events.

We covered quite a lot here, so let me recap what the steps are to add a new domain event to this framework:

1. Create a new domain event object. This will be used as the container for the inbound event. We demonstrated this earlier when we created the `ProcessEvent` class (listing 8.1).
2. Create a new implementation of `StatementSubscriber`. This class serves two purposes: (a) using it to register EPL statements associated with the new event you're setting up, and (b) creating an anonymous inner class to receive the output generated by the EPL statements as they process the inbound events. The EPL statements you create will reference the event object(s) created in step 1.
3. Add the class created in step 2 to the `StatementManagerImpl` object's `initializeStatements` method. This will enable the class to be properly registered so that it can process the inbound events.
4. Add a new service method in the `EsperManager` and its implementation class `EsperManagerImpl`. This will expose the method as a SOAP operation.
5. Restart SCA.

Obviously, there are improvement opportunities available for this framework. We cited some previously, such as instrumenting the classes for JMX management, but other ideas might include better declarative support using Spring so that Java code changes aren't as necessary (that is, building a plug-in model). Esper can now be integrated using web services. Next, we'll explore how you can test this web service using soapUI.

8.7.4 Testing with soapUI

Once Tuscany is running, the service can be testing using soapUI (a soapUI project is included in this section's sample code). With soapUI, you start a new project by reading in an existing WSDL. It will then interrogate that WSDL and create a sample request you can edit. For example, you could enter the following:

```
<soapenv:Envelope xmlns:soapenv="http://schemas.xmlsoap.org/soap/envelope/"
 xmlns:esp="http://esper.opensoa"
 xmlns:xsd="http://event.jbpm.esper.opensoa/xsd">
  <soapenv:Header/>
  <soapenv:Body>
    <esp:sendProcessStartEndEvent>
      <esp:param0>
        <xsd:processInstanceId>1</xsd:processInstanceId>
        <xsd:processName>SalesOrder</xsd:processName>
        <xsd:processVersion>1</xsd:processVersion>
        <xsd:props>
          <xsd:key>totalPrice</xsd:key>
          <xsd:value>55.43</xsd:value>
        </xsd:props>
        <xsd:state>2</xsd:state>
      </esp:param0>
    </esp:sendProcessStartEndEvent>
  </soapenv:Body>
</soapenv:Envelope>
```

When you click the submit button, the request will then be sent to the Esper service we instantiated previously. You can use soapUI to test a variety of requests, and even develop test suites and cases with the tool (some features are only available in the Enterprise edition, however). It's a useful tool for testing. As a convenience, the sample code also includes an SCA client called `JBPMClientMain` that you can use for submitting test requests.

8.8 Summary

This chapter introduced the principles behind complex event processing and its important role within SOA. A SOA environment, because of its distributed nature, presents some unique challenges insofar as management and monitoring. ESP addresses those concerns by evaluating and analysis events, in real time, that can be generated automatically by SOA services and BPM processes. The ability to detect subtle (or not-so-subtle) changes in the operational, day-to-day workings of your organization is becoming both a regulatory and a competitive requirement. ESP, working in conjunction with BAM for presentation and dissemination, provides powerful operational insights.

Until recently, there were no open source ESP solutions available. Fortunately, that changed with Esper. Esper is an ESP engine that provides comprehensive event correlation, aggregation, and analysis capabilities. Using an SQL-like syntax called EPL, a user can create queries, views, and patterns by which inbound events are evaluated.

Although Esper doesn't offer a web services front-end to its engine, using Apache Tuscany and SCA, we introduced a framework for how this can be accomplished. The combination of SCA, BPM through jBPM, and Esper creates a compelling SOA solution. In the next chapter, we'll turn to Apache Synapse, which is a lightweight ESB that can augment the capabilities we've described so far.

9 Enterprise integration and ESBs

This chapter covers

- Common features of an ESB
- Introducing Apache Synapse
- Service mediation with Synapse

An *enterprise service bus* (ESB) is a strange bird. The term first burst upon the scene in 2002, followed by a flurry of products that proclaimed themselves as ESBs. However, what constitutes an ESB has always been a matter of debate. At a minimum, most would agree that an ESB is an enterprise messaging system that primarily relies on the exchange of XML messages. These messages, in turn, can be intelligently routed and transformed through a decentralized architecture.

The emergence of ESBs has roughly coincided with the increasing standardization of web service and messaging protocols such as Java Messaging System (JMS) and SOAP. Indeed, the initial group of vendors who released ESBs tended to be those who had existing JMS-based middleware offerings, and included the likes of Sonic Software (now Progress) and Fiorano. Soon thereafter, open source ESBs began to appear, with Mule and ServiceMix leading the charge. Later, other open source ESBs emerged, such as Apache Synapse, JBoss ESB, Sun's OpenESB, and Apache Camel (though Camel eschews positioning itself as an ESB).

Clearly, the wide choice of available ESBs, both commercial and open source, is a testimony to their popularity within the enterprise. A need exists that the ESB is fulfilling. However, a debate rages on as to whether an ESB is an essential part of SOA. Let's take a closer look at the relationship between an ESB and SOA.

9.1 The relationship between ESB and SOA

Some view an ESB as merely a temporary stepping-stone that can be used to SOA-enable legacy services or applications. The criticism most often leveled at ESBs is that they're too often positioned as a shortcut for achieving SOA, when in reality they're simply one of several *technology* tools in your SOA arsenal. As Bobby Woolf points out, "An ESB by itself produces no business value. An ESB is a means to an end, not the end itself." He further equates it to electrical wiring, which by itself does nothing, but in tandem with a light produces value [Woolf]. After the initial hype of ESBs simmered down, a general consensus has emerged that Woolf's categorization is likely spot-on.

Treating ESB technology as a SOA enabler doesn't, by any stretch, relegate it to a bit player in the SOA equation. In particular, even if all of your services are exposed in ways consistent with SOA, there likely remains a compelling case for using an ESB. Up until now, we've discussed how to build composite-style services using Apache Tuscany and you've seen how to use those services when building business processes with JBoss jBPM. Throughout the lifecycle of a business process, critical events or milestones occur. Our coverage of Esper, a complex event processor (CEP), described how those events can be consumed and analyzed in real time to spot important business activities or trends. Thus, the previous chapters were primarily internally focused within the enterprise. However, nearly every mid- to large-size organization must support electronic interchange of documents with external partners or customers. In all likelihood, the interfaces with these entities will be across the board, insofar as the protocols (SOAP, POX, CSV files, etc.) and transports (HTTP(s) FTP, sFTP, etc.) being used. This is the real sweet spot for an ESB, as it comes with prebuilt adapters or connectors for these various protocols and transports.

If Apache Tuscany supports protocols such as JMS and SOAP, why not just expose your services directly to your partners using it? Well, it's generally considered unwise to expose such services directly within your intranet because of security reasons. Instead, an ESB container can serve as the front-line service manager within an extranet, thereby shielding your services and other internal electronic assets from direct access. As you'll see in the next chapter, the ESB can also nimbly manage transport switching, so you can use it to receive a service request, say through SOAP-over-HTTPs, and reroute to JMS for internal processing. (JMS is considered a more robust protocol than HTTP because of its facilities for guaranteed delivery, among other factors.) ESBs also support a broad range of transports, something that Tuscany or other frameworks like Spring don't do.

In this first of two chapters on ESB technology, we'll define what it means to be an ESB. Further, we'll identify appropriate and inappropriate uses of the technology.

Lastly, we'll introduce Apache Synapse, which as you'll recall is our ESB of choice for our Open SOA Platform. In the next chapter, we'll explore implementation using Synapse, and you'll see a real-life case study with numerous examples that demonstrate how to integrate it with our other Open SOA Platform products.

Let's get started by examining the history of how ESBs emerged and became such a force in the marketplace. This is relevant as it will help frame our understanding of where the ESB is best utilized.

9.2 Historical foundations of ESB

The heritage of ESBs is derived from *enterprise application integration* (EAI), which emerged nearly 30 years ago. EAI, sometimes known as integration brokers, arose with the advent and adoption of enterprise resource planning (ERP) applications. These big-ticket software packages were intended to run all aspects of an enterprise's business: manufacturing, supply chain management, human resources, and customer relationship management (CRM). Obviously, that's a pretty tall order, and inevitably, some companies chose to mix-and-match ERP software components to achieve a "best-of-breed" solution. Other companies had multiple divisions or organizations, many of which had different solutions in place. Thus arose the need to integrate these disparate systems, and EAI emerged to meet that need.

Vendors such as TIBCO, Vitria, SeeBeyond, webMethods, and IBM all provided EAI-type offerings. Unfortunately, they were highly proprietary and expensive in nature, since few standards existed at the time, and building adapters to the ERP products was a complex undertaking. The solutions themselves, in addition to being costly, were also difficult to implement. According to one report in 2001, average EAI integrations projects took 20 or more months to complete, with a success rate of less than 35 percent [Forrester]. Since the solutions were highly proprietary, skills didn't easily translate from one project to another, which, in part, attributed to the high cost and long delays.

Most of the early EAI implementations relied on what is known as a hub-and-spoke topology. This consists of a centralized hub that accepts requests from multiple sources or applications, all of which are connected as spokes using various prebuilt adapters. Over time, many of the EAI solutions began morphing into more of a bus-style topology leveraging message-oriented middleware (MOM). MOM is a messaging infrastructure, or bus, that, instead of using a hub/spoke approach, uses *message channels* as a way to distinguish between messages of different types. Reliability features ensure that delivery of messages is guaranteed and arrives at its destination with integrity (that is, it was received in the same form it was sent).

When using MOM as the backplane for EAI, one or more integration brokers are connected to the bus to provide EAI services such as routing and transformation. Individual applications or services can be attached to the bus via adapters or connectors. Figure 9.1 depicts this style of EAI.

The advantage to this approach is that it offers a decentralized approach. In figure 9.1, the partners are connected via lightweight adapters that enable the

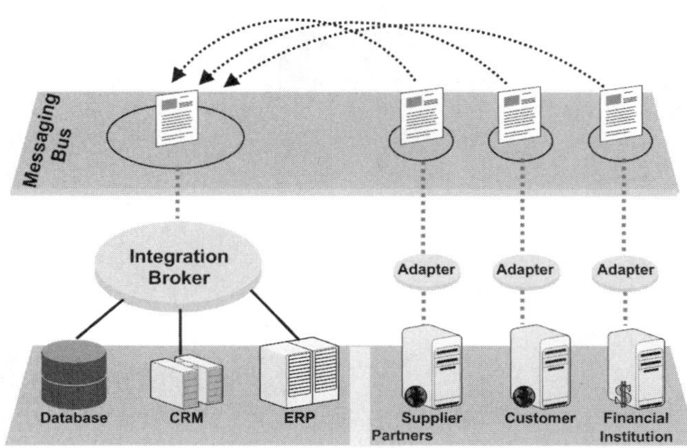

Figure 9.1 EAI architecture using a messaging bus topology. Notice the adapters required by external partners.

messages to be transmitted directly to a distributed messaging bus. However, this too is not ideal, as it requires EAI software components to be installed in the partner's system. If you're a big Fortune 500 firm, such a request is likely to be granted—if not, you're likely dead in the water. This bus-style topology laid the foundation for the emergence of ESBs.

NOTE You can think of a messaging bus as sort of like a stream, where you can toss a message in a bottle, but with confidence that it will end up in the correct hands. A hub and spoke architecture is more like your home router, where everything plugs directly into it and it carries the responsibility for managing the connectivity between your various computing devices.

The bus topology assumes a central role within an ESB (as the last word of the term suggests). In the Java world, the bus is most often predicated on a JMS messaging backbone. Messages are deposited on the bus, with routing rules and transformations then applied to navigate the message to the proper endpoint service. Although ESBs often provide adapters for proprietary systems, the preferred approach for working with partners is through XML over HTTP (be it SOAP, plain-old XML, or REST). This eliminates the requirement for custom software to be installed remotely. Indeed, XML is the lingua franca of ESBs, and is the preferred method for all message exchanges. We'll get into more of the specifics of what constitutes an ESB shortly; in the meantime, figure 9.2 shows the ESB alternative to the EAI diagram depicted in figure 9.1.

In figure 9.2, notice that the *service adapters* shown are all supporting standards-based protocols. In part, it's this protocol standardization that paved the way for ESBs to emerge. A multitude of open source libraries exists that support these standards, and they can be easily embedded into the solutions of both open source and commercial vendors (depending on licensing restrictions). This is a somewhat unspoken secret of commercial ESB vendors and changed the cost dynamics for commercial ESBs, which were typically priced about one-fourth as much as traditional EAI software.

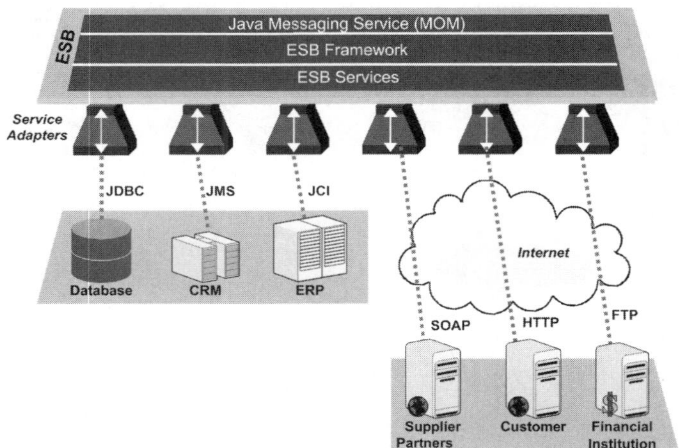

Figure 9.2 Typical ESB architecture example leveraging standards-based protocols (SOAP, FTP, etc.) instead of propriety adapters

In figure 9.2, *ESB Framework* and *ESB Services* represent the core functionality provided by the ESB. The services represent the supported protocol adapters and ancillary functions such as transformation services and content-based routing. The framework itself represents the ESB application, and includes cross-cutting features such as logging, auditing, and management. Let's take a deeper look at the core capabilities that are typically associated with ESB products, as this will help us understand the appropriate role an ESB can play within SOA.

9.2.1 *Core ESB capabilities*

When looking at the product sheets for most ESBs, you'll probably be a bit overwhelmed by the features offered—it may seem like everything but the kitchen sink. When you separate the wheat from the chaff, what generally remains for most ESBs are protocol adapters, message-oriented middleware, XML-based messaging, intelligent routing, message transformation, tasks/timers, monitoring, and an extendable API. Let's take a brief look at these features so that we have a foundation on which to build our use case in the next chapter.

PROTOCOL ADAPTERS

ESBs typically provide a multitude of adapters, sometimes referred to as components or services, that enable the ESB to easily interface with communications protocols or transports such as HTTP, FTP, POP3/SMTP (email), and file systems. Connectivity is at the core of any ESB and represents its greatest value proposition. You typically configure an adapter by editing XML configuration files, but sometimes a wizard-style interface is provided to simplify the task. The following example shows an XML configuration used to define an HTTP client adapter for Apache ServiceMix:

```
<http:endpoint service="testBasicAuth:MyProviderService"
  endpoint="myProvider"
  role="provider"
  locationURI="https://localhost:8193/Service/">
  <http:basicAuthentication>
    <http:basicAuthCredentials username="testuser" password="testpass" />
  </http:basicAuthentication>
</http:endpoint>
```

As you can see, such a declarative style configuration is easy to use and is common among most ESBs. In this example, a new HTTP client adapter is configured so that when it receives a message, it will post that message to the `@locationURI` attribute value that was assigned.

NOTE Most open source and commercial ESBs use the Apache Commons set of libraries to provide connectivity. This is a real benefit, because these libraries have been widely used for years, and are very robust and performance optimized. See http://commons.apache.org/.

An ESB adapter typically works as either a server or client. So, for instance, you can set up an HTTP listener/consumer to receive inbound requests or to act as a client making an outbound HTTP request. While the same standard set of adapters is present in nearly all ESBs, there are subtle but important differences in the extent to which a protocol's various options are supported. For example, not all ESBs offer full support for the various SOAP-related WS-Security standards.

MESSAGE-ORIENTED MIDDLEWARE

We've defined MOMs earlier in our discussion of EAI typologies that support a messaging bus. Java-based ESBs use JMS, and often it's embedded within the very fabric of the ESB application. In some ESB implementations, JMS can also be used internally for managing message flows or as an interface for integrating with external services that support the protocol. Indeed, JMS is usually the means by which an ESB can be distributed in a decentralized fashion.

JMS supports two types of messaging models or channels: *publish and subscribe* (pub/sub), and *point-to-point*. As figure 9.3 illustrates, the difference between the two is that in a pub/sub model, multiple consumers, known as subscribers, can subscribe to and receive published messages, whereas in a point-to-point typology, only a single consumer/receiver may receive the message (on a first-come, first-serve basis).

Of the two models, the queue, or point-to-point, approach is more prevalent because you often don't want processing to occur multiple times for a given message. However, having multiple receivers that are capable of lifting and processing the message, such as shown in figure 9.3, is useful for load balancing or clustering; if any one receiver goes down, another will simply pick up the messages if they're registered as a listener.

When is the pub/sub model appropriate? Often it's used in tandem with an event-based computing model. For example, say you have an order entry system. When an

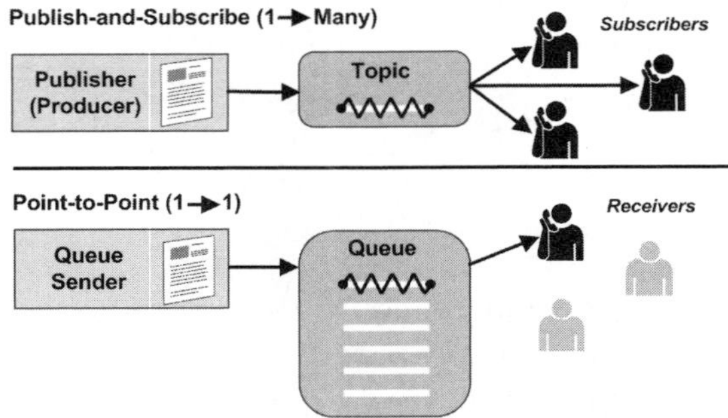

Figure 9.3 JMS messaging using queue and pub/sub models

order is submitted, it should publish result notifications to an accounts receivable system in addition to a CRM for updating a summary of account activity.

You can consider JMS to be the backplane for Java-based ESBs, with XML the common message dialect, which is our next topic.

XML-BASED MESSAGING

While most ESBs are capable of dealing with non-XML data such as binary files, the clear preference is to work with XML. Why? Most recently developed services are usually exposed using XML-based protocols—this includes SOAP, XML over HTTP, and REST. The benefits of using XML are probably obvious to you by this point. They include greater interoperability, the self-describing and human-readable nature of XML, extensibility, and schema-based validation capabilities. ESBs are designed for interrogating the content of XML messages for any variety of operations, including routing, aggregation, enrichment, and validation.

One often-overlooked benefit of using XML is the implication it has for operational monitoring. If all (or most) of the messages flowing in and out of the bus are XML, the streams of data can be analyzed in real time via a complex event processor (the topic of the previous chapter). Figure 9.4 depicts how an ESB wiretap pattern can be used to facilitate such real-time monitoring.

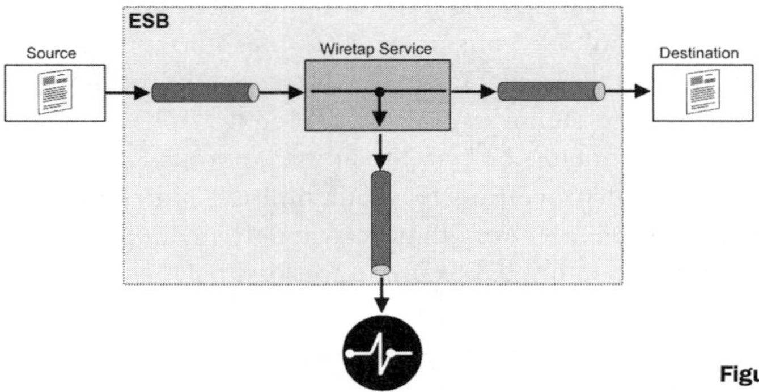

Figure 9.4 Wiretap pattern used for operation monitoring via CEP

In figure 9.4, an inbound message enters the ESB, and a wiretap operation is applied to the inbound message. The wiretap pattern leaves the message intact but forwards a copy of it to the Esper engine for real-time analysis.

NOTE The definitive guide to integration patterns can be found in Hohpe and Woolf's book, *Enterprise Integration Patterns* [HohpeWoolf]. The book's influence is often cited by the developers of many of the open source ESBs.

When messages arrive in XML, they can be easily transformed and routed by the ESB. Let's look at routing next.

INTELLIGENT ROUTING AND DISTRIBUTION

An ESB acts as an intermediary for the communications that occur between the various services that connect to it. Thus, systems and applications that leverage an ESB should rely on it to route messages to the appropriate locations or endpoints. The routing rules used by an ESB depend on the message content (in which case it's dynamic), or they can be established in a static fashion using a fixed pipeline pattern.

Although routing is an easy concept to understand, there are several permutations for how it can be implemented, and various ESBs may manage it differently. Table 9.1 depicts the various possible approaches and highlights some of the pros and cons of each.

Table 9.1 Approaches to ESB routing

Pattern	Description	Pros	Cons
Processing pipeline	A predefined sequence of steps or nodes is defined that a given message must follow. You define this pipeline up front, and any message entering the channel will adhere to the pipeline rules.	Simple to configure and debug.	Can impose a performance penalty, since some nodes within the pipeline may not be required for processing by all inbound messages. So, filtering must be provided.
Routing slip	An initial component assigns a route, called a *routing slip*, to the inbound message. The slip identifies what services must be invoked and is attached as a property to the message.	Efficient message flow, since only the required steps are performed. Supports highly decentralized computing, so it's highly scalable.	A routing table is typically immutable once it has been created and assigned, so downstream processing can't alter it. Also, assignment of routing rules up front can be complex to define.
Centralized router	A super-router is used that defines how messages should be processed. After a message exits each node, return is handed back to the router to determine its next step.	Fairly simple to administer and debug. Enables very complex process flows to be defined.	As the name suggests, control is managed by a central process, which can impose scalability and performance penalties.

Table 9.1 Approaches to ESB routing *(continued)*

Pattern	Description	Pros	Cons
Content-based routing	A router (perhaps several) examines the message content and routes the message to a different channel or node based on some content in the message body.	Dynamically determines message flow so only required steps are called. When using XML, XPath expressions make configuring straightforward.	Confined to evaluating a single message at a time. Building a process flow with multiple steps becomes difficult to manage and debug.
Component-based routing	Each node (usually implemented as a component), regardless of its function, determines where the message goes next. In a sense, each component contains CBR-type responsibilities.	Supports a highly decentralized computing model. Components participating in flow can reside anywhere access to the bus is provided.	Can result in proliferation of running component/node instances, resulting in large memory requirements.

As you can see, no single routing approach is without some drawbacks. Many of the open source ESBs support multiple routing methods; which one you use is in part dependent on your requirements. My experience suggests that if you're building complex flows, a better alternative is to use BPM and strive to keep ESB-based process flows fairly simple in design. In that case, content-based routing is likely sufficient.

NOTE An implementation of BPM using jBPM is the topic of chapters 5–7.

One last note regarding routing: an ESB can often be used as a proxy for web mediation. This capability can be supported by deriving routing rules based on the endpoint Uniform Resource Locator (URI) that's specified (a URI is just an address for a given resource, just as a URL is used for accessing web pages). For instance, to facilitate service abstraction, you may choose to use an ESB as a proxy where it can intercept inbound requests and redirect them based on the URI that was specified. WS-Addressing is a SOAP-based standard designed explicitly for such purposes (all inbound requests could share the same URI, but be redirected internally based on the WS-Addressing values provided with the SOAP header). We'll discuss more about this in the next section when we explore service virtualization.

Distribution is a somewhat similar concept to routing, but more generally refers to when you want to split a message into several messaging channels, or, alternatively, hold and aggregate messages based on some criteria. The latter can become challenging as you must base the aggregation rules on some sort of message correlation value.

We've covered over half of the core capabilities of an ESB, but some of the most beneficial features lie ahead of us, beginning with one of the most common uses of an ESB: message transformation.

MESSAGE TRANSFORMATION

One of the clear benefits in working with XML is the ease with which it can be transformed from one XML vocabulary to another. For instance, if you're a manufacturer dealing with large retailers and you're fortunate enough that they support XML, it's unlikely the XML is the same format you support internally. For example, your ERP system may have web service capabilities but only in the cXML format (an early e-commence XML vocabulary). Your partner, however, may only support the more recent OASIS UBL format. Using an ESB, you can easily incorporate an XSLT transformation that will convert from one to the other.

Many ESBs may also support transformation tools for use with dialects other than XML. For example, they may support features to convert EDI or CSV into XML. In such cases, it can be beneficial to chain or pipeline together a sequence of transformations, such as converting CSV into some normalized XML format and then into the designed final form. By using chaining, you can better reuse certain transformations and simplify development and debugging (we'll demonstrate such a scenario in the next chapter).

TASKS/TIMERS

Often you need to poll or fetch data from an external source based on some trigger. For instance, polling is generally a built-in feature of an ESB's FTP consumer adapter, since it must periodically check the FTP location to identify any new files that may have been deposited. Other common uses are for extract, transform, and load (ETL) techniques in which you need to periodically fetch data for batch operations based on some event trigger.

Nearly all ESBs support some sort of timer capability, and it's sometimes categorized as *tasks*. Figure 9.5 illustrates a timer used to initiate a web service call; the results are then transformed and inserted into a database.

The configurability of timers can obviously vary. Some offer capabilities reminiscent of Unix/Linux cron, which is highly flexible. Others are more limited in functionality and only support interval-based configurations.

Let's next look at an increasingly ESB role: *quality of service* (QoS) processing.

QUALITY OF SERVICE/WEB MEDIATION

This category of ESB functionality is an emerging field—early ESB implementations didn't often focus on QoS or web mediation. As companies have increased their web service presence through the use of publicly available APIs, the need has arisen to improve performance, availability, and service discrimination. What do I mean by the latter? For instance, many search engines provide web service APIs, but usually with a restriction that limits the number of connections that can be made within a period of

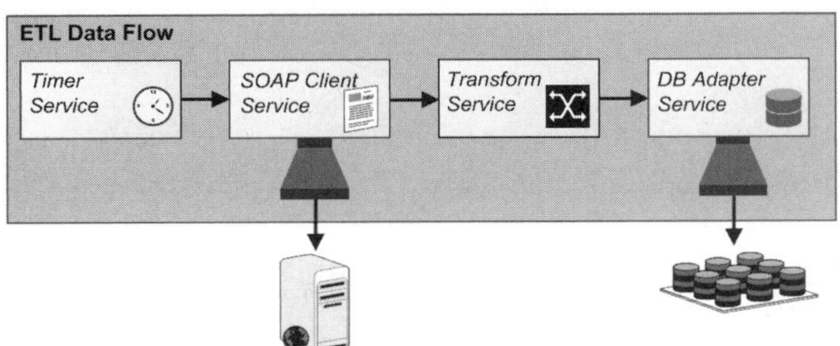

Figure 9.5 Example of using a timer service to initiate a SOAP request

time. This is done to ensure that all users get an acceptable level of performance, but perhaps more importantly, it's a way to monetize their investment. Many search engines provide a pay-based licensing model that removes these metering restrictions. In other words, they're discriminating their service levels based on whether you're a paying customer. An ESB with web mediation features that can be used for QoS enforcement can manage such requirements.

Another common scenario that we're seeing with increasing frequency involves content filtering based on the security profile of the client. For example, a hosted Applicant Tracking System (ATS) may provide their customers with an API so that they can retrieve an applicant's application data through a web service. This is useful, for instance, when integrating the ATS data with a local HR or ERP system. Since the ATS data may contain sensitive personal information (SPI) such as birth date or government ID, the ATS may not be willing to make such data available unless the client adheres to certain security requirements. For example, the ATS might require the use of SSL or message-level signatures or encryption using WS-Security. For those clients who can't provide such security, only non-SPI data will be transmitted. An ESB can be used to filter out outbound data to enforce such policy rules. Figure 9.6 illustrates both of these scenarios.

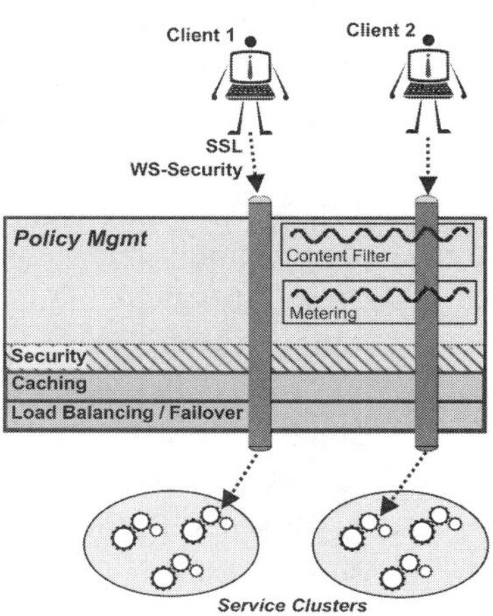

Figure 9.6 Using an ESB for policy management to discriminate service levels

As you can see in figure 9.6, Client 2's service request passes through two levels of filtering since they're using nonencrypted transport and messaging. The content filter removes data that they aren't entitled to view, and the metering filter verifies that they haven't exceeded their allocation of requests for a given time period. On the other hand, no filtering restrictions are applied to Client 1. Also in figure 9.6, notice the reference to caching and load balancing and failover. This is also considered part of QoS, as caching and load balancing address performance, with availability positively impacted by the use of failover provisions. Not all ESBs specifically address these issues in the fashion I've described, but many can accommodate these requirements in some way or another.

MONITORING AND ADMINISTRATION

Given the critical role that an ESB plays within the enterprise, it should come as no surprise that monitoring and administration are important considerations for an ESB. Most Java-based ESBs, both open source and commercial, have begun to build monitoring tools using Java Management Extensions (JMX). JMX is a technology designed specifically for monitoring and real-time management of Java applications. Several generic-type consoles exist, including JConsole, which ships standard with Java's JDK. Using JMX, you can monitor an application's resources and attributes, and even invoke method operations (if they're configured for JMX support).

The types of metrics relevant to an ESB include

- Messages received
- Number of faults
- Average processing time
- Number of messages processed per transport
- Queue size
- Messages processed per endpoint or proxy

NOTE Advanced management features have generally been a weak area for most open source ESBs. Some, like Mule, do provide sophisticated monitoring tools, but in Mule's case, it's a commercial product (Mule Saturn).

The last common feature shared among most ESBs is the ability to create your custom components or services using their API framework.

EXTENDABLE API

Most popular open source ESBs are well architected, and include several means by which you can extend their functionality. One of the most straightforward ways is to use one of the supported scripting languages. Choices include Groovy, JRuby, JavaScript (Rhino), or Jython (Python). Using a scripting language allows you to embed required programming logic within the definition of the ESB XML configuration files (or via a reference to a scripting resource that contains the code).

You can also create custom components or services by using a Java API. This is supported in all popular Java-based ESBs. Often, you can accomplish this by simply implementing one of their available classes intended for this purpose. Generally, you must implement a few required methods, then place the class in the appropriate location, and you are ready to rock 'n' roll.

As you can now probably appreciate, ESBs offer a lot of functionality. As we've shown here, when you carve away all of the marketing and technology spin, they tend to all share the same underlying core functionality. Obviously, some offer additional features and are stronger in some areas than others. One of the big challenges when working with an ESB is identifying where its use is most appropriate. Because of the flexibility ESBs provide, the technology can be subject to misuse and may violate your SOA objectives. In the next two sections, we'll identify the areas in which an ESB is most appropriate, and where it can be counterproductive when better alternatives exist.

9.2.2 Appropriate uses of an ESB

What are the areas where an ESB is most beneficial in a SOA environment? The answer partially depends on your specific environment. However, experience suggests that it's best suited for the following roles: service enablement, service virtualization, asynchronous communications, and protocol bridging. Let's consider each in more detail.

SERVICE ENABLEMENT

As we alluded to briefly already, ESBs can effectively be used to service enable existing application functionalities. For example, you may have an existing business application, such as an order entry system, that doesn't provide service interfaces (or perhaps only rudimentary interfaces). Using an available ESB adapter such as JDBC, you may be able to quickly create a SOAP-based web service. This effectively creates a reusable service and eliminates each interested client from having to code such interfaces manually when connectivity is required. This approach can extend your existing IT investments.

SERVICE VIRTUALIZATION

The term *virtualization* is a fairly loaded word in the IT vocabulary. Most think of it within the context of OS virtualization products such as XEN and VMware. However, when coupled with services, it has a somewhat different meaning. *Service virtualization* refers to the ability to logically define abstract service endpoints instead of using actual physical addresses. In some respects, it's akin to how your telephone service works. When you make a call, the number you dial isn't a physical location of where the responder resides. Rather, that determination is somehow managed behind the scenes by the telephone company. For example, in many instances you can now keep your same cell number from one carrier to another, so that you don't have to get a new phone number when you dump your carrier to buy that shiny new iPhone 3G. Service virtualization is a similar concept for the services you wish to expose.

Using an ESB, you can assign a logical or abstract address for your service clients, and the ESB will manage the routing for how it gets to the physical address where the service resides. Standards such as WS-Addressing can also be used in tandem with this when working with SOAP (more on this later). This is an important feature when managing for a SOA environment, as it makes things far less brittle—by using a physical address, when any network changes occur, all clients accessing that server will be impacted.

ASYNCHRONOUS COMMUNICATIONS

In chapter 2, we discussed how earlier distributed computing models based on remote procedure calls (RPCs) resulted in a tightly coupled architecture that made any sort of service reuse very problematic. Also, RPC's reliance on synchronous communications meant that, if the remote service was down or nonresponsive, the application would cease to function. Early implementations of web services using SOAP also relied heavily on RPC-style communications. As the limitations of using RPCs became apparent, best practices in web services eschewed RPCs and moved toward a document-centric approach. More recently, the use of asynchronous-style web services has grown in popularity. Asynchronous messaging allows communications to occur in a more standalone fashion and is less susceptible to communication hiccups that may arise between the two services. Further, if using message-oriented middleware like JMS, the store-and-forward capabilities mean that the message can be sent to the middleware bus, with the client system free to continue processing. When the target is back online, the middleware will ensure that it receives the queued message. Nearly all Java-based ESBs rely on JMS middleware, and by virtue, inherently support asynchronous communications. While JMS alone could be used, an ESB load-balancing or service detection feature can be used in conjunction with a cluster of services to redirect when one service isn't operable. Figure 9.7 depicts the general concept behind asynchronous messaging when combined with an ESB.

In the scenario shown in figure 9.7, the caller routine initiates an asynchronous call to the callee through a message channel or queue, which is managed by the ESB. The caller then continues processing. Eventually, the callee completes the operation and issues the results back by way of the replyTo queue. The caller then picks up the processed message and continues processing. Notice in this case the service virtualization features were also used, as the caller doesn't directly communicate to the callee but does so by way of a message channel.

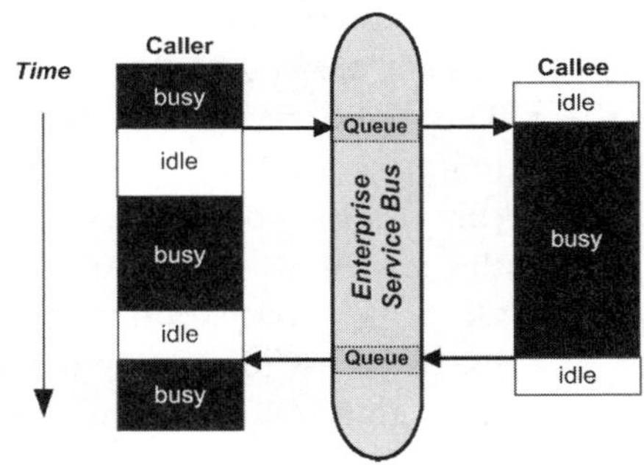

Figure 9.7 Basic concept of asynchronous messaging using a callback

Obviously, there are scenarios where asynchronous processing isn't feasible, such as when someone is placing an order through a website and anticipates immediately receiving a confirmation with an order number. The fundamental point to remember is to, when at all possible, use asynchronous communications augmented by the capabilities provided by the ESB.

PROTOCOL BRIDGING

A common scenario encountered when dealing with external partners is the need to bridge from one protocol to another. Let's look at a common use case. Say your partner only supports batch-style integration, whereby they send nightly FTP files using CSV (comma-separated values) file formatting. Internally, the preference is XML over JMS. This sort of scenario is the sweet spot for an ESB. A simple ESB processing pipeline can lift the inbound FTP file, transform it from CSV to XML, and then deposit it to the appropriate JMS queue. Since ESBs typically come with a wide variety of adapters, this is generally a straightforward exercise. I'm sure you can think of many such bridging scenarios within your enterprise.

The areas just covered identify some of the appropriate uses for where an ESB can best be utilized. However, because of an ESB's flexibility, it can often be used inappropriately. Like the old saying goes, when you're a hammer, everything looks like a nail. In part, there's the temptation to use an ESB for everything, but doing so can be harmful to your long-term SOA goals. Let's examine some of these areas where an ESB shouldn't be used.

9.2.3 *Inappropriate uses of an ESB*

ESB evangelists may take some issue with some of the areas we believe are inappropriate uses of the technology. The basis for making this determination is my experience with implementing several commercial and open source ESBs in a variety of projects. Initially, I fell victim to the early hype surrounding ESBs and felt they were a Swiss army knife for implementing SOA. Over time my enthusiasm tempered as best practices emerged. The areas in which I believe an ESB shouldn't be used include service composition, orchestrations, high-throughput processing, and business rules.

SERVICE COMPOSITION

The ability for an ESB to easily bridge between different protocols can lead to the temptation to code your services to a specific message protocol and let the ESB take care of any protocol bridging. Since we just spoke about an ESB's strong capability in this regard, why is this a problem? For example, perhaps your team has decided that all of the services you're developing will use XML over JMS. If a .NET or Ruby client needs access to one of your services, the ESB can wrapper the service and expose it through SOAP, for instance. This is certainly doable, but I strongly recommend against it. Your service code should not contain protocol-specific logic or libraries. That approach limits the audience of your service and requires you to develop and maintain ESB wrapper scripts. Further, since technology changes rapidly, do you really want to hard-wire protocol-specific logic into your service? What's the alternative?

In chapters 3 and 4, we described how service composition and assembly can be done using the Apache Tuscany framework, which is an SCA implementation. With Tuscany, you declaratively define, at runtime, how your components will be exposed as services. When developing your components using SCA, you don't code for any protocol. Instead, the XML-based assembly model defines how the service is exposed. This declarative approach to protocol binding is superior as it future-proofs your code and provides greater flexibility. In cases where the supported protocol isn't available through Tuscany, an ESB-based wrapper solution is obviously a sound choice (or, as in our example, when batch-style integration is required).

If you're using SCA, you may wonder why you should use an ESB at all. A good justification is that, when you're working with external partners and clients, prudent network security demands using some sort of extranet environment for their access. Directly exposing services running within your main internal network is never a good idea. An extranet-based ESB can act as a service proxy (granted, network devices can perform the same role). By using ESB as a proxy in the extranet, you can support protocols such as FTP and email. The inbound data is transformed by the proxy ESB into the proper XML Schema and transmitted to the internal network via JMS. Once the inbound request is received by the internal ESB, it can then be routed to the proper service endpoints. This sort of configuration is shown in figure 9.8.

In figure 9.8, we show inbound requests coming in by way of three different protocols. The ESB transforms the requests as necessary, and deposits the message to JMS, where it's then received by the internal ESB and routed to the appropriate endpoint service. If the endpoint service is using Tuscany, any of the supported protocols could be used that are supported by Tuscany. This sort of typology is consistent with SOA best practices, such as service abstraction/virtualization and loose coupling (see

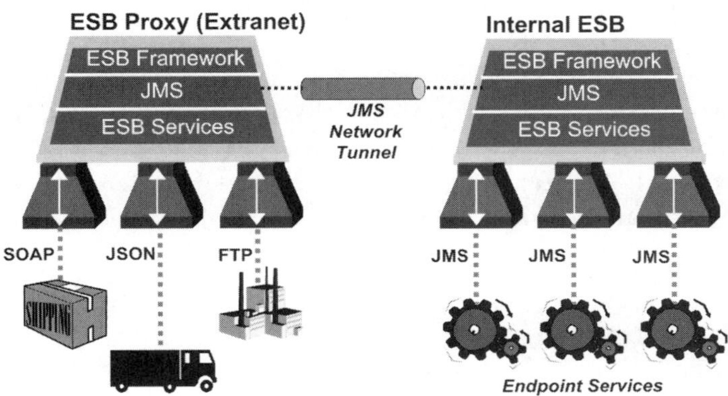

Figure 9.8 An example of a secure network ESB configuration

chapter 1). The key consideration here is that the services themselves are running in whatever container or app server is appropriate for the framework being used, and not directly hosted in the ESB container. This is a decentralized, distributed environment that can scale as needed since the services can be located anywhere in your computing grid.

ORCHESTRATIONS AND ESBS

As you may recall, in chapter 5 we briefly contrasted an ESB's pipeline or data flow capabilities with the features provided by a BPM. Most ESBs provide some means to sequence together several steps into what's sometimes referred to as an itinerary, or micro-flow. This is necessary when several things must be done to process an inbound message, such as receiving it using one protocol, transforming it, possibly enriching it with additional data, and finally, routing. These sorts of sequences are what we refer to as data flows.

NOTE Some people use the term *process flow* in lieu of *data flow*, but that term can be confusing since the term *process* is also widely used with BPM.

An ESB's data flow capabilities should be limited to simple sequences of steps, and not serve as a substitute for BPM orchestrations. Data flows don't inherently support the concept of long transactions. So if any human-in-the-loop action is required, or service callouts with unpredictable response times occur, data flows become untenable because ESBs don't include the ability to persist long-running transactions to a database (in BPM terms, this is referred to as hydration/dehydration). Further, BPM orchestrations are intended to convey a *business process* that can be visually understood and even edited by subject matter experts. An ESB's data flow is developer-tool designed to simplify creating multistep operations. We've witnessed firsthand elaborate ESB data flow sequences that quickly became unmanageable when you have to factor in exception handling and alternative flows. A BPM's language constructs, such as BPEL or jPDL in the case of jBPM, are designed for creating elaborate workflows. Attempting to replicate these features in an ESB is akin to trying to make a car fly by attaching wings.

SYNCHRONOUS HIGH THROUGHPUT DISTRIBUTED PROCESSING

In certain scenarios, using an ESB when high-throughput messaging is required can result in performance bottlenecks. While it's unfair to generalize across all ESB products, many use internal JMS queues to facilitate distributed processing of nodes in a data flow. Although this has the advantage of enabling distribution of load, it can also result in unanticipated bottlenecks. Such a bottleneck occurs when one service in a data flow takes longer than the others. Messages back up while waiting on that service, and a backlog can quickly build, adversely affecting quality of service. This scenario is illustrated in figure 9.9.

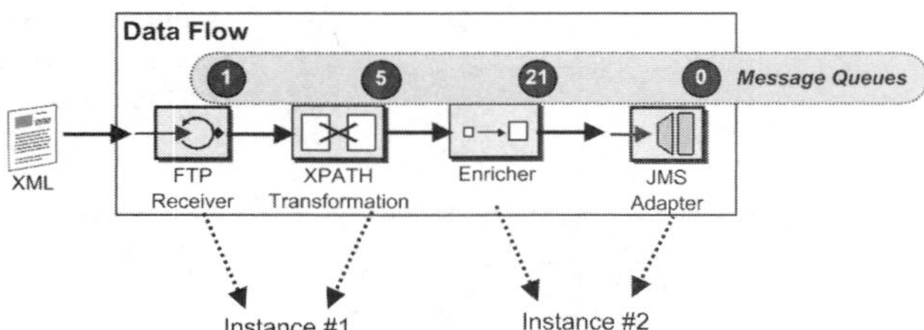

Figure 9.9 Queue buildup effect in ESB data flow

In figure 9.9, the Enricher service is responsible for querying data from an external data source to augment the inbound XML (for example, retrieving a customer name based on a customer ID). However, it's slow, and as a result, a backlog of messages quickly builds when a high volume of messages flow through the system. In this case, 21 messages are waiting to be processed so that the next message received will have to wait for the preceding ones to be completed before its processing is done. If this were a real-time system with a requirement for a synchronous request/response, you can imagine that this would result in unacceptable delays.

NOTE Always bear in mind that an ESB is another technology tool for implementing SOA, but SOA encompasses more than technology, and includes governance, process, and even culture.

Congratulations! We've covered a lot of material, starting with the heritage of ESB, to its core capabilities, to its proper usage. Now we'll switch gears a bit (you might be thankful after so much theory!), and begin looking at the ESB we selected in chapter 2 for our Open SOA Platform: Apache Synapse.

9.3 Introducing Apache Synapse

Apache Synapse has suffered from somewhat of an identity crisis. The initial proposal for Apache positioned Synapse as a "robust, lightweight implementation of a highly scalable and distributed service mediation framework on Web services specifications" [Synapse2005]. By the time of the 1.0 release, it was repositioned more as a full-fledged ESB, and was described as an "easy-to-use and lightweight XML and Web Services management and integration broker that can form the basis of a Service Oriented Architecture (SOA) and Enterprise Service Bus (ESB)" [Synapse2007].

NOTE Apache Synapse became an Apache Top-Level Project (TLP) with the 1.1.1 release in February 2008. This was an important milestone for Synapse, as it reflects the growing interest in the product and the designation carries with it important prestige value.

Like a lot of open source projects, Synapse is largely sponsored by a single commercial entity that seeks to monetize on the investment it makes in supporting development. Synapse is no different, with the main contingent of developers coming from WSO2, an open source middleware company.

WSO2 does rebrand Synapse as WS02 ESB. While the same core product remains Synapse, WSO2's ESB sports a slick user interface that simplifies management. In our coverage of Synapse, we'll focus on Apache's version, which relies on manually editing the configuration files necessary to run the ESB. If you're anything like me, you prefer to first understand the essentials of the Synapse configuration XML instead of working with the "black-box" approach provided by WSO2's ESB (which uses a web-based configuration approach, though it doesn't preclude manual editing). This decision isn't intended to reflect negatively on WSO2's product—they've done a very nice job. In particular, some of the management features the product introduces are definitely worthwhile, and I encourage you to check them out.

Synapse, which is Java based and supports all major platforms, runs as a service and listens for incoming messages. It can then process messages using a variety of actions, and then returns the results to the calling client. The overall concept is shown in figure 9.10.

In figure 9.10, we show several inbound message protocols (these are only representative; there are more) that are sending messages to the listener/mediator. From there, one or more of the available actions, such as transformations or transport switching, can be applied to the message. Once the actions are completed, the endpoint service exposed to the ESB will be invoked. You can configure Synapse to act as a *proxy service*, whereby it accepts inbound requests on behalf of the service to be called. Each proxy defines an in/out *sequence* that's called to perform transformations, validation, logging, routing, and so forth. Once the actions associated with the sequence are performed, the *endpoint* where the target service resides is called. The response

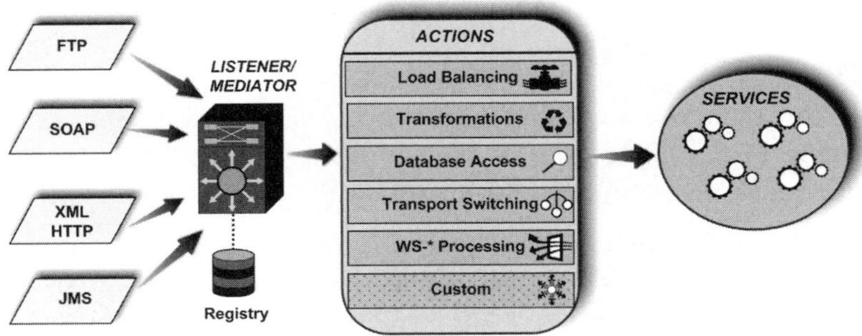

Figure 9.10 Overview of Synapse architecture

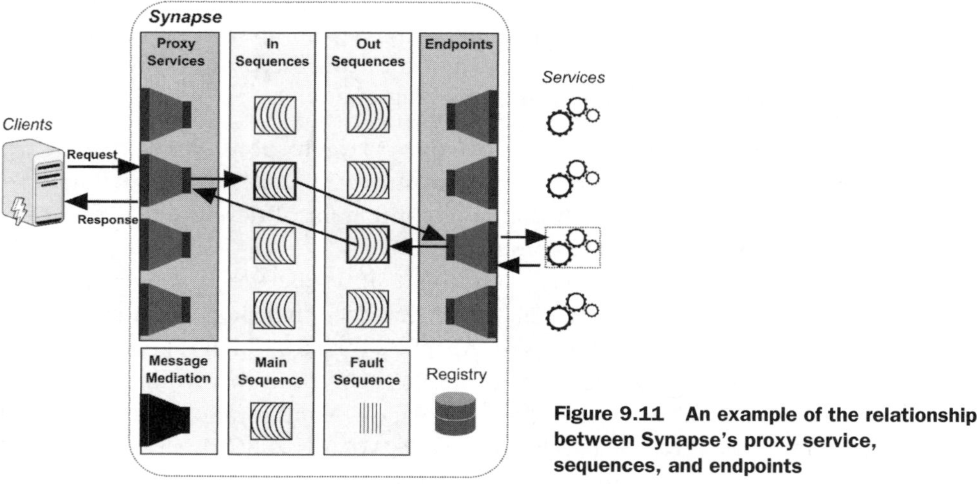

Figure 9.11 An example of the relationship between Synapse's proxy service, sequences, and endpoints

received by the endpoint, if synchronous in nature, then runs through the associated out sequence prior to returning the results to the client. Figure 9.11 illustrates an example of this flow.

In the example shown in figure 9.11, a client issues a request by specifying a Synapse endpoint URI location. At this point, the *in* sequence defined for the given proxy name is invoked, and the request is then redirected to the target endpoint service. The response then flows back through the *out* sequence associated with the defined proxy. You'll notice in figure 9.11 that *message mediation* can also be the recipient of an inbound request. How does this differ from a proxy service? We'll get into this in more detail later, but the main distinction is that, when using a proxy, the client specifies a Synapse URI as the endpoint. When using Synapse as the message mediator, you can use it as a client HTTP proxy—it will perform ESB services in a fashion transparent to the client. Also, when using SOAP with WS-Addressing in conjunction with a message mediator, it will automatically route the message to the appropriate endpoint location (this is considered a *smart client* in the Synapse samples). Before we plunge into the examples in the next chapter, let's take a look at how Synapse supports the main functionalities required by an ESB, beginning with transport/communication protocols.

9.3.1 Protocol adapters

Synapse is largely built around the Apache Axis 2 web services engine. As you might expect, its support for SOAP-based web services (SOAP 1.1 and 1.2) is outstanding. In particular, it offers excellent support for the following WS-* set of standards:

- *WS-Addressing*—A standard for communicating addressing information in a transport-neutral way, it's defined using the SOAP header extension mechanism. Without WS-Addressing, many SOAP implementations required the use of a `SOAPAction` HTTP header as a way of communicating which endpoint to use.

However, this is obviously bound to the HTTP protocol and doesn't work when using SOAP over JMS, for example. The support and use of WS-Addressing is growing significantly.

- *WS-ReliableMessaging*—This is a SOAP standard for reliable delivery of messages. Depending on the need, different *Delivery Assurances* can be specified, such as `ExactlyOnce`, which can be used to guarantee the message was successfully delivered to exactly one receiving service. Using this protocol can significantly increase the amount of network chatter, but when message reliability is paramount, it's an excellent solution.
- *WS-Security*—A transport-neutral standard for securing web services. Message integrity, which ensures that a given message hasn't been tampered with, can be done by signing the message using a `BinarySecurityToken` profile. This is most often accomplished with an X.509 certificate, which can be used to both sign a given message and verify user identity. If you just want to verify user credentials, you can use a `UsernameToken` profile. Credentials can be passed in plain text (`PasswordText`) or encrypted through the use of a digest (`PasswordDigest`). Like WS-Addressing, this is a standard that's really achieving critical mass in the marketplace (thanks, in large part, to Microsoft's excellent.NET support—see, I'm not always critical of the Redmond behemoth).
- *WS-Policy*—A specification for defining, in XML, how policies such as WS-Security and WS-Addressing are applied to a given web service. It's also extendable and is used by Synapse for managing throttling rules, which we'll cover in the next chapter.

While many ESBs proclaim support for these standards, they are often not fully implemented. Synapse's support is unmatched in this area.

NOTE Synapse uses nonblocking HTTP(s) so that web services using that protocol benefit from exceptional performance and high-concurrency capabilities. This, in part, is why Synapse is considered the fastest open source ESB.

Common protocols such as JMS, TCP, HTTP, HTTPS, and email (POP3, SMTP, IMAP) are also fully supported by Synapse, as are a variety of others through Synapse's integration with the Apache Commons Virtual File System (VFS). This pseudo-protocol provides support for accessing files in a local file system or via S/FTP. Additionally, it provides compression support, such as ZIP, JAR, TAR, and GZIP.

9.3.2 Message-oriented middleware

Synapse can be configured to work with any JMS-compatible messaging system. JMS implementations that have been tested include TIBCO, IBM's WebSphere MQ, FioranoMQ, and Apache's ActiveMQ. Using JMS, you can create a highly distributed ESB architecture, where multiple instances of Synapse can be running concurrently and communicating via JMS topics or queues. Synapse includes support for JMS binary, plain text, XML, or SOAP messages.

9.3.3 XML-based messaging

As I pointed out earlier, Synapse's engine is built on Apache Axis 2. XML is thus, by default, assumed to be the messaging protocol. Synapse's strong XML support includes services such as a validation mediator, which can be used to validate XML against a defined schema for both inbound or outbound XML messages. When using XML, Synapse can switch transports in a transparent fashion—taking an HTTP SOAP message and depositing the message on a JMS queue, for example. As with most ESBs, XML support is managed using Apache Xerces libraries, which are robust and efficient.

For those instances where you need support for binary data, Synapse supports *Message Transmission Optimization Mechanism* (MTOM), which is a binary optimization mechanism for web services. MTOM uses a standard called *XML-Binary Optimized Packaging* (XOP) for transmitting binary data. Using MTOM is easier and more efficient than using MIME attachments for SOAP.

9.3.4 Intelligent routing and distribution

Synapse provides several ways to facilitate routing using what are known as selection mediators. You can use a simple filter based on regular or XPath expressions, or in conjunction with a switch-style statement. The basis for the evaluation can be the message body, message properties, or the URI. As I mentioned earlier, full support for WS-Addressing also exists, which enables SOAP messages to be directed to the appropriate endpoint service.

Routing rules can also be configured for faults, which is essential for proper error handling. For example, you can configure a fault sequence that will be invoked if a timeout occurs while Synapse is attempting to call a remote service. You can even redirect the message to an alternative service. Achieve more sophisticated routing by using one of the available scripting languages such as Groovy or Ruby by modifying message properties that will redirect the message.

Message distribution features include the ability to clone a message so that it can be sent to multiple recipients in parallel. You can also split the message into multiple fragments, with each portion sent to a different service. Alternatively, messages can be aggregated together using an XPath expression that defines the correlation rule used to associate the messages as they arrive.

9.3.5 Message transformation

Like all popular ESBs, Synapse supports XSLT-based transformations that can be applied to in- or outbound messages. You can selectively identify, via an XPath expression, which portion of the message you wish to transform. More sophisticated transformations can be performed using the XQuery mediator, which also enables you to enrich a message based on an external XML document or supported XQuery data source. In conjunction with fault processing, you can generate a SOAP fault, thereby transforming a response when an unexpected value is received. Lastly, scripting can be used to transform a message.

9.3.6 *Tasks/timers*

New in the Synapse 1.1 release is support for tasks, which represent triggers that can be invoked in a continuous fashion. A task class determines the action that will occur when a trigger is fired. Synapse comes out of the box with a message injector that will deposit an arbitrary message into the ESB for processing. For example, you could set up a recurring timer to call an exchange rate service that you will then use for deriving currency calculations. Undoubtedly many scenarios come to mind. You can also create your own timer implementation classes that perform other actions.

When configuring a Synapse task, you can define how many times it should be called and how frequently it should be invoked by setting a timing interval. Support for more sophisticated scheduling features similar to Unix/Linux cron is also available.

9.3.7 *Quality of service/web mediation*

In the introduction to section 9.2, we alluded to the fact that Synapse has gone through some subtle repositioning. Initially, the focus was on web mediation, so it should come as no surprise that Synapse excels in this area. In particular, Synapse offers unique functionality in how it supports load balancing, failover processing, and message throttling/metering. While hardware routers have long provided load balancing and failover rule logic, Synapse supports it at the message instead of just the transport level (granted, some hardware routers do support message interrogation, but that's usually far more complicated).

Message throttling, or metering, refers to the ability to establish policies that determine how frequently a client can call a managed ESB service. Frequency can be based on the concurrent number of connections or maximum allowable calls within a given time interval. Restrictions can also be based on the inbound IP address or hostname of the client, so in effect, it acts as a firewall. Throttling directly relates to QoS, because it enables you to better enforce service-level agreements. While the old saying goes that everyone should be treated equally, as the animals in Orwell's *Animal Farm* discovered, some are more equal than others [Orwell].

9.3.8 *Monitoring and administration*

Synapse provides JMX monitoring support, though this is a fairly new addition to the product and further enhancements are needed to provide a complete solution. As it stands, a basic level of functionality is provided. This includes operations for stopping and restarting Synapse, as well as basic statistics about usage activity and faults.

9.3.9 *Extendable API*

Creating your own custom mediators in Synapse is surprisingly easy. You simply extend one of the available interface classes designed for such purposes and implement a handful of required methods. The Synapse documentation provides several examples, and you can also review the code or existing mediators to provide guidance, since they too implement the same interfaces.

This brief overview of Synapse's features demonstrates that, vis-à-vis standard ESB functionality, it has all of the bases covered. In particular, Synapse web services support with SOAP is unmatched when factoring in its support for many WS-* standards and QoS capabilities. Amazingly, it manages to accomplish all of this while retaining a lightweight footprint coupled with exceptional performance. At this point, you're probably eager to get your hands dirty. Let's take our first hands-on look at Synapse by introducing what it refers to as *message and service mediation*. This will lay the groundwork for the next chapter's detailed use case that we'll use to familiarize ourselves with many of Synapse's capabilities.

9.4 Basic Apache Synapse message and service mediation

As a gentle introduction to Synapse, let's create a simple configuration that receives an inbound request for a hypothetical web service called `CreateOrderService` and returns no SOAP response. We'll demonstrate both the message and service mediation approaches; learn the distinctions in the accompanying sidebar.

Understanding Synapse's message and service mediation

One of the more confusing aspects of using Synapse is understanding the differences between what is called *service* and *message* mediation. With *service mediation*, Synapse refers to configuring a specific endpoint URL that's serviced by Synapse. This is defined through Synapse using the proxy element definition. In other words, you are explicitly defining a URL endpoint in the Synapse configuration. On the other hand, *message mediation* is more transparent to the client. An example would be where you use Synapse as a conventional HTTP type proxy server. For instance, the client may be calling a remote endpoint URL, but has configured Synapse as the network HTTP(s) proxy. Synapse will then intercept the request and optionally perform actions on the service. Even if no direct routing or transformations are required, this could be beneficial for purposes of logging or BAM. Another possible scenario for message mediation is where a client specifies a generic Synapse endpoint address but uses WS-Addressing to inform Synapse of the ultimate endpoint location.

So what guidelines exist for determining which to use? That's a good question, as each can be used to perform similar functions. If your clients support WS-Addressing, I suggest using message mediation and specifying the SOAP URL as the Synapse ESB container. Synapse can then use addressing to determine the final destination target. Message mediation is also appropriate if you already have applications utilizing web services and don't want to alter their URL destinations. Instead, you can specify Synapse as an HTTP proxy, and likely won't have to make any direct code changes. Sending the requests through Synapse allows for uniform logging, error handling, and activity monitoring (cross-cutting type concerns). Using service mediation makes sense if you're exposing web services to external clients that aren't using WS-Addressing. You can provide them with a Synapse-based URL endpoint, without revealing any details to the customer as to the actual endpoint being used—this is consistent with the principles of service transparency.

9.4.1 Simple message mediation example

Listing 9.1 shows a simple "hello world" style configuration, provided as synapse_sample_opensoa_1.xml in the example code (see the README.txt file in the chapter's source code examples).

Listing 9.1 Simple message mediation example, which outputs called service to log

```
<definitions xmlns="http://ws.apache.org/ns/synapse">        ❶
  <sequence name="main">                                ❷
    <log level="custom">                          ❸
      <property name="Text" value="Service called was"/>
      <property name="service: " expression="get-property('To')"/>
    </log>
    <in>                    ❹
      <drop/>
    </in>
  </sequence>
</definitions>
```

All Synapse configurations begin with the `definitions` document root element ❶ which has the default namespace as shown (`http://ws.apache.org/ns/synapse`). The permissible child elements can then include `registry`, `localEntry`, `sequence`, `endpoint`, `proxy`, and `task`, all of which we'll cover moving forward. In this case, we're using message mediation, which is defined through the `sequence` element ❷. The `sequence` element with the `@name` attribute value set to `main` has special meaning: it's the entry point for all messages that arrive when using message mediation. In other words, this sequence will always be encountered, and can be thought of as analogous to a Java class with a static `main()` method.

In listing 9.1, Synapse logging is illustrated using a custom level ❸, which in this case prints out a static string value followed by outputting the value of the `To` property associated with the inbound message (properties are described in the *Apache Synapse ESB – Configuration* [SynapseLanguage]). The `@expression` attribute is used to print out a valid XPath expression, which in this case uses a custom extension function called `get-property()`. The `property` element itself can also be used independent of logging to set and unset properties (you'll see examples of this in the next chapter).

NOTE In addition to the `get-property` extension, you can also use those defined in the extensive Jaxen XPath function library, documented at http://jaxen.codehaus.org/apidocs/index.html. For example, to change the service name to uppercase, you could use `<property name="service-upper-case: " expression="fn:upper-case(get-property('To'))"/>`.

Finally, in the example in listing 9.1, you'll notice the `in` element ❹. This element identifies what mediators to perform when executing the request. In this case, we're simply stopping any further processing of the message in order to keep this example simple. Normally, a corresponding `out` element is also present, which is used to perform mediator actions on the response received from the `in` element's processing (we'll expand on this functionality shortly). If you submit a SOAP request and specify the URL as the Synapse ESB port (such as sending to http://localhost:8280, which is the default port for Synapse), you'll see console output that prints out the property values specified. If you change the `log @level` attribute to `full` (and remove the child elements) and submit a request, you'll see the inbound SOAP message printed to the Synapse console, along with various property values (this is a good way to discover what possible properties exist).

NOTE To simulate an inbound SOAP order, you can use soapUI (http://www.soapui.org/) and import the soapUI project called `soapui-inbound.xml` located in the sample code in the Chapter9/src/soapUI directory. Then select any sample request and run it—the results will appear in the Synapse console window.

You might now be wondering how you can differentiate between incoming messages so that you can process them accordingly. When using message mediation, you can most easily do this by using either the `filter` or `switch` mediator. Let's first look at how the filter element can be used with the example shown in listing 9.2.

Listing 9.2 Example of filter mediator and reusable sequence

```
<definitions xmlns="http://ws.apache.org/ns/synapse">
  <sequence name="main">
    <log level="full"/>
    <in>
      <filter source="get-property('To')"
        regex=".*/CreateOrderService">            ❶ Matches URL using regular expression
        <sequence key="CreateOrderService"/>     ❷ Invokes named sequence
      </filter>
    </in>
  </sequence>

  <sequence name="CreateOrderService">          ❸ Defines sequence
    <log level="custom">
      <property name="Text" value="Inside CreateOrderService"/>
    </log>
    <in>
      <drop/>
    </in>
  </sequence>
</definitions>
```

In this example, the `filter` element's `@source` attribute identifies the property value to be evaluated, followed by the `@regex` attribute, which represents the regular expression used to interpret the value's results (a boolean comparison, as shown in ❶. For example, if the `To` address of the SOAP URL endpoint was http://localhost:8280/CreateOrderService, the filter shown (`.*/CreateOrderService`) would evaluate to `true`, thereby processing the filter's child elements (when received by Synapse, the transport and host portion of the URL is stripped, leaving /Create-OrderService). If the filter criteria aren't met in listing 9.2, such as when a URL doesn't end with /CreateOrderService, no further processing occurs.

NOTE Another form of the filter element also exists, which only accepts a single @xpath attribute that must evaluate to a boolean result. So this <filter xpath="fn:contains(get-property('To'), '/CreateOrderService')"> is roughly equivalent to the example shown in listing 9.2.

The other notable difference between listing 9.2 and listing 9.1 is that in 9.2, a separate sequence node with the @name attribute of CreateOrderService was defined ❸. If the filter expression shown evaluates to true, that sequence is called, identified by looking up the corresponding value of the @key attribute of the child sequence ❷. This allows you to create more modular, and reusable, sequence definitions.

Let's take a look at how the switch element can be used to accomplish much the same effect. While we're at it, we'll introduce a few new wrinkles. Listing 9.3 shows this alternative approach using switch.

Listing 9.3 Example of switch mediator and introduction to fault processing

```
<definitions xmlns="http://ws.apache.org/ns/synapse">
  <sequence name="main">
    <log level="full"/>
    <in>
      <switch source="get-property('To')">        ❶ Evaluates inbound URL
        <case regex=".*/CreateOrderService">
          <sequence key="CreateOrderService"/>
        </case>
        <default>                                  ❷ Defaults if no match
          <sequence key="NotFound"/>
        </default>
      </switch>
    </in>
  </sequence>
  <sequence name="CreateOrderService">
    <log level="custom">
      <property name="Text" value="Inside CreateOrderService"/>
    </log>
    <in>
      <drop/>
    </in>
  </sequence>
  <sequence name="NotFound">                       ❸ Prints console output
    <log level="custom">
      <property name="Text" value="Service not supported/found"/>
    </log>
    <in>
      <property name="RESPONSE" value="true"/>    ❹ Indicates manual response
      <makefault>                                  ❺ Creates a SOAP fault
        <code value="tns:Receiver"
          xmlns:tns="http://www.w3.org/2003/05/soap-envelope"/>
        <reason value="Service not found"/>
```

```
        </makefault>
        <send/>
      </in>
    </sequence>
</definitions>
```

As you can see, the switch statement is now used in lieu of filter. The switch element takes a single attribute, @source, that identifies the value evaluated against in the child case element's @regex attribute. The switch construct ❶ offers additional flexibility since you can evaluate multiple case statements against it. Also, the optional default element ❷ can be used, as shown, to catch any messages that don't meet the existing case criteria. In this example, the sequence with a @name of NotFound is used for the default option if no match is found.

In the corresponding NotFound sequence ❸, notice that we also introduce some new features. In particular, we use the makefault element ❺ to force a SOAP fault to be returned to the client. This would thus be returned if the URL of the inbound SOAP message (stored in the To property) didn't evaluate to the regex value of .*/CreateOrderService. The SOAP response would be

```
<soapenv:Envelope
  xmlns:soapenv="http://schemas.xmlsoap.org/soap/envelope/">
  <soapenv:Body>
    <soapenv:Fault>
      <faultcode
       xmlns:tns="http://www.w3.org/2003/05/soap-envelope">tns:Receiver
      </faultcode>
      <faultstring>Service not found</faultstring>
    </soapenv:Fault>
  </soapenv:Body>
</soapenv:Envelope>
```

You may be wondering what we accomplish by setting the RESPONSE property value to true in listing 9.3 ❹. This value instructs the processing engine that the response to the service call has been completed, and tells the engine to use, in this case, the results of the makefault element as the response. In other words, you're bypassing the default behavior of executing the service request and returning the provided response instead. We could also use this same approach with the CreateOrderService sequence, so instead of currently returning no response, we could mock up a canned reply by replacing the in element node with the following:

```
<in>
   <property name="RESPONSE" value="true"/>
   <header name="To" action="remove"/>
   <script language="js"><![CDATA[
    mc.setPayloadXML(
       <CreateOrderResponse xmlns="uri:opensoa.chapter09.order">
          <Status>200</Status>
          <Message>Ok</Message>
       </CreateOrderResponse>);
    ]]></script>
   <send/>
</in>
```

In this example, a JavaScript script snippet is used to generate a canned SOAP response. We'll cover the use of scripts in greater depth in the next chapter, but for now, note that the script uses a handle to the message context, which is accessed through the object variable called `mc`. This object includes the `setPayloadXML` method, which can be used to set the response value returned. Notice that, in addition to setting the `RESPONSE` property to `true`, as we did in the previous example, a `header` element is also present (`header name="To" action="remove"`). The `header` element is used to manage the SOAP header envelope properties. The `to` property, which is used in conjunction with WS-Addressing, is removed so that no attempt is made to deliver the message to its destination endpoint. This wasn't required when generating the SOAP fault in listing 9.3, since the `makefault` mediator automatically removed that header value.

Testing Synapse as an HTTP proxy

As pointed out previously, one of the main reasons for using message mediation is that you can introduce it by using an HTTP proxy without requiring any modifications to your existing web service clients. To test this feature, use the soapUI project associated with this section, soapui-inbound.xml, and then when running soapUI, select File > Preferences. Then choose the Proxy Settings tab. In the Host field, enter localhost, and in the Port field, enter 8280. You can then enter a bogus URL endpoint, such as http://foo.com/bogus, and submit a request. You'll see in the Synapse ESB console that the message was received by the ESB and processed according to the rules specified in your configuration XML.

While we've spent a little time going through this message mediation example, much of what you learned will be used again as we proceed, so these are important building blocks. Let's now compare how service mediation contrasts with what we've seen with message mediation.

9.4.2 *Simple service mediation example*

In service mediation, unlike with message mediation, you explicitly configure an endpoint URL address in the configuration. This approach has the benefit of eliminating the need for the types of `switch` and `filter` statements we used with message mediation. Let's look at the sample shown in listing 9.4.

Listing 9.4 Simple example of service mediation

```
<definitions xmlns="http://ws.apache.org/ns/synapse">
  <proxy name="CreateOrderService" transports="http">     <-- 1 Uses proxy mediation now
    <target>
      <inSequence>                    <-- 2 Defines inbound mediator
        <log level="full"/>
        <property name="RESPONSE" value="true"/>
        <header name="To" action="remove"/>
```

```
        <script language="js"><![CDATA[
          mc.setPayloadXML(
           <CreateOrderResponse xmlns="uri:opensoa.chapter09.order">
             <Status>200</Status>
             <Message>Ok</Message>
           </CreateOrderResponse>);
        ]]></script>
        <send/>
      </inSequence>
    </target>
  </proxy>
</definitions>
```

In listing 9.4, the `proxy` element ❶ is now used instead of the `sequence name="main"` to indicate that service mediation will be used. The term *proxy* is used by Synapse because this form of mediation indicates that Synapse is *acting as a proxy* on behalf of a service that's being called. It's analogous to when you grant the power of attorney to someone; that individual is authorized to act on your behalf. In this case, you're letting the Synapse configuration manage how the ultimate endpoint service is to be called.

NOTE The URL for submitting a request against the configuration shown in listing 9.4 would resemble http://localhost:8280/soap/CreateOrderService, with a sample provided in the soapUI project.

The `target` element accepts three child elements: `inSequence`, `outSequence`, and `endpoint`. `inSequence` ❷ is used for inserting mediators on the outbound/request message. In other words, you could use this element to modify the outbound message prior to it being sent to its destination. In this example, we're mocking up a response directly, so we aren't forwarding the message. `outSequence` is used when you want to mediate the response received by the outbound service. In this example, there's no response to mediate, because we forced a response in `inSequence` by setting the property `RESPONSE` to `true`. Finally, the `endpoint` is used to specify the destination for the request. To demonstrate the use of `endpoint` and `outSequence`, let's create a mock web service that can be called. It will return the same XML as shown in listing 9.4, but will be a stand-alone service. That way, when `CreateOrderService` is called, it will forward the request to this mock web service. Listing 9.5 thus illustrates a more typical use of the proxy configuration.

Listing 9.5 Example of invoking a web service from within a proxy

```
<definitions xmlns="http://ws.apache.org/ns/synapse">
  <endpoint name="mock">                                          ❶ Defines reusable endpoint
    <address uri="http://localhost:8280/soap/mockEndpoint"
      format="soap11"/>
  </endpoint>
  <proxy name="CreateOrderService" transports="http" trace="enable">
    <target>
      <endpoint key="mock"/>                                      ❷ Uses defined endpoint
```

```
      <inSequence> <log level="full"/> </inSequence>
      <outSequence>
        <log level="full"/>
        <send/>                    ❸ Requires send
      </outSequence>
    </target>
  </proxy>
  <proxy name="mockEndpoint" transports="http">      ❹ Defines mock service
    <target>
      <inSequence>
        <property name="RESPONSE" value="true"/>
        <header name="To" action="remove"/>
        <script language="js"><![CDATA[
          mc.setPayloadXML(
          <CreateOrderResponse xmlns="uri:opensoa.chapter09.order">
            <Status>200</Status>
            <Message>Ok</Message>
          </CreateOrderResponse>);
        ]]></script>
        <send/>
      </inSequence>
    </target>
  </proxy>
</definitions>
```

In listing 9.5, the new mock web service we've created is defined within the proxy element named mockEndpoint ❹. The ability to easily create such mock services is also useful for testing purposes (see [Godage] for an excellent article on using this approach). The use of reusable endpoints is also demonstrated in the listing, where the mock endpoint is defined at the root level of the configuration ❶. The @format attribute is used to identify the message protocol we're using, in this example SOAP v1.1. If @format is omitted, the format will be assumed to be the same as the incoming request. This endpoint defined in ❶ is then referenced, by way of the @key attribute ❷, from within the CreateOrderService proxy definition (alternatively, we could have specified the full URL by using the @uri attribute instead of the @key attribute). Because this endpoint is defined as a child element of target, there's no need to explicitly issue a <send/> from within inSequence (indeed, doing so will cause looping issues). An equivalent target configuration is

```
<target>
  <inSequence>
    <send><endpoint key="mock"/></send>
  </inSequence>
  <outSequence> <log level="full"/> <send/></outSequence>
</target>
```

Here, the endpoint has been moved from a child of target to a child of send.

Let's turn now to the outSequence element in listing 9.5. Since it's present, a <send/> must be explicitly issued ❸. If the logging mediator weren't needed as shown, the entire outSequence could have been left out, since no other mediation on the response message is being performed.

NOTE Although we've been talking about inbound SOAP requests, we could've just as well been using plain old XML (POX). The only difference is that the inbound request from the client would need to have an HTTP `Content-Type` header value set to `application/xml`, not `text/xml`, along with omitting the SOAP envelop. The POX example in the soapUI project demonstrates a simple XML request.

Now that we've covered some of the basics of configuring Synapse, the next chapter will introduce you to more detailed examples using a significant portion of Synapse functionality distilled through a real-life case study.

9.5 Summary

An enterprise service bus (ESB) is probably one of the most confusing technology categories to get your head around. In part, this is because an ESB is both a framework and a tool, and its capabilities can vary significantly from product to product. However, we did isolate what are considered to be the key functionalities found in any full-featured ESB, and we then identified the most appropriate uses of the technology in a SOA environment. Because ESBs are so flexible, they can be subject to misuse, so we touched on some examples of where this can occur.

In the second portion of this chapter, we introduced Apache Synapse, which we selected as the ESB for our Open SOA Platform. Synapse was chosen based on its complete feature set, lightweight footprint, performance, and simplicity. It provides the basic ESB functionality, and offers some unique features related to load balancing, failover, and message metering.

Now that we've got a solid understanding of the functionality and role of an ESB, we can turn to the fun stuff: examples of implementing Synapse with an emphasis on how it can be integrated with our other Open SOA products. This is our focus for the next chapter.

10 ESB implementation with Apache Synapse

This chapter covers

- Implementing a real-life case study
- Using multiple protocols with Synapse
- Advanced service mediation

In chapter 9 we introduced the enterprise service bus (ESB) and described its role in service-oriented architecture (SOA). While there is some debate as to exactly what constitutes an ESB, at its core it's messaging middleware that provides such services as message routing, transformation, and connectivity/bridging for a variety of protocols. In the open source community, there are several outstanding ESB choices, including Mule, Apache ServiceMix, and OpenESB, among others. For our Open SOA Platform, we've selected Apache Synapse. Although you've seen a brief hands-on introduction to Synapse, we haven't explored the specifics of using the product. We'll cover those specifics in this chapter and place special emphasis on integrating Synapse with the other products making up our Open SOA Platform.

The documentation that comes with Synapse is fairly sparse, but a fairly comprehensive set of examples exists (70 examples, as of this writing). The examples are well documented and easy to try out.

NOTE WSO2, the principal sponsor of Synapse, packages a Synapse-based product called *WSO2 ESB* and has set up a portal website called the *ESB Site*, located at http://esbsite.org. The site offers articles, code examples, blogs, custom mediators, and video tutorials on Synapse and WSO2's ESB; it's an excellent resource.

The examples that come with Synapse are purposely kept very simple so that they're easy to follow. This serves the purpose of introducing the user to the various Synapse functionalities but often doesn't reflect more real-world usage scenarios. We'll bridge that gap in this chapter by building a case study that becomes increasingly rich as the chapter progresses. In addition, we'll integrate Synapse with the other Open SOA products we've discussed and demonstrate the synergies that can be achieved. Let's begin by looking at our hypothetical case study.

10.1 Learning Synapse through a case study

Our case study revolves around a sales order process for receiving electronic orders from partners or customers. Orders can be received through a variety of communication protocols such as HTTP (SOAP or XML) or FTP, and then forwarded internally to a jBPM business process. Once the order has been processed, a reply message is sent to the order originator/customer. I chose this scenario as it is a fairly common process used by service and manufacturing organizations alike. In the past, such a process would typically be accomplished by adopting an electronic data interchange (EDI) solution. However, the cost and complexity of EDI limited its appeal to all but the largest of organizations. Fortunately, with the advent of standards-based web services leveraging the ubiquitous connectivity provided by the internet, small and medium-sized businesses (SMBs) can now enjoy the benefits of such automation.

The case study is broken into four phases, with each phase layering in some new Synapse functionality. First I'll provide an overview of the phases; when we get into the details of each, you'll see flow diagrams that describe the process we're modeling.

10.1.1 Phase 1: typical web service mediation using error handling, routing, and transport switching

In phase 1, we'll configure Synapse to receive an inbound SOAP order using the OASIS Universal Business Language (UBL) vocabulary [UBL]. UBL is one of the increasingly popular business document libraries intended to standardize electronic communications between companies (other popular vocabularies include RosettaNet, the Open Applications Group Integration Specification [OAGIS], and Electronic Business XML, or ebXML). Once the UBL order is received, the XML is validated and converted into a simplified XML format that's more suitable for internal use. The transformation includes adding a SOAP envelope that is then used for instantiating a jBPM business process. You may recall that in chapter 7 we created a SOAP interface to jBPM, and we used it as the basis for this example. The SOAP message used for instantiating the jBPM process is transmitted via JMS, as this is a more robust protocol than HTTP, but is suitable only for internal communications.

The features of Synapse that we'll use in phase 1 of the case study include

- SOAP over HTTP, configured as a Synapse proxy
- XML validation mediator, which will be used to verify that the inbound UBL order conforms with the UBL schema
- The XSLT mediator to convert the UBL order into a format suitable for instantiating a new jBPM business process
- Protocol switching from SOAP over HTTP to SOAP over JMS for internal messaging

10.1.2 Phase 2: protocol/transport bridging and event propagation

In the second phase of the case study, we'll demonstrate a scenario where a customer is supplying the order in a comma-separated values (CSV) format over FTP. This remains a common scenario, but unlike the SOAP solution described in phase 1, it introduces some unique challenges, such as converting the CSV data file into XML and for managing error handing, since it's an asynchronous batch operation. As part of this phase, we'll also describe how to interface with Esper, the event stream processor (ESP) we described in detail in chapter 8.

In addition, one of the main advantages of using an ESB is that, as the central point for all internal messaging, it's ideally positioned as a propagator of business events. We can employ a wiretap style mediator to simultaneously send events to Esper as they flow through the bus.

In all, the Synapse features we'll demonstrate in phase 2 are

- Use of a file system transport to pull files from either FTP or a local file system
- Introduction of a custom mediator to process the CSV data file into XML
- Use of the mail transport to email the customer if errors are encountered in validating the data
- Use of the clone mediator, which is a wiretap message pattern implementation used to send a copy of the order to Esper

A frequent use of an ESB is supporting legacy-style protocols, such as the ones we're using with this example. The unfortunate fact remains that many companies only support these old "file-drop" style integrations, so it's important that we demonstrate how this can be supported within Synapse.

10.1.3 Phase 3: using tasks, scripting, and database integration

In phase 3 we'll introduce some of the more advanced features of Synapse, such as tasks, database integration using the database mediator, and message splitting. You'll learn how a task can be used to periodically poll another web service for information, such as a sales order. Use of the database mediator will be demonstrated by using it to look up customer details after an order has been received, and we'll incorporate this information to enrich the in-transit XML so that when it's received internally, it has all of the required information present.

To summarize, we'll cover the following Synapse features:

- Synapse tasks using the `MessageInjector` class
- Database lookups using the DB mediator
- Message splitting pattern implementation using the iterator mediator

By the end of this phase, you'll have the essentials necessary to begin using Synapse as a truly enterprise-class ESB.

10.1.4 Phase 4: quality of service mediation

In the last phase, we'll focus on Synapse's QoS features, which include WS-Security support and what Synapse refers to as *throttling*. Like a lot of standards, WS-Security was slow to be embraced, but it's now gathering a fair amount of industry support. Widespread adoption was predicated on the release of libraries such as Apache's Rampart, which has subsequently been rolled into many open source and commercial web service products, including Apache Axis 2.

Synapse's concept of throttling pertains to the ability to offer different service levels for different clients, based on criteria such as the incoming IP address (or hostname) associated with the request. You can use it to restrict access altogether, or for capping the total number of requests allowed in a given period. This is a powerful feature, particularly for organizations wanting to adopt a Software as a Service (SaaS) product offering.

NOTE Probably the most well-known SaaS offering is from Salesforce.com, which provides a platform for building web-based business applications that are remotely hosted. Salesforce offers a comprehensive SOAP-based API that allows its clients to access, via service calls, nearly every aspect of the application. Other well-known SaaS vendors include RightNow Technologies (CRM), Taleo (applicant tracking), HireRight (background screening), and SuccessFactors (performance and talent management).

Throughout the course of these examples, we'll demonstrate most of the Synapse configuration language constructs, and also illustrate how to use the local and remote registry capabilities. When completed with all phases of the case study, you'll have a solid understanding of how to use Synapse in your enterprise, and you'll be armed with some real-life examples from which to build on.

10.2 Phase 1: simple web service mediation

In phase 1 of the project, an inbound SOAP order is received by a customer (the role we're playing, as a supplier), validated, transformed, and deposited on a JMS queue for arrival into a new jBPM process instance. The diagram in figure 10.1 shows an overview of the process.

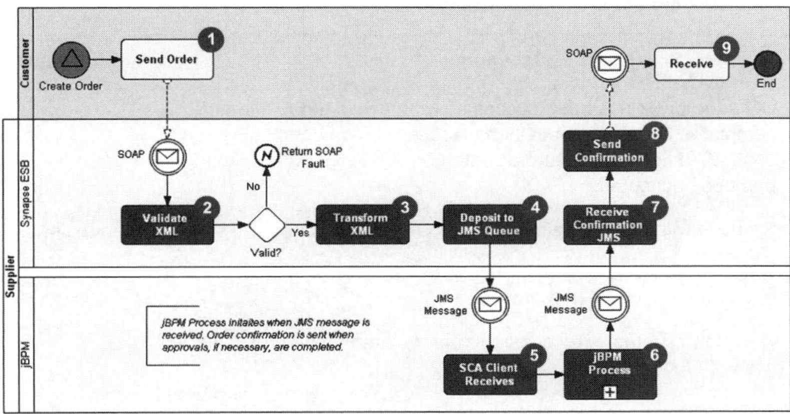

Figure 10.1 Phase 1 case study process diagram

Each step in the process is described in table 10.1, cross-referenced using the sequence number shown in the diagram.

Table 10.1 Phase 1 project steps

Step #	Description	Synapse feature
1	A customer places a sales order request using the UBL-Order-2.0 XML Schema. The message protocol is using SOAP, over an HTTP transport. We'll simulate this traffic using the soapUI testing tool (open source).	
2	The inbound SOAP request is received by Synapse, which then validates the XML against the UBL schema. When using XML-based web services, this is always a prudent step to ensure the message content adheres to what was mutually agreed.	SOAP endpoint proxy and validate mediator
3	Once validated, the next step is to transform the UBL XML format into a simplified internal XML sales order format. The ultimate recipient of the new order will be a jBPM process instance, so we're also wrapping the order document within the web service wrapper we created in chapter 7.	XSLT mediator
4	Internally, JMS is used as the preferred transport, due to its reliability and ease by which we can set up multiple queue listeners for simple load balancing. We'll use Synapse's transport-switching ability to deposit the internal SOAP message into a JMS queue.	Transport switching from SOAP over HTTP to SOAP over JMS
5	The jBPM web service interface developed in chapter 7 using SCA/Synapse will be used to lift the incoming SOAP-over-JMS message and start a new jBPM business process instance.	

Table 10.1 Phase 1 project steps *(continued)*

Step #	Description	Synapse feature
6	Once the order has been successfully received and fulfillment completed in the jBPM business process, an outbound message will be generated to the customer, verifying that the order has been accepted.	
7	Synapse will receive the inbound JMS message.	JMS endpoint
8	Synapse will use protocol switching to convert the message into an outbound HTTP message.	HTTP sent using SOAP format
9	The client/customer receives the order confirmation message (we will stub this out).	

Let's start by examining the inbound message that initiates the process.

10.2.1 Sales order initiation

To make this case study reflective of a real-life scenario, we'll transmit the sales order using the UBL business document schema. UBL doesn't, by itself, provide a SOAP envelope for transmitting messages, so I crafted a simple WSDL and created a single-service operation called `CreateOrder`. A depiction of the schema appears in figure 10.2 (you can find the complete WSDL, called `ubl_order.wsdl`, in chapter 10's sample code). In figure 10.2 under the `CreateOrderPortType`'s `CreateOrder` operation, you can see that the input XML is represented by the `order:CreateOrder` element. Investigate the actual WSDL code, and you'll see that this points to a UBL schema (which I trimmed to make our example easier to follow) that corresponds to the UBL `Order` document. This WSDL can then be shared with the hypothetical business partner so that they can place an order.

Now that we have a WSDL that describes our web service, we can move on to the fun stuff—creating a Synapse project definition that configures the ESB to receive the inbound SOAP message.

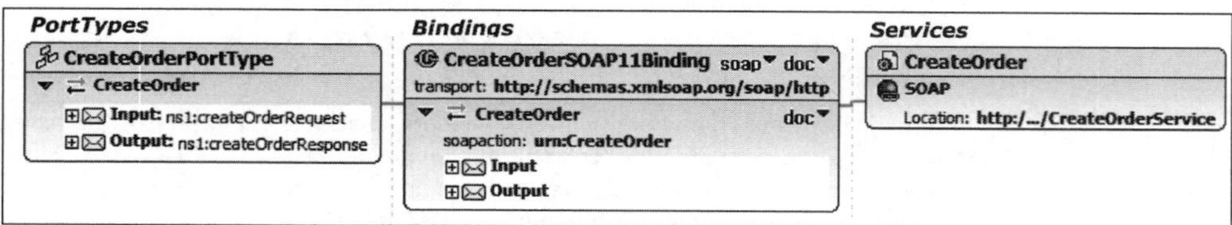

Figure 10.2 The WSDL used for capturing inbound sales order from a hypothetical customer

10.2.2 *Configuring the service mediation proxy and using validation mediation*

As shown in figure 10.1, we'll configure Synapse to receive the inbound order so that it can then perform various actions on the request. Let's begin by configuring a service mediator (proxy) that includes a validation of the inbound XML, as shown in listing 10.1.

Listing 10.1 Service mediation using XML validation and remote registry

```
<definitions xmlns="http://ws.apache.org/ns/synapse">
  <registry
     provider="org.apache.synapse.registry.url.SimpleURLRegistry">
    <parameter name="root">
     file:./repository/conf/opensoa/resources/
    </parameter>
    <parameter name="cachableDuration">150000</parameter>
  </registry>
  <endpoint name="mock">
    <address uri="http://localhost:8280/soap/mockEndpoint"/>
  </endpoint>
  <proxy name="CreateOrderService" transports="http" >
    <target>
      <endpoint key="mock"/>
      <inSequence>
        <log level="full"/>
        <validate source="//*[local-name()='Order']">
          <schema key="schemas/ubl.xsd"/>
          <on-fail>
            <makefault>
              <code value="tns:Receiver"
               xmlns:tns="http://www.w3.org/2003/05/soap-envelope"/>
                <reason value="Invalid Order Request"/>
            </makefault>
            <property name="RESPONSE" value="true"/>
            <header name="To" action="remove"/>
            <send/><drop/>
          </on-fail>
        </validate>
      </inSequence>
    </target>
  </proxy>
  <proxy name="mockEndpoint" transports="http">
    <target inSequence="sequence/mockProxy.xml"/>
  </proxy>
</definitions>
```

1. Defines registry
2. Identifies XPath location
3. Identifies XSD used for validation
4. Defines fault behavior
5. Terminates processing
6. Defines mock proxy
7. Invokes named sequence

Some of what's shown in listing 10.1 we covered in the previous section, but we've introduced some new functionality. The `registry` node ❶ is used to define a remote registry that's used by the configuration (though in this case it's just referring to a local file system location). Many of the definitions and artifacts used by a configuration can reside in a registry, which simplifies maintenance and promotes reuse. The `@provider` attribute identifies the class used to manage the registry. In this case, we're using a URL-based registry that comes with Synapse, but you can add your own, if necessary. The `SimpleURLRegistry` can cache registry entries, with the refresh period specified through the `@cachableDuration` parameter. The `root` parameter identifies the root location for the resources that can be loaded; that way, subsequent references to those resources can be conveniently set as path fragments appended to that location (we'll see this used in a moment).

What are we storing in the registry? We're using it to store the location of the UBL XSD schema that's used to validate the inbound `CreateOrderService` request (to refresh your memory, the OASIS Order document is used to represent the inbound order schema we're using in the case study). The schema validation is performed using the `validate` mediator, which is defined in ❷. The `scheme` child element's `@key` attribute is used to locate the XSD file ❸ using the registry's root path element (`schemas/ubl.xsd`). The `@source` attribute of the `validate` element identifies, via an XPath expression, where the validation should begin within the XML. In this case, we're specifying the `Order` element as the root. An example order can be found in the soapUI project in this section's source code, but for those eager for a glimpse, figure 10.3 shows a little fragment of what the order resembles.

Continuing with the example from listing 10.1, the `validate` statement accepts an optional `on-fail` element ❹. This identifies what actions to take in the event that the validation fails. One or more mediators can be included here, but for now we're only calling the `makefault` mediator to force generation of a SOAP fault. Finally, the fault response is sent back to the client and further processing of the message is terminated ❺.

The last thing to point out is the definition of the `mockEndpoint` ❻ proxy. You may remember from listing 9.5 in the previous chapter that we used `mockEndpoint` to simulate, or mock, a SOAP response. In this case, its full definition has been removed from the configuration and placed in a file accessible to the repository called sequence/mockProxy.xml. The contents of that file are as follows:

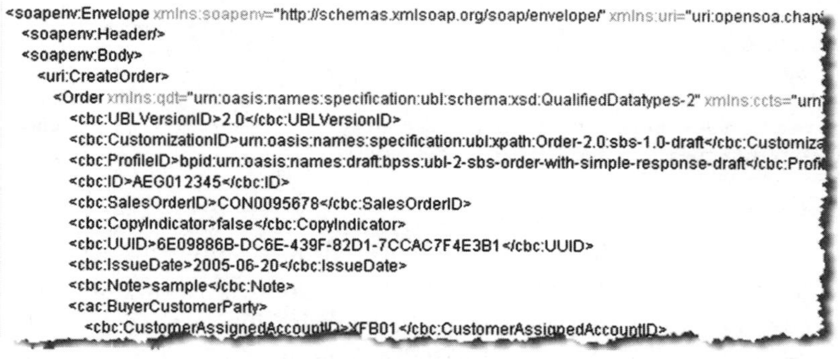

```
<soapenv:Envelope xmlns:soapenv="http://schemas.xmlsoap.org/soap/envelope/" xmlns:uri="uri:opensoa.chap
  <soapenv:Header/>
  <soapenv:Body>
    <uri:CreateOrder>
      <Order xmlns:qdt="urn:oasis:names:specification:ubl:schema:xsd:QualifiedDatatypes-2" xmlns:ccts="urn
        <cbc:UBLVersionID>2.0</cbc:UBLVersionID>
        <cbc:CustomizationID>urn:oasis:names:specification:ubl:xpath:Order-2.0:sbs-1.0-draft</cbc:Customiza
        <cbc:ProfileID>bpid:urn:oasis:names:draft:bpss:ubl-2-sbs-order-with-simple-response-draft</cbc:Profi
        <cbc:ID>AEG012345</cbc:ID>
        <cbc:SalesOrderID>CON0095678</cbc:SalesOrderID>
        <cbc:CopyIndicator>false</cbc:CopyIndicator>
        <cbc:UUID>6E09886B-DC6E-439F-82D1-7CCAC7F4E3B1</cbc:UUID>
        <cbc:IssueDate>2005-06-20</cbc:IssueDate>
        <cbc:Note>sample</cbc:Note>
        <cac:BuyerCustomerParty>
          <cbc:CustomerAssignedAccountID>XFB01</cbc:CustomerAssignedAccountID>
```

Figure 10.3 Example of an inbound `CreateOrderService` SOAP request

```
<sequence name="mockProxy" xmlns="http://ws.apache.org/ns/synapse">
  <property name="RESPONSE" value="true"/>
  <header name="To" action="remove"/>
  <script language="js"><![CDATA[
    mc.setPayloadXML(
    <CreateOrderResponse xmlns="uri:opensoa.chapter10.order">
      <Status>200</Status>
      <Message>Ok</Message>
    </CreateOrderResponse>);
  ]]></script>
  <send/>
</sequence>
```

This code does differ slightly from the code in listing 9.5 since we're defining a `sequence` and not a `proxy`. In this case, the `proxy` definition ❼ in listing 10.1 specifies the `inSequence` as a named sequence available through the registry path provided. You could, for example, choose not to use a registry and instead include the `sequence` node directly within the configuration; then you'd reference it by the name assigned the sequence, `mockProxy`.

When using an external file, a final, but important, note is the namespace declaration that is used in the stand-alone file containing the `sequence` (`xmlns=http://ws.apache.org/ns/synapse`). This is required, and if omitted, the sequence will fail when invoked (with little reason provided as to why it failed, so be warned).

The next step, once the message has passed validation, is to transform the UBL order XML into the simplified XML used internally for processing orders. This requires the XSLT mediator.

10.2.3 Configuring XSLT mediation

One of the most frequent uses of an ESB is to transform an in- or outbound message from one XML format or vocabulary into another. Synapse makes doing so a straightforward endeavor. In our case study, a hypothetical order arrives in the UBL XML format, and we want to transform it into a simple schema—one without the namespaces and complex structure of UBL documents. We won't go through the process of developing the XSLT file, as that's beyond the scope of this book. The XSLT file I developed for this example is called mapUBLOrder.xslt, and you can find it in the source code for this section.

In listing 10.1 we demonstrated the use of a remote registry. This time around, we'll use a local registry and illustrate how it can be used. The main distinction between a local and a remote registry is that, when using a local registry, you're limited to specifying a file within the file system that Synapse is running under. A local registry is specified using the `localEntry` element, which is defined at the main root level of the configuration (where registry was located in listing 10.1). For example:

```
<localEntry key="xslt-key"
   src="file:repository/conf/opensoa/resources/xslt/mapUBLOrder.xslt"/>
```

Then you can reference that key within the `xslt` mediator definition, which in this case is located immediately following the `validate` node, since we want to run the transformation only if the inbound XML is valid. The `xslt` statement is defined as

```
<xslt key="xslt-key" source="//*[local-name()='CreateOrder']"/>
```

As you can see, the `@key` value (`xslt-key`) corresponds to the `localEntry` we just defined. The `xslt` element's optional `@source` attribute serves the same purpose as it did in the `validate` element: to identify the child node where the XSLT processing should begin. In this example, we use the XPath `local-name` function so that we don't have to fuss with the namespace of the `CreateOrder` element. Otherwise, you could use this:

```
<xslt key="xslt-key" source="//order:CreateOrder"
  xmlns:order="uri:opensoa.chapter10.order"/>
```

NOTE The sample configuration that demonstrates the `xslt` mediator is called synapse_sample_opensoa_7.xml. It can be invoked using the run.example.07 ant target and tested by submitting a request using the sample soapUI project. You should see the modified XML in the Synapse console.

The XML transformation not only converts the order into the proper internal format, but it also prepares the message for consumption by the service that will be used to instantiate a new jBPM business process instance. You learned about the web service interface in chapter 7.

Let's now demonstrate how Synapse can easily bridge multiple transports.

10.2.4 Transport switching from HTTP to JMS

To run the examples for this section, you'll need an instance of JMS running, and you'll need to configure Synapse to support JMS. The README.txt file in the source code describes how to configure Apache ActiveMQ as the JMS server. The setting changes required in Synapse to interact with it are minimal. To keep things simple, we'll mock the jBPM JMS service (though in this section's code samples, you can run a complete end-to-end test). This approach has the added advantage of showing you how to configure a JMS listener in Synapse. Let's start by first creating the mock JMS service, which will simulate the jBPM process receiving the inbound message, and then we'll tackle configuring the ESB to submit a message on a JMS queue.

CONFIGURING A MOCK JMS SERVICE PROXY

You'll be surprised at the ease with which you can set up a JMS proxy service that Synapse can use to listen to a queue for inbound messages. Since the JMS configuration properties are defined in the axis2.xml file, Synapse will automatically associate the name (the `@name` attribute) assigned to the `proxy` to the JMS queue it's listening on (see listing 10.2).

Listing 10.2 Example of JMS proxy listener configuration

```
<proxy name="CreateProcessInstanceService"          ← Defines new
  transports="jms">                                    ❶ proxy
  <target>
    <inSequence>
      <property action="set" name="OUT_ONLY"        ← Requires property
        value="true"/>                                 ❷ for JMS
      <property name="RESPONSE" value="true"/>
      <script language="js">
        <![CDATA[mc.setPayloadXML(
          <createProcessInstanceResponse
            xmlns="http://vo.sca.opensoa-ch10/xsd">
            <processInstanceId>1001</processInstanceId>
          </createProcessInstanceResponse>);]]>
       </script>
       <send/>
    </inSequence>
  </target>
</proxy>
```

As you can see in listing 10.2, the name assigned to the `proxy` definition is `CreateProcessInstanceService` ❶; that's also the queue name it will be listening for. Synapse knows to use JMS since the `@transports` attribute is assigned to `jms`. Beyond that, the only difference between this and the SOAP previous mock service is the creation and setting of the property called `OUT_ONLY` ❷. This property is used to indicate that the message processing doesn't expect a response since we're generating the response manually. Pretty simple, huh? Let's look at the modified proxy service that will then submit requests to the JMS queue that we're subscribing to in listing 10.2.

CONFIGURING THE PROXY TO SUBMIT THE JMS MESSAGE

In listing 10.1 we defined the proxy `CreateOrderService`, the service that receives the inbound UBL order from the customer or partner. Now we need to make a few changes to the proxy. Previously, we configured `CreateOrderService` to validate, transform, and ultimately send the request to a SOAP-over-HTTP endpoint. Let's replace the endpoint definition with the assigned name of `mock` in listing 10.1 with the following, which is now using JMS to interface with the mock endpoint we created in listing 10.2:

```
<endpoint name="MockCreateProcessInstanceService">
  <address uri="jms:/CreateProcessInstanceService?
  ➥transport.jms.ConnectionFactoryJNDIName=QueueConnectionFactory&amp;
  ➥java.naming.factory.initial=
  ➥org.apache.activemq.jndi.ActiveMQInitialContextFactory&amp;
  ➥java.naming.provider.url=tcp://localhost:61616&amp;
  ➥transport.jms.DestinationType=queue" format="soap11"/>
</endpoint>
```

The `@uri` attribute value has now been configured to send the message to the same JMS queue that we assigned in the proxy mock service in listing 10.2. (The other parameter value settings are typical ActiveMQ configuration settings and aren't unique to Synapse.) The only other change is updating the endpoint key to `<endpoint key="MockCreateProcessInstanceService"/>` in the `proxy` definition for `CreateOrderService` (see synapse_sample_opensoa_8.xml in the source code).

These are all the changes necessary to perform the transport switch from receiving as SOAP over HTTP to sending to an endpoint as SOAP over JMS. There's one minor improvement we can make related to manageability. Specifying the endpoint address in the ESB configuration file isn't always desirable, since it can be dynamically determined by interrogating the WSDL associated with the SOAP service. How can this be accomplished? The first step is to modify the SOAP's WSDL so that it includes binding and service definitions for JMS (a lot of people assume that a WSDL is only used in conjunction with SOAP over HTTP, but a WSDL is actually transport neutral). In chapter 7 we created a WSDL for the jBPM web services we developed, but that only included HTTP bindings. Listing 10.3 is an example of an added JMS binding.

Listing 10.3 Example of WSDL JMS binding configuration

```
<wsdl:binding name="CreateProcessInstanceJMSBinding"
    type="ns1:CreateProcessInstancePortType">
  <soap:binding style="document"
    transport="http://schemas.xmlsoap.org/soap/jms"/>      ❶ Specifies JMS as transport type
  <wsdl:operation name="createProcessInstance" >
    <soap:operation soapAction="" style="document"/>       ❷ Sets soapAction to ""
     <wsdl:input><soap:body use="literal"/></wsdl:input>
     <wsdl:output><soap:body use="literal"/></wsdl:output>
  </wsdl:operation>
</wsdl:binding>
```

The main difference between listing 10.3 and the standard HTTP binding we defined earlier is the `soap:binding`'s `@transport` attribute value, which identifies it as JMS ❶. The `@soapAction` attribute has also been set to `""` ❷, since that value is most typically passed as an HTTP header property, which isn't directly relevant in JMS. Obviously, this doesn't specify the endpoint URL JMS address—we do this using the `soap:address` element in the `wsdl:service` definition, as shown in listing 10.4.

Listing 10.4 Setting up a WSDL service for use with JMS binding

```
<wsdl:service name="CreateProcessInstance">
  <wsdl:port name="SOAP"                                     ❶ Specifies SOAP binding
     binding="ns1:CreateProcessInstanceSOAP11Binding">
    <soap:address
      location="http://localhost:8085/CreateProcessInstanceService"/>
  </wsdl:port>
  <wsdl:port name="JMS"                                      ❷ Specifies JMS binding
    binding="ns1:CreateProcessInstanceJMSBinding">
    <soap:address location=                                  Defines JMS parameters
    ➥"jms:/CreateProcessInstanceService?
    ➥transport.jms.ConnectionFactoryJNDIName=
    ➥QueueConnectionFactory&amp;
    ➥java.naming.factory.initial=
    ➥org.apache.activemq.jndi.ActiveMQInitialContextFactory&amp;
```

```
➥java.naming.provider.url=
➥tcp://localhost:61616?wireFormat.maxInactivityDuration=0"/>
  </wsdl:port>
</wsdl:service>
```

In listing 10.4, the `wsdl:service` definition includes the original `wsdl:port` definition for the HTTP binding ❶, but now it has an additional `wsdl:port` node ❷ for the new JMS binding we created in listing 10.3. This node has the same JMS URL specified in the `@location` attribute that we specified earlier in the ESB configuration file. The WSDL now includes provisions for both HTTP and JMS. You might be wondering whether this is worth the trouble, so let's see how this WSDL can now be used in the ESB configuration.

Until now, the `endpoint` nodes we've defined have all used the `address` child element (see listing 10.1). However, you can also specify a `wsdl` element in lieu of the `address` element. `wsdl` enables you to define the endpoint URL by referencing (or looking up) the service in a WSDL file. For example, to reference the service we defined in listing 10.4, we'd use this:

```
<endpoint>
  <wsdl uri="file:repository/conf/opensoa/resources/wsdl/jbpm-ch10.wsdl"
    service="CreateProcessInstance" port="JMS"/>
</endpoint>
```

Now we no longer have to specify the URL address in the Synapse configuration file. If the URL changes in the WSDL (for example, the JMS queue name is used), no changes would be have to be made in the ESB configuration. When managing lots of services, this strategy is clearly advantageous.

So what have we done up to this point in our case study? We've configured steps 1–4 shown in figure 10.1. We've set up an ESB proxy service to receive the inbound order, validate the XML, transform the XML, and deposit the message to a JMS queue. So we've accomplished a great deal! What remains are steps 5–9, where the jBPM service receives the inbound JMS message, creates a jBPM process instance, and sends a confirmation back to the hypothetical customer. Since we're focusing on Synapse now, we'll skip steps 5–6, which pertain to creating the jBPM process instance. The README.txt associated with this chapter's examples demonstrates how to set up this part, and it builds on what we developed in chapter 7. Let's skip ahead to steps 7–9, where the Synapse ESB will receive a JMS message sent through the jBPM process instance and send a confirmation of the order back to the customer.

10.2.5 Transport switching from JMS to HTTP

Figure 10.4 shows an example of the XML response that's sent by the jBPM process instance upon approval of the sales order. It's obviously a simple XML document. The UBL order response, which is a bit more involved, appears in the foreground in the figure.

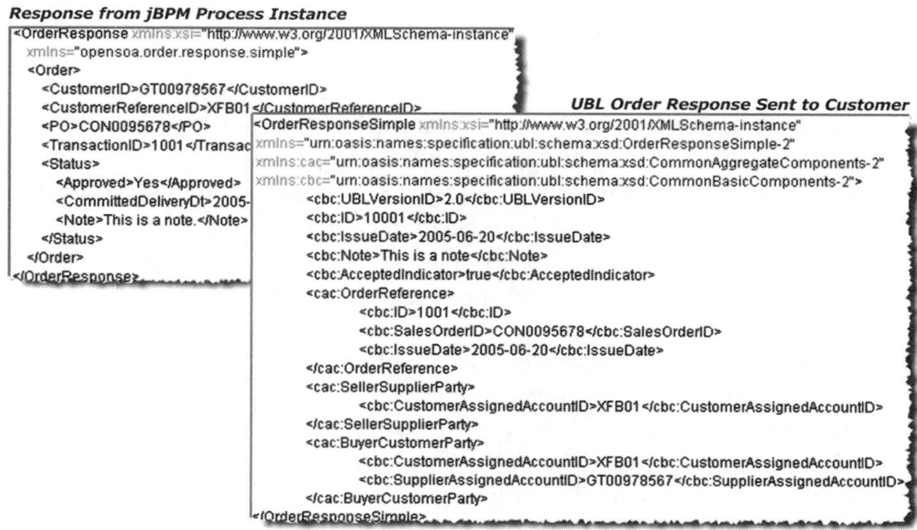

Response from jBPM Process Instance

```
<OrderResponse xmlns:xsi="http://www.w3.org/2001/XMLSchema-instance"
  xmlns="opensoa.order.response.simple">
  <Order>
    <CustomerID>GT00978567</CustomerID>
    <CustomerReferenceID>XFB01</CustomerReferenceID>
    <PO>CON0095678</PO>
    <TransactionID>1001</Transac
    <Status>
      <Approved>Yes</Approved>
      <CommittedDeliveryDt>2005-
      <Note>This is a note.</Note>
    </Status>
  </Order>
</OrderResponse>
```

UBL Order Response Sent to Customer

```
<OrderResponseSimple xmlns:xsi="http://www.w3.org/2001/XMLSchema-instance"
xmlns="urn:oasis:names:specification:ubl:schema:xsd:OrderResponseSimple-2"
xmlns:cac="urn:oasis:names:specification:ubl:schema:xsd:CommonAggregateComponents-2"
xmlns:cbc="urn:oasis:names:specification:ubl:schema:xsd:CommonBasicComponents-2">
        <cbc:UBLVersionID>2.0</cbc:UBLVersionID>
        <cbc:ID>10001</cbc:ID>
        <cbc:IssueDate>2005-06-20</cbc:IssueDate>
        <cbc:Note>This is a note</cbc:Note>
        <cbc:AcceptedIndicator>true</cbc:AcceptedIndicator>
        <cac:OrderReference>
                <cbc:ID>1001</cbc:ID>
                <cbc:SalesOrderID>CON0095678</cbc:SalesOrderID>
                <cbc:IssueDate>2005-06-20</cbc:IssueDate>
        </cac:OrderReference>
        <cac:SellerSupplierParty>
                <cbc:CustomerAssignedAccountID>XFB01</cbc:CustomerAssignedAccountID>
        </cac:SellerSupplierParty>
        <cac:BuyerCustomerParty>
                <cbc:CustomerAssignedAccountID>XFB01</cbc:CustomerAssignedAccountID>
                <cbc:SupplierAssignedAccountID>GT00978567</cbc:SupplierAssignedAccountID>
        </cac:BuyerCustomerParty>
</OrderResponseSimple>
```

Figure 10.4 An example of XML sent by the jBPM process instance and ultimately to the hypothetical customer

Thus, in addition to receiving the message via JMS from jBPM, we need to convert the XML to the external UBL `OrderResponseSimple` document type. This is a simple mapping for an XSLT style sheet, as you can see in figure 10.5.

With the style sheet in hand, we can now configure the ESB to listen for the JMS message sent from jBPM and forward it as a UBL `OrderResponseSimple` response to the customer. This follows closely with what we learned earlier. The first thing we'll do is create a mock web service that simulates the one we'd expect to be hosted by the customer receiving the order response.

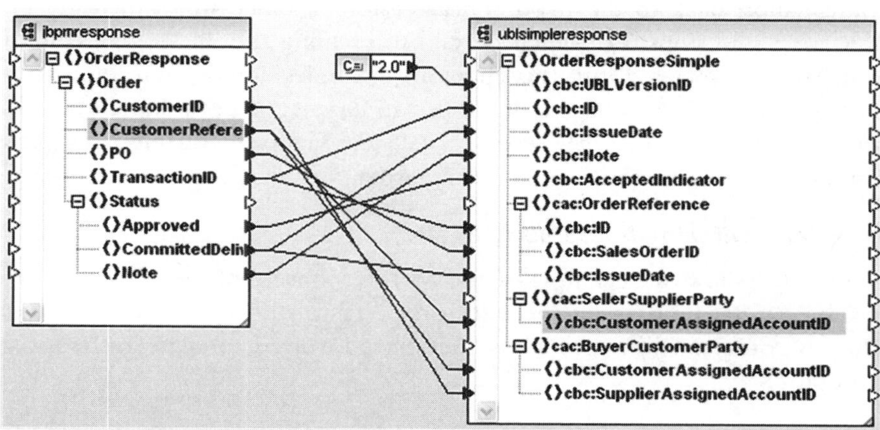

Figure 10.5 Mapping between internal and external order responses (response.xslt in the sample)

CREATING A MOCK WEB SERVICE FOR THE CUSTOMER ORDER RESPONSE SERVICE

The endpoint name we'll assign for the mock service is `OrderResponseService`. To keep our configuration file clean, we'll use the registry feature and reference the configuration from an external file. Here's the definition of the service in the main ESB configuration:

```
<proxy name="OrderResponseService" transports="http">
  <target inSequence="sequence/mockProxyResponse.xml"/>
</proxy>
```

The contents of the file sequence/mockProxyResponse.xml look like this:

```
<sequence name="mockProxyResponse" xmlns="http://ws.apache.org/ns/synapse">
  <property name="RESPONSE" value="true"/>
  <header name="To" action="remove"/>
  <script language="js"><![CDATA[
    mc.setPayloadXML(
    <AckOrderResponse xmlns="uri:opensoa.chapter10.order">
      <Status>200</Status>
      <Message>Ok</Message>
    </AckOrderResponse>);]]></script>
  <send/>
</sequence>
```

By this point, this likely all looks very familiar. We're simply generating a hard-coded mock response, so when you submit a request locally to the ESB using a URL such as http://localhost:8280/soap/OrderResponseService, you'll receive the XML reply shown in the `setPayloadXML` method. We now have our service that simulates a response we'd anticipate receiving from a customer. Next, we'll develop the service to receive the JMS message from jBPM, transform it, and send it to the mock service we just developed.

CREATING A JMS RECEIVER SERVICE AND TRANSPORT SWITCHER

To complete the exercise for this section (steps 7 and 8), we'll create the JMS receiver/listener service, which receives the response message from jBPM and then sends it as a UBL response, as shown in figure 10.1. We'll begin with defining the proxy service:

```
<proxy name="SendOrderResponse" transports="jms">
  <target inSequence="sequence/jmsOrderReceiver.xml">
    <endpoint>
      <address uri="http://localhost:8280/soap/OrderResponseService"
        format="soap11"/>
    </endpoint>
  </target>
</proxy>
```

Since the proxy service is receiving a JMS message, we set the `@transports` attribute to `jms`. The endpoint address is set to the mock `OrderResponseService` we defined in the previous step.

NOTE You can specify multiple transports for a given proxy definition, so you could, for instance, specify `@transports="jms,http,https"`.

Let's now look at the definition for the sequence associated with the SendOrder-Response proxy, which is located in sequence/jmsOrderReceiver.xml:

```
<sequence name="mockProxyResponse" xmlns="http://ws.apache.org/ns/synapse">
   <log level="custom">
      <property name="Text" value="jmsOrderReceiver.xml was invoked"/>
   </log>
   <property action="set" name="OUT_ONLY" value="true"/>
   <xslt key="xslt-key-resp" source="//*[local-name()='OrderResponse']" />
</sequence>
```

The xslt element's @key attribute value (xslt-key-resp) references a localEntry defined in the main ESB configuration (localEntry definitions are global, and thus visible in the entire configuration). localEntry is defined as

```
<localEntry key="xslt-key-resp"
  src="file:repository/conf/opensoa/resources/xslt/response.xslt"/>
```

This code will transform the XML response from the jBPM process instance into the formal UBL response required by the customer.

This completes the configuration required for phase 1. What remains is to test the JMS response we just configured. Since the JMS message initiates the outbound order response, we can manually create the message using the ActiveMQ web console and admin facility (if you're using 5.0 or above). To do so, you simply navigate to the admin URL (assuming you are running it locally) at http://localhost:8161/admin, and then select Queues from the menu bar. This will return a list of queues that have been defined for that instance. For each queue, a list of operations appear; these include Send To, Purge, and Delete. Choose Send To, and enter the contents of the file ExampleOrderResponseFromjBPM.xml into the Message Body text area. Then click Send to submit the message to the JMS queue, where it will be picked up by the ESB's SendOrderResponse proxy service.

If you glance back to figure 10.1, you'll see that we've accomplished a great deal in this section. You now have a pretty solid understanding of how Synapse works. In the process of building our case study, we covered many of the basics of using the ESB. The most typical uses of an ESB include validation, routing, transformation, and transport switching. You've seen all of these functions put to good use.

Consider for a moment what would be required programmatically if you did all these things the old-fashioned way, by just coding everything in custom Java classes. I think you'll find that you'd have spent considerably more development and QA time; the solution you'd end up with would be mostly *one-off* in nature, and it wouldn't likely be as easily reconfigured and maintained through declarative XML files.

In the rest of this chapter, we'll continue to expand the scope of the case study, and in the process, cover several other important ESB functions. This includes using FTP, additional mediators, and scripting support.

10.3 Phase 2: VFS, CSV, email, and message wiretap

In phase 2, we're demonstrating some additional features of Synapse, such as Apache Commons VFS support (used for FTP and local file system support); SMTP; and the use of a wiretap-style messaging pattern to forward a message to multiple recipients. Figure 10.6 shows the changes introduced in this phase.

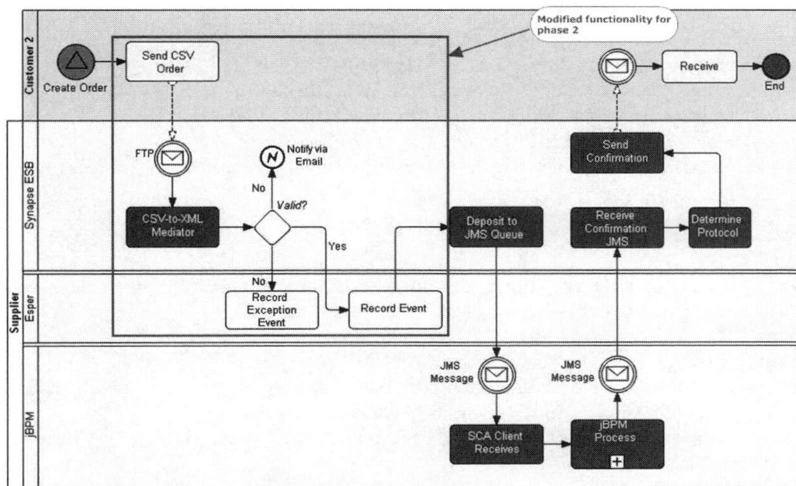

Figure 10.6 Phase 2 of the new order case study

As figure 10.6 shows, the order will now arrive over a file system in CSV format. If any errors occur while validating the order, an email will be sent to the support team for troubleshooting. In addition, a copy of the inbound order (or error exception) will be forwarded to Esper, the event stream processor (ESP) we discussed in chapter 8. Let's start by configuring the Apache VFS transport, which is used for FTP and local file access.

10.3.1 Using the VFS transport

Apache VFS is part of the Apache Commons project [Commons], which provides highly regarded Java libraries for a variety of common tasks. VFS (short for Virtual File System) provides a single API for accessing various file systems [ApacheVFS]. These include FTP, local files, HTTP/HTTPS file retrieval, and SFTP, as well as a variety of compression-related file types such as ZIP, TAR, and JAR. Synapse has taken Commons VFS and wrapped it as a supported ESB transport type, so it supports all VFS-related file systems. While our diagram in figure 10.6 alluded to FTP, to simplify things we'll use local files, but the setup is nearly identical to that of FTP (and sample 254 that comes with Synapse illustrates FTP). We'll begin by using a SOAP XML file for retrieval, and then in the next section, we'll move to CSV. Listing 10.5 shows the initial proxy service definition.

Listing 10.5 Example VFS proxy service configuration

```
<proxy name="VFSFileReceiverService" transports="vfs">            ❶
  <parameter name="transport.vfs.FileURI">
    file://tmp/synapsevfs/in                         ❷
  </parameter>                                                              ❸
  <parameter name="transport.vfs.ContentType">text/xml</parameter>
  <parameter name="transport.vfs.FileNamePattern">.*\.xml</parameter>   ❹
  <parameter name="transport.PollInterval">15</parameter>
  <parameter name="transport.vfs.MoveAfterProcess">
    file://tmp/synapsevfs/original</parameter>                   ❺      ❻
  <parameter name="transport.vfs.MoveAfterFailure">
    file://tmp/synapsevfs/original</parameter>
  <parameter name="transport.vfs.ActionAfterProcess">MOVE</parameter>
  <parameter name="transport.vfs.ActionAfterFailure">MOVE</parameter>

   <target>
    <endpoint>
      <wsdl
       uri="file:repository/conf/opensoa/resources/wsdl/jbpm-ch10.wsdl"
       service="CreateProcessInstance" port="JMS"/>
    </endpoint>
    <outSequence>
      <property name="transport.vfs.ReplyFileName"             ❼
        expression="fn:concat(fn:substring-after(
        get-property('MessageID'), 'urn:uuid:'), '.xml')"
        scope="transport"/>
      <send>
        <endpoint>                                             ❽
          <address uri="vfs:file:////tmp/synapsevfs/out"/>
        </endpoint>
      </send>
    </outSequence>
  </target>
</proxy>
```

The basic principle used by the VFS transport is that you define a file system location that will be periodically polled for incoming files. When a file exists that matches the filter criteria, the contents will be lifted from it, and can thereby be sent to an endpoint location for processing. The first thing to notice when setting up the proxy in listing 10.5 is that `vfs` is identified as the transport ❶. The set of parameters that follow are, as the `@name` attributes value suggests, VFS transport specific. First, the location of where to poll for the incoming files is identified through the parameter `transport.vfs.FileURI` ❷. Since we're using a local file system, the location is prefaced by `file://[`*absolute-path*`]`, but if you were using FTP, it would follow the format of `ftp://[`*username*`[:` *password*`]@]`*hostname*`[:`*port*`][`*absolute-path*`]`.

NOTE When testing in your own environment, you'll want to set up your own local directory structure and modify those places in listing 10.5 where the `file://` protocol is specified.

The `transport.vfs.ContentType` parameter ❸ is used to identify the type of file being processed. The Synapse language guide [SynapseLanguage] lists the possible values for this, and the selection you make is important as it determines how the file's contents will be read (we'll revisit this when we start using an actual CSV file). In this case, since we're starting with SOAP/XML, `text/xml` is used as the MIME type. The next parameter ❹, `transport.vfs.FileNamePattern`, is used as an inclusion filter to determine which files are eligible for processing. In this case, we're just processing files that end in *.xml*. The interval for how often to read the file system is controlled through the `transport.PollInterval` parameter ❺. In this example, we're asking the ESB to check every 15 seconds.

The remaining parameters ❻ deal with how to manage processed and failed files, and descriptions can be found in the Synapse language configuration guide. Related to this is the setting of `transport.vfs.ReplyFileName`, which occurs in the `outSequence` ❼. What does the `@expression` attribute value shown here accomplish? Every message that flows through the ESB is assigned a globally unique identifier (GUID), which is automatically assigned to the `MessageID` message context property. The value of `MessageID` is appended with .xml, and this is used as the processed file's name when it's stored once the file has successfully been processed. The directory location where it's stored is specified in the `outSequence`'s endpoint address ❽.

To test this out, you can simply drop a valid SOAP XML file into the location assigned to the property `transport.vfs.FileURI`. You'll then see activity in the ESB console if configured properly. Of course, this isn't entirely what we want in this case study, as we're anticipating a CSV file, not a SOAP XML file.

10.3.2 Working with CSV files

Out of the box, Synapse doesn't include a specific mediator for working with CSV files. While some creative XSLT can be used for such purposes, creating such a style sheet can be a little tedious. Fortunately, WSO2's esbsite.org provides a free marketplace where other Synapse users can submit their own custom mediators (you can also create your own mediator fairly easily; learn how at http://wso2.org/library/2936). One such custom mediator that has been submitted is called *OpenCSV Mediator* [CSVMediator], and it will be used in this demonstration.

NOTE To install OpenCSV Mediator, copy the two provided JAR files (csv.jar and opencsv-1.8.jar) to the Synapse home's lib directory.

When using a custom mediator, you use the class element to define the full class name (including the package) of the custom mediator you're invoking (the author can also create an XML configuration domain-specific language [DSL], but this is optional). In this case, the custom mediator is invoked using

```
<class name="org.apache.synapse.contrib.OpenCSVtoXML"/>
```

The OpenCSV library on which this mediator is based (http://opencsv.sourceforge.net/) has numerous options for parsing a CSV. By default, it will use the first row to identify the column names, and we'll adhere to that format for this example (a sample file called CSVOrder.csv is provided in this chapter's example code). Let's modify the code from listing 10.5 to use this new custom mediator (see listing 10.6).

Listing 10.6 Example of using CSV custom mediator in tandem with VFS

```
<proxy name="VFSFileReceiverService" transports="vfs">
 <parameter name="transport.vfs.FileURI">
   file://tmp/synapsevfs/in</parameter>
 <parameter name="transport.vfs.ContentType">          ❶ Requires content type for CSV
   application/octet-stream</parameter>
 <parameter name="transport.vfs.FileNamePattern">
    .*\.csv                                             ❷ Defines filename pattern
 </parameter>
 <!-- other properties same as listing 10.5 -->
 <target>
   <endpoint>
    <wsdl
      uri="file:repository/conf/opensoa/resources/wsdl/jbpm-ch10.wsdl"
      service="CreateProcessInstance" port="JMS"/>
   </endpoint>
   <inSequence>
    <class
     name="org.apache.synapse.contrib.OpenCSVtoXML"/>   ❸ Uses custom mediator class
   </inSequence>
   <!-- outSequence as same as listing 10.5 -->
 </target>
</proxy>
```

In listing 10.6 we've changed the `transport.vfs.ContentType` to `application/octet-stream` ❶. We did this because the CSV mediator was designed to receive binary data, not `text/plain`. We also modified the inclusion filter, which now is expecting files with the extension of .csv instead of the previously configured .xml ❷. Finally, we included the mediator definition inside the `inSequence` phase ❸. The resulting XML that appears when the CSV file is processed resembles this:

```
<csv xmlns="http://ws.apache.org/synapse/ns/csv">
   <col-defn n="17">
      <col name="TransactionID"/>
      <col name="SalesOrderId"/>
      <!-- other columns here -->
   </col-defn>
   <data>
      <row n="1">
         <col name="TransactionID">AEG012345</col>
         <col name="SalesOrderId">CON0095678</col>
         <!-- other columns here -->
      </row>
   </data>
   </csv>
```

As you can see, the `col-defn` node shows the column locations and names based on the first row's column title data. The `data` node then includes row entries for each `row` of data found in the file, along with the name identifier to show which column's value is being output. While outputting in XML is good, it's obviously not of the correct format required by `CreateProcessInstanceService` (covered previously in section 10.2). Thus, an XSLT style sheet is used to transform the CSV-derived XML format to the simple order XML used as part of the jBPM `CreateProcessInstanceService`. The following was added to the `outSequence` following the custom mediator to accomplish this transformation:

```
<xslt key="xslt-key-csv2order" source="//*[local-name()='csv']"/>
```

`xslt-key-csv2order` is defined as a `localEntry` at the root level as

```
<localEntry key="xslt-key-csv2order"
 src="file:repository/conf/opensoa/resources/xslt/CSVtoSimpleOrder.xslt"/>
```

Thus, the flow we've seen so far includes

- Reading the CSV file in via the VFS transport
- Using the custom CVS to XML mediator to convert the CSV file into XML
- Transforming the XML output from the custom mediator into the XML format required by the `CreateProcessInstanceService`, which is responsible for kicking off a new jBPM process instance

The next step, as shown in figure 10.6, is to add some exception handling that will fire off an email to a support distribution list so that the team can be alerted that a message failed to process successfully.

10.3.3 Exception handling and SMTP transport

In section 10.2.2, we demonstrated the use of the `validate` mediator to verify the validity of the incoming XML against a defined XSD schema. We'll impose a similar check on the CSV-converted XML file, and in the event validation fails, we'll configure an outbound email that can be sent, for instance, to the support team to alert them of the error (we'll also demonstrate some additional fault handling in the next section, 10.4). This is our first look at using the mail transport.

NOTE You must configure Synapse for SMTP mail support by editing some property values in the axis2.xml configuration file. For more details, see http://synapse.apache.org/Synapse_Samples_Setup.html#mailsender.

As with our other examples, the best way to illustrate its use is through some code samples. Listing 10.7 shows the validation block that has been added to the `VFSFileReceiverService` proxy defined in listing 10.6.

Listing 10.7 Example of using an email transport in tandem with a `validate` mediator

```
<validate source="//*[local-name()='csv']">
  <schema key="schemas/CSVOrder.xsd"/>
  <on-fail>
    <property
     name="Subject" value="Errors occurs when processing order"/>    ❶
```

```
      <xslt key="xslt-key-email" source="//*[local-name()='csv']">
        <property name="filename" expression="$trp:FILE_NAME"/>
      </xslt>
      <send>
        <endpoint>
          <address uri="mailto:someone@someplace.com" format="pox"/>
        </endpoint>
      </send>
      <drop/>
    </on-fail>
  </validate>
```

The `on-fail` node begins with the definition of the property named `Subject` ❶, which is used for setting the subject line of the outbound email message. This is followed by an `xslt` element, used to generate the body contents of the message ❷. Notice in this example we're dynamically passing an XSLT property ❸. In this case, we're passing a property called `filename` that represents the value of the expression `$trp:FILE_NAME`. This expression is interpreted by Synapse as the name of the inbound VFS file being processed.

NOTE The Javadocs list the static field constants that can be used for retrieving `$trp:[`*`property`*`]` expression values.

The style sheet assigned to the key `xslt-key-email` (`file:repository/conf/open-soa/resources/xslt/Email.xslt`) uses the `filename` XSLT parameter to identify which inbound file failed so that you can identify and resolve the issue. Finally, the email is sent using the `mailto:` transport prefix ❹, followed by the email address to use. As you can see, using SMTP transport is simple, with the only real effort involving the creation of the style sheet to format the body of the outbound message (if we left this out, the raw contents of the XML message would be sent). The last step in phase 2 of the case study is to generate events that can be consumed by Esper. We'll demonstrate how the wiretap message pattern can be implemented by Synapse.

10.3.4 Using the wiretap message pattern

In the wiretap pattern, we use a fixed recipient list with two outputs so that when a message is consumed off the input channel, it's then broadcast to both output channels simultaneously [WireTap]. This approach is ideal for publishing events to Esper, as it is nonintrusive and doesn't impact the actual processing of the message. Instead, it just fires off a separate copy to the ESP engine. In chapter 8, we described a framework for service-enabling Esper. We used Apache Synapse/SCA in a way similar to how we service-enabled jBPM. In the source code for this chapter, a complete end-to-end example is provided, but for purposes of keeping our focus on Synapse, we'll mock the Esper service.

The mock Esper service we'll use is defined here:

```
<proxy name="EsperService" transports="http">
  <target>
```

```
    <inSequence>
      <property name="RESPONSE" value="true"/>
      <header name="To" action="remove"/>
      <property action="set" name="OUT_ONLY" value="true"/>
      <drop/>
    </inSequence>
  </target>
</proxy>
```

By this point, you probably need little explanation. The only interesting part of this code is that, since this will be an asynchronous call, no response is returned, which is why the property `OUT_ONLY` is set to `true`. We'll use the wiretap in two places: one for generating a message when a validation exception occurs, and the other when normal processing is followed. Since we just discussed the exception handling used with sending an email notification, let's target that first.

When sending a notification to Esper, metadata about the file being processed should also be included. You've already seen how we can access some of the VFS-related transport metadata by referencing properties such as `$trp:FILE_NAME`. Let's include some of this information in the SOAP header itself. Why consider this approach? You may want, for logging and/or auditing purposes, to store each inbound message in a database or archive. This message context information can be useful when interrogating the archives. Using the `header` element, you can create or delete SOAP message header elements (when creating headers, you're limited to simple elements). In our example, we'll capture the filename, modified date, and file length VFS metadata:

```
<header name="vfs:filename" expression="$trp:FILE_NAME" action="set"/>
<header name="vfs:datestamp" expression="$trp:LAST_MODIFIED" action="set"/>
<header name="vfs:filesize" expression="$trp:FILE_LENGTH" action="set"/>
```

These elements are added directly following the `inSequence` definition for the `VFS-FileReceiverService` proxy service. This will result in a SOAP header that resembles the following as the message proceeds through its processing lifecycle:

```
<soapenv:Header xmlns:vfs="uri:open-soa/chpt10/vfs">>
  <vfs:filename>faulttest.csv</vfs:filename>
  <vfs:datestamp>1218758847000</vfs:datestamp>
  <vfs:filesize>404</vfs:filesize>
</soapenv:Header>
```

You may have noticed the namespace definition in the SOAP message (`xmlns:vfs="uri:open-soa/chpt10/vfs"`). This appears because we defined the namespace alias in the root of the ESB configuration file, with the alias then referenced when the header was defined (e.g., `header name="vfs:filename"`). We can now create the wiretap (see listing 10.8) by using the `clone` mediator, which is defined in the first child node in the `on-fail` element (see listing 10.7 earlier for reference).

Listing 10.8 An example of the wiretap message pattern using the clone mediator

```
<clone continueParent="true">                    ❶
  <target >
    <sequence>        ❷
      <xslt key="xslt-key-esper-csv-err"
        source="//*[local-name()='csv']">
        <property name="filename"                ❸
          expression="//vfs:filename"/>
        <property name="errorType" value="XML Validation Error"/>
      </xslt>
      <send>                                      ❹
        <endpoint>
          <address format="soap12"
            uri="http://localhost:8280/soap/EsperService"/>
        </endpoint>
      </send>
    </sequence>
  </target>
</clone>
```

The first thing to note with the `clone` statement is the presence of the `@continueParent` attribute ❶, which is set to `true`. If set to `false`, message processing won't continue after the `clone` mediator is completed (in this respect, it's analogous to using a `<drop/>`). In our example, we do want processing to continue. What follows in the `clone` definition is similar to what we've seen elsewhere where the `target` element is used. The only distinction is that, since a wiretap is by nature an asynchronous activity (it's firing a copy of the message off for processing elsewhere), an `outSequence` makes no sense. Hence, in lieu of an `inSequence` and `outSequence`, we use a single `sequence` element ❷. Within that element, other mediators can be specified—for example, using the `xslt` mediator to transform the message en route to its destination. In listing 10.8, this is demonstrated with the two parameter values sent to the style sheet ❸. Of particular note is the `filename` property, which is assigned using an XPath expression based on the header values we set previously. Lastly, we use the `send` node to direct the message to its endpoint location ❹.

The purpose of the code in listing 10.8 is to send Esper a notification upon a validation error, but we also want to send Esper a copy of the message in the event it was processed successfully. The only difference between this `clone` definition and the one in listing 10.8 is that it uses a different style sheet. Rather than duplicate this entire code block, a more prudent approach is to combine the definitions and use the switch mediator to dynamically select the appropriate style sheet that needs to be called. This new definition can then be managed as a separate registry entry (i.e., stand-alone file) so that it can be reused where appropriate. The new clone definition is shown in listing 10.9.

Listing 10.9 Using the switch mediator to create a reusable clone block

```
<sequence name="esper" xmlns="http://ws.apache.org/ns/synapse"
  xmlns:vfs="uri:open-soa/chpt10/vfs">                  ❶ Evaluates VFS
  <switch source="//vfs:status">                          processing status
```

```
      <case regex="SUCCESS">
        <xslt key="xslt-key-esper-csv" source="//*[local-name()='Order']">
          <property name="filename" expression="//vfs:filename"/>
        </xslt>                                            ❷ Specifies case
      </case>                                                 conditions
      <case regex="FAILED">
        <xslt key="xslt-key-esper-csv-err"
           source="//*[local-name()='csv']">
          <property name="filename" expression="//vfs:filename"/>
          <property name="errorType" value="XML Validation Error"/>
        </xslt>
      </case>
    </switch>
    <send> <!-- endpoint not shown for brevity, but is just EsperService -->
    </send>
  </sequence>
```

The switch statement in listing 10.9 uses the value from the XPath expression //vfs:status ❶ to determine which xslt mediator to call ❷. Earlier code listings didn't create that header value, so we'll illustrate in a moment where it's derived from. Beyond that, the sequence definition is identical to what you saw in listing 10.8.

Since we've covered a great deal in this section, you may be wondering what the complete definition looks like for the VFS/CSV proxy. Figure 10.7 shows the configuration that comprises the solution (you'll also notice the vfs:status property header is set).

This concludes phase 2 of the case study. In it, we learned how to use the VFS transport, which supports various file system protocols such as FTP, SFTP and local file systems. The majority of partner and customer integrations in place today use older, legacy protocols such as FTP rather than HTTP, and the ability to support them is

Figure 10.7 The complete solution described in phase 2 of the case study

essential for an ESB. When working with external entities, the opportunity to rip-and-replace is seldom feasible, so introducing an ESB must be done transparently.

Also in this section, you learned how to use a custom mediator as part of the CSV processing we performed. You saw how Synapse can be augmented rather easily with new capabilities when needed. Finally, we explored how the wiretap message pattern is used to send out duplicate messages and events when needed for consumption by an ESP processor like Esper.

What remains to discuss are some advanced features of Synapse. While you may be tempted to skim through the next section, I suggest sticking with it, as you'll come to appreciate some of the unique capabilities Synapse has to offer. I use these capabilities frequently, and you'll likely do the same as you begin to fully leverage all that Synapse can provide. Let's dive into phase 3, where we'll use Synapse tasks, the DB mediator, and the message splitter pattern.

10.4 Phase 3: tasks, DB mediator, and iterator

Let's recap: In phase 1, we set up a SOAP-based interface to receive inbound sales orders. In doing so, we explored many of the core features of Synapse, such as transformations, routing, and protocol switching. In phase 2, we added a file system interface and supported receiving orders in CSV data file format. Now, in phase 3, we'll demonstrate a pull-based approach for receiving sales orders. In this process, we'll use a Synapse task to periodically poll a remote web service for any queued orders that might be present. We'll also use the DB mediator to enrich the inbound order(s) with some additional data, and we'll use a message splitter pattern to process multiple orders. Figure 10.8 shows the revised and the new functionality we'll introduce in this section.

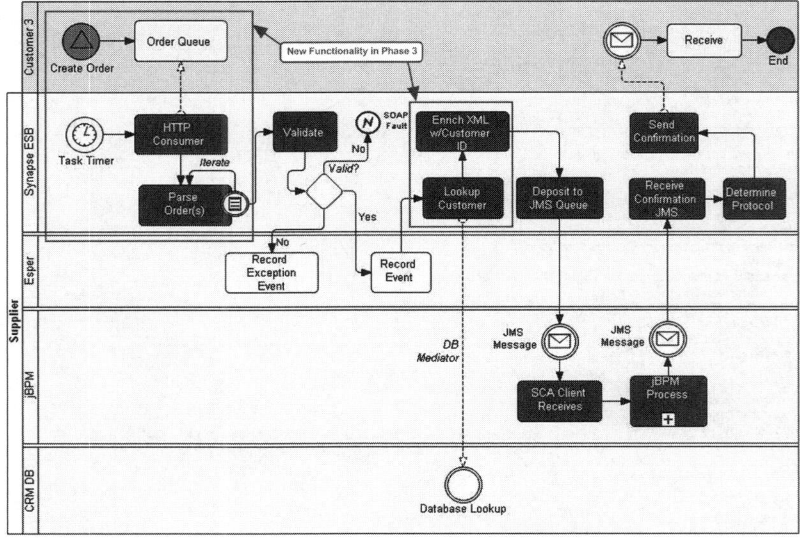

Figure 10.8 Phase 3 case study enhancements

We'll tackle this phase in three steps:

1 Configure a Synapse task to poll a mock web service for queued orders.
2 Use an iterator mediator to split the order if more than one exists in the message.
3 Enrich the order with information from a database.

10.4.1 Configuring Synapse tasks

The scenario for this phase of the case study assumes that the customer will queue up orders that can then be received by using a SOAP-based web service call. Why would a supplier (whose shoes we're wearing) advocate using this approach? Posting messages, as we demonstrated in phase 1, can be somewhat challenging to implement. For one, some companies, especially in the financial sector, have policies that severely restrict allowing inbound requests within their firewall. However, such restrictions usually aren't in place for outbound calls. Another reason might be that a customer, if they work with many suppliers (we're playing the role of a supplier in the case study), may find it easier to support a queue-based pull model. Otherwise, posting orders to many supplier web services may require more extensive setup and monitoring.

To simulate a customer order queue web service, we'll create another simple Synapse mock proxy. This web service will simply receive a request and return a static SOAP message that contains two UBL orders (you may recall from phase 1 that the inbound orders were using the UBL order specification). Listing 10.10 shows the mock service configuration.

Listing 10.10 Mock service definition representing queued customer orders

```
<proxy name="CustomerOrderQueueService" transports="http">
  <target>
    <inSequence>
      <property name="RESPONSE" value="true"/>
      <header name="To" action="remove"/>
      <xslt key="xslt-key-dummyOrders"/>          <- 1 Uses XSLT to generate output
      <send/>
    </inSequence>
  </target>
</proxy>
```

The mock service shown in listing 10.10 is very similar to the others we've defined, with the exception that we're using an `xslt` mediator to generate the sample response instead of a script ❶. We did this because of the size of the response message, which contains two UBL orders. The key used to reference the style sheet, `xslt-key-dummy-Orders`, is defined as follows:

```
<localEntry key="xslt-key-dummyOrders"
  src="file:repository/conf/opensoa/resources/xslt/dummyUBLOrders.xslt"/>
```

The next step is to create the Synapse task to periodically call this service to receive the orders. A task, in simple terms, is basically just an internal timer that runs a Java class that implements the `org.apache.synapse.startup.Task` interface. Listing 10.11 shows the configuration we'll begin with for setting up the task.

Listing 10.11 Example of Synapse task configuration

```
<task                                                        ❶
  class="org.apache.synapse.startup.tasks.MessageInjector"
  name="FetchOrders">
  <property name="to"                ❷
   value="http://localhost:8280/soap/QueuedOrderRequestor"/>
  <property name="soapAction" value="urn:getOrders"/>
  <property name="message">                                  ❸
   <getOrders xmlns="uri:opensoa.chapter10.order">
     <customerId>1001</customerId>
   </getOrders>
  </property>
  <trigger interval="30"/>        ❹
</task>

<in>        ❺
   <send/>
</in>

<proxy name="QueuedOrderRequestor"        ❻
   transports="http">
   <target>
     <endpoint>
       <address uri="http://localhost:8280/soap/CustomerOrderQueueService"
         format="soap11"/>
     </endpoint>
   </target>
</proxy>
```

The `task` statement/element requires the `@class` and `@name` attributes. The `@class` attribute is used to identify the Java class that implements the `Task` interface. While you can easily create your own implementation (see [Tasks]), Synapse comes with one called `MessageInjector` that will suit our needs ❶. This class simply takes the XML message defined in the property called `message` ❸ and sends it to the SOAP web service associated with the `property` called `to` ❷. The frequency by which the message is sent is managed using the `trigger` element's `@interval` attribute and is specified in seconds. In the example in listing 10.11, we configured the interval for every 30 seconds ❹. It's worth noting that each task implementation class may require a different set of property values, depending on its implementation.

When using tasks we must specify a default message mediator block, as shown in ❺. The outbound task message needs this to be present in order to send the out message.

NOTE As a convenience, you can use the `<in>` block as the default message mediator rather than wrapping it with `<sequence name="main">`. In chapter 9 we discussed the differences between message and service mediation.

The service that's receiving the task-generated message is an internal service called QueuedOrderRequestor ❻. This service merely receives the message and, in turn, forwards it to the mock service CustomerOrderQueueService (listing 10.10). Why not just invoke the mock proxy service directly from within the task? That's a good question! The reason is that we'll want to interject some mediators into the response received from the mock service. Including that logic in the mock service itself wouldn't be an accurate simulation, since in any real-life scenario, we wouldn't be able to do that (the service would be hosted on the customer's site, not ours). If you run this example (synapse_sample_opensoa_17.xml), the Synapse console will show the UBL orders being displayed that were generated by the mock service. Since the XSLT style sheet that we're using to generate the mock orders is creating multiple orders, we now want to split the orders apart, since when we forward the message to the jBPM web service, it's only designed to process one order at a time.

10.4.2 Using the iterator mediator to split messages

The Synapse iterator mediator implements the enterprise integration pattern known as *Splitter*. It's used to "break out the composite message into a series of individual messages each containing data to one item" [Splitter]. The iterator mediator is straightforward to use, as demonstrated in listing 10.12.

Listing 10.12 Example Synapse iterator mediator to split apart a message

```
<proxy name="QueuedOrderRequestor" transports="http">
  <target>
    <endpoint><address
      uri="http://localhost:8280/soap/CustomerOrderQueueService"
      format="soap11"/>
    </endpoint>
    <outSequence>
      <iterate expression="//uri:CreateOrder/ublord:Order"      ❶
        preservePayload="true"      ❷
        attachPath="//uri:CreateOrder"      ❸
   xmlns:ublord="urn:oasis:names:specification:ubl:schema:xsd:Order-2"
        xmlns:uri="uri:opensoa.chapter10.order">
        <target>
          <sequence>
            <log level="full"/>
          </sequence>
        </target>
      </iterate>
    </outSequence>
  </target>
</proxy>
```

The iterator element has two required attributes: @expression and @preservePayload. The @expression attribute is used to identify the XPath location for splitting the messages. In our example UBL order, repeating Order nodes can be present and so this is where we want to split the XML message. In listing 10.12, you can see how this

XPath expression is defined ❶. The `@preservePayload` attribute, which can be either `true` or `false`, is set to `true` in the listing ❷. When `true`, it instructs Synapse to include the prior parent XML specified through the XPath provided in the `@attachPath` attribute ❸. If the value is set to `false`, the `@attachPath` must not be set, since it's only applicable when `@preservePayload` is set to `true`. Figure 10.9 illustrates the differences between the various options using the order example through one iteration of processing.

Figure 10.9 An example of the `iterate` mediator and use of the `@preservePayload` attribute

In figure 10.9, the original message is shown with two orders present. After one iteration where the split occurs on the `Order` element, when `@preservePayload` is set to `true` with a corresponding `@attachPath` XPath, you can see that the message is kept intact, except that a single `Order` is now being processed. Conversely, when `@preservePayload` is `false`, the `CreateOrder` element is now omitted, so the split message being processed has a modified message structure. Obviously, which you choose depends on your needs, but for the case study, we want to preserve the payload.

The last step in this phase is to demonstrate the use of the DB mediator. This mediator allows queries to be made against a relational database.

10.4.3 Using the DB mediator

As you may recall from phase 1, the UBL order that we're working with will be transformed into an internal format better suited for use by the jBPM web service we created in chapter 7. Let's assume now that we want to add some data elements to the XML that's being passed—the sales representative's name and email address associated with the customer placing the order. This information could be beneficial to the jBPM process, as it could then be used for assigning tasks to that representative as it pertains to the order processing (for example, perhaps a large order requires approval by the sales rep). The Synapse DB mediator (`dblookup`) provides the ability to invoke a database query (or insert/update using `dbrecord`). The result is then made available for incorporation into the message being processed. For our illustration, we'll query against a customer table in an Apache Derby database (see the README.txt file found in the chapter's sample code for setup instructions). We'll use the `customerId` associated with the incoming order and then look up the associated sales rep information. The sales rep's name and email will subsequently be inserted into the message sent to the jBPM web service.

Without further ado, let's take a look at the code in listing 10.13.

Listing 10.13 Example of using the `dblookup` mediator

```
<dblookup>
  <connection>                    <-- 1
    <pool>        <-- 2
      <driver>org.apache.derby.jdbc.ClientDriver</driver>
      <url>jdbc:derby://localhost:1527/synapsedb;create=false</url>
      <user>synapse</user><password>synapse</password>
    </pool>
  </connection>
  <statement>
    <sql>select * from salesrep sr     <-- 3
     join customer c on sr.salesContactId = c.salesContactId
     where c.customerId = ?</sql>      <-- 4
    <parameter        <-- 5
     expression="//cac:BuyerCustomerParty/cbc:SupplierAssignedAccountID"
     type="VARCHAR"/>
    <result name="salesrep-name" column="name"/>          6
    <result name="salesrep-email" column="email"/>
  </statement>
</dblookup>
```

The `dblookup` node, shown in listing 10.13, begins with the definition of the database connectivity parameters ❶. The `pool` child element can be used to directly specify the database connection properties ❷, or optionally use a data source lookup (illustrated in sample 363 in the Synapse examples). Apache DBCP is used on the backend for pooling, so it's efficient and doesn't require reestablishing a connection for every request.

Once the connection-related definition is completed, the `statement` section follows. As you can see in listing 10.13, we created a SQL statement that performs a lookup against the salesrep table using a join with the customer table ❸. The SQL query uses the `?` character to define a parameter that will be populated at runtime, which in this case is a comparison value for looking up the `customerId` ❹. One or more `parameter` elements can then be present, which are used for dynamically assigning a value for each `?` specified (based on the ordinal values of the parameters). In our example, we have just one dynamic value assignment, so a single parameter element is used, with an XPath expression used to assign the value ❺. Finally, we use the result element to assign the results of the query to the specified property identified by the @name attribute ❻. If the query returns no results, the properties will have a null value assignment.

Now that we've identified the sales rep's name and email and have assigned them to the properties salesrep-name and salesrep-email, respectively, we can reference them within the XSLT style sheet that's responsible for converting the UBL orders into the simplified internal format. For example, the values can be passed as style sheet parameters:

```
<xslt key="xslt-key" source="//*[local-name()='CreateOrder']">
  <property name="salesrep-name"
    expression="get-property('salesrep-name')"/>
  <property name="salesrep-email"
    expression="get-property('salesrep-email')"/>
</xslt>
```

You can find the complete example in synapse_sample_opensoa_19.xml, and you'll see the dblookup mediator statement in the iterate element. Thus, the database query is performed for each split message being processed.

Congratulations! We've now completed phase 3 of the case study. In this phase, we demonstrated how to use Synapse tasks to initiate an outbound message, and then illustrated using the iterator to split apart messages based on an XPath expression. We concluded the section by using the dblookup mediator to perform a database query, and then incorporated the query results into the message being processed by using style sheet parameter values.

10.5 Phase 4: QoS using Synapse

In this final phase, we'll turn our attention to Synapse's quality of service–related functionality. While you may be able to cobble together some pieces of this functionality with other ESBs, with Synapse it represents a particular area of emphasis that's unique to the product. Your investment in learning this capability will pay rich rewards as you develop your own enterprise-ready web services. We'll illustrate how you can use Synapse to easily incorporate WS-Security on inbound SOAP requests, and explore the capabilities provided via the throttle mediator, which can be used for a variety of purposes, such as restricting or metering access based on inbound IP addresses or domain. Figure 10.10 shows the new functionality we'll be adding to our case study.

As you can see in figure 10.10, we've added WS-Security. WS-Security is not a single standard, but rather a set of specifications for adding encryption, digital signatures, and other security-related enhancements to web services (the book *SOA Security* [Kanneganti] provides comprehensive coverage of the standard). The WS-Security we'll implement for the case study is known as *Web Services Security UsernameToken Profile 1.0* [WSS]. This standard can be used for passing the username and password as part of the SOAP header. We'll use the *PasswordDigest* approach to create a hash value so that the password isn't sent in clear text. Fortunately, we don't have to worry about the underlying mechanics of implementing the standard, since Synapse will do this for us, as we'll see next.

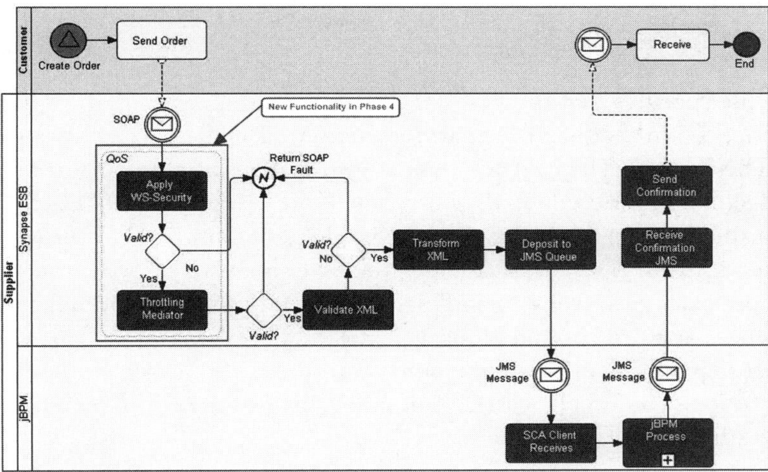

Figure 10.10 Phase 4 case study enhancements

10.5.1 Implementing WS-Security

Synapse, like most recent applications or tools that support WS-Security, uses WS-Policy assertions to express the security requirements for a web service. Describing the configuration of a WS-Policy file is beyond the scope of this book, but the official specification does provide an excellent overview [WSPolicy]. Since we're just using WS-Security for implementing username/password credentialing, the policy file is straightforward. Things become a bit more complex when using encryption or X.509-based signatures. Listing 10.14 shows the policy configuration for this example.

Listing 10.14 WS-Policy configuration file used for username/password credentialing

```
<wsp:Policy wsu:Id="UTOverTransport"><!--namespaces omitted for brevity -->
  <wsp:ExactlyOne>
    <wsp:All>
      <sp:SignedSupportingTokens>
        <wsp:Policy>
          <sp:UsernameToken
             sp:IncludeToken="omitted for brevity">
            <wsp:Policy>
             <sp:HashPassword/>
          </wsp:Policy>
          </sp:UsernameToken>
        </wsp:Policy>
      </sp:SignedSupportingTokens>
      <ramp:RampartConfig xmlns:ramp="http://ws.apache.org/rampart/policy">
           <ramp:passwordCallbackClass>
            samples.userguide.PWCallback
          </ramp:passwordCallbackClass>
      </ramp:RampartConfig>
```

❶ Specifies profile to use

❷ Uses password hash style

❸ Defines callback class

```
    </wsp:All>
  </wsp:ExactlyOne>
</wsp:Policy>
```

The policy file specifies that the `UsernameToken` profile is to be used for authenticating the service ❶. In that profile, a further assertion is made that a password hash, or digest, is to be used ❷. The callback class, shown in ❸, is used to perform the lookup to authenticate the user credentials. Currently, we're using the `PWCallback` class, as it comes with the Synapse examples. In your implementation, you'd obviously want to replace this with your own callback code (the code for `PWCallback.java` is available in the Synapse examples, so it's a good place to start). In this case, the callback accepts two username/password combinations, `Ron/noR` or `joe/eoj`.

The next step is to incorporate the policy within the ESB proxy configuration. This part of the process couldn't be easier, as demonstrated in the sample test proxy service defined in listing 10.15.

Listing 10.15 Illustration of how to configure WS-Security in the proxy definition

```
<proxy name="TestWSSecurityService" transports="http" trace="enable">
  <target>
    <inSequence>        <-- 1
      <property name="RESPONSE" value="true"/>
      <header name="To" action="remove"/>
      <script language="js"><!-- omitted for brevity --></script>
      <send/>
    </inSequence>
  </target>
  <publishWSDL          <-- 2
   uri="file:repository/conf/opensoa/resources/wsdl/ublOrder.wsdl"/>
  <policy key="sec_policy"/>          <-- 3
  <enableSec/>          <-- 4
</proxy>
```

In listing 10.15, we have a mock service that simply returns a canned XML response. This is similar to what we've already used several times, and is defined in the `inSequence` block ❶. The `publishWSDL` is a new construct we haven't used before ❷. It serves multiple purposes: (a) it exposes a WSDL via a URL for the service in question (which can be accessed locally on your instance at `http://localhost:8280/soap/TestWSSecurityService?wsdl`), and (b) it's used in conjunction with WS-Addressing to determine which service to invoke. In most cases, WS-Addressing is used in tandem with WS-Security, but this isn't a specification requirement, although it's implemented that way in Synapse (this will be addressed in the next release of Synapse, which will remove this requirement). Currently, you *must* use `publishWSDL` when using WS-Security in Synapse.

The next step is to associate the policy file with the proxy. In listing 10.15, we specify the key `sec_policy` ❸, which is previously defined in the configuration (not shown in the listing) as

```
<localEntry key="sec_policy" src="file:repository/conf/opensoa/resources/
  policy/usernametoken.xml"/>
```

Finally, the `enableSec` statement is used to instruct Synapse to use WS-Security for this proxy web service ❹. This completes the security configuration, and you can now submit a request against the service using the included soapUI project (`Chapter10WSSecurity-soapui-project.xml`). The SOAP header used will resemble that shown in listing 10.16.

Listing 10.16 Example of WS-Security SOAP header using password digest

```
<!-- namespace omitted for brevity, see source -->
<soapenv:Header>
  <wsse:Security soapenv:mustUnderstand="1">
    <wsse:UsernameToken wsu:Id="UsernameToken-11716351">
    <wsse:Username>Ron</wsse:Username>                              ❶
    <wsse:Password Type="omitted">8wvdegivxnBfo7</wsse:Password>        ❷
      <wsse:Nonce>OoUUiImpi/d/Q0O1eNIqqA==</wsse:Nonce>                ❸
      <wsu:Created>2008-08-19T15:59:06.895Z</wsu:Created               ❹
    </wsse:UsernameToken>
  </wsse:Security>
  <wsa:MessageID>urn:uuid:96E62098B11B3B51371213289387794
  </wsa:MessageID>                                                     ❺
  <wsa:Action>urn:CreateOrder</wsa:Action>
</soapenv:Header>
```

Unfortunately, the code in listing 10.16 can be a bit tedious to read because of the lengthy namespaces used by WS-Security. However, you can see in ❶ that `Username` is passed in plain text. `Password` ❷ is a digest value derived from concatenating the provided password (`noR`) + nonce value ❸ + created timestamp ❹ and applying an MD5 hash. That hash is then reproduced by the recipient to ensure the signature is valid. The WS-Addressing headers are also present ❺, as required by Synapse when using security.

You now know how to add WS-Security to an inbound SOAP request. You can also use Synapse to add WS-Security to an outbound request. The process is similar, as you activate security with the `enableSec` element present in the endpoint definition of the remote service (see example 100 in the Synapse samples). We'll also be using policies in conjunction with our next topic, which is using Synapse's throttling/message metering capability.

10.5.2 Using Synapse throttling mediator

The throttling mediator is one of the unique features of Synapse, and it can perform multiple functions that are important in a SOA environment. It can be used for the following based on the inbound IP address or domain:

- Restricting access to services
- Limiting the number of requests or concurrent requests within a given period of time
- Redirecting inbound requests to different endpoint services

The ability to restrict access by inbound IP address or domain filtering is a function normally performed by network administrators via firewall or routing rules. However, those can be cumbersome to change and often involve a lot of bureaucracy. The ability to limit or restrict the number of requests allowed within a period of time can be important for several reasons. For one, it allows you to give preferential treatment to certain customers. Second, it is important from a security perspective, as you can block usage patterns that might indicate suspicious activity (such as a customer that normally makes no more than ten service requests per hour suddenly submitting thousands). The redirection feature is handy from a versioning perspective. Some customers may be using older versions of a service, and you can effectively reroute those requests to the appropriate internal endpoint without having to burden them with changing their public endpoint URL (service virtualization).

While these are powerful features, they can be a bit more challenging when testing, since doing so usually requires having a distributed environment. With that in mind, I'll try to keep the examples fairly simple, so that you can easily test them if you have at your disposal at least one other machine from which you can submit a SOAP request using soapUI.

As we briefly discussed, Synapse's throttling implementation uses WS-Policy assertions to define the rules. This should not come entirely as a surprise, since WS-Policy, though typically only used for security definitions, is designed as a "general purpose model and corresponding syntax to describe the policies of a Web Service" [WSPolicy]. Let's begin by examining the simple policy we'll use for this example, shown in listing 10.17.

Listing 10.17 Example of WS-Policy used for Synapse throttling

```
<wsp:Policy xmlns:wsp="http://schemas.xmlsoap.org/ws/2004/09/policy"
  xmlns:throttle="http://www.wso2.org/products/wso2commons/throttle">   ❶
  <throttle:ThrottleAssertion>                  ❷
    <throttle:MaximumConcurrentAccess>10          ❸
    </throttle:MaximumConcurrentAccess>
    <wsp:All>
      <throttle:ID throttle:type="IP">other</throttle:ID>       ❹
        <wsp:ExactlyOne>
          <throttle:IsAllow>false</throttle:IsAllow>      ❺
        </wsp:ExactlyOne>
    </wsp:All>
    <wsp:All>
      <throttle:ID throttle:type="IP">192.168.0.104</throttle:ID>     ❻
      <wsp:ExactlyOne>
        <wsp:All>
          <throttle:MaximumCount>2</throttle:MaximumCount>       ❼
          <throttle:UnitTime>500000</throttle:UnitTime>       ❽
          <throttle:ProhibitTimePeriod          ❾
             wsp:Optional="true">500000
          </throttle:ProhibitTimePeriod>
        </wsp:All>
      <throttle:IsAllow>true</throttle:IsAllow>
```

```
      </wsp:ExactlyOne>
    </wsp:All>
  </throttle:ThrottleAssertion>
</wsp:Policy>
```

One of the first things you may have noticed in listing 10.17 is the namespace alias `throttle`, which is short for `http://www.wso2.org/products/wso2commons/throttle` ❶. There's currently no standard for throttling assertions, so we're using one developed by the team at WSO2. The top-level element for the throttle-related policies is the `ThrottleAssertion` node ❷, and within that node, there are just a few allowable choices. The `MaximumConcurrentAccess` element is used ❸ to define the overall number of concurrent incoming messages allowed for the service in question, regardless of the inbound IP address or host in question. What follows are the IP address or host-specific settings. In the first example shown (`ID` element), the use of the special `other` value is used to indicate a catchall category, which all IPs or domains not explicitly defined elsewhere will use ❹. In this instance, the `isAllow` element is set to `false` ❺, which means that any IP or domains that fall into this category won't be permitted access to the service. When `isAllow` is set to `false`, no other throttling properties should be present.

The next `ID` node specifies an IP address ❻, and in this case, a maximum number of requests permitted within 50 seconds (500,000 milliseconds) ❼ is 2 ❽. If the maximum count is exceeded within that time period, then the client must wait for the duration specified in `ProhibitedTimePeriod` if that element's `@Optional` attribute is set to `true`. In this case, the client would have to wait 50 more seconds before attempting any further requests ❾. As you can see, this provides a great deal of control over metering incoming traffic. Let's now look at how we associate this policy with the proxy service.

There are a few steps involved in the configuration. The first thing we'll do is define the proxy (see listing 10.18).

Listing 10.18 Proxy definition using throttling policy

```
<proxy name="ThrottledProxy" transports="http">
  <target>
    <inSequence>
      <throttle          ❶
        onReject="throttle-fault"       ❷
        onAccept="mockEndpoint" id="A">      ❸
        <policy key="policy/throttle_policy.xml"/>      ❹
      </throttle>
    </inSequence>
    <outSequence>
      <throttle id="A"/>      ❺
      <send/>
    </outSequence>
  </target>
  <!-- publishWSDL, policy and enableSec not shown for brevity -->
</proxy>
```

The proxy node in listing 10.18 includes the additional `throttle` element, which is positioned as a child of `inSequence` ❶, to indicate that throttling will be used with this service. The `@onReject` ❷ and `@onAccept` ❸ attributes are used for calling a named sequence in the event that the request fails or is permitted. The `@id` attribute has relevance when using the `MaximumConcurrentAccess` assertion (as we did in listing 10.18), since it acts as a trigger for keeping track of currently in-progress requests and must be referenced in the `outSequence` in order for it to work properly ❺. The policy file itself is referenced through the registry in ❹.

NOTE You can include the throttle policy definition inline rather than using an external policy file, if you so desire.

The two sequences referenced from the `@onReject` and `@onAccept` attributes are just normal sequence definitions and don't contain anything specific to the throttle policy configuration (they can be seen in the sample synapse_sample_opensoa_21.xml). For example, here's the rejection sequence:

```
<sequence name="throttle-fault" trace="enable">
  <makefault>
    <code value="tns:Receiver"
      xmlns:tns="http://www.w3.org/2003/05/soap-envelope"/>
      <reason value="**Access Denied**"/>
    </makefault>
  <property name="RESPONSE" value="true"/>
  <header name="To" action="remove"/>
  <send/><drop/>
</sequence>
```

According to the rules we've defined, if you attempted to access this service from your local machine using http://localhost/soap/ThrottledProxy, you'd receive this unwelcome response:

```
<soapenv:Fault>
  <faultcode xmlns:tns="http://www.w3.org/2003/05/soap-envelope">
    tns:Receiver
  </faultcode>
  <faultstring>**Access Denied**</faultstring>
</soapenv:Fault>
```

You'd also receive that message if you attempted to submit more than two requests within 50 seconds from IP address 192.168.0.104. Although not done for this example, using the clone mediator to fire off a copy of the message to Esper would also be prudent, so you can monitor any unusual activity in real time.

This ability to restrict access and/or meter usage by IP address or domain is one of the most novel features of Synapse. If your organization is considering or adopting the SaaS model, this sort of capability is a must-have.

We've covered a lot of mileage in this chapter, and if you've been able to stick with it, I think you'll be as excited about Synapse as I am. Let's recap what we've learned and learn what's next.

10.6 Summary

In chapter 9, we introduced the ESB and described the core functionality typically associated with this product category. This chapter focused on implementation using Apache Synapse. We used a real-life case study that we built in four phases. In this process, we revealed most of Synapse's functionality, including standard ESB-type features such as message transformations and routing along with connectivity adapters for various protocols and transports. In addition, we demonstrated many of Synapse's more advanced, and unique, features, such as database querying, message throttling, and custom mediators. Lastly, we touched on how WS-Security can be managed by Synapse, along with message patterns such as wiretap and splitter. I think you'll agree with me that Synapse, while easy to use and configure, is extremely powerful and can save your organization countless hours of development time.

We're approaching the end of our journey, but we do have two important topics remaining: business rule management and asset registry (the registry chapter can be downloaded separately as a bonus chapter at http://www.manning.com/davis). Business rules are the heart of any enterprise, and leveraging a Business Rule Management System (BRMS) will improve your organization's agility, reduce maintenance costs, and better engage your subject matter experts. With a SOA approach, these rules can be exposed as readily reusable services that can be accessed from multiple applications or business processes.

Part 5

Enterprise decision management

Regardless of what enterprise you are in, there are undoubtedly a multitude of business rules that influence all aspects of your organization. Traditionally, these rules are often hard-coded within the context of a given business application, or more loosely understood within the minds of subject matter experts. Thus, when either the application or individual possessing such knowledge retires or moves on, the organization is left scrambling to fill in the gaps. Enterprise decision management aims to avoid such perils by treating business rules as true corporate assets, where they're managed independently of applications or individuals. While this has long been a goal for many organizations, SOA is the catalyst that makes it possible. Why? Because it's now possible to create stand-alone decisions services that can be easily integrated into applications or processes. Rules can be centrally managed through a business rule management system, and then exposed through standard protocols such as SOAP, JMS, JSON, and so forth. This final part of the book will explain how to use JBoss Rules, most commonly referred to as Drools, for managing, integrating, and executing business rules. As you'll discover, implementing a business rules approach can profoundly impact your organization's agility and competiveness.

11 Business rules using JBoss Drools

This chapter covers

- Understanding business rules
- Introducing Drools
- Using the Drools language

Decisions, in the form of rules, represent the brains behind your business. Whether you sell products or services, engage in a nonprofit venture, or even make movies, every step along the way involves decisions. Some decisions are more strategic in nature, such as deciding when to develop and introduce a new product. Others are more tactical or operational in nature, such as deciding whether to extend credit terms to a new customer. The quality of the strategic decisions impacts the long-term viability of your organization; the operational ones greatly influence bottom-line profitability.

This chapter and the next will focus on how to use a rules engine for centrally managing operational decisions in the context of a SOA environment. We'll describe the benefits and drivers behind adopting a rules engine, explore its common characteristics, introduce the Drools rules engine, and describe the features and functionality of Drools using a Hello World example (the next chapter will cover implementation strategies for using Drools). By the conclusion of this chapter, you'll understand why a rules engine represents such a powerful addition to SOA.

As you'll recall from chapter 2, we chose JBoss Rules (Drools) as the open source rules engine for our Open SOA Platform. The product, while mature and robust, continues to undergo significant enhancements due to the substantial investments made by JBoss and the Drools community. Because the benefits of using a rules engine are becoming more visible within the industry, Drools is a very "hot" project, as witnessed to by the increasing number of downloads and mailing list activity.

NOTE JBoss Rules is more commonly known as Drools, which was the name of the product before it became part of the JBoss family of products. Since the development project at JBoss also refers to it by the Drools moniker, this is the name we'll use moving forward.

Before we delve too deeply into what constitutes a rules engine, let's first develop a common concept of its foundation: business rules.

11.1 Understanding business rules

At its most basic, a business rule is a statement that conforms to a when/then type construct, or is sometimes framed as conditions/consequence. Examples include the following:

- When a premium customer places an order, give them free shipping.
- When hiring new employees, send them an email invitation to sign up for the 401(k) plan.
- When a customer complaint is received, always follow up *x* days after the issue is resolved to ensure they are satisfied.

While categorizing business rules as any when/then statement is easy to understand, it does lack richness in conveying some of the essential properties that make up a well-crafted business rule. Ian Graham nails it in his definition:

> *A business rule is a compact, atomic, well-formed, declarative statement about an aspect of a business that can be expressed in terms that can be directly related to the business and its collaborator, using simple, unambiguous language that is accessible to all interested parties: business owner, business analyst, technical architect, customer, and so on. This simple language may include domain-specific jargon. [Graham]*

Let's clear up some of the less obvious terms he uses in his definition:

- *Atomic*—This means that the rule is completely stand-alone in nature, and result is a boolean (`true/false`) outcome.
- *Well-formed*—The rule follows the constructs of the when/then form, and when used by a rules engine, adheres to the specified language requirements.
- *Declarative*—Rules aren't expressed in a procedural, code-driven fashion and instead are expressed using a statement-style vocabulary.

- *Domain-specific jargon*—Rules can be written using a custom vocabulary that's targeted at nontechnical individuals. In other words, rules are written using a business, not programmatic, nomenclature.

While not specifically addressed in this definition, it's also important to stress that business rules ought to be owned and managed by business users, not programmers and other technical team members. As a developer, I find this is a somewhat painful assertion to make, but failure to embrace this foundational concept will greatly limit the benefits that you can otherwise achieve by introducing this solution to your enterprise.

Where do business rules come from, and how are they harvested? They are often scattered throughout the organization, from those codified in applications to those informally held in the minds of subject matter experts. Figure 11.1 illustrates some of the sources of business rules.

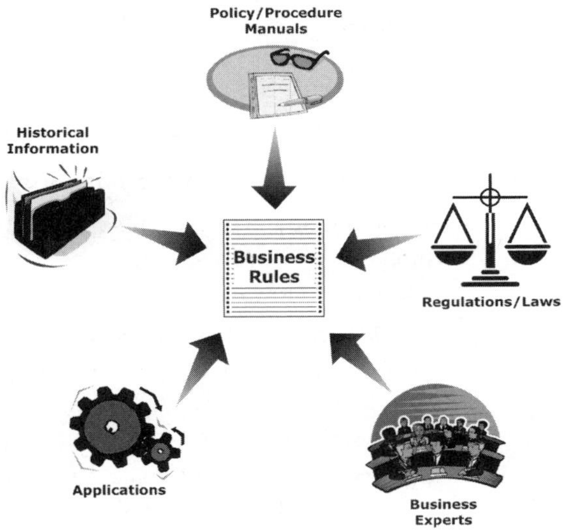

Figure 11.1 Sources of business rules

Harvesting rules from the various sources generally requires a business analyst. Further, like with most initiatives, the process doesn't need to be completely thorough in order to begin reaping the benefits of using a rules engine. The formal process of collecting, categorizing, and then incorporating business rules into a centralized repository for management and execution is sometimes referred to as the *business rules approach.* Barbara von Halle defines this as "a formal way of managing and automating an organization's business rules so that the business behaves and evolves as its leaders intend" [VonHalle]. The purpose of managing these assets through a central repository is that it provides greater visibility of the rules throughout the organization, and thereby facilitates faster responsiveness as changes are needed.

Armed with our knowledge of what a business rule is, we can then define the role of a business rule service, or sometimes more elegantly called a *decision service.* Like any SOA service, it encapsulates a stand-alone, autonomous component or operation but is tailored for making operational business decisions. As such, the inputs represent the material facts necessary for the decision to be rendered. Since some rules may require substantial fact sets on which to base the decision, it may not be practical or feasible to include all facts required for the decision in each call. Instead, the service may preload fact data upon startup, and periodically refresh it at certain intervals (in the next chapter, you'll learn an approach for achieving this). Hence, only the minimal amount of contextual information is passed with each service call.

> **What are facts?**
> Facts are the data necessary for the decision to be rendered. In Drools, the working memory is used to store these facts. The fact data may be seeded from a database, real-time events, or event logs. When a doctor diagnoses an illness, she evaluates it based on the input provided by the patient, her own experiences, and familiarity and knowledge of the disease symptoms. These inputs represent the facts required to intelligently diagnose the condition.

Now that we've defined what constitutes a business rule, let's examine why introducing a rules engine is so beneficial.

11.1.1 Benefits and drivers of the business rule approach

We have already touched on some of the benefits that can be achieved by adopting a business rules approach, such as greater agility, but there are many more. They include the following:

- *Reduction in development costs*—Using a rules engine can reduce complexity in developing software components because building rules in a rules engine is far easier than writing them in conventional code. A decision service can then be called, when necessary, by the application code.
- *Reduction in maintenance costs*—When business rules are embedded into procedural code, even the slightest modification incurs recompilation, testing, and redeployment costs. In part, this is why software maintenance costs are estimated to be as high as 70 percent of total development costs.
- *Rule longevity and sharing*—If rules are embedded in code, when the application is retired, so too are the valuable rule assets. When rules are managed centrally, they outlive the individual application, and can be shared and reused. This also helps preserve retention so that knowledge doesn't walk out the door when key individuals do.
- *Performance*—Rules engines typically offer very high performance, using highly optimized algorithms such as Rete that can filter through vast numbers of rule sets at lightning speed. Replicating such abilities using conventional coding techniques is challenging (and expensive).
- *Consistent framework*—Although not often cited as a benefit of using decision services, this approach allows us to use a standard framework for invoking business rules. Frameworks simplify maintenance and improve quality and consistency. We'll demonstrate such a framework in the next chapter.
- *Auditability and compliance*—In many industries, such as financial, health care, and transportation, regulations play an important role. All public U.S.

companies also face increasing regulations in the form of Sarbanes-Oxley Act (SOX) compliance. In many cases, it's not sufficient to simply introduce controls; instead you must demonstrate that your organization is compliant throughout the day-to-day operations of the business. Using a rules engine facilitates this process since decision services can incorporate cross-cutting concerns such as logging and event notifications while improving the visibility to centrally managed organizational rules.

- *Improved software quality*—In the absence of a rules engine, the interpretation of rules is left to the developers. Although their intentions may be sound, mistakes are inevitable due to the translations required from functional specifications to code. As Taylor and Raden point out, "Embedding business expertise in the system is hard because those who understand the business can't code, and those who understand the code don't run the business" [TaylorRaden].

Other benefits include improvements in customer service, especially when decisions that were otherwise being made by individuals can now be applied more consistently within applications or business processes. Along similar lines, personalization features unique to each customer can be more easily supported and maintained. If you've ever developed or supported SaaS applications, you have no doubt experienced the need to perform custom modifications demanded by an important customer. Soon you find that your code is littered with exceptions. Using a rules engine can help avoid those perils. Finally, as we pointed out in the previous section, any delay in aligning operational decisions with strategic ones represents an opportunity cost that may not be recoverable in our fast-moving landscape.

If you weren't already convinced of the merits of a rules engine, you should be by now. However, you might still wonder how the business rule approach fits with a service-oriented architecture. We'll cover this topic next.

11.1.2 Relationship to SOA

In the introduction to section 11.1, we touched on the notion of exposing rules as decision services. Doing so effectively requires a SOA-based approach as it provides the foundational elements necessary for services to be designed, consumed, and monitored. By exposing rules engine functionality as a service you are significantly increasing the likelihood that the rules can be reused by numerous applications or business processes. In that respect, decision services are simply other services among many. In the past, rules engines failed to gain much traction due to the complexity involved in embedding the rules engine libraries within standard applications—the learning curve could be substantial. By using a SOA-based approach, the developers using decision services follow the same programming practices used with other web services. If using SOAP, the required inputs and outputs are well defined, and using a product like Apache Tuscany (the subject of chapters 3 and 4) greatly simplifies client access to the services. As Ian Graham points out, "Service oriented architectures and business rules management systems are an essential component of modern agile businesses. They vastly reduce the problems associated with the evolution of complex and volatile business strategies and policies. SOA and BRMS are parallel and complementary technologies" [Graham].

Apart from a SOA approach being required for decisional services, rules can also provide logic for how the various services in a SOA environment can be integrated. As an example, let's say you have a decision service that calculates pricing for an inbound order. In addition to calculating the price, the rules engine may further instruct the calling client that shipping and currency services need to be called in order to complete the pricing calculation. When using a BPM product (see chapters 5 through 7 for coverage of JBoss jBPM), a rules engine can be used to drive the workflow paths being followed, particularly when BPM's rather rudimentary if/then/while conditional capabilities prove inadequate. Indeed, decision services can be thought of as the brains behind building composite applications.

Let's take a closer look at some of the key characteristics of a rules engine.

11.1.3 Characteristics of a rules engine

To achieve the performance demanded of them, rules engines inevitably use some type of pattern-matching algorithms for processing rules. Depending on the product selected, a rules engine may use Rete, TREAT, LEAPS, or any number of other algorithms. While covering these are beyond the scope of this chapter, the most popular algorithm, and the one used by popular open source rules engines such as Drools (the later subject of this chapter), Jess (http://herzberg.ca.sandia.gov/), and Soar (http://sitemaker.umich.edu/soar/home) use Rete. To vastly oversimplify things, Rete works by building a tree (or network of nodes) from the rules, and when a new fact is introduced, it works its way down the tree, matching conditions until leaf nodes are encountered. In the absence of this sort of approach, every set of conditions for each rule would have to be evaluated each time, making processing very inefficient. Instead, pattern matching is used to rapidly isolate which rules can be fired, or *activated.*

NOTE Rete, which is Latin for *net,* was an algorithm developed in 1974 by Charles Forgy and later became the subject of his PhD. It has subsequently undergone numerous revisions, some of which are in the public domain.

Rules, as you know, can be thought of as simply when/then type constructs. We'll refer to them as *conditions* or *consequences.* A condition can be any arbitrarily complex expression, but must evaluate to *true* or *false* (boolean). The data, or facts, used for evaluating a given rule is contained within the *working memory,* which can be thought of simply as an in-memory type of database (or working cache). The facts are representations of real-world objects, such as a purchase order or customer record, for instance.

Once a rule's conditions are evaluated and found true, then an *action* (the consequence) is triggered. An action can be anything you want. It may be an event that's fired, a database update, or even the insertion or updating of new facts into the working memory. The latter, in turn, may then trigger a new set of rules that are activated as a result of the new or updated information. Figure 11.2 shows the relationship between the rules engine, facts, and actions.

The figure in 11.2 shows how new or updated facts can result in rule activation. It also, perhaps artificially, delineates between what we refer to as volatile versus nonvolatile facts. A *nonvolatile* fact is one that's generally preloaded when the rules engine is instantiated, and then periodically refreshed. It represents the historical information that's often culled from a database into the working memory. In the next chapter, we'll create a sample rule service that's used for product pricing. The nonvolatile facts, in this case, are the product and pricing catalog data required for performing the calculation (various discounts can be applied to the order, depending on customer classification). The *volatile* facts, on the other hand, represent the instance data that will trigger the rules engine to fire. In the product pricing example cited, the instance data is a quote request that, upon completion of the rules engine's firing, will return a pricing calculation.

Backward chaining

Drools and other Rete-based products are generally most suitable for what's called *forward chaining*, which is what we'll demonstrate throughout our examples. Drools uses the facts at hand to decide an outcome. Conversely, some rules engines also support *backward chaining*, where you instead start with a condition or goal and work backward through a logic chain to identify a cause. For example, diagnosing a computer or automotive problem often uses backward chaining, since the outcome is known but the cause is not. We won't explore backward chaining in our examples, as Drools support for it remains experimental—read more at http://www.jboss.org/community/docs/DOC-9132.

We've now defined what constitutes a business rule, the role of a rules engine in executing the rule logic, and how it can be exposed as a SOA-based service. However, you might be asking yourself, "How can I manage all of these newly created rules that I'm busily creating?" Well, that leads us to our next topic: a business rules management system.

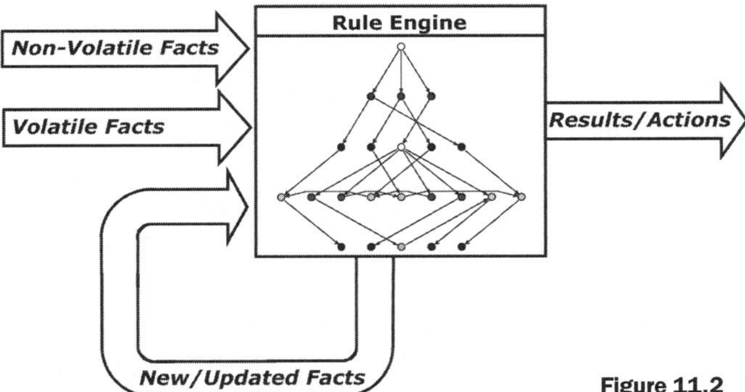

Figure 11.2 Facts and actions in a rules engine

11.1.4 Business rules management systems

A *Business Rule Management System* (BRMS) is a system that is used to manage, deploy, and monitor business rules from within a centralized repository. In many respects, it's analogous to a database management system (DBMS), but it's tailored for business rules. A rules engine can exist independently of a BRMS, as exemplified by Jess and earlier versions of Drools, which didn't incorporate such features (the developer was left to devise a solution for the management and maintenance of the rules). The main benefits of a BRMS include the following:

- *Centralized repository*—The ability to store and view rules via a centralized location improves visibility to them by the business stakeholders and subject matter experts. The ability to reference them in a single location, rather than having the rules scattered about and embedded within various apps or processes, will greatly improve the adoption of a business rules approach in your enterprise.
- *Versioning controls*—Most BRMSs feature automatic versioning and snapshot/baselining capabilities so that you can easily manage the packaging, release, and promotion process of rules. While tools such as Subversion (http://subversion.tigris.org/) offer powerful version control features, they are generally targeted toward developers or other technical types, not the sort of business user who is the main audience of a BRMS.
- *Accessibility*—Nearly all BRMSs typically can be accessed via a web browser and don't require any specialized software to be installed on the client's box. This makes access convenient and reduces the friction required for working with these important corporate assets.
- *Zero-client authoring*—Related to the previous point, most modern BRMSs now use some type of web 2.0–style interface that enables authoring of the rules to take place entirely within the browser. There is no need for installing software and the attendant headaches that process introduces.
- *Archiving and availability*—Perhaps an often-overlooked benefit, centralizing the management of rules makes it much easier to employ robust backup-and-recovery procedures of these assets. Having rules assets centrally located can improve availability.

Although it may not be necessary to use a BRMS when first dipping your toes into the business rule approach, when widespread adoption begins to take hold it becomes essential (we discuss *Guvnor*, the Drools BRMS, in the next chapter).

How does a BRMS integrate with the notion of decision services that we've been discussing? The BRMS is used for the management of the rules, with the rules engine then tapping into the rules maintained through the BRMS repository. Figure 11.3 shows the interplay among the decision service, BRMS, rule repository, and client applications.

In figure 11.3, you can also see the business users who are responsible for authoring the rules through the BRMS. Obviously, there would also be some formal QA and release process, such as tagging the rules for production deployment.

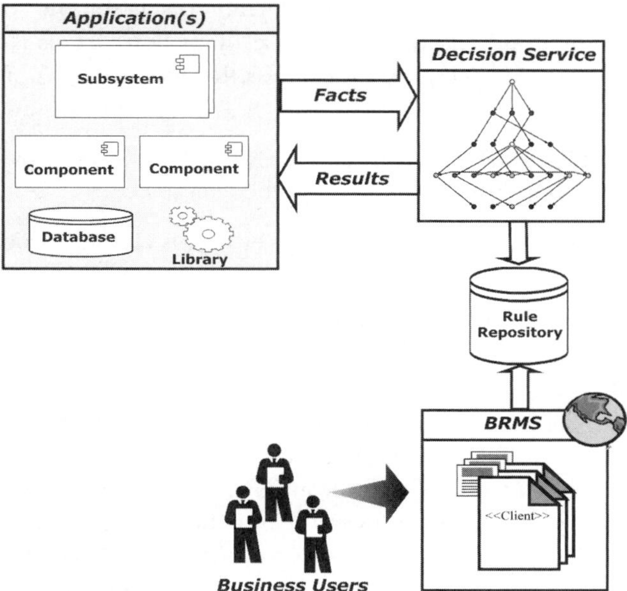

Figure 11.3 Relationship between the rules engine and the BRMS

> **Enterprise decision management (EDM)**
> EDM, a fairly new acronym, can be thought of as the formal application of the business rule approach to the entire enterprise. That is, it's about harvesting business rules, primarily those operational in nature, and centralizing their management through a BRMS. Like enterprise architecture, it's an attempt to introduce a uniform approach throughout an organization for managing business rule assets. Whereas a BRMS or rules engine can be thought of as tangible applications, EDM is more of a philosophy than a product.

Now that you have some context for understanding what constitutes a rules engine and BRMS, along with its complementary role in SOA, we can start cutting our teeth on JBoss Rules/Drools—the real fun begins now!

11.2 Introducing Drools

Unlike some of the other applications we've profiled in this book, such as Esper or Apache Synapse, Drools has been around for a comparatively long time. The first production-ready release was the 2.1 version, which appeared near the end of 2005. In the following year, the Drools product and team became affiliated with JBoss, which followed on the heels of the 3.0 release. While it offered substantial performance improvements and a revised rules language, the 4.0 product was even more significant and included BRMS functionality. Several dot releases of the 4.0 product have since appeared, and as of this writing, the 5.0 version is in late beta. This book will focus on this forthcoming release, as it offers many BRMS enhancements. Given the continuous improvements in the product and its popularity, it's evident that Drools is a centerpiece of the JBoss middleware stack (known officially as the *JBoss Enterprise Middleware* [JEMS]).

NOTE The README.txt file found in this chapter's sample code provides instructions on how to set up Drools and run the examples.

The main features of Drools, many of which we'll cover as this chapter proceeds, are as follows:

- *Rules engine*—Based on the Rete algorithm, it offers outstanding performance; flexible Java-based API; temporal (time-based) and dynamic rule management; and carries a lightweight footprint.
- *Authoring*—The Drools Rule Language (DRL) offers a very rich vocabulary for expressing rules. It's extensible through its support for custom Java functions, and provides the ability to create natural-language rules via its *domain-specific language* (DSL) capabilities. It also comes with an Eclipse plug-in that includes a rule editor and other developer tools designed to simplify rule creation. Lastly, it includes support for decision tables using Excel or Open Office.
- *BRMS*—As you know from an earlier section, BRMS was added new in the 4.0 release (Guvnor), and provides the ability for centrally managing rules through support of a built-in repository (most major DBMSs can be used for this backend). It includes a full authoring environment that's suitable for use by business users.
- *Platform*—The JBoss rules engine can be run stand-alone with any JDK 1.4 or greater release. The BRMS can be run within most Java web or application servers such as Tomcat, JBoss App Server, IBM WebSphere, and Oracle WebLogic.

As you see, Drools offers a full range of features, and when coupled with its outstanding performance and robustness, provides a compelling solution. We'll begin our examination of how to use Drools with a customary Hello World example.

11.2.1 Hello World, Drools!

Fact objects are a central concept when you're working with Drools. These objects are used by the engine to perform conditional expressions. If an expression evaluates to true, the engine triggers a consequence, or action. To begin our simple example, let's create a POJO-style Java class that will contain a `Person` object that we'll use to say hello. This fact class is shown in listing 11.1.

Listing 11.1 `Person` fact object

```
package opensoa.drools.hellodrools;
public class Person {
   private String name;
   private String gender;
```

```
   private int age;
   public Person(String name, int age, String gender) {
      super();
      this.age = age;
      this.name = name;
      this.gender = gender;
   }
      /* standard getters/setters not shown */
}
```

As you can see, the Person class is just a container object, similar to what's sometimes referred to in the Java world as a *data transfer object* (DTO) (see [DTO] for more information). For now, let's assume that we'll instantiate this fact using

```
Person person = new Person ( "John Doe", 22, "M" );
```

With our fact populated (in a moment you'll learn how this is done in Drools), let's create a Hello World rule using the Drools language (DRL). See listing 11.2.

Listing 11.2 Simplistic Hello World rule

```
package opensoa.drools.hellodrools;                  ❶
import opensoa.drools.hellodrools.Person;            ❷

rule "HelloBasic"                                    ❸
   when
      Person();                                      ❹
   then
      System.out.println("HelloBasic: Hello World"); ❺
end
```

The first thing you'll notice is the package declaration ❶. The notion of a package is similar to how it's used in Java, and it allows you to logically group rule assets, such as rule files and rule flows, together (more on rule flows in section 11.7). Packages are often used to group rules hierarchically by domain area. For example, a top-level group may be finance, followed by more granular classifications such as finance.sales-order.pricing. *All rule files must have a package declaration.* Next is the import statement ❷, which is used to include the Person fact class we created in listing 11.1.

The rule definition begins with the keyword rule, followed by a descriptive name (which must be unique) that's assigned to the rule ❸. The when, or condition clause, states that if one or more Person fact objects exist ❹, then the criteria of the rule have been satisfied, and the commands listed in the then portion of the rule will be activated.

NOTE For Java developers, the notation of Person() may seem to imply that it's a constructor used for creating a new instance of Person. That's not the meaning it holds when used within the conditional/when part of the rule definition, which is one of filtering.

So in listing 11.2 the statement "HelloBasic: Hello World" would print out on the console when the engine is fired ❺.

Let's now add a new, slightly modified rule that, rather than just printing out "Hello World", uses the person's name. This can easily be accomplished by creating an *alias* (think *handle*) to the `Person` object, as shown here:

```
rule "HelloBasic2"
   when
      person : Person();
   then
      System.out.println("HelloBasic2: Hello " + person.getName());
end
```

We create the alias called `person` by specifying the alias name, followed by a colon (:) and the fact object being assigned. In this example, we then use the `person` alias for printing out the individual's name when the rule is activated (i.e., "HelloBasic2: Hello John Doe").

If both this rule and the previous rule created in listing 11.2 are present when run, each will be fired (activated), as rules aren't, by default, mutually exclusive. Most likely, the last rule defined will fire first, but that can't be guaranteed. Instead, if want to manage the order in which rules are fired when more than one may be activated, you can do so by using the `salience` keyword before the `when` statement, followed by numeric value indicating priority (higher `salience` values will fire before lower ones). Listing 11.3 illustrates this and also introduces a new condition that will limit the rule from being fired unless the person's `gender` is `M` (male).

Listing 11.3 Example of using the `salience` keyword and fact qualifier

```
rule "HelloMr"
   salience 30                        <-- 1 Assigns salience
   when
      person : Person ( gender == 'M');        <-- 2 Matches pattern
   then
      System.out.println("Hello Mr. " + person.getName());
end
```

Listing 11.3 illustrates how you can add qualifiers to the fact object (in this case `Person`) to limit or restrict the condition based on the fields within a fact object (sometimes referred to as fact patterns). In this case, `gender == 'M'` restricts the rule from firing except where that condition evaluates to `true` ❷. Notice as well the `salience` keyword definition, which assigns a weight of `30` to this rule ❶.

Agenda

When working with Rete-based rules engines such as Drools, you'll occasionally see reference to what is called the agenda. An agenda is created by the rules engine when instructed to execute, and is the internal mechanism used for determining which rules will be activated, and in which order. Rule properties such as salience factor into the construction of the agenda through the rules engine's conflict resolution strategies.

Before we wrap up this quick introduction to Drools, let's create one additional rule in listing 11.4—this one will fire only if the `Person` is male *and* under `25`. If the rule criteria are met, we'll then print "Hello Dude!"

Listing 11.4 Illustration of using *and*–style logical operator

```
rule "HelloDude"
   salience 40                       <-- 1 Assigns salience
   when
      person : Person ( gender == 'M', age < 25 );   <-- 2 Matches two conditions
   then
      System.out.println ("Hello Dude!");
end
```

In the rule shown in listing 11.4, `salience` is set to `40` (1), which means it will fire before the last one we'd defined (listing 11.3), which had a `salience` value of `30`. Then we add the constraint to the `Person` fact by specifying `age < 25` (2). You can comma-separate the constraints, which is an implicit and, or explicitly define using `&&` instead.

This is great, but while we can control the order in which rules are fired, we still have multiple rules that are triggered, displaying multiple console messages. While we've demonstrated how to add constraints to facts to limit when a rule is triggered, in some cases it's not desirable to do so. Instead, we'd just rather suppress Rule X from being fired when Rule Y is triggered previously. We'll get into some ways that this can be managed, but for now, the easiest thing to do using our Hello World example is to just remove the `Person` fact object from working memory. That way, the other rules that otherwise trigger downstream would no longer do so, since the rule conditions no longer apply (there's no more `Person` object in working memory). We can accomplish this very easily by using the `retract` keyword within the `then` (consequence) clause. For example, let's assume that if the "`HelloDude`" rule is fired, we don't want the others to fire at all. Here's the modified rule definition that will accomplish this:

```
rule "HelloDude"
   salience 40
   when
      person : Person ( gender == 'M', age < 25 );
   then
      System.out.println ("Hello Dude!");
      retract ( person );
end
```

The only distinction between this and the earlier example is the addition of the `retract(person)` line. If this consequence is invoked, the `Person` fact object is removed from the working memory, and thus any other rules dependent on that object would subsequently not fire. Now that we've defined our rules, let's see what's needed to run them within the rules engine.

11.2.2 Running Hello World, Drools!

The Java code shown in listing 11.5 contains the logic used to run the rules we've defined in the previous section. When you create a new Drools project in Eclipse, a sample DRL is created along with a corresponding Java class that closely resembles listing 11.5.

Listing 11.5 Java Main for running Hello World example rules

```
package opensoa.drools.hellodrools;
import java.io.*;
import org.drools.*;
import org.drools.compiler.PackageBuilder;
import org.drools.rule.Package;
public class HelloDroolsMain {
  public static final void main(String[] args) {
    try {
      RuleBase ruleBase = readRule();                          ❶
      WorkingMemory workingMemory =
        ruleBase.newStatefulSession();                         ❷
      Person person = new Person ( "John Doe", 22, "M" );      ❸
      workingMemory.insert( person );                          ❹
      workingMemory.fireAllRules();                            ❺
    } catch (Throwable t) {
      t.printStackTrace();
    }
  }
  private static RuleBase readRule() throws Exception {
   Reader source = new InputStreamReader                       ❻
     (HelloDroolsMain.class.getResourceAsStream("/HelloDrools.drl"));
   PackageBuilder builder = new PackageBuilder();              ❼
   builder.addPackageFromDrl( source );                        ❽
   Package pkg = builder.getPackage();                         ❾
   RuleBase ruleBase = RuleBaseFactory.newRuleBase();          ❿
   ruleBase.addPackage( pkg );                                 ⓫
   return ruleBase;
  }
}
```

As you can gather from listing 11.5, most of the code deals with initially configuring the `RuleBase`. Perhaps at the risk of oversimplifying things, the `RuleBase` can be thought of as the runtime container where one or more rule packages are loaded (packages can be dynamically modified during runtime operations). To create our `RuleBase`, an internal method called `readRule()` is called ❶. That method first identifies and reads in the DRL file that contains the rules we created ❻. The next step is to instantiate a `PackageBuilder` ❼ whose `addPackageFromDrl()` method ❽ is then used for loading the rules associated with the package specified in the DRL. This step will also parse the DRL file and compile it into executable code. The `PackageBuilder.getPackage()` method is then used to create a new `Package` object ❾ that can be consumed by the `RuleBase` ⓫ (as noted, a `RuleBase` may contain one or more packages). The `RuleBase` itself is instantiated using the `RuleBaseFactory`.❿ A factory is used because a `RuleBase` is thread safe and can be shared across multiple threads in your application.

NOTE The `RuleBase` is thread safe and serializable, which means that it can be cached for use within a web application or web service. Caching eliminates the need for continuously regenerating the `RuleBase`, which is a relatively expensive operation.

Once the `RuleBase` is created, you can then use it to instantiate a new `WorkingMemory` instance ❷. Interestingly, you can create more than one `WorkingMemory` instance, if you so desire. For example, you may want a separate working memory area per `RuleBase` package, though this is somewhat artificial, since you can't specifically identify which package is associated with each working memory instance. To populate the working memory with some fact objects, a `Person` is instantiated, using its constructor to create the individual assigned with the name `John Doe` ❸. The `Person` is then added to the `WorkingMemory` using its `insert` method ❹.

Now that we've created the `RuleBase` and `WorkingMemory`, we're ready to fire up the engine to run. We do this using the `WorkingMemory.fireAllRules()` method ❺. This instructs the rules engine to process the rules using whatever fact data exists within the working memory.

NOTE You can find this example in the sample code associated with this chapter.

Now that you have for a good grasp of how things work using Drools, let's take a closer look at the Drools programming language. This is the vocabulary by which rules are expressed and that forms the foundation for creating our SOA-based decisional services.

11.3 Drools Rule Language (DRL) overview

Based on the Hello World example we created in the previous section, you may be left with the impression that the DRL language is simplistic and perhaps not very powerful. However, you can create quite sophisticated pattern matching statements for the rule conditions. We also only mentioned one rule attribute, the `salience` keyword, but many others are available. It's outside the scope of this chapter to provide in-depth coverage of the entire language; the official Drools documentation is outstanding in this regard [Drools]. Instead, I'll provide an overview, with code samples that demonstrate how to craft rules using the Drools language. We'll explore the most important constructs, so you are aware of Drools' capabilities and can investigate further.

Figure 11.4 shows the language components that you can use in a DRL file.

In figure 11.4, we group several of the items together into what we're calling *header elements*. The reason for doing this is because they must appear at the start of any DRL file, before the rules or queries are configured. Thus, they are more supporting type in nature, and are subsequently used by either rules or query definition. We'll examine these language elements first.

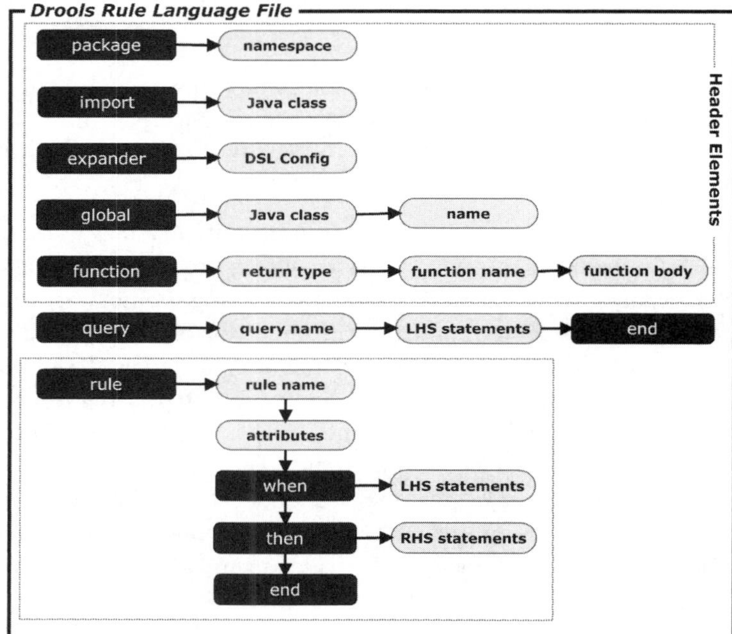

Figure 11.4 Overview of Drools language components and constructs

11.4 Drools header elements

The components that we're considering as header elements are `package`, `import`, `expander`, `global`, and `function`. Every rule file must have a package defined, and it must be the first declaration in the file (in that respect, it is similar to an XML root element). Let's look at `package` first.

11.4.1 package

The `String` value assigned as a `package` represents a namespace analogous in concept to how the similarly named construct exists within Java. However, unlike in Java, it can be any arbitrary value; it's not related in any way to the folder and file structure being used. Although you do not have to use a dot-notation style name (i.e., `opensoa.drools.example`), this type of naming convention is generally followed, since it's familiar in style to that used by Java developers and is also commonly used within XML for namespace definitions. The dot notation can also be useful from a categorization standpoint, allowing logical hierarchies to be defined (such as `hr.benefits` and `hr.benefits.401k`).

11.4.2 import

The `import` statement is used when you want to reference Java objects within the DRL. To do so, you must reference the complete Java package plus the class name. Java primitives such as String are automatically imported, so there's no need to import them. You'll likely find you use this most often when working with your custom fact objects, such as that demonstrated in listing 11.2 with the Person class.

11.4.3 expander

The expander keyword is necessary when using the Drools DSL capabilities. This keyword will identify the template file used for defining your custom DSL vocabulary. We'll explore this in section 11.8.

11.4.4 global

global is a global variable that's used primarily within the consequence portion of a rule definition. A global variable isn't stored within working memory, and can't be used for pattern-matching purposes (except when used with an eval, which we discuss in section 11.5.2). A global that's defined within a DRL file must first have been instantiated when your Drools session is created. In that respect, you aren't instantiating the global variable within the DRL but are instead receiving a handle to one that was created when the Drools session was initiated.

In chapter 8 we discussed Esper, the open source CEP that we selected for our Open SOA Platform. Using a global variable, we could obtain a handle to the Esper EPServiceProvider object and use it to send events to Esper when a rule has been fired. For example, let's update our earlier example to include an event posting to Esper:

```
global com.espertech.esper.client.EPServiceProvider epService;
rule "HelloDude"
   salience 40
   when
      person : Person ( gender == 'M', age < 25 );
   then
      System.out.println ("Hello Dude!");
      epService.getEPRuntime().sendEvent(
         new ProcessEvent("PersonDrools", "HelloDude",
              person.getName()));
      retract ( person );
end
```

Here, we're using global to receive a handle to EPServiceProvider and assigning it to the variable epService. In the consequence portion of the rule, we're then firing off a new event to the Esper engine. Obviously, some up-front work is required for setting up Esper, but the concept should be clear.

The Esper example is the type of use for which a global is intended. You can also use globals for callbacks, whereby a method could be called on a service that invoked the engine. We'll conclude our coverage of the header elements by looking at functions.

11.4.5 function

function is simply a way of including procedural code directly within DRL files. functions are written in Java, and when the DRL is compiled, helper classes are automatically generated. In you turn back to listing 11.3, you'll remember the example we created to print out Hello World with the person's name prefaced with a salutation. Let's create a function that performs the determination of whether to use "Mr." or "Mrs.", and we'll also convert the name to uppercase.

```
function String salutationGenerator( Person person ) {
  if ( person.getGender().equals("M") )
    return "Mr. " + person.getName().toUpperCase();
  else if ( person.getGender().equals("F") )
    return "Mrs. " + person.getName().toUpperCase();
  else
    return "";
}
```

Now let's use this function in a new rule:

```
rule "HelloFunction"
   salience 35
   when
     person : Person ( );
   then
     System.out.println( salutationGenerator( person ) );
end
```

The highlighted code shows `function` being called. Generally, `functions` aren't used within conditional (when) statements, except when a function returns a `Boolean`, in which case an `eval` can be used when calling the `function`.

In lieu of using a helper `function`, you could create a Java helper class with a static method to achieve the same results. I think this is a better idea, as intermixing code and rules in the same file runs contrary to one of the main tenets of using a rules engine: separating the concerns. Further, you may want a different configuration management lifecycle with code than you do for rules, which coincidently is our next topic of conversation.

11.5 Defining rules in Drools

We've already explored some basic functionality of rules, but we've only skimmed the surface. We'll begin by looking at rule attributes. We used one earlier, `salience`, to manage the priority for how rules are fired, but there are many more.

11.5.1 Modifying rule behavior with attributes

Rule attributes can be thought of primarily as a way of influencing how and when rules are fired. Without them, the sole determination is left to the conditional patterns defined for the rule. However, there are times when you want additional control and to simplify rule maintenance. We'll describe each of the available rule attributes next.

ACTIVATION-GROUP

You may recall from our Hello World example that, in order to prevent the other rules from firing after the `HelloDude` rule (listing 11.4), we retracted the `Person` object from working memory. This may not always be a desired option if you still want the fact object in the working memory. This is where you can use `activation-group`. The attribute takes a single `String` value, and when two or more rules have the same value, the rules will fire exclusively. In other words, if one rule in the activation group fires, none of the others will. You can also use `salience` to control the order and activation of rules.

AGENDA-GROUP

Agenda groups represent a way to manage flow control. For an example, see figure 11.5.

```
package opensoa.drools.hellodrools;
import opensoa.drools.hellodrools.Person;

rule "MrFlow"
    when
        Person( gender == 'M');
    then
        System.out.println("MrFlow: Setting to agend-group 'Mr'");
        drools.setFocus( "Mr" );
end
rule "MrsFlow"
    when
        Person( gender == 'F');
    then
        System.out.println("MrsFlow: Setting to agend-group 'Mrs'")
        drools.setFocus( "Mrs" );
end

rule "HelloMr"
    agenda-group "Mr"
    when
        person : Person ();
    then
        System.out.println("Hello Mr. " + person.getName());
        retract ( person );
end
rule "HelloMrs"
    agenda-group "Mrs"
    when
        person : Person ();
    then
        System.out.println("Hello Mrs. " + person.getName());
        retract ( person );
end
```

Figure 11.5 Use of agenda-group in action

In figure 11.5, the rules titled `MrFlow` and `MrsFlow` are used in a fashion akin to a distributor. If the conditions specified for the rule apply, the `drools.setFocus()` method is used to direct processing of the rule to the assigned `agenda-group`. All rules associated with that `agenda-group` will then be processed, and will fire based on whether the specified condition criteria are satisfied. In the example in figure 11.5, if the `Person` is male (`gender == 'M'`), the rule `MrFlow` is activated, and then sets the `agenda-group` focus to the one titled `'Mr'`, which in turns triggers the `HelloMr` rule to fire (since that rule's conditions are met).

AUTO-FOCUS

In figure 11.5 we used the `drools.setFocus()` directive to activate an `agenda-group`. The `auto-focus` attribute (which is a `Boolean`) can be used to accomplish the same feat, since it will activate a given `agenda-group` if the rule condition is met. Here's an example:

```
rule "MrFlow"
  auto-focus true
  agenda-group "Mr"
  when
    Person( gender == 'M');
  then
end
```

This MrFlow rule can replace the one shown in figure 11.5 and has the same effect.

DATE-EFFECTIVE

As the name suggests, using this attribute means that the rule can only be fired after the date and time specified. For example:

```
rule "DateEffectiveTest"
   salience 100
   date-effective "01-Nov-2009T01:01:01"
   when
     Person( );
   then
     System.out.println("DateEffectiveTest triggered");
end
```

This rule will only fire on or after November 1, 2009 at 1:01:01 AM (you can optionally leave the time off).

DATE-EXPIRES

When date-expires is used, a rule won't be triggered if the current date and time is past the value specified for this attribute. You can use this with date-effective to create a date range:

```
rule "DateExpiresTest"
   salience 100
   date-effective "01-Aug-2009T01:01:01"
   date-expires "01-Nov-2009T01:01:01"
   when
     Person( );
   then
     System.out.println("DateExpiresTest triggered");
end
```

Here, we're limiting the rule from firing between 01-Aug-2009 and 01-Nov-2009. This approach is useful when, for example, you're applying a pricing discount over a holiday period timeframe (for example, "Mother's day sale!").

DIALECT

The dialect attribute is used to determine which syntax is being used for the rule's conditions (when) and consequence (then) statements. Possible values are java or mvel (the default is java). Learn more about MVEL at http://mvel.codehaus.org/.

DURATION

The duration attribute will delay the firing of the rule for the specified time value (in milliseconds). After the timer has expired, the rule is re-evaluated to see whether the condition remains true. Here's an example:

```
rule "DurationTest"
  duration 60000
  when
    Person( );
  then
    System.out.println("DurationTest triggered");
end
```

Here, if the `Person` fact was subsequently removed from working memory between the time that this rule was first qualified and the completion of its duration timer, the rule would no longer be `true` and the system out message never printed. What's an example of where using `duration` could be useful? One scenario that comes to mind is where you want to discriminate service levels by customer. For example, perhaps you have various rules for how to process inbound customer service requests. Customers who have a "gold" status would be escalated immediately, but those with a status of "silver" would only be escalated after a specified period of time.

LOCK-ON-ACTIVE

The `lock-on-active` attribute is another way of managing rule activations, but it's only used with `agenda-group` or `ruleflow-group`. When set to `true`, `lock-on-active` will block any future activations of that rule from occurring (until the `ruleflow-group` is no longer active or the `agenda-group` loses focus). For example, in figure 11.5 we depicted the following rule:

```
rule "HelloMr"
   agenda-group "Mr"
   when
      person : Person ();
   then
      System.out.println("Hello Mr. " + person.getName());
      retract ( person );
end
```

If we were to use `update` instead of `retract`, the fact object would be refreshed in working memory, and the rule would continually fire in an endless (recursive) loop. This looping behavior could be avoided by using the `lock-on-active` attribute, as shown here:

```
rule "HelloMr"
   agenda-group "Mr"
   lock-on-active true
   when
      person : Person ();
   then
      System.out.println("Hello Mr. " + person.getName());
      update ( person );
end
```

This behavior can be beneficial, in particular when rules are performing calculations, where any reactivations resulting in a new calculation wouldn't be desirable.

NO-LOOP

The no-loop attribute, when set to true, will help prevent recursive (looping) reactivations that can result from modifying working memory as a result of an activation firing. We'll see this attribute in use in many of the examples that follow.

RULEFLOW-GROUP

Drools offers some fairly sophisticated ways in which to manage the order, or agenda, in which rules are activated. However, managing this using an agenda-group can still be rather tedious, especially when dealing with potentially hundreds of rules. The RuleFlow mechanism allows you to manage groups of rules and the order in which they can be activated. A String name assigned to the ruleflow-group attribute corresponds to a sequence node within a RuleFlow diagram. We'll demonstrate this capability in section 11.7 and in the case study in the next chapter.

SALIENCE

You've seen how the salience attribute can be used to manage the priority of rule activation. The value must be assigned an integer, which can be positive or negative. Higher numbers indicate higher rule priority. By default, if the attribute isn't specified, a salience value of 0 is assigned to the rule.

Let's now turn our attention to where the fun actually begins: the construction of the rules themselves. This begins with the conditional, or "when," portion of a rule definition.

11.5.2 Conditional part of rule statement (when part)

We've already explored some simple conditions as part of our Hello World, Drools example in section 11.2.1. Drools supports a rich set of constructs that can be used for building conditions. As we'll discover, conditions represent an essential part of the rules engine, as they directly impact your ability to craft sophisticated rules. Conditions work using pattern matching, so we'll begin by examining that concept in more detail.

PATTERNS AND CONSTRAINTS

In the Hello World example, we demonstrated a few types of patterns. The first pattern, in listing 11.2, matched whether the object Person existed in working memory. The when clause simply read: Person(). We later included some additional constraints to qualify the rule based on the Person attributes of age and gender, such as

```
Person ( gender == 'M', age < 25 );
```

The use of the comma is synonymous with an implicit *and*, which can be expressed using &&. Similarly, an *or* constraint can be added by using ||. So the following would match if the person is male *or* less than 25 years old:

```
Person ( gender == 'M' || age < 25 );
```

Using parentheses, you can also control the evaluation priority, the same as with any mathematical equation. So, for example, this rule would match if the person was a male under 25, or a female under 30:

```
Person ( ( gender == 'M' && age < 25 ) || ( gender == 'F' && age < 30 ) );
```

NOTE If using parenthetical phrases, you can't use a comma in lieu of `&&`.

As you probably noticed, as long as you're working with standard JavaBean type objects, it isn't necessary in conditional statements to use accessor methods when referencing fields. Using introspection, Drools will automatically add the appropriate *getXXX* or *isXXX* when attempting to resolve the field. Supported field types include numerics, `Date`, `String`, and `Boolean`. The date format, by default, is `'dd-mmm-yyyy'`, but this can be modified using the `drools.dateformat` system property. When using a primitive `Boolean`, you don't have to provide quotes around the `true` or `false` value.

You may be wondering how collections such as an `ArrayList` can be used. You can reference individual elements by using the index location (other ways in which collections can be used will be covered later in this section). For example, let's modify the `Person` class to include a new field called `interests` that's an `ArrayList` of `String` values representing an individual's hobbies. Using Drools' *nested accessor* support, we could create a rule such as the following:

```
rule "NestedAccessors"
   when
      person : Person ( interests[1] == 'Golf' )
   then
      System.out.println("NestedAccessors " + person.getName());
end
```

In this rule, we're checking whether the first indexed value of the `interests ArrayList` is equal to `Golf`. Keep the following in mind when working with nested accessors: working memory isn't directly aware of these values, and thus when they're changed, rules will be activated accordingly. Instead, you should remove and re-assert the parent reference of the accessor.

Let's now look at how we can use a variety of operators when comparing values used for pattern matching.

PATTERN OPERATORS

The default expression language for defining rules uses MVEL (as defined using the `dialect` header property). While Java-based and similar in style, it does offer some conveniences, particularly in operator comparisons, that aren't native to Java. In our `Person` example, we used the equality operator ('==') with a `String` value to compare the `interests` indexed value. This obviously isn't standard Java syntax, but it's a more intuitive approach for writing rules since the same operators can be used regardless of type. Other standard operators include '<', '>', '<=', '>=', and '`!=`'. While these are self-explanatory, there are some additional ones that you likely haven't encountered (shown in table 11.1).

You can also combine standard operators such as '==', '<', '>' into a shorthand form called *multiple restrictions*. For example, notice the condition within this rule:

```
rule "MultiRestrictions"
   when
      person : Person ( age (> 20 && < 25) )
   then
end
```

In this example, we're checking whether an individual's age is between 20 and 25. Multiple restrictions require that you group the conditions within parentheses, and you're limited to using && or || as logical operators. In certain scenarios, alternatives to using multiple restrictions exist for comparing a given value against a list of possible hits, which can simplify your rule definition—our next subject.

Table 11.1 Drools' extended operators

Operator Description	Example

`contains`
Used to check whether a `Collection` or array field contains the value specified. In the example shown, an `ArrayList` called `interests` consists of `String` values representing the `interests` of a `Person`, and we're checking whether one of their interests is `"Golf"`.
	`rule "Contains"`
	`when`
	`person: Person`
	`(interests contains "Golf");`
	`then`
	`end`

`not contains`
The opposite of `contains`, this checks whether the `Collector` or array list values do not contain the specified value.
	`rule "NotContains"`
	`when`
	`person: Person`
	`(interests not contains "Golf");`
	`then`
	`end`

`memberOf`
Somewhat analogous to `contains`, but checks whether a single field's value is located within the `Collection` or array specified. However, the comparison collection must be a variable. In the example shown, a global variable called `topInterests` is prepopulated with values such as "`Golf`" and "`Tennis`". The field value being compared is a `String` value representing the favorite interest of a `Person`.
	`rule "MemberOf"`
	`when`
	`person: Person`
	`(favoriteInterest memberOf`
	`topInterests);`
	`then`
	`end`

`matches`
Compares a single field value against any valid Java regular expression. In the example shown, a comparison match exists if the name of the `Person` is `"<any-first-name> Doe"`.
	`rule "Matches"`
	`when`
	`person : Person`
	`(name matches "(.*?)( )[Dd]oe");`
	`then`
	`end`

`not matches`
The opposite of `matches`, this checks whether the field value does not match the provided regular expression.
	`rule "NotMatches"`
	`when`
	`person : Person`
	`(name not matches`
	`"(.*?)( )[Dd]oe");`
	`then`
	`end`

Table 11.1 Drools' extended operators *(continued)*

Operator Description	Example

`soundslike`
Checks whether a word has the same phonetic sound as the provided value. For instance, in the example shown, if a `favoriteInterest` of a `Person` is "`Golf`", then "`Gulf`" would match using `soundslike` (which is a form of soundex).
	`rule "Soundslike"`
	` when`
	`  person : Person`
	`   (favoriteInterest soundslike`
	`      'Gulf' )`
	`  then`
	`end`

Note: These examples can be found in the sample code for this chapter.

GROUP-RELATED EVALUATORS

The official Drools documentation [Drools] refers to comparing a field value against a list of one or more possible values' *compound value restrictions.* If you use SQL, the *in* operator is likely familiar to you. Table 11.2 describes how `in` and `not in` are supported.

Table 11.2 Group evaluators

Conditional Description	Example

`in`
An evaluator that compares a single value against a list of possible values. In the example, a `String` field called `favoriteInterest` is compared against two possible choices (`'Golf'`, `'Biking'`). If the field value is either value listed within the `in` parenthetical, the rule will fire. Rather than using literals, as shown, you could also use a return value or variable.
	`rule "In"`
	` when`
	`  person : Person (`
	`favoriteInterest`
	`       in ('Golf', 'Biking' ) )`
	`  then`
	`end`

`not in`
The negative of using just `in`. So in the example to the right the rule would fire only if `favoriteInterest` *is not* `'Golf'` or `'Biking'`.
	`rule "NotIn"`
	` when`
	`  person : Person (`
	`favoriteInterest`
	`       not in ('Golf', 'Biking' ) )`
	`  then`
	`end`

Note: These examples can be found in the sample code for this chapter.

We've now completed our discussion of comparison-based operators and evaluators. Let's turn our attention for the remainder of this section to how you can logically construct statements that are composed of these operators and evaluators. We'll begin by looking at what we term *logical conditionals.*

LOGICAL CONDITIONALS

When constructing conditional phrases, you often find it necessary to combine various statements together to form the pattern required for the rule. Our Hello World example was purposely kept as simple as possible, so these logical conditions weren't used. But now let's expand the use case so that we can illustrate some of these features. In particular, we'll add a new property to the `Person` class called `homeZip`. It will be an integer field, and as the name suggests, it'll store the home zip code for the individual. Then we'll add a new `ZipCode` class. Its fields are `(int) zipcode`, `(String) city`, `(String) state`. For example purposes, we'll populate several `ZipCode` entries into the working memory so that we can compare `Person.homeZip` against `Zipcode.zipcode` to retrieve the state and city in which the individual resides.

The conditionals are listed in table 11.3, with descriptions and examples for each.

Table 11.3 Logical conditionals

Conditional Description	Example

`and`
The `and` conditional is used to group together other conditional statements or elements. It's one of the most frequently used conditionals, and several permutations are supported, as shown in the examples.
In each example, we're simply matching a `ZipCode` against a `Person` using the `ZipCode.zipcode` and `Person.homeZip` field values as the join criteria. In the first example, an implicit `and` is used, as it is the default behavior for joining one or more statements. In the second case, what's called a `prefixAnd` is used, which has the format of `(and <statements>)`. In the last example, we used an `infixAnd`, where conditional element statements are specifically tied together using an explicit `and`.
	`rule "ImplicitAndConditional"`
	` when`
	`  person : Person ($zip : homeZip);`
	`    zipCode : ZipCode (zipcode ==`
	`$zip);`
	`  then`
	`end`
	Is the same as:
	`rule "PrefixAndConditional"`
	` when`
	`  (and`
	`    (person : Person ($zip :`
	`homeZip ))`
	`    (zipCode : ZipCode (`
	`      zipcode == $zip)) )`
	` then`
	`end`
	Is the same as:
	`rule "InfixAndConditional"`
	` when`
	`  (person : Person($zip : homeZip))`
	` and`
	`  (zipCode : ZipCode(zipcode ==`
	`$zip))`
	` then`
	`end`

Table 11.3 Logical conditionals *(continued)*

Conditional Description	Example

`or`
A conditional grouping that will result in rule activation for each true statement. This is often a source of great confusion. When used, the Drools engine will actually split the rule apart internally into one or more subrules. What's confusing is that, depending on your authoring, a rule using an `or` may then fire multiple times, because multiple rules are created behind the scenes for each statement.
In the first example shown, if the `Person` is older than `20` but younger than `30`, the rule will fire twice, since both statements are true. In the second example, the rule will only fire once if the individual's `homeZip` is one of the two values shown.
	Uses the `prefixOr` format.
	`rule "PrefixOrConditional"`
	`when`
	`(or person : Person (age > 20)`
	`person : Person (age < 30) )`
	`then`
	`end`
	Uses the `infixOr` format.
	`rule "InfixOrConditional"`
	`when`
	`person :`
	`(Person (homeZip == 80012)`
	`or Person (homeZip == 80920))`
	`then`
	`end`

Note: There is no support for an implicit `or`, as this would be interpreted instead as an implicit `and`.	

`not`
This will check for the nonexistence of something within the working memory. So in the example shown the rule will fire if no `Person` has a `homeZip` of `83822`.
	`rule "Not"`
	`when`
	`not Person (homeZip == 83822);`
	`then`
	`end`

`exists`
Related in concept to `not`, `exists` will check whether one or more facts within the working memory qualify using the pattern presented. In the example shown, the rule will fire only once if one or more `Persons` has a `homeZip` of `80920`.
	`rule "Exists"`
	`when`
	`exists (Person (homeZip ==`
	`80920));`
	`then`
	`end`

`eval`
This is a flexible construct that allows any code that returns a `Boolean` to be used within a pattern. In the example, the `ArrayList` size of the `interests` field is used to determine whether the rule will fire. You could also call Drools functions or other Java methods, as long as they return a primitive boolean.
	`rule "Eval"`
	`when`
	`person : Person ( $age : age );`
	`eval`
	`(person.getInterests().size()`
	`>= 2 );`
	`then`
	`end`

Note: These examples can be found in the sample code for this chapter.

You'll likely find that you'll be using these conditionals on a frequent basis, especially as your rules go beyond trivial. The last set of conditionals we'll look at relate to using iterators and collections.

ITERATOR- AND COLLECTION-RELATED CONDITIONALS

As you begin to build more complex rule patterns using more complex fact object structures, you'll likely encounter the need to use one of the conditionals shown in table 11.4.

Table 11.4 Collection-related conditionals

Conditional Description	Example

`forall`
Somewhat akin to an iterator pattern matcher, `forall` is constructed in two parts. The first is a pattern that returns a set of facts, with the second part iterating through those facts to determine whether the pattern provided is true. If all are true, the rule will fire. So in the first example we're pattern-matching all `Person` fact objects, then for each matching fact object we evaluate whether they are over the age of 18.
In the second example, we're using the negative form of `forall`. In this case, we're checking all to see that all `Person` facts have a valid `zipcode`, based on the `homeZip` field value.
	`rule "Forall"`
	` when`
	`  forall(person : Person ()`
	`   Person (this == person,`
	`        age > 18) )`
	` then`
	`end`
	Using a `not` form of `forall`:
	`rule "ForallNot"`
	` when`
	`  not`
	` (forall(person : Person ()`
	`   ZipCode(zipcode ==`
	`       person.homeZip)))`
	` then`
	`end`

`from`
The `from` conditional allows you to specify a source for patterns to reason over. It can be data either in working memory or returned from a function, bound variable, etc. In the example, we're first iterating through the global variable called `topInterests`. Then we're iterating through the `ArrayList` of `Person interests`, matching against the iterated values returned from `topInterest`. *The rule will fire for each matching interest.*
	`rule "From"`
	` when`
	`  person : Person ();`
	`  String (val : toString)`
	`     from topInterests;`
	`  foundInterest : String`
	`    (toString == val)`
	`     from person.interests;`
	`  then`
	`end`

`collect`
The `collect` conditional will return a collection for any matched pattern objects. In the example shown, an `ArrayList` is returned for all matching `ZipCode` facts (no pattern is provided, so all are returned), with the size of the `List` printed out in the consequence portion of the rule.
	`rule "Collect"`
	` when`
	`  collection : ArrayList ()`
	`from`
	`    collect ( ZipCode () );`
	` then`
	`  System.out.println("Collect "`
	`    + collection.size());`
	`end`

Table 11.4 Collection-related conditionals *(continued)*

Conditional Description	Example
`accumulate` This conditional is a more powerful form of a `collect`, and allows you to iterate over a collection of objects while performing individual actions on each element encountered. It's ideally suited for things such as performing summary calculations. We'll examine this conditional in more detail in our use case study, which is covered in the next chapter.	See the next chapter's use case for a detailed examination of using this conditional.

Table 11.4 represents the last of the conditionals, and as you can see, they're very powerful constructs. Knowledge of these conditionals will prove indispensible as you begin creating your own rules, especially as they grow more complex in nature. We'll conclude this section on the conditional elements of rules with a look at variable binding. As you'll see, binding becomes important when working on the consequence portion of the rule definition (which represents the decisions and action to be undertaken when a rule is matched).

VARIABLE BINDING

In several of our Hello World examples, we demonstrated the use of variable binding. In listing 11.3, for example, we assigned the `Person` fact handle to a variable called `person`. That was done so we could print out the individual's name in the consequence part of the rule when it's activated. Rather than assigning the variable to the entire object, you could create one that just captures the individual's name—in other words, only a `String` object would be created. Let's rewrite that example to demonstrate this (listing 11.6).

Listing 11.6 Listing 11.6 Use of variable binding in field-level assignment

```
rule "HelloMr2"
   salience 30
   when
     Person ( $name : name, gender == 'M');    <-- 1
   then
      System.out.println("Hello Mr. " + $name);    <-- 2
end
```

In listing 11.6, the name of the person is assigned to the variable `$name` ❶ (the `$` prefix is optional but helps avoid confusion when the variable name is the same as the fact object field's name). That name is subsequently printed out in the consequence portion of the rule ❷. Notice that it's not necessary to cast the variable to the appropriate type, as this is handled transparently by Drools through reflection techniques.

This completes our coverage of the conditional portion of a rule definition. We'll tackle the consequence, or action part, next. Unlike with the conditional part, the language constructs are minimal for the consequence—so hang in there!

11.5.3 Consequence part of rule statement (then part)

The main purpose for the consequence portion of a rule is to *insert*, *retract*, or *update* data in the working memory. When using rules as a service, the findings should be returned to the client. To preserve a loose coupling between services, I don't recommend that the consequence directly execute application code. Instead, *the purpose of the rules engine is to render a decision, not execute code.* There are three main actions that can be performed on working memory: update, insert, and retract. We'll discuss each in turn.

NOTE The consequence part of a rule is sometimes referred to as the *right-hand side* (whereas the conditional part is the *left-hand side*). This terminology is derived from its Rete heritage. While I generally avoid using this terminology, it's worth noting since you'll see it used often throughout the official Drools documentation [Drools].

UPDATE

The signature for this method is `update (<object>)`, where the `<object>` is the fact you're modifying. When you trigger an update, take care to avoid a recursive loop, as the rule may be reactivated. To illustrate how `update` can be used, consider this example:

```
rule "HelloDudeUpdate"
   salience 50
   no-loop true
   when
      person : Person ( gender == 'M', age < 25 );
   then
      System.out.println ("Hello Dude2!");
      person.setSalutation ( "Hello Dude" );
      update ( person );
end
```

Here, the `salutation` field of `Person` (added for purposes of this illustration) is set to `"Hello Dude"` using the `setSalutation` method. Then the `person` fact object variable is updated to reflect the change in working memory. If the `no-loop true` header weren't set, a recursive condition would occur, since the rule conditions would again evaluate to `true` (the update results in rules being re-fired). As an aside, in lieu of using `no-loop`, you could add an additional condition to the pattern, as in `(salutation == null, gender == 'M', age < 25)`.

INSERT AND INSERTLOGICAL

The `insert` method, which takes an object as its single parameter, will add the object as a fact into working memory. The `insertLogical` method also inserts an object into working memory, but has one important distinction: the inserted object will be removed (retracted) from working memory when the pattern conditions that activated the rule are no longer true. A simple example will help clarify this behavior. Consider the following rule:

```
rule "HelloInsert"
   salience 20
   when
      person : Person ();
   then
      insertLogical ( new String ( "test" ) );
end
```

If a `Person` object exists in memory, this rule will fire, and a `String` will be inserted into working memory using `insertLogical`. Now, if a subsequent rule fires that retracts the `Person` object that was used to activate this rule, the `String` object added via `insertLogical` will be removed. Similarly, consider this rule scenario:

```
rule "HelloInsert"
   salience 20
   when
      person : Person( name == "John Doe" );
   then
      insertLogical ( new String ( "test" ) );
      person.setName("Jane Doe");
      update ( person );
end
```

What's interesting about this rule is that it will only fire if the `Person.name` equals `"John Doe"`, and once fired, the `insertLogical` method is invoked to add the `String` object into working memory. However, within the consequence part, the `Person.name` is modified and updated, which results in this rule no longer being fire-able. Since the rule conditions are no longer satisfied as a result of this update, *the inserted object is removed immediately*. Thus, you should clearly understand the behavior of `insertLogical` before electing to use it.

RETRACT

The `retract` method accepts a single object representing a handle to a fact that's to be removed from working memory. If your sole desire for using `retract` is to avoid other rules from being fired, it sometimes makes more sense to instead create a flag-type field that can be set and then subsequently checked that it's not null. Obviously, it depends on whether it's useful to preserve the object in working memory.

As you can see, the consequence portion of the rule definition is about altering the facts within the working memory. Granted, nothing precludes you from making Java method calls to perform some action logic. However, I advise against going in this direction, because the notion of using rules as a decision service means that it should be limited to rendering a judgment. In other words, it doesn't perform an action but instead informs the client consumer that calls the service of its decision. This preserves the loose coupling that's essential for a SOA environment and makes the service far more reusable by other client systems.

There's one final piece of functionality we haven't touched on: queries. Using a query, which basically resembles a rule but only contains the conditional part, you can search on facts residing in the working memory.

11.6 Querying facts in Drools

A query provides a means to search working memory and stores the results under a named value. Then, within the Java code used to fire the rules, the working memory can be queried using the assigned name. For example, let's create a query to return all `Person` facts within working memory:

```
query "PersonQuery"
  person : Person ( )
end
```

Any bound variables, such as `person`, will be stored within the query. To retrieve the contents of the query from within Java, use a fragment such as

```
Person person = null;
QueryResults results =
  workingMemory.getQueryResults ("PersonQuery" );
System.out.println ("Number of Person objects: " + results.size());
for (QueryResult qresult : qresults) {
 person = (Person) qresult.get("person");
 System.out.println("Person is: " + person.getName());
}
```

Queries can be a convenient way of passing information back to the calling client, without having to resort to inserting objects into working memory, which may not always be desired.

Congratulations! We've covered the language essentials for creating business rules in Drools. You can now create the condition and consequence portions of the rule, query working memory, and use the various rule attributes to influence the order in which rules are activated. As you may recall from section 11.5.1, one of the rule attributes we spoke about was `ruleflow-group`. This is used to logically group the order in which rules are evaluated. This feature has been significantly expanded in the 5.0 release of Drools, and we'll consider its capabilities next.

11.7 Drools RuleFlow for rule orchestration

Drools RuleFlow, originally introduced in version 4 of the product, allows users to create a graphical flow chart that defines the order in which rules should be evaluated. The Drools Eclipse IDE includes a graphical editor for constructing the flows, as shown in figure 11.6.

Why would you consider using this feature? There are several possible reasons:

- *Managing large rulesets*—If you're working with a large number of rules, managing the order in which they fire using `salience` or `agenda-groups` can become challenging. RuleFlow simplifies this process by allowing you to graphically describe the proper sequence of steps. Further, you can easily add sophisticated branching logic using RuleFlow.
- *Wait states and work items*—With RuleFlow, you can define wait states within your flow that will pause processing until a given constraint is satisfied. Similarly, you

can create work items, whereby processing is suspended until a certain action is completed. These capabilities share some common features typically found in a BPM solution (indeed, RuleFlow is based on the jBPM engine).

- *Integration*—With RuleFlow, you can use an action to invoke custom Java code at points within the flow. This enables you to more easily integrate with external applications or services.

A significant amount of functionality is available using RuleFlow, and it's beyond the scope of this book to entirely do it justice (the Drools 5.0 documentation on RuleFlow is vastly superior to what was provided in the 4.0 release). However, we'll create a simple example that demonstrates its capabilities (and the next chapter will also use RuleFlow extensively in a use case).

In figure 11.6, we show a depiction of a RuleFlow that builds on the Hello World example we've been using throughout this chapter. In this example, a splitter node labeled `Gender` is used to evaluate the `Person` object's `gender` property and, depending on the results, direct the flow to either the `Male` or `Female` node. The behavior of the splitter is defined based on the constraints identified in its property view. For example, the path flowing from `Gender` to `Male` has a constraint of `Person (gender == "M")`. The `Male` node is a `RuleFlowGroup` component. A `RuleFlowGroup` node has a similarly named `String` property (`Id`) that identifies which rules to use based on the `ruleflow-group` assigned to the rules (which, in this case, is a value of `'male'`). This will become clearer when we look at one of the rules assigned to that `RuleFlowGroup` (see listing 11.7)

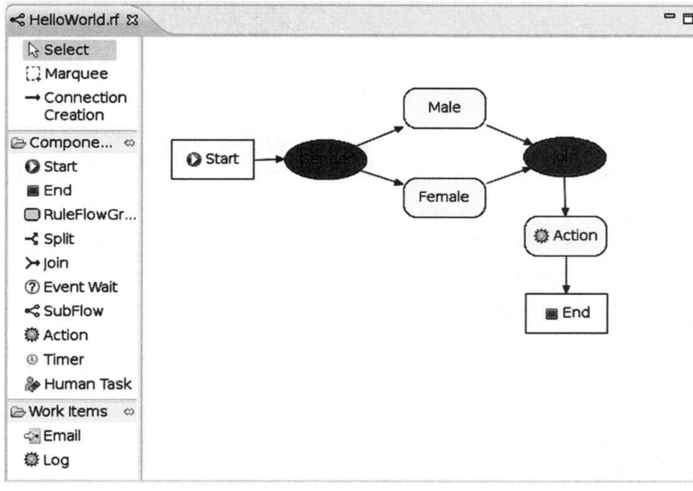

Figure 11.6 Drools Eclipse RuleFlow editor

Listing 11.7 Example of using `ruleflow-group`

```
rule "HelloWorldMaleFlow"
   ruleflow-group 'male'                    <-- ❶ Assigns RuleFlowGroup name
   no-loop true
   when
      man : Person ( )
   then
      man.setSalutation ( "Mr." );
      update ( man );
      System.out.println ( "HelloWorldMaleFlow fired: "
        + man.getName() );
end
```

As you can see in listing 11.7, the rule header's `ruleflow-group` attribute is set to `'male'` ❶, which is the same value assigned in the `RuleFlowGroup` node for the `Male` node in figure 11.6. Since the splitter was used to differentiate based on `gender`, there was no need to add that constraint to the rule defined in listing 11.7. Not shown is a query that was also defined that simply captured all `Person` objects in working memory. This query is referenced downstream in the `Action` node shown in figure 11.6. An `Action` is simply any MVEL or Java script snippet that you define. In this example, it prints out the `Person` objects captured from the query.

NOTE The full RuleFlow example can be found in the source code for this chapter.

Up until now, we've defined our rules exclusively using the DRL. While I think you'll agree it's fairly intuitive, it does remain more targeted to the developer than the business user. In light of that, let's examine the other means of creating rules: *domain-specific language* (DSL) and *decision tables.*

11.8 Alternatives to using Drools Rule Language

One of the major challenges facing all rules engine vendors is how to make the definition of rules more like natural language. Since the intention is for business users to craft rules, this is considered an important requirement. It has been met with varying degrees of success, since the vocabulary for rules is often very domain specific. The Drools approach to this conundrum is to use a templating mechanism that allows developers to create DSLs that can be language specific to the context or domain in which they're used. Let's create a simple DSL for our Hello World example, and you'll see how straightforward the process is.

RuleFlow vs. jBPM

You may have seen some similarities between RuleFlow and jBPM, which we covered in chapters 5–7. Indeed, as Mark Proctor, the JBoss Drools lead, states, RuleFlow is "an integration of rules and processes" [Proctor]. This obviously begs the question, why not just use Drools with RuleFlow instead of jBPM? I'm not completely convinced that tightly coupling rules and processes is always advantageous. For one, it breaks

> **RuleFlow vs. jBPM *(Continued)***
> one of the central tenets of SOA—namely, loosely couple services. By merging them as one, we are assuming the lifecycles of rules and processes are the same, when in fact, they're often different. Further, while a BPM process undoubtedly uses rules, that's not its central foundation. The RuleFlow functionality in Drools is also not currently as rich as jBPM, so it may not be suitable in all instances. My recommendation is to use RuleFlow to simplify the management of complex rulesets, but for true business process modeling and execution, stick with jBPM.

11.8.1 Using DSLs for business user authoring

The easiest approach we've found for creating a DSL is to start with an existing rule or rules, and then consider how the rule's syntax can be made to resemble natural language. In listing 11.4, we defined a rule with a pattern that identified a `Person` whose age was less than 25 and who was a male. The when condition was specified as

```
person : Person ( gender == 'M', age < 25 )
```

Obviously, building this condition assumes some fairly detailed knowledge about the fact object, and would be rather confusing for a business type to understand. It would be much more readily understandable to business users if it were expressed using something like this:

```
There is a person who is > than age 25, and that person is male.
```

While you could create a template that would allow precisely that language to be expressed, it would be so specific that it might not be very reusable when crafting other rules. A better approach would be something like this:

```
There is at least one person
The person is > than age 25
The person is Male.
```

We can define such a vocabulary using the DSL template definition shown in listing 11.8.

Listing 11.8 Example of DSL definition

```
[when]There is at least one person=person: Person ();
[when]The person is {oper} than {age}=Person ( age {oper} {age});      <-- 1
[when]The person is male=Person ( gender == 'M' );
[when]The person is female=Person ( gender == 'F' );
```

Each template line begins by specifying whether you're defining a `condition` or `consequence`, wrapped within brackets (`[]`). This is followed by an empty set of brackets, and then the natural language statement. Data that needs to be captured by the rule author is specified via tokens that are surrounded by curly brackets (`{}`). The template part that begins following the equal sign (=) is then the rule expression, in DRL syntax. Any token placeholders captured in the natural language part can then be referenced in the DRL definition (the part that follows the =). A good example in listing 11.8 of a template definition is where the age of the person is used as the rule pattern ❶. In this case, two tokens are defined: one for the comparison operator (`{oper}`) and the other the age (`{age}`). What's interesting about this definition is that it illustrates that token replacement can be used not just for fact conditions, but also for Drools language elements, such as for the comparison operator.

To simplify creation of complex rules that can include one or many possible constraints, you can use a shortcut to define a variety of possible constraints to a single rule definition. In listing 11.8, the author is required to add several independent rules to achieve the desired definition. For example, a complete rule might resemble this:

```
rule "DSL2"
   when
      There is at least one person
      The person is >= than 20
      The person is male
   then
      Log : "DSL2"
      Print the name of the person
end
```

Here, the three conditional statements all correspond to separate DSL templates, and the actual resulting rule when compiled into DRL would be

```
rule "DSL2"
   when
     person: Person ();
     Person ( age >= 20);
     Person ( gender == 'M' );
   then
     System.out.println("DSL2");
     System.out.println("Person is: " + person.getName());
end
```

As you can see, this is a fairly inefficient definition, since the `Person` fact is referenced and constrained in three separate statements. Instead, the template can be rewritten to avoid this by specifying field constraints in a separate template line that begins with a dash (`-`). Take a look at listing 11.9.

Listing 11.9 Example of DSL definition

```
[when]There is a  person=person:Person()
[when]- age is greater or equal to {age}=age >= {age}
[when]- age is less than or equal to {age}=age <= {age}
[when]- gender is male=gender=='M'
[when]- gender is female=gender=='F
```

Each template definition that starts with the dash will add the constraint identified on the right-hand side of the equals to the parent fact object. So, if the constraint `gender is male` is selected, it would result in the constraint `gender=='M'` being added to the People fact pattern. In other words, what would result in the translated DRL is

```
person: Person (gender=='M');
```

NOTE When using the Eclipse rule editor, you can see the translated DRL by clicking on the *DRL Viewer* tab that appears on the bottom left in the editor panel.

The real power behind using DSLs becomes most evident when using the Drools' Eclipse rule editor (or editing within Guvnor, discussed in the next chapter). When editing, code expansions can be used to select a predefined template, and the author can then just replace the tokens with actual values. Figure 11.7 shows the editor in use; I pressed Ctrl+Spacebar to access the pop-up list of template options.

If you're just adding a field constraint, you can filter just those lines by first entering - prior to hitting Ctrl+Spacebar.

In listing 11.5, we showed you how to run the Hello World example from within Java. To use a DSL, only a minor change is required: you must load the DSL configuration file (the template), and then use the alternative method signature for PackageBuilder. addPackageFromDrl(<DRLFileSource>, <DSLFileSource>). So if the DSL configuration is helloworld.dsl, and the corresponding DRL file is called HelloWorld.dslr (notice the different file extension, .dslr instead of .drl, to indicate it's a DSL-based rule file), then it would be loaded using

```
Reader source = new InputStreamReader(
  HelloDroolsMainDSL.class.getResourceAsStream( "/HelloWorld.dslr" ) );
Reader DSLsource = new InputStreamReader(
  HelloDroolsMainDSL.class.getResourceAsStream( "/helloworld.dsl" ) );
PackageBuilder builder = new PackageBuilder();
builder.addPackageFromDrl( source, DSLsource );
```

The remainder of the code used in listing 11.5 remains valid.

The DSL capabilities are definitely worth exploring if you want to extend the authoring environment to regular business users. Another way of expressing rules is a decision table, which we'll cover next.

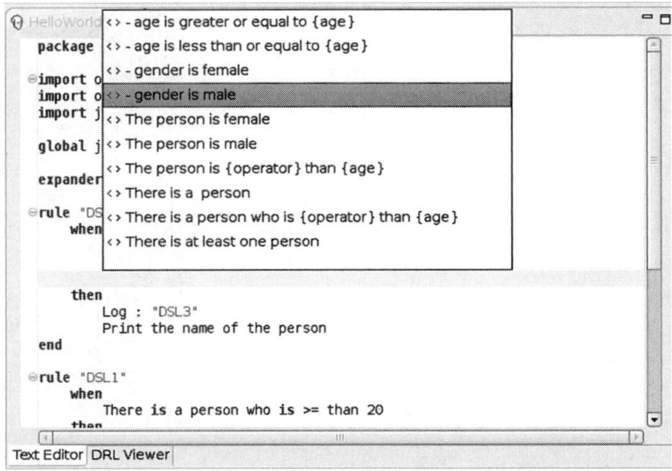

Figure 11.7 An example of the Eclipse rule editor using DSL

11.8.2 Defining rules using decision tables

Decision tables are a way of collecting conditional logic through a spreadsheet. Columns within the spreadsheet represent rule conditions or consequences (actions), while rows represent individual rules generated by the data entered therein. Decision tables are ideally suited when you have a limited number of rule parameters but many rule conditions.

A surprising amount can be accomplished using decision tables, but it's beyond the scope of this book to cover all possible configurations (the official documentation does offer excellent coverage of this feature). However, figure 11.8 conveys some sense of how decision trees are constructed, using our Hello World, Drools example.

As you can see in figure 11.8, the columns that include the keywords of CONDITION or ACTION are used to represent the condition or consequence portion of a rule. The next row after that is used to identify the working memory objects you're working with (notice the two columns are merged, so that object applies to both columns), with the row after that identifying the rule templates that apply to those objects. Following that row is just a column description, which isn't used in rule execution. Once the template information is set up, then the actual rule data itself can be specified, which is what follows.

In the example shown in figure 11.8, we created a salutation based on the `Person` object's `age` and `gender` fields. The `age` is specified as a range (`age >=$1, age <= $2`), with the `$1` and `$2` being replaced by the values within the data columns (when you're

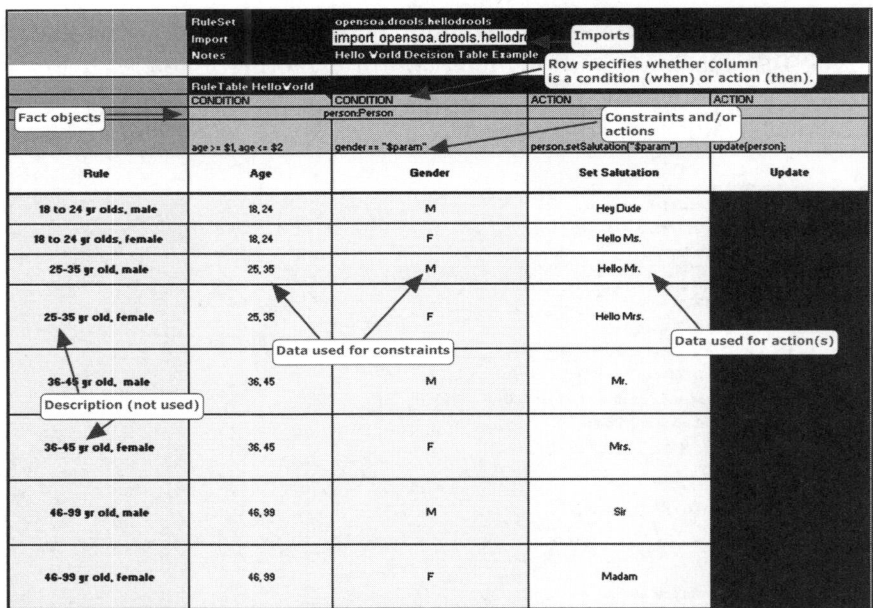

Figure 11.8 An example decision table

working with multiple values, the form of `$1`, `$2`, `$3` can be used, which correspond to the comma-separated data used in the rule row data). For example, if the `Person` is between the ages of `46` and `99` and is a male, then the salutation is set to `Sir`.

Decision tables are a convenient way for business users to maintain rulesets. Spreadsheet applications such as Excel or Open Office are familiar territory, and thus the training is minimal. However, if highly complex and varied rules are required, decision tables may not be a workable choice.

We've covered a lot of material in this chapter, and hopefully you have a fairly solid understanding of how Drools works and are as excited as I am about its potential.

11.9 Summary

The operational decisions that are made by any organization on a day-to-day basis represent its key intellectual property. Using a rules engine, these decisions can be extracted from specific applications or domain experts where they often reside and managed independently as assets. In this fashion, they can be more readily understood, maintained, and modified to reflect changes in the business environment. Further, complexity is reduced, since rules engines offer powerful constructs for creating and expressing rules that can be otherwise very difficult to code within conventional programming languages such as Java.

JBoss Rules, known as Drools by most folks, is a mature, fast, highly capable rules engine that continues to undergo significant enhancements from release to release. This chapter introduced you to the key functionality of Drools, while providing many examples of how to craft rules using the product. The next chapter will focus on implementation, and will cover *Guvnor*, the Drools Business Rules Management System (BRMS), while presenting a real-life use case to further build on what you've learned in this chapter. I'll also describe how to create stateless decision services through integration with Apache Tuscany.

12 *Implementing Drools*

This chapter covers

- Using Drools in a real-life case study
- Using Drools Guvnor BRMS
- Implementing a decision service

In the previous chapter we discussed what constitutes business rules and how they can be used with a rules engine in a SOA environment to significantly improve the reusability of these assets and promote greater agility within your organization. We then explored JBoss Rules (most commonly called *Drools*), which will serve as the rule engine for our Open SOA Platform. We spent the latter part of chapter 11 describing many examples that illustrated the key language constructs of Drools. For your less technical users, we covered some of the alternative ways in which rules can be expressed, such as through decision tables and domain-specific languages. What we didn't discuss, and what's the initial focus of this chapter, was how to use the Drools *Business Rule Management System* (BRMS), known as *Guvnor.* By the time you complete this chapter, you'll share my enthusiasm for this exciting capability—it truly unlocks the power of rules to your business audience.

The last thing we'll cover before concluding this chapter is how we can combine the capabilities of Drools with the service component framework of Apache Tuscany (an implementation of the *Service Component Architecture*, or SCA), which we covered in chapters 3 and 4. You'll learn how to create *decision services* that can be a key foundation for SOA-enabling your enterprise. We'll demonstrate why decoupling rules from their historically intertwined role within application logic transitions them into corporate assets that can be reused across many solutions and processes. As we talked about in the previous chapter, the decisions a company makes are what determines its success. Centralizing these decisions, represented as rules, through Guvnor and exposing them as services, will allow them to become substantial contributors to your journey to SOA.

To introduce Guvnor and the decision services that follow, we'll create a real-life case study.

12.1 Case study overview

One of the most common, and often complex, requirements for a company is developing a pricing engine that can be used to calculate the price of products or services being quoted to a customer. This is a challenge because you may want the prices to vary depending on any number of factors, such as customer classification, size of order, shipment options selected, promotional sales, or product availability. Many ERP systems include sophisticated capabilities to assist in product pricing, but you're still limited to whatever parameters they support. Of course, if you don't have a million-dollar ERP system in place, determining pricing can be a much more manual and tedious process. The case study we'll examine describes how a pricing engine can be developed using Drools, and then exposed as services that can be readily utilized by a number of applications. Obviously, given the ubiquity of rules, the notion of services central to the premise of SOA can act as a catalyst toward achieving your SOA objectives.

The premise behind the case study is to create a service that, upon receiving a request that contains order details, will return a computed cost for the products selected. The variables that will impact the pricing calculation include the following:

- Customer classification, such as whether they are a Gold, Silver, or Standard customer
- Volume discounts based on item count
- Shipment calculations based on the carrier selected

In order for the pricing and rules engine to perform its calculations, it requires a substantial amount of data in its working memory. For example, it must know the weight of the products to calculate shipping costs, it must be able to look up the classification of a customer, and it must have access to the pricing of the individual products.

Listing 12.1 shows an example, depicted in XML, of an inbound request.

Listing 12.1 Example of XML inbound request for rule engine calculation

```
<Order>
   <header>
      <orderId>2020322</orderId>
      <partyId>WA-23923</partyId>        <-- (1) Identifies customer
```

```
        <partyContactId>1006</partyContactId>
        <currency>USD</currency>                 ❷ Identifies
        <shipping>                                  shipping carrier
          <carrier>USPS</carrier>
          <method>STANDARD</method>                 Identifies shipment
        </shipping>                              ❸ method
    </header>                      ❹ Lists order line
    <lines>                           items
        <product>
          <lineId>2020322-1</lineId>
          <productId>GZ-1004</productId>
          <cnt>1</cnt>                            Orders line
        </product>                                itemsest
        <product>
          <lineId>2020322-2</lineId>
          <productId>GZ-1001</productId>
          <cnt>12</cnt>
        </product>
    </lines>
</Order>
```

As you can see, the inbound request includes a customer identifier ❶ that can be used to look up the customer classification; shipping details such as which carrier to use ❷ along with delivery type (standard ground, overnight, etc.) ❸; and a breakdown of the line item products ❹ and their quantity. Once processed by the rules engine, an XML rendering of the results would look like this:

```
<DecisionResponse>
   <orderId>2020322</orderId>
   <salePrice>72.97</salePrice>
   <shippingPrice>12.5</shippingPrice>
   <totalPrice>60.47</totalPrice>
 </DecisionResponse>
```

In order to populate the Drools working memory with the data needed to perform the calculations, a set of DTOs must be created and populated, which can then be referenced when creating the Drools business rules.

An overview of the DTO objects used within the case study is shown in figure 12.1.

The objects shown in figure 12.1 contain no business logic and are simply containers for capturing the required data needed by Drools. The methods, which aren't shown in the figure, are simply getters and setters (accessor methods) for each of the class member variables. The `Order` and `OrderProduct` classes represent the instance (volatile) data used to represent an inbound request, and are the class manifestations of the XML shown in listing 12.1 (in other words, these classes are the input used by the rule engine to calculate the pricing).

NOTE The complete Java classes for all the classes shown in figure 12.1, plus all samples that follow in this chapter, can be found in the chapter 12 example code.

Let's now take a look at some of the rules used in our case study. You'll become familiar with some nontrivial type examples that truly illustrate the power of Drools.

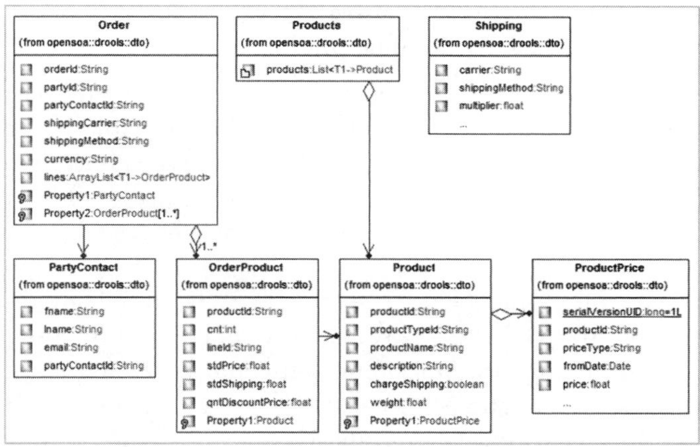

Figure 12.1 Case study DTO fact classes intended for use by the Drools working memory

12.1.1 *Defining the DRL rules*

Because of the number of rules that we'll use to perform the pricing calculation, it represents an ideal scenario for applying the Drools RuleFlow feature. As you may recall from section 11.5 in the previous chapter, you use RuleFlow when you want to manage the sequence by which rules can be activated. Further, it allows you to more logically group rules together, thereby simplifying ongoing maintenance. The Rule-Flow diagram used for our case study is shown in figure 12.2.

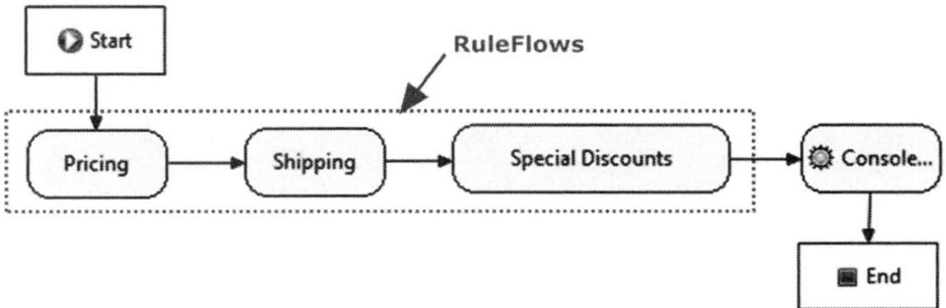

Figure 12.2 Case study RuleFlow diagram illustrating the grouping logic of the rules

As you can see in figure 12.1, three RuleFlow groups are shown:

- *Pricing*—This set of rules is used to calculate base prices for each of the product line items. As we'll show in a moment, the price varies depending on customer classification or whether volume discounts apply.
- *Shipping*—These rules calculate the shipping costs associated with the order estimate. A variety of factors influence how this is calculated. At the most basic level, the choice of delivery method is the main factor.

- *Special Discounts*—This is where special pricing rules can be applied, and this group, as the last, also calculates the final pricing estimate.

Since the complete DRL rules can be found in the example code for this chapter, out of respect for your time, we won't visit each of them individually. However, let's take a look at a sample or two from each RuleFlow group, so you have some context as we move forward. We'll first look at the `Discount-LineItemPrice` rule, which is used to determine whether discounts can be applied based on customer classification.

DISCOUNT-LINEITEMPRICE RULE

The `Discount-LineItemPrice` rule belongs to the `Pricing` RuleFlow group (the actual `id` assigned for this group is `price-calc`). This RuleFlow group is used for rules that determine line item pricing (the line items are captured in the `OrderProduct` class, which has a one-to-many relationship to `Order`). In this rule example, the discount price of the product, as captured from the `ProductPrice` object, is applied to all customers who are classified as either `GOLD` or `SILVER`. In natural language pseudocode, the rule can be described as: "*When the customer is either* `SILVER` *or* `GOLD`*, then use the product discount price for calculating the cost for each of the line items in the order.*" In DRL form, this is expressed as shown in listing 12.2.

Listing 12.2 Rule for calculating line item discounts

```
rule "Discount-LineItemPrice"
  ruleflow-group 'price-calc'
  salience 20
  when
    order : Order();                                          ❶
    item : OrderProduct ( itemCnt : cnt, stdPrice == 0 )
      from order.getLines();                                  ❷
    party : Party ( partyId == order.partyId,                 ❸
      partyTypeId in ( Party.SILVER, Party.GOLD ) );
    ProductPrice ( price : price,                             ❹
      productId == item.productId,
      priceType == ProductPrice.DISCOUNT_PRICE);
   then
    item.setStdPrice ( price * itemCnt );                     ❺
    update ( order );                                         ❻
end
```

Let's examine listing 12.2 in a bit more detail. The first thing we're doing is identifying the inbound quote request (`Order`) we're working with by assigning that object to the alias `order` ❶. From there, we're using the `from` iterator (see chapter 11) to assign each product line item to the alias called `item` ❷ (behind the scenes, this will cause the rule to fire a specified number of times based on the number of line items present in the order). We then restrict this rule based on the pattern of whether the customer (represented by `partyId`) is classified as either `GOLD` or `SILVER` ❸ (without this clause, the discount would be applied to all customers). The last statement in the conditional portion of the rule then looks up the individual discount price for each object ❹.

The `OrderProduct` (represented by the alias `item`) includes the class member variable `stdPrice`. When the instance fact representing the order pricing request is received by Drools, this value is `null`. However, this field gets assigned a value in the consequence portion of the rule ❺, where it's calculated as the discount price times the number of units specified (represented by the alias `itemCnt`). Finally, the order object is updated in working memory ❻, which in turn also updates the associated line items since `OrderProduct` is associated as a child to `Order`. Now let's look at a rule that tallies up the total price and applies any quantity-based discounts, if applicable.

TOTALENDPRICE RULE

When 10 or more units are ordered for a particular line item, we also want to apply a quantity-based discount. If this condition occurs, the `OrderProduct` member variable called `qntDiscountPrice` is assigned as the line item price. So if the standard price of item X is $9.99, and 10 units were specified, then the `qntDiscountPrice` would be set to $99.90 with a 5 percent discount applied to that value, leaving a total of $94.90. When computing the order's total (minus shipping), this volume discount is then factored into an equation, as we see in the business rule shown in listing 12.3. This rule also happens to be the last one run for the `Pricing` RuleFlow group (this is controlled by using its `salience` value, which is set to a low-value of `5`).

Listing 12.3 Rule to calculate total price based on aggregated line items

```
rule "TotalEndPrice"
  ruleflow-group 'price-calc'
  salience 5
  no-loop true
  when
    order : Order();
    totalPrice : Float() from accumulate (                    ❶
      OrderProduct ( disprice : qntDiscountPrice,
         stdprice :  stdPrice > 0 ) from order.getLines(),          ❷
         init ( float total = 0; ),
         action ( total += (disprice > 0 ? disprice : stdprice); ),      ❸
         result ( new Float(total) )
     );                                                      ❹
  then
    TotalPrice tot = new TotalPrice();
    tot.setTotalPrice ( totalPrice );                    ❺
    tot.setOrderId ( order.getOrderId() );                  ❻
    insert ( tot );
end
```

In the `TotalEndPrice` rule (listing 12.3), the `accumulate` conditional is used to iterate through the `OrderProduct` line items ❶, which includes a pattern restriction specifying that the `stdPrice` must be greater than 0. What this means is that a line item total must have previously been calculated ❷; otherwise this rule will not qualify for firing. Then the `action` statement of `accumulate` is used ❸ to compute the total order cost. If `qntDiscountPrice` has been assigned, that value is used for the calculation; otherwise the `stdPrice` is used for computing the total. The result of the `accumulate` statement is therefore the total price estimate of the order, which gets assigned to the `totalPrice` alias variable.

Turning to the consequence part of the rule shown in listing 12.3, a new instance of `TotalPrice` is instantiated ❹, with a member variable assigned (`tot`) to represent the computed price for the order ❺ and is thereafter inserted into the working memory ❻ (this object will be used in the two remaining RuleFlow groups that are called).

The examples shown in listings 12.2 and 12.3 are good illustrations of nontrivial type rules. If you've been able to successfully follow the logic of these rules, you have a strong command of how rules can be fashioned using Drools. If you're struggling a bit, I suggest reviewing chapter 11 to refresh your understanding.

The remaining rules associated with the `Shipping` RuleFlow are fairly straightforward and follow a pattern similar to those we've just discussed (that is, primarily iterating through the individual line items to establish an item's weight, then applying a multiple based on the carrier selected along with assigning a minimum charge, if appropriate). Let's move on to examining one last rule, this one from the last RuleFlow group, in which we print out the final total price and update the `TotalPrice` object within the working memory. This final rule is shown in listing 12.4.

Listing 12.4 `FinalTotals` rule used to calculate final pricing order estimate

```
rule "FinalTotals"
  ruleflow-group 'special-calc'
  activation-group 'final-price'
  salience 50
  when
    price : TotalPrice ( salePrice == 0.0);          ❶
    order : Order (orderId == price.orderId);          ❷
  then
    price.setSalePrice (                ❸
       FunctionHelper.currencyConverter(order.getCurrency(),
       price.getShippingPrice() + price.getTotalPrice() ));
    System.out.println ( "** FINAL TOTALS **" );
    System.out.println ( "  Order Id: " + price.getOrderId());
    System.out.println ( "  Price:    " + price.getTotalPrice());           ❹
    System.out.println ( "  Shipping: " + price.getShippingPrice());
    System.out.println ( "  Sale Price:" + price.getSalePrice() +
          " ( " + order.getCurrency() + " )");
    update ( price );          ❺
end
```

As you can see in listing 12.4, the conditions for activating this rule are minimal—if the `TotalPrice.salePrice` value is 0 ❶ (meaning it hasn't previously been calculated) and the `TotalPrice.orderId` matches the `Order.orderId` ❷, we can proceed to the consequence portion of the rule.

In the consequence (then) portion of the rule, we first set the `TotalPrice.salePrice` variable as the sum of `TotalPrice.totalPrice` and `TotalPrice.shippingPrice` ❸. The summed value is then sent to the `FunctionHelper.currencyConverter` method, which will compute the currency-adjusted price. Then, what follows are some console outputs that display details about the results produced by the rules engine ❹. Finally, the `TotalPrice` object, represented by the `price` alias, is updated in working memory ❺.

What's the upshot of all of this? The `TotalPrice` object updated by the rule now contains the computed values that represent the output to be returned to the calling client. The question now becomes, how do we retrieve this data from working memory so that it can be returned to the client application/user? There are a couple of options to achieve this:

- We could iterate through the working memory *fact handles* using the method `WorkingMemory.iterateFactHandles()`, and then check the class name to locate the `TotalPrice` object that contains the computed estimate.
- We could store the `TotalPrice` in a named query so that the method `WorkingMemory.getQueryResults(<string>)` could be used to locate the results.

The latter option is more straightforward, so let's use this approach. We defined the following query in the DRL file associated with the `Special Discounts` RuleFlow group:

```
query "FinalPrice"
  total : TotalPrice ( salePrice > 0.0 );
  order : Order (orderId == total.orderId);
end
```

This query is activated when the two consequence statements are true. Notice that the first one checks whether a `TotalPrice.salePrice` has been assigned (that is, `salePrice > 0`). As you recall from a moment ago, this `salePrice` was set during the rule shown in listing 12.4. So only after this rule is activated will this pattern be satisfied. In the next section you'll see how this query is retrieved.

Now that we have our rules defined, let's explore the process for invoking them.

12.1.2 Running as an embedded engine

There are several approaches for how Drools can be used. The most common is using it in an embedded fashion. Using this approach, you can incorporate the rule engine directly within your application code. We'll describe later in section 12.3 what's likely a better approach—exposing Drools as a *decision service*. However, since the decision service approach shares much in common with how it can be used as an embedded engine, it's worthwhile to begin with the embedded approach.

If you use the Eclipse IDE for creating a new Drools project, it will optionally create some example, starter-style classes that you can begin building on. I recommend trying this, because it will shed much light on how Drools can be run using an embedded style setup. We'll expand on what's automatically generated via the Eclipse plug-in and refactor it to make it more suitable for reuse.

Let's begin by providing an overview of the steps required for running Drools in an embedded fashion:

> **Using Apache Commons Digester for populating working memory objects**
>
> One of the first challenges you'll likely encounter when using Drools is how to populate the classes destined for working memory with data. While you could obviously create some methods to populate the data directly from a database, this does tightly bind your solution to the underlying data model, so that if the database schema changes, your solution will break. In other words, this is a fairly fragile approach. For purposes of this case study, we took a different tack. We generated our data using XML, which is obviously very amenable to hand authoring, and then used Apache Commons Digester (http://commons.apache.org/digester/) to unmarshal the data from XML into the appropriate classes. Obviously, the use of Digester is outside the scope of this chapter, so we won't go into specific details as to how this is done, but the example code for this chapter and the Digester home page are excellent resources.

1. Create the RuleFlow and rules (rule assets). We tackled this in the previous section, and have our rule DRL files and flows created.
2. Create and populate the `RuleBase`. This Drools class is used to load, parse, and store the rule assets.
3. Create a `WorkingMemory` session from the `RuleBase`. This creates a working memory container for populating the fact data required by the rules engine for processing.
4. Load the `WorkingMemory`. Populate the working memory with fact data.
5. Start the RuleFlow process. If a RuleFlow process is used, it must be started using `WorkingMemory.startProcess(<processId>)`.
6. Activate the rules. This is done using the method `WorkingMemory.fireAllRules()`. This will run the rule engine using the rule assets and working memory.
7. Query the results from the named query. We covered in the previous section how query results can be retrieved, and this represents the last step in the process (we'll review it in context with the rest of the code for completeness).

Since we already created step 1, let's jump right to step 2, and see how to create a `RuleBase`.

STEP 2: CREATING AND POPULATING THE RULEBASE

To break things into more discrete functions, we've created a *helper* class called `SessionHelper` that we can use to perform the individual steps and also simplify the code. The first static method we'll create in this class is for instantiating the `RuleBase` (see listing 12.5).

Listing 12.5 Static method used to create and populate Drools' `RuleBase`

```
private static RuleBase readEmbeddedRules() throws Exception {

  PackageBuilder builder = new PackageBuilder();          <-- 1
  Package pkg = builder.getPackage();                            <-- 2
  RuleBase ruleBase = RuleBaseFactory.newRuleBase();                 <-- 3
```

```
  Reader source = new InputStreamReader(
   SessionHelper.class.getResourceAsStream("/CalculatePriceFlow.drl" ));
  Reader shippingSource = new InputStreamReader(
   SessionHelper.class.getResourceAsStream("/CalculateShippingFlow.drl") );
  Reader specialDiscSource = new InputStreamReader(
   SessionHelper.class.getResourceAsStream
   ("/CalculateSpecialDiscountFlow.drl" ));
  Reader flowsource = new InputStreamReader(
   SessionHelper.class.getResourceAsStream("/PriceCalculator.rf"));
  builder.addProcessFromXml(flowsource);

  builder.addPackageFromDrl( source );
  builder.addPackageFromDrl( shippingSource );
  builder.addPackageFromDrl( specialDiscSource );

  ruleBase.addPackage(pkg);          <-- 5
  return ruleBase;          <-- 6
}
```

Loads rule assets from files into Readers

Adds RuleFlow to PackageBuilder

4

The first statement shown in listing 12.5 is used to create an instance of PackageBuilder ❶. That in turn is used to create a new Package ❷. A Package can be thought of as a container for DRLs. A RuleBase consists of compiled packages, so an instance of it is created in ❸ so that downstream we can add populated packages to it. From there, we're simply creating a Reader for each of the DRL and RuleFlow processes so that they can be read from disk. Each of the Readers is then used by the PackageBuilder for loading, parsing, and compilation ❹. The Package, which was derived by the PackageBuilder, is then added to the RuleBase ❺. The RuleBase object is populated with all compiled rule assets, and is returned to the caller ❻. The next step (❸ in our sequence) is to use the RuleBase object to instantiate the WorkingMemory.

NOTE Instead of hard-coding the rule file assets within the readEmbeddedRules() method in listing 12.5, you could make the method far more reusable by passing them dynamically as a Map to the method, but to keep things simple, we didn't go this route.

STEP 3: CREATING THE WORKING MEMORY

Now that a RuleBase has been created from the prior step, we can use it to create a WorkingMemory session. To do this, we'll use the RuleBase.newStatefulSession() method (you can optionally create a stateless session, where the working memory isn't preserved after the rules fire). The static method SessionHelper.getEmbeddedSessionURL() used to create the WorkingMemory is shown in listing 12.6.

Listing 12.6 Method used for instantiating WorkingMemory from a RuleBase

```
public static StatefulSession getEmbeddedSessionDRL() {

  if ( rulebase == null ) {
    try {
      rulebase = readEmbeddedRules();          <-- 1
    } catch (Exception e) {
```

```
      e.printStackTrace();
    }
  }

  session = rulebase.newStatefulSession();        ❷

  session.addEventListener(                    ❸
    new DefaultAgendaEventListener() {
  public void afterActivationFired(AfterActivationFiredEvent event,
   WorkingMemory workingMemory) {
     super.afterActivationFired( event, workingMemory );
     System.out.println( "Event: " +
     event.getActivation().getRule().getName()) ;
   }
  });

  return session;        ❹
}
```

The first order of business is to call the readEmbeddedRules() method we created in listing 12.5 ❶. Since, depending on usage, rulebase may have previously been instantiated, we first check to see if it is null prior to making the method call. Once the RuleBase instance is populated, we can then use its method to create a StatefulSession ❷, which implements the WorkingMemory interface. For logging and diagnostic purposes, we then add a listener to the session so that we can easily track, mostly for troubleshooting purposes, which rule was activated ❸. Finally, we return the WorkingMemory session to the calling client ❹. As you can see, this is all a pretty straightforward process.

Now that we have the WorkingMemory instantiated, we can use it to populate the facts necessary for the rule engine to perform its magic.

STEP 4: LOADING THE WORKING MEMORY WITH NONVOLATILE FACTS

The process of loading the fact data into the working memory is very simple. To do so, you call WorkingMemory.Insert(<*object*>). In our case study, we're using the LoadData class to unmarshal XML files into Java data objects using Apache Commons Digester. Once the objects are populated via this class, we create another method called loadNVWorkingMemory() in the SessionHelper class that loads each of the objects required for the pricing calculation. Here's an example of the ProductPrice objects being loaded into working memory from within the loadNVWorkingMemory() method:

```
ArrayList<ProductPrice> prices = ld.loadPrices();
for (ProductPrice price:prices) {
  workingMemory.insert(price);
}
```

The loadNVWorkingMemory() method only is responsible for loading what we term the *nonvolatile* facts—that is, those facts that aren't altered by the rules and don't frequently change (such as a product catalog). We'll see in a moment how we load the volatile, or instance facts, just prior to invoking the engine. However, before we do this, we have one last housekeeping chore to attend to: loading the RuleFlow process.

STEP 5: STARTING THE RULEFLOW PROCESS

As you recall, we used the RuleFlow process feature in this case study to more easily manage the sequence by which rules can be activated. While you can often do without it, the visual nature of the RuleFlow process diagrams can aid in maintenance and assist rule authors in devising the proper rule activation sequences. You identify the correct RuleFlow process to use by calling the `WorkingMemory.startProcess(`*`<rule-flow-process-id>`*`)` method. The *`<rule-flow-process-id>`* value represents the `id` assigned when developing the Eclipse IDE RuleFlow process (the Properties view is generally always present when working in the Java perspective, but if not, you can add it to your current perspective by choosing Window > Show View). You can display the process properties by clicking in the main diagram window, and the properties should appear similar to what is shown in figure 12.3.

NOTE You don't need to use the Eclipse plug-in to create a RuleFlow—you can do it manually since it's just an XML file.

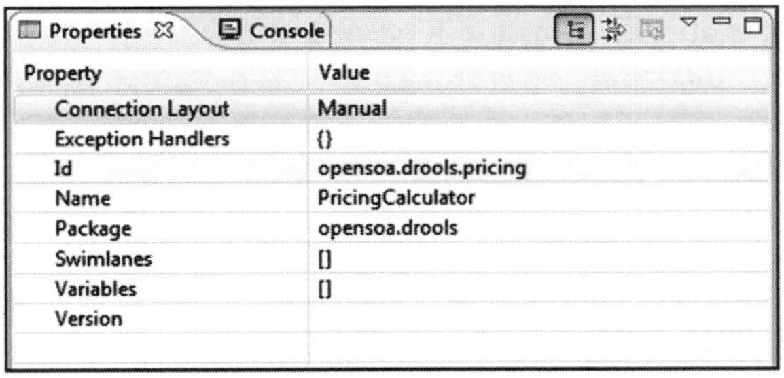

Properties ☒ Console

Property	Value
Connection Layout	Manual
Exception Handlers	{}
Id	opensoa.drools.pricing
Name	PricingCalculator
Package	opensoa.drools
Swimlanes	[]
Variables	[]
Version	

Figure 12.3 RuleFlow properties window, highlighting the process ID

So the statement needed to start up the RuleFlow looks like this:

```
workingMemory.startProcess("opensoa.drools.pricing");
```

We'll show this in context next when we discuss activating the rule engine.

STEP 6: ACTIVATING THE RULE ENGINE

You activate the rule engine with a single method call, `WorkingMemory.fireAllRules()`. However, first we need to populate the instance data, which represents the input to the rule engine. This instance data is also just working memory objects, but is transitory in nature and will generally be removed once the rules are processed (unlike the nonvolatile working memory, which is persisted). So in our case, the instance data is represented by the `Order` (and includes an association with one or more `OrderProduct` classes that represent the individual line items of the order). For testing purposes, you'll find in the example code for this chapter a Java main class called `EmbeddedDrools`. Listing 12.7 shows the method that's used to invoke the engine.

Listing 12.7 Activating the rules engine to process the results

```
private static void runEngine (String orderFile,
  WorkingMemory workingMemory) throws Exception {

  LoadData ld = new LoadData();                          ❶
  Order order = ld.loadOrders(orderFile);
  workingMemory.insert( order );
                                                          Identifies
  workingMemory.startProcess("opensoa.drools.pricing");  <-- RuleFlow process

  workingMemory.fireAllRules();     <-- ❷

  SessionHelper.showResults(workingMemory);
  }
}
```

The `runEngine()` method shown in listing 12.7 requires two parameters: an XML file to be loaded using Commons Digester, representing the instance data (listing 12.1, for example), and the `WorkingMemory` instance we created in step 3. The instance data is then processed into working memory ❶, and the rule engine is ready for activation using the `fireAllRules()` method ❷. This method instructs the rule engine to run, and once completed, the results that were stored into the named query can be retrieved, which we cover next.

STEP 7: QUERYING THE RESULTS FROM THE NAMED QUERY

As you may recall from section 12.1.1, we created a named query called `FinalPrice` in the last RuleFlow group that contained the pricing results derived from running the rules engine. The static method `SessionHelper.showResults()`, shown in listing 12.7, is used to process the query results. Let's examine this in more detail in listing 12.8, as it contains the results of the rule engine processing.

Listing 12.8 Method used to return results from the rules engine

```
public static TotalPrice showResults (WorkingMemory workingMemory) {

  QueryResult result;              Initializes
  TotalPrice price = null;         variables
  Order ord = null;

  QueryResults results =
    workingMemory.getQueryResults("FinalPrice");      <-- ❶

  for (QueryResult qresult : results) {     <-- ❷
    result = (QueryResult) qresult;
    price = (TotalPrice) result.get("total");          ❸
    ord = (Order) result.get("order");
  }

  FactHandle priceFH = workingMemory.getFactHandle(price);   ❹
  FactHandle ordFH = workingMemory.getFactHandle(ord);

  workingMemory.retract(priceFH);           ❺
  workingMemory.retract(ordFH);
  return price;                   <-- ❻
}
```

The purpose of the `showResults()` method is to retrieve the query results from the engine, locate the referenced objects returned by the query, clean up the working memory of the results, and return the results to the caller of the method. The `WorkingMemory.getQueryResults(<named-query>)` method is used to retrieve a named query from the engine. Here the query is named `FinalPrice` ❶. Once the query results are retrieved, you can access any facts associated with the aliases that were defined in the query. As you recall, our query was defined as

```
query "FinalPrice"
  total : TotalPrice ( salePrice > 0.0 );
  order : Order (orderId == total.orderId);
end
```

Returning to our code in listing 12.8, since we have just a single query with this name, we can safely assume that the first returned `QueryResult` resulting from the `QueryResults` iterator is the object we need ❷. With the `QueryResult` in hand, we can then use the alias name assigned in the query definition to retrieve that object ❸. The `TotalPrice` object is most relevant here as it contains the computed results (the alias assigned to it is called `total`).

What remains is to remove the instance facts from working memory, since they're no longer needed and would cause future complications if left in memory (that is, once the order is estimated, there's no need to keep them in working memory). To remove the instance fact, we use the objects retrieved as a signature to create a `FactHandle` ❹. The `FactHandle` can be passed as a parameter to the `WorkingMemory.retract()` method, which flushes that item from working memory ❺. (Of course, this wouldn't be necessary if it were a stateless session, whereby the working memory must be reconstituted from scratch for each request.) Although it no longer exists in working memory, `price` remains unaffected and is returned by the method ❻.

Let's recap what we've accomplished so far. We went through the end-to-end process of creating the rules, running them, and then retrieving the results. At this point, we have a completely operational rules engine solution, albeit one that could only be embedded within a given application. Before we wrap up this section, let's consider how things might work using the DSL capability of Drools instead of the DRLs we've created. In the previous chapter, we explained how this works, so we'll assume that you've read that material and won't revisit the basics of how it works. The objective is to reinforce what you learned previously about DSLs by applying them to a real-world type scenario. This will also help contrast the differences between standard DRL rules and the more natural language–like DSL-based rules.

12.1.3 User-friendly rules using a DSL

The main impetus behind using the DSL capability is that you can craft more natural-language representations of your rules. This is particularly relevant when you want to give subject matter experts in your organization the responsibility of rule authoring—something they're often enthusiastic about assuming. Nontechnical users might find it challenging to create DRL rules, as the process assumes a high degree of knowledge of the Drools language. However, as we'll see, DSL-based rules are much easier for the average user to understand, and thus increase the likelihood of their participation in managing them (anytime developers have to translate user requirements to code, there's always an opportunity for subtle errors to be introduced because of the translation that must occur).

For example, let's consider the rule used to determine whether a quantity-based discount can be applied. In DRL format, this rule was defined as follows:

```
rule "Quantity-Discount"
ruleflow-group 'price-calc'
salience 30
  when
    order : Order();
    item : OrderProduct ( qntDiscountPrice == 0, price : stdPrice,
      cnt >= 10, stdPrice > 0 ) from order.getLines();
  then
    item.setQntDiscountPrice ( price * .90f );
    update ( order );
end
```

In pseudo-code, this rule is stating that "If an order exists, and no quantity discount has currently been applied but a standard price has been computed and the unit count is >= 10, then apply a 10 percent discount." While a trained eye could read the DRL rule and interpret it the same way, a far more readable representation, in DSL, is

```
rule "Quantity-Discount-dsl"
ruleflow-group 'price-calc-dsl'
salience 30
  when
    There is an order
    Retrieve calculated order items which exceed a quantity of 10
  then
    Log : "Applying volume discount"
    Apply line item discount of .10 to previously calculated price
    Update the order
end
```

The pricing.dsl template file, located in the example code for this chapter, contains the definitions that make this DSL feasible. For example, the second condition statement is defined using this template (shown word-wrapped, but normally it's not):

```
[when]Retrieve calculated order items which exceed a quantity of
{x}=item : OrderProduct ( qntDiscountPrice == 0, price : stdPrice, cnt >=
{x}, stdPrice > 0 ) from order.getLines();
```

As you can see, the only parameter replacement required by the author is to specify the number of items that qualify for a discount (represented by `item`). However, this statement does require a prior condition (such as the DSL statement defined as `"There is an order"`) in order to receive a handle to the `order` alias referenced in the right-hand side of this template for retrieving the order items. The complete example can be found in the source code.

The only difference when using a DSL from what we described in the previous section is that the DSL template must be specified as an additional parameter to the `PackageBuilder.addPackageFromDRL()` method. Consider this example:

```
Reader DSLsource = new InputStreamReader(
  DroolsTestDSL.class.getResourceAsStream( "/pricing.dsl" ) );
Reader source = new InputStreamReader(
  DroolsTestDSL.class.getResourceAsStream( "/CalculatePriceFlow.dslr" ) );
builder.addPackageFromDrl( source, DSLsource );
```

As you can see, we read the DSL template file (pricing.dsl) and DSL rule file (CalculatePriceFlow.dslr) into a Java `Reader`, both of which are then passed as parameters to the method `addPackageFromDRL()`. In other words, when loading a DSL file, you also need to specify the DSL template (by convention, it ends with the .dsl extension). That's the only distinction in what we covered in the last section.

We've now explored the basics of the case study, and this real-life example builds on the knowledge you gained in the previous chapter. With this foundation in place, we can now move toward discussing the Drools Business Rule Management System (BRMS), otherwise known as Guvnor. This feature is essential for enterprise adoption of the business rules approach, since it allows for centralized management of rule assets. It also is the foundation for building SOA-style decision services, which we'll cover in section 12.3.

12.2 Rules management using Drools Guvnor

One of the most exciting developments that occurred with the 4.0 release of Drools was the introduction of the Guvnor BRMS. This multiuser web application can be used to centrally house all of your business rules, provide tools for management and editing of the rules, and support versioning and lifecycle management. A fair amount of criticism was leveled against the first release, claiming that it lacked essential functionality such as user management. However, it's important to bear in mind that this was the first release of the BRMS component, and I can happily report that the 5.0 release appears to address many of the cited deficiencies (for our examples, we're using the 5.0CR1 release, which is a beta version).

The official documentation provides an excellent resource for how to install and maintain the BRMS [DroolsUserGuide], so our focus will be on introducing key functionality so that you can assess whether it's an appropriate solution for your environment. Let's start by taking a look at the main navigational hierarchy of Guvnor, which will provide a good overview of its functionality.

12.2.1 Guvnor functionality overview

The Drools team has done an outstanding job of developing the user interface for Guvnor. Built using Google's GWT toolkit, it offers a rich, "thick client–like" interface that's highly intuitive. When first logging into the web application, you'll be presented with the screen shown in figure 12.4.

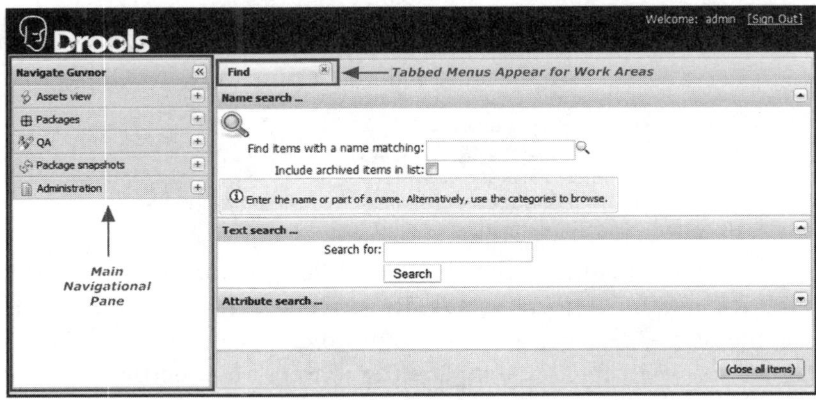

Figure 12.4 You'll see the Drools Guvnor main menu when logging in as an administrator.

As the screenshot in figure 12.4 illustrates, several different audiences might use the solution. For rule authors, it's anticipated they'll spend the bulk of their time within the *Assets view* module. Developers, on the other hand, will be focused on the *Packages* and *Package snapshots* modules. Those maintaining the system will primarily work within the *Administration* module, with quality assurance and testing working within the *QA* module. Let's take a look into each module so we can understand its purpose and usage.

ASSETS VIEW MODULE

The Assets view module is primarily where rule authors and business users will operate. It serves two purposes: it's a means of navigating through categories of existing rule assets, and it provides the ability to create new rules or potentially archive existing ones. Guvnor includes a categorization capability that lets you define your own custom categories and assign rule assets to one or more of them (it's similar in concept to tagging, though you can't dynamically create new ones since that must be done via the Administration module). A category can be considered more of a logical view of rule assets, as opposed to how they're physically grouped within packages. For example, you may have categories that correspond to your main business functions, such as HR and Finance. These categories can also be used to manage visibility of the rules, since you can specify which groups have rights to view the category tree (the user logged in for the figure 12.4 snapshot has full admin rights, so everything appears). Figure 12.5 shows the Assets view module when a category has been selected that contains rules (in this example, a business user is logged in with restricted module options using the pricing estimator case study rules we've been working with in this chapter).

As figure 12.5 shows, if a category contains rules, it will appear in the rule pane listing on the right. If you double-click on a rule, it will take you into the rule editor, which we'll cover in a moment. Users with permission may also be able to navigate through the rules by rule status. As with categories, rule statuses are defined by the

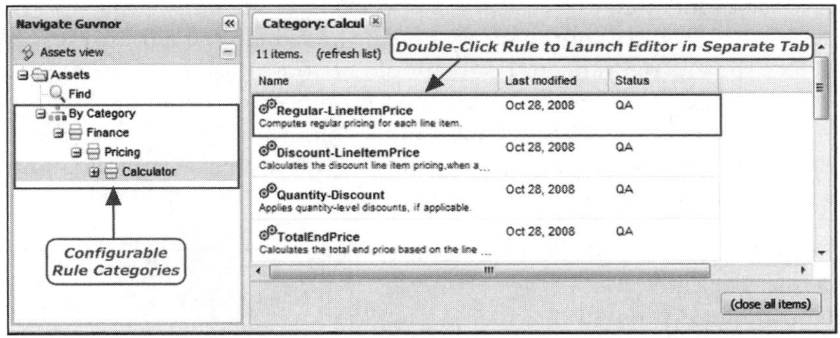

Figure 12.5 Example of Asset view category listing

administrator, and typically are values such as Production, QA, Development, and the like. Statuses are used as part of the workflow release cycle, which is why they aren't, by default, made visible to normal business users and authors. If users have the appropriate permission, a pull-down menu will appear below the Asset view that enables them to create a new rule asset, as shown in figure 12.6.

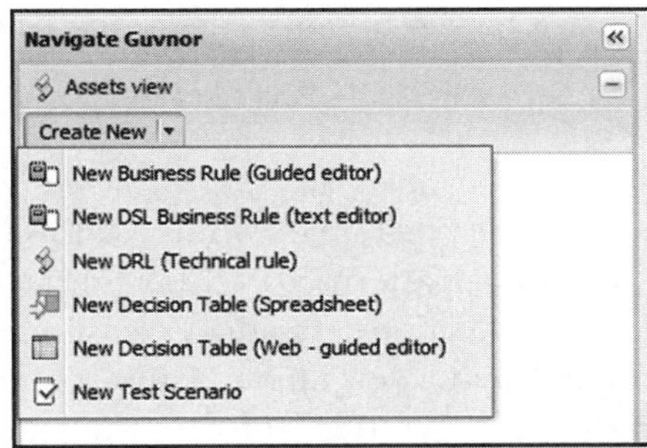

Figure 12.6 Selecting which type of business rule asset to create using the Create New pull-down

Let's now take a look at the Packages module, which is used by administrators for setting up new rule domains.

PACKAGES MODULE

In chapter 11's Hello World, Drools example, we briefly touched on what a rule package means within Drools. All rule assets are associated with a given package. Similar to Java, it can be thought of as analogous to a namespace, so that similarly named rules can exist in multiple locations without conflicting with one another. In Guvnor, it also plays an important role in rule authoring, as a model of the working memory facts must be loaded into Guvnor so that it can use the objects within its rule editor. So one of the first steps required when using Guvnor for a new rule domain such as our pricing estimator is for the administrator to create a new package where the fact model and rules can then be loaded and associated.

NOTE I recommend that you use the same package naming conventions for both your Java working memory objects and their related business rules where they're referenced. For example, if you're using the rule package of `mycompany.finance.pricing`, then use the same name prefix for your related Java classes. This becomes more important as you move toward a decision services paradigm, where many rule domains may be running within a single rules engine instance.

When logged in as an administrator and selecting the Packages model, you'll see a Create New pull-down menu like the one in figure 12.6. The menu includes an option to create a new package. Once you create the package, a classification of asset types appears in a tree fashion associated with the new package, as shown in figure 12.7.

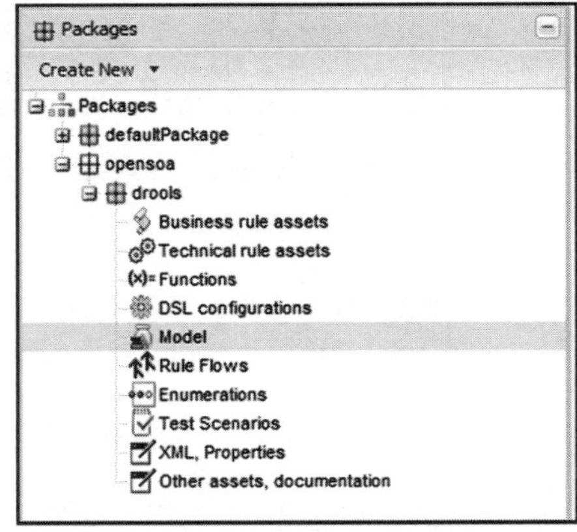

Figure 12.7 Package assets types

When you click on a given asset type such as Business rule assets, you'll then see a listing of the associated items belonging to that type. Using the Create New pull-down, you can add items to any of the type categories shown.

The first thing you do when configuring a new package is add a new model, which is a standard JAR file containing the working memory fact objects. You use this file when authoring rules so that you can build condition patterns based on the fact objects loaded into the model (think of it as a form a reflection). To add an existing DRL rule file, select the New Package option from the Create New menu. You can then specify the package name (such as `opensoa.drools`, as we used in our case study), and then select a DRL file to upload. If the package already exists in Drools, it will simply append the rules to the existing package as Technical rule assets without creating a new package. Once you have a package and at least one category defined, you can begin authoring rules using Guvnor.

The various asset types associated with a package are discussed in table 12.1.

Table 12.1 Package asset types

Asset type	Description
Business rule assets	When you're creating business rules using Guvnor's guided DRL or DSL editor, they'll appear within this classification. See section 12.2.2 on creating rules using the guided editors.
Technical rule assets	When you're importing existing DRL rule assets or when creating them in Guvnor as a "technical rule - text editor," they'll appear here.

Table 12.1 Package asset types *(continued)*

Asset type	Description
Functions	You can upload DRL functions, which will then appear as items in this list. Generally, I recommend instead creating Java helper-style classes since it promotes greater reusability.
DSL configurations	You can create new DSL mapping templates using this asset type.
Model	You can upload one or more JAR files that represent the fact model used by the particular package you're working within.
Rule Flows	When you upload a new RuleFlow it will appear in this list when selected.
Enumerations	Enumerations are used in the guided editor to restrict field values to certain values. For example, in our case study, we spoke about `STANDARD`, `GOLD`, or `SILVER` customer classifications—an enumeration could be created restricting choices to these values. We'll illustrate how enumerations are used in section 12.2.2.
Test Scenarios	Drools 5.0 introduced a new testing framework for testing rules. With it, you can create testing scenarios that will appear in this list. You'll see a service-based approach in section 12.3.4 that I believe is superior to this framework.
XML, Properties	As of the 5.0 release, it wasn't entirely clear what this asset type is for—there doesn't appear to be a Create New option to create this asset type (this will presumably change by the final release).
Other assets, documentation	You can upload virtually any supporting file, such as Word documentation, and it will appear in this listing. You can create these asset types by selecting Create New > New File.

The Package view module, as you may have deduced, is intended for administrators, and allows for quick-and-easy access to all assets that constitute a given package. As we pointed out, it also plays an essential role for DSL language developers, as this is where the DSL templates are managed.

One last piece of important functionality available through this module is the ability, when you click a specific package, to view the configuration details of the package such as imported class types and global definitions (you can click Advanced View to modify imports). The Build and validate section, shown in figure 12.8, allows you to validate that the package is error-free—you'll want to perform this periodically to ensure you can successfully build a binary package.

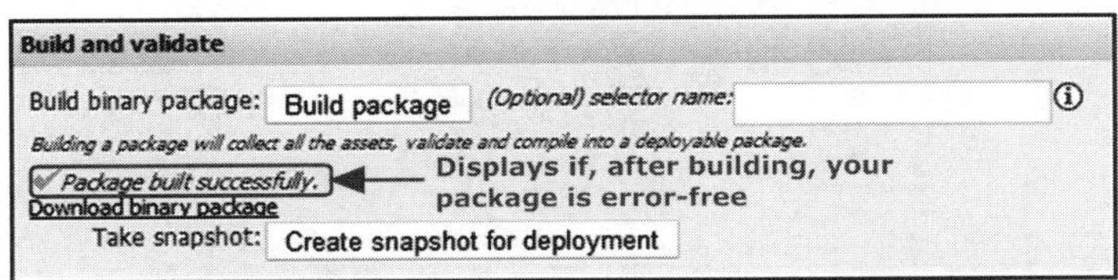

Figure 12.8 Verifying package is error-free using build and validate package

As you can see, in addition to building a binary package, you can download it. But what exactly is a binary package? It combines all rule assets together in a single file that can then be loaded using the Rule Agent capability (which we'll describe how to use in section 12.3). This is a very convenient feature, because it eliminates the need to load the rule assets manually as we had to do in our prior examples, such as in listing 12.5. We'll discuss binary packages more next in our coverage of the Package snapshots module.

NOTE What happened to the *QA* module? We elected to not cover this functionality as it was very much a work-in-progress at the time of this writing and had little supporting documentation. In our experimentation with this feature, we found it lacking for creating anything beyond the most simple type tests.

PACKAGE SNAPSHOTS MODULE

This module serves an important purpose: it creates binary deployment snapshots. A snapshot can be considered a *point-in-time* code freeze. Once a snapshot is made, any other current in-progress or future changes won't affect it. Indeed, internally the snapshot version is moved into a different location in the Java content repository (which coincidentally, uses Apache Jackrabbit). There are only a few possible actions you can take in this module, as shown in figure 12.9.

Using the Deploy pull-down menu shown in figure 12.9, you can create new deployment snapshots. When doing so, you can choose an existing snapshot name, in which case it will override it with the new one. Alternatively, you can specify a new unique name, thereby creating an entirely new snapshot. Each new snapshot will result in a new tree node displayed below the package tree. When you click on a specific snapshot, a new tab will appear on the right, which when you expand the node, will display all the rule assets associated with that particular snapshot, reflecting the

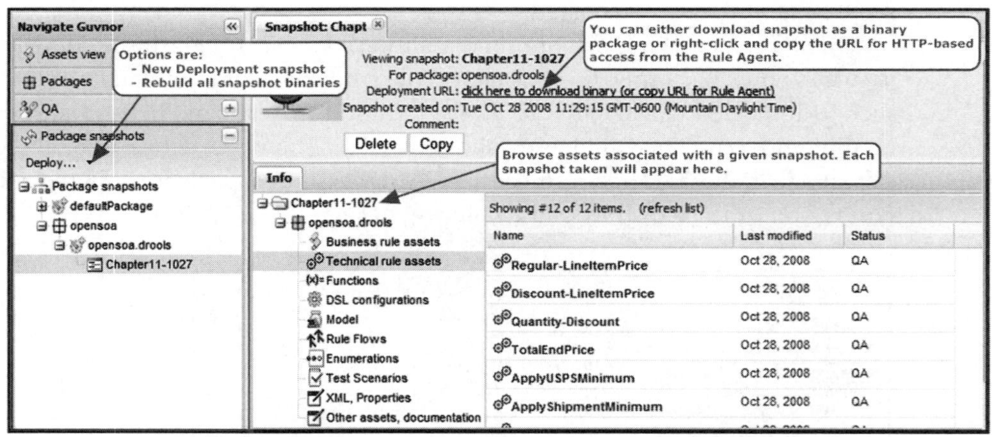

Figure 12.9 Package snapshot module displaying available options

point in time in which the snapshot was taken (remember, a snapshot is a point-in-time freeze of all rule assets associated with the package).

The objective of taking a snapshot is for use by the Rule Agent for loading rule-related assets. As shown in figure 12.9, once a snapshot is generated you can either download a binary package of the snapshot, or right-click on the Deployment URL link to capture the URL (as you'll see in section 12.3, the Rule Agent can be configured to work with a binary file or HTTP URL).

The snapshot capability will likely have significant implications for your enterprise deployment of Drools. With it, you can more effectively manage the release process associated with your rules. If you so choose, you can version the binary using a package such as CVS or Subversion. Creating snapshots also enables rule authors and testers to modify rule assets without inadvertently affecting your production environment. I strongly recommend using it.

NOTE Binary packages can also be generated through Ant tasks, which is demonstrated in the example build scripts which accompany this chapter's source code.

We're nearing the end of our functionality tour overview. These features lay the foundation for our coverage of decision services for SOA, which follow in section 12.3. The last module is Administration, and it's used for a combination of housekeeping, code list management, and user permissions.

ADMINISTRATION MODULE

The Administration module has options for managing the subnodes identified in table 12.2.

Table 12.2 Administration subnodes

Node	Description
Categories	In the Assets view module, we described how categories are used for logically grouping rule assets. These categories are set up using this node, and it is intuitive and easy, so we won't describe the process here.
Archive items	For most rule assets, there's an option to archive items that are no longer desired or used, rather than deleting them outright. When this node is selected, you can view all archived items, and they're categorized by type, such as archived snapshots and rules.
Status	You can manage the available statuses that can be assigned to rule assets using this node option.
Import/Export	As of the 5.0 release, this seems something of a work in progress. You can create a zip-based export of your entire repository or of a single package, but there are only options to import from an XML file (oddly, you can't export to XML). Instead, for backing up Guvnor, I suggest reading the section on data management in the Guvnor User's Guide.
Error log	Log messages that are defined as using INFO or ERROR are displayed in this view. They pertain only to actions performed as part of Guvnor's usage, and not to specific rule assets.

Table 12.2 Administration subnodes *(continued)*

Node	Description
User permission mappings	New with the release 5.0, this enables you to create users and assign them predefined roles, such as admin, analyst, and package admin. It's designed for managing authorization, not authentication. That is, you can define a user, but your authorization must be configured using Java Authentication and Authorization Service (JAAS). This is outside the scope of this chapter, but is covered in the official Guvnor User's Guide.

You'll likely use the Administration module only infrequently and only if you're responsible for managing the overall BRMS. During the initial setup, however, statuses and categories will need to be configured.

We've now covered all the main navigation options available through Guvnor, but haven't really touched on the main purpose of the system: to manage the creation of rules. Before concluding this section on Guvnor, let's spend some time on this important area.

12.2.2 Rule authoring using Guvnor

In addition to providing a centralized location to house your business rule assets, one of the main reasons for adopting a BRMS is to allow business users to author and manage their domain rules, ideally through a "zero-install" client such as a web interface. While the Eclipse IDE Drools plug-in offers nice authoring functionality, rolling this solution out to a significantly sized user base is problematic, not to mention the learning curve involved in using Eclipse for nondeveloper types, issues of source code control (which is managed transparently in Guvnor), and... well, you get the picture.

As we'll see, Drools Guvnor, while aiding the rule author with many useful features intended to lower the technical barrier in creating rules, is still far removed from being a tool that can simply be handed off to the average business user. Instead, there's often a subset of business users or analysts in any organization who are fairly technology competent, and Guvnor is intended for these power users (you know the type—those users who become experts at Excel macros or Visual Basic scripting and can cause headaches for IT groups). Our experience is that these individuals, with some training and/or handholding, can quickly become proficient in rule authoring.

To provide the greatest flexibility in rule authoring, you can create rules in Guvnor in one of these five ways:

- *Business rule (using a guided editor)*—Probably the most popular of the five, the guided editor presents the user with a wizard-like approach for creating rules, based on the model objects that have been loaded as part of the package. This approach is suitable for technical business users.
- *DRL rule (technical rule using text editor)*—The author is presented with a basic text area where he or she can edit a rule in a freehand fashion. The model fact

objects are shown as a convenience, but authoring is done by hand. This approach is aimed at advanced users who understand the Drools language.

- *Business rule using a DSL (text editor)*—This approach is suitable when using a DSL, and the author can then use hints for constructing the various rule phrases. This approach is suitable for technical business users.
- *Decision table (web using guided editor)*—Enables the rule author to dynamically create decision tables. You define the columns that represent the facts and actions, and then use rows to specify the various rule conditions. Decision tables are used when you have a lot of possible rules but a fairly small set of fact objects with little variability in conditions.
- *Decision table (spreadsheet)*—Allows the user to upload a spreadsheet file that contains the decision table spreadsheet. The spreadsheet template must adhere to the format, as described in chapter 11.

As you can see, quite a few options are available, and selecting which authoring type to use largely depends on your audience and the type of rules you're working with. Although we won't go into specific details on using each of the editor methods, let's take a look at some of the common features you'll find regardless of the type of authoring you're using.

COMMON EDITOR FEATURES

Figure 12.10 depicts authoring using a DRL rule (technical rule using the text editor).

As you can see, the editor consists of three main panels. The first is the editing window, where the rule author in figure 12.10 is editing the DRL rule by hand. Notice below the editing panel is a *Validate* option. This allows you to check the rules syntax for errors—which is a very handy feature. The notes area is a documentation mechanism, and to the right is the metadata panel, which is present in all DRL and DSL

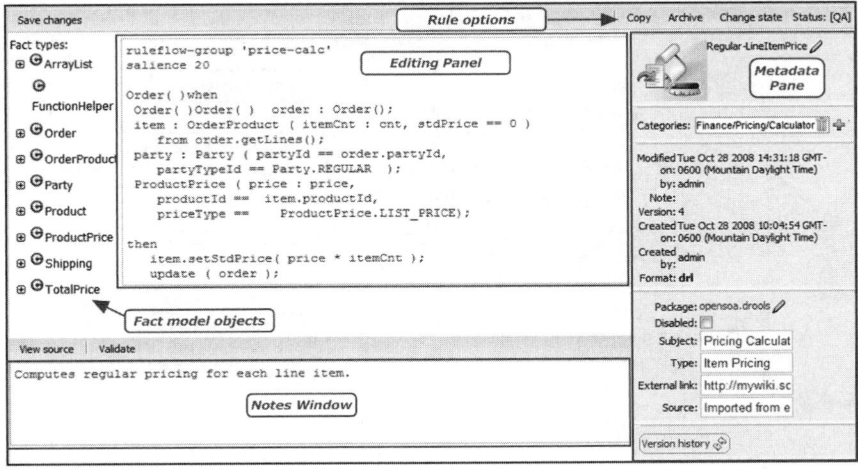

Figure 12.10 Authoring using a DRL rule

editors. In that window, you can assign or modify which category the rule is assigned, and edit any tag-related keywords such as subject and type, which is beneficial for later searching. You can even assign external links that can be used for additional documentation. Also in the metadata pane, you can see automatically assigned metadata such as the version number, author ID, and the dates the rule was first created and last modified. Related is the Version history button link, which allows you to go back to previous versions of a rule, and even restore it, if need be. This function can be useful when you're troubleshooting errors that may have been inadvertently introduced in later releases of the rule.

The two most common types of editors your users will likely use are the guided business rule and DSL editors. Let's take a brief tour of their capability before concluding our section on Guvnor.

CREATING BUSINESS RULES USING THE DRL GUIDED EDITOR

The DRL guided editor represents a novel approach for creating business rules. Using the fact models associated with each package, and any defined enumerations, it lets you create fairly sophisticated rules without requiring in-depth understanding of the Drools language (and you don't have to set up a DSL). An example of the editor is shown in figure 12.11.

When you first launch the editor, only the *WHEN*, *THEN* and *(options)* portions of the rule are shown. You build each of these respective sections by clicking the large green plus sign to the right of each section. A wizard-style dialog opens where you identify the fact objects along with other part-specific options. Figure 12.11 shows a rule used for assigning minimal shipping amounts where the shipment carrier is `DHL` and the shipment method is `STANDARD`. Notice both of these are pull-down values, as we created an enumeration for these values (see the Guvnor User's Guide for instructions on setting up enumerations). When creating conditions, you can also assign variables, as shown in the third condition in the example, where `orderId` is

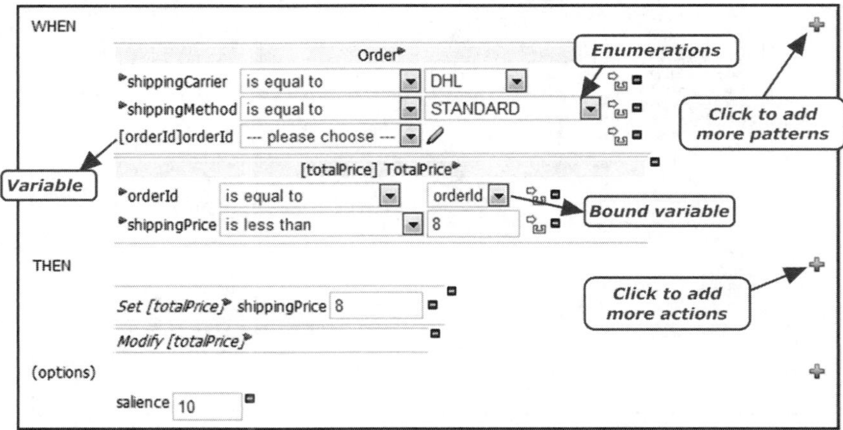

Figure 12.11 Example of using the DRL guided editor

assigned. These bound variables can then be used downstream in other conditions (such as for associating the `TotalPrice` fact object) or in the consequence/then portion of the rule. Not shown in the figure is an option that lets you view the source associated with the guided rule. In this case, the source is shown as

```
rule "DSLExample"
salience 10
dialect "mvel"
when
   Order( shippingCarrier == "DHL" ,
     shippingMethod == "STANDARD" , orderId : orderId)
     totalPrice :
       TotalPrice( orderId == orderId , shippingPrice < "8" ) then
   totalPrice.setShippingPrice( 8 );
   update( totalPrice );
end
```

As you might imagine, it's far easier for business users to use the guided editor rather than crafting the rules by hand. Even easier still is using the DSL editor, which we'll address next.

CREATING BUSINESS RULES USING THE DSL EDITOR

In chapter 11, we discussed how the DSL functionality works in Drools, and showed how you can use it to create business rules using a nomenclature specific to the domain area in which you're working. The Eclipse IDE plug-in offers excellent support for this feature, and so too does Guvnor. Before using the DSL editor, you must create the DSL template file, which defines the language constructs. Doing this in Guvnor is identical to what we described in the previous chapter. For example:

```
[when]There is an Instance with field of "{value}"=
  i: Instance(field=="{value}")
```

Once you've defined the DSL templates, you're ready to use the DSL editor. Figure 12.12 shows an example of the DSL editor in use within Guvnor.

Figure 12.12 shows the context-sensitive rule-tip mechanism. If you're editing either the `when` or `then` portion of a rule and press Ctrl+Spacebar, a pop-up will

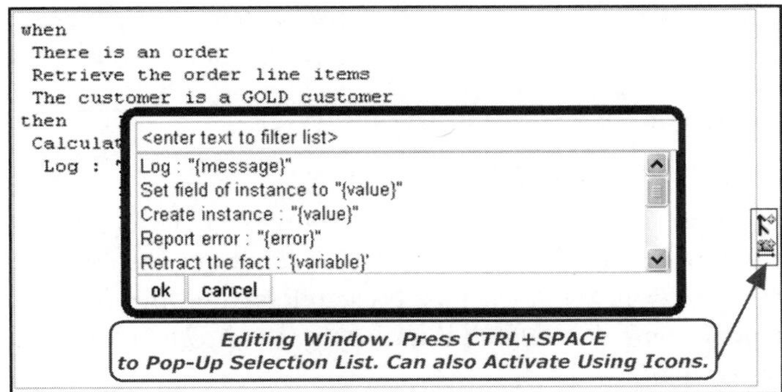

Figure 12.12 Example of DSL editor in use within Guvnor

appear (you can also invoke the pop-up by clicking one of the icons to the right of the editor, as highlighted in the figure). From there, you can select one of the various phrases that are defined with the DSL template file. The phrases are contextually sensitive, so `when` statements will only appear when working on the conditional portion of the rule. This approach makes things particularly easy for those not versed at all in the Drools language, but does entail some setup by an expert to create the DSL template phrases.

In the last two sections, we've introduced you to the specifics of our pricing estimator case study, and then demonstrated how the rules can be managed in tandem with Guvnor, the Drools BRMS. We've laid the groundwork for what comes next: creating decision services using Drools.

12.3 Developing decision services

The term *enterprise decision management* (EDM) has recently entered into the lexicon of famous IT terms, joining other popular new concepts such as *cloud* and *utility* computing. What exactly does EDM mean? While you may get different answers depending on who you ask (it's the same with SOA), at its core EDM is the automation of operational decisions that drive an organization's business. It includes the management and rule repository features we've described in our discussion of the Guvnor BRMS. More importantly, it's a philosophy that dictates that the critical decisions that drive your enterprise be separated from the application code or BPM processes.

Why is this separation important? It's because business rules and decisions often change much more frequently than business processes, and hard-coding them within applications is one major reason why ongoing software maintenance costs are such a substantial portion of total IT software budget on a year-to-year basis. Further, when rules are centralized using a decision services approach, they can be leveraged and reused across multiple applications, and form the basis for ongoing business optimization and improved agility. As James Taylor points out, "Treating decision logic as a manageable enterprise resource in this way means that you can reuse it across multiple applications in many different operational environments" [Taylor]. He later equates this approach to providing the brains for creating composite applications, a key tenet of SOA—the rules (or decision) services approach.

What are the central tenets of a decision service? We'll examine these next.

12.3.1 What are decision services?

A decision service has the following characteristics:

- *Stateless*—The decision service should be stateless—each call to it is self-contained and not dependent on any prior call. This facilities scalability and simplifies service virtualization. While each call is stateless, the working memory itself may contain persistent, nonvolatile data, such as a product catalog, which is periodically refreshed.

- *Virtualized*—Client systems utilizing the service should do so through a logical URI, so that they need not be aware of the actual specific endpoint used to fulfill the service. This is where a web mediation service such as Apache Synapse can play such an important role, since it can manage directing each service call to the proper endpoint address (Synapse was the topic of chapters 9 and 10).
- *Autonomous*—The decision service itself should not be dependent on any specific application, with working memory populated through an abstraction layer independent of its source location. We'll illustrate how this can be done using a cache solution such as PojoCache by JBoss.
- *Protocol and transport neutral*—Ideally, the decision service should be accessible via a variety of protocols, such as SOAP over JMS or HTTP, EJB, or REST.
- *Auditable*—Each call to the decision service should be auditable so that calls can be analyzed for business optimization and compliance. For example, each call should result in events being generated that can then be processed by an event stream processor (ESP) such as Esper, the topic of chapter 8.

Now that you have a good idea of what constitutes a decision service, let's consider how it can be implemented using the Open SOA Platform stack. We can create the service components using Apache Tuscany and the SCA implementation (which was the topic of chapters 3 and 4), and expose them using any of the available protocols and bindings supported (which include SOAP, JSON, EJB, and RSS/ATOM). The overall architecture is depicted in figure 12.13.

As you can see from the diagram, the service is defined using a WSDL, which enables easy consumption by diverse platforms such as Java and .NET. Guvnor's role is the management and repository of the business rules, and when snapshots are published through Guvnor, the updated rules are reflected in the production decision service.

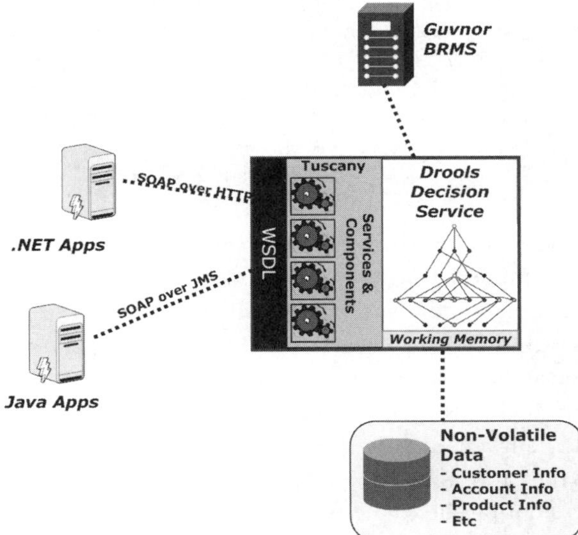

Figure 12.13 Top-level architecture of decision services, illustrating the role of Apache Tuscany

For the remainder of this chapter, we'll describe how to create such a decision service using our case study as the basis. Let's begin by tackling the overall design and introducing a new technology intended to address challenges in populating the Drools working memory.

12.3.2 Designing the decision service

One of the thorniest issues regarding a decision service is how to populate the nonvolatile data into the Drools working memory. In many cases, this will entail a substantial number of data classes. In our pricing engine case study we introduced in section 12.1, this was exemplified by the product, pricing, and shipping objects that were required by the rules engine to determine a pricing estimate. It's not practical, in many scenarios, to use a web service to populate working memory, because the volume of data required is too substantial. Instead, the approach we'll advocate uses JBoss Cache, PoJo edition [POJOCache] as the vehicle by which to transmit nonvolatile working memory data to the decision service. Let's examine this approach more closely since we haven't previously discussed this technology.

USING JBOSS CACHE FOR WORKING MEMORY PROPAGATION

JBoss Cache is officially described as a tree-structured, clustered, transactional cache. It's used extensively in JBoss products, such as in their application server for clustering support, and is very mature and proven. You could think of it as a simplistic, distributed in-memory database, but instead of using SQL-style query statements, you use fully qualified names (FQNs) derived from a tree-style navigation hierarchy. While this all may sound complicated, as you'll see, it's just the opposite and is very straightforward.

> **Using XAware to create data services**
>
> Another approacha for populating nonvolatile working memory is to use XAware [XAware] to build data services that can be tapped to fetch the required data. Using XAware, you build an XML abstraction layer that can expose data from a variety of relational databases and/or file systems. XAware lets you create XML views that harvest data from disparate systems and combine it into a single XML document. For example, you can grab customer a database from an Oracle database and combine it with CRM data originating from a SQL Server database.

How do we envision using JBoss Cache for populating the Drools working memory? When the decision service is launched, it will create a new cache. Then that cache will be populated with Java data objects that ultimately will be loaded into the Drools working memory associated with the decision service. Who and how those data objects get deposited will depend on your environment. For example, in our case study the nonvolatile working memory includes product, pricing, and shipping cost information. This information would likely be harvested from an ERP-type system using an ESB like Synapse to periodically poll and populate or update the cache. In section 12.3.3, we'll show an example of populating the cache using standard Java code.

Once the cache is populated, some trigger would still be necessary for the Drools decision service to grab the cached objects and populate them into its working memory session (as you'll see in a moment, a `Load` operation can be used for this purpose). Figure 12.14 shows how the process to harvest and populate working memory objects might look.

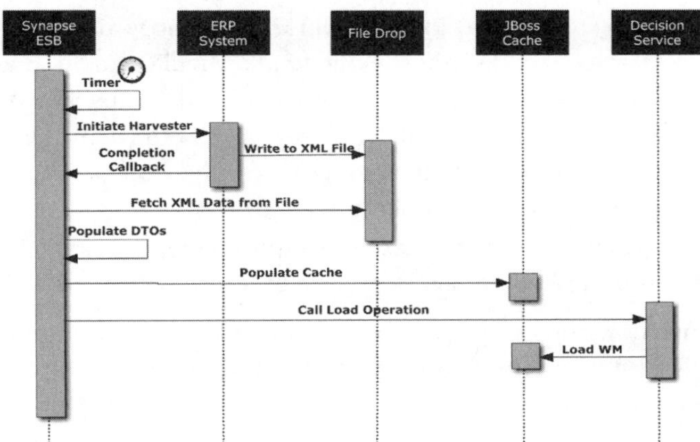

Figure 12.14 A process to harvest and populate working memory objects

As you can see, a few steps are involved, and they'd vary depending on where the working memory data originated. However, once such a pattern is identified, it can be reused. For purposes of our case study, we'll pick things up where the Java data transfer objects (DTOs) are being populated into JBoss Cache. We've already briefly discussed the `Load` operation, but let's take a high-level look at the WSDL to see how it defines all of the various operations required by the decision service we're creating.

TOP-DOWN WSDL DESIGN FOR OUR DECISION SERVICE

When working with Apache Tuscany, you can approach things in two basic ways:

- A top-down approach in which you define your WSDL first and then generate the components for each operation
- A bottom-up approach in which you first create your components and then use Tuscany's ability to autogenerate the WSDL

Although the second approach can often be easier and faster, a top-down approach yields a WSDL that's likely more intelligently defined and extensible. For these reasons, I always advocate a top-down approach, which is how I went about constructing the WSDL for the decision service. The first thing I did was identify the necessary operations.

Since our intention is to create a flexible WSDL that's not entirely specific to our case study, I defined operations using a set of verbs that are generic in nature:

- `Decision`—The main operation, `Decision` is called by clients who want a decision rendered. The instance data that's passed is obviously specific to the domain, so in our case study, it represents the details of the order in which the pricing estimate is performed.
- `Load`—As previously mentioned, `Load` is used to update the Drools working memory using the objects culled from JBoss Cache. As currently designed, this is a global operation, and will reload all working memory objects associated with the decision service (that is, not specific to a particular rule domain).
- `Suspend`—A global operation, `Suspend` sets a flag to indicate that the service shouldn't respond to any inbound queries. `Suspend` would typically be called prior to the `Load` operation so that erroneous results don't occur while the working memory is in the process of being loaded.
- `Resume`—The opposite of `Suspend`, `Resume` simply changes a status flag to indicate that the decision service can again receive inbound requests.

You may be wondering how the `Decision` operation can work if the intention is to support multiple rule domains (our case study is an example of a specific rule domain, whereas something like claims processing would be a different domain). Using XML Schema's extension mechanism, an inbound request for the pricing estimator case study would resemble that shown in listing 12.9.

Listing 12.9 Example SOAP request for pricing engine calculation

```
<!-- soap envelop not shown for brevity -->
<urn:DecisionRequest
  xsi:type="so:PriceCalculatorRequest"
  xmlns:so="urn:opensoa.drools.salesorder">
  <Order xmlns="urn:opensoa.drools.salesorder">
    <header>
      <orderId>2020322</orderId>
      <partyId>WA-23923</partyId>
      <partyContactId>1006</partyContactId>
      <currency>USD</currency>
      <shipping>
        <carrier>USPS</carrier>
        <method>STANDARD</method>
      </shipping>
     </header>
    <lines>
      <!-- line items would go here -->
    </lines>
  </Order>
</urn:DecisionRequest>
```

In listing 12.9, I've highlighted the `DecisionRequest` element. Notice how it contains the `@xsi:type` attribute, whose value is set to `so:PriceCalculatorRequest`. If you look at the schema associated with this object in the sample code for this chapter (the parent WSDL is called DroolsService.wsdl, and it includes Order.wsdl, which is where this element is defined), you'll see this definition:

```
<xs:complexType name="PriceCalculatorResponse">
  <xs:complexContent>
    <xs:extension base="drools:DecisionResponseType">
      <xs:sequence>
        <xs:element name="orderId" type="xs:string"/>
        <xs:element name="salePrice"  type="xs:float"/>
        <xs:element name="shippingPrice" type="xs:float"/>
        <xs:element name="totalPrice" type="xs:float"/>
        <xs:element name="comments" type="xs:string" minOccurs="0"/>
        <xs:element name="currency" type="xs:string"/>
      </xs:sequence>
    </xs:extension>
  </xs:complexContent>
</xs:complexType>
```

The extension base `drools:DecisionResponseType` is the element type defined for `DecisionRequest`. The upshot of this approach is that all `decision` operations will use that same element, but what will differ for each domain area is the corresponding `@xsi:type` value and subsequent child elements. What's the alternative to this approach? You'd end up creating a multitude of domain-specific operations such as `getPricingEstimate`, which seems less than desirable. Granted, for each decision domain or package supported, custom code will be required on the backend, as you'll see in a moment.

The WSDL consists of a high-level parent WSDL, which uses the `wsdl:import` mechanism to load the domain-specific schema elements. In this fashion, the only change required in the parent WSDL for each new domain that's added is to include a `wsdl:import` statement like this:

```
<wsdl:import namespace="urn:opensoa.drools.chapter12"
     location="Order.wsdl"/>
```

The end result for the decision service is a WSDL that looks like the one shown in figure 12.15.

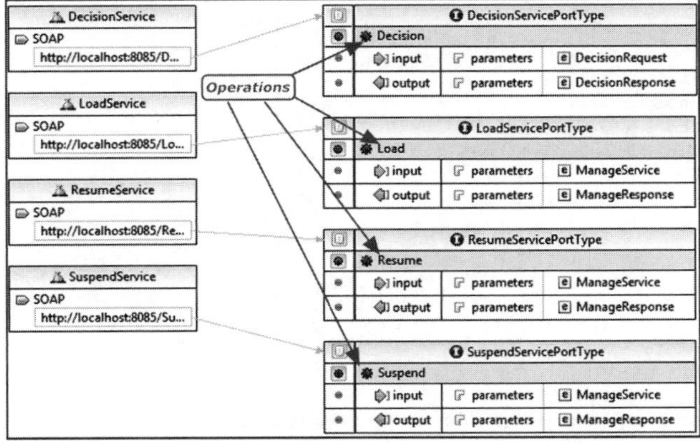

Figure 12.15 Graphical depiction of the decision service WSDL

As figure 12.15 shows, separate services such as `LoadService` and `ResumeService` are defined, as opposed to grouping all of the operations under a single service. This is done to simplify the components used by Tuscany's SCA implementation, which we'll explore next.

TUSCANY SCA COMPONENT OVERVIEW

To keep our example as straightforward as possible, we'll only define a SOAP over HTTP binding for the decision service.

NOTE We cover adding bindings, such as for JMS, in chapter 3.

The SCA implementation consists of only two components: one (`DroolsDecisionComponent`) for handling the inbound SOAP requests, and the other (`SessionManager`) for handling the Drools and JBoss Cache sessions (for efficiency reasons, new working memory isn't instantiated for each inbound request but is persisted across the life of the service or until reloaded using the `Load` operation). A single SCA service called `DroolsDecisionService` is used, and it includes the four web service bindings that correspond to the services shown in the WSDL in figure 12.15. The SCA service and two components can be viewed graphically when using the SOA Tools plug-in available for Eclipse (http://www.eclipse.org/stp/). Figure 12.16 shows one of the available views, in this case a tree-style depiction of the SCA service, components, and properties that comprise the decision service.

Figure 12.16 shows the various property values that are passed in declaratively through the composite XML file (Drools.composite). You'll learn what these are in the next section, but suffice it to say that they identify for the `SessionManagement` component what rule packages to use and the JBoss Cache configuration details.

Now that we have a WSDL in place and a high-level definition of the SCA configuration, we can turn to the fun stuff: code!

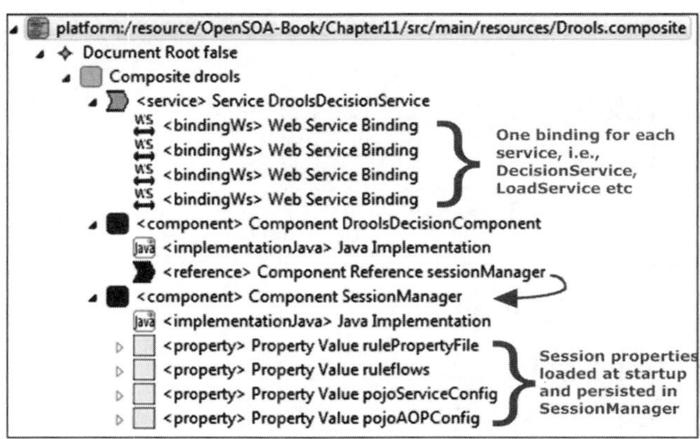

Figure 12.16 Tree depiction of the decision service using SOA Tools Eclipse plug-in

12.3.3 Implementing the decision service using Tuscany and Drools

Since we developed the WSDL first as part of our top-down design philosophy, we can use it to generate the Java classes that represent the inputs and outputs for the web service operations. Two schemas are used in the WSDL. The first, defined in the main WSDL file DroolsService.wsdl, uses a namespace of `urn:opensoa.drools` and is used for defining the various operation parameters. The second, defined in the `Orders.wsdl` imported file, uses the namespace of `urn:opensoa.drools.salesorder`. Since we have two schemas located in different files, we'll call the Tuscany tool `XSD2JavaGenerator` on each respective WSDL file. This will generate Java classes for each of the elements and attributes present in the schemas. Calling this tool is easiest from within Ant; listing 12.10 shows an Ant target configured to generate the classes based on the WSDL files.

Listing 12.10 Ant target used to generate Java classes from WSDL

```
<target depends="init" name="generate.classes.from.wsdl">
  <java classname="org.apache.tuscany.sdo.generate.XSD2JavaGenerator"
      fork="true">                                          ❶
    <arg value="-targetDirectory"/>                                 ❷
    <arg value="src/main/generated/wsdl2javasource"/>
    <arg value="-noContainment"/>                       Defines code
    <arg value="-noUnsettable"/>                        generator options
    <arg value="src/main/resources/DroolsService.wsdl"/>     ❸
    <classpath>
      <fileset dir="${tuscany.lib.10}">                Specifies classpath
        <include name="*.jar"/>                        for SCA libraries
      </fileset>
    </classpath>
  </java>
  <!-- omitted Order.wsdl java block, which is functionally
      identical to the above -->
</target>
```

The Ant target uses a Java task to run the `XSD2JavaGenerator` ❶, which has a variety of usage arguments (for a description of all of the options, see [Generator]). The required argument `-targetDirectory` is used to specify the path location of the generated files ❷. This is followed by some optional arguments. Then we specify the location of the WSDL file that contains the XML Schema ❸. These classes will now be used as we build the individual operations, beginning with `Load`.

LOAD OPERATION

The reason we tackled this operation first is because it invokes the same methods that are used at startup for the decision service. When the service starts, the working memory must be populated in order for the rules engine to function. Additionally, we want to keep the working memory session active, so that it doesn't have to be reconstituted for every request. For these reasons, we created the `SessionManagerBRMSImpl` class, which implements `SessionManager` and uses the conversational capabilities of SCA to keep this class stateful for the duration of the decision service (see chapter 4). This class receives, via SCA properties, three property values:

- `rulePropertyFile`—The Drools Rule Agent mechanism relies on a property file to indicate how to load a rule package. For an example, see the rule.properties file in the source code for this chapter. You can either load the rule package directly from the Guvnor repository using the `url` property, or download the .pkg file locally and reference it via the `file` property. In either case, you can specify multiple packages to load by comma-delimiting the location of each package.
- `pojoServiceConfig`—The JBoss Cache version we're using is referred to as POJO Cache (it provides some additional functionality above-and-beyond regular JBoss Cache), and it uses an XML configuration file to specify network connectivity settings. For more information on the various setting options, see [POJOCache].
- `pojoAOPConfig`—This property specifies another configuration XML file required by POJO Cache and the specification for its contents are described in the official documentation. In all likelihood, no changes will be needed to this file, and the out-of-the-box configuration will suffice.

The final result is this component SCA definition:

```
<component name="SessionManager">
   <implementation.java
      class="opensoa.drools.service.impl.SessionManagerBRMSImpl"/>
   <property name="rulePropertyFile">/rule.properties</property>
   <property name="pojoServiceConfig">replSync-service.xml</property>
   <property name="pojoAOPConfig">pojocache-aop.xml</property>
</component>
```

With these properties now available to `SessionManagerBRMSImpl`, it can proceed to (a) start a new Drools working session instance using the package(s) specified in the `rulePropertyFile`, and (b) populate the working memory with the objects seeded into the cache.

Loading the rule package involves only a few lines of code, as this method from `SessionManagerBRMSImpl` illustrates:

```
private static RuleBase loadRuleBaseFromRuleAgent(String rulePropertyFile) {
  RuleAgent agent = RuleAgent.newRuleAgent( rulePropertyFile );
  RuleBase rulebase = agent.getRuleBase();
  return rulebase;
}
```

The returned `RuleBase` can then be used to create the working memory session using its method `newStatefulSession()`. With the handle to the working memory, the objects in the cache can be loaded. The method used to do so is displayed in listing 12.11.

Listing 12.11 Method to populate Drools working memory

```
private void loadWM () {
  boolean toStart = true;                    ❶
  PojoCache pcache =                  <─┘
    PojoCacheFactory.createCache(pojoServiceConfig, toStart);

  Map workingObjs = pcache.findAll("/opensoa/drools/salesorder/");      <─❷

  Iterator it = workingObjs.entrySet().iterator();
  while (it.hasNext()) {                          <─┐
Map.Entry pairs = (Map.Entry) it.next();             ❸
workingMemory.insert(pairs.getValue());
  }
}
```

The first step in loading the objects is to create an instance of the cache. This is done with the `PojoCacheFactory.createCache()` method ❶, which accepts as its two parameters the location of the service configuration (passed as a parameter populating the `pojoServiceConfig` variable) and a `Boolean` to indicate whether to immediately start the instance. This configuration assumes that you've already started the cache, which you can do by using the `run.pojoServer` target in the project's Ant build file. This will start an instance of the cache and seed it with the data objects. Once the cache is started, a map of the loaded objects in the cache is acquired in the `loadWM()` method shown in listing 12.11 using the FQN `"/opensoa/drools/salesorder/"` ❷. This could obviously be made more generic and flexible—for example, by passing the FQN via an SCA property—but we're trying to keep things simple here, so we've just hard-coded it. Finally, we iterate through all returned objects in the cache and load them into the working memory ❸.

The `Load` operation's SOAP request is very terse:

```
<soapenv:Envelope> <!-- namespaces not shown -->
  <soapenv:Body>
    <urn:ManageService/>
  </soapenv:Body>
</soapenv:Envelope>
```

You might be wondering how the service knows that this call pertains to the `Load` operation. As you may remember, separate WSDL services were configured for each operation (shown in figure 12.15), so the actual URL that this is posting to is what reveals the operation: `http://localhost:8085/LoadService`.

The component responsible for fielding the incoming SOAP requests is implemented by way of the class `PriceCalculatorResponseImpl`. It includes a method that corresponds to the SOAP operation signature, as shown in listing 12.12.

Listing 12.12 Load method used for responding to inbound SOAP requests

```
public ManageResponseTypeImpl Load(ManageServiceTypeImpl service)
  throws RemoteException, Exception {

  sessionManager.setStatus(false);     <─❶
```

```
    scope = SDOUtil.createHelperContext();          Initializes SDO
    dfactory = DroolsFactory.INSTANCE;               for response
    DroolsFactory.INSTANCE.register(scope);

    ManageResponseTypeImpl response =                                      Initializes SDO
      (ManageResponseTypeImpl) dfactory.createManageResponseType();         for response
    response.setResultCode(200);                                            ❷
    response.setResult("SUCCESS");

    sessionManager.initialize();           ❸
    sessionManager.setStatus(true);            ❹
    return response;                       ❺
}
```

First we set the `SessionManager.status` (implemented by `SessionManagerBRMSImpl` to `false` ❶. As you recall, the `SessionManager` was injected as an SCA `COMPOSITE` scoped reference when the class was first created. The `status` flag is used to notify any clients who attempt a request that the decision service is currently unavailable. After that, we perform some SDO initialization tasks (SDO is discussed in chapter 4) so that we can prepare a response to the method (granted, this could be improved to include error handling, but we'll keep things simple).

NOTE You may be wondering why the method name, `Load`, doesn't follow the standard Java method convention of starting with a lowercase letter. This is because it's patterned to match the operation name in the WSDL. (We could change the WSDL, but SOAP naming conventions are often different than Java.) The parameter object and return value are both generated by `XSD2JavaGenerator`.

Derived from the WSDL code generation, `ManageResponseTypeImpl` represents the return value that's expected. We populate it with a response that represents what will be returned from the SOAP call ❷. In step ❸, we call the `initialize()` method of the `SessionManage` implementation. This method, which we haven't shown before, just invokes the two methods (`loadBaseFromRuleAgent()` and `loadWM()`) we previously had created in the `SessionManagerBRMSImpl` class. In effect, this disposes of the existing Drools working memory session, creates a new session, and populates it with the objects from the JBoss Cache. Finally, we set the `status` back to `true` (on) ❹, and return the response we created ❺.

Whew, that's a lot of stuff we covered. Fortunately, since we've discussed the `SessionManager` implementation, the remaining operations will be simple in comparison. Let's look at how the main operation, `Decision`, is implemented.

DECISION OPERATION

The `Decision` operation, unlike the other three, is specific to the rule domain or package being called. For example, in our case study we're just dealing with the rules concerning the calculation of an order's price (listing 12.9 depicted an example inbound SOAP request). Thus, the implementation we'll show is unique to this domain, and an implementation must be provided for each rule domain you're incorporating into the decision service. This becomes clearer as we look at the method used for processing the Decision operation for the pricing engine calculator:

```
public PriceCalculatorResponseImpl Decision(PriceCalculatorRequestImpl
  order) throws Exception {

  if (sessionManager.isStatus() == false) {
    throw (new Exception("Service unavailable"));
  }

  PriceCalculatorProcessor processor =
    new PriceCalculatorProcessor(order);

  return processor.process(sessionManager);
}
```

The method signature for this Decision operation, which receives a Price-CalculatorRequestImpl object, clearly illustrates that it's specific to the pricing calculator. You'd create additional Decision methods with their own unique signatures for each rule domain you set up. In the Decision method, you see that we're checking the status, and if it's set to false, we return an error to the client. Such a scenario occurs when the Load operation is called to refresh the working memory, or when the service has been suspended using the Suspend operation. The heart of the processing occurs in the PriceCalculatorProcessor class. This class, which we'll show next, is responsible for invoking the rule engine by its process() method and for preparing a response of its findings.

The PriceCalculatorProcessor.process()method is shown in listing 12.13.

Listing 12.13 Method responsible for processing the pricing engine domain rules

```
public PriceCalculatorResponseImpl process(SessionManager sessionManager) {

  workingMemory = sessionManager.getWorkingMemory();       <-- 1
  Order dorder = convertToBaseObj();                  <-- 2

  PriceCalculatorResponseImpl response = null;
  try {
    response = runRules(dorder);                    <-- 3
  } catch (Exception e) {
    e.printStackTrace();
  }
  return response;          <-- 4
}
```

The first thing we do in the process() method is receive a handle to the Drools working memory session ❶. The workingMemory object is a class variable, and the passed SessionManager is used as a factory to reference it. The stateful SessionManager was provided by way of the calling class, DroolsManagerImpl. The next step ❷ is to convert the SDO object that was automatically populated by the SOAP request into the working memory fact object that we'd prepared earlier when creating the case study (this step could be eliminated if you designed the working memory instance objects up front for use by the decision service). Since this is just an exercise in object mapping, we won't bother showing it here, but you can find it in the source code. We then invoke the `runRules()` method ❸, which is responsible for calling the engine. The last step is to return the results to the calling class ❹.

The `runRules()` method is where the real work resides, as shown in listing 12.14.

Listing 12.14 Method that invokes the rule engine and prepares a response

```
private PriceCalculatorResponseImpl runRules(Order order) throws Exception {

  workingMemory.insert( order );                                        ❶

  workingMemory.startProcess("opensoa.drools.pricing");                 ❷

  workingMemory.fireAllRules();                                         ❸

  TotalPrice total = SessionHelper.showResults(workingMemory);          ❹

  PriceCalculatorResponseImpl response = (PriceCalculatorResponseImpl)
   salesFactory.createPriceCalculatorResponse();                        ❺
  response.setOrderId(total.getOrderId());
 // other setters not shown

 return response;          ❻
}
```

Using the `workingMemory` class variable, which represents the Drools session, we insert the object representing the SOAP request into the working memory ❶. Since the case study uses a RuleFlow, that process is started next ❷, using the named identifier assigned to the RuleFlow. Then the rule engine is fired using the `fireAllRules()` method ❸, and the results are gathered by the `SessionHelper.showResults()` method ❹. With the results now present in the `TotalPrice` object, they need to be converted into the SDO object that's used for the service response ❺. With the response in hand, it can be returned to the caller ❻, where it eventually gets passed back as the actual SOAP response.

Since we've covered a lot here, let's recap in figure 12.17 the overall process for fulfilling an inbound `Decision` operation request.

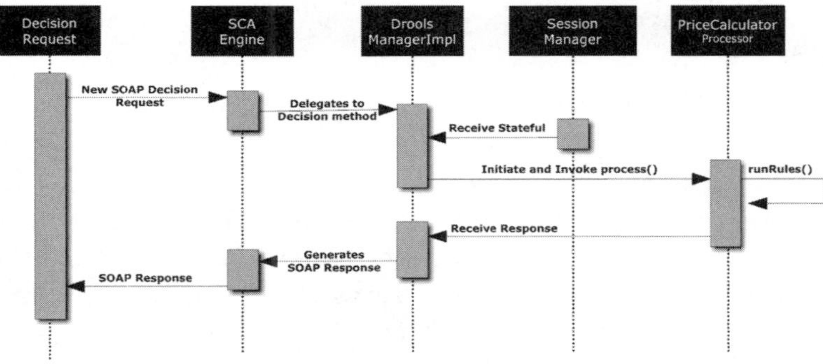

Figure 12.17 Process for fulfilling an inbound `Decision` operation request

When introducing a new rule domain, the only change necessary is to create a new process type class similar to `PriceCalculatorProcessor`, create a new method signature in `DroolsManagerImpl`, and then call the processor from within the new method. Using Spring, a solution could be wired together more elegantly still, but we didn't want to further complicate our example by introducing another technology (while many of you are familiar with Spring, some may not be).

SUSPEND AND RESUME OPERATIONS

The `Suspend` and `Resume` operations are intended for circumstances where you want to temporarily suspend (and eventually resume) the decision service, but don't necessarily just want to turn it off entirely, which would result in network timeout errors. The only thing these operations do is change the stateful `SessionManager.status` `Boolean` flag, since that's checked before the service will process any decision request. For example, here's the `Suspend` method's implementation:

```
public ManageResponseTypeImpl Suspend(ManageServiceTypeImpl service) throws
  RemoteException, Exception {
  sessionManager.setStatus(false);
  scope = SDOUtil.createHelperContext();;
  dfactory = DroolsFactory.INSTANCE;
  DroolsFactory.INSTANCE.register(scope);
  ManageResponseTypeImpl response =
    (ManageResponseTypeImpl) dfactory.createManageResponseType();
  response.setResultCode(200);
  response.setResult("SUCCESS");

  return response;
}
```

As you can see, we haven't introduced anything new, so let's turn to how we can test our new decision service.

12.3.4 Testing

Most Java developers are already familiar with unit testing tools such as JUnit or TestNG. These are essential tools in any Java developer's toolbox. However, one of the main drivers behind adopting a BRMS is so that business users can author their own rules, tapping into the considerable business expertise they posses. Such users are obviously not skilled enough to perform unit testing using conventional Java testing tools. In recognition of this, Guvnor is being enhanced to support a testing framework, but it remains a work in progress as of this writing. Instead, I suggest deploying soapUI for testing by rule authors and subject matter experts. Figure 12.18 shows soapUI used for testing our case study's pricing engine rule service.

As figure 12.18 shows, a variety of authoring views are available. The one shown in the figure is the Outline view, but a Form view is also available that derives a form based on the WSDL. Similarly, the response can be viewed in a variety of fashions, from Raw XML to the Overview layout shown in figure 12.18. The capabilities of soapUI extend far beyond what is shown, and it can be used to create comprehensive testing suites that can be run for regression-style automated testing. Used in tandem with

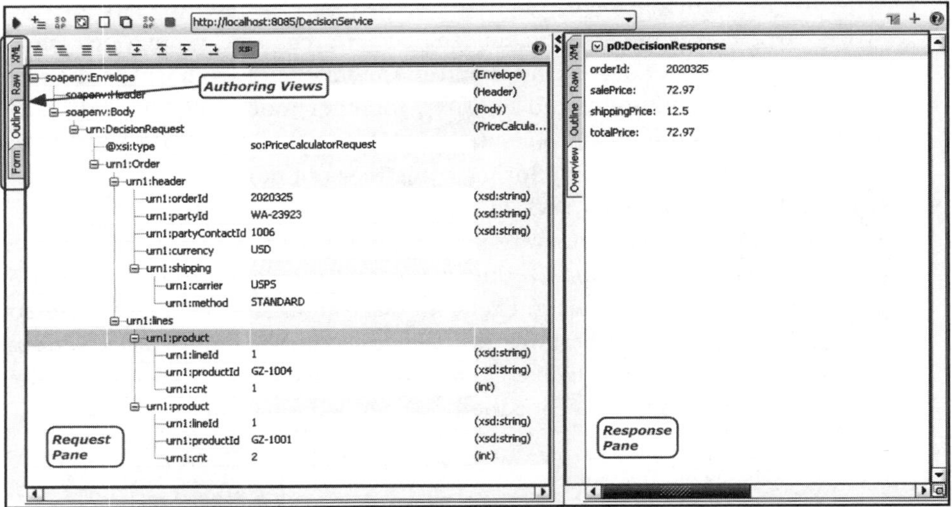

Figure 12.18 soapUI is used for testing the decision service.

Guvnor, a true end-to-end solution can be created that includes authoring, rule management, and testing.

The decision service we've created using the pricing estimator case study has demonstrated the powerful combination of using Apache Tuscany and JBoss Drools. You've seen how Apache Synapse can play a central role in a real-life environment for harvesting the data necessary for the rule engine to perform its inference logic. You can imagine a scenario where the Esper ESP could be beneficial, in particular as a way to optimize decision yield and spot abnormal or unusual trends.

12.4 Summary

The purpose of this chapter was to build on what you learned in chapter 11, where we introduced the Drools rule engine and many of its essential capabilities. In this chapter, we constructed a real-life type case study that consisted of 15 rules with activation sequencing managed via the Drools RuleFlow capability. We then migrated these rules into Guvnor, the Drools BRMS, and explored many of its features. Most significant is the ability Guvnor provides for business users to author and manage business rules, which impact their area of domain expertise. In providing this capability, rules truly become unlocked from their historical binding deep within an application's code and instead become business assets that can be managed and shared across multiple applications or business processes.

We concluded the chapter by describing how a decision service can be created using Apache Tuscany that exposes these rules as web services that can be easily consumed by a multitude of client applications. Thorny issues that have plagued the adoption of decision services, such as how to populate the facts required for the service to perform its logic, were addressed using a distributed cache technology built on

JBoss Cache. A framework resulted that can be extended and built on within your enterprise.

Drools is one of the exciting technologies we covered in the Open SOA Platform, and its adoption promises a new paradigm—a business rules approach that reduces development costs and dramatically improves organizational agility!

resources

[ActiveMQ] ActiveMQ open source JMS server. Available at http://activemq.apache.org/.

[ApacheVFS] Apache Commons VFS. Available at http://commons.apache.org/vfs/filesystems.html.

[Baeyens] Baeyens, Tom. 2008. "Process Component Models: The Next Generation in Workflow?" Available at http://www.infoq.com/articles/process-component-models.

[BEA] BEA white paper. 2005. "Domain Model for SOA: Realizing the Business Benefit of Service-Oriented Architecture." Available at http://eudownload.bea.com/uk/events/soa/soa.pdf.

[Bernhardt]Bernhardt, Thomas and Vasseur, Alexandre. April 2008. "Complex Event Processing Made Simple Using Esper." Available at http://www.theserverside.com/news/thread.tss?thread_id=48954.

[BPMBasics]BPM Basics: BPM Glossary. Available at http://www.bpmbasics.com/introduction/glossary.jsp.

[BSF] Bean Scripting Framework. Available at http://jakarta.apache.org/bsf/.

[Camel] "Apache Camel." Available at http://activemq.apache.org/camel/.

[CEPInterest] Complex Event Processing Interest. Available at http://www.eventstream processing.com.

[Choicepoint] Swartz, Nikki. 2007. "ChoicePoint Lessons Learned." Available at http://find articles.com/p/articles/mi_qa3937/is_200709/ai_n21100514.

[Commons] Apache Commons. Available at http://commons.apache.org/.

[Cooper] Cooper, Peter. 2007. *Beginning Ruby: From Novice to Professional.* New York: Apress.

[CSVMediator] Open CSV Mediator. Available at http://esbsite.org/resources.jsp?path=/mediators/paulfremantle/OpenCSV%20Mediator.

[Drools] Drools Documentation. Available at http://downloads.jboss.com/drools/docs/4.0.7.19894.GA/html/index.html.

[DroolsUserGuide] JBoss Rules User Guide. Available at http://downloads.jboss.com/drools/docs/4.0.7.19894.GA/html_single/index.html.

[DTO] "Core J2EE Patterns: Data Transfer Objects." Available at http://java.sun.com/blueprints/corej2eepatterns/Patterns/TransferObject.html.

[Eckerson] Eckerson, Wayne W. 2006. *Performance Dashboards: Measuring, Monitoring and Managing Your Business.* Hobokon, NJ: John Wiley & Sons, Inc.

[Erl2005] Erl, Thomas. 2005. *Service-Oriented Architecture: Concepts, Technology and Design.* Upper Saddle River, NJ: Pearson Education, p. 54.

[Erl2007] Erl, Thomas. 2007. *SOA: Principles of Service Design.* Boston: Prentice Hall.

[Fingar] Smith, Howard and Fingar, Peter. 2003. *Business Process Management—The Third Wave.* Tampa, FL: Meghan-Kiffer Press.

[Forrester] Chappell, David. 2004. Enterprise Service Bus. References "Reducing Integration Costs." Forrester Research. 2001.

[Generator] Static Code Generator. Available at http://wiki.apache.org/ws/Tuscany/TuscanyJava/SDO_Java_Overview#generator.

[Godage] Godage, Upul. "Mock Web Services with Apache Synapse to Develop and Test Web Services." Available at http://www.ibm.com/developerworks/webservices/edu/ws-dw-ws-synapse.html.

[Graham] Graham, Ian. 2007. *Business Rules Management and Service Oriented Architecture.* Hoboken, NJ: John Wiley & Sons.

[HBR] Merrifield, Ric and Stevens, Dennis. 2008. "The Next Revolution in Productivity." *Harvard Business Review,* June.

[Hinchcliffe] Hinchcliffe, Dion. 2008. "What Is WOA? It's the Future of Service-Oriented Architecture (SOA)." Available at http://hinchcliffe.org/archive/2008/02/27/16617.aspx.

[HohpeWoolf] Hohpe, Gregor, and Woolf, Bobby. 2004. *Enterprise Integration Patterns.* New York: Addison-Wesley.

[IW] Smith, Roger. 2008. "A Simpler Approach to SOA." Available at http://www.informationweek.com/news/software/soa/showArticle.jhtml?articleID=209904293.

[jBPMGettingStarted] JBoss.org jBPM Getting Started. Available at http://www.jboss.org/community/docs/DOC-11142.

[JSR-223] JSR 223: Scripting for the JavaTM Platform. Available at http://www.jcp.org/en/jsr/detail?id=223.

[Kanneganti] Kanneganti, Ramarao, and Chodavarapu, Chodavarapu. 2007. *SOA Security.* Greenwich, CT: Manning Publications.

[Luckham2002] Luckham, David. 2002. *The Power of Events: An Introduction to Complex Event Processing in Distributed Enterprise Systems.* New York: Addison-Wesley Professional.

[MargolisSharpe] Margolis, Ben, and Sharpe, Joseph. 2007. *SOA for the Business Developer. Concepts, BPEL and SCA.* Lewisville, TX: MC Press.

[McAfeeBrynjolfsson] McAfee, Andrew and Brynjolfsson, Erik. "Investing in the IT That Makes a Competitive Difference." *Harvard Business Review,* July–August 2008, Vol. 86, No. 7.

[Orwell] Orwell, George. 1945. *Animal Farm.* London: Secker and Warburg.

[OSGi] Web Services Interoperability Organization (WS-I). Available at http://www.ws-i.org/.

[POJOCache] POJO Cache: User Guide. Available at http://www.jboss.org/file-access/default/members/jbosscache/freezone/docs/3.0.0.GA/pojo/userguide_en/html_single/index.html.

[Pointillism] "Pointillism." Available at http://en.wikipedia.org/wiki/Pointillism.

[Prahalad] Prahalad, C.K., and Krishnan, M.S. 2008. *The New Age of Innovation.* New York: McGraw-Hill.

[Proctor] "A Vision for Unified Rules and Processes." Available at http://blog.athico.com/2007/11/vision-for-unified-rules-and-processes.html.

[Ranadivé] Ranadivé, Vivek. 2006. *Power to Predict.* New York: McGraw-Hill, pp. 182, 183.

[RESTvsSOAP] Roch, Eric. 2006. "SOAP versus REST." Available at http://blogs.ittoolbox.com/eai/business/archives/soa-versus-rest-debate-9225.

[SCAWS] "SCA Web Services Binding V1.00." Available at http://www.osoa.org/download/attachments/35/SCA_WebServiceBinding_V100.pdf?version=2.

[SmithFinger] Smith, Howard, and Finger, Peter. 2003. *Business Process Management—The Third Wave.* Tampa, FL: Meghan-Kiffer Press, p. 21.

[Splitter] Hophe, Gregor, and Woolf, Bobby. "Enterprise Integration Patterns – Splitter." Available at http://www.enterpriseintegrationpatterns.com/Sequencer.html.

[Synapse] "Leading SOA Vendors Announce Synapse Project to Develop Web Service Mediation Framework." Available at http://findarticles.com/p/articles/mi_m0EIN/is_2005_August_22/ai_n14929275.

[Synapse2005] Synapse Proposal (Incubator Wiki). Available at http://wiki.apache.org/incubator/SynapseProposal.

[Synapse2007] Apache Synapse. Available at http://web.archive.org/web/20070716152006rn_1/ws.apache.org/synapse/.

[SynapseLanguage] Apache Synapse ESB – Configuration. Available at http://synapse.apache.org/Synapse_Configuration_Language.html.

[Tasks] Godage, Upul. "Writing a Task in WSO2 ESB." Available at http:/wso2.org/library/2900.

[Taylor] Taylor, James. 2007. "What You Need to Know about Decision Services." Available at http://www.edmblog.com/weblog/2007/03/what_you_need_t.html.

[TaylorRaden] Taylor, James, and Raden, Neil. 2007. Smart Enough Systems: How to Deliver Competitive Advantage by Automating Hidden Decision. Boston: Pearson Education, Inc.

[UBL] OASIS Universal Business Language (UBL). Available at http://www.oasis-open.org/committees/tc_home.php?wg_abbrev=ubl.

[VonHalle] Von Halle, Barbara. 2002. *Business Rules Applied.* Hoboken, NJ: John Wiley & Sons.

[VonHalleGoldberg] Von Halle, Barbara and Goldberg, Larry. 2006. *The Business Rule Revolution.* Cupertino, CA: Happy About.

[WADL] "Web Application Description Language." Available at https://wadl.dev.java.net/.

[WIKI] Wikipedia. "Event-driven architecture." Available at http://en.wikipedia.org/wiki/Event_Driven_Architecture.

[WireTap] Wire Tap Enterprise Integration Patterns. Available at http://www.eaipatterns.com/WireTap.html.

[Woolf] Woolf, Bobby. "ESB-Oriented Architecture: The Wrong Approach to Adopting SOA." Available at http://www.ibm.com/developerworks/library/ws-soa-esbarch/index.html.

[WSAddressing] Linker, Beth. 2005. "Introduction to WS-Addressing." Available at http://www.fpml.org/_wgmail/_bpwgmail/pdfdz3oYx1M9e.pdf.

[WSDL] "WSDL Essentials." Available at http://www.developer.com/services/article.php/1602051.

[WSPolicy] Web Services Policy 1.2 – Framework (WS-Policy). Available at http://www.w3.org/Submission/WS-Policy/.

[WSS] OASIS. "Web Services Security UsernameToken Profile 1.0." Available at http://docs.oasis-open.org/wss/2004/01/oasis-200401-wss-username-token-profile-1.0.pdf.

[XAware] XAware.org, at http://www.xaware.org/.

index

A

F

K

L

M

N

O

P

T

X

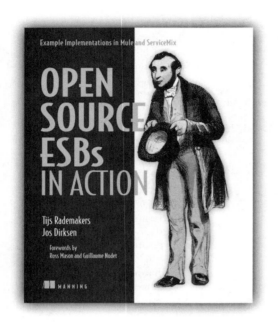

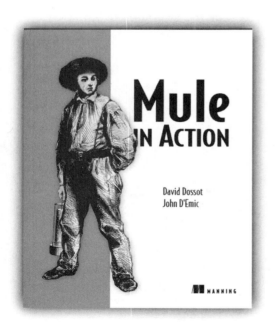